NOTES ON THE TRANSLATION

OF THE

NEW TESTAMENT.

NOTES ON THE TRANSLATION

OF THE

NEW TESTAMENT

BEING THE

OTIUM NORVICENSE (PARS TERTIA)

BY THE LATE

FREDERICK FIELD, M.A., LL.D.

FORMERLY FELLOW OF TRINITY COLLEGE, CAMBRIDGE

REPRINTED WITH ADDITIONS BY THE AUTHOR

Hendrickson Publishers, Inc. edition

ISBN: 1-56563-080-7

This edition is a reprint of the 1899 Cambridge University Press edition.

First Printing — March 1994

Printed in the United States of America

PREFACE.

THE greater number of these notes appeared in 1881 as *Pars Tertia* of the *Otium Norvicense*. They are here reprinted, with additions which may be classified under two heads : first, notes which Dr Field at his death left in the final stages of their preparation for publication, and, secondly, supplementary illustrations from classical sources which he had jotted down in the margin of his own copy of the *Otium*. Additions of the first class will be found in their due order marked by asterisks, while those of the second class are placed as footnotes and enclosed in square brackets.

For aid in the selection of these additions, and in the verification of references, I owe many thanks to the Reverend J. Armitage Robinson, D.D., late Norrisian Professor of Divinity in this University, now Canon of Westminster ; to W. Aldis Wright, Esq., M.A., Vice-Master of Trinity College ; and to the Reverend C. A. Phillips, M.A., of King's College ; but I am, of course, myself responsible for all errors which may be found in the reproduction of the notes or the verification of the references.

I ought also to acknowledge gratefully the kindness of the Delegates of the Clarendon Press, which has made it

b 2

possible to reprint the interesting autobiography prefixed by Dr Field to his edition of the Hexapla of Origen. Lastly, the skill and patience of the readers and workmen of the Pitt Press deserve thankful recognition from one who is a slow novice in the work of seeing a book such as this through the press.

A. M. KNIGHT.

GONVILLE AND CAIUS COLLEGE,
  CAMBRIDGE.
     May, 1899.

THE following autobiography is reprinted from Dr Field's edition of the Hexapla of Origen.

QUOD Germanis literatis moris est, ut ad summos in philosophia honores rite capessendos vitae et studiorum rationes reddant, id mihi semper visum est senescenti quam adolescenti aetati, et absoluto quam vixdum inchoato curriculo, magis consentaneum esse. Cum igitur, Deo favente, ad finem ultimi mei laboris literarii tanquam ex longa navigatione in portum pervenerim, peto indulgentiam tuam, L. B., dum quid in vita ultra communem terminum producta peregerim, et quibus studiorum inceptorumque meorum auctoribus et fautoribus, breviter expono.

Natus sum Londini anno MDCCCI mensis Julii die XX in vico cui nomen a Nova Porta, in quo pater meus HENRICUS FIELD, et ante eum pater ejus, et post eum frater meus natu maximus per longam annorum seriem medicam artem exercuerunt. Avus meus JOANNES FIELD uxorem duxit ANNAM filiam THOMAE CROMWELL, negotiatoris Londinensis, viri humili conditione, sed stirpe illustri, quippe qui patrem habuerit HENRICUM CROMWELL, Majorem (qui dicitur) in exercitu Reginae Annae; avum autem HENRICUM CROMWELL, Hiberniae Dominum deputatum, filium natu minorem OLIVERII CROMWELL, Reipublicae Angliae, Scotiae et Hiberniae Protectoris. Sed stemmatum satis. Redeo ad patrem meum, virum strenuissimum, integerrimum, piissimum, cujus memoriam nunquam eo quo par est amore et veneratione prosequi potero. Is, dum sextum annum agebam, cooptatus est in medicum Orphanotrophei Christi a Rege Edvardo VI fundati, quo eventu patuit mihi aditus gratuitus ad scholas dicti Orphanotrophei grammaticas, primum sub disciplina viri optimi et amabilissimi, LANCELOTTI PEPYS STEPHENS, A.M., scholae inferioris magistri; donec, aetate paulo provectior, transii in scholam superiorem ab ARTHURO

GULIELMO TROLLOPE, S.T.P., tunc temporis gubernatam, quo praeceptore, nulli coaetaneorum suorum secundo, a pueritia usque ad annum aetatis duodevigesimum literis Latinis, Graecis, Hebraeis sedulo imbutus sum.   E schola egressum anno MDCCCXIX excepit me Collegium SS. Trinitatis apud Cantabrigienses, cujus post sex menses Discipulus factus sum.   Tutores habui in disciplinis mathematicis JOANNEM BROWN, A.M., et GULIELMUM WHEWELL, A.M.; in eruditione autem classica (quae dicitur) JACOBUM HENRICUM MONK, S.T.B., Graecarum literarum Professorem Regium; quorum praelectiones diligenter attendens, privato tutore facile carere potui. Elapso triennio (cujus disciplinae quotidianae jucundissimam memoriam recolo) anni MDCCCXXIII mense Januario in gradum Baccalaurei Artium admissus sum, quo tempore in tripode (quem vocant) mathematico primae classis decimum locum obtinui.   Ejusdem anni mense Martio numisma aureum a Cancellario Universitatis pro profectu in studiis classicis quotannis propositum reportavi. Vix bimestri spatio elapso, tertium in arenam descendi, et exhibitione a Roberto Tyrwhitt, A.M., ad eruditionem Hebraeam promovendam instituta dignatus sum.   Proximo anno, Octobris die primo, culmine votorum meorum potitus sum, in Sociorum celeberrimi Collegii ordinem post examinationem habitam cooptatus.   Collegas honoris habui tres: THOMAM BABINGTON MACAULAY, Poetam, Oratorem, Historicum; HENRICUM MALDEN, in Collegio Universitatis Londini Graecarum literarum Professorem; et GEORGIUM BIDDELL AIRY, Astronomum Regium.   Anno MDCCCXXVIII a JOANNE KAYE, S.T.P., Episcopo Lincolniensi, sacris ordinibus obligatus sum.   Ex eo tempore S. Scripturae et Patrum Ecclesiae studio me addixi, nullo tamen publice edito fructu, donec anno MDCCCXXXIX S. Joannis Chrysostomi Homilias in Matthaeum ad fidem codicum MSS. et versionum emendatas et annotationibus illustratas non modico sudore ac sumptu evulgavi.   Non multo post almae matri meae valedixi, et curam pastoralem Saxhamiae Magnae in agro Suffolciensi per tres annos administravi.   Anno MDCCCXLII beneficium ecclesiasticum Reephamiae cum Kerdistone in agro Norfolciensi, cujus collatio ad Collegium SS. Trinitatis pertinet, jure successionis mihi obtigit.   In hoc viculo amoenissimo annos unum et viginti non inutiliter consumpsi, partim in cura animarum non ita multarum mihi commissarum, partim in studiis eis sectandis, quae gloriam Dei illustrare, et Ecclesiae ejus adjumento esse possent. Ne longior fiam, per id tempus Chrysostomi, deliciarum mearum,

Homiliarum in Divi Pauli Epistolas novam recensionem, septem voluminibus inclusam, in gratiam Bibliothecae Patrum Ecclesiae a presbyteris quibusdam Oxoniensibus inceptae edidi. Praeterea, rogatu venerabilis Societatis de Promovenda Doctrina Christiana, Veteris Testamenti juxta LXX interpretes recensionem Grabianam denuo recognovi ; cujus operis, quamvis ad aliorum modulum et praescriptum conformati, merita qualiacunque candide agnovit Tischendorfius in *Prolegomenis ad V. T. juxta LXX interpretes*, Lipsiae, 1869, quartum editis. Vixdum hoc pensum finieram, cum in mentem mihi venit cogitatio operis, quod ad priora illa quasi cumulus accederet, hoc est, ORIGENIS HEXAPLORUM novae et quae nostri saeculi votis satisfaceret editionis ; quod tamen ut ad felicem exitum perducerem, quantulum mihi restaret tam vitae quam vigoris in hunc unum laborem impendendum esse sensi. Resignato igitur beneficio meo, e cujus amplis reditibus jam omnibus bonis affluebam, anno MDCCCLXIII Norvicum me contuli, unde anno sequenti, prolusionis gratia, OTIUM meum NORVICENSE, sive *Tentamen de Reliquiis Aquilae, Symmachi et Theodotionis e lingua Syriaca in Graecam convertendis*, emisi. In animo habebam librum per subscriptiones (quas vocant) publicare, sed in hac bonarum literarum despicientia res tam male mihi successit, ut spem omnem operis edendi abjecissem, nisi peropportune Delegati Preli Oxoniensis Academici, interveniente ROBERTO SCOTT, S.T.P., Collegii Balliolensis Magistro, omnem novae editionis impensam in se suscepissent ; quibus pro sua in me, exterae Academiae alumnum, benevolentia gratias quam maximas ago.

Quod superest quam brevissime potero conficiam. Fidem catholicam, ab Ecclesia Anglicana reformata expositam, firmiter teneo. Errores ac novitates, qui in tot annorum decursu alter alteri supervenerint, sive Evangelicalium (qui nominantur), sive Rationalistarum, sive (quod novissimum ulcus est) Ritualistarum et Papizantium, praeveniente Dei gratia feliciter evasi. Jus fasque tum in privatis tum in publicis rebus impense amavi ; injurias et aggressiones, sive regum delirantium, sive plebeculae tyrannidem affectantis, immitigabili odio ac detestatione prosecutus sum. Vitam umbratilem et otiosam semper sectatus sum, non ut desidiae indulgerem, sed ut iis negotiis, in quibus me aliquid proficere posse senserim, vacarem. Per quadraginta fere annos in bonis literis excolendis, praecipue eis quae ad Verbi Divini illustrationem pertinent, sine patrocinio, sine emolumento, sine honore desudavi.   Nunc senio confectus, et rude donatus, nihil antiquius habeo quam ut juniores competentioresque in eodem campo decurrentes, dum vivo et valeo, consiliis, adhortationibus, facultatibus adjuvem.

Scribebam Norvici die XVI Septembris, A. D. MDCCCLXXIV

To this autobiography a few extracts may be added from a notice of Dr Field which was written by an intimate friend for the *Cambridge Review* of May 6, 1885[1].

"In 1870 he was invited to become a member of the Old Testament Revision Company, and although his deafness precluded him from taking part in the discussions, and he was never present at any of the meetings of the Company, he regularly contributed the most valuable suggestions, which like everything that he did were marked by a ripe and sober judgment.   It was one of the few regrets which could have shadowed a life of such blameless simplicity that he did not see the completion of a work in which he was so profoundly interested.   In a letter written on the 2nd of April (1885), in serene expectation of his approaching end, he said, 'Although I should have been glad to see this part offspring of my brain completed and given to the public (as I have most providentially been spared to see other important "opera" of mine brought to their desired consummation), yet I am aware that this is a matter mostly beyond all human calculation, and that I have no right to expect that uniform success should be dealt out to me by a higher power.'

"In 1881, after the appearance of the Revised Version of the New Testament, and to some extent in consequence of it, he printed and circulated privately a third part of the *Otium Norvicense*, containing 'Notes on Select Passages of the Greek Testament, chiefly with reference to recent English Versions.'...This was written when he had already entered upon his eighty-first year.

---

[1] For permission to use this notice my thanks are due to the Editor of the *Cambridge Review*.

The reading which he had undertaken in view of this work (see note on p. xvii.) "is one proof among many that the *vita umbratilis et otiosa* which he desired was not idly spent.

"Although he sought no honours for himself, his great merits were recognised by the University, and in 1875 the honorary degree of Doctor of Laws was conferred upon him. In the same year he was elected to an honorary fellowship in his own College.

"At the ripe age of 83 he died on the 19th of April [1885], at his residence, 2, Carlton Terrace, Norwich.

"It is fitting that these short and simple annals of the life of a scholar of the antique type should be placed on record, that others may be encouraged by the example it affords of single-minded devotion to a lofty object."

AUTHOR'S PREFACE TO THE THIRD PART OF THE *OTIUM NORVICENSE.*

THE following pages, from the desultory and fragmentary character of their contents, have no claim to be considered as anything more than the Author's contribution to the common stock of materials for the right understanding of that part of the Word of God to which they relate. Ὁ ἔσχεν, ἐποίησεν. The study of the original text has lately received a notable impulse from the publication of the Revised New Testament, as well as from the intelligent interest taken therein by all classes of the Anglo-Christian body, and the criticism which it has received at the hands of a number of more or less competent judges. In the three or four months which have elapsed since the memorable 17 May 1881, much has been written in approval or depreciation of the general style of the Revised version, and its treatment of particular passages ; and it cannot yet be affirmed that a sound public opinion has been pronounced for or against its adaptation to the purposes of private study ; still less its adoption as a substitute for the venerable translation now "appointed to be read in Churches." Speaking for himself, as an original member of the O. T. Revision Company, the present Writer would say that nothing short of this latter consummation, as the ultimate, however distant, end of his labours, entered into his view, in agreeing to bear his humble part in the prosecution of so arduous an undertaking. A new version of the Bible for the use of students who could follow the original tongues, might safely be left to the ordinary purveyors of sacred literature, and to private speculation. The solemn acceptance of the completed work by the English-speaking portion of the Church of Christ, its authorized introduction into the reading-desk and pulpit, its ascendancy in our schools, families, and closets, is the sole worthy aim, the *dignus vindice nodus*, which should gather so large an assembly of scholars and divines, for ten or fifteen years at stated intervals, round the table of the Jerusalem Chamber, to compare together the results of so many hours of laborious investigation, conducted in their respective studies at home.

Whether the departure from precedent in the issue of a portion of the Revised version as soon as completed, without waiting till the HOLY BIBLE in its integrity, "the Law, the Prophets and the Psalms," together with their counterparts in the teachings of Christ and his Apostles, could be presented to a Church built upon the foundation of both, was a judicious step, may admit of a doubt. One consequence of it, which might have been anticipated, has taken place ; namely, that it has drawn down upon the devoted heads of the first adventurers a hail of criticism, some part of which might have been diverted to that other band of heroes which has yet to stand on its defence. When the time comes for the O. T. Company to bespeak a share of the public attention, it is to be feared that its utterances will fall somewhat flat upon the exhausted energies of reviewers and correspondents. On the other hand it may be taken as an undoubted gain, that by this mode of publication an experiment has been made, the results of which may furnish useful suggestions for the future conduct of the undertaking. The *pulse* of the patient has been felt; and the doctors will do well to make a note of it. From the nature of the reception accorded to the Revised N. T. two important facts may be considered as placed beyond all reasonable doubt : *first*, that public opinion has declared itself unmistakably in favour of REVISION ; a question on which, before the inception of the work, learned men, including, perhaps, some of the Revisers themselves, were not agreed; and *secondly*, that the same public opinion which sanctions the undertaking, and does not question the competence of those who have been entrusted with it, reserves to itself the right of the freest discussion of the manner in which it has been executed. This right it has not scrupled to exercise on that portion of the work which has been submitted to it; and the result is, underlying a strong feeling of appreciation of the sterling merits of the Revision, equally strong marks of dissatisfaction with certain unlooked-for, and (it might be thought) uncalled-for innovations, both in the general principles of translation adopted by the Revisers, and in their handling of particular (so to speak) *crucial* passages. The latter class of objections cannot here be discussed; as to the former, it is alleged that in construing the leading "Rule" prescribed to them by the Committee of Convocation—"To introduce as few alterations as possible into the text of the A. V. consistently with FAITHFULNESS"—the Revisers have understood by this word, not (as was evidently intended) faithfulness to the sense and spirit of the original, but to its grammatical and etymological proprieties; the effect of which has been, not only to introduce needless and finical changes[1], which jar upon the ear, but also to throw over the general style an air of pedantry and punctiliousness, which cannot but be distasteful to the reader who has been "nourished up" in the plain, homely, and idiomatic English of the men of 1611.—*Non nostrum est tantos componere lites;* but that they will be *composed*, and that the final result will be, in conjunction with the revised Hebrew Scriptures, a work worthy to take its place as the English Bible of the future, we have no doubt. That the N. T. Company are not inaccessible to suggestions from without, the Author is personally able to avouch, having

---

[1] As an instance, take the exclusion of "the *uttermost* farthing" in favour of "the *last* farthing," than which no single verbal alteration has met with such general reprobation.

had occasion to bring under their notice two papers, on "Conversion" (Matt. xiii. 15) and on "The first recorded utterance of Jesus Christ" (Luke ii. 49), which materially influenced the final revision of those two passages. A third paper, on Acts xx. 24, in defence of the *Textus receptus* against the mutilation (as he conceives) proposed to be inflicted upon it, was not so fortunate[1].

And this leads him to say a word upon the subject of the reformed *Greek text* adopted by the Revisers in deference to what are generally conceded to be the oldest MSS. extant, which were not accessible to the Translators of 1611. That these "ancient authorities" are deserving of the greatest respect, cannot and need not be denied. Still, as all MSS. are liable to be affected by the errors, and, occasionally, the caprices of their transcribers, the interests of truth require that even the oldest and best of them should be continually checked by a reference to the other great branch of the critical art, the *internal evidence* of the good sense and propriety of the passage itself. This is a far more delicate criterion than the former, and requires a longer apprenticeship to attain to eminence in the application of it; for which very reason, perhaps, it has not received its due share of attention. With every respect for great names and well-earned reputations, we cannot ignore the fact, that our foremost biblical critics are *not* the men whom, from their distinguished attainments in philological studies, or their successful exercise of the critical faculty on works of less transcendent difficulty and importance, we should, *a priori*, have thought most fitted for the task. Such qualifications can only be developed by early training, and a life-long study of the grand monuments of ancient learning, which (we devoutly believe) have been providentially preserved to us for this, among other reasons, that by the light reflected from the pages of the poets, historians, and philosophers of a

---

[1] Of these three papers the second will be found in its due order, the first and third are printed at the end of the notes. ED.

bygone race and religion, we might be better able to interpret
the records of our own imperishable faith. In making these
remarks, it is not by any means the wish of the Writer, that
documentary proofs should have one grain less than their
due weight in the constitution of the sacred text; but only
that considerations of internal evidence should have FAIR
PLAY; and whenever the preponderance of the former in-
clines to what is absurd in sense or impossible in construction,
that *then* the latter should be allowed to turn the scale. The
former may not inaptly be compared to the *direct* proofs of
guilt in criminal jurisprudence; while the latter partake more
of the nature of what is called *circumstantial* evidence. The
analogy holds good also in regard to the *cogency* of either
description of proof, lawyers invariably insisting, in favour of
the latter, on the point of its being comparatively exempt
from the danger of error or falsification, to which the testimony of alleged eye-witnesses must always be subject.

The foregoing remarks may suffice as an apology for the
greater part of the present work, which is taken up with a
comparison of the venerable A. V. with its more modern
competitors. For the remainder, which is of a more miscel-
laneous character, the Author's excuse must be that the
study of the Greek language and literature, especially in
connexion with the interpretation of the Holy Scriptures of
the Old and New Testaments, has been not so much the
pursuit as the *passion* of a life protracted far beyond the
ordinary limits. In particular, in the illustration of the
phraseology of the writers of the Greek Testament from
classical sources he has found a never-failing fund of delightful
occupation, a small portion of the fruits of which, in the hope
of meeting with a few readers like-minded with himself, he
has included in the following pages. This was a favourite
exercise of the biblical scholars of the eighteenth century,
but has lately fallen into unmerited neglect. Indeed, after
the researches of L. Bos (1700), Hombergk (1712), Heupelius
(1716), Elsner (1720), Alberti (1725), Ottius (from Josephus,

1741), Raphelius (from Xenophon, Polybius, Arrian, and Herodotus, 1747), Ger. Horreus (1749), Palairet (1752), Kypke (1755), Munthe (from Diodorus Siculus, 1755), Krebs (from Josephus, 1755), Koehler (1765), Loesner (from Philo Judaeus, 1777); and especially after the immense collection (partly borrowed, but to a great extent original) of J. J. WETSTEIN (1751), it might be thought that little remained to be gleaned in regard to a comparison of the style of the writers of the Greek Testament with that of classical authors. Still a *spicilegium* there is, as will appear from a cursory glance at the following pages; in which most of the quotations from the Greek classics (unless expressly assigned to Wetstein and others) are due to the Author's own reading of the last three or four years[1], and are now for the first time (as far as he is aware) applied to the elucidation of the sacred text. Being extracted in full, carefully printed, with occasional assistance to the better understanding of them, it is hoped that they will afford no little gratification to the reader, who, in his riper years, has retained, or desires to recover, the fruits of his early culture at school and college.

---

[1] This has embraced the *whole* of the following: Diodorus Siculus, Dionysius Hal. Antiq. Rom., Stobaei Florilegium ed. Gaisford, Alciphron, Achilles Tatius, Antoninus Liberalis, Andocides, Babrii Fabulae, Charito Aphrodisiensis, Philostrati Heroica and Imagines; also parts of Herodotus (VIII), Thucydides (VII, VIII), Lucian (Tom. I, II, III, V, VIII, IX, ed. Bipont.), Plutarchi Vitae (Vol. I, pp. 1-312, Vol. II, pp. 1-393, Vol. III, pp. 1-178, ed. Schaefer.), Diogenes Laert. Lib. I-VI, Pausaniae Corinth., Messen., Lacon.

NORWICH, *September* 14, 1881.

NOTE.

Where 'the Syriac Versions' are quoted in these notes the lately discovered 'Sinaitic' Syriac of the Gospels is not included.   ED.

NOTES ON SELECT PASSAGES

OF THE

GREEK TESTAMENT.

ST MATTHEW.

*Chap. I. 18 : **μνηστευθείσης κ.τ.λ.**] A. V. 'When as his mother Mary was espoused to Joseph.' *When as* or *Whenas* is a good old English combination, though our great Lexicographer has described it as obsolete. He gives examples from Spenser, 'This *when as* Guyon saw,' and Milton, ' *When as* sacred light began to dawn '; but has not noticed the biblical use of it, here and Ecclus. xxxiii. 7 : 'Why doth one day excel another, *when as* all the light of every day in the year is of the sun ?'

The elimination of this 'innocent archaism' is said to be owing to a suggestion of the 'American committee'; though neither set of Revisers appear to have stumbled at the cognate form *while as* in Heb. ix. 8 : 'while as the first tabernacle was yet standing.'

I. 21 : **αὐτὸς γὰρ σώσει**] A. V. 'For he shall save.' The Revised Version, 1881 [R. V.] renders : 'For it is he that shall save.' But this would seem to require αὐτὸς γάρ ἐστιν ὁ μέλλων σώζειν. Compare Matt. xi. 14 : αὐτός ἐστιν Ἠλίας ὁ μέλλων ἔρχεσθαι. Luke xxiv. 21 : ὅτι αὐτός ἐστιν ὁ μέλλων λυτροῦσθαι τὸν Ἰσραήλ. The proposed correction takes for granted that there would be a Saviour, which the Greek does not.

*I. 22 : **τοῦτο δὲ ὅλον γέγονεν**] A. V. 'Now all this was done.' R. V. ' Now all this is come to pass.' The substitution of the perfect tense for the aorist is probably due to the influence of Prof. Lightfoot (*Fresh Revision of N. T.* ed. 1891, p. 101) who fancies he sees in the former ' the freshness of the earliest catechetical narrative, when the narrator was not so far removed from the fact that it was unnatural for him to say, 'This *is* come to pass.' A less ingenious, but, perhaps for that very reason, more probable account of the matter is, that St Matthew, as being ἰδιώτης τῷ λόγῳ, ἀλλ' οὐ τῇ γνώσει, had fallen into a habit of using the perfect tense, in this particular phrase, instead of the aorist (compare ch. xxi. 4, xxvi. 56).

There is little or no choice between 'was done' and 'came to pass'; but the A. V. is amply defended by Luke xiv. 22 : γέγονεν ('it is done') ὡς ἐπέταξας. John xix. 36 : ἐγένετο ('were done') γὰρ ταῦτα. Exod. xxxiv. 10 : ποιήσω ἔνδοξα ἃ οὐ γέγονεν ('such as have not been done') ἐν πάσῃ τῇ γῇ. Dan. ix. 12 : οἷα οὐ γέγονεν (as before) ὑποκάτω παντὸς τοῦ οὐρανοῦ. Also by classical usage, as Plut. *Vit. Anton.* XIV : ἡ δὲ σύγκλητος ἐκύρωσε ταῦτα, καὶ τῶν ὑπὸ Καίσαρος γεγονότων ἐψηφίσατο μηδὲν ἀλλάττειν.

II. 4 : ἐπυνθάνετο παρ' αὐτῶν] A. V. 'He demanded of them.' We accept the R. V. 'he enquired of them'; though Mr Davies has shown (*Bible English*, p. 121) that there was not, in old English, that *peremptoriness* in the use of the word 'demand,' which is now conveyed by it. So in Luke iii. 14, the soldiers 'demanded of him, saying, What shall we do?' where the Greek is simply ἐπηρώτων. And in the Office for Baptism, the priest says, 'I demand therefore, Dost thou in the name of this child' &c.

With the incident related by St Matthew it is interesting to compare Dion. Hal. *Ant.* IV. 59 : συγκαλέσας δὲ (Tarquinius) τοὺς ἐπιχωρίους μάντεις, ἐπυνθάνετο παρ' αὐτῶν, τί βούλεται σημαίνειν τὸ τέρας;

*III. 4 : εἶχε τὸ ἔνδυμα αὐτοῦ ἀπὸ τριχῶν καμήλου] Mark i. 6 : ἐνδεδυμένος τρίχας καμήλου. In Joseph. *B. J.* I. 24, 3, the sons of Mariamne, when they see Herod's other wives exhibiting themselves in her clothes, threaten ὡς ἀντὶ τῶν βασιλικῶν, ἐν τάχει περιθήσουσιν ἑαυταῖς ἐκ τριχῶν πεποιημένας; or, as the same incident is otherwise related by the same historian *Ant. Jud.* (ed. Hudson) XVI. 7, 3, ἀντὶ τῆς παρούσης ἀβρότητος ἀπειλεῖν ὡς τριχέσιν ἠμφιεσμέναι καθειργοῦνται; the former expression coinciding exactly with St Matthew's, the latter with St Mark's.

The error of painters in attiring the Baptist with *a camel's skin* has been pointed out by Sir Thomas Browne (*Vulgar Errors* V. 15), De Rohr (*Pictor errans* p. 11. 2, 9) and others. From Eustath. *ad Il.* τ, p. 1249, 52 : μήπω ἐσθήτων εὑρημένων, περιβλήμασιν ἐχρῶντο τοῖς ἐκ τριχῶν, ἢ καὶ τετριχωμέναις δοραῖς, it plainly appears that a garment ἐκ τριχῶν is *not* a skin with the hair on (τετριχωμένη δορά), in contradiction to C. F. A. Fritzsche's suggestion : 'Might not John wear a camel's skin, and still be clothed in camel's hair?'

St Chrysostom (T. VII. p. 674 D) speaking of the austerity of the monks of his time says that their clothes were made, some of goat's hair (ἀπὸ τριχῶν αἰγῶν), others of camel's hair (ἀπὸ τριχῶν καμήλων) ; adding εἰσὶ δὲ οἷς καὶ ΔΕΡΜΑΤΑ ἤρκεσε μόνον.

*IV. 24 : πάντας τοὺς κακῶς ἔχοντας] A. V. 'all sick people.' R. V. 'all that were sick.' A good Greek phrase, often played upon by the Comic writers, as Stob. *Flor.* T. c. 5 : πολὺ μεῖζόν ἐστι τοῦ κακῶς ἔχειν κακὸν | τὸ καθ' ἕνα πᾶσι τοῖς ἐπισκοπουμένοις | δεῖν τὸν κακῶς ἔχοντα, πῶς ἔχει, λέγειν. *Id.* T. CII. 6 : τίς οὗτός ἐστ'; ἰατρός. ὡς κακῶς ἔχει | ἅπας ἰατρός, ἂν κακῶς μηδεὶς ἔχῃ. Anglicè : 'It is ill with the physician, when nobody is ill.'

V. 22 : 'But whosoever shall say, Thou fool (μωρέ), shall be in danger of hell fire (εἰς τὴν γέενναν τοῦ πυρός).' 'It may be interesting,' says Dean Stanley[1], 'for those who can follow the original, to know that it is not, as is often supposed, a Greek word, nor does it, perhaps, mean *fool*. It is a Hebrew or Syriac word, *moreh*, like the other word *raca* ; and though it, probably, gains an additional strength of meaning from its likeness to the Greek word *morè, fool*, its own proper signification is *rebel* or *heretic*, one who wilfully breaks the laws of his church or country, one who would presume to teach his own teachers. It is the same word which Moses (Num. xx. 10) uses to the Israelites : "Hear now, ye *rebels*." It was, according to the Jewish tradition, for using this offensive word to God's people, that he was forbidden to enter the promised land.'

If, as is here strangely asserted, μωρέ is not a Greek word, then *of course*, not *perhaps*, it does not mean *fool* ; nor, if a Hebrew or Syriac word, can it possibly derive any additional strength from its accidental resemblance to the Greek word. Moreover, Hebrew and Syriac being different languages[2], or agreeing only in particular instances (of which the present is *not* one), it is not enough to describe it as a Hebrew OR Syriac word, but it should be distinctly stated for which of the two languages the claim is preferred.

(1) There is a Syriac word *morè* (ܡܳܪ), and a very common one, as common as κύριος in Greek, or *dominus* in Latin, for which words it is the equivalent, as the emphatic form ܡܳܪܝܐ is for ὁ Κύριος, or *Dominus*. But this honourable title can have no place in our Lord's denunciation ; and, in fact, no other objector to the common interpretation ever suggested that μωρέ is a Syriac word, but always a Hebrew one.

(2) There is a Hebrew word *moreh* (מֹרֶה) which means *contumax, rebellis*, as in the passage from Numbers, and many others. But if μωρέ were intended to represent this, it would enjoy the distinction of being the *only* pure Hebrew word in the Greek Testament (ἀλληλουΐα, ἀμήν, and

---

[1] *The Christian Rule of Speech.* A Sermon preached in Westminster Abbey, July 4, 1869.

[2] Any one may convince himself of this by turning to Gen. xxxi. 47: 'And Laban [the Syrian] called it Jegar-sahadutha (ܣܗܕܘܬܐ ܝܓܪ, *The heap of witness*), but Jacob [the Hebrew] called it Gal-eed' (גַּל־עֵד, *The heap of witness*).

σαβαώθ, as being taken from the LXX., belong to a different class), all other foreign words being indisputably Aramaic, as *raca, talitha kumi*[1], *maran atha*, &c., which, as might have been expected, are retained by the authors of the Syriac versions without alteration. Not so μωρέ, for which both the Peschito and Philoxenian versions have *lelo* (ܠܠܐ), which is also put for μωρός in Matt. vii. 26 (Philox.), and Deut. xxxii. 6, Psal. xciii. 8, and Jerem. v. 21 (all in the Syro-hexaplar version)—a plain proof that these learned Syrians took it for an exotic, and not, like ῥακά, a native word.

As there is no reason for disturbing the A. V. in regard to this word *fool*, so neither can we accept the same learned writer's suggestion as to the remaining part of the sentence—the penalty assigned to the person committing this offence. The use of this term, he says, 'deserves as much shame and reproach as belongs to those whose carcases were thrown out into the Valley of Hinnom—Gehenna, as it was called— where they were burnt up in the fires which consumed all the offal of the city. This is the meaning of the words, which we translate in this place *hell fire*. It is the fire, the funeral pile, the burning furnaces of that dark valley, the Smithfield (?), the slaughter-house, the draught-house of Jerusalem.' The pollution of the Valley of Hinnom, the scene of the horrid rites of Moloch, by Josiah, as related in 2 Kings xxiii. 10, 13, 14, and its subsequent appropriation to the most ignominious purposes, may be accepted as historical facts ; though the additional circumstance of 'burning furnaces,' perpetually maintained for the consumption of the bodies of criminals, carcases of animals, and other *ejecta* of a great city, does not appear to rest on sufficient evidence, but was probably invented *after* the application of the name of this valley to denote *the place of eternal torment*. At all events it is in the latter sense, and in that alone, that the word *Gehenna* is used by our Lord. Indeed, the *applied* sense being once established in the religious nomenclature of the Jews, it is very improbable that the valley itself should continue to be called by the same name, גֵּיהִנֹּם, γέεννα ; nor can any instance be produced of either of these words being so used.

The unusual construction ἔνοχος εἰς τὴν γ. has been variously explained : e.g. by supposing an ellipsis of βληθῆναι (Homberg, Kuinoel) or, according to modern phraseology, a *pregnant construction* for ἔνοχος ὥστε βληθῆναι εἰς τὴν γ. (Alford) ; or by taking εἰς in the sense of ἕως εἰς,

---

[1] Although *talitha* (ܛܠܝܬܐ) is the ordinary Syriac word for 'damsel,' and is so interpreted by St Mark (ὅ ἐστι μεθερμηνευόμενον, τὸ κοράσιον), a writer in the "Sunday at Home" for March 1881, having met with the poetical word טָלֶה, 'a lamb,' in Isai. lxv. 25, not content with suggesting that there may be an etymological connexion between the two, actually translates our Lord's words, 'My lamb—my pet lamb— arise !' Truly, 'A little learning is a dangerous thing.'

usque ad (C. F. A. Fritzsche). But since εἰς is perpetually interchanged with ἐν[1], there seems no objection to take it so here, and then we may compare such examples as Andocid. π. μ. 79 : εἰ δὲ μή, ἔνοχον εἶναι τὸν παραβαίνοντα ταῦτα ἐν τοῖς αὐτοῖς, ἐν οἷσπερ οἱ ἐξ ᾿Αρείου πάγου φεύγοντες.

* The notion of μωρέ being a Syriac or Hebrew word seems to be of recent and, probably, English origin, as it is not mentioned by Wolf, Schleusner, Kuinoel, De Wette &c. It is quoted in Bowyer's *Critical Conjectures*, Lond. 1782, from a work of Sykes on the *Connexion of Natural and Revealed Religion*, p. 426 ; on which Dr Owen remarks : 'This observation is certainly just ; and yet the Syriac interpreter did not take the word in this sense, for he retains *Raka* untranslated, yet he renders *Moreh* by a word that signifies *fool*.'

It is generally understood that Dean Stanley, in taking the view which we have now combated, was under the influence of his friend the late Emmanuel Deutsch of the British Museum ; against whose authority I am now able to set that of Dr A. Neubauer of the Bodleian, who has favoured me with the following communication dated Nov. 24, 1881 : 'You are certainly right for the word μωρέ. But I may be allowed to draw your attention to the fact that this Greek word was much in use with the Jews at the time of Christ. The *Midrash Tanhuma* explains the word המורים (Num. xx. 10): מהו לישנא דמורה אמר ר׳ ראובן כהדין (μωρός) לישנא יונית צווחין לשטיא מורים. In the same *Midrash Tanhuma* Sect. חקת this word is explained (μωροί) בכרכי הים קורין לשוטין מורי. The feminine also is mentioned : (μωρά) לשין יוני צווחין לשטיתא מורא[2].'

* VI. 2, 5 : ἀπέχουσι τὸν μισθὸν αὐτῶν] R. V. 'they have received their reward,' i.e. (says one of the American Revisers) 'they have received all the reward they sought from men, and need not expect any more.' The Greek word by no means implies that human applause was all the reward they sought, but only that it was all they would get ; and this could not be more significantly expressed than by the emphatic 'they HAVE their reward.' In making the change, the Revisers, no doubt, were influenced by the A. V. of Luke vi. 24 'ye have received your

---

[1] Compare v. 35 : (μὴ ὀμόσαι) ἐν τῇ γῇ...μήτε εἰς Ἱεροσόλυμα: where some would render 'toward Jerusalem,' referring to 1 Kings viii. 30, Dan. vi. 10. But in those places the person praying is in a foreign land. [In Luke iv. 44 : 'And he preached in their synagogues' (ἐν ταῖς συν. T. R.), the Revisers have adopted εἰς τὰς σ., but retain 'in.']

[2] Of these quotations Mr Schechter points out that the first is from the *Pesikta d' Rab Kahana*, ed. Buber, p. 118 b : the second is from the *Tanchuma* on Num. xx. 10: and the third is to be found in the Introduction to *Midrash Echah Rabbah* § 31. Mr Schechter also remarks that R. Reuben to whom this interpretation is attributed lived late in the third century after Christ. Ed.

consolation'; but there still remains Philip. iv. 18 (in both versions) 'I HAVE all, and abound[1].'

VI. 27 : 'Which of you by taking thought can add unto his ἡλικία one ———?' The word ἡλικία is ambiguous, signifying either *age* or *stature*; in classical Greek more frequently *age*, in biblical *stature*. We therefore wait for the concluding word to clear up the doubt. Shall it be a measure of *time*, as *year* (Isai. xxxviii. 5 : προστίθημι πρὸς τὸν χρόνον σου δεκάπεντε ἔτη) or of *length*? The answer is conclusive : ΠΗΧΥΝ μίαν. Πῆχυς is not only *a* measure of length, but that by which a man's *stature* was properly measured[2]. Euthymius on this place remarks : καὶ μὴν οὐδὲ σπιθαμήν (half a cubit), οὐδὲ δάκτυλον (a 24th part): λοιπὸν οὖν πῆχυν εἶπε, διότι κυρίως μέτρον τῶν ἡλικιῶν ὁ πῆχύς ἐστι[3]. Thus a short man is τρίπηχυς, a tall man τετράπηχυς (as Aristoph. *Vesp.* 553 : ἄνδρες μεγάλοι καὶ τετραπήχεις. Philostr. *Imag.* I. 24 : καὶ καλούς, καὶ τετραπήχεις ἐκ μικρῶν). We read in the Martyrdom of St Eusignius (Montfaucon, *Pal. Gr.* p. 27): ἀποδύσαντες οὖν αὐτὸν οἱ στρατιῶται εἰσήγαγον· καὶ ἰδοὺ ἦν ὁ ἀνὴρ τριῶν ἥμισυ πηχῶν (a medium height). Above four cubits the stature became gigantic, as Diodorus Siculus (I. 55) says of the statue of Sesostris, τῷ μεγέθει τέτταρσι παλαισταῖς μείζονα τῶν τεττάρων πηχῶν, adding, ἥλικος (*qua statura*) ὢν καὶ αὐτὸς ἐτύγχανεν (4⅔ cubits)[4] ; and Plutarch (*Vit. Alex.* 60) of Porus, τὸν Πῶρον ὑπεραίροντα τεσσάρων πηχῶν σπιθαμῇ τὸ μῆκος (4½ cubits). Of scriptural examples we have 1 Chron. xi. 23 an Egyptian, ἄνδρα ὁρατὸν πεντάπηχυν, slain by Benaiah ; and Goliath of Gath, 1 Sam. xvii. 4, whose height was ἐξ πήχεων καὶ σπιθαμῆς. To which may be added the bedstead of Og (Deut. iii. 11), 'nine cubits was the length

---

[1] Philologians do not seem to have appreciated the Hebrew phrase בָּא אֵלַי, *pervenit ad me*, addressed (1) by Joseph's steward to his brethren (Gen. xliii. 23): 'Your money came to me'; and (2) by the representatives of the 2½ tribes to Moses (Num. xxxii. 19): 'We will not inherit with them on yonder side Jordan ...because our inheritance is fallen to us (בָּאָה אֵלֵינוּ) on this side Jordan east- ward.' In both cases it seems to be implied, that the speaker had no further claim on the person addressed, an idea which is also suggested by the A. V. of the former place, 'I HAD your money.' Now it is remarkable that the 'Penta- teuch Company' of the LXX. (who were in an especial degree *docti utriusque linguae*) have in both places used the very word, which best expresses this idea : in the first, τὸ ἀργύριον ὑμῶν 'ΑΠΕΧΩ ; in the second, ὅτι 'ΑΠΕ- ΧΟΜΕΝ τοὺς κλήρους ἡμῶν ἐν τῷ πέραν τοῦ 'Ιορδάνου ἐν ἀνατολαῖς.

[2] [Cf. Aristaen. *Ep.* I. 5 : ἔτι δὲ εὐμήκης ἡλικία.]

[3] Cf. Aristot. *Metaph.* 9 (p. 183 Bekker): ὥσπερ ἂν εἰ ἄλλου ἡμᾶς με- τροῦντος ἐγνωρίσαμεν πηλίκοι ἐσμὲν τῷ τὸν πῆχυν ἐπὶ τοσοῦτον ἡμῖν ἐπιβάλλειν.

[4] Herodotus (II. 106) says of the same statue, in his peculiar manner, μέγαθος πέμπτης σπιθαμῆς (4½ cubits); and Eusebius (from Manetho) πηχῶν δ παλαιστῶν γ δακτύλων β (4¹⁷/₃₂ cubits). But such precision in the measure- ment of stature is of very rare occurrence.

thereof, and four cubits the breadth of it, after the cubit of a man'; and Nebuchadnezzar's image of gold (Dan. iii. 1) 'whose height was threescore cubits, and the breadth thereof six cubits.'

The other interpretation, *age*, would, probably, never have been thought of, had it not been for the place in Psal. xxxix. 5 (where Symmachus inserts ὡς before παλαιστάς, and so both our English versions); which does not at all defend the present text: first, because in the Psalm there is no ambiguous word to be guarded against; and, secondly, because we are not required, as here, to solve the curious problem 'Find the sum of so many years + one cubit.'

* It may be interesting to the admirers of *conjectural criticism* to give one more instance of πῆχυς as a measure of stature from a fragment of Alcaeus preserved by Strabo (XIII. 2. 3), if only to show *quantum criticus critico praestet.* The geographer's text has corruptly κτείνοντ' ἄνδρα μαχαιτάν, ὥς φησι, βασιλήων παλαιστάν, ἀπολιπόντα μόνον ἀνίαν τ' ἀχέων ἀποπέμπων. Bishop Blomfield (*Mus. Crit.* I. 444) proposes to read κτείνων ἄνδρα μαχαιτάν; βασιλῆα παλαιστάν, ἀπὸ λοιγόν τ' ἀμύνων, ὀνίαν τ' ἀχέων ἀποπέμπων. Now compare with this 'prentice-work the hand of a master (O. Müller): παλαιστὰν ἀπολείποντα μόνον μίαν παχέων ἄπο πέμπων, '(in stature) wanting only one span of five cubits.' Compare Herod. I. 60: (γυνὴ) μέγαθος ἀπὸ τῶν τεσσέρων πηχέων ἀπολείπουσα τρεῖς δακτύλους.

* VIII. 3: θέλω, καθαρίσθητι] A. V. 'I will, be thou clean.' 'This,' says Jeremiah Markland, 'seems to be as strong an instance of the sublime, as that more noted one in Genesis i. "Let there be light[1]."' One is tempted to ask, is anything gained in respect to faithfulness in the R. V. 'I will; be thou made clean,' to compensate for the appreciable loss of sublimity?

* VIII. 14: βεβλημένην καὶ πυρέσσουσαν] A. V. 'laid, and sick of a fever.' R. V. 'lying sick of a fever.' This is Tyndale's version. Cranmer's, 'lying in bed, and sick of a fever,' is to be preferred, as distinguishing between the two conditions of the woman, (1) as 'keeping her bed' (Exod. xxi. 18), and (2) as 'being in a fever.' See on Luke xvi. 20.

* XI. 28: κοπιῶντες] '*that labour*,' or, 'are weary,' as the version of Geneva. Both meanings are undoubted, but the use of the LXX. is in favour of the latter, of which good examples are 2 Kings (Sam.) xvii. 2: 'I will come upon him,' καὶ αὐτὸς κοπιῶν (יָגֵעַ) καὶ ἐκλελυμένος τὰς χεῖρας 'while he is weary and weak-handed.' Isai. xl. 30: πεινάσουσι γὰρ νεώτεροι, καὶ κοπιάσουσι νεανίσκοι. I add S. Chrysost. T. XI. p. 106 A: οὐχ ἁπλῶς ἡμᾶς ἐργάζεσθαι βούλεται, ἀλλ' ὥστε κοπιᾶν, ὥστε ἑτέροις μεταδιδόναι, where Hales has a note 'Lege ἀλλὰ κοπιᾶν. Nam quid est ἐργάζεσθαι ὥστε κοπιᾶν?' But compare the same T. IX. p. 700 A: ἀλλὰ τοσαῦτα ἐβάδιζεν, ὥστε καὶ κοπιᾶσαι (alluding to Joh. iv. 6).

[1] [Cf. Bowyer's *Critical Conjectures*, ad loc. Ed.]

* XI. 29 : ἄρατε τὸν ζυγόν μου ἐφ᾽ ὑμᾶς...καὶ εὑρήσετε ἀνάπαυσιν ταῖς ψυχαῖς ὑμῶν] Canon Farrar remarks (*Life of Christ*, ed. 1888, p. 90) 'It is probable, though not certain, that he (Christ) was acquainted with the un-canonical books,' comparing this passage of St Matthew with Sirac. li. 26, 27 : τὸν τράχηλον ὑμῶν ὑπόθετε ὑπὸ ζυγόν...ὅτι ὀλίγον ἐκοπίασα, καὶ εὗρον ἐμαυτῷ πολλὴν ἀνάπαυσιν ; also Luke xiv. 28 : τίς γὰρ ἐξ ὑμῶν, θέλων πύργον οἰκοδομῆσαι κ.τ.λ. with 2 Macc. ii. 29 : καθάπερ γὰρ τῆς καινῆς οἰκίας ἀρχιτέκτονι τῆς ὅλης καταβολῆς φροντιστέον, τῷ δὲ ἐγκαίειν καὶ ζωγραφεῖν ἐπιχειροῦντι τὰ ἐπιτήδεια πρὸς διακόσμησιν ἐξεταστέον κ.τ.λ. In the former example a slight verbal coincidence may be conceded, in the latter none at all. A much better than either is Sirac. xxviii. 2 : ἄφες ἀδίκημα τῷ πλησίον σου, καὶ τότε δεηθέντος σου αἱ ἁμαρτίαι σου λυθήσονται compared with Matth. vi. 12. Outside the Gospels Prof. Plumptre (Farrar l. c.) 'has observed that James "the Lord's brother" certainly makes allusions to the Apocrypha (cf. James i. 6, 8, 25 with Ecclus. vii. 10; i. 28; xiv. 23).' In all these the resemblance is of the very slightest, in the last consisting in the single word παρακύπτειν, which, moreover, the apocryphal writer uses in its proper sense (of *looking in through the window*), the canonical in a figurative one. Here also a better example might have been found in close proximity to the others, viz. James i. 19 : ταχὺς εἰς τὸ ἀκοῦσαι, which is a palpable reminiscence of Ecclus. v. 11 : γίνου ταχὺς ἐν ἀκροάσει σου.

XIII. 12 : δοθήσεται καὶ περισσευθήσεται] A. V. 'To him shall be given, and he shall have more abundance (R. V. have abundance).' But περισσευθήσεται, like δοθήσεται, is *impersonal*, and may be resolved into περισσῶς δοθήσεται, 'and given in abundance.' Compare John x. 10 (R. V.): 'I came that they may have life, and may have it abundantly (ἵνα ζωὴν ἔχωσιν, καὶ περισσὸν ἔχωσιν).'

XIII. 15 : καὶ ἐπιστρέψωσι] A. V. 'And should be converted.' R. V. 'And should turn again.' In the LXX., wherever we find ἐπιστρέψαι in an intransitive sense, the A. V. is 'turn,' 'return,' or 'turn again,' with the single exception of the place here quoted by our Lord (Isai. vi. 10), where we read, 'and convert.' Any one of these is to be preferred to that which the Translators of the N.T. have three times, in quoting the words of Isaiah, substituted for it, 'and be converted,' an expression not in harmony with the voluntary acts of seeing, hearing, and under-standing, with which it is joined, and which, moreover, from its being popularly used in the present day in a different sense, is liable to misconstruction[1]. The same objection does not apply to the intransitive

---

[1] A notable instance of such mis-construction is Matt. xviii. 3 : 'Except ye be converted,' &c., where it is im-possible to believe that our Translators would have employed this term, if they had supposed that it would ever be understood (as it is now universally understood by common readers) of the

form 'to convert,' as used by A. V. in Isai. vi. 10, and elsewhere by the older translators. Thus Coverdale, 2 Kings xxiii. 25: 'Which so *converted* unto the Lord with all his heart'; and Nehem. ix. 28: 'So they *converted*, and cried unto thee'; and Cranmer, Acts iii. 19: 'Repent and *convert.*' See other examples in Davies, *Bible English*, p. 70. If this term, now obsolete, had been adopted in all places instead of the other, the question so often asked among a certain class of religious persons would no longer have been, '*Are* you converted?' but '*Have* you converted?'

*XIII. 36 : τότε ἀφεὶς τοὺς ὄχλους] A. V. 'Then Jesus sent the multitude away.' R. V. 'Then he left the multitudes.' Also Mark iv. 36 : καὶ ἀφέντες τὸν ὄχλον. A. V. 'And when they (the disciples) had sent away the multitude.' R. V. 'And leaving the multitude.' Dean Burgon in defence of the A. V. remarks (*Revision Revised*, p. 194 sq.): 'It is found to have been our Saviour's practice to "send away" the multitude whom he had been feeding or teaching, in some formal manner...The word employed to designate this practice on two memorable occasions is ἀπολύειν (Matt. xiv. 15, 22, 23; xv. 32, 39; Mark vi. 36, 45; viii. 9; Luke ix. 12); on the other two (see above) ἀφιέναι. This proves to have been perfectly well understood as well by the learned authors of the Latin version of the N. T. as by the scholars who translated the Gospels into the vernacular of Palestine.' The Latin version, in all cases, is *dimissis* (not *relictis*) *turbis*; but both Syriac versions agree in distinguishing ἀφιέναι from ἀπολύειν, rendering the former by ܐܘܒܩ (ἀφῆκε, κατέλιπε, εἴασε), and the latter by ܫܪܐ (ἀπέλυσε). While protesting, as strongly as the Dean himself, against the 'pedantic striving after uniformity of rendering' of the same Greek word (ἀφείς) by the same English one, we must insist upon dealing with every case on its merits. Now in the former of the two texts at the head of this note, Jesus 'went out of the house, and sat by the sea side, and there were gathered unto him great multitudes,' who stood on the beach, while he taught them from a boat. His discourse being ended, he 'left (ἀφείς) the multitudes, and went into the house,' some of them, no doubt, attending him to the very door, and then, without any formal dismissal, each returning to his own home. Here is no 'sending the multitudes away,' the utmost pressure that can be put on ἀφείς being that he 'let them go.' Still less, in the other case, is there a question of any formal dismissing or leave-taking; for there it is our Lord himself who proposes to his disciples to 'go over unto the other side'; and his disciples who 'take him with them, even as he was, in the boat'; which they could not do

general 'conversion' of a sinner, and not of a specific change in the temper and disposition of those to whom it was addressed: 'Except ye *turn*, and become as little children,' &c.

without 'leaving the multitude' on this side; though to 'send them away' to their respective homes, would seem perfectly needless, whether on his part, or (still more) on theirs.

We do not deny that the general sense of 'dismissal' is common to both words, but not without a certain distinction, which may best be illustrated by an example. The president of a public meeting, when the business is finished, 'dismisses the assembly' (Acts xix. 41 : ἀπέλυσε τὴν ἐκκλησίαν), which disperses its several ways. A schoolmaster also, when the clock strikes, 'dismisses' his juvenile charge, who scamper away to their sports. Here then seems to be an occasion for the less formal and official term of the two. And it is at hand. In English, 'the playful children' are not 'just *dismissed*,' but 'just LET LOOSE from school.' And in Greek (Aelian *V. H.* XII. 9), Timesias παρῄει διὰ (*praeter*) διδασκαλείου, οἱ δὲ παῖδες ᾿ΑΦΕΘΕΝΤΕΣ ὑπὸ τοῦ διδασκάλου ἔπαιζον.

In Matthew l. c. of the older English translators, only Wickliff has 'left'; in Mark 'leaving' is supported by Wickliff, Tyndale, Cranmer and Geneva.

XIII. 54 : **εἰς τὴν πατρίδα αὐτοῦ**] '*into his own country.*' The word 'country' carries with it to the English reader the idea of a man's *native land*, instead of his *native place* or *town*, which is the proper meaning of the Greek word, both in the N. T. and in profane authors. From the latter we may instance Stob. *Flor.* T. XLIV. 21 (from the laws of Zaleucus): πόλιν δὲ φιλαιτέραν μηδεὶς ἄλλην ποιείσθω τῆς αὐτοῦ πατρίδος. Appian. VI. 38 : ἐς πόλιν ἦν ἀπὸ τῆς ᾿Ιταλίας ᾿Ιταλικὴν (Italica in Spain) ἐκάλεσε (Scipio), καὶ πατρίς ἐστι Τραϊανοῦ τε καὶ ᾿Αδριανοῦ. Ach. Tat. I. 3: ἐμοὶ Φοινίκη γένος, Τύρος ἡ πατρίς[1]. 'Into their own country' is the rendering of εἰς τὴν χώραν αὐτῶν, ch. ii. 12.

XIV. 6 : ὠρχήσατο...ἐν τῷ μέσῳ] A. V. 'before them.' R. V. 'in the midst.' ᾿Εν τῷ μέσῳ is *in publico, coram omnibus*, as in the well-known phrases ἐν μέσῳ στρέφεσθαι, εἰς μέσον προελθεῖν, &c.[2] With the present example I compare Lucian. *De Morte Peregr.* 8 : τί γὰρ ἄλλο, ἔφη, ὦ ἄνδρες, χρὴ ποιεῖν...ὁρῶντας ἄνδρας γέροντας, δοξαρίου καταπτύστου ἕνεκα, μονονουχὶ κυβιστῶντας ἐν τῷ μέσῳ; (dancing on their heads in public)[3].

[1] [Cf. Ael. *V. H.* XII. 54: ἐξ ὧν καὶ τὴν πατρίδα (Stagira) κατῴκισε κατεσκαμμένην ὑπὸ Φιλίππου (Aristoteles).]

[2] [Cf. Mark iii. 3: ἔγειρε εἰς τὸ μέσον. Both A. V. and R. V. have 'stand forth,' but R. V. in margin 'Gr. arise into the midst.']

[3] [Cf. Plut. *Vit. Caesar* XXVIII: οἱ μὲν ἀρχὰς μετιόντες ἐν μέσῳ θέμενοι τραπέζας ἐδέκαζον ἀναισχύντως τὰ πλήθη.

Mox: πολλοὶ δ᾿ ἦσαν οἱ καὶ λέγειν ἐν μέσῳ τολμῶντες. *Id. Vit. Tim.* v : ἔγνω ζῆν καθ᾿ ἑαυτὸν ἐκ μέσου γενόμενος, XIV: διαπληκτιζόμενον ἐν μέσῳ τοῖς ἀφ᾿ ὥρας ἐργαζομέναις γυναιοῖς. Dio. Chrys. XXXIII. p. 395, 33: τῶν καλουμένων ἰατρῶν, οἳ προκαθίζοντες ἐν τῷ μέσῳ..., LXVI. p. 604, 14: οὐδένα ἀνθρώπων βούλεται λανθάνειν, ἀλλ᾿ ἐν μέσῳ ταῦτα ποιεῖ.]

XIV. 8: προβιβασθεῖσα ὑπὸ τῆς μητρός] A. V. 'Being before instructed of her mother.' R. V. 'Being put forward by her mother.' This latter is objectionable, because the damsel, even if she had retired from the banquet, must have *come forward* of her own accord to signify her choice of a gift. Other proposed renderings are 'set on,' 'urged on,' &c. But when we consider that προβιβάζειν is used by the LXX. in a very similar manner (e.g. Deut. vi. 7 : προβιβάσεις αὐτὰ τοῖς υἱοῖς σου) we shall see no reason for departing from the Vulgate *praemonita*, from which the A. V. is taken. But instead of 'before instructed' perhaps 'instructed' would be sufficient, the instruction necessarily preceding the action. Compare Ach. Tat. VII. 1: ἔμελλε δ' ἐκεῖνος, ὑπὸ τοῦ Θερσάνδρου δεδιδαγμένος, κ.τ.ἑ.[1] In Acts xix. 33: ἐκ δὲ τοῦ ὄχλου προεβίβασαν Ἀλέξανδρον, 'They brought Alexander out of the multitude,' the Revisers have given as an alternative version, 'Some of the multitude *instructed* Alexander[2].'

XVI. 5 : καὶ ἐλθόντες οἱ μαθηταὶ αὐτοῦ εἰς τὸ πέραν, ἐπελάθοντο ἄρτους λαβεῖν] A. V. 'And when his disciples were come to the other side, they had forgotten to take bread.' R. V. 'And the disciples came to the other side, and forgot to take bread.' But the omission having taken place before they set out on their voyage (Mark viii. 14), though not discovered till they were come to the other side, the A. V. has rightly used the *plusquam perfectum*, 'they had forgotten', *per breviloquentiam* for 'they found that they had forgotten.' So the best expositors, both ancient and modern ; as Beza, 'viderunt se oblitos fuisse'; Bois, 'senserunt se oblitos fuisse'; Fritzsche, 'Audire tibi videaris ipsos admirantes, *Non cibos nobiscum tulimus.*' Again in v. 7, the A. V. 'Saying, *It is* because we have taken no bread,' is, for the English reader, a more correct version of the Greek, λέγοντες, Ὅτι ἄρτους οὐκ ἐλάβομεν, than the R. V. 'Saying, We took no bread.'

XVI. 21 : τῇ τρίτῃ ἡμέρᾳ] The phrases used in the N.T. to indicate the day of our Saviour's resurrection in respect to that of his crucifixion are *three*. (1) τῇ τρίτῃ ἡμέρᾳ. (2) μετὰ τρεῖς ἡμέρας. (3) Once (Matt. xii. 40) it is intimated that he should be in the grave τρεῖς ἡμέρας καὶ τρεῖς νύκτας.

(1) The first of these is by far the most common, being found eight times in the Gospels, and once (1 Cor. xv. 4) in St Paul. It has long been taken as certain and indisputable that the interval between the days on which the Church has from the beginning commemorated these two

---

[1] [Cf. Plut. *Vit. Crass.* v: ὡς δ' ἀπεκρίναντο δεδιδάχθαι (' as they had been instructed'). *id.* II. 256: ἡ κόρη παρῆγεν αὐτὸν ὑπὸ τῆς μητρὸς διδασκομένη, καὶ ἀνέπειθεν ἐλευθεροῦν τὴν πόλιν.]

[2] From a note made in his copy of the *Otium Norvicense* it is evident that

Dr Field considered the Revisers to have translated συνεβίβασαν in the text, and προεβίβασαν in the margin of their version. According to Dr Scrivener (*The Parallel New Testament Greek and English*) the Revisers read συνεβίβασαν in either case. Ed.

events is that indicated by τῇ τρίτῃ ἡμέρᾳ, of which phrase the others are merely variations. But as it has been lately questioned, 'whether there are not grounds for doubting the correctness of the common opinion[1],' it may be as well to show, by examples both from sacred and profane authors, that when a speaker uses the phrase τῇ τρίτῃ ἡμέρᾳ or only τῇ τρίτῃ, he invariably means *the next day but one*, and not *the next day but two*. If there were the smallest ambiguity in the use of the phrase, if it could possibly indicate *either* of the two days, as the occasion might require, then the familiar use of it must be given up altogether; I could not ask my friend to dine with me τῇ τρίτῃ, unless we both perfectly understood what day was intended.

'To-day, to-morrow, the day after to-morrow.' In Greek, σήμερον, αὔριον, τῇ τρίτῃ. Examples: Luke xiii. 32: ἰάσεις ἐπιτελῶ σήμερον καὶ αὔριον, καὶ τῇ τρίτῃ τελειοῦμαι. (In the next verse for τῇ τρίτῃ, *the third day*, is substituted τῇ ἐχομένῃ, *the next day*.) Acts xxvii. 18, 19: τῇ ἑξῆς ἐκβολὴν ἐποιοῦντο· καὶ τῇ τρίτῃ αὐτόχειρες τὴν σκευὴν τοῦ πλοίου ἐρρίψαμεν. Exod. xix. 10, 11: ἅγνισον αὐτοὺς σήμερον καὶ αὔριον...καὶ ἔστωσαν ἕτοιμοι εἰς τὴν ἡμέραν τὴν τρίτην. 1 Sam. xx. 12: מָחָר הַשְּׁלִשִׁית, for which LXX. have only τρισσῶς (omitting מָחָר altogether), but in the Hexapla after τρισσῶς there is an insertion: αὔριον καὶ εἰς τρίτην. Epict. *Arr.* IV. 10: ὅτι αὔριον ἢ εἰς τὴν τρίτην δεῖ ἢ αὐτὸν ἀποθανεῖν ἢ ἐκεῖνον. Plut. *Vit. Phoc.* XXII: 'When many rushed to the βῆμα, crying out that the report was true, and that Alexander was dead, οὐκοῦν, εἶπεν, εἰ σήμερον τέθνηκε, καὶ αὔριον ἔσται καὶ εἰς τρίτην τεθνηκώς, so that we need not be in a hurry.' Id. *Vit. Lys.* X: τῇ δ' ὑστεραίᾳ πάλιν ἐγίνοντο ταυτά, καὶ τῇ τρίτῃ μέχρι τετάρτης. Xenoph. *Cyrop.* VIII. 7, 5: ὡς δὲ καὶ τῇ ὑστεραίᾳ συνέβαινεν αὐτῷ ταυτα, καὶ τῇ τρίτῃ, ἐκάλεσε τοὺς παῖδας κ.τ.ἑ. Aristoph. *Pax*, 894: ἔπειτ' ἀγῶνα δ' εὐθὺς ἐξέσται ποιεῖν | ταύτην (*Pacem*) ἔχουσιν αὔριον καλὸν πάνυ...τρίτῃ δὲ μετὰ ταῦθ' ἱπποδρομίαν ἄξετε. Antiph. Περὶ τοῦ Χορευτοῦ, p. 145, 19: οὗτοι γὰρ τῇ μὲν πρώτῃ ἡμέρᾳ ᾗ ἀπέθανεν ὁ παῖς, καὶ τῇ ὑστεραίᾳ ᾗ προέκειτο, οὐδ' αὐτοὶ ἠξίουν αἰτιᾶσθαι ἐμέ...τῇ δὲ τρίτῃ ἡμέρᾳ ᾗ ἐξεφέρετο ὁ παῖς κ.τ.ἑ. (There was a law of Solon ἐκφέρειν τὸν ἀποθανόντα τῇ ὑστεραίᾳ ᾗ ἂν προθῶνται.) We may add the express testimony of Porphyrius (*Quaest. Hom.* 14) quoted by Wetstein on Matt. xii. 40: καὶ γὰρ ὁ ληγούσης ἡμέρας ἐπιδημήσας, καὶ τῆς τρίτης ἕωθεν ἐξιών, τῇ τρίτῃ ἀποδημεῖν λέγεται, καίτοι μίαν τὴν μέσην ὅλην ἐτέλεσεν[2].

---

[1] Westcott, *Introduction to the Study of the Gospels*, p. 348 (6th ed.). In a note at p. 349 the author, after enumerating the phrases above named and one or two others, remarks: 'It will scarcely be denied that the obvious meaning of these phrases favours the longer interval which follows from the strict interpretation of Matt. xii. 40.' *Obvious*, that is, to an English reader, who is not familiar with other ways of reckoning besides his own. To a scholar, as to a native Hebrew or Greek, the obvious meaning not only *favours* the shorter interval, but *makes any other impossible*.

[2] [So a *tertian* fever is one that returns every other day. Lucian. *Philops.* 19: ὁπότε μ' ἰάσατο διὰ τρίτης ὑπὸ τοῦ ἠπιάλου ἀπολλύμενον.]

As might be expected, the same rule was observed in reckoning backward: 'To-day, yesterday, *the day before yesterday* (τῇ τρίτῃ).' Thus Xenoph. *Cyrop.* VI. 3, 11: καὶ ἐχθὲς δὲ καὶ τρίτην ἡμέραν τὸ αὐτὸ τοῦτο ἔπραττον. Antiphon[1] in Lex. Reg. (MS.) ἐχθὲς μετὰ πέντ' ἔπινον, ἡμέραν τρίτην μεθ' ἑπτά. Lucian. *Halc.* 3: ἑώρακας, Χαιρεφῶν, τρίτην ἡμέραν (*nudius tertius*) ὅσος ἦν ὁ χειμών; To this agrees the Hebrew idiom בִּתְמוֹל שִׁלְשׁוֹם, ὡσεὶ χθὲς καὶ τρίτην ἡμέραν (Gen. xxxi. 2; Exod. v. 7).

(2) The phrase μετὰ τρεῖς ἡμέρας is only another form for τῇ τρίτῃ ἡμέρᾳ, with which it is interchanged Mark viii. 31; Matt. xxvii. 63, 64. So Gen. xlii. 17, 18, Joseph 'put his brethren into ward ἡμέρας τρεῖς, and he said unto them τῇ ἡμέρᾳ τῇ τρίτῃ.' In 2 Chron. x. 5: πορεύεσθε ἕως τριῶν ἡμερῶν, καὶ ἔρχεσθε πρὸς μέ is otherwise expressed v. 12: ἐπιστρέψατε πρὸς μὲ τῇ ἡμέρᾳ τῇ τρίτῃ. And lastly, in Hos. vi. 2: ὑγιάσει ἡμᾶς μετὰ δύο ἡμέρας, ἐν τῇ ἡμέρᾳ τῇ τρίτῃ ἐξαναστησόμεθα, the former note of time cannot mean *after two complete days*, or it would be identical with 'on the third day,' but must be understood as equivalent to ἐν τῇ ἡμέρᾳ τῇ δευτέρᾳ. So of years: Shalmaneser came up against Samaria and besieged it in the *fourth* year of King Hezekiah, 'and *at the end of three years* (ἀπὸ τέλους τριῶν ἐτῶν) they took it, even in the *sixth* year of Hezekiah' (2 Kings xviii. 9, 10).

(3) The remaining passage (Matt. xii. 40) will not detain us long. The particular form of speech, *three days and three nights*, there used to express the same interval with the two former, is evidently accommodated to the language of the O.T. narrative of the history of Jonah. Even in that narrative it is not at all certain that the words are to be construed according to the strict literal meaning of them, the *usus loquendi* in all languages admitting of a certain laxity in such cases, which being well understood is not liable to misapprehension. We have a similar case in the book of Esther (iv. 16), who sends word to Mordecai, 'Go, gather all the Jews that are present in Shushan, and fast ye for me, and neither eat nor drink *three days night or day;* I also and my maidens will fast likewise, and so will I go in unto the king.' Yet it is certain that she did not herself fast, according to the strict letter of the prescribed term, *three days, night and day;* for we read in the next chapter (v. 1): 'Now it came to pass *on the third day* (ἐν τῇ ἡμέρᾳ τῇ τρίτῃ) that Esther put on her royal apparel, and stood in the inner court of the king's house.'

XVII. 27: καὶ ἀνοίξας τὸ στόμα αὐτοῦ εὑρήσεις στατῆρα] 'And when thou hast opened his mouth, thou shalt find a piece of money.' It would seem impossible to twist these words into any meaning but that which they would convey to a child, who might be told to do the same thing at the present day. Yet they have been tampered with even by writers who do not deny the possibility of miracles in general, or of this in particular; and who would probably repudiate such an interpretation of them as that

---

[1] See Ruhnken, *Diss. de Antiph. Graec.* III. p. 156. Ed. p. 248, and Meineke, *Frag. Com.*

given by Paulus and others, whose day is long since past : 'Postquam piscem hami vinculo liberaveris, staterem eo vendito lucraberis.' What else can be the meaning of Canon Farrar's remark (*Life of Christ*, Chap. XXXVIII.) : 'The literal translation of our Lord's words may most certainly be, "on opening its mouth, thou shalt get, or obtain, a stater"'? Yet *finding* and *getting* are not the same thing. I *find* what I sought or looked for, in the present case, a piece of money in a fish's mouth : but if, in the ordinary course of business, I take a fish to market, and sell it for the same sum, I *get*, but I cannot be said, either in Greek or English, to *find* it. That εὑρήσεις is properly used in the former case is evident from the similar incident (except that it was fortuitous, not miraculous) related by Herodotus (III. 42) : τὸν δὲ ἰχθὺν τάμνοντες οἱ θεράποντες εὑρίσκουσι ἐν τῇ νηδύϊ αὐτοῦ ἐνεοῦσαν τὴν Πολυκράτεος σφρηγῖδα. And it is also true that the same verb is used, by a peculiarity of the Greek language, of *selling*; but in that case it is not the seller, but the article sold, which *finds* (or, as we should say, *fetches*) the price for which it is sold. Thus Charit. Aphrod. I. 10 : λυσιτελέστερον εἶναι πωλῆσαι τὴν γυναῖκα· τιμὴν γὰρ εὑρήσει διὰ τὸ κάλλος. Theophr. *Char.* XV. 1 : καὶ πωλῶν τι, μὴ λέγειν τοῖς ὠνουμένοις, πόσου ἂν ἀποδοῖτο, ἀλλ' ἐρωτῶν, τί εὑρίσκει (what is it worth?).

XVIII. 25 : μὴ ἔχοντος δὲ αὐτοῦ ἀποδοῦναι] A. V. 'But forasmuch as he had not to pay.' R. V. 'had not *wherewith* to pay.' The same phrase recurs Luke vii. 42, where A. V. less correctly : 'when they had nothing to pay[1].' In all such cases we may take ἔχω as not differing in sense from δύναμαι, 'he was not able to pay.' So, without the infinitive, Mark xiv. 8 : ὃ ἔσχεν ἐποίησε, 'she hath done what she could.' This use of ἔχειν is common in the best authors, but generally in the same connexion of *paying*; e.g. Plut. *Vit. Cato Maj.* XV : (mulctam) ἦν οὐκ ἔχων ἐκεῖνος ἀπολύσασθαι, καὶ κινδυνεύων δεθῆναι, μόλις ἐπικλήσει τῶν δημάρχων ἀφείθη. Id. *Vit. Pericl.* XXII : τὸν μὲν βασιλέα χρήμασιν ἐζημίωσαν, ὧν τὸ πλῆθος οὐκ ἔχων ἐκτῖσαι, μετέστησεν ἑαυτὸν ἐκ Λακεδαίμονος. Lucian. *Chronos.* 15 : καὶ τὸ ἐνοίκιον, οἵτινες ἂν καὶ τοῦτο ὀφείλοντες καταβαλεῖν μὴ ἔχωσι. Diod. Sic. T. X. p. 145 ed. Bip. (quoted by Wetstein) : ἐνστάντος δὲ τοῦ ὁρισθέντος (χρόνου) καὶ μὴ ἔχων ἀποδοῦναι, πάλιν ἔταξε λ' ἡμερῶν προθεσμίαν (where *dele* καί)[2].

*XIX. 11 : οὐ πάντες χωροῦσι τὸν λόγον τοῦτον] A. V. 'All men cannot receive this saying.' A writer in the *Expositor* for April, 1882, says : 'An inaccuracy for "All men receive not," though the fact that it is not indefensible is shewn by its acceptance by our Revisers.' But since χωρεῖν is not to *receive*, but to *contain*, i.e. *be capable of receiving*, the rendering objected to is perfectly correct.

[1] [Cf. Luke xiv. 14: οὐκ ἔχουσιν ἀνταποδοῦναί σοι. R. V. 'they have not *wherewith* to recompense thee.']

[2] [Cf. Lucian. *Hist. Conscr.* 42: ὡς, εἴ ποτε καὶ αὖθις τὰ ὅμοια καταλάβοι, ἔχοιεν, πρὸς τὰ προγεγραμμένα ἀποβλέποντες, εὖ χρῆσθαι τοῖς ἐν ποσί.]

XIX. 27 : τί ἄρα ἔσται ἡμῖν ;] In an anonymous version published by
G. Morrish, London (no date), these words are rendered : 'What then
shall happen to us?' But the phrase is classical as well as biblical, to
signify, 'What reward shall we have?' Wetstein quotes two good
examples from Xenophon, *Anab.* I. 7, 8 : ἀξιοῦντες εἰδέναι, τί σφισιν ἔσται,
ἐὰν κρατήσωσι. II. 1, 10 : λεγέτω τί ἔσται τοῖς στρατιώταις, ἐὰν αὐτῷ ταῦτα
χαρίσωνται. I add 1 Kings (Sam.) xvii. 26 : τί ποιηθήσεται τῷ ἀνδρὶ ὃς ἂν
πατάξῃ τὸν ἀλλόφυλον ἐκεῖνον; as quoted from memory by St Chrysost.
T. IX. p. 734 D : εἰ δὲ λέγει, τί ἔσται τῷ ἀνελόντι τὸν ἀλλόφυλον τοῦτον ; οὐ
μισθὸν ἀπαιτῶν ἔλεγεν κ.τ.ἑ.[1]

XXI. 13 : σπήλαιον λῃστῶν] 'a den (or cave) of robbers.' The phrase
is taken from Jerem. vii. 11 : μὴ σπήλαιον λῃστῶν ὁ οἶκός μου...ἐνώπιον
ὑμῶν; The propriety of the comparison will be better seen, if we take
into the account John ii. 14, where besides the moneychangers and
sellers of doves are specially mentioned 'those that sold oxen and sheep,'
a characteristic feature of the interior of those spacious caverns in which
brigands were wont to house, not themselves only, but the droves of
cattle which formed the chief produce of their successful raids. Thus we
read in Dion. Hal. *Ant.* I. 39 that Hercules, when he had slain the
robber Cacus, and recovered the stolen cattle from the cave to which
they had been driven, ἐπειδὴ κακούργων ὑποδοχαῖς εὔθετον ἑώρα τὸ χωρίον,
ἐπικατασκάπτει τῷ κλωπὶ τὸ σπήλαιον (buried the thief in the ruins of his
own cave).

XXI. 42 : παρὰ κυρίου ἐγένετο αὕτη] Literally : 'This was from the
Lord.' But both here and in Psal. cxviii. 23 the thoroughly English
rendering, 'This is the Lord's doing,' so admirably represents the sense
of the Hebrew and Greek originals, that it seems almost an act of
sacrilege to disturb it, especially if it should turn out that the O.T.
revisers have abstained from doing so[2]. Still more objectionable is the
attempt of Fritzsche, Meyer and others to account for the gender of αὕτη
by making its antecedent to be κεφαλή, 'This (head of the corner) was
from the Lord,' when every Hebrew scholar knows that the pronoun
זֹאת, αὕτη, though properly feminine, is also used for the neuter τοῦτο, and
ought so to have been translated by the LXX. in this and other places :
e.g. 1 Sam. iv. 7 : οὐαὶ ἡμῖν, ὅτι οὐ γέγονε τοιαύτη (כָּזֹאת) ἐχθὲς καὶ τρίτην.
1 Kings xi. 39 : καὶ κακουχήσω τὸ σπέρμα Δαυὶδ διὰ ταύτην (זֹאת לְמַעַן) πλὴν
οὐ πάσας τὰς ἡμέρας, where after ταύτην Cod. 247 interpolates τὴν πλάνην.

---

[1] [Cf. Aesop. *Fab.* 356: τί μοι ἔσται
πρώτῃ σοι εἰπούσῃ;]

[2] [Cf. Gen. xxiv. 50: παρὰ Κυρίου
ἐξῆλθε τὸ πρᾶγμα τοῦτο. 1 Kings xii.
24: ὅτι παρ' ἐμοῦ γέγονε τὸ ῥῆμα τοῦτο.

Liban. I. 225: αὐτὸ τοῦτο τὸ νῦν ἐμὲ καὶ
ζῆν καὶ λέγειν...παρὰ τῆς Ἀρτέμιδός
μοι σαφέστατα, ὦ ἄνδρες. App. *B. C.*
III. 65: καὶ τάδε μοι παρ' ὑμῶν, ὦ συ-
στρατιῶται, γέγονεν.]

*XXII. 2 : ἐποίησε γάμους. 8 : ὁ μὲν γάμος ἕτοιμος] There does not seem to be any distinction between the plural and the singular, though γάμοι is generally used by good writers, when the marriage *feast* is principally intended : e.g. Diog. L. *Vit. Plat.* II : τελευτᾷ δ', ὥς φησιν Ἕρμιππος, ἐν γάμοις δειπνῶν. Xenoph. Eph. II. 7 : ὁ δὲ Ἄψυρτος ἐποίει τῆς θυγατρὸς τοὺς γάμους, καὶ ἑώρταζον πολλαῖς ἡμέραις. Diod. Sic. XIII. 84 : Ἀντισθένης...γάμους ἐπιτελῶν τῆς θυγατρός, εἱστίασε τοὺς πολίτας ἐπὶ τῶν στενωπῶν ὧν ᾤκουν ἕκαστος. Aelian, *Ep. penult.* : ἐγὼ μὲν ἔθυον γάμους (τοῦ υἱοῦ) ὁ χρυσοῦς μάτην, καὶ περιῄειν ἐστεφανωμένος οὐδὲν δέον. Ach. Tat. V. 14 : καὶ ὄνομα μὲν ἦν τῷ δείπνῳ γάμοι, τὸ δὲ ἔργον (*concubitum*) συνέκειτο ταμιεύεσθαι. But the plural is sometimes used for *marriage* in the abstract, as Lucian *Am.* 51 : γάμοι μὲν ἀνθρώποις βιωφιλὲς πρᾶγμα. Plut. II. p. 27 A : ἅτε δὴ τρυφῶσα καὶ γάμων ὥραν ἔχουσα. On the other hand γάμος in the singular is often found in the Greek Bible for a marriage feast, as Gen. xxix. 22 : συνήγαγε δὲ Λάβαν πάντας τοὺς ἄνδρας τοῦ τόπου, καὶ ἐποίησε γάμον (Heb. מִשְׁתֶּה, *convivium*). I Macc. x. 58 : καὶ ἐξέδοτο αὐτῷ Κλεοπάτραν τὴν θυγατέρα αὐτοῦ, καὶ ἐποίησε τὸν γάμον αὐτῆς ἐν Πτολεμαΐδι...ἐν δόξῃ μεγάλῃ. In the passage before us the most suitable English word both for γάμοι and γάμος will be found to be 'a wedding,' which includes both the actual ceremony, and the festivities thereupon.

*XXII. 23 : προσῆλθον αὐτῷ ΣαδδουκαῖΟΙ, ΟΙ λέγοντες μὴ εἶναι ἀνάστασιν] Here, in deference to the principal uncials and other authorities, later Editors omit οἱ, according to which reading we must understand that they came to him, saying that there is no resurrection. But this is absurd. Their opinions on this subject were well known to our Lord, and any formal statement of them would have been impertinent. But as they might not be so well known to the reader, the writer himself inserts a parenthetical remark, which prepares his readers for what was to follow, and what the Sadducees really 'came to him saying.' So Mark xii. 18 : οἵτινες λέγουσιν ἀνάστασιν μὴ εἶναι, and Luke xx. 27 : οἱ ἀντιλέγοντες ἀνάστασιν μὴ εἶναι. The cause of the omission is patent.

*XXII. 27 : ὕστερον δὲ πάντων] A. V. 'And last of all.' This is better, perhaps, for the English reader than the more literal rendering, (R. V.) 'And after them all.' Ὕστερον is here used as a preposition, as in Dion. Hal. v. 1 : ὀλίγαις ἡμέραις ὕστερον τῆς ἐκβολῆς τοῦ τυράννου. Jerem. xxxi. 19 : ὅτι ὕστερον αἰχμαλωσίας μου μετενόησα, καὶ ὕστερον τοῦ γνῶναί με ἐστέναξα.

*XXII. 36 : ποία ἐντολὴ μεγάλη ἐν τῷ νόμῳ] Here no MS. supplies the article ἡ after ἐντολή ; yet it is certain that we must either suppose it to have been accidentally omitted by a transcriber, or we must take μεγάλη in the sense of μεγίστη. The rendering, adopted by Dean Alford and others, 'What commandment is great in the law?' is perfectly

unmeaning.   C. F. A. Fritzsche, who denies the use of μεγάλη for
μεγίστη, arrives at the same result by a roundabout way, explaining
ἐντολὴ μεγάλη to mean 'a law, which you may rightly and truly call great,
so that the others, be they ever so great in themselves, appear small in
comparison with it.'   What is this but THE GREAT COMMANDMENT?

*XXIII. 4 : 'For they bind heavy burdens...and lay them on men's
shoulders, but they themselves will not move them with their finger
(αὐτοὶ δὲ τῷ δακτύλῳ αὐτῶν οὐ θέλουσι κινῆσαι αὐτά).'   The scope of this
charge, forming part of a general denunciation of the hypocrisy of the
scribes and Pharisees, can hardly (one would suppose) admit of a doubt.
It is the same thought as that which is expanded by St Paul in
Rom. ii. 21—23 : 'Thou therefore that teachest another' &c.   But a
writer in the *Leisure Hour* for August 1881, criticizing certain passages
of the R. V. 'chiefly from the Jewish point of view,' upsets all this
by simply denying the truth of the accusation, as thus understood.   'The
passage cannot, therefore, mean that the Pharisees laid on others burdens
which they did not touch ; nor yet, as has been suggested, that they did
not sympathize with, or help others in their burdens.'   The latter
suggestion may be safely put aside ; as to the former, if the common
understanding is not the true one, we would fain know what is.   This
our critic proceeds to show.   The Pharisees, he says, claimed the power
of 'binding and loosing,' and what they are here charged with is that
they exercised this power of 'binding,' or laying heavy burdens on the
shoulders of their disciples, but made no use of the 'loosing' or
'dispensing' power, when occasion required, in spite of one of the
special warnings given them in the Talmud.   'A more heavy burden
ought not to be laid on a congregation, unless the larger part of it is able
to bear it.'   Our Lord, therefore, in this passage, must be understood to
charge the Pharisees with uncharitableness, because they bound heavy
burdens &c. *while with their finger they would not move them away ;* in
other words, remove, as they might have done, even the slightest part of
them.   Thus far the 'Jewish' point of view, to reconcile which with the
'grammatical' we are informed that κινεῖν means not only to 'move,' but
also to 'remove,' as in Rev. ii. 5 : 'I will remove (κινήσω) thy candlestick
out of its place'; where, however, the addition of ἐκ τοῦ τόπου αὐτῆς
makes it a matter of indifference whether we translate 'move,' as the
Revisers, or 'remove,' as A. V.   But κινεῖν in connexion with a heavy
weight, and in contrast with the act of bearing it upon the shoulders, can
only be understood of a simple *moving* or *stirring* of it, especially when
it is added 'with the finger,' or, as the phrase is varied in Luke xi. 46 :
'Ye touch not (οὐ προσψαύετε) the burdens with one of your fingers,'
recalling the familiar Greek proverb ἄκρῳ τῷ δακτύλῳ ἅψασθαι, for *leviter
attingere.*   So we find it used in a Scholium on Lucian, *De conscrib.
Hist.* 34, where one Titormus a herdsman, in a trial of strength with Milo

of Crotona, takes the biggest stone he can find, and after sundry manipulations with it, τέλος ἀράμενος ἐπὶ τῶν ὤμων ἔφερεν ὡς ἐπ' ὀργυιὰς ῡ, καὶ ἔρριψεν αὐτόν; while his antagonist, a professed athlete, μόγις τὸν λίθον ᾽ΕΚΙΝΗΣΕΝ.

*XXIII. 25 : γέμουσιν ἐξ ἁρπαγῆς καὶ ἀκρασίας] This seems to be a *locutio praegnans* for γέμουσι τῶν ἐξ ἁρπαγῆς καὶ ἀκρασίας συνειλεγμένων. The full phrase is found in Lucian. *Tim.* 23 : ἄχρις ἂν...ἐν ἀκαρεῖ τοῦ χρόνου ἄθλιος ἐκχέῃ τὰ κατ' ὀλίγον ἐκ πολλῶν ἐπιορκιῶν καὶ ἁρπαγῶν καὶ πανουργιῶν συνειλεγμένα.

XXIII. 38 : 'Your house is left unto you desolate.' I would print 'Your House' (comparing Isai. lxiv. 11 : 'Our holy and beautiful House, where our fathers praised thee'), and in Luke xi. 51 : 'which perished between the altar and the House' [A. V. 'temple,' R. V. 'sanctuary']. Other explanations of ὁ οἶκος ὑμῶν have been proposed[1], but none so simple, and to Jewish ears so familiar. Theophylact and Euthymius are quoted for this sense, but not St Chrysostom, although there is no doubt he so understood the words. In his exposition of St Matthew he rather assumes than declares it; but in another passage (*Hom.* LXV. on St John, p. 389 E) he is very clear : 'But even thus [after the High Priesthood had been made an affair of purchase] the Spirit was still present. But when they lifted up their hands against the Messiah, then he left them, and transferred himself to the Apostles. And this was indicated by the rending of the veil, and the voice of Christ, which said, "Behold, your House is left unto you desolate."' There is, however, no foundation for the gloss which Dean Alford puts upon the phrase, 'no more God's, but *your* house.' It rather means 'the house you are so proud of.'

XXIV. 4 : μή τις ὑμᾶς πλανήσῃ] A. V. 'That no man deceive you.' R. V. 'That no man lead you astray.' Again, John vii. 12 : πλανᾷ τὸν ὄχλον, the same versions give respectively, 'He deceiveth the people,' and 'He leadeth the multitude astray.' There is really no sound reason for the change, nor have those who introduced it attempted to carry it out uniformly. Thus in 2 Tim. iii. 13 they retain 'Deceiving and being deceived.' In Matt. xxvii. 63 ἐκεῖνος ὁ πλάνος is still 'that deceiver,' and in Rev. xii. 9 ὁ πλανῶν τὴν οἰκουμένην ὅλην, 'the deceiver of the whole world.' The glossaries give Πλανᾷ· ἀπατᾷ. Πλάνος· ἀπατεών.

*XXIV. 45 : Τίς ἄρα ἐστὶν ὁ πιστὸς δοῦλος κ.τ.ἑ.] 'A question asked *that each one may put it to himself*—and to signify the high honour' of such an one'—*Alford*. Rather, to intimate the *rarity* of such a

---

[1] Alford characteristically : '*Your house*—said primarily of the temple— then of Jerusalem—and then of the whole land in which ye dwell.'

character. S. Basil, T. III. p. 7 B (*De Sp. Sancto* V) : Τίς ἔγνω νοῦν κυρίου, καὶ τίς σύμβουλος αὐτοῦ ἐγένετο; Τὸ γὰρ, τίς, ἐνταῦθα οὐχὶ τὸ ἄπορον παντελῶς, ἀλλὰ τὸ σπάνιον δηλοῖ, ὡς ἐπὶ τοῦ, Τίς ἀναστήσεταί μοι ἐπὶ πονηρευομένους; καὶ, Τίς ἐστιν ἄνθρωπος ὁ θέλων ζωήν; καὶ, Τίς ἀναβήσεται εἰς τὸ ὄρος τοῦ κυρίου;

XXV. 8 : αἱ λαμπάδες ἡμῶν σβέννυνται] Here the rendering of R. V. 'are going out' is greatly to be preferred to that of A. V. 'are gone out.' Compare Prov. xxxi. 18 : οὐκ ἀποσβέννυται ὅλην τὴν νύκτα ὁ λύχνος αὐτῆς. Charit. Aphrod. I. 1 : ὥσπερ τι λύχνου φῶς ἤδη σβεννύμενον ἐπιχυθέντος ἐλαίου πάλιν ἀνέλαμπε.

*XXV. 21 : 'Thou hast been faithful ἐπὶ ὀλίγα, over a few things.' If it were ἐπὶ ὀλίγων, we might explain the preposition from the clause which immediately follows, 'when set over a few things.' As it is, ἐπὶ seems to have the force of *quod attinet ad*, as in 1 Cor. vii. 36 : εἰ δέ τις ἀσχημονεῖν ἐπὶ τὴν παρθένον αὐτοῦ νομίζει. If so, it may be not improperly rendered 'in a few things,' which is the construction in Luke xix. 17 : ἐν ἐλαχίστῳ πιστὸς ἐγένου ; and xvi. 10 : ὁ πιστὸς ἐν ἐλαχίστῳ καὶ ἐν πολλῷ πιστός ἐστι. But perhaps 'over a few things' may be defended by Heb. iii. 6 : Χριστὸς δὲ (πιστὸς) ὡς υἱὸς ἐπὶ τὸν οἶκον αὐτοῦ.

XXV. 27 : καὶ ἐλθὼν ἐγὼ ἐκομισάμην ἂν τὸ ἐμὸν σὺν τόκῳ] 'And at my coming I should have received (back) mine own with usury.' In Luke xix. 23 for ἐκομισάμην the word is ἔπραξα, 'I should have demanded (lit. *exacted*) it.' Instead of ἐλθών, in this sense, we should rather have expected ἐπανελθών, especially in St Luke (compare v. 15 : καὶ ἐγένετο ἐν τῷ ἐπανελθεῖν αὐτὸν λαβόντα τὴν βασιλείαν). This objection, however, is not conclusive against the A. V., because we find ἐλθών so used in good writers, as Plut. *Vit. Pomp.* XLVII : τότε δὲ Καῖσαρ ἐλθὼν ἀπὸ στρατείας ἥψατο πολιτεύματος. Dion. Hal. *Ant.* VIII. 57 : εἰ μὲν εὖ πράξας ὁ Μάρκιος ...ἔλθοι[1]. But it is remarkable that in both Gospels the pronoun ἐγώ is so used as if it were intended to be *emphatic*, as it certainly was understood to be by St Chrysostom on St Matthew (T. VII. p. 754 B) : αὐτὸς δὲ οὐχ οὕτως· ἀλλὰ ΣΕ ἔδει καταβαλεῖν, φησί, καὶ τὴν ἀπαίτησιν ΕΜΟΙ ἐπιτρέψαι. If we accept this view of the parable, we must translate : 'And I should have gone (to the bank) and received back mine own (or demanded it) with interest.' Compare Matt. ii. 8 : ὅπως κἀγὼ ἐλθὼν προσκυνήσω αὐτόν. viii. 7 : ἐγὼ ἐλθὼν θεραπεύσω αὐτόν.

XXVI. 15 : οἱ δὲ ἔστησαν αὐτῷ τριάκοντα ἀργύρια] A. V. 'And they covenanted with him for (R. V. and they weighed unto him) thirty pieces of silver.' Hieron.: *At illi constituerunt ei triginta argenteos.* So both Syriac versions (ܘܩܡܘ ܠܗ); and this explanation of the phrase,

---

[1] [Cf. Dio Chrys. *Or.* XI. p. 171.   μήτε πρότερον μήτε ὕστερον, ἐλθὼν ἀπ' 36 : καὶ γὰρ ἦν δεινὸν, εἰ Νέστωρ μὲν,   Ἰλίου....]

which is that of Theophylact (οἱ δὲ ἔστησαν λ̄ ἀργύρια, ἀντὶ τοῦ συνεφώνησαν, ἀφώρισαν δοῦναι, οὐχ ὡς οἱ πολλοὶ νοοῦσιν, ἀντὶ τοῦ ἐζυγοστάτησαν), Grotius, Bois, Elsner, and others, still finds its advocates in the present day (e.g. Alford (who relies chiefly on the ἐπηγγείλαντο of Mark, and the συνέθεντο of Luke), Fritzsche ('non tam ob locos parallelos Marci et Lucae, quam ob verba τί θέλετέ μοι δοῦναι—αὐτόν; quibus bene respondent, *illi autem triginta siclos se daturos ei polliciti sunt*') and others). But this use of στῆσαι cannot be proved. In Gen. xxiii. 17: ἔστη ὁ ἀγρὸς...τῷ ᾿Αβραὰμ εἰς κτῆσιν, nothing is said about the price, and in v. 20, for the very same Hebrew, in the Greek is ἐκυρώθη ὁ ἀγρὸς τῷ ᾿Αβραάμ, 'the field *was made sure* to him,' which is a very different thing from agreeing about the price. On the other hand, the biblical use of ἔστησαν ἀντὶ τοῦ ἐζυγοστάτησαν is undoubted. Besides the place of Zechariah (xi. 12) καὶ ἔστησαν τὸν μισθόν μου λ̄ ἀργυροῦς, 'So they weighed for my hire thirty pieces of silver,' we have in Jeremiah (xxxii. 9) the identical construction of St Matthew: καὶ ἔστησα αὐτῷ τὸ ἀργύριον, ἑπτὰ σίκλους καὶ δέκα ἀργυρίου. We find the same construction, only with *telling* instead of *weighing*, in profane authors, as Dion. Hal. *Ant.* IV. 62: ἐκέλευσαν ἀπαριθμῆσαι τῇ γυναικὶ τὸ χρυσίον ὅσον ᾔτει. And even in the present transaction, we need not suppose that actual scales and weights were introduced, but only that the older form of speech remained in use long after the practice had become obsolete.

XXVI. 50: ἐφ' ὃ πάρει] A. V. 'Wherefore art thou come?' R. V. '*Do* that for which [or, *wherefore*, as Acts x. 21] thou art come.' So the words are rightly explained by Euthymius: δι' ὃ παραγέγονας· ἤγουν τὸ κατὰ σκοπὸν πρᾶττε, τοῦ προσχήματος ἀφιέμενος. The sentiment is the same as in John xiii. 27, where also the traitor is addressed: ὃ ποιεῖς, ποίησον τάχιον. The phrase ἐφ' ο πάρει may be illustrated from Ach. Tat. VIII. 16: ἀγνοοῦσαν τὴν ἀλήθειαν ἐφ' ὃ παρῆν. Lucian. *Pseudomant.* 53: ἐρωτηθεὶς γὰρ ἐφ' ὅ τι ἧκε, θεραπείαν, ἔφη, αἰτήσων πρὸς ὀδύνην πλευροῦ. Aelian. *V. H.* VI. 14: καὶ δριμὺ ἐνιδών, τί οὖν οὐ δρᾶτε τοῦτο, εἶπεν, ἐφ' ὃ καὶ ὡρμήσατε;[1]

XXVI. 61: διὰ τριῶν ἡμερῶν] Not 'in three days' (ἐν τρισὶν ἡμέραις, Ch. xxvii. 40, John ii. 19); nor 'within three days' (A. V. Mark xiv. 58); but 'after three days.' So Mark ii. 1: δι' ἡμερῶν, 'after some days'; Acts xxiv. 17: δι' ἐτῶν πλειόνων, 'after many years'; Gal. ii. 1: διὰ δεκατεσσάρων ἐτῶν, 'after fourteen years'; Deut. xv. 1: δι' ἑπτὰ ἐτῶν (מִקֵּץ שֶׁבַע־שָׁנִים). Classical usage agrees: e.g. Stob. *Flor.* T. XLIV. 41: Σαυρομάται διὰ τριῶν ἡμερῶν σιτοῦνται εἰς πλήρωσιν. Aelian. *V. H.* XIII. 42: οἰκίσαι δὲ Μεσσήνην δι' ἐτῶν τριάκοντα καὶ διακοσίων[2].

---

[1] [Cf. Soph. *Oed. Col.* 1280: λέγ', ὦ ταλαίπωρ', αὐτὸς ὢν χρείᾳ πάρει.] πόσου χρόνου φοιτᾷν ταῖς πόλεσιν εἰώθεν. Ὁ δὲ ἔφη, διὰ μ̄ ἐτῶν, ἐνίοτε δὲ καὶ διὰ λ̄ (῞Ορκος loquitur).]

[2] [Cf. Aesop. *Fab.* 372: ἠρώτα διὰ

XXVII. 3: ἀπέστρεψε τὰ λ ἀργύρια τοῖς ἀρχιερεῦσι] For ἀπέστρεψε, 'he brought back,' the uncials BLא read ἔστρεψε, which is supposed to be not different in sense from the other. But this is not so. Examples of ἀποστρέφειν, to bring back, are very common; as Gen. xliii. 12: τὸ ἀργύριον τὸ ἀποστραφὲν ἐν τοῖς μαρσίπποις ὑμῶν ἀποστρέψατε μεθ᾽ ὑμῶν. Deut. xxii. 1: 'If thou seest thy brother's ox...go astray, ἀποστροφῇ ἀποστρέψεις αὐτὰ τῷ ἀδελφῷ σου.' But the simple verb στρέφω has no such meaning; and the only instance referred to by Dean Alford, Isai. xxxviii. 8: ἐγὼ στρέφω (הֵשִׁיב) τὴν σκιάν, 'I will cause the shadow to return,' is quite different, though even there ἀποστρέφω would be more appropriate, and is so used in the very same verse.

XXVII. 24: ὅτι οὐδὲν ὠφελεῖ] 'that he prevailed nothing.' John xii. 19: ὅτι οὐκ ὠφελεῖτε οὐδέν, 'how ye prevail nothing.' This sense of 'prevail' for 'to be of use' seems to require confirmation. Somewhat similar is 1 Kings xxii. 22: 'Thou shalt persuade him, and prevail also'; but there the Greek is καίγε δυνήσῃ. In James v. 16 we read: 'The prayer of a righteous man availeth much'; but there also the word is ἰσχύει, not ὠφελεῖ. There seems to be no reason why we should not keep close to the Greek: 'When Pilate saw that he did no good'; 'Perceive ye how ye do no good at all.' Compare Job xv. 3: 'With speeches wherewith he can do no good' (ἐν λόγοις οἷς οὐδὲν ὄφελος)[1]. In classical Greek (e.g. Thucyd. II. 87: τέχνη ἄνευ ἀλκῆς οὐδὲν ὠφελεῖ) the phrase is current, generally of things; of persons, οὐδὲν ἀνύει, or οὐδὲν ὀνίνησι is preferably employed[2]. St Matthew goes on: ἀλλὰ μᾶλλον θόρυβος γίνεται, 'but that rather a tumult was made.' This is the generally received rendering; for which one might prefer with Fritzsche (since the tumult had already begun) 'but that the tumult was increasing,' were it not for the absence of the article, which such a construction would seem to require. Thus Thucyd. VII. 25: καὶ τὸν ἐκεῖ πόλεμον μᾶλλον ἐποτρύνωσι γίγνεσθαι (should be carried on more vigorously).

XXVII. 28—31. With this irony of the Roman soldiery it is interesting to compare a grim jest which was wont to be played off by the Mediterranean pirates, of whose unbounded insolence many anecdotes are recorded by Plutarch in his life of Pompey XXIV. 'But the most contemptuous circumstance of all was, that when they had taken a prisoner, and he cried out that he was a Roman (Civis Romanus sum), they pretended to be struck with terror, smote their thighs, and fell upon their knees (προσέπιπτον αὐτῷ) to ask his pardon; and that his quality might no more be mistaken, some put calcei on his feet, others threw a toga around him (οἱ μὲν ὑπέδουν τοῖς καλτίοις αὐτόν, οἱ δὲ τήβενναν περιέ-

---

[1] [Cf. Tobit ii. 10: 'I went to the physicians and they helped me not,' οὐκ ὠφέλησαν.]

[2] [Cf. περαίνειν: Plut. Vit. Tim. x: τί γὰρ ἂν καὶ περαίνειν ἀπειθῶν;]

βαλλον), the official costume of a Roman citizen. When they had made game of him (κατειρωνευσάμενοι αὐτόν) for some time, they let down a ladder into the sea, and bade his worship go in peace ; and if he refused, they pushed him off the deck, and drowned him.'

*XXVII. 48: ἐπότιζεν αὐτόν] 'gave him to drink.' An honoured correspondent (not a divine) writes to me : 'There is a point (of which I have seen no notice) which appears to me to shew that at least two of the evangelists were eye-witnesses of the crucifixion. It is *the sudden-ness of death after drinking.* In speaking of *impalement*, which, in a physiological sense (destruction by fretting of branch-nerves, without injury to any vital organ) appears to resemble crucifixion, Lord Byron says :

> "Oh water ! water !—smiling hate denies
> The victim's prayer ; for if he drinks, he dies."'

On which we remark : (1) that there is no mention of *water* through-out the narrative of the crucifixion ; (2) that the first offer (ἔδωκαν, ἐδίδουν) of drink (Matt. xxvii. 34, Mark xv. 23), 'wine mingled with gall' or 'myrrh,' was the act of the soldiers before the crucifixion, and was refused by their victim (γευσάμενος οὐκ ἤθελε πιεῖν, οὐκ ἔλαβε) : (3) that the second offer (a sponge full of vinegar), from one of the bystanders, took place immediately after the exclamation 'My God &c.' Whether this was accepted by the sufferer, is not quite clear, as the word in both evangelists (Matt. xxvii. 48, Mark xv. 36) is ἐπότιζεν, which may mean only that they offered him this refreshment. According to both these evangelists his last outcry and death followed immediately. St John (xix. 28—30) agrees, with the additional circumstance that our Lord invited the refreshment, and, when it was offered, accepted it : ὅτε οὖν ἔλαβε τὸ ὄξος Ἰησοῦς, εἶπε, Τετέλεσται κ.τ.έ.

XXVIII. 3 : ἦν δὲ ἡ ἰδέα αὐτοῦ (A. V. 'his countenance.' R. V. 'his appearance') ὡς ἀστραπή] There seems no sufficient reason for the change. A man's ἰδέα is his *form* or *aspect*, which, as distinguished from his raiment, is chiefly shown in his *countenance.* Compare Dan. i. 15 : 'And at the end of ten days their countenances (αἱ ἰδέαι αὐτῶν) appeared fairer and fatter in flesh than all the children which did eat the portion of the king's meat.' The classical usage of the word does not differ from the biblical, e.g. Diod. Sic. III. 8 : The Ethiopians ταῖς μὲν χρόαις εἰσὶ μέλανες, ταῖς δὲ ἰδέαις σιμοί (flat-nosed), τοῖς δὲ τριχώμασιν οὖλοι. Plut. *Vit. Flamin.* 1 : ἰδέαν μὲν ὁποῖος ἦν πάρεστι θεάσασθαι τοῖς βουλομένοις ἀπὸ τῆς ἐν Ῥώμῃ χαλκῆς εἰκόνος. Philostr. *Her.* p. 160 ed. Boiss. : ἢ οὐδὲν περὶ τῆς ἰδέας αὐτοῦ ὁ Πρωτεσίλεως ἑρμηνεύει ;[1]

---

[1] [Cf. Plut. *Vit. Brut.* 1 : ἀναφέρειν ἐνίους πρὸς τὸν ἀνδριάντα τοῦ Βρούτου τὴν ὁμοιότητα τῆς ἰδέας. Paus. X. 19, 2 : Some fishermen drew up πρόσωπον, made of olive wood—τοῦτο ἰδέαν παρέσχετο φέρουσαν μὲν εἰς τὸ θεῖον ξείνην

XXVIII. 14 : ἐὰν ἀκουσθῇ τοῦτο ἐπὶ τοῦ ἡγεμόνος] 'If this come to the governor's ears.' R. V. in margin : 'Or, *come to a hearing before the governor*.' So Dean Alford : 'Not only *come to the ears of the governor*[1], but, *be borne witness of before the governor*, come before him officially.' But this supposed judicial sense of ἀκουσθῇ seems rather to be suggested by the vernacular idiom (according to which we speak of a cause being 'ripe for hearing,' being 'part heard') than by the usage of the Greek word[2]. Compare John vii. 51, Acts xxv. 22, where it is the *accused* that is heard, not the *cause*. And the usual understanding of the passage is quite unobjectionable : 'If this be heard (talked of) before the governor.' Compare Mark ii. 1 : 'It was noised (ἠκούσθη) that he was in the house.'

δὲ.... Plut. *Vit. Demetr.* 11 : μεγέθει μὲν ἦν τοῦ πατρὸς ἐλάσσων, ἰδέᾳ τε καὶ κάλλει προσώπου θαυμαστὸς καὶ περιττός. Id. *Vit. Galbae* 9 : καὶ μᾶλλον ἐδόκει κάθ᾽ ὁμοιότητα τῆς ἰδέας ἐκείνῳ προσήκειν. But Plut. 11. p. 257 E : περίβλεπτον μὲν ἰδέᾳ σώματος καὶ ὥρᾳ.]

[1] [The literal Greek version of the English idiom is found in Liban. 1. 195 : ἕως εἰς ὦτα τοῖς βασιλεῦσιν ἀφίκοιτο.]

[2] In Acts xxv. 21 Paul 'appeals to be reserved unto the *hearing* of Augustus,' but there the Greek is διάγνωσις (R. V. 'decision').

ST MARK.

*Chap. I. 7 : λῦσαι τὸν ἱμάντα τῶν ὑποδημάτων αὐτοῦ] In one word ὑπολῦσαι αὐτόν, a servile office. Compare Plat. *Symp.* p. 213 B: ὑπολύετε, παῖδες, Ἀλκιβιάδην. Plut. *Vit. Pomp.* LXXIII : ἰδὼν ὁ Φαώνιος, οἰκετῶν ἀπορίᾳ, τὸν Πομπήϊον ἀρχόμενον αὐτὸν ὑπολύειν, προσέδραμε, καὶ ὑπέλυσε, καὶ συνήλειψε, where Langhorne *oscitanter*, 'to wash himself'…'washed him.'

*I. 27 : τί ἐστι τοῦτο; τίς ἡ διδαχὴ ἡ καινὴ αυτη; ὅτι κατ' ἐξουσίαν κ.τ.έ.] This is the T. R. which is supported by AC, the Vulgate and both Syriac versions. A shorter reading is that of BLℵ : τί ἐστι τοῦτο; διδαχὴ καινὴ κατ' ἐξουσίαν κ.τ.έ. for which Tischendorf gives : 'What is this? A new doctrine with authority! He commandeth' &c. Dean Alford : 'What thing is this? It is a teaching new and with authority. He commandeth' &c. R. V. 'What is this? a new teaching! with authority he commandeth' &c. This last is to be preferred so far as it separates κατ' ἐξουσίαν from διδαχή, and joins it with ἐπιτάσσει, which is confirmed by Luke iv. 36 : ὅτι ἐν ἐξουσίᾳ καὶ δυνάμει ἐπιτάσσει κ.τ.έ. ; but the clumsy device of putting the two words διδαχὴ καινή *extra constructionem*, by interpolating a note of admiration after them, is tantamount to a confession that the reading, as a whole, cannot be construed. If the speaker had intended to utter an exclamation of surprise, he would have said, ὡς (or τί) καινὴ ἡ διδαχή! or ὦ τῆς καινῆς διδαχῆς! or, without the interjection, τῆς καινῆς διδαχῆς![1] One is surprised to be told by Dean Alford, that the shorter reading 'seems to have been the original, and to have been variously conformed to the parallel place in St Luke,' who has only τίς ὁ λόγος οὗτος, ὅτι ἐν ἐξουσίᾳ κ.τ.έ. We should rather have supposed that the T. R. of St Mark had been conformed to Acts xvii. 19 : δυνάμεθα γνῶναι, τίς ἡ καινὴ αὕτη ἡ ὑπὸ σοῦ λαλουμένη διδαχή; if it could be proved that the copyists were in the habit of interpolating the Gospels from the Acts, as well as from one another.

---

[1] Babr. *Fab.* XCIII : καινῆς γε ταύτης, εἶπε, τῆς μεσιτείας! where the note of admiration is mine.

I. 30 : κατέκειτο πυρέσσουσα] 'lay sick of a fever.' Rather, 'kept her bed (A. V. Exod. xxi. 18), being sick of a fever.' Compare Plut. *Vit. Cic.* XLIII : (being summoned to a meeting of the Senate) οὐκ ἦλθεν, ἀλλὰ κατέκειτο, μαλακῶς ἔχειν ἐκ τοῦ κόπου σκηπτόμενος[1].

II. 23 : ἤρξαντο ὁδὸν ποιεῖν τίλλοντες τοὺς στάχυας] 'They began, as they went, to pluck the ears of corn.' R. V. adds in margin : ' Gr. *began to make* their *way plucking.*' The explanation, that the disciples made themselves a road through the corn by plucking the ears, is usually attributed to Meyer, but was long ago noticed and refuted by Rosenmüller, who rightly objects that such a wanton act of mischief would have been unlawful on any day, let alone the Sabbath. It is even as old as Euthymius, who, in his commentary on the parallel place of St Matthew, says : Ὁ δὲ Μάρκος εἶπεν . . . . ἐπεὶ γὰρ μέσον τῶν σπορίμων διήρχοντο, ἅμα μὲν ἀνέσπων τοὺς στάχυας, ἵνα προβαίνειν ἔχοιεν, ἅμα δὲ ἤσθιον τοὺς ἀνασπωμένους. But though the distinction between ὁδὸν ποιεῖν (= ὁδοποιεῖν) 'to make a road,' and ὁδὸν ποιεῖσθαι 'to make a journey,' holds good in Classical Greek[2], some latitude must be allowed for the writers of the N. T., whose style was confessedly modified by their familiarity with the Greek version of their Scriptures. Now the usage of the LXX. is clearly proved from Jud. xvii. 8 : 'And he came to mount Ephraim to the house of Micah, *as he journeyed*' (Heb. *in making his way;* LXX. : τοῦ ποιῆσαι τὴν ὁδὸν αὐτοῦ).

III. 10 : ὥστε ἐπιπίπτειν αὐτῷ] 'Insomuch that they pressed upon him.' R. V. in margin : 'Gr. *fell.*' The examples of ἐπιπίπτειν quoted by Kypke, Elsner, and Wetstein are in favour of the meaning, *to fall upon, attack suddenly, assault,* which is not suitable to this place. A better one from Thucydides (VII. 84) seems to have been overlooked : ἄθροοι γὰρ ἀναγκαζόμενοι χωρεῖν ἐπέπιπτόν τε ἀλλήλοις καὶ κατεπάτουν.

III. 21 : οἱ παρ' αὐτοῦ] A. V. 'his friends. Or, *kinsmen.*' Hieron. *sui.* Theophylact and Euthymius explain οἱ οἰκεῖοι αὐτοῦ, though the former adds : τυχὸν οἱ ἀπὸ τῆς αὐτῆς πατρίδος, ἢ καὶ οἱ ἀδελφοὶ αὐτοῦ. Οἱ παρά τινος, in Greek writers, are generally *legati ab aliquo missi,* a sense which does not suit this place. Of the examples adduced in support of the sense οἱ οἰκεῖοι αὐτοῦ, many are irrelevant; but after rejecting these, there still remain several *indubitatae fidei.* (1) Prov. xxxi. 21 : πάντες γὰρ

---

[1] [So *cubo* in Latin. Horace, *Epist.* II. ii. 68 : cubat hic in colle Quirini.]

[2] Kypke (*Observ. Sacr.* T. I. p. 154) to defend ὁδὸν ποιεῖν, *iter facere,* from the charge of being a Latinism, gives four examples from Xenophon, Dion. Hal., Josephus and Dio Cass. ; but in

all of them it is ποιεῖσθαι, not ποιεῖν. Even in his quotation from Libanius, ὑπὲρ ἀδελφοῦ τὴν ὁδὸν Ὑπερέχιος ἔφη ταυτηνὶ πεποιῆσθαι, where (he says) the use of the passive implies that the active might be so used, πεποιῆσθαι is *not* passive, but middle.

οἱ παρ' αὐτῆς ἐνδιδύσκονται δισσά. (Heb. כָּל־בֵּיתָהּ.) Fritzsche objects:
'E codd. reponendum οἱ παρ' αὐτῇ,' but the other is undoubtedly the true
reading, being found in II, III, and the Syro-hex. ܗܠܝܢ ܕܒܒܝܬܗ.
(2) Susan. 33: ἔκλαιον δὲ οἱ παρ' αὐτῆς (Hieron. *sui*) καὶ πάντες οἱ ἰδόντες
αὐτήν. (3) 1 Macc. xiii. 52: καὶ προσωχύρωσε τὸ ὄρος τοῦ ἱεροῦ τὸ παρὰ τὴν
ἄκραν, καὶ ᾤκει ἐκεῖ αὐτὸς καὶ οἱ παρ' αὐτοῦ (A. V. 'his company,' Vulg.
qui cum eo erant, against Fritzsche, who would understand *posteri ejus*,
but gives no example of such an usage). (4) Joseph. *Ant.* I. 10, 5: καὶ
῎Αβραμος μὲν ἐπὶ τούτοις εὐχαριστήσας τῷ θεῷ, περιτέμνεται παραυτίκα, καὶ
πάντες οἱ παρ' αὐτοῦ, καὶ ὁ παῖς Ἰσμάηλος. Some good examples of this use
of παρά, from Polybius and others, may be found in Wetstein, to which
may be added Diod. Sic. XIX. 53: τὸ μὲν πρῶτον τῶν Θηβαίων τοῦ παρ'
αὐτῶν ἔθνους (*suae gentis*) προστάντων, μετὰ δὲ ταῦτα τῆς τῶν Ἑλλήνων
ἡγεμονίας ἀμφισβητησάντων.

IV. 1. For συνήχθη the reading συνάγεται is followed by R. V.:
'There *is gathered* unto him a very great multitude, so that he *entered*
into a boat, and *sat* in the sea.' But in that case the Greek, ὥστε αὐτὸν
ἐμβάντα . . . καθῆσθαι, should also be rendered in the present tense, 'so
that he *entereth* . . . and *sitteth*.'

IV. 29: ἀποστέλλει τὸ δρέπανον, ὅτι παρέστηκεν ὁ θερισμός] A. V. 'He
putteth in the sickle.' R. V. 'He putteth forth the sickle. Or, *sendeth
forth*.' Comparing Joel iv. (iii.) 13: ἐξαποστείλατε δρέπανα, ὅτι παρέστηκεν
ὁ τρυγητός, there can be no doubt that the Evangelist (or the speaker
himself) had the words of the prophet, *as rendered by the LXX.* (for in the
Hebrew the verb in the second clause is not קָרַב, or any other word
which might fitly be rendered by παρέστηκε, but בָּשַׁל, *coctus est*) in his
mind. Now the Hebrew שָׁלַח, besides its ordinary meaning *to send*, has
also a special one, *to put forth*, generally *the hand*, but also *a rod* (Jud.
vi. 21, 1 Sam. xiv. 27), *a branch* (Ezek. viii. 17), here *a sickle*. In all
such cases (about forty in number) the LXX. have employed the proper
Greek word ἐκτείνειν, with the single exception of Joel iv. 13. We must
therefore understand ἐξαποστέλλειν in that place, as well as in St Mark,
in the sense of *putting forth*. The marginal rendering can only be
admitted on the assumption that 'the sickle' may be taken for 'the
reapers,' which on the other supposition is unnecessary.

V. 4: ἴσχυε δαμάσαι] A.V. 'could tame him.' R.V. 'had strength to
tame him'; perhaps to indicate that it is not the same word as that used
in *v.* 3 (ἠδύνατο). But ἰσχύω followed by an infinitive occurs sixteen times
in the Greek Testament; in all of which (exc. Luke xvi. 3) the Revisers
have left *I can*, or *I am able;* even in John xxi. 6, where bodily strength is

required: 'they were not able to draw the net for the multitude of fishes[1].'
In the next verse κατακόπτων ἑαυτὸν λίθοις, for 'cutting himself' I would
recall the rendering of Wicliff, Tyndale and Cranmer, 'beating himself,'
contundens, not (as Hieron.) *concidens*. Compare Ach. Tat. V. 23: ἑλκύσας
δὲ τῶν τριχῶν, ἀράσσει πρὸς τοὔδαφος, καὶ προσπίπτων κατακόπτει με πληγαῖς[2].
The word is also used of *beating the breast, head*, &c. in mourning: as St
Chrysost. T. X. p. 544 C: οἱ ἐν ἀκμῇ τοῦ πένθους μηδενὸς ἀνεχόμενοι πατέρες,
καὶ κατακόπτοντες ἑαυτούς. T. XI. p. 468 B: εἰ δὲ τὸ ἀλγεῖν ἐπὶ τοῖς ἀπελθοῦσιν
ἐθνικῶν, τὸ κατακόπτεσθαι, καὶ καταξαίνειν παρειάς, τίνων ἄρα ἐστίν, εἰπέ μοι;

V. 26: **πολλὰ παθοῦσα ὑπὸ πολλῶν ἰατρῶν**] Wetstein quotes Menander
[p. 338 ed. Meineke]: Πολλῶν ἰατρῶν εἴσοδός μ' ἀπώλεσε. Plin. *Hist. Nat.*
XXIX. 5: 'Hinc illa infelicis monumenti inscriptio, *turba se medicorum
periisse.*' Compare Diod. Sic. T. X. p. 61 ed. Bip.: καὶ δεινῶν ἀλγηδόνων
ἐπιγενομένων, συνεκλήθη πλῆθος ἰατρῶν.

ibid.: **καὶ δαπανήσασα τὰ παρ' αὐτῆς πάντα**] 'And had spent all that
she had[3].' Good examples of this phrase are quoted by Kypke from
Josephus, namely: *Ant.* VIII. 6, 6 (of the Queen of Sheba): καὶ ἡ μὲν...ὧν
προειρήκαμεν τυχοῦσα, καὶ μεταδοῦσα πάλιν τῷ βασιλεῖ τῶν παρ' αὐτῆς, εἰς τὴν
οἰκίαν ὑπέστρεψεν. *B. J.* II. 8, 4 (of the Essenes): οὐδὲν δὲ ἐν ἀλλήλοις οὔτε
ἀγοράζουσιν οὔτε πωλοῦσιν, ἀλλὰ τῷ χρῄζοντι διδοὺς ἕκαστος τὰ παρ' αὐτοῦ, τὸ
παρ' ἐκείνου χρήσιμον ἀντικομίζεται. Hence in Lucian *Phal.* II. 13: καὶ
ἀναλίσκοντα καὶ καταδαπανῶντα παρ' αὐτοῦ, we should probably read καταδαπανῶνΤΑ ΤΑ παρ' αὐτοῦ.

V. 30: **ἐπιγνοὺς ἐν ἑαυτῷ τὴν ἐξ αὐτοῦ δύναμιν ἐξελθοῦσαν**] A.V. 'Knowing in himself that virtue had gone out of him.' R.V. 'Perceiving in himself that the power *proceeding* from him had gone forth.' Is it not rather
a *locutio praegnans*, for τὴν ἐν αὐτῷ δύναμιν ἐξελθοῦσαν ἐξ αὐτοῦ? and if so,
does not the A.V. (which presupposes that a healing virtue resided in
him) give the sense as clearly and faithfully as could be desired? Dean
Alford and others translate: 'Knowing in himself the power which had
gone forth from him.' But it was not the power itself that he knew
(or recognized), but the fact that it had gone forth from him.

V. 36: **εὐθέως ἀκούσας τὸν λόγον λαλούμενον**] A.V. 'As soon as he heard
the word that was spoken.' For εὐθέως ἀκούσας the uncials BL∆ℵ read

---

[1] [But in Luke xvi. 3: σκάπτειν οὐκ
ἰσχύω, the R.V. has 'I have not strength
to dig.']

[2] [Cf. Plut. II. p. 260 B: ὡς δ'
ᾔσθετο τῇ φωνῇ κάτω (at the bottom
of the well) γεγονότος, πολλοὺς μὲν
αὐτὴ τῶν λίθων ἐπέφερε πολλοὺς δὲ

καὶ μεγάλους αἱ θεραπαινίδες ἐπεκυ-
λίνδουν, ἄχρις οὗ κατέκοψαν αὐτὸν καὶ
κατέχωσαν.]

[3] [Cf. Luke x. 7: ἐσθίοντες καὶ πίνοντες τὰ παρ' αὐτῶν, 'such things as
they give.']

παρακούσας, which has been variously rendered by 'overhearing' (Alford and margin of R. V.), 'having casually heard' (Tischend.), 'not heeding' (R. V. in text). The proper meaning of παρακούειν is 'to hear carelessly' (*oscitanter*), or 'incidentally' (*obiter*), without heeding what one hears, or even intending to hear at all. This will include all the senses given above, and also that of *refusing to hear*, which is required in Matt. xviii. 17. But there is yet another meaning which seems very suitable to this place, namely, *to pretend not to hear*. 'Jesus, making as though he heareth not the word spoken, saith' &c. Compare Hex. ad Psal. xxxviii. 13: אַל־תֶּחֱרַשׁ. Ο'. μὴ παρασιωπήσῃς. 'Α. μὴ κωφεύσῃς. Σ. μὴ παρακούσῃς (*do not make as though thou hearest not*). In this sense it is often joined with παρορᾶν or παριδεῖν, as in the following examples. Plut. *Vit. Philop.* XVI: Diophanes, the general of the Achaeans, would have punished the Lacedaemonians for some offence committed against the confederacy of which they formed a part; but Philopoemen remonstrated with him, urging that when King Antiochus and the Romans were threatening Greece with such powerful armies, it was to them that he should turn his attention, τὰ δ' οἰκεῖα μὴ κινεῖν, ἀλλὰ καὶ παριδεῖν τι καὶ παρακοῦσαι τῶν ἁμαρτανομένων. Id. *De Curiosit.* XIV (T. II. p. 522 B): τοῦτο δὴ τὸ ἔθος ἐπάγων τῇ πολυπραγμοσύνῃ, πειρῶ καὶ τῶν ἰδίων ἔνια παρακοῦσαί ποτε καὶ παριδεῖν[1].

*V. 40 : ἐκβαλὼν ἅπαντας] Compare Charit. Aphrod. III. 2 : καὶ εἰσελθοῦσα εἰς τὸν νεών, πάντας ἐκβαλοῦσα, ταῦτα εἶπε πρὸς τὴν θεόν. *Id.* v. 8 (varying the phrase) : βασιλεὺς δέ, μεταστησάμενος ἅπαντας, ἐβουλεύετο μετὰ τῶν φίλων.

VI. 14. For ἔλεγεν 'some ancient authorities' (including the Vatican MS.) read ἔλεγον. This variation, though not supported by the ancient versions, has great merit, when taken in connexion with the following verses. Read and point the whole passage thus : 'And king Herod heard *thereof*; (for his name had become known: and they said, John the Baptist is risen from the dead, and therefore do the powers work in him. But others said, It is Elijah ; and others said, It is a prophet, as one of the prophets). But Herod, when he heard *thereof*, said, John, whom I beheaded, the same (οὗτος. See Matt. xxi. 42, John iii. 26) is risen.' Here, after the words καὶ ἤκουσεν ὁ β. Ἡρ. (*v.* 14), the sentence is suspended, in order to introduce the opinions of the people, and taken up again at *v.* 16: ἀκούσας δὲ ὁ Ἡρώδης κ.τ.έ.

VI. 19 : ἐνεῖχεν αὐτῷ] A. V. 'had a quarrel (Or, *an inward grudge*) against him.' R. V. 'set herself against him.' Against the Vulg. *insidiabatur illi*, and Beza's *imminebat ei*, Bois rightly argues that these are the

[1] [Cf. Lucian. *Ep. Sat.* 39: καὶ διὰ τοῦτο παρακούει αὐτων τὰ πολλά, 'turns a deaf ear.']

effects of malevolence, not the ill-feeling itself, which the writer intended to express, and could not have better expressed than by ἐνεῖχεν, *had a grudge against him*. [The epithet *inward* was probably added by A. V. to express the preposition in ἐνέχειν, but is not necessary.] There is no example of this use of the word in classical writers, except in Herodotus, with the addition of χόλον, which is necessary to bring out the proper force of ἐνέχειν, *to hold* or *keep within, to cherish an inward feeling;* e.g. Herod. VI. 119 : ἐνεῖχέ σφι δεινὸν χόλον. VIII. 27 : ἅτε σφι ἐνέχοντες αἰεὶ χόλον. By long usage (as Fritzsche remarks) the ellipsis was forgotten, as that of νοῦν after ἐπέχειν, and of אף after נטר (Psal. ciii. 9 : 'neither will he keep (his anger) for ever.' O'. οὐδὲ εἰς τὸν αἰῶνα μηνιεῖ). But the very best example for our purpose is the LXX. version of Gen. xlix. 23 : καὶ ἐνεῖχον αὐτῷ (Joseph) κύριοι τοξευμάτων. The same Hebrew word (שׂטם) occurs in two other places in Genesis (xxvii. 41, l. 15), where the same admirable translators (the Pentateuch Company, as we may call them, who were equally 'well seen' in Hebrew and Greek) have translated : καὶ ἐνεκότει Ἡσαῦ τῷ Ἰακὼβ περὶ τῆς εὐλογίας, and μήποτε μνησικακήσῃ ἡμῖν Ἰωσήφ. These three words, ἐνέχειν, ἐγκοτεῖν and μνησικακεῖν, mutually illustrate one another, and are in favour of Bois's emendation of Hesychius, Ἐνέχει· μνησικακεῖ, ἐγκοτεῖ (for ἔγκειται), were it not more probable that μνησικακεῖ refers to Mark vi. 18, and ἔγκειται to Luke xi. 53 : ἤρξαντο οἱ γραμματεῖς καὶ Φαρισαῖοι δεινῶς ἐνέχειν, where a different meaning must be sought for the word, not the *ira alta mente reposta* which is required in this place.

VI. 20 : καὶ ἀκούσας αὐτοῦ πολλὰ ἐποίει] For ἐποίει, which is supported by all the ancient versions except Memph., R.V. adopts the reading of BLℵ ἠπόρει, 'he was much perplexed,' in favour of which it has not (I think) been suggested that this use of πολλὰ for *vehementer* is very characteristic of this Evangelist : e.g. Ch. iii. 12 : πολλὰ ἐπετίμα αὐτοῖς. v. 23 : παρεκάλει αὐτὸν πολλά. xv. 3 : κατηγόρουν αὐτοῦ πολλά. On the other hand it will hardly be denied that the proposed change introduces a jarring note into the description of Herod's feelings towards the Baptist. He feared him, he respected his character, he kept him safely, he 'heard him gladly' (or 'with pleasure,' as Philip heard Aeschines, πράως καὶ ἡδέως ἤκουεν αὐτοῦ (Aelian, *V. H.* VIII. 12)). This last especially seems inconsistent with a perplexed and doubtful state of mind[1]. Take, for example, the case of Felix, who 'sent for Paul to hear him concerning the faith in Christ.' Of the Roman governor and his prisoner, it might be truly said, καὶ ἀκούσας αὐτοῦ πολλὰ ἠπόρει, but certainly not, καὶ ἡδέως αὐτοῦ ἤκουε.

In noticing this case, the 'Two Members of the N. T. Company' (p. 47)

---

[1] Bishop of Lincoln's *Address*, &c. p. 14 : 'People are not wont to hear gladly those by whom they are much perplexed.' Xenophon (*Anab.* I. 3, 8) joins τούτοις ἀπορῶν τε καὶ λυπούμενος.

ask, 'What are the "many things" that Herod did after he had heard St John the Baptist? Meyer tells us that they were the many things which he heard from St John, though how this can be elicited from the words we do not clearly see.' But is not this (to use the fashionable phraseology) to 'miss the point' altogether? When Demosthenes (p. 658, 12) says of a certain king who was threatened with hostilities by a neighbouring power, πρέσβεις πέμπων ΑΠΑΝΤΑ ποιεῖν ἕτοιμος ἦν, we understand this of an unconditional surrender on the part of the sender of the embassage. But suppose the message had been ΠΟΛΛΑ ποιεῖν ἕτοιμος ἦν, would not the alteration imply that there was something reserved, some concession that he was unwilling to make? It is easy to perceive how this applies to Herod, and his relations to the Baptist, as his spiritual adviser. The remark is as old as Elsner *ad loc.* 'πολλὰ ἐποίει, at non primarium illud quod Joannes urserat : *fratris uxorem non dimisit.*'

If ἠπόρει is (as we think) a *correction*, it is an easy matter to trace the origin of it. Herod 'was much perplexed' (διηπόρει) on another occasion (Luke ix. 7), though still in connexion with the Baptist. His perplexity in regard to the character and claims of Jesus was not unnaturally transferred to those of his forerunner.

VI. 26 : οὐκ ἠθέλησεν αὐτὴν ἀθετῆσαι] 'He would not *reject* her.' Perhaps, 'he would not *disappoint* her.' Compare the LXX. version of Psal. xiv. (Heb. xv.) 4 : ὁ ὀμνύων τῷ πλησίον αὐτοῦ, καὶ οὐκ ἀθετῶν. The Hebrew is different, but the Prayer-book translation follows the LXX. : 'He that sweareth unto his neighbour, and *disappointeth* him not.'

VI. 40 : καὶ ἀνέπεσον πρασιαὶ πρασιαί] 'And they sat down in ranks.' A marginal note might be added : 'Gr. *garden plots.*' Canon Farrar (*Life of Christ*, Chap. XXIX.) would translate : 'They reclined in *parterres*,' supposing the word to be suggested by 'the gay red and blue and yellow colours of the clothing which the poorest Orientals wear.' But πρασιαί are not *flower-beds* only or chiefly, but also plots of leeks (πράσον) and other vegetables (λάχανα) ; and the allusion is not to the 'gay colours,' but to the regularly-formed groups, with spaces between, in which the companies were ranged, reminding the spectator of the square or oblong beds in a garden. So Hesychius : Πρασιαί· αἱ ἐν τοῖς κήποις τετράγωνοι λαχανιαί ; and Euthymius, absurdly enough, makes the distinction between συμπόσια and πρασιαί to be, that the former were arranged in circles, and the latter in squares.

VII. 3 : πυγμῇ] A. V. 'oft,' and in margin : ' Or, *diligently*: in the original, *with the fist* : Theophylact, *up to the elbow.*' The rendering 'diligently,' or 'carefully,' is supported by both[1] Syriac versions, which have ܐܠܝܠܐܩ (elsewhere put for the Greek ἐπιμελῶς and ἀκριβῶς). But the later Syriac has a note in the margin, ܐܡܠܘ ܐܪܩ;ܣܩܡ?

---

[1] viz. the Peshito and Philoxenian. Ed.

ܘܣܐܚܕܨ, i.e. according to White, p. 593 : *qui se oblectant digitos suos aqua* (abluendo). But *oblectavit se* is the meaning of the Ethpaal ܐܠܦܨܐ, not of the Pael ܠܦܨܐ, to which (on the authority of this marginal note) J. D. Michaelis would assign the sense of *humectavit, perfudit*. In confirmation of this sense, I find in Geopon. p. 115, 13 :

ܕܢܣܩܘܦܐ ܐܠܦܨ ܕܦܨ ܠܘܐ, for the Greek, εἶτα διαψύξας καὶ ἀποκλύζων τὸ στόμα (gallinae); which would give for the Philoxenian scholium (probably a translation from the Greek) Πυγμῇ· ἀποκλύζοντες τῷ ὕδατι τοὺς δακτύλους αὐτῶν.

VII. 18 : οὕτως καὶ ὑμεῖς ἀσύνετοί ἐστε ;] 'Are ye so without understanding also?' Perhaps it would be better to take οὕτως (*adeone, siccine*) as in Matt. xxvi. 40, rendering : 'What, are ye also void of understanding?'

VII. 19 : καὶ εἰς τὸν ἀφεδρῶνα ἐκπορεύεται, καθαρίζον (καθαρίζων ABℵ) πάντα τὰ βρώματα] A.V. 'And goeth out into the draught, purging all meats.' It would be a waste of time to notice and to refute the various explanations that have been given of the clause καθαρίζον πάντα τὰ βρώματα, all of them equally repugnant to grammar and common sense. Take Dean Alford's as a specimen. He reads καθαρίζων (rightly, as we shall presently see), and adds: 'The masc. part. applies to ἀφεδρῶνα, by a construction of which there are examples, in which the grammatical *object* of the sentence is regarded as the logical *subject*, e.g. λόγοι δ' ἐν ἀλλήλοισιν ἐρρόθουν κακοί, | φύλαξ ἐλέγχων φύλακα, Soph. *Antig.* 259.' In my schoolboy days, we were taught to call this the *nominative absolute*, for φύλακος ἐλέγχοντος φ. He goes on: 'What is stated is *physically* true. The ἀφεδρών is that which, by the removal of the part carried off, purifies the meat; the portion available for nourishment being in its passage converted into chyle, and the remainder (the κάθαρμα) being cast out.' But surely, assuming the Dean's physiology to be correct, it is the *actus egerendi* which purifies what is left, not the *egesta* themselves, still less the ἀφεδρών which is merely the passive receptacle of them. But the whole thing is a mistake, arising from taking καθαρίζων π. τ. β. to be part of our Lord's discourse, not (as it really is) a remark of the Evangelist founded upon it. Grammatically, καθαρίζων depends on καὶ λέγει αὐτοῖς, v. 18: but since it is separated from it by the intervention of a discourse consisting of several sentences, it may be necessary in translating to help out the construction by the insertion of a few words, as : '*This he said*, cleansing all meats,' *cleansing* being here taken in the same sense as in Acts x. 15: 'What God hath *cleansed*, that call not thou common.' This simple explanation of a difficult passage will, probably, be objected to on the ground of its being *novel*; but that also is a mistake. It is as old as Origen, who in commenting on the parallel place in St Matthew (Tom. III.

p. 494 D) says: καὶ μάλιστα ἐπεὶ κατὰ τὸν Μάρκον ἔλεγε ταῦτα ὁ σωτήρ, καθαρίζων πάντα τὰ βρώματα. He is followed by St Chrysostom (T. VII· p. 526 A): ὁ δὲ Μάρκος φησίν, ὅτι καθαρίζων τὰ βρώματα ταῦτα ἔλεγεν[1]. This explanation also accounts for the repetition of ἔλεγε δὲ in the following verse, in which the Evangelist takes up the continuation of our Lord's discourse after his own explanatory remark. We have a similar incidental remark in ch. iii. 30, after our Lord's denunciation of the sin against the Holy Ghost: 'Because they said, He hath an unclean spirit,' where we might also supply: ' This he said, because' &c. And the following from Xenophon (*Anab.* VII. 1, 22) only differs from our construction of this passage of St Mark's in the length of the intervening discourse: ὁ δ' ἀπεκρίνατο· ἀλλ' εὖ τε λέγετε, καὶ ποιήσω ταῦτα· εἰ δὲ τούτων ἐπιθυμεῖτε, θέσθε τὰ ὅπλα ἐν τάξει ὡς τάχιστα· βουλόμενος αὐτοὺς κατηρεμίσαι[2].

*VIII. 24 : βλέπω τοὺς ἀνθρώπους, ὡς δένδρα, περιπατοῦντας] We may compare the proverbial expression, οὐδὲ ἀνθρώπους ἑώρων τοὺς ἀνθρώπους, said of persons suddenly thrown into a state of excitement bordering on delirium, e.g. of criminals pardoned at the foot of the gallows (S. Chrysost. T. XI. p. 479 F). On this principle, Mill's reading βλέπω τοὺς ἀνθρώπους, ὅτι ὡς δένδρα ὁρῶ περιπατοῦντας, though scarcely intelligible, may be explained from the confusion existing in the mind of the blind man. The same excuse will not avail for what follows in *v.* 25, according to the sadly confused reading of BC¹LΔℵ thus rendered by R.V.: 'Then again he laid his hands upon his eyes; and he looked stedfastly (καὶ διέβλεψεν,

[1] Dean Burgon (*Last xii verses of St Mark*, p. 179, note u) adds from Gregory Thaumaturgus (Routh, *Rel. Sacr.* III. 257), a disciple of Origen: καὶ ὁ σωτήρ, ὁ πάντα καθαρίζων τὰ βρώματα, οὐ τὸ εἰσπορευόμενον, φησί, κοινοῖ τὸν ἄνθρωπον, ἀλλὰ τὸ ἐκπορευόμενον.

[2] The *history* (so to speak) of the above interpretation may be worth recording. The places of Origen and St Chrysostom had escaped the notice of all critics and commentators till Matthaei in his critical edition of the N. T. (Riga 1788) T. II. p. 117 referred to the former in these disparaging terms: 'Sine sensu Orig. III. 494 D laudat καθαρίζων, quasi referre voluerit ad σωτὴρ, *quod plane absurdum est.*' Again, in his minor edition (Wittenb. 1803) T. I. p. 211 he refers for the reading καθαρίζων to St Chrysost. VII. 526 A; but gives his opinion in

favour of καθαρίζον, as explained by Euthymius, καθαρὰ ἀπολιμπάνον. From that time nothing more was heard of this interpretation till the year 1839, when the present writer, in editing St Chrysostom's Homilies on St Matthew, drew attention to it in a note (T. III. pp. 112 sq.). He was not, however, fortunate enough (so far as he is aware) 'to catch the eye' of even one of the many critics and expositors of the Greek Testament, English and foreign, from that time till the appearance of the work of Dean Burgon quoted in the preceding note; in which highly favourable mention is made of the writer's attempt to restore the true interpretation of this passage. Shortly after he had the gratification of seeing it adopted, without any marginal variation, by the Company of Revisers of the N. T.

instead of the T. R. καὶ ἐποίησεν αὐτὸν ἀναβλέψαι) and was restored, and saw all things clearly (τηλαυγῶς)[1].' On the last word Bois has a remark, which is worthy of the attention of translators in general, and of those of the Bible in particular: 'Vetus, *clare*; alii [Beza] *procul et dilucide*, nimis enucleate, et ut sic loquar, paedagogice. Origines verborum enucleare paedagogis potius quam interpretibus convenit. Interpres officio suo abunde functus est, si sensum recte et fideliter exprimat, id quod a vetere hic interprete praestitum nemo, opinor, negabit.'

IX. 11 : καὶ ἐπηρώτων αὐτὸν λέγοντες, "Οτι (A.V. 'Why') λέγουσιν οἱ γραμματεῖς...*v.* 28: ἐπηρώτων αὐτὸν κατ' ἰδίαν "Οτι (as before) ἡμεῖς οὐκ ἠδυνήθημεν...]

The use of ὅτι for τί, when the interrogation is *indirect*, is sanctioned by the practice of the best writers; as Herod. III. 78: εἴρετο ὅτι (*curnam*) οὐ χρᾶται τῇ χερί. Thucyd. I. 90: ὁπότε τις αὐτὸν ἔροιτο τῶν ἐν τέλει ὄντων, ὅτι οὐκ ἐπέρχεται ἐπὶ τὸ κοινόν. Lucian. *Asin.* 32: τοῦτον, δέσποτα, τὸν ὄνον οὐκ οἶδ' ὅτι βόσκομεν, δεινῶς ἀργὸν ὄντα καὶ βραδύν. Joseph. *Ant.* VII. 7, 1: γνοὺς τοῦτο ὁ βασιλεὺς ἀνέκρινεν αὐτὸν (Uriam) ὅτι μὴ πρὸς αὐτὸν εἰς τὴν οἰκίαν ἔλθοι[2]. These examples do not defend the same usage in a *direct* interrogation, which cannot be proved from classical writers, and scarcely from biblical. Of the two instances, Gen. xii. 18 and 1 Chron. xvii. 6, where ὅτι corresponds to the Hebrew לָמָּה, the former is doubtful, according as we point, τί τοῦτο ἐποίησάς μοι; ὅτι (*quare*) οὐκ ἀπήγγειλάς μοι...or, τί τοῦτο ἐποίησάς μοι, ὅτι (*quod*) οὐκ ἀπήγγειλάς μοι... The latter is more to the purpose: 'Spake I a word to any of the judges of Israel, saying, ὅτι (*quare*) οὐκ ᾠκοδόμηκατέ μοι οἶκον κέδρινον;' Still, even if no authority could be found for this usage, these two instances, occurring in the same chapter of St Mark, must be held mutually to support and sanction each other. And the only alternative renderings: 'And they asked him, saying, The scribes say that Elias must first come'; and 'His disciples asked him privately, saying, We could not cast it out,' are simply intolerable.

*X. 19 : μὴ ἀποστερήσῃς] 'Defraud not.' In biblical Greek this word is appropriated to the act of *keeping back the wages* of an hireling, as Mal. iii. 5, James v. 4 ; from which the classical use differs only in the thing kept back being money or goods deposited with another for safe keeping, as the ten talents of silver which Tobit left in trust with Gabael at Rages of Media. So the Schol. on Aristoph. *Plut.* 373 : ἀποστερῶ ἐστιν, ὅταν παρακαταθήκην τινὸς λαβὼν εἰς διαβολὴν χωρήσω, καὶ οὐκ ἐθέλω

---

[1] "Απαντα alone of this reading seems preferable to the ἅπαντας of the T. R. Compare Lucian. *Contemp.* 7 : κἀπειδὰν εἴπω τὰ ἔπη, μέμνησο μηκέτι ἀμβλυώττειν,

[2] [Cf. Plut. *Vit. Arat.* 30: καθάπερ τῷ κόκκυγί φησιν Αἴσωπος ἐρωτῶντι τοὺς λέπτους ὄρινθας ὅτι φεύγοιεν αὐτόν.]

ἀλλὰ σαφῶς πάντα ὁρᾶν.

διδόναι αὐτῷ ἃ ἔλαβον. As striking at the root of the commercial integrity of those times, it was a grievous offence, and punished accordingly. Porphyr. *A. A.* IV. 10: 'I have worshipped the gods, honoured my parents,' τῶν τε ἄλλων ἀνθρώπων οὔτε ἀπέκτεινα, οὔτε παρακαταθήκην ἀπεστέρησα, οὔτε ἄλλο οὐδὲν ἀνήκεστον διεπραξάμην. Stob. *Floril.* T. XLIV. 41 : Apud Pisidas ἡ μεγίστη κρίσις ἐστὶ παρακαταθήκης· τὸν δὲ ἀποστερήσαντα θανατοῦσιν. It is distinguished from κλέπτειν: *Ibid.* T. LXXIX. 51 : κελευόμενος ὑπ' αὐτοῦ κλέπτειν ἢ παρακαταθήκην ἀποστερεῖν. Plut. *Vit. Lyc.* IX: τίς γὰρ (if men used iron money) ἢ κλέπτειν ἔμελλεν, ἢ δωροδοκεῖν, ἢ ἀποστερεῖν, ἢ ἁρπάζειν ;

The precept μὴ ἀποστερήσῃς is generally considered as coming under the Tenth Commandment, but it may also be referred to the preceding one, inasmuch as the person denying the deposit was obliged to purge himself by an oath to that effect. So Aesop. *Fab.* CCCLXXII, ed. de Fur. : Παρακαταθήκας τις λαβὼν φίλου ἀποστερεῖν διενοεῖτο. καὶ δὴ προσκαλουμένου αὐτὸν ἐκείνου ἐπὶ ὅρκον...ὤμοσε μὴ εἰληφέναι τὴν π.

X. 21 : 'And Jesus looking upon him, loved him (ἠγάπησεν αὐτόν).' Perhaps we might translate 'caressed him,' comparing Plut. *Vit. Pericl.* I : ξένους τινὰς ἐν Ῥώμῃ πλουσίους κυνῶν τέκνα καὶ πιθήκων ἐν τοῖς κόλποις περιφέροντας καὶ ἀγαπῶντας (*fondling*) ἰδὼν ὁ Καῖσαρ...ἠρώτησεν εἰ παιδία παρ' αὐτοῖς οὐ τίκτουσιν αἱ γυναῖκες.

*Cf. Plut. *Anton.* 70. (Timon the misanthrope) Ἀλκιβιάδην νέον ὄντα καὶ θρασὺν ἠσπάζετο καὶ ἐφίλει προθύμως. Lightfoot *ad loc.* quotes examples of Jewish Doctors getting up and kissing their disciples when they were pleased with them, and adds :—'Quid si ipsissimo hoc gestu usus fuerit Salvator erga hunc juvenem? Aptiusque cum coram eo flexis genibus provolveretur. Aliquo saltem gestu usus est quo et ipsi juveni et astantibus planum fuit, juvenem et interrogatione sua et responsione non parum placuisse.' But his examples of ἀγαπᾶν in this sense are naught, especially Jos. *Ant.* VI. 14, 6: ἀγαπήσειν δὲ σεσωσμένας τὰς γυναῖκας ἀπολαμβάνοντας ἔλεγον.

XI. 3 : καὶ εὐθέως αὐτὸν ἀποστελεῖ ὧδε] (St Matthew has only εὐθέως δὲ ἀποστελεῖ αὐτούς.) The question raised on these words is, whether the nominative to ἀποστελεῖ is τις or ὁ κύριος ; in other words, whether they are a continuation of our Lord's speech to the two disciples, or of that of the two disciples to the owner of the colt. We should have little hesitation in deciding in favour of the former interpretation, were it not that in St Mark the uncials BCDLΔℵ after ἀποστελεῖ (or ἀποστέλλει) insert πάλιν, 'he will send him *back* hither.' Origen has the same reading ; and his *exegesis* of both Evangelists, though highly allegorical, seems to assume the *sending back* of the animals εἰς τὸν τόπον ὅθεν ἐλύθη πρότερον, though no longer ἐπὶ τοῖς ἔργοις τοῖς προτέροις. But in defence of the T. R. and of the generally received interpretation, it may be urged (1) that εὐθέως (or εὐθύς) is far more properly said of the promptness of the owners in giving up the colt than of the expedition of the borrower in returning it, which could only take place after a certain interval of time ; and (2) that the effect of the authoritative requisition, ' The Lord hath need of him,' upon the minds of the owners would be weakened rather than strengthened by the addition, 'and will be sure to return him.'

XI. 19: καὶ ὅτε ὀψὲ ἐγένετο, ἐξεπορεύετο ἔξω τῆς πόλεως] 'And when even was come, he went out of the city.' We learn from St Luke (xxi. 37) that this was his daily custom ; but can St Mark's words be explained so as to convey the same information? Those who translate 'And every evening [Gr. whenever evening came] he went forth out of the city,' evidently thought so, reading ὅταν ὀψὲ ἐγένετο with BCKLℵ. The solecism is probably due to St Mark himself, who writes ὅταν ἐθεώρουν ch. iii. 11, and ὅταν στήκετε in this chapter. The imperfect ἐξεπορεύετο (for which St Matthew has ἐξῆλθε) might appear to intimate a repetition of the action, but in this particular verb it does not seem to be necessarily so. Thus 1 Kings (Sam.) xvii. 35 : καὶ ἐξεπορευόμην ὀπίσω αὐτοῦ, καὶ ἐπάταξα αὐτόν. 2 Kings (Sam.) xix. 19 : ἡμέρᾳ ᾗ ἐξεπορεύετο ὁ κύριός μου ὁ βασιλεὺς ἐξ Ἱερουσαλήμ[1]. And the connexion in St Mark's narrative is decidedly in favour of a single action, especially when contrasted with the clear and explicit terms in which St Luke indicates the general practice : ἦν δὲ τὰς ἡμέρας ἐν τῷ ἱερῷ διδάσκων· τὰς δὲ νύκτας ἐξερχόμενος ηὐλίζετο εἰς τὸ ὄρος τὸ καλούμενον ἐλαιῶν.

XII. 4 : κἀκεῖνον λιθοβολήσαντες ἐκεφαλαίωσαν, καὶ ἀπέστειλαν ἠτιμωμένον] Or, according to the shorter reading of BDLΔℵ and Vulg. κἀκεῖνον ἐκεφαλαίωσαν καὶ ἠτίμασαν. In favour of the latter is the distinction laid down by Ammonius, p. 26 : ἀτιμοῦται καὶ ἀτιμάζεται διαφέρει· ἀτιμοῦται μὲν γάρ τις ὑπὸ τῶν νόμων ὁλοσχερεῖ ἀτιμίᾳ· ἀτιμάζεται δὲ ὁ ὑβριζόμενος ἔν τινι πράγματι. But the difficulty, common to both readings, is in the word ἐκεφαλαίωσαν, which it has been attempted, in various ways, to explain without departing from the proper meaning of the word, to sum up; but with so little success, that nearly all the commentators have been forced to acquiesce in the rendering of the Vulgate, et illum in capite vulnerarunt. Both Syriac versions (following the T. R.) have : ܘܣܩܠܘܗܝ ܘܨܥܪܘܗܝ ܒܪܝܫܗ where ܣܩܠܘܗܝ is simply vulnerarunt, ἐτραυμάτισαν, without regard to the part wounded. While it is acknowledged that no example can be adduced, in which κεφαλαιοῦν has this meaning[2], the legitimacy of

---

[1] [But cf. Tobit vii. 11 : ('I gave her to seven husbands,') καὶ ὁπότε ἐὰν εἰσεπορεύοντο πρὸς αὐτήν, ἀπέθνησκον ὑπὸ τὴν νύκτα. R. V. 'And whensoever they came in unto her they died in the night.']

[2] Rev. W. Trollope, in his Notes on the Gospel of St Mark, fancied that he

it is asserted from the analogy of γαστρίζειν (=τὸ εἰς γαστέρα τύπτειν), γναθοῦν (=τὸ εἰς γνάθους τύπτειν), and a few others. But as κορυφή makes κορυφοῦν, not κορυφαιοῦν, so (according to this analogy) the derivative from κεφαλή would be not κεφαλαιοῦν, but κεφαλοῦν ; and St Mark should have written ἐκεφάλωσαν, a *vox nihili*, it is true, but which would have been accepted without hesitation in the only sense which could have been assigned to it. The reading of BLℵ, ἐκεφαλίωσαν, does not help us much. We can only conjecture that the Evangelist adopted ἐκεφαλαίωσαν, a known word in an unknown sense, in preference to ἐκεφάλωσαν, of which both sound and sense were unknown.

That κεφαλαιοῦν must be referred to κεφάλαιον, not to κεφαλή, was rightly understood by Alberti (*Observ. Philol.* pp. 174—183), who is also successful in showing that κεφάλαιον is sometimes used for the *thick end* or *knob* of *roots, bones,* &c., why not therefore of *a club* (in fact, Phavorinus defines κορύνη to be πᾶσα ῥάβδος κεφαλαιωτή, from κάρα, *caput*)? But when he goes on, by the help of the figure *synecdoche*, from the *knob* to the *club* itself, and from κεφάλαιον, *a club* (?) to κεφαλαιοῦν, *to beat with clubs*, we confess that we cannot follow him. A *knob* is not a *knobbed stick.* If the English reader were to meet with such a sentence as this, 'and him they *knobbed*, and shamefully handled,' we rather think he would understand it in a sense not very different from that to which we are finally brought back, 'they wounded him in the head.'

*XII. 21 : R. V. 'Leaving no seed *behind* him': reading ἀπέθανε μὴ καταλιπὼν σπέρμα for ἀπέθ. καὶ οὐδὲ αὐτὸς ἀφῆκε σπέρμα. In Mark xii. 19, where καταλίπῃ is used of the wife,—'leave behind.' But in the parallel, Luke xx. 31, 'left' (κατέλιπον); and so *constanter* (18 passages out of 24) for καταλ.

*XII. 28: ποία ἐστὶν πρώτη πάντων (T. R. πασῶν) ἐντολή ;] The neuter πάντων, *omnium rerum*, is undoubtedly correct, though it may be difficult to find an exactly similar instance. Thucyd. IV. 52 is usually quoted, καὶ ἦν αὐτῶν ἡ διάνοια, τάς τε ἄλλας πόλεις τὰς Ἀκταίας καλουμένας...ἐλευθεροῦν, καὶ πάντων μάλιστα (*above all*) τὴν Ἄντανδρον. Fritzsche quotes as 'plane gemellus' Aristoph. *Av.* 471: οὐδ' Αἴσωπον πεπάτηκας | ὃς ἔφασκε λέγων κορυδὸν πάντων πρώτην ὄρνιθα γενέσθαι | προτέραν τῆς γῆς. But this is not an instance in point, because the speaker means to assert, not that the lark was the most ancient of the birds, but that the birds in general (he takes a particular one, the lark) were older than all other creatures; so that πασῶν would have been intolerable. A better example is St Chrysost. T. VII. p. 108 B : ψυχὴ ὑπὸ πονηρίας ἀλοῦσα πάντων ἀνοητοτέρα γίνεται.

had discovered a clear instance of this use of the word in Aristoph. *Ran.* 854 : ἵνα μὴ κεφαλαιῶ τὸν κρόταφόν σου ῥή-ματι. But a reference to the place will show that κεφαλαίῳ (not κεφαλαιῶ) is an adjective agreeing with ῥήματι, and that for the verb we must go to the next line, θένων ὑπ' ὀργῆς.

XII. 37: ὁ πολὺς ὄχλος] A. V. 'the common people.' Alford and others prefer 'the great multitude,' or 'the mass of the people.' There is not much to choose between these; but both biblical and classical usage is in favour of the older version. Thus Levit. iv. 27 'the common people' is in Hebrew and Greek עַם־הָאָרֶץ, ὁ λαὸς τῆς γῆς, a term used by Rabbinical writers in a disparaging way. Elsner quotes from Plut. *Vit. Rom.* XXVII: ἐν δὲ τούτῳ (the occurrence of celestial portents during an assembly of the people) τὸν μὲν πολὺν ὄχλον σκεδασθέντα φυγεῖν, τοὺς δὲ δυνατοὺς συστραφῆναι μετ' ἀλλήλων. I add Pausan. *Messen.* XIV. 1: ὁ δὲ ὄχλος ὁ πολὺς κατὰ τὰς πατρίδας ἕκαστοι τὰς ἀρχαίας ἐσκεδάσθησαν. Dio Chrys. *Or.* IV. p. 72. 30: ὁ πολὺς καὶ ἀμαθὴς ὅμιλος. Id. *Or.* LXXII. p. 629. 30: καὶ θαυμάζεσθαι ὑπὸ τοῦ πολλοῦ ὄχλου, καὶ περιβλέπεσθαι. Lucian. *De Luctu* 2: ὁ μὲν δὴ πολὺς ὅμιλος, οὓς ἰδιώτας οἱ σοφοὶ καλοῦσιν[1]. Diod. Sic. T. X. p. 216 ed. Bip.: ὁ δὲ πολὺς λεώς (distinguished from οἱ ἐπιφανέστατοι καὶ δραστικώτατοι) ἐξέπεσεν εἰς τὴν νῦν καλουμένην Ἰουδαίαν.

*XIII. 8: 'There shall be earthquakes in divers places; there shall be famines.' After λιμοὶ T. R. adds καὶ ταραχαί, which is not very appropriately coupled with λιμοί, and is wanting in BDLℵ. Dean Alford retains it, because 'no possible reason can be given for the interpolation of the clause.' But if the original reading was λιμοὶ καὶ λοιμοὶ (as in Luke xxi. 11 and the T. R. of Matt. xxiv. 7) and καὶ λοιμοὶ had been accidentally omitted, then it was very natural that some one should have attempted to restore the equilibrium (so to speak) of the construction, by the addition of some other particular, corresponding with St Luke's ἀκαταστασίαι. But if καὶ ταραχαὶ is to be eliminated, we think a strong case is made out for the insertion of καὶ λοιμοί, even though unsupported by MSS. or versions. Λιμοὶ καὶ λοιμοὶ have been connected ever since Hesiod (*Op.* 242): Τοῖσιν δ' οὐρανόθεν μέγ' ἐπήγαγε πῆμα Κρονίων | λιμὸν ὁμοῦ καὶ λοιμόν, ἀποφθινύθουσι δὲ λαοί.

*XIII. 28: γινώσκετε] Dean Alford here most uncritically adopts γινώσκεται from AB²DLΔ, evidently an error of the scribe, since the very same MSS. have it in *v.* 29 also, where it is impossible; and in St Matthew all the MSS. read γινώσκετε in both places. Fritzsche also adopts γινώσκεται in all three Gospels[2], otherwise (he says) the opposition οὕτω καὶ ὑμεῖς...γινώσκετε is 'prorsus absona.' But (1) γινώσκετε in *v.* 28 is general, not personal, 'one knows,' and (2) the impersonal γινώσκεται,

---

[1] [Cf. Lucian. *Hermot.* 72: καὶ ὅμως ὁ πολὺς λεὼς πιστεύουσιν αὐτοῖς . . . διὰ τὸ ξένα καὶ ἀλλόκοτα εἶναι. Id. *Harmon.* 2: ὁ γάρ τοι πολὺς οὗτος λεώς, αὐτοὶ μὲν ἀγνοοῦσι τὰ βελτίω κ.τ.έ. Id. *Rhet. Praecept.* 17: οὕτω γάρ σε ὁ λεὼς ὁ πολὺς ἀποβλέψονται. Id. *Hist. Conscr.*

[2] In Luke xxi. 30 for βλέποντες ἀφ' ἑαυτῶν γινώσκετε the same intrepid critic would read 'e Codd.' (?): ὅταν προβάλωσιν ἤδη, ἀπ' αὐτῶν (τῶν δένδρων) γινώσκεται κ.τ.έ.

10: ἢν μὴ τὸν συρφετὸν καὶ τὸν πολὺν δῆμον ἐπινοήσαις.]

38 ST MARK. XIV. 2

'it is known,' does not occur in the N. T. (Matt. xii. 33, ἐκ τοῦ καρποῦ τὸ δένδρον γινώσκεται, is quite another thing), nor yet in the O. T. (unless Eccles. vi. 10, καὶ ἐγνώσθη ὅ ἐστιν ἄνθρωπος, can be so considered).

In the same verse (=Matt. xxiv. 32) the Edd. and MSS. (such of them as have accents) are divided between the transitive ἐκφύῃ 'putteth forth,' and the intransitive ἐκφυῇ, 'spring forth' (Hieron. et nata fuerint folia). The latter is the more likely, as in the other case we should have expected the aorist ἐκφύσῃ. Thus Euthymius (commenting on Matt. xxiv. 32) explains ὅταν προβάλωσιν in St Luke by ὅταν ἐκφύσῃ τὰ φύλλα. Cf. Symmachus on Psa. ciii. 14: εἰς τὸ ἐκφῦσαι τροφὴν ἀπὸ γῆς.

*XIV. 2: μήποτε ἔσται θόρυβος τοῦ λαοῦ] A. V. 'lest there be an uproar of the people.' R. V. 'lest haply there shall be a tumult of the people.' To the same class belong Col. ii. 8: βλέπετε μή τις ὑμᾶς ἔσται ὁ συλαγωγῶν, 'Take heed lest there shall be any one that maketh spoil of you': and Heb. iii. 12: βλέπετε μήποτε ἔσται ἔν τινι ὑμῶν, 'Take heed lest haply there shall be in any one of you.' In most cases μήποτε is sufficiently rendered by 'lest,' though, occasionally, the addition of 'haply' or 'at any time,' may be an improvement. But what we strongly protest against is the literal translation of μήποτε ἔσται, 'lest there shall be,' instead of the only grammatically correct English rendering, 'lest there be.' We appeal unto CRUDEN. Under 'lest' we find about a hundred examples from both Testaments, of which all but six belong to the form 'lest there be,' 'lest he fall,' &c. In the exceptions, the form is 'lest there should be,' which in five out of the six examples is correct, the verb in the preceding clause being in the past tense; as 2 Cor. xii. 7: 'There was given me a thorn in the flesh, lest I should be exalted above measure.' In the other exception, Heb. ii. 1: 'We ought to give the more earnest heed to the things which we have heard, lest at any time we should let them slip' (μήποτε παραρρυῶμεν), 'we let them' would be more grammatical, and the Revisers have made this very correction. 'Lest there shall be' is not to be found at all. Grammarians have taken subtle distinctions between μήποτε ᾖ and μήποτε ἔσται, but it is doubtful whether the ἰδιῶται καὶ ἀγράμματοι, to whom we are indebted for the four Gospels, knew anything about them. Thus St Matthew writes, ἵνα μὴ θόρυβος γένηται: and it is not at all improbable that the true reason why we find μήποτε ἔσται in the instances quoted, is because the verb εἰμὶ has no aorist, which is the tense required in the present case[1].

XIV. 10: εἷς τῶν δώδεκα] Recent editors have adopted ὁ εἷς τῶν δ. on the authority of BC (ut videtur) LM and ℵ (ex corr.). But ὁ εἷς τῶν δ. can mean nothing but 'the first (No. 1) of the twelve,' which is absurd.

[1] Such a construction as μήποτε ᾖ θόρυβος would not be justified by ἵνα μὴ ᾖ σχίσμα (1 Cor. xii. 25) because a tumult is a single incident, whereas schism is an abiding condition.

R. V. in marg. 'Gr. *the one of the twelve*'; and in text, 'he that was one of the twelve,' which would require ὁ ὢν εἷς τῶν δ. The English reader might surely have been left in ignorance of such *quisquiliae* as these.

XIV. 15: 'A large upper room *furnished* (ἐστρωμένον).' The Greek word signifies 'spread with carpets (στρώματα),' not that the floor of the room, but that the couches (κλῖναι) on which the guests reclined, were so spread. Compare Ezek. xxiii. 41: καὶ ἐκάθου ἐπὶ κλίνης ἐστρωμένης. The articles necessary for the furnishing of a banquet-room are thus described by Aristoph. *Ach.* 1089: τὰ δ' ἄλλα πάντ' ἐστὶν παρεσκευασμένα, | κλῖναι, τράπεζαι, προσκεφάλαια, στρώματα[1]. When, therefore, it is said that the two disciples were shown 'a large upper room ἐστρωμένον,' it is implied that all the other requisites, κλῖναι, τράπεζαι, &c. had been previously provided, the spreading of the στρώματα being the last thing attended to before the arrival of the guests.

XIV. 36: παρένεγκε] A. V. 'Take away.' R. V. 'Remove.' More precisely, 'Turn aside, cause (or suffer) to pass by.' Compare Plut. *Vit. Pelop.* IX: τοῦ δὲ Φυλλίδου παραφέροντος τὸν λόγον, 'letting the remark pass without notice,' not, as Langhorne, 'endeavouring to turn the discourse.' *Ibid.* X: ἐπὶ δὲ τοῦ πρώτου παραφερομένου (while the first storm was passing away) δεύτερον ἐπῆγεν ἡ τύχη χειμῶνα τοῖς ἀνδράσιν. So Buttmann (*Excurs.* III. *ad Demosth. c. Mid.* p. 531, 15) explains τὰς ὥρας παρηνέγκατε (*praeterire sivistis*) τῆς θυσίας καὶ τῆς θεωρίας. To prove the sense of 'take away,' the following passage from Xenoph. *Cyrop.* II. 2, 4 is usually relied on: κἀκεῖνος ἔλαβε μετ' ἐμὲ δεύτερος. ὡς δ' ὁ τρίτος ἔλαβε, καὶ ἔδοξεν αὐτῷ μεῖζον ἑαυτοῦ λαβεῖν, καταβάλλει ὃ ἔλαβεν, ὡς ἕτερον ληψόμενος· καὶ ὁ ἄρταμος (the cook) οἰόμενος αὐτὸν οὐδὲν ἔτι δεῖσθαι ὄψου, ᾤχετο παραφέρων πρὶν λαβεῖν αὐτὸν ἕτερον: where, however, παραφέρων is not *auferens*, but *praeterferens*, 'passing on the dish to the next person[2].'

XIV. 41: ἀπέχει] 'It is enough.' Hieron. *sufficit.* Hesych. Ἀπέχει· ἀπόχρη, ἐξαρκεῖ. In Pseud-Anacreon. *Od.* XXVIII. 33 the poet gives instructions to a painter for the portrait of his mistress, and concludes: Ἀπέχει· βλέπω γὰρ αὐτήν· | τάχα, κηρὲ, καὶ λαλήσεις. 'Enough—the girl herself I view; So like, 'twill soon be speaking too.' These seem to be the only authorities for this use of the word; for in the passage quoted from St Cyril on Hagg. ii. 9 (in the old editions) by Wetstein, Fritzsche, and Dean Alford, ἀπέχει, καὶ πεπλήρωμαι, καὶ δεδέημαι τῶν τοιούτων οὐδενός, the true reading is ἀπέχω, as printed by P. E. Pusey ὁ μακαρίτης in his edition of St Cyril on the XII Prophets, Oxon. 1868.

---

[1] [Cf. Plut. II. p. 181 F: εἰ δέ ποτε δειπνίζοι τοῖς τῶν φίλων ἐχρῆτο, μεταπεμπόμενος ἐκπώματα καὶ στρώματα καὶ τραπέζας.]

[2] [Cf. Athen. (ed. Dind.) XI. 3, p. 464: οἶνος αὐτοῖς ᾠνοχοεῖτο καὶ τραγήματα παρεφέρετο.]

*XIV. 51: περιβεβλημένος σινδόνα ἐπὶ γυμνοῦ] The σινδὼν or 'sheet' is well illustrated from Diog. Laert. VI. 90, where Crates the Cynic philosopher being censured by the magistrates (ἀστυνόμοι) at Athens ὅτι σινδόνα ἠμφίεστο, replies: καὶ Θεόφραστον ὑμῖν δείξω σινδόνα περιβεβλημένον; and when they would not believe him, ἀπήγαγεν ἐπὶ κουρεῖον, καὶ ἔδειξε κειρόμενον. Perhaps the rendering 'cast about his body' conveys an idea of hurry and want of preparation, not in the original word, which is usually rendered 'clothed' or 'arrayed,' and in the above quotation is interchanged with ἠμφίεστο. We should prefer 'having a sheet *wrapped about* his naked body'; and in Acts xii. 8 (where the whole narrative negatives the idea of a hasty flight) for περιβαλοῦ τὸ ἱμάτιόν σου, '*wrap* thy garment about thee.'

XIV. 53: συνέρχονται αὐτῷ (sc. τῷ ἀρχιερεῖ)] These words may mean, either 'there come with him,' or, 'there come together unto him,' not, as A. V., 'with him were assembled,' nor, as R. V., 'there come together with him.' We prefer taking αὐτῷ as equivalent to πρὸς αὐτόν[1]. The High Priest was already in his house; the others came together on receiving a summons from him. So both Syriac versions, ܥܠܘܗܝ ܐܬܟܢܫܘ. There is the same ambiguity in John xi. 33, where the former sense is the more probable one.

XIV. 65: ῥαπίσμασιν αὐτὸν ἔβαλλον] For ἔβαλλον or ἔβαλον the oldest MSS. read ἔλαβον (ABCℵ) or ἐλάμβανον (DG). With the last agrees the Philoxenian Syriac (ܡܩܒܠܝܢ ܗܘܘ). Dean Alford explains ἔλαβον 'took him in hand,' 'treated him'; Meyer, 'took him into custody'(!); R. V. 'received him with blows of their hands (Or, *strokes of rods*),' as if he was now for the first time handed over to the officers, instead of having been in their custody from his apprehension. There is a verbal correspondence between the Greek ῥαπίσμασι λαβεῖν τινα, and an expression of Cicero's (*Tusc.* II. 14): 'Spartae vero pueri ad aram sic *verberibus accipiuntur*, ut multus e visceribus sanguis exeat.' But such a rude reception on the occasion of their first introduction to Diana Orthia is something very different from the present case; and if such a sense had been intended, the Greek would probably have been μετὰ ῥαπισμάτων αὐτὸν ἐδέξαντο. On the other hand, supposing ἔβαλον to have been the original reading, the phrase βάλλειν ῥαπίσμασι may have appeared a καινῶς ῥηθέν to a transcriber accustomed only to such combinations as βάλλειν λίθοις, βέλεσι, &c., who might therefore have thought ἔλαβον (the

---

[1] [A good example is Plut. *Vit. Timol.* XXV. The Syracusans were so terrified at the greatness of the Carthaginian armament—ὥστε μόλις τῷ Τιμο- λέοντι (their commander) τρισχιλίους ἀπὸ τοσούτων μυριάδων ὅπλα λαβόντας τολμῆσαι συνελθεῖν.]

two words being constantly interchanged with one another) more likely to be the true reading. On ῥαπίσμασιν see on John xviii. 22.

XIV. 72: καὶ ἐπιβαλὼν ἔκλαιε] A. V. 'And when he thought thereon, he wept. Or, *he wept abundantly*, or, *he began to weep.*' The first of these is retained by R. V. in the text, the third in the margin.

Of these three versions, the *first* is, probably, taken from Beza, who, while giving the preference to another translation, *cum erupisset, cum sese foras prorupisset*, adds : 'The words might, perhaps, be rendered *cum hoc animadvertisset*, as if he had been suddenly roused out of a deep sleep by Christ's looking upon him [which, however, St Mark does not mention] and the crowing of the cock.' The *second* version, 'he wept abundantly,' is arrived at by taking ἐπιβαλών in the sense of προσθείς (as Luke xix. 11 : προσθεὶς εἶπε) q. d. *adjiciens, superaddens, vehementer flebat*. So, it is argued, the word is used in such phrases as ἐπιβαλών φησι, ἐπιβαλὼν ἐρωτᾷ (Theophr. *Char.* VIII), where, however, the meaning rather seems to be *subjiciens, sermonem excipiens, taking up the discourse*. The *third* version, 'he began to weep,' is that of the Vulgate and both Syriac versions (Pesh. καὶ ἤρξατο κλαίειν; Philox. καὶ ἀρξάμενος ἔκλαιε, the former of which has found its way into the text of Cod. D, and the latter is one of the alternative explanations given by Theophylact, ἢ ἀρξάμενος (ἢ) μετὰ σφοδρότητος). And if the Greek had been καὶ ἐπέβαλε κλαίειν, this rendering would have been less open to criticism on grammatical grounds than any other. But there is one objection common to all three renderings, namely, that they are frigid and lifeless ; they present no new idea ; instead of enlivening the description, they rather enfeeble it. Especially is this true of the first, 'when he thought thereon, he wept.' The chord was struck, the sluices were opened, when ' Peter called to mind the word that Jesus had said unto him, Before the cock crow twice, thou shalt deny me thrice.' Then, say St Matthew and St Luke, ' Peter went out, and wept bitterly.' Instead of the epithet St Mark introduces an additional action, ἐπιβαλὼν ἔκλαιε, 'he *did something*, and wept.' He might have done many things to show the intensity of his grief. He might have thrown himself on the ground (as Xenoph. Ephes. p. 22 (ed. Londini, 1726): καταβαλόντες ἑαυτοὺς ἔκλαιον: or p. 50: αὐτὸν ἐπὶ τῆς εὐνῆς ῥίψας ἔκλαιεν); he might have 'turned himself about,' like Joseph (Gen. xlii. 24: ἀποστραφεὶς δὲ ἀπ᾽ αὐτῶν ἔκλαυσε)[1]; he might have covered his face, like David mourning for Absalom (2 Sam. xix. 4)[2]. Any of these actions would have expressed in a lively manner the ἔκλαυσε πικρῶς of the other Evangelists; and the last, ' he covered his head and wept,' besides its characteristic propriety, may be shown to be not unsupported on linguistical grounds.

[1] [Cf. Aristaen. I. *Ep.* 22 : ἐδάκρυέ τε ἀστακτὶ μεταστραφεὶς ἐπὶ θάτερα.]

[2] [Or, fleeing from Jerusalem, 2 Kings (Sam.) xv. 30 : ἀναβαίνων καὶ κλαίων καὶ τὴν κεφαλὴν ἐπικεκαλυμμένος.]

The custom of covering the head in weeping is well known. Women did so, that they might indulge their grief more freely. Thus Charit. Aphrod. I. 1: ἔρριπτο ἐπὶ τῆς κοίτης, ἐγκεκαλυμμένη καὶ δακρύσασα. 3: ταῦτα εἰποῦσα ἀπεστράφη, καὶ συγκαλυψαμένη δακρύων ἀφῆκε πηγάς. In the case of men there was an additional reason for so doing, tears in the sterner sex being considered as undignified, and even unmanly[1]. There are many indications of this feeling both in sacred and profane writers, some of which may be quoted for the sake of the variety of expressions used in this connexion. Thus Eurip. *Orest.* 280: ξύγγονε, τί κλαίεις, κρᾶτα θεῖσ' ἔσω πέπλων; *Iph. Aul.* 1547: ὡς δ' ἐσεῖδεν 'Αγαμέμνων ἄναξ | ἐπὶ σφαγὰς στείχουσαν εἰς ἄλσος κόρην, | ἀπεστέναξε, κἄμπαλιν στρέψας κάρα | δάκρυα προῆγεν, ὀμμάτων πέπλον προθείς[2]. Plat. *Phaed.* p. 117 C: ἀλλ' ἐμοῦ γε βίᾳ καὶ ἀστακτὶ ἐχώρει τὰ δάκρυα, ὥστε ἐγκαλυψάμενος ἀπέκλαιον ἐμαυτόν. Plut. *Vit. Timol.* IV: ὁ μὲν Τιμολέων ἀποχωρήσας μικρὸν αὐτῶν καὶ συγκαλυψάμενος εἱστήκει δακρύων[3]. It appears, therefore, that if St Mark had written καὶ ἐγκαλυψάμενος ἔκλαιε (the very expression which occurs in Isocr. *Trapez.* p. 362 B: ἐπειδὴ ἤλθομεν εἰς ἀκρόπολιν, ἐγκαλυψάμενος ἔκλαιε), there could have been no doubt of his meaning; and Dean Alford would hardly have ventured on the remark: 'This explanation of ἐπιβαλών, although it suits the sense very well, appears *fanciful.*' The only question is, whether ἐπιβαλών would be likely to convey the same idea to a Greek reader as ἐπικαλυψάμενος or συγκαλυψάμενος. It certainly did so to Theophylact, who explains it by ἐπικαλυψάμενος τὴν κεφαλήν. It is no objection to this sense of the word that it requires ἱμάτιον or some such word to be mentally supplied; since that is the case with ἐπικαλυψάμενος (the full phrase being τῷ ἱματίῳ τὴν κεφαλὴν ἐπικ. or ἐγκ. as Plut. *Vit. Brut.* XVII). In Charit. Aphrod. I. 3 we meet with the elliptical expression καὶ περιρρηξάμενος ἔκλαιε, where the action intended is equally clear. In 1 Cor. xi. 4 the phrase κατὰ κεφαλῆς ἔχων, in connexion with praying or prophesying, has never occasioned any perplexity[4]; nor even the still harsher ellipsis in the Greek version of Esth. vi. 12: 'Αμὰν δὲ ὑπέστρεψεν εἰς τὰ ἴδια λυπούμενος κατὰ κεφαλῆς (Heb. *operto capite*). In all these instances the association of ideas between *sorrowing,* and *covering the head,* or *rending the clothes,* supplies the missing link, and enables the

---

[1] [Cf. Aristaen. I. *Ep.* 10: κλαίειν γὰρ αἰδούμενος τὴν ἡμέραν, τὸ δάκρυον ἐταμιεύετο ταῖς νυξί.]

[2] This seems to be the most probable explanation of the veiling of Agamemnon in Timanthes' picture of the Sacrifice of Iphigenia, and not the one commonly given, that the painter had exhausted his skill on the other figures.

[3] [Cf. Plut. *Vit. Cleom.* XXV: πολὺν

μὲν χρόνον ἔκλαιε τὴν χλαμύδα θέμενος πρὸ τοῦ προσώπου. Id. *Caes.* XLI: ἀπῆλθεν ἐγκαλυψάμενος καὶ καταδακρύσας (Cato on seeing the number of slain of the enemy). Id. *Phoc.* XXXIV: οἱ μὲν βέλτιστοι τῶν πολιτῶν ὀφθέντος τοῦ Φωκίωνος ἐνεκαλύψαντο καὶ κάτω κύψαντες ἐδάκρυον.]

[4] [Cf. Plut. II. p. 200 E: καὶ τῆς νεὼς ἀποβάς, ἐβάδιζε κατὰ κεφαλῆς ἔχων τὸ ἱμάτιον.]

reader or hearer to choose, out of a great variety of possible meanings, that which the writer or speaker had in his mind. That ἐπιβαλεῖν may be properly said of the wearing of apparel is not denied. Thus Lev. xix. 19: ἱμάτιον ἐκ δύο ὑφασμένον οὐκ ἐπιβαλεῖς σεαυτῷ. Aristoph. *Eccles.* 536: ἐπιβαλοῦσα τοὔγκυκλον. Eurip. *Elect.* 1221: ἐγὼ μὲν ἐπιβαλὼν φάρη κόραις ἐμαῖσι. It may have been a *trivial* or *colloquial* word, such as would have stirred the bile of a Phrynichus or a Thomas Magister, who would have inserted it in their *Index expurgatorius* with a caution, Ἐπιβαλὼν μὴ λέγε, ἀλλὰ ἐγκαλυψάμενος ἢ ἐπικαλυψάμενος. But in this, as in most of the examples of vulgar or non-Attic words and phrases stigmatized by those grammatical purists, *Magna est* ἡ συνήθεια, *et praevalebit;* popular usage is more than a match for critical canons. We shall only add that the two Greek scholars who have most elaborately discussed the point in question, Salmasius in the early days of classical learning, and C. F. A. Fritzsche in our own time, have unhesitatingly come to the same conclusion; the former (*De Foenore Trapezitico*, p. 272) adding 'Quae sola expositio vera est, ceterae omnes falsae'; the latter (*Comment. in Evang. Marci*, p. 664) 'Omnes veritatis numeros eorum rationem habere existimo, qui transferunt, *Et veste capiti injecta flevit.*'

XV. 6: ἀπέλυεν αὐτοῖς ἕνα δέσμιον, ὅνπερ ᾐτοῦντο] A. V. 'whomsoever they desired.' R. V. 'whom they asked of him.' The latter represents ὃν παρῃτοῦντο, which is the reading of ABℵ, but has no support from the versions (Vulg. *quemcunque petiissent*, Syr. ‎ܐ‎‎ܝ‎‎ܢ‎ ‎ܙ‎‎ܒ‎‎ܐ‎‎ܠ‎‎ܐ‎‎ܢ‎), the preposition being represented by the addition 'of him.' To this it may be objected (1) that the word παραιτεῖσθαι in the N. T. bears an entirely different meaning, *to refuse, decline, avoid, deprecate*, conformably with the usage of good Greek writers. (2) By the latter παραιτεῖσθαί τινα is occasionally used for ἐξαιτεῖσθαι, *to beg off* (as one condemned to death), which would be very suitable in Matt. xxvii. 20: 'But the chief priests and elders persuaded the multitude that they should ask for (αἰτήσωνται) Barabbas, and destroy Jesus.' But what is wanted here is some word expressive of the *will* or *choice* of the people in regard to the object of their accustomed privilege. So St Matthew: 'Now at that feast the governor was wont to release unto the people a prisoner, *whom they would* (ὃν ἤθελον).' And St Luke: 'And he released unto them him that for sedition and murder was cast into prison, whom they desired (ὃν ᾐτοῦντο).' We therefore adhere to the T. R.

*XV. 24: τίς τί ἄρῃ] 'What each should take.' Gr. *who should take what*. Compare Luke xix. 15: ἵνα γνῷ τίς τί διεπραγματεύσατο. The construction has been traced up to Homer's τίς πόθεν εἰς ἀνδρῶν; but that is different, being merely an omission of the copula. Better examples are Xenoph. *Mem.* II. 2, 3: τίνας οὖν ὑπὸ τίνων εὕροιμεν ἂν μείζονα εὐηργετημένους ἢ παῖδας ὑπὸ γονέων; Plat. *Phaedr.* p. 259 c: ἐλθὸν παρὰ Μούσας ἀπαγγέλλειν τίς τίνα αὐτῶν τιμᾷ τῶν ἐνθάδε. Charit. Aphrod. I. 8: τίνα τίς ἄγγελον πέμψει; Philostr. *Vit. Apoll.* III. p. 114 (ch. xxiv. ed. Didot): τίς τί ἄγοι. Euseb. *H. E.* v. 18: τίς οὖν τίνι χαρίζεται τὰ ἁμαρτήματα;

*XV. 36. **καθελεῖν αὐτόν**] This is the technical word for the operation here described. Wetst. quotes Polyb. I. 86: τοῦτον μὲν οὖν παραχρῆμα πρὸς τὸν τοῦ Σπενδίου σταυρὸν ἀγαγόντες...ἐκεῖνον μὲν καθεῖλον, τοῦτον δ' ἀνέθεσαν ζῶντα. I add Charit. Aphrod. VIII. 8: ἐκέλευσε καθαιρεθῆναί με τοῦ σταυροῦ, σχεδὸν ἤδη πέρας ἔχοντα. Philo *De Legg. spec.* T. II. p. 324: μὴ ἐπιδύετω ὁ ἥλιος ἀνεσκολοπισμένοις, ἀλλ' ἐπικρυπτέσθωσαν γῇ πρὸ δύσεως καθαιρεθέντες. Plut. *Vit. Themist.* XXII: οὗ νῦν τὰ σώματα τῶν θανατουμένων οἱ δήμιοι προβάλλουσι, καὶ τὰ ἱμάτια καὶ τοὺς βρόχους τῶν ἀπαγχομένων (of those who hang themselves?) καὶ καθαιρεθέντων ἐκφέρουσι (Langhorne: 'of such as have been strangled, or *otherwise put to death*(?)'). Anton. Lib. XIII: ὤμοσεν ὅτι πρότερον τίσεται τὸν τύραννον, ἢ τὸ σῶμα καθαιρήσει τὸ τῆς ἀδελφῆς (she hanged herself). Plut. *Vit. Agis* XX: ὡς δὲ ἐθεάσατο τὴν μητέρα νεκρὰν ἐκ τοῦ βρόχου κρεμαμένην, ἐκείνην μὲν αὐτὴ τοῖς ὑπηρέταις συγκαθεῖλε.

XV. 43: **τολμήσας εἰσῆλθε πρὸς Πιλᾶτον**] 'Went in boldly unto Pilate.' So Vulg. (*audacter introivit*) and all other English versions that I know of, except an anonymous one (Lond., G. Morrish) which has 'emboldened himself,' for which the more biblical English would appear to be 'took courage' (2 Chron. xv. 8). And this is the rendering of Casaubon, Schleusner, and Fritzsche, who, however, do not give any examples except the Homeric, θαρσήσας μάλα εἶπε. H. Steph. quotes Herodian. VIII. 5, 22: τολμήσαντες οὖν (*sumpta audacia*) ἐπίασι τῇ σκηνῇ αὐτοῦ. I add Plut. *Vit. Cam.* XXXIV: οἱ μὲν οὖν πολιορκούμενοι θαρρήσαντες (taking heart) ἐπεξιέναι διενοοῦντο καὶ μάχην συνάπτειν. *Ibid.* XXII: ἐπεὶ δὲ τολμήσας τις ἐξ αὐτῶν (Gallorum) ἐγγὺς παρέστη Παπειρίῳ Μανίῳ, καὶ προσαγαγὼν τὴν χεῖρα, πράως ἥψατο τοῦ γενείου. Langhorne: 'At last one of them ventured to go near Papirius Manius, and advancing his hand, gently stroked his beard.' This last example, which has hitherto escaped notice, seems to be conclusive in favour of the rendering, 'took courage, and went in unto Pilate[1].'

*XVI. 8: **εἶχε δὲ αὐτὰς τρόμος καὶ ἔκστασις**] 'For they trembled and were amazed.' R. V. 'for trembling and astonishment had come upon

---

[1] [Cf. Lucian. *Philops.* 24: ἐγὼ δὲ θαρσήσας ἐπέκυψα. App. *B. C.* III. 13: καὶ τὸ δόγμα ἔφη γενέσθαι μηδενός πω τοὺς ἀνδροφόνους διώκοντος· ἀλλ' ὁπότε θαρσήσας τις διώκοι.... Plut. *Vit. Demetr.* XLIV: τέλος δὲ τῷ Δ. τολμήσαντές τινες προσελθεῖν. 'Had the as-surance to go to D.' Langhorne. Babr. XXXI. 12: καί τις γαλῆν μῦς προυκαλεῖτο θαρσήσας. XXV. 8: καί τις (leporum) εἶπε θαρσήσας. They were going to drown themselves as being the weakest of animals, but found the frogs fled from them.]

them.' Literally, 'had hold of them, possessed them.' It is nearly the same as ἔλαβε, which is 'had taken hold of,' Luke v. 26, vii. 16, Plut. *Vit. Crass.* XI: ἐφοβήθη μὴ λάβοι τις ὁρμὴ τὸν Σπάρτακον ἐπὶ τὴν Ῥώμην ἐλαύνειν, or κατέσχε, Jerem. vi. 24: θλῖψις κατέσχεν ἡμᾶς. Ἔχειν is so used in the best Greek Authors from Homer and Herodotus down to Plut., *Vit. Popl.* VII: ἔκπληξις εἶχε καὶ φρίκη καὶ σιωπὴ πάντας ἐπὶ τοῖς διαπεπραγμένοις. Id. *Vit. Pomp.* XXXVIII: αὐτὸν δέ τις ἔρως καὶ ζῆλος εἶχε Συρίαν ἀναλαβεῖν. Ach. Tat. I. 4: πάντα δέ με εἶχεν ὁμοῦ, ἔπαινος, ἔκπληξις, τρόμος, αἰδώς, ἀναίδεια.

ST LUKE.

Chap. I. v. 37: ὅτι οὐκ ἀδυνατήσει παρὰ τῷ θεῷ πᾶν ῥῆμα] A. V. 'For with God nothing shall be impossible.' We may compare, for παρὰ τῷ θεῷ, Matt. xix. 26: παρὰ ἀνθρώποις τοῦτο ἀδύνατόν ἐστιν, παρὰ δὲ θεῷ πάντα δυνατά. But the text, being undoubtedly a reminiscence of (if we may not say, a quotation from) Gen. xviii. 14 in the LXX. μὴ ἀδυνατήσει παρα τῷ θεῷ ῥῆμα, must be considered with reference to that place[1]. The Hebrew is הֲיִפָּלֵא מֵיְהֹוָה דָּבָר, 'Is any thing too wonderful (=hard) for the LORD?' where מֵיְהֹוָה should have been translated ὑπὲρ τὸν θεόν, not παρὰ τῷ θεῷ (or, as the Cod. Cotton. and one or two cursives read, παρὰ τοῦ θεοῦ, which *may have been* the reading of the Vatican and Sinaitic MSS. when perfect, and which certainly represents the usual force of the Hebrew preposition better than the other). Another text bearing on the question under discussion is Jerem. xxxii. 17, where the LXX. taking the Hebrew word in another meaning (as our Translators have done in Deut. xxx. 11, 'It is not *hidden* from thee'), have rendered οὐ μὴ ἀποκρυβῇ ἀπὸ σοῦ οὐδέν, for which Aquila gives οὐκ ἀδυνατήσει ἀπὸ σοῦ πᾶν ῥῆμα (observe that this translator always renders מִן by ἀπό, even when it is clearly ὑπέρ), and Symmachus οὐκ ἀδυνατήσει σοι (compare Matt. xvii. 20: καὶ οὐδὲν ἀδυνατήσει ὑμῖν[2]). Returning to the text, we observe that the very same variation παρὰ τοῦ θεοῦ is found in BDLא[1] (against ACא[3]), which circumstance, taken in conjunction with the disputed reading of Gen. xviii. 14, certainly makes out a strong case against the received text, although perfectly unobjectionable in itself, and supported by the Vulgate and both Syriac versions. Supposing then that St Luke wrote ὅτι οὐκ ἀδυνατήσει παρὰ τοῦ θεοῦ πᾶν ῥῆμα, how is this to be explained? The translation adopted by the Revisers is, 'For no word from God shall be void of power.' On which we remark (1) that it seems to require some word connecting πᾶν ῥῆμα with παρὰ τοῦ θεοῦ; as, in English, 'no word *which proceedeth* from God'; or, in Greek, παρὰ τοῦ θεοῦ ἐκπορευόμενον πᾶν ῥῆμα; or, if not, a different arrangement of the words, ὅτι οὐκ ἀδυνατήσει πᾶν ῥῆμα παρὰ τοῦ θεοῦ

---

[1] This reading (ἀδυνατήσει) is adopted by Holmes and Parsons in their edition of the LXX. In his own edition

Dr Field reads ἀδυνατεῖ. Ed.
[2] [Cf. also Job xlii. 2: ἀδυνατεῖ δέ σοι οὐδέν.]

(as 1 Kings (Sam.) xvi. 14: καὶ ἔπνιγεν αὐτὸν πνεῦμα πονηρὸν παρὰ κυρίου. Lam. ii. 9: καίγε προφῆται αὐτῆς οὐκ εἶδον ὅρασιν παρὰ κυρίου). And (2) that ἀδυνατεῖν never has the meaning, 'to be void of power[1]'; but either (of things) 'to be impossible,' or (of persons) 'to be unable,' in which latter case it is invariably followed by a verb in the infinitive mood. To afford the sense proposed, the Greek should have been οὐκ ἀσθενήσει, or οὐκ ἀνενέργητον ἔσται. This last objection, however, might be obviated by translating, 'For from God no word (or, nothing) shall be impossible.'

II. 7, 12: 'Wrapped in swaddling clothes' (ἐσπαργανωμένον). Ch. xxiv. 12: 'the linen clothes' (ὀθόνια). John xi. 44: 'bound hand and foot with grave clothes' (κειρίαι). xx. 5, 6, 7: 'linen clothes' (ὀθόνια). Since the distinction between *cloths* (plural of *cloth*) and *clothes* (plural without a singular) has long been established, both in spelling and pronouncing, there seems no reason why the English reader of the N. T. should not have the benefit of it. The Revisers have accepted this suggestion in the second and fourth examples, but have left the two others unaltered[2]. In the present text all room for misunderstanding would be taken away by the use of the biblical term 'swaddlingbands.' Compare Job xxxviii. 9: 'And thick darkness a swaddlingband for it,' where LXX.: ὀμίχλῃ δὲ αὐτὴν ἐσπαργάνωσα; and the well-known Christmas Hymn, 'All meanly wrapped in swathing bands.'

II. 9: ἄγγελος κυρίου ἐπέστη αὐτοῖς] A. V. 'came upon them.' R. V. 'stood by them[3].' In Ch. xxiv. 4 both versions have 'Behold, two men stood by them.' The word properly signifies any *sudden* or *unexpected arrival*, or *coming* of one party *upon* another[4]. So 1 Thess. v. 3: τότε αἰφνίδιος αὐτοῖς ἐφίσταται ὄλεθρος, ὥσπερ ἡ ὠδὶν τῇ ἐν γαστρὶ ἐχούσῃ. In the present instance the A. V. fairly represents the Greek; but in v. 38 ἐπιστᾶσα is not 'coming in,' for she was probably in the temple before; nor yet 'standing near' (Scholefield, *Hints for an Improved Translation of the N. T.*, p. 22), for that would imply that she had been present during the preceding incident; but (as rightly R. V.) 'coming up.' We read in the life of Myson (Diog. Laert. I. 108) that that philosopher once fell a-laughing when he was in a perfect solitude: ἄφνω δέ τινος ἐπιστάντος, καὶ πυθομένου διὰ τί μηδενὸς παρόντος γελᾷ, φάναι· δι' αὐτὸ τοῦτο.

*II. 12: 'Ye shall find (εὑρήσετε) a babe,' 16, 'they found (ἀνεῦρον) both M. and J. and the babe.' It is singular that the Revisers should have failed to distinguish the simple and compound verbs. The former indicates no more than coming upon a thing, as in Luke xxiv. 23, 24: 'and

---

[1] [Except Lev. xxv. 35 (of a person): καὶ ἀδυνατήσῃ ταῖς χερσὶν παρὰ σοί, where many MSS. read ἀδυναμήσῃ.]

[2] [Except that in John xi. 44 they suggest 'grave-bands' in the margin.]

[3] [But in Luke xxi. 34, R.V. 'come on': A.V. 'come upon.']

[4] [Cf. Lucian. *De Gymn.* 34: καὶ ἄδηλον ὁπότε τις ἐπιστάς, κοιμώμενον κατασπάσας ἀπὸ τῆς ἁμάξης φονεύσειεν.]

when they *found* not his body'...'we went to the sepulchre, and *found* it even so as the women had said.' The latter implies a previous search, 'they found out' or 'discovered,' as in Acts xxi. 4: ἀνευρόντες δὲ τοὺς μαθητάς, 'and having *found out* the disciples.' Take a few examples. Herod. IV. 127: τυγχάνουσι ἡμῖν ἐόντες τάφοι πατρώϊοι· φέρετε, τούτους ἀνευρόντες, συγχέειν πειρᾶσθε αὐτούς. Plut. *Vit. Marcel*. XIX: τὸν αὐτόχειρα τοῦ ἀνδρὸς (Archimedes) ἀπεστράφη καθάπερ ἐναγῆ, τοὺς δ' οἰκείους ἀνευρὼν ἐτίμησεν. Id. *Vit. Cam*. XXXII. (in searching the ruins of the Hut of Mars) τοῦτο δὴ τότε (the *lituus* of Romulus) τῶν ἄλλων ἀπολωλότων ἀνευρόντες διαπεφευγὸς τὴν φθοράν. 'The word ἀνευρίσκειν, peculiar to St Luke...is employed by the medical writers of finding out the seat of a disease[1].'

II. 14: ἐν ἀνθρώποις εὐδοκία] 'Good will toward men.' For 'good will' it would be better, perhaps, to substitute 'good pleasure.' Εὐδοκεῖν and εὐδοκία, which answer to the Hebrew רָצָה and רָצוֹן, are especially used in Scripture of the *favour* or *feeling of complacency* with which God regards his people. Thus LXX. Psa. cxlvi. 11: εὐδοκεῖ κύριος ἐν τοῖς φοβουμένοις αὐτόν. Psa. cv. 4: μνήσθητι ἡμῶν, κύριε, ἐν τῇ εὐδοκίᾳ τοῦ λαοῦ σου. Sym. Prov. xiv. 9: καὶ ἀναμέσον εὐθέων εὐδοκία. Hardly to be distinguished from these are חָפֵץ and חֵפֶץ, generally rendered by θέλειν and θέλημα; e.g. Psa. xvii. 20: ῥύσεταί με, ὅτι ἠθέλησέ με. Eccles. v. 3: οὐκ ἔσται θέλημα (sc. θεοῦ) ἐν ἄφροσι. On a consideration of these and similar passages we shall have no difficulty in understanding by εὐδοκία the *favour* or *good pleasure of God*, shown *towards men* (ἐν ἀνθρώποις) by the birth of the Saviour of mankind. We may measure (humanly speaking) the intensity of the divine benevolence displayed on this occasion, by comparing it with that which he himself expresses towards the chosen instrument of it: 'This is my beloved Son, in whom I am well pleased (ἐν ᾧ εὐδόκησα).' From henceforth men will be εὐαρεστοῦντες τῷ θεῷ, and God will be εὐδοκῶν ἐν αὐτοῖς[2].

With respect to the force of the preposition, we adhere to the A. V. No doubt, in good Greek, 'good will toward men' would be εὔνοια πρὸς τοὺς ἀνθρώπους, as Plut. *Vit. Lucull.* 1: τῆς δὲ πρὸς τὸν ἀδελφὸν αὐτοῦ Μάρκον εὐνοίας πολλῶν τεκμηρίων ὄντων κ.τ.λ.[3] But the regular construction of the Hebrew verbs and nouns aforesaid being with the preposition בְּ of the object, the corresponding Greek terms εὐδοκεῖν, θέλειν, εὐδοκία, θέλημα follow the same rule; and in the present case, the object of the 'good

---

[1] Hobart (W. K.), *On the medical language of St Luke*, p. 99.

[2] St Chrysost. T. XI. p. 347 B: Δόξα κ.τ.έ. ἰδού, φησί, καὶ ἄνθρωποι ἐφάνησαν εὐαρεστοῦντες λοιπόν. τί ἐστιν, εὐδοκία; ΚΑΤΑΛΛΑΓΗ. We are reminded of another Christmas Hymn:

'Peace on earth and mercy mild; God and sinners RECONCILED.'

[3] [Εὔνοια is said of men; εὐμένεια more correctly of divine favour. Lucian. *De Gymn.* 33: ὡς δὲ νῦν ἔχετε, θεῶν τινος εὐμενείᾳ σώζεσθαί μοι δοκεῖτε.]

pleasure' being 'men,' ἐν ἀνθρώποις εὐδοκία is rightly translated 'good pleasure in men,' or 'good will toward men,' not, as in the margin of R. V., 'good pleasure among men.'

The Revisers, as might have been foreseen, have followed the reading of the principal uncials and the Latin Vulgate, καὶ ἐπὶ γῆς εἰρήνη ἐν ἀνθρώποις εὐδοκίAC, 'And on earth peace among men in whom is well pleased.' To which it may be (briefly) objected, (1) that it ruins the *stichometry*; (2) that it separates ἐν from εὐδοκία, the word with which it is normally construed; (3) that 'men of good pleasure' (אַנְשֵׁי רָצוֹן) would be, according to Graeco-biblical usage, not ἄνθρωποι εὐδοκίας, but ἄνδρες εὐδοκίας[1]; (4) that the turn of the sentence, ἐν ἀνθρώποις εὐδοκία, very much resembles that of the second clause of Prov. xiv. 9: וּבֵין יְשָׁרִים רָצוֹן, rendered (as we have seen) by Symmachus: καὶ ἀναμέσον εὐθέων εὐδοκία.

*Other renderings of ἐν ἀνθρώποις εὐδοκίας have been proposed, as 'among men of his counsel for good,' or 'of his gracious purpose' (*Contemp. Rev.* Dec. 1881, p. 1003), 'among men of contentment,' or 'contented men' (!). It has even been suggested that 'there is no need to take εὐδοκίας as distinguishing certain men from the rest: the phrase admits likewise the more probable sense, "in (among and within) accepted mankind."' (Westcott and Hort, App. p. 56.) But although, taken alone, ἐν ἀνθρώποις can only mean ἐν τῷ ἀνθρωπίνῳ γένει, yet the assumption of an epithet has the immediate effect of defining and marking off a select portion of mankind, to which the particular description applies. In fact ἄνθρωποι εὐδοκίας or εὐδοκητοί is exactly equivalent to ἄνθρωποι ἐκλογῆς or ἐκλεκτοί, and 'accepted mankind' is almost as great an absurdity as 'selected mankind.'[2]

II. 37: καὶ αὐτὴ χήρα ὡς ἐτῶν ὀγδοήκοντα τεσσάρων] 'And she *was* a widow of about fourscore and four years.' For ὡς the uncials ABLℵ[1] read ἕως, which the Vulgate renders, *Et haec vidua usque ad annos*

---

[1] I have examined all the instances of similar combinations in the O. T., and cannot find a single one in which ἄνθρωπος is so used. The following are the principal ones: 2 Sam. xvi. 7: אִישׁ הַדָּמִים. O'. ἀνὴρ αἱμάτων. *Ibid.* xviii. 20: אִישׁ בְּשֹׂרָה. O'. ἀνὴρ εὐαγγελίας. Psa. lxxx. 18: עַל־אִישׁ יְמִינֶךָ. O'. ἐπ' ἄνδρα δεξιᾶς σου. Psa. cxix. 24: אַנְשֵׁי עֲצָתִי. 'A. ἄνδρες βουλῆς μου. Jerem. xv. 10: אִישׁ רִיב. O'. ἄνδρα δικαζόμενον. 'A. ἄνδρα μάχης. Dan.

x. 11: אִישׁ־חֲמֻדוֹת. O'. ἀνὴρ ἐπιθυμιῶν. Obad. 7: אַנְשֵׁי בְרִיתֶךָ. O'. οἱ ἄνδρες τῆς διαθήκης σου. *Ibid.*: אַנְשֵׁי שְׁלֹמֶךָ. O'. ἄνδρες εἰρηνικοί σου. [Prov. xxix. 10: אַנְשֵׁי דָמִים. O'. ἄνδρες αἱμάτων. 2 Sam. viii. 10: אִישׁ מִלְחֲמוֹת. 'A.Σ. ἀνὴρ πολέμων.]

[2] [εὐδοκίας at the end of a line would differ from εὐδοκία only by the addition of the smallest possible c, little more than a point, for which it might have been intended—thus εγΔοκιαᶜ.]

octoginta quatuor, and R. V. 'And she had been a widow even for fourscore and four years'; which number of years, being added to those of her maiden and married state, would make her at this time upwards of a hundred years old, an improbable, though not incredible age. We may compare what is recorded of Judith (xvi. 22, 23), that she remained a widow (οὐκ ἔγνω ἀνὴρ αὐτήν) all the days of her life, from the day that her husband Manasses died; and she increased more and more in greatness, καὶ ἐγήρασεν ἐν τῷ οἴκῳ τοῦ ἀνδρὸς αὐτῆς ἑκατὸν πέντε ἔτη. It should, however, be borne in mind, that ΕΩC might very easily have been written instead of ʳΩC (especially when followed by a noun in the genitive case), and that the phrase χήρα ἕως ἐτῶν seems to require confirmation. Both Syriac versions read ὡς.

The phrase ἀπὸ τῆς παρθενίας αὐτῆς has not yet been illustrated, as it might be, from classical authors; e.g. J. Pollux, III. 39: ἡ δὲ ἐκ παρθενίας τινὶ γεγαμημένη πρωτόποσις ἐκαλεῖτο. Plut. *Vit. Pomp.* LV: οὐ παρθένον, ἀλλὰ χήραν ἀπολελειμμένην νεωστὶ Ποπλίου τοῦ Κράσσου, ᾧ συνῴκησεν ἐκ παρθενίας. Id. *Vit. Brut.* XIII: εἶχε δ' αὐτήν...οὐκ ἐκ παρθενίας, ἀλλὰ τοῦ προτέρου τελευτήσαντος ἀνδρός. Charit. Aphrod. III. 7: ἐμὸς ἀνὴρ ἐκ παρθενίας[1].

*II. 49 : Τί ὅτι ἐζητεῖτέ με; οὐκ ᾔδειτε ὅτι ἐν τοῖς τοῦ πατρός μου δεῖ εἶναί με;] It is unfortunate that the very first words which can be certainly known to have been uttered by our blessed Lord are of *doubtful interpretation*; not, indeed (as we hope to show in this paper)[2], intentionally ambiguous on the part of the speaker, nor even actually such as to fail to convey their intended meaning to the minds of the hearers, but yet so framed as to afford matter of disputation to after times, when Greek should cease to be a spoken language, and the exact force of particular idioms, instead of being seized intuitively, would have to be investigated by the research of learned men, trained to such enquiries, and applying to the conduct of them the accumulated critical stores of preceding ages. Thus, in the case before us, the words ἐν τοῖς τοῦ πατρός μου have been held by competent authorities, down to our own times, to admit of two different meanings, 'about my Father's business,' and 'in my Father's house'; yet it is certain that only one of these was in the mind of the artless child, from whose lips they fell, and that *that* meaning was rightly apprehended by those who heard them. We are told, indeed, that his parents 'understood not the saying which he spake unto them'; but this remark refers not to any difficulty in its grammatical construction, but to its appropriateness in the mouth of the speaker, and its bearing on the actual circumstances. So when, at a later period, our Lord told his disciples that 'the Son of Man should be delivered unto the Gentiles, and they should scourge him, and put

---

[1] [Cf. App. *B. C.* II. 99: Μαρκίᾳ γέ τοι, τῇ Φιλίππου, ξυνὼν ἐκ παρθένου.]

[2] Dr Field printed this note in the form of a pamphlet, January 1879. Ed.

him to death, and the third day he should rise again'; although there could be no possible misunderstanding of the plain grammatical meaning of the words, we read that 'they understood none of these things, and this saying was hid from them, neither knew they the things which were spoken[1].'

We have said that *two* interpretations have been attributed by learned men to the expression here used, only *one* of which (in this place at least) can be the right one. Attempts, indeed, are sometimes made to include *both*; but such comprehensions are usually resorted to by that class of critics whose distrust of their own judgment makes them unwilling to reject any interpretation which may *possibly* be the true one. Thus Dean Alford *ad loc.*: 'Primarily, *in the house of my Father*; but we must not exclude the wider sense, which embraces *all places and employments of my Father*. The best rendering would, perhaps, be, *among my Father's matters[2].*' We shall ask the reader to weigh the evidence which we shall set before him, and to pronounce an unhesitating verdict in favour of one or other of the two renderings now to be discussed.

I.   The first is that of the Authorized Version (A. V.), with which we are all familiar: 'Wist ye not that I must be about my Father's business?'

No example has been produced of the entire phrase, $\epsilon\hat{i}\nu\alpha\iota$ $\dot{\epsilon}\nu$ $\tau o\hat{i}s$ $\tau\iota\nu os$, *to be about a person's business*; although there is no reason why it should not bear that meaning, if clearly required by the context. The authority most strongly urged in favour of this rendering is 1 Tim. iv. 15, where St Paul, after charging Timothy to attend to reading, exhortation, and doctrine, adds: $\tau\alpha\hat{v}\tau\alpha$ $\mu\epsilon\lambda\acute{\epsilon}\tau\alpha$, $\dot{\epsilon}\nu$ $\tau o\acute{v}\tau o\iota s$ $\ddot{\iota}\sigma\theta\iota$. Here the only question is as to the degree of interest and occupation intended to be conveyed by the expression, *being in* the things alluded to, whether ordinary or to the the exclusion of all other objects. The latter seems to be the view of A. V., 'Meditate upon these things, *give thyself wholly to them*'; and of those commentators who compare with St Paul's phrase Horace's *omnis in hoc sum* and *totus in illis*, where, however, the *omnis* and *totus* make a notable difference[3]. If this view were correct, then the phrase, as used

---

[1] Luke xviii. 34.

[2] So Cappellus, though he decides for 'my Father's house,' adds *negotiis videlicet non exclusis;* and Philip Doddridge, the most learned and candid of non-conformists, '*Did ye not know that I ought to be at my Father's?* and that wherever I was, I should be so employed in his service as to be secure of his protection?'

[3] The corresponding Greek phrase,

$\ddot{o}\lambda os$ $\epsilon\hat{i}\nu\alpha\iota$ $\dot{\epsilon}\nu$ $\tau\iota\nu\iota$ $\pi\rho\acute{a}\gamma\mu\alpha\tau\iota$, occurs in a passage of Plutarch (II. p. 342 B), which affords an interesting parallel to this incident of our Lord's childhood. The youthful Alexander, we are told, conversing with the ambassadors of the King of Persia, asked no childish questions (as, for instance, about the Golden Vine, or the Hanging Gardens, or how the king was dressed), $\dot{a}\lambda\lambda$' $\ddot{o}\lambda os$ $\dot{\epsilon}\nu$ $\tau o\hat{i}s$ $\kappa\upsilon\rho\iota\omega\tau\acute{a}\tau o\iota s$ $\hat{\eta}\nu$ $\tau\hat{\eta}s$ $\dot{\eta}\gamma\epsilon\mu o\nu\iota\alpha s$,

by the child Jesus, might appear to be too strong for the occasion, and the example would prove too much. But, in fact, such an entire absorption does *not* seem to be implied, either in St Paul's use of the expression, or in other instances which may be quoted from profane authors. Of these latter we may set aside such as relate to the *general pursuit* or *mode of life* of the persons spoken of, and not to their *actual employment* at the time. 'Nihil est frequentius,' says Jeremiah Markland[1], 'locutione ἔν τινι εἶναι ἐπιστήμῃ, scientiam aliquam tractare, ἐν φιλοσοφίᾳ, ἐν μούσαις εἶναι.' Thus Herod. II. 82 : οἱ ἐν ποιήσει γενόμενοι. Aelian, *V. H.* I. 31 : ἅτε δὴ ὄντες ἐν γεωργίᾳ, καὶ περὶ γῆν πονούμενοι. To which we may add Soph. *Oed. Tyr.* 562 : τότ᾽ οὖν ὁ μάντις οὗτος ἦν ἐν τῇ τέχνῃ ; i.e. 'Did he at that time profess the art of divination?' Making these deductions, we have remaining Xenoph. *Cyrop.* IV. 3, 23 : οἱ μὲν δὴ ἐν τούτοις τοῖς λόγοις ἦσαν. Thucyd. VIII. 14 : πάντες ἐν τειχισμῷ ἦσαν καὶ παρασκευῇ πολέμου. Dion. Hal. VI. 17 : ἐν ἑορταῖς τε καὶ θυσίαις ἦσαν (after a victory). Plut. I. p. 656 B (quoted by Wetstein) : ἐν τούτοις μὲν οὖν ὁ Καῖσαρ ἦν, which seems to be rightly understood by the English translator, 'While Caesar was thus employed.' We need not be surprised if examples of this usage are rare, because the ordinary Greek formula for *occupari in aliqua re* is not εἶναι ἔν τινι πράγματι, but εἶναι περί τι πρᾶγμα, corresponding with the English idiom *to be about any business.* Of this use one or two authors alone will furnish sufficient examples. Thus Diod. Sic. IV. 28 : τοῦ δ᾽ Ἡρακλέους περὶ ταῦτα ὄντος. XII. 84 : Ἀθηναῖοι μὲν οὖν περὶ ταῦτα ἦσαν. XIV. 25 : ὄντων δὲ αὐτῶν περὶ ταῦτα. 57 : περὶ ταῦτα δ᾽ ὄντων αὐτῶν. Dion. Hal. I. 82 : ἐν ᾧ δὲ οὗτοι περὶ ταῦτα ἦσαν. V. 40 : οἱ μὲν δὴ περὶ ταῦτα ἦσαν. So with γίνεσθαι, διατρίβειν, ἀσχολεῖσθαι, &c. As Diod. Sic. XI. 22 : περὶ τὴν θυσίαν γινομένῳ. *Ibid.* 75 : οὗτοι μὲν οὖν περὶ τὰς παρασκευὰς ἐγίνοντο. XII. 51 : τοῦ δὲ Σιτάλκου περὶ ταῦτα διατρίβοντος. *Ibid.* 59 : τῶν δὲ Ἀθηναίων περὶ ταῦτα ἀσχολουμένων[2].

The conclusion from this part of the enquiry seems to be, that if the child Jesus had intended to convey the meaning that 'he must be about his Father's business,' he *might* have said, ἐν τοῖς τοῦ πατρός μου δεῖ

enquiring in what the power of the Persians consisted, what was the king's post in battle, which were the shortest roads from the coast to the interior ; insomuch that the strangers were astonished (ἐκπεπλῆχθαι) &c.

[1] Ad Max. Tyr. XXI. (p. 396 ed. Reiske). Markland was, as we shall presently see, a strong advocate for the other interpretation, 'in my Father's house.' [The words quoted in the text are not to be found in the note by Markland to which Dr Field here

refers, nor have I been able to trace them elsewhere. Ed.]

[2] A later usage seems to have been εἶναι πρός τινι, as Synes. *Ep.* IV. p. 165 B : καὶ οἱ μὲν ἦσαν πρὸς τούτοις. Pausan. *Messen.* XXVII. 7 : καὶ τὴν μὲν τότε ἡμέραν πρὸς θυσίαις τε καὶ εὐχαῖς ἦσαν. Lucian. *D. D.* XIX. 2 : καὶ ὅλως πρὸς τῷ τοιούτῳ ἐστίν. Stob. *Flor.* p. 370, 31 : ὅσα μὲν γὰρ ἔργα πάνυ ἐντείνει τὸ σῶμα καὶ κάμπτει, ταῦτα καὶ τὴν ψυχὴν ἀναγκάζει πρὸς αὐτοῖς εἶναι μόνοις.

εἶναί με, though it is doubtful whether his hearers would have so understood him, considering that the more familiar meaning of this expression was (as will hereafter be shown) something quite different. It is, therefore, more probable that he would have said, περὶ τὰ τοῦ πατρός μου, which is quite free from ambiguity, and more in accordance with the Greek idiom. It is true that we have no other example of this identical combination in the Greek Testament; but St Luke's μεριμνᾷς καὶ τυρβάζῃ περὶ πολλά (Ch. x. 41) and his τοὺς περὶ τὰ τοιαῦτα ἐργάτας (Acts xix. 25) are hardly to be distinguished from it.

Another, and more obvious, form of speech, which might have been employed to express the same idea, would have been, οὐκ ᾔδειτε ὅτι τὰ τοῦ πατρός μου δεῖ πράττειν με; (comparing πράσσειν τὰ ἴδια, 1 Thess. iv. 11). There is also our Lord's own formula, after he had entered upon his real work, τὰ ἔργα τοῦ πατρός μου δεῖ ἐργάζεσθαί με; which, however, might be thought too grave and solemn for the childish incident here recorded.

II. We pass on to the alternative meaning which has been assigned to this passage, 'that I must be *in my Father's house.*'

The omission of the word *house* is common in all languages, both ancient and modern. Thus, such phrases as εἰς Καυκῶνος ἀφίκετο (Ael. V. H. I. 24), εἰς Ἀρκελάου ποτὲ ἀφίκοντο (II. 21), ἐφοίτα εἰς Λαμίας τῆς ἑταίρας (XII. 17), παρῆλθεν εἰς πανδοκέως (XIV. 48), ἐν Φαρναβάζου γενόμενος (IV. 15), ἐν Σύρφακος ἐστιώμενος (Appian VI. 30), might be paralleled in the familiar discourse of our own country[1]. Sometimes the singular article is prefixed to the possessive case of the noun, as ἐν τῷ καπήλου, ἐν τῷ Κηφέως[2], where οἴκῳ may be understood. But what we are now concerned with is the peculiarly Greek usage, by which the article in the neuter plural (τὰ) is utilized for the same purpose. Grammarians invite us to supply οἰκήματα or δώματα, but unnecessarily. Τά τινος are, properly, a person's *things* or *belongings* (as πάντα τὰ τοῦ πατρὸς ἡμῶν Gen. xxxi. 1), and came to be used specially of his *house,* either as being the chief of his possessions, or as being an aggregate of various parts, offices, or *premises.* However this may be, the use itself is certain, and not liable to be misunderstood. Common instances of it are Theocr. *Id.* II. 76: ᾇ τὰ Λύκωνος (where Schol. ὅπου εἰσὶ τὰ οἰκήματα τὰ Λ.); Aristoph. *Vesp.* 1440: παράτρεχ' εἰς τὰ Πιττάλου; Artem. *Onir.* V. 82: ἔθος μὲν γὰρ τοῖς συμβιώταις καὶ εἰς τὰ τῶν ἀποθανόντων εἰσιέναι καὶ δειπνεῖν. This last phrase, εἰς τὰ τοῦ ἀποθανόντος εἰσιέναι, is also quoted by Demosthenes, *c. Macart.* (p. 1071, 6) from one of Solon's laws, as forbidden to women, except those above a certain age, or within a certain degree of relationship. Other examples require a special notice.

1. A clear instance, and one much relied on by those who take this

---

[1] Even the Comic poet's ἥκετ' οὖν εἰς ἐμοῦ, ἴτω εἰς ἐμοῦ (*Lys.* 1063, 1211) exactly correspond with the East Anglian vernacular, 'Come to *mine*,' 'I called at *yours.*'

[2] Lobeck. ad Phryn. p. 100.

view of the text, is Lys. *c. Eratosth.* p. 195 ed. Taylor. 'They overtake us at the very door, and ask us whither we are going ; whereupon my companion replies : εἰς τὰ τοῦ ἀδελφοῦ τοῦ ἐμοῦ, ἵνα καὶ τὰ ἐν ἐκείνῃ τῇ οἰκίᾳ σκέψηται.' On which Markland has this note : 'Hinc illustratur Luc. ii. 49, ἐν τοῖς τοῦ πατρός μου, *in domo patris mei.* Sic Joseph. *Ant.* XVI. 10, 1 : ἦν δ' αὐτῷ καταγωγὴ ἐν τοῖς Ἀντιπάτρου, *hospitio autem Antipatri domo utebatur.* Sic ἐγγὺς τῶν Πυθοδώρου Demosth. *adv. Conon* [p. 1258, 25]. Miror aliquos hunc Lucae locum aliter interpretari et vertere.'

2. Another good example is furnished by St Chrysos. *Hom.* LII. *in Gen.* (*Opp.* T. IV. p. 507 B) : 'Whither dost thou send away the just man (Isaac)? Knowest thou not that wherever he may chance to go, he *must* be in his Master's house (ἐν τοῖς τοῦ δεσπότου ἑαυτοῦ εἶναι αὐτὸν ἀνάγκη)?' This place is quoted by Joh. Boisius (Boys), Canon of Ely[1] ; but was first indicated by Nicolas Fuller (*Miscel. Sacr.* IV. 17) ; on which the Canon remarks : 'Qui amant bonas literas, studiisque cultioribus dediti sunt, multum debent Nicolao propter loci istius indicationem.' I add, from the same author (*Opp.* T. XI. p. 259 B) : ποῖος γὰρ, εἰπέ μοι, υἱὸς, ἐν τοῖς τοῦ πατρὸς πονῶν, καὶ ἑαυτῷ πονῶν, γογγύζει;

3. The LXX. version of the Old Testament, besides Esth. vii. 9 : ἐν τοῖς Ἀμάν, supplies Job xviii. 19, where, after the Hebrew, 'He shall have neither son nor nephew among his people, nor any remaining in his dwellings,' the translator adds *de suo,* ἀλλ' ἐν τοῖς αὐτοῦ ζήσονται ἕτεροι. But the most notable example from this version is Gen. xli. 51 : ὅτι ἐπιλαθέσθαι με ἐποίησεν ὁ θεὸς πάντων τῶν πόνων μου, καὶ πάντων τῶν τοῦ πατρός μου. The latter clause *might* be construed by borrowing πόνων from the former ; but besides the impropriety of Joseph's forgetting his father's troubles, the Hebrew וְאֵת כָּל־בֵּית אָבִי is conclusive in favour of 'and all my father's house[2].'

4. In another class of examples, a plural adjective is used instead of the noun to denote the person whose house it is. Thus Sirac. xlii. 10 : καὶ ἐν τοῖς πατρικοῖς αὐτῆς ἔγκυος γένηται (for ἐν τοῖς τοῦ πατρὸς αὐτῆς). Dion. Hal. VIII. p. 526 (ch. 57), ἀπέλυσαν ἐπὶ τὰ οἰκεῖα. *Ibid.* p. 531 (ch. 63): ἀπῄεσαν ἑκάτεροι ἐπὶ τὰ σφέτερα (for ἐπὶ τὰ ἑαυτῶν). In the Greek Testament itself we find John xvi. 32 : ἕκαστος εἰς τὰ ἴδια (A. V. 'every man to his own, or, *his own home*'). Acts xxi. 6 : ὑπέστρεψαν εἰς τὰ ἴδια (A. V. 'they returned home again'). In the A. V. of John i. 11, 'He came unto *his own,* and *his own* received him not,' an English reader would suppose that the Greek word was the same in both clauses ; which is not the case. In the former it is εἰς τὰ ἴδια, *to his own home* ; in the latter οἱ ἴδιοι, *his own people.*

Besides philological grounds the testimony of the ancient versions, and of the Greek expositors, may be briefly referred to.

---

[1] *Vet. Interpretis cum Beza aliisque recentioribus Collatio* &c. Lond. 1655.

[2] This capital example seems to

have been first pointed out by Pet. Keuchen (*Annotata in omnes N. F. libros,* Lug. Bat. 1775).

With respect to the former, the Vulgate, Arabic, and Ethiopic translate literally, *in his quae patris mei sunt,* which is not decisive in favour of either interpretation. But the Syriac Peschito is clear for *in domo patris mei*; and this being the vernacular idiom both of parents and child, it is highly probable that in the text of this very ancient version, ܩܘܐ ܐ ܠܐ ܒ ܐܘܠ ܐܢܘܐ, we have the identical sounds which fell from the lips of the divine child. The Greek translator may have preferred ἐν τοῖς τοῦ π. μ. to ἐν τῷ οἴκῳ τοῦ π. μ. as being more *trivial,* and therefore more natural in the mouth of a child. Of Greek commentators, to the names of Origen (Cent. III)[1], Theophylact (XI), and Euthymius (XII), which are commonly appealed to in favour of this rendering, we may add Epiphanius (IV)[2] and Theodoret (V)[3].

On a review of the arguments on both sides, the reader will, probably, be inclined to think that the preponderance is greatly in favour of the second interpretation. But if any doubt should remain, an appeal to the connexion in which the words are found will be sufficient to turn the scale. Mary had complained of her son's conduct, on the ground that she and her husband had suffered much anxiety in *seeking* for their lost child. He replies, 'How is it that ye *sought* me? Missing me, ye ought to have certainly known where to look for me. Where should the child be, but in his Father's house?' All here is in logical sequence. Not so, if we adopt the other explanation. He might be 'about his (heavenly) Father's business,' and they might have been sure that he was so, without their knowing exactly where to find him. At a later period of his life, during his public ministry, he was always 'about his Father's business,' but not always in the Temple, or in the midst of the doctors. During the three days that he was missing, he, probably, found shelter in the house of some one or other of his parents' friends, with whom they had lodged during the feast. Of some of these friends we may suppose that the parents made their first enquiries; though we cannot agree with those who assume that the greater part of the third day (the day which followed that on which they made their return journey) was spent in the fruitless search for him. For aught that appears on the face of the narrative[4], they might have begun their search

---

[1] *Opp.* T. III. p. 954: '*Nescitis quia in his quae sunt Patris mei oportet me esse?* Ubi sunt haeretici impii atque vesani, qui asserunt non esse Patris Jesu Christi legem et prophetas? Certe Jesus in templo erat, quod a Salomone constructum est, et confitetur templum illud Patris sui esse, quem nobis revelavit, cujus filium esse se dixit.'

[2] *Haeres.* I. 30 (ch. 29): Ἐν τοῖς τοῦ

πατρός μου· σημαίνων ὅτι ὁ ναὸς εἰς ὄνομα θεοῦ, τουτέστι, τοῦ αὐτοῦ πατρὸς, ᾠκοδομήθη. εἰ τοίνυν ἀπὸ νηπίου οἶδε τὸν ναὸν καὶ τὸν πατέρα, οὐκ ἄρα ψιλὸς ἄνθρωπος ὁ γεννηθεὶς Ἰησοῦς.

[3] *Opp.* T. v. p. 1063: Ὁ δὲ εἶπε· τί ὅτι ἐζητεῖτέ με; οὐκ ᾔδειτε ὅτι ἐν τῷ οἴκῳ τοῦ πατρός μου δεῖ με εἶναι;

[4] The phrase μετὰ τρεῖς ἡμέρας is only another form for τῇ τρίτῃ ἡμέρᾳ, with which it is interchanged Mark

by a visit to the Temple, as a likely place to find the divine child. But even so, since they would have gone thinking only that he *might be* there, there would still have been room for the mild expostulation, 'How is it that ye sought me? Wist ye not that I *must be* in my Father's house?'

III. 14: στρατευόμενοι] 'soldiers.' R. V. in margin: 'Gr. *soldiers on service.*' Alford: 'Properly, *men on march.*' 'The expression used by St Luke is not "soldiers" (στρατιῶται), but the participle στρατευόμενοι, i.e. "men under arms," or men "going to battle."'—J. D. Michaelis, *Introduction to N. T.*, Vol. I. p. 51. The latter finds in this form a proof of the authenticity of the N. T. 'Whence these persons came, and on what particular account, may be found at large in the history of Josephus (*Ant.* XVIII. 5, 1). Herod the tetrarch of Galilee was engaged in a war with his father-in-law Aretas, a petty king in Arabia Petraea, at the very time in which John was preaching in the wilderness.... The army of Herod, then, in its march from Galilee passed through the country in which John baptized, which sufficiently explains the doubt, who the soldiers were.' But as this war did not break out till A.U.C. 789, and John began to preach A.U.C. 781, this ingenious explanation falls to the ground. Nor is it required. Στρατευόμενος is 'one who serves in the army,' whether engaged in actual warfare or not, not therefore distinguishable from στρατιώτης. Here the advice given to them seems rather to point to soldiers at home, mixing among their fellow-citizens, than to those who were 'on the march' in an enemy's country. And so in 2 Tim. ii. 4, οὐδεὶς στρατευόμενος is hardly 'no man that warreth' (A. V.), or even 'no soldier on service' (R. V.); otherwise he would be precluded by the necessity of the case from 'entangling himself in the affairs of (civil) life.'

St Chrysostom uses στρατευόμενοι in the same way to denote a class in the following passage (T. VII. p. 466 D): καὶ γὰρ καὶ γέροντες καὶ νέοι, καὶ γυναῖκας ἔχοντες, καὶ παῖδας τρέφοντες, καὶ τέχνας μεταχειριζόμενοι, καὶ στρατευόμενοι, κατώρθωσαν τὰ ἐπιταχθέντα ἅπαντα.

*III. 14: μηδένα διασείσητε] A. V. 'Do violence to no man' (or, *put no man in fear*). This case answers to the *concussio* of the Roman jurists, i.e. extorting money by threats, or under pretence of authority. Thus Chrysologus, *Serm.* XXVI. (de bono milite): 'Si paruit imperatis, si *concussit* neminem.'

The other clause, μηδὲ συκοφαντήσητε is more correctly rendered

viii. 31, ix. 31. Even the 'three days and three nights,' which proved such a stumbling-block to 'Herman Heinfetter' that he could only get over it by keeping 'Good Thursday' instead of 'Good Friday,' is satisfied, according to Biblical usage, by a *few hours* of one νυχθήμερον, the *whole* of a second, and *less than half* of a third.

by A. V. 'neither accuse any falsely,' than by R. V. 'neither exact *any thing* wrongfully.' Again in Ch. xix. 8: εἴ τινός τι ἐσυκοφάντησα, 'if I have taken anything from any man by false accusation,' R. V. renders, 'if I have wrongfully exacted aught of any man,' again ignoring the *false accusation*, which is of the essence of the word. So Choricius ap. Villois. *Anecd.* II. p. 50: τοιοῦτόν ἐστι συκοφαντία· τὸ προστυχὸν ἀεὶ πρόφασιν ποιεῖτε (ποιεῖται) διαβολῆς.

IV. 13: **πάντα πειρασμόν**] A. V. 'all the temptation,' which would require the article. R. V. 'every temptation.' Rather, 'every kind of temptation.' So A. V. Matt. xii. 31: πᾶσα ἁμαρτία καὶ βλασφημία, 'all manner of sin and blasphemy.' Dion. Hal. *Ant.* v. 48: κράτιστος τῶν τότε Ῥωμαίων κατὰ πᾶσαν ἀρετὴν νομισθείς. St Chrysostom (T. VII. p. 172 B) thus comments upon the text: καὶ πῶς ὁ Λουκᾶς φησιν, ὅτι πάντα συνετέλεσε πειρασμόν; ἐμοὶ δοκεῖ, τὰ κεφάλαια τῶν πειρασμῶν εἰπών, πάντα εἰρηκέναι, ὡς καὶ τῶν ἄλλων ἐν τούτοις περιειλημμένων. τὰ γὰρ μυρία συνέχοντα κακὰ ταῦτά ἐστι· τὸ γαστρὶ δουλεύειν, τὸ πρὸς κενοδοξίαν τι ποιεῖν, τὸ μανίᾳ χρημάτων ὑπεύθυνον εἶναι. And so Beza (ed. 1598) ad loc.: 'Vix enim reperiatur ulla tentationis species, quae vel ad diffidentiam de Deo, vel ad rerum caducarum studium, vel ad vanam sui ostentationem non referatur.'

V. 7: **τοῦ ἐλθόντας συλλαβέσθαι αὐτοῖς**] The grammarians give: Συλλαμβάνει ὁ δεῖνα τῷ δεῖνι· ἤγουν βοηθεῖ; of which examples from the best Greek authors may be found in Wetstein. The use of the middle voice in this sense is more recent; and the instances from older writers, to which the Lexicographers send us, are not to be relied on[1]. As examples from later Greek we may take Diod. Sic. XVI. 65: ὃ (which circumstance) συνελάβετο αὐτῷ πρὸς τὴν τῆς στρατηγίας αἵρεσιν[2]. Dion. Hal. *Ant.* IV. 76: καὶ τοὺς θεοὺς εὐχαῖς λιτανεύσαντες συλλαβέσθαι σφισίν. Anton. Lib. 12: εὔξατο συλλαβέσθαι αὐτῷ τὸν Ἡρακλέα. It may be worth while to compare with St Luke's narrative two cases of an extraordinary 'draught of fishes' from profane authors. The first is from Alciphron's Epistles (I. 17), quoted by Wetstein: καὶ ἡμεῖς (on the report of a shoal of tunny fish) πεισθέντες τῇ σαγήνῃ μονονουχὶ τὸν κόλπον ὅλον περιελάβομεν· εἶτα ἀνιμώμεθα, καὶ τὸ βάρος μεῖζον ἦν ἢ κατὰ φορτίον ἰχθύων (it was, in fact, a dead camel). ἐλπίδι οὖν καὶ τῶν πλησίον τινὰς ἐκαλοῦμεν, μερίτας ἀποφαίνειν ἐπαγγελλόμενοι, εἰ συλλάβοιντο ἡμῖν καὶ συμπονήσαιεν. The other is described by Philostratus (*Imag.* I. 13): βοὴ δὲ ἦρται τῶν ἁλιέων, ἐμπεπτωκότων ἤδη τῶν ἰχθύων ἐς τὸ δίκτυον...ἀμηχανοῦντες δὲ ὅ τι χρήσονται τῷ πλήθει, καὶ παρανοίγουσι τοῦ

---

[1] E.g. Herod. III. 49, where συλλαβέσθαι τοῦ στρατεύματος is '*to take part in* the expedition.' Xenoph. *Ages.* II. 31, where συλλήψεται is the future of συλλαμβάνειν, not of συλλαμβάνεσθαι.

[2] [Cf. Plut. *Vit. Sertor.* XIII: ὁρῶν δὲ τοὺς Λαγγοβρίτας οὐ μικρὰ τῷ Σερτωρίῳ συλλαμβανομένους....]

δικτύου, καὶ ξυγχωροῦσιν ἐνίους διαφυγεῖν καὶ διεκπεσεῖν· τοσοῦτον ἐς τὴν θήραν τρυφῶσιν[1].

*VI. 1: ἐγένετο δὲ ἐν σαββάτῳ (δευτεροπρώτῳ)] The last word is wanting in BLℵ, 1. 33, al. Pesch. Copt. Ethiop. Those critics who have attempted to give a probable explanation of the epithet, and those who have offered ingenious speculations to account for its insertion, have both egregiously failed. At the risk of adding another name to the latter class, I offer the following solution. I suppose that in the original reading, ἐγένετο δὲ ἐν σαββάτῳ διαπορεύεσθαι αὐτὸν διὰ τῶν σπορίμων, there was an accidental transposition in one of the MSS. (as D still has αὐτὸν before ἐν σ. διαπορεύεσθαι). The error being indicated in the usual manner, the text might have stood thus: ἐγένετο δὲ ἐν σαββάτῳ αὐτὸν διαπορεύεσθαι διὰ τῶν σπορίμων. From these two superimposed numerals, I think it just possible that δεύτερον πρῶτον, slightly altered in deference to the construction, may have made its way into the text in the form of δευτεροπρώτῳ, as an epithet of σαββάτῳ. Si quid novisti, &c.

VI. 3: οὐδὲ τοῦτο ἀνέγνωτε ὃ ἐποίησε Δαβίδ] A. V. 'Have ye not read so much as this (R. V. even this) what David did.' As if it were τί ἐποίησε, as in the other two Gospels. The Vulgate recognizes the distinction by rendering, in the latter, Nonne legistis quid fecerit, but in St Luke, Nec hoc legistis quod fecit, 'this that David did.'

VI. 16: ὃς [καὶ] ἐγένετο προδότης] 'Which [also] was the traitor.' In the other Gospels we read, ὃς καὶ παρέδωκεν αὐτόν; and it is to be noted that when the verb is used, it is always παραδιδόναι, not προδιδόναι; when the noun, always προδότης (this of necessity, as the noun παραδότης is not in use). But why 'the traitor'? He is never so stigmatized in the Gospels, 'Judas the traitor,' but always described by a periphrasis, Ἰούδας ὁ παραδιδοὺς αὐτόν. In the text ὃς καὶ ἐγένετο προδότης must be taken to express neither more nor less than ὃς καὶ παρέδωκεν αὐτόν, 'which also became a traitor,' as the American R. V., or, as we say, 'turned traitor.' Compare Acts vii. 52: 'Of whom ye have now become betrayers and murderers' (προδόται καὶ φονεῖς γεγένησθε). Eurip. Phoen. 996: προδότην γενέσθαι πατρίδος ἤ μ' ἐγείνατο. Diod. Sic. XIV. 70: καὶ γὰρ τὸ πρότερον Ἀρέτης ὁ Λακεδαιμόνιος, ἀντιλαμβανόμενος αὐτῶν τῆς ἐλευθερίας, ἐγένετο προδότης. XV. 91: οὗτος δέ, παραλαβὼν τὴν ἡγεμονίαν, καὶ χρήματα πρὸς ξενολογίαν ...ἐγένετο προδότης τῶν πιστευσάντων.

---

[1] [Cf. Lucian. Hermot. 65: ὥσπερ οἱ ἁλιεύοντες πολλάκις καθέντες (for χαλάσαντες) τὰ δίκτυα, καὶ βάρους τινὸς αἰσθανόμενοι ἀνέλκουσιν, ἰχθὺς παμπόλλους γε περιβεβληκέναι ἐλπίζοντες, εἶτα ἐπειδὰν κάμωσιν ἀνασπῶντες, ἢ λίθος τις ἀποφαίνεται αὐτοῖς, ἢ κεράμιον....]

VI. 35: καὶ δανείζετε, μηδὲν ἀπελπίζοντες] A. V. 'And lend, hoping for nothing again.' It has been attempted to retain the classical use of ἀπελπίζειν, 'never despairing' (or, with μηδένα, 'despairing of no man'), which is explained by Dean Alford, 'without anxiety about the result.' But such a state of mind (which would be more aptly expressed by μηδὲν μεριμνῶντες) belongs to the creditor who lends 'hoping for nothing again,' not to him who, however impoverished his debtor may be, does not despair of being repaid at last. No doubt this use of the word is nowhere else to be met with; but the context is here too strong for philological quibbles. 'If ye lend to them παρ' ὧν 'ΕΛΠΙΖΕΤΕ 'ΑΠΟλαβεῖν, what thank have ye?' Then follows the precept: 'Lend, μηδὲν 'ΑΠΕΛΠΙΖΟΝΤΕΣ,' which can by no possibility bear any other meaning than μηδὲν ἐλπίζοντες ἀπολαβεῖν.

Dean Alford mentions a third rendering of ἀπελπίζων, 'causing no one to despair, i.e. refusing no one' (reading μηδένα), and adds: 'So the Syr. renders it.' But (1) this transitive sense of the word is almost as un-exampled as the other, resting on a single quotation from the Anthology (T. II. p. 325 Brunck) where ἄλλον ἀπελπίζων (said of an astrologer, who had predicted that a certain person had only nine months to live) may as well mean 'despairing of another' (giving him over) as 'causing him to despair'; and (2) the Syriac ⲁⲗⲁ ⲁ ⲟⲟⲙⲟⲗ ⲗ ⲗⲟ is the ordinary periphrasis for ἀπελπίζειν τινά in its usual sense of 'despairing of any person.' Thus in Ecclus. xxii. 21: ἐπὶ φίλον ἐὰν σπάσῃς ῥομφαίαν, μὴ ἀπελπίσῃς· ἔστι γὰρ ἐπάνοδος, for μὴ ἀπελπίσῃς Paul of Tela has ⲡ ⲗⲟⲟ ⲟⲟⲙⲟⲗ. All that can be inferred, therefore, from this version is that it read μηδένα (not μηδέν).

*Canon Norris (Public Opinion, July 30, 1881) states that 'never despairing' would be, according to Hellenistic usage, μηδὲν ἀπηλπισμένοι. He quotes Isai. xxix. 19: οἱ ἀπηλπισμένοι τῶν ἀνθρώπων, in the sense of 'the despairing among men.' But both in Hellenistic and classical Greek οἱ ἀπηλπισμένοι can be nothing else than 'the despaired of' or 'given over'; and the version of the LXX. is a free translation of אֶבְיוֹנֵי אָדָם, 'the poor among men.' In Judith ix. 11 God is called ἀντιλήπτωρ ἀσθενούντων, ἀπεγνωσμένων σκεπαστής, ἀπηλπισμένων σωτήρ. Add from non-Hellenistic writers Diog. Laert. VIII. 69: Πάνθειαν ἀπηλπισμένην ὑπὸ, τῶν ἰατρῶν. St Chrysost. T. v. p. 202 C: ἰδοὺ ἡ πόλις αὕτη, ἡ ἀπεγνωσμένη. ἡ ἀπηλπισμένη, ἡ ἐρείπιον οὖσα, πῶς ἐπὶ λαμπρότερον ἐπανῆλθε σχῆμα; Diod. Sic. I. 25: καὶ πολλοὺς μὲν ὑπὸ τῶν ἰατρῶν διὰ τὴν δυσκολίαν τοῦ νοσήματος ἀπελπισθέντας ὑπὸ ταύτης (Iside in somniis assistente) σώζεσθαι.

VII. 30: τὴν βουλὴν τοῦ θεοῦ ἠθέτησαν εἰς ἑαυτούς] A. V. 'Rejected (Or, frustrated) the counsel of God against themselves.' Comparing Psa. xxxii. (Heb. xxxiii.) 10: καὶ ἀθετεῖ βουλὰς ἀρχόντων, we prefer the marginal version, 'frustrated (or made void) the counsel of God.' So Gal. ii. 21: 'I do not frustrate (ἀθετῶ) the grace of God.' Then, as the frustration

could be only apparent, there is room for a qualification, such as, 'as far
as in them lay,' or 'as far as concerned themselves,' which might be expressed in a variety of ways, as τὸ ἐξ ὑμῶν (Rom. xii. 18); ὅσον ἐφ' ἑαυτοῖς
(Dion. Hal. *Ant.* V. 51); ὅσον ἐπ' αὐτῷ (Plut. *Vit. Pericl.* XVIII); or (still
nearer to the text) τό γ' εἰς ἑαυτόν (Soph. *Oed. T.* 706); τὸ μὲν γὰρ εἰς ἐμέ
(Eurip. *Iph. T.* 691). If we could get over the absence of the article (τὸ
εἰς ἑαυτούς), we should have no hesitation in adopting this view. As the
text stands, we have no difficulty in translating 'made void the counsel of
God concerning themselves,' comparing 1 Thess. v. 18: τοῦτο γὰρ θέλημα
θεοῦ ἐν Χριστῷ Ἰησοῦ εἰς ὑμᾶς, which seems exactly parallel, both as relates
to the *hyperbaton,* and also to the absence of the article τὴν before εἰς
ἑαυτούς. The R. V. 'rejected for themselves the counsel of God,' seems
to be liable to the objection before mentioned, that it would require τὸ εἰς
ἑαυτούς.

IX. 11: **καὶ τοὺς χρείαν ἔχοντας θεραπείας ἰάσατο**] 'And healed them
that had need of healing.' The repetition of the same word might be
considered not inelegant, as in Diod. Sic. XII. 16: διορθοῦν δὲ συνεχώρησε
(Charondas) τὸν χρείαν ἔχοντα διορθώσεως (νόμον). But since θεραπεύειν
and ἰᾶσθαι are clearly distinguishable, it is better, if possible, to preserve
the distinction in the rendering. So Vulg.: *et qui cura indigebant,
sanabat.* In English, we have to choose between 'He cured them that
had need of healing,' and 'He healed them that had need of cure.' The
latter seems preferable, because θεραπεία answers to the Latin *curatio,* the
treatment of a disease, its *cure,* in the sense in which we use that word,
when we speak of the 'cure of souls,' the 'water-cure' (ἡ δι' ὕδατος
θεραπεία). Compare Diod. Sic. XVII. 89: ὁ Πῶρος, ἔμπνους ὤν, παρεδόθη
πρὸς Ἰνδους πρὸς τὴν θεραπείαν[1]. Plut. *Vit. Alex.* LXI: ἐκ δὲ τῆς πρὸς Πῶρον
μάχης καὶ ὁ Βουκεφάλας ἐτελεύτησεν, οὐκ εὐθύς, ἀλλ' ὕστερον, ὡς οἱ πλεῖστοι
λέγουσιν, ὑπὸ τραυμάτων θεραπευόμενος (where, perhaps, we should read ἀπὸ
τραυμάτων, comparing Diod. Sic. XIV. 26: ὁ δὲ βασιλεὺς βέλτιον ἔχων ἀπὸ
τοῦ τραύματος, LXX. 4 Kings viii. 29: τοῦ ἰατρευθῆναι ἐν Ἰεζραὲλ ἀπὸ τῶν
πληγῶν). Aesop. Fab. CCXXIV. ed. de Fur.: ἰατρὸς νοσοῦντα ἐθεράπευε·
τοῦ δὲ νοσοῦντος ἀποθανόντος, κ.τ.έ.

IX. 12: **ἐπισιτισμόν**] 'victuals.' So the word is rendered by A. V.
Jos. i. 11, ix. 11; but by 'provision' Gen. xlii. 25, xlv. 21, Jos. ix. 5; in
all which places it is used in its proper sense of 'provision for a journey.'
Hesych. Ἐπισιτισμόν· ἐφοδιασμόν. Diod. Sic. XIII. 95: λαβόντες ἐπισιτ-
ισμὸν ἡμερῶν λ͞. As our English term 'victuals' does not seem to include
this idea, and is also of the plural form, it might be better to render it

---

[1] [Cf. Plut. II. p. 208: προστάττον-
τος δέ τινος αὐτῷ ἰατροῦ περιεργοτέραν
θεραπείαν καὶ οὐχ ἁπλῆν.... Id. *Vit.
Otho* 8: οὐ παρῆν μὲν ἀλλ' ἐθεραπεύετο
πεπτωκὼς ἀφ' ἵππου. Id. *Vit. Arat.* 33:
τὸ σκέλος ἔσπασε (sprained)...καὶ τομὰς
ἔλαβε πολλὰς θεραπευόμενος.]

here by 'provision,' and βρώματα in the next verse by 'victuals' (as A. V. Lev. xxv. 37, Matt. xiv. 15).

IX. 25 : ἑαυτὸν δὲ ἀπολέσας ἢ ζημιωθείς] A.V. 'And lose himself, or be cast away.' R. V. 'And lose or forfeit [i.e. lose by some offence or breach of condition—*Johnson*] his own self.' Dean Alford: 'And destroy or lose himself.' None of these renderings of ζημιωθείς seems satisfactory. In the A. V. of the Epistles, ζημιωθῆναι (*absolute positum*) is either to 'suffer loss,' or to 'receive damage,' which come to the same thing[1]. If ἑαυτόν is to be taken in connexion with both verbs, we may understand ἀπολέσας of a *total*, and ζημιωθείς of a *partial* loss : 'And lose, or receive damage in, his own self.'

X. 30 : λῃσταῖς περιέπεσεν] 'fell among thieves (robbers).' Rather, 'fell in with,' 'met with,' since the same verb is often joined with a noun in the singular number, as περιέπεσε χειμῶνι, πάθει (Thucyd.), τῷ Πανὶ (Herod.), Stob. *Flor.* T. CVIII. 81 : ἢ λῃσταῖς διὰ τοῦτο μέλλοντες περιπεσεῖν, ἢ τυράννῳ. And Polybius (quoted by Raphel) makes the robbers 'fall in with' the other party : τούτους (legatos) λῃσταί τινες περιπεσόντες ἐν τῷ πελάγει διέφθειραν[2]. But in v. 36 ἐμπεσὼν εἰς τοὺς λῃστάς is rightly rendered 'fell among.'[3] On ἡμιθανής Schleusner *Lex. in N. T.* says : 'Phavor. Ἡμιθνὴς μὲν λέγεται ὁ ψυχαγωγῶν, καὶ ἤδη τὸ ἥμισυ θανών. Idem tradit Tzetzes in Lycophr. p. 511.' He should have noticed that Tzetzes for ψυχαγωγῶν gives the correct reading ψυχορραγῶν. To the few examples quoted by the Lexicographers I add Dion. Hal. *Ant.* x. 7 : τὸν μὲν ἀδελφόν μου νεκρόν...ἐμὲ δὲ ἡμιθανῆ, καὶ ἐλπίδας ἔχοντα τοῦ ζῆν ὀλίγας. Alciphr. *Ep.* III. 7 : ἡμιθνῆτα, μᾶλλον δὲ αὐτόνεκρον θεασάμενος, φοράδην ἀνελὼν ἤγαγεν εἰς ἑαυτὸν οἴκαδε. So far, and throughout this beautiful narrative, all is as classical as the most determined Anti-Hellenistic would require. But the phrase πληγὰς ἐπιθέντες (here and Acts xvi. 23) seems to be a Latinism, *plagas imponere,* for which the Greek would be πλ. ἐντείναντες, as Stob. *Flor.* T. LXXIX. 39 : χαλεπήναντος γὰρ αὐτῷ τοῦ πατρός, καὶ τέλος πληγὰς ἐντείναντος...[4].

---

1 [Cf. Aristaen. II. 18: νῦν δὲ πικρῶς ὀλοφυραμένη ἦν ἐζημίωται σωφροσύνην, 'perditam honestatem.']

2 [Cf. Liban. *Argum. ad Dem. c. Timocr.*: πλέοντες ἐν τριήρει, περιπεσόντες Ναυκρατίταις ἀνθρώποις ἐμπόροις, ἀφείλοντο αὐτῶν τὰ χρήματα. Ael. *V. H.* XIII. 25 : Πίνδαρος...ἀμαθέσι περιπεσὼν ἀκροαταῖς.]

3 [Cf. Plut. II. p. 194 : εἰπόντος δέ τινος τῶν στρατιωτῶν · 'Ἐμπεπτώκαμεν εἰς τοὺς πολεμίους. Τί μᾶλλον, εἶπεν, ἢ εἰς ἡμᾶς ἐκεῖνοι; Cf. also περιτυχεῖν.

Ibid. II. p. 234: περιτυχόντες τινὲς Λάκωσι καθ' ὁδὸν, εἶπον· Εὐτυχήκατε, ἀρτίως ἐντεῦθεν λῃστῶν ἀπιόντων. Οἱ δὲ, οὐ μὰ τὸν Ἐννάλιον, ἀλλ' ἐκεῖνοι, μὴ περιτυχόντες ἡμῖν.]

4 [Cf. Lucian. *D. D.* XI. 1 : πληγὰς αὐτῷ ἐνέτεινα...τῷ σανδάλῳ. We find also πλ. ἐμβαλεῖν, Plut. *Vit. Cor.* 17 : τοῖς δὲ ἀγορανόμοις καὶ πλ. ἐνέβαλον; ἐπιβαλεῖν, Xen. *Lac.* II. 8 : τί δῆτα... πολλὰς πλ. ἐπέβαλε τῷ ἁλισκομένῳ; ἐντρίψαι, Ael. *V. H.* XIII. 38 : ἐντρίψας αὐτῷ κόνδυλον εὖ μάλα στερεόν.]

X. 32: γενόμενος κατὰ τὸν τόπον, ἐλθὼν καὶ ἰδὼν ἀντιπαρῆλθεν] This is the reading of the T. R. with which apparently agree A (with αὐτὸν after ἰδών), C and others, and the Philoxenian Syriac: ܠܐܬܪܐ ܘܚܙܐ ܗܘܐ ܟܕ

ܘܥܒܪ ܠܗ. Other 'ancient authorities' omit ἐλθών, as D (with ἰδὼν αὐτόν), the Vulgate, the Curetonian Syriac, and St Chrysostom (om. ἐλθὼν καί). Lastly, the uncials BLXΞ and א³ (א¹ omits the whole verse) omit γενόμενος. This last is the reading, κατὰ τὸν τόπον ἐλθὼν καὶ ἰδών, which is adopted by the Revisers, 'when he came to the place, and saw him'; against whose decision it may be urged:

1. That γενόμενος κατὰ τὸν τόπον is a choice Greek idiom, quite in St Luke's style, and wholly unaccountable as an after-insertion by a corrector. Take a few examples. Acts xxvii. 7: μόλις γενόμενοι κατὰ τὴν Κνίδον. Herod. III. 86: ὡς κατὰ τοῦτο τὸ χωρίον ἐγένοντο. Stob. Flor. T. VII. 65: γενόμενος δὲ κατὰ γέφυραν ποταμοῦ Σάρδωνος. Thucyd. VIII. 86: ἐπειδὴ ἐγένοντο πλέοντες κατ᾽ Ἄργος. Xenoph. H. G. IV. 6, 14: κατὰ τὸ Ῥίον (not, as quoted by Schleusner, Lex. N. T. s. v. κατά, κατὰ τόπον) ἐγένετο. Lucian. D. D. XI. 1: ὁπότ᾽ ἂν κατὰ τὴν Καρίαν γένῃ (Luna). Ach. Tat. VIII. 15: ἐπειδὴ κατὰ τὸν Φάρον ἐγεγόνει. Pausan. Messen. XVI. 5: ὡς κατὰ τὴν ἀχράδα ἐγένετο. Aesop. Fab. IV. ed. de Furia: ὡς ἐγένετο κατὰ τὸ αὐτὸ φρέαρ. LVI: ὡς ἐγένετο κατά τινα ποταμὸν πλημμυροῦντα. LXIV: ἐγένετο κατά τι σπήλαιον[1].

2. Another good Greek phrase is that which occurs in v. 33, ἦλθε κατ᾽ αὐτόν (of persons), answering exactly to the English 'came where he was.' So Plut. II. p. 235 (said of an old man looking for a seat in the amphitheatre at Olympia): ὡς δὲ κατὰ τοὺς Λακεδαιμονίους ἧκεν (when he came to where they were sitting). Ach. Tat. V. 9: εἴτε ἐλεήσαντες, εἴτε καὶ τὸ πνεῦμα αὐτοὺς κατήγαγεν, ἔρχονται κατ᾽ ἐμέ, καί τις τῶν ναυτῶν πέμπει μοι κάλων (throws me a rope)[2].

3. There remains the phrase ἐλθὼν κατὰ τὸν τόπον (of places) for πρὸς τὸν τόπον, of which I have not been able to find a single example[3].

On the whole, the most probable solution seems to be that St Luke wrote γενόμενος κατὰ τὸν τόπον καὶ ἰδών, and that ἐλθών was originally a gloss on γενόμενος, which found its way into the text, as it now appears in T. R. This produced an apparent tautology, which was remedied by the expunction of γενόμενος.

---

[1] [Cf. Plut. Vit. Agis XIX: ἐκτροπὴν δέ τινα τῆς ὁδοῦ ἐχούσης, ὡς ἐγένοντο κατ᾽ αὐτὴν βαδίζοντες. Dio Chrys. Or. I. 15, 37 (p. 68): ἐπεὶ κατιόντες ἐγένοντο κατὰ τὴν τυραννικὴν εἴσοδον. Lucian. Philops. 25: ἐπεὶ δὲ κατὰ τὸ δικαστήριον ἐγενόμην.]

[2] [Cf. Lucian. Herod. 5: λοχῶντι ἔοικεν, ὡς φοβήσειεν αὐτούς, ὁπότε κατ᾽

αὐτὸν γένοιντο σύροντες. Plut. Vit. Aemil. XXI: κατὰ τούτους δὲ (where they were) μέγας ἦν ἀγών.]

[3] [Cf. Plat. Phaedr. p. 229 A: κατὰ τὸν Ἰλισσὸν ἴωμεν. Acts xvi. 7: ἐλθόντες δὲ κατὰ τὴν Μυσίαν. A. V. 'after they were come to Mysia.' R. V. 'when they were come over against Mysia.']

X. 37: πορεύου, καὶ σὺ ποίει ὁμοίως] Without wishing to stand between
the English reader and a form of words so natural and familiar to him, as
'Go, and do thou likewise,' we may remark that, philologically, any
translation of the Greek must be faulty, which separates καὶ from σύ, or
reduces καὶ to a mere copula. 'Go, and do thou likewise' would be
πορεύου, καὶ ποίει σὺ ὁμοίως. 'Go thou, and do likewise,' πορεύου σύ, καὶ
ποίει ὁμοίως[1]. But καὶ σὺ is 'thou also,' and answers to the Latin *tu
quoque*, and the Hebrew אַתָּה־גַם. Compare 2 Kings (Sam.) xv. 19: ἱνατί
πορεύῃ καὶ σὺ μεθ' ἡμῶν; Obad. 11: καὶ σὺ ἦς ὡς εἷς ἐξ αὐτῶν. Matt. xxvi.
69: καὶ σὺ ἦσθα μετὰ Ἰησοῦ τοῦ Γαλιλαίου[2]. This being assumed, we may
either point πορεύου καὶ σύ, ποίει ὁμοίως, 'Go thou also, do likewise,' or
πορεύου, καὶ σὺ ποίει ὁμοίως, 'Go, do thou also likewise.' In the former
case we rather seem to require a copula before ποίει, and so the words
are actually quoted by St Chrysostom (T. XII. p. 109 B): πορεύου οὖν, φησί,
καὶ σύ, καὶ ποίει ὁμοίως. In the latter πορεύου is merely a *formula hortantis*,
like πορευθέντες μάθετε, and need not be coupled with ποίει. But, as we
have already hinted, such *minutiae* as these do not fall within the scope
of a revision of the A. V. such as the proposers of it intended, and the
English public will accept.

X. 40: περὶ πολλὴν διακονίαν] 'about much serving.' Those who would
restrict the meaning of this term to waiting at table, and serving up the
dishes (as Ch. xxii. 27, John xii. 2) suppose that Mary sat at Jesus' feet,
while the meal was going on. But διακονία can be shown to include the
preparations for the feast, even to the cleaving of the wood for cooking,
as appears from a story told by Plutarch in his life of Philopoemen, which
will remind the reader of a similar passage in English history. A woman
of Megara, being told that the general of the Achaeans was coming to
her house, ἐθορυβεῖτο παρασκευάζουσα δεῖπνον, her husband happening to
be out of the way. In the meantime Philopoemen came in, and as his
habit was ordinary, she took him for one of his own servants, and desired
him to assist her in the business of the kitchen (τῆς διακονίας συνεφά-
ψασθαι). He presently threw off his cloke, and began to cleave some
wood (τῶν ξύλων ἔσχιζεν), when the master of the house came in and
recognized him. It is worth remarking that Martha's expression ἵνα μοι
συναντιλάβηται is explained by Euthymius, ἵνα μοι συνεφάψηται τῆς διακονίας, the identical phrase used in the extract from Plutarch.

X. 42: ἑνὸς δέ ἐστι χρεία...τὴν ἀγαθὴν μερίδα] In both these terms there
seems to be a passing allusion to the feast which was in preparation,
which was probably, as usually happens on such occasions, περιττὴ τῆς
χρείας (Plut. *Vit. Syll.* XXXV) including not only τὰ πρὸς τὴν χρείαν, but

---

[1] [Cf. Plut. *Vit. Otho* XVII: ἴθι τοίνυν,
ἔφη, σύ, καὶ ποίει τοῖς στρατιώταις ἐμ-
φανῆ σεαυτόν.]

[2] [Cf. 2 Tim. iii. 5: καὶ τούτους
ἀποτρέπου. R. V. 'from these also....']

τὰ πρὸς τὴν τρυφήν. Μερίς also (at all events, let it be Englished by 'portion,' not 'part') is well known as a convivial term, both from biblical (Gen. xliii. 34, 1 Reg. (Sam.) i. 4, ix. 23, Nehem. viii. 12) and classical writers. As Wetstein gives numerous examples from the latter, in all of which μερίς is *portio caenae*[1], we will add a few in which it is used in the higher sense. Synes. p. 25 A: οὓς λυπῶ, προσχωρήσας τῇ μερίδι τῇ κρείττονι. Dion. Hal. *Ant*. VIII. 30: ἐξὸν γὰρ ἑλέσθαι τὴν κρείττω μερίδα (in republica), τὴν χείρονα εἵλου[2].

XI. 53: δεινῶς ἐνέχειν] A. V. 'to urge *him* vehemently.' R. V. 'to press upon *him* vehemently. Or, *to set themselves vehemently against* him.' The only authorities for this use of ἐνέχειν appear to be the Vulg. *graviter insistere*, and a gloss of Hesychius: Ἐνέχει· μνησικακεῖ, ἔγκειται. For the latter word Bois and others have conjectured ἐγκοτεῖ; but ἔγκειται may be defended, either by supposing the Lexicographer to indicate two different senses of the word, one belonging to Mark vi. 19, and the other to Luke xi. 53; or else by taking ἔγκειται in the sense of *inhaerere*, in which ἐνέχειν is occasionally used, e.g. Plut. *Vit. Pomp*. LXXI: ὠθεῖ διὰ τοῦ στόματος τὸ ξίφος, ὥστε τὴν αἰχμὴν περάσασαν ἐνσχεῖν κατὰ τὸ ἰνίον (the nape of the neck)[3]. In our note on Mark vi. 19, while strongly maintaining the sense of μνησικακεῖν as eminently suited to that place, we hinted that for δεινῶς ἐνέχειν in St Luke it might be necessary to look out for some other meaning of the word; and if so, none seems to have a better claim than that of Budaeus, *acriter instare*, or of the A. V. 'to urge *him* vehemently.' But after all, it may still be a question, whether the notion of *angry feeling* be not suitable to this place as well as to the other. 'The scribes and Pharisees began to be very angry.' So at least Euthymius: Ἐνέχειν, ἤγουν ἐγκοτεῖν, ὀργίζεσθαι; and the Philoxenian Syriac ܘܣܪܟܘ ܥܡܗ, using the very same word ܥܡ as Paul of Tela for ἐνέχειν Gen. xlix. 23, and for ἐγκοτεῖν Psa. liv. 4. The older Syriac version, though somewhat free, is to the same effect: 'they began ܘܣܪ ܘ̈ܣܪܝܢ, *aegre ferre, et irascebantur.*'

XII. 19: 'Soul, thou hast much goods,' &c.] Compare Charit. Aphrod. III. 2: καρτέρησον, ψυχή, προθεσμίαν σύντομον, ἵνα τὸν πλείω χρόνον ἀπολαύσῃς ἀσφαλοῦς ἡδονῆς. And, for the whole parable, Lucian. *Navig*. 25:

---

[1] [Cf. Plut. *Vit. Cato Min*. VI: ἐν δὲ τοῖς δείπνοις ἐκληροῦτο περὶ τῶν μερίδων. εἰ δέ τις ἀπολάχοι....]

[2] [Plut. *Vit. Brut*. 53: ἐγώ σοι, ὦ Καῖσαρ, ἀεὶ τῆς βελτίονος καὶ δικαιοτέρας τιμῆς καὶ μερίδος ἐγενόμην.]

[3] For ἐνσχεῖν G. H. Schaefer prints ἀνασχεῖν from a conjecture of Coraës,

who compares *Vit. Caes*. XLIV: ἀνακόπτεται ξίφει πληγεὶς διὰ τοῦ στόματος, ὥστε καὶ τὴν αἰχμὴν ὑπὲρ τὸ ἰνίον ἀνασχεῖν. But though the incident is the same, the difference in the prepositions makes one hesitate to accept the correction as certain.

ἈΔΕΙΜΑΝΤΟΣ. Τοῦτον ἐβουλόμην βιῶναι τὸν βίον, πλουτῶν ἐς ὑπερβολὴν καὶ τρυφῶν, καὶ πάσαις ἡδοναῖς ἀφθόνως χρώμενος. ΛΥΚΙΝΟΣ. Τίς γὰρ οἶδεν, εἰ ἔτι παρακειμένης σοι τῆς χρυσῆς τραπέζης...ἀποφυσήσας τὸ ψυχίδιον ἄπει, γυψὶ καὶ κόραξι πάντα ἐκεῖνα καταλιπών;

XIII. 1: **παρῆσαν δέ τινες...ἀπαγγέλλοντες**] 'There were present...some that told him.' Rather, as Dean Alford, 'There came some...that told him[1].' See for this use of πάρειμι Matt. xxvi. 50, John xi. 28, Acts x. 21, Coloss. i. 6. Wetstein quotes a strikingly similar example from Diod. Sic. XVII. 8: περὶ ταῦτα δ' ὄντος αὐτοῦ, παρῆσάν τινες ἀπαγγέλλοντες πολλοὺς τῶν Ἑλλήνων νεωτερίζειν. We may also compare Gen. xiv. 13: παραγενόμενος δὲ τῶν ἀνασωθέντων τις ἀπήγγειλεν Ἀβραὰμ τῷ περάτῃ[2].

XIII. 9: **εἰς τὸ μέλλον**] A. V. '*then* after that.' R. V. 'thenceforth.' The true rendering of εἰς τὸ μέλλον was pointed out by Jeremiah Markland in his *Expl. Vet. Auct.* p. 286[3], namely, 'next year.' Here ἔτος occurs in the preceding verse, but, even without that, the idiom is well established. Plutarch frequently uses it of magistrates *designate*, as *Vit. Caes.* XIV: τὸν δὲ Πείσωνα κατέστησεν ὕπατον εἰς τὸ μέλλον[4]. Another good example (also quoted by Markland) is Joseph. *Ant.* I. 11, 2: ἥξειν ἔφασαν εἰς τὸ μέλλον, καὶ εὑρήσειν αὐτὴν ἤδη μητέρα γεγενημένην, compared with Gen. xviii. 10: κατὰ τὸν καιρὸν τοῦτον εἰς ὥρας, 'about this time next year,' for which we also find νέωτα or εἰς νέωτα. So the Lexicographers, as Moeris, p. 268: Νέωτα, Ἀττικῶς· τὸ μέλλον ἔτος, Ἑλληνικῶς. Hesychius: Νέωτα· εἰς τὸ ἐπιὸν ἢ νέον ἔτος. We need not translate 'against next year,' the preposition being redundant, as in εἰς αὔριον, εἰς τὴν τρίτην. But 1 Tim. vi. 19, 'laying up...against the time to come' (εἰς τὸ μέλλον) is different[5].

*XIII. 9: 'and if it bear fruit afterward —.' Dean Alford remarks : 'After καρπὸν, λείπει τὸ εὖ ἔχει, Euthym.: but not without reason : to fill up the *aposiopesis*, did not belong to the purpose of this parable.'

An *aposiopesis* is a rhetorical figure, 'by which the speaker through some affection (as sorrow, bashfulness, fear, anger, or vehemency) breaks off his speech before it be all ended.' In the present case, if such a figure were found, it would be in the second, or minatory clause : 'but if not —.' But this is not a *rhetorical*, but a *grammatical* figure, very common in Greek, from Homer downwards (but strictly appropriated to this particular construction, κἂν μὲν—εἰ δὲ μήγε), and not without

---

[1] [So παρουσία, 'coming.' 2 Thess. ii. &c., where the Revisers always put in the margin 'Gr. presence.']

[2] [Cf. Synes. p. 232 C: ἦκε δέ τις ἀγγέλλων ὡς....]

[3] *Eurip. Supplices...cum expl. loc... ex auct. Gr. et Lat. Londini*, 1763. Ed.

[4] [Cf. Appian. *B. C.* II. 5: Σιλανὸς... ὃς ἐς τὸ μέλλον ᾕρητο ὑπατεύειν. Also ἐς τοὐπιόν, *Ibid.* II. 26; Plut. *Vit. Caes.* LVII.]

[5] [Cf. Appian. *B. C.* III. 17: ἐς δὲ τὸ μέλλον, Ἀντώνιε..., 'quod superest.']

examples in Hebrew. Of the two places referred to in the margin, Luke xix. 42 does not belong to this idiom. In the other, Exod. xxxii. 32, our translators have retained the ἀνανταπόδοτον: 'Yet now, if thou wilt forgive their sin—and if not,' probably because the introduction of an expression of approval or acquiescence might have appeared irreverent; but in Dan. iii. 15 and this place, they have rightly supplied *well.*

*XIII. 24: ἀγωνίζεσθε εἰσελθεῖν] Examples of this word with an infinitive being very rare, note the following from Diod. Sic. Tom. x. p. 25 ed. Bip.: ὥστε ὁ μὲν πατὴρ ἐξίστασθαι τῆς ὅλης ἀρχῆς ἠγωνίζετο τῷ παιδί. Plut. *Vit. Cic.* 1: λέγεται νεανιευσάμενος εἰπεῖν, ὡς ἀγωνιεῖται τὸν Κικέρωνα τῶν Σκαύρων καὶ τῶν Κάτλων ἐνδοξότερον ἀποδεῖξαι.

XIII. 33: πλὴν δεῖ με σήμερον καὶ αὔριον—καὶ τῇ ἐχομένῃ πορεύεσθαι] This is the arrangement approved by the Greek commentators, the ἀποσιώπησις to be marked by the voice, making a pause at αὔριον, and closely joining καὶ τῇ ἐχ. πορεύεσθαι. After αὔριον the Syriac Peschito supplies ἐργάζεσθαι, Euthymius ἐνεργῆσαι ἃ εἶπον, others ἐκβάλλειν δαιμόνια. But Theophylact prefers the more natural method described above. Μὴ νοήσῃς, he says, ὅτι δεῖ με σήμερον καὶ αὔριον πορεύεσθαι, ἀλλὰ στῆθι ἄχρι τοῦ σήμερον καὶ αὔριον, καὶ οὕτως εἰπὲ τὸ τῇ ἐχ. πορεύεσθαι. He goes on to illustrate the construction from common parlance: Ἐγὼ κυριακῇ, δευτέρᾳ—καὶ τρίτῃ ἐξέρχομαι. So the unhappy debtor in Aristophanes (*Nub.* 1131) counts the intervening days to the last day of the month, when the interest was to be paid:—

> Πέμπτη, τετράς, τρίτη, μετὰ ταύτην δευτέρα·
> εἶθ᾽ ἣν ἐγὼ μάλιστα πασῶν ἡμερῶν
> δέδοικα καὶ πέφρικα καὶ βδελύττομαι,
> εὐθὺς μετὰ ταύτην ἔστ᾽ ἔνη τε καὶ νέα.

In that case, πορεύεσθαι would be *discedere ex vita,* as in Ch. xxii. 22; and ὑπάγειν Matt. xxvi. 24.

XIV. 10: προσανάβηθι ἀνώτερον] 'Go up higher.' Here no account is taken of the preposition πρός. It must have one of two values; either of *addition,* 'Adscende *adhuc* superius' (Bois) as 2 Macc. x. 36: ἕτεροι δὲ ὁμοίως προσαναβάντες (in addition to those who first mounted the wall); or, of *motion towards* a place, 'Ascende *huc* superius,' as Exod. xix. 23: οὐ δυνήσεται ὁ λαὸς προσαναβῆναι πρὸς τὸ ὄρος τὸ Σινᾶ. The latter seems to be the case here. The host comes into the room[1] (ὅταν ἔλθῃ ὁ κεκληκώς σε, not as in *v.* 9, ἐλθὼν ἐρεῖ σοι), takes his place at the head of the table, and calls to the guest whom he intends to honour, 'Friend, *come* up higher[2].' This view is remarkably confirmed by the passage in

---

[1] [Cf. Aristaen. *Ep.* v: πάντων οὖν εἰς ταὐτὸν ἀθροιζομένων τῶν δαιτυμένων, ὁ χρυσοῦς ἑστιάτωρ εἰσῄει.]

[2] [But ἡ ἀνωτάτω κλίνη was lowest in point of honour, as in Plut. *Vit. Brut.* XXXIV: μαρτυρομένου δὴ Βρούτου

Prov. xxv. 7, which our Lord undoubtedly had in his mind: κρεῖσσον γὰρ τὸ ῥηθῆναί σοι, ἀνάβαινε πρὸς μέ, ἢ ταπεινῶσαί σε ἐν προσώπῳ δυναστοῦ.

XIV. 17: ὅτι ἤδη ἕτοιμά ἐστι πάντα] So A, Vulg. Philox. and (with a transposition, πάντα ἕτοιμά ἐστιν) D, Pesch. In Bℵ¹ πάντα is wanting. We shall first give a few examples of the more familiar phrase, 'All things are ready.' Matt. xxii. 4: πάντα ἕτοιμα. Plut. *Vit. Pyrrh.* xv: γενομένων δὲ πάντων ἑτοίμων. Thucyd. VII. 65: καὶ ἐπειδὴ πάντα ἕτοιμα ἦν. Babr. *Fab.* LXXV: ἕτοιμα δεῖ σε πάντ᾽ ἔχειν· ἀποθνήσκεις. *Ibid.* cx: πάνθ᾽ ἕτοιμά σοι ποιεῖ¹. With εὐτρεπῆ for ἕτοιμα we have Lucian. *D. Mar.* x. 2: σὺ δὲ ἀπάγγελλε τῷ Διὶ πάντα εἶναι εὐτρεπῆ. Id. *Asin.* 20: ἀλλὰ πάντα, εἶπεν ἡ γραῦς, εὐτρεπῆ ὑμῖν, ἄρτοι πολλοί, οἴνου παλαιοῦ πίθοι, καὶ τὰ κρέα δὲ ὑμῖν τὰ ἄγρια σκευάσασα ἔχω. Diod. Sic. XVIII. 54: ὡς δὲ εὐτρεπῆ πάντα ἦν αὐτῷ τὰ πρὸς τὴν ἀποδημίαν. *Ibid.* 70: ταχὺ δὲ πάντων εὐτρεπῶν γενομένων. The curious expression, ὅτι ἤδη ἕτοιμά ἐστιν, 'for things are now ready,' is not defended by Paus. *Messen.* XV. 1: ὡς δὲ τὰ ἄλλα ἐς τὸν πόλεμον ἕτοιμα ἦν αὐτοῖς; nor yet by Plut. *Vit. Thes.* XIX: γενομένων δὲ ἑτοίμων (sc. τῶν νηῶν, which may be assumed from ναυπηγίᾳ). But the following clear instances from Thucydides, namely, II. 98: Σιτάλκης...παρεσκευάζετο τὸν στρατόν· καὶ ἐπειδὴ αὐτῷ ἕτοιμα ἦν, ἄρας ἐπορεύετο κ.τ.έ.; and VII. 50: καὶ μελλόντων αὐτῶν, ἐπειδὴ ἕτοιμα ἦν, ἀποπλεῖν, seem to establish a peculiar usage with regard to ἕτοιμα, which is in accordance with the reading of the most generally approved MSS. in this place².

XIV. 21: ἀναπήρους] The uncials (here and *v.* 13) vary between ἀναπείρους and ἀναπίρους, which is the commonest of all faults of spelling. Yet Dean Alford (and, perhaps, other modern editors) have actually printed ἀναπείρους! How would such preposterous sticklers for uncial infallibility deal with the witty saying of Diogenes: ἀναπήρους ἔλεγεν, οὐ τοὺς κωφοὺς καὶ τυφλούς, ἀλλὰ τοὺς μὴ ἔχοντας πήραν?

XIV. 31: πορευόμενος συμβαλεῖν ἑτέρῳ βασιλεῖ εἰς πόλεμον] The A. V. 'Going to make war against another king,' conveys to the English reader the idea which would be expressed by the Greek μέλλων πρὸς ἕτερον βασιλέα πόλεμον ἄρασθαι, instead of the true sense, 'on his way to fight a battle with another king.' There need be no hesitation in

---

μὴ κεκλημένον αὐτὸν ἥκειν καὶ κελεύοντος ἀπάγειν ἐπὶ τὴν ἀνωτάτω κλίνην, βίᾳ παρελθὼν εἰς τὴν μέσην κατεκλίθη. See Smith's *Dict. of Gr. and Rom. Antiq.* s. v. triclinium.]
    ¹ [Cf. also App. *B. C.* I. 56: ὡς δὲ αὐτῷ πάντα ἕτοιμα ἦν. *Ibid.* II. 50: ὡς δέ οἱ πάντα ἦν ἕτοιμα. *Ibid.* 77: ὡς δέ σφισιν ἕτοιμα πάντα ἦν. Plut. *Vit.*

Nic. XXIII: ὡς δὲ ἦν ἕτοιμα ταῦτα πάντα. Id. *Vit. Arat.* XXI: ἐπεὶ δ᾽ ἦν ἕτοιμα πάντα. Id. *Vit. Cleom.* XXII: πάντων οὖν ἑτοίμων γενομένων.]
    ² [Cf. Thuc. II. 3: ἐπεὶ δὲ ὡς ἐκ τῶν δυνατῶν ἕτοιμα ἦν. Compare also ὡς δὲ ἦν ἄπορα (Plut. *Vit. Caes.* XXXVIII), ὡς ἦν ἄφυκτα (Id. *Vit. Mar.* XLVI).]

rendering πόλεμον by 'battle' here as well as in 1 Cor. xiv. 8, Rev. ix. 9 (in both which places the A. V. has been injudiciously altered by the Revisers), because the Greek noun is employed in both senses (Passow says that in Homer and Hesiod the idea of *battle* prevails, in later writers, especially Attic, that of *war*), and the verb συμβαλεῖν is decisive in favour of 'battle.' Compare the phrases συμβαλεῖν τινι εἰς μάχην, εἰς χεῖρας, συμβαλεῖν τοῖς πολεμίοις (Herod.), and συμβολή, *praelium*[1]. Even in the phrase ποιῆσαι πόλεμον μετά τινος (Rev. xi. 7, xii. 17) a single conflict seems to be intended.

In what follows the use of ἐν for μετά will offend no one who will take the trouble to compare Num. xx. 20: καὶ ἐξῆλθεν Ἐδὼμ ἐν ὄχλῳ βαρεῖ καὶ ἐν χειρὶ ἰσχυρᾷ; or Jude 14: ἰδοὺ ἦλθε κύριος ἐν μυριάσιν ἁγίαις αὐτοῦ. Those who suggest that the difference of prepositions indicates that the 10,000 were the entire force at the disposal of the one king, and the 20,000 only so many as the other belligerent thought sufficient for the occasion, may be dismissed with the equivocal compliment *Subtilius quam verius.*

*For πόλεμος in the sense of μάχη may be quoted from 'later writers' Lucian. *De Conscr. Hist.* 29: τῶν ἀκριβῶς εἰδότων ὅτι μηδὲ κατὰ τοίχου γεγραμμένον πόλεμον ἑωράκει. Also the following, which mutually illustrate each other. 3 Reg. xxxii. 34: ἐξάγαγέ με ἐκ τοῦ πολέμου ὅτι τέτρωμαι. Lucian. *Dial. Mort.* XIV. 5: εἴ ποτε τρωθείης, καὶ βλέποιέν σε φοράδην τοῦ πολέμου ἐκκομιζόμενον, αἵματι ῥεόμενον. Dion. Hal. *Ant.* VI. 12: ἀποκομισθέντων δ᾽ ἀμφοτέρων ἐκ τῆς μάχης.

*XV. 13: συναγαγὼν ἅπαντα, *subaudi* εἰς ἀργύριον: in one word ἐξαργυρίσας, 'having sold all off.' Compare Plut. *Vit. Cat. Min.* VI: καὶ κληρονομίαν δ᾽ αὐτῷ προσγενομένην ἀνεψιοῦ Κάτωνος ρ ταλάντων εἰς ἀργύριον συναγαγών, παρεῖχεν ἄνευ τόκων χρῆσθαι τῷ δεομένῳ τῶν φίλων. Id. *Vit. Alcib.* V: οὐ πολλὰ κεκτημένον, ἀποδόμενον δὲ πάντα, καὶ τὸ συναχθὲν εἰς ρ στατῆρας τῷ Ἀλκιβιάδῃ προσφέροντα, καὶ δεόμενον λαβεῖν. Xen. Ephes. III. 2: πάντα ὅσα ἦν μοι χρήματα ἀποδόμενος, συλλέξας ἄργυρον εἰς Βυζάντιον ἔρχομαι. Diog. Laert. IV. 47: ὃς καὶ ἀποθνήσκων κατέλιπέ μοι πάντα· κἀγὼ κατακαύσας αὐτοῦ τὰ συγγράμματα, καὶ πάντα συγξύσας (having scraped all together) Ἀθήναζε ἦλθον καὶ ἐφιλοσόφησα. If the prodigal had 'gathered all his goods together,' and taken them with him, the proper word would have been συσκευασάμενος ἅπαντα, as Dion. Hal. *Ant.* III. 46: συνεσκευασμένος τὴν οὐσίαν ὅσην οἷός τ᾽ ἦν, ᾤχετο πλέων ἐκ τῆς Κορίνθου, and a little further on, τά τε χρήματα πάντα συσκευασάμενος (on moving from one place to another).

XV. 13: ζῶν ἀσώτως] 'With riotous living.' Why not, 'with prodigal living,' with reference to the familiar English title of the parable, 'The

[1] [Cf. Plut. *Vit. Dion.* XLIX: ἀναγκασθεὶς συνέβαλε καὶ ἡττήθη.]

prodigal son¹'? Aristotle (*Eth. Nic.* IV. 1, 3) defines the word : τοὺς γὰρ ἀκρατεῖς καὶ εἰς ἀκολασίαν δαπανηροὺς ᾿ΑΣΩΤΟΥΣ καλοῦμεν. *Profuse expenditure* seems to be the leading idea of the word, other ideas, as those of profligacy, debauchery, and riotous living, coming in by way of association. Plutarch (T. II. p. 463 A) gives us a glimpse of the life of such an one (quoted in a garbled form by Wetstein) : διὸ τῶν μὲν ἀσώτων ταῖς οἰκίαις προσιόντες, αὐλητρίδος ἀκούομεν ἑωθινῆς, καὶ πηλόν, ὥς τις εἶπεν, οἴνου, καὶ σπαράγματα στεφάνων, καὶ κραιπαλῶντας ὁρῶμεν ἐπὶ θύραις ἀκολούθους. Compare Archbishop Trench's *Synonyms of the N. T.*, p. 52, ed. 9.

XV. 30, 32 : ὁ **υἱός σου οὗτος**...ὁ **ἀδελφός σου οὗτος**] To give the full force of οὗτος we might almost venture to translate, 'This *precious* son of thine,' 'This *dear* brother of thine.' Wetstein compares Aristoph. *Nub.* 60 : μετὰ ταῦθ᾽ ὅπως νῷν ἐγένεθ᾽ υἱὸς οὑτοσί, where the Scholiast directs the reader to stop at υἱός, and then, after a pause, add οὑτοσί, ὡς ἀχθομένου αὐτοῦ τῇ γενέσει.

XVI. 1 : **καὶ οὗτος διεβλήθη αὐτῷ ὡς διασκορπίζων τὰ ὑπάρχοντα αὐτοῦ**] '*Διεβλήθη*—not *wrongfully*, which the word does not imply necessarily— but *maliciously*, which it does imply.'—*Alford*. It means properly *being accused behind one's back²*. So Herod. VII. 10, 7 : ὁ μὲν γὰρ διαβάλλων ἀδικέει, οὐ παρεόντος κατηγορέων. Lucian. *De Calum.* 8 : ὁ δὲ τῇ διαβολῇ κατὰ τῶν ἀπόντων λάθρα χρώμενος. St Luke's construction, διεβλήθη τινί (or πρός τινα) ὡς ποιῶν τι, is that of the best Greek authors; e.g. Stob. *Flor.* T. XLII. 13 : Πελοπίδας, ἀνδρείου στρατιώτου διαβληθέντος αὐτῷ, ὡς βλασφημήσαντος αὐτόν. Lucian. *De Calum.* 29 : τὸν Σωκράτην τὸν ἀδίκως πρὸς τοὺς ᾿Αθηναίους διαβεβλημένον, ὡς ἀσεβῆ καὶ ἐπίβουλον. Dion. Hal. *Ant.* VIII. 49 : ἔπειτα διαβληθεὶς πρὸς αὐτούς, ὡς συμπράττων πάλιν τοῖς τυράννοις τὴν κάθοδον.

XVI. 19 : **εὐφραινόμενος καθ᾽ ἡμέραν λαμπρῶς**] The Revisers have done right in retaining the A. V., except that for 'faring' they might with advantage have substituted 'feasting.' So the Vulg. *et epulabatur quotidie splendide*. But in the margin they propose another rendering : 'living in mirth and splendour every day.' Here the luxurious living of the rich man is presented to us under two different aspects : *mirth*, which we may suppose to consist in eating and drinking, and *splendour*, which suggests elegance of house and furniture. But the Greek word

---

¹ The title of this κεφάλαιον in Greek is, Περὶ τοῦ ἀποδημήσαντος εἰς χώραν μακράν; but a more appropriate one would be, Περὶ τοῦ υἱοῦ τοῦ ἀσώτου. [Note, that in *v.* 22, the insertion of ταχὺ before ἐξενέγκατε is supported by

a fragment of the Curetonian Syriac published by Professor Wright in 1872.]

² [For διαβολή we commonly use 'suspicion,' in the well-known saying of Caesar : ὅτι τὴν Καίσαρος γυναῖκα καὶ διαβολῆς δεῖ καθαρὰν εἶναι.]

εὐφραινόμενος only contains the former idea, that of merry-making[1], which is qualified by the adverb λαμπρῶς, *laute*, 'sumptuously.' Thus Theophylact: Λαμπρῶς· ἀσώτως καὶ πολυτελῶς. And we often find this epithet in connexion with feasting: e.g. Ecclus. xxix. 22 : ἐδέσματα λαμπρά. Diod. Sic. XIV. 108 : τὸ μὲν πρῶτον ἐφ' ἡμέρας τινὰς ἐχορήγουν τὰς τροφὰς λαμπρῶς. XVII. 91 : τὴν δύναμιν ἅπασαν λαμπρῶς εἱστίασε. 93 : ξενισθεὶς λαμπρῶς[2].

XVI. 20: ἐβέβλητο] 'was laid.' Dean Alford *improves* upon this, already too literal, version : 'ἐβέβλητο, *was*, or *had been, cast down*, i.e. was placed there on purpose to get what he could of alms.' In that case we should have expected ἐτίθετο, as in the account of the impotent man καθ' ἡμέραν πρὸς τὴν θύραν τοῦ ἱεροῦ. But ἐβέβλητο is merely 'lay,' and differs from ἔκειτο only as it is used of sick persons[3]. See Matt. viii. 6. Nor can we agree with the Dean in thinking that ἀλλὰ καὶ in the next verse seems to imply that he got the crumbs ; or that the dogs licked his sores *in pity* (not, as Bengel, *dolorem exasperantes*). This latter incident is introduced to show the utter helplessness and friendlessness of the beggar, who had no one that cared for him even so much as to drive away the dogs that took advantage of his impotence. So Theophylact : ἀλλὰ καὶ ἔρημος τῶν θεραπευσόντων· οἱ γὰρ κύνες ἔλειχον τὰ ἕλκη αὐτοῦ, οἷα μηδενὸς ὄντος τοῦ ἀποσοβήσοντος αὐτούς. We may compare the fable of *The Flies*, as told by Josephus (*Ant.* XVIII. 6, 5): Τραυματίᾳ τινὶ κειμένῳ μυῖαι κατὰ πλῆθος τὰς ὠτειλὰς περιέστησαν· καί τις τῶν παρατυχόντων, οἰκτείρας αὐτοῦ τὴν δυστυχίαν, καὶ νομίσας ἀδυναμίᾳ μὴ βοηθεῖν [sc. ἑαυτῷ] οἷός τε ἦν ἀποσοβεῖν αὐτοὺς παραστὰς κ.τ.λ.

*XVI. 31. οὐδὲ, ἐάν τις ἐκ νεκρῶν ἀναστῇ, πεισθήσονται] So both Scrivener and Palmer point the words, differing from the common editions, which have either no commas at all, or the latter one only. The change was required to justify the rendering of both versions, 'Neither will they be persuaded, though one rose (R. V. if one rise) from the dead.' But οὐδὲ ἐάν (or οὐδ' ἐάν, as ABD) are closely connected, in the sense of 'not even if'; and though the A. V. fairly represents the Greek, and may claim to keep its place by right of prescription, the more correct rendering would be, retaining the order of the original, 'not even if one rise from the dead, will they be persuaded.' Compare Hom. *Il.* A 90: οὐδ' ἦν Ἀγαμέμνονα εἴπῃς. Alciphr. II. 4 (quoted by Wetstein): οὐδ' εἰ βοῦς μοι, τὸ λεγόμενον, φθέγξαιτο, πεισθείην.

---

[1] [Cf. 3 Kings iv. 20: ἔσθοντες καὶ πίνοντες καὶ εὐφραινόμενοι, 'making merry.']

[2] [Cf. App. *B. C.* II. 69: καὶ οἱ θεράποντες αὐτοῖς δαῖτα λαμπροτάτην ἐπόρσυνον. Plut. *Vit. Ant.* LXXXV: Cleopatra before killing herself—λουσαμένη δὲ καὶ κατακλιθεῖσα λαμπρὸν ἄριστον ἠρίστα.]

[3] [Cf. Aesop. *Fab.* CCLVII: Λύκος ὑπὸ κυνῶν δηχθεὶς, καὶ κακῶς πάσχων, ἐβέβλητο.]

XVII. 21. A. V. 'The kingdom of God is within you. Or, *among you.*' The Greek is ἐντὸς ὑμῶν, which some explain in the sense of ἐν ὑμῖν, or ἐν μέσῳ ὑμῶν, and compare Ch. xi. 20: ἄρα ἔφθασεν ἐφ' ὑμᾶς κ.τ.έ. But no *sound* example has yet been adduced of ἐντός so used. The only apparent one, which has been handed down from Raphel to Dean Alford, is Xenoph. *Anab.* I. 10, 3: οὐ μὴν ἔφυγόν γε, ἀλλὰ καὶ ταύτην (Cyrus's Milesian concubine) ἔσωσαν, καὶ ἄλλα ὁπόσα ἐντὸς αὐτῶν καὶ χρήματα καὶ ἄνθρωποι ἐγένοντο, πάντα ἔσωσαν; where, however, ἐντὸς αὐτῶν is not simply 'among them,' but 'within their position,' and does not differ from ἐντὸς τοῦ τείχους γενέσθαι, *to get safe within the wall.* The generally received version is supported by the invariable use of ἐντός (compare Psa. xxxviii. 4, cii. I: ἡ καρδία μου ἐντός μου—πάντα τὰ ἐντός μου) as well as by similar sentiments in the Apostolic writings (e.g. Rom. xiv. 17). Though the kingdom of God was not, in any sense, in the hearts of the Pharisees, who were immediately addressed, nor is, in its fullest sense, in the hearts of the greater number of professed Christians, yet *that* is where it is to be sought: ταύτην, says Theophylact, τὴν ἀγγελικὴν κατάστασιν καὶ διαγωγὴν ἐντὸς ἡμῶν ἔχομεν, τουτέστιν, ΟΤΑΝ ΒΟΥΛΗΘΩΜΕΝ. 'Let every man retire into himself, and see if he can find this kingdom in his heart; for if he find it not there, in vain will he find it in all the world besides[1].'

XVIII. 5: ἵνα μὴ εἰς τέλος ἐρχομένη ὑπωπιάζῃ με] A. V. 'Lest by her continual coming she weary me.' R. V. 'Lest she wear me out (Gr. *bruise me*) by her continual coming.' Dean Alford seems to incline towards Meyer's 'literal interpretation'—'lest at last she should become desperate, and come and strike me in the face' (!). It may be conceded that εἰς τέλος admits of either signification, 'continually,' or 'at last,' as may be most suited to the context. Here, where it is closely joined with a present participle, we prefer the former, in which sense it is constantly interchanged with the Hebrew לָנֶצַח, *in perpetuum,* as we might say, 'She is *for ever* coming and wearying me.' With this also agrees the *tense* of the verb, ὑπωπιάζῃ, not ὑπωπιάσῃ, which necessarily implies a *recurring* action, such as wearying a person by continual solicitation, not something which is to be done 'at last,' that is, once only. This distinction is rightly insisted on by St Chrysostom in a somewhat similar place, 2 Cor. xii. 7: ἄγγελος Σατᾶν ἵνα με κολαφίζῃ; on which he remarks: ὥστε ΔΙΗΝΕΚΟΥΣ δεῖσθαι τοῦ χαλινοῦ· οὐ γὰρ εἶπεν, ἵνα κολαφίσῃ, ἀλλ' ἵνα κολαφίζῃ. Meyer's interpretation is, therefore, doubly erroneous; as it would require, to satisfy the plainest rules of grammar, ἵνα μὴ εἰς τέλος ἐλθοῦσα ὑπωπιάσῃ με. Need it be added, that what the unjust judge dreaded, was not a sudden burst of fury, which he would know how to deal with, but the trouble and annoyance of the woman's coming day after day, and preferring the same suit, which he, being under no restraints, human or divine, had no mind to grant?

[1] John Hales' *Golden Remains.*

XVIII. 7: καὶ μακροθυμῶν ἐπ' αὐτοῖς] A. V. 'Though he bear long with them.' R. V. 'And he is long-suffering over them'; reading μακρο-θυμεῖ with all the uncials. There can be little doubt that this is the true construction of the passage, joining καὶ μακροθυμεῖ not with οὐ μὴ ποιήσῃ, but with τῶν βοώντων, which, in sense, is equivalent to οἱ βοῶσιν. Then the copula exerts the same force as in Psa. xxii. 2: 'Lord, I cry unto thee, and thou hearest not.' Comparing Prov. xix. 11 (in the LXX. and A. V.) I would translate: 'who cry unto him day and night, and he *deferreth his anger* on their behalf.' This sense of μακροθυμεῖν, though not a very common one, is sufficiently supported by the very similar text (Bois says, *Non est ovum ovo similius*) in Ecclus. xxxv. 18, speaking of the prayers of the poor: 'For the Lord will not be slack (οὐ μὴ βραδύνῃ), neither will the Mighty be patient towards them (οὐδὲ μὴ μακροθυμήσῃ ἐπ' αὐτοῖς).' I add two good examples from St Chrysostom, T. IV. p. 451 A: οὐκ οἰκτείρει τὸ γύναιον...ἀλλὰ μακροθυμεῖ, βουλόμενος τὸν λανθάνοντα θησαυρὸν ...κατάδηλον ποιῆσαι. T. VII. p. 333 E: καὶ μετὰ ταῦτα πολλάκις ἀφῆκεν αὐτοὺς εἰς χαλεπωτέρους χειμῶνας πραγμάτων ἐμπεσεῖν, καὶ ἐμακροθύμησε.

Of course there is no contradiction between the tardiness implied in this verse, and the speedy vengeance denounced in the next. For (as Bois remarks) 'Tarditas est κατὰ τὸ φαινόμενον, et ex opinione eorum quibus etiam celeritas, ut dicitur, mora est: at celeritas est κατὰ τὸ ἀληθές, et ex rei veritate.'

*XVIII. 9: καὶ ἐξουθενοῦντας τοὺς λοιπούς] A. V. 'and despised others.' R. V. 'and set all others (Gr. *the rest*) at nought.' There seems no reason for the change, except the etymological one. Suidas: ἐξουθενῶ σε· ἀντ' οὐδενός σε λογίζομαι. The A. V. is retained by the Revisers in 1 Cor. i. 28, xvi. 11, Gal. iv. 14, 1 Thess. v. 20. In Rom. xiv. 3, 10, where A. V. 'despise...set at nought,' the latter rendering might be made conformable to the former, instead of (as R. V.) the former to the latter. In the present case, a good Greek writer would, perhaps, have said, καὶ ὑπερ-φρονοῦντας, or καὶ κατεπαιρομένους (τῶν λοιπῶν).

*XVIII. 12: R. V. 'I give tithes of all that I *get*' (κτῶμαι not κέκτημαι). The change (especially in so correct a writer as St Luke) may be accepted without difficulty, although the distinction is sometimes overlooked in later Greek; e.g. Aesop. *Fab.* LXXXI. ed. de Fur.: A trumpeter says πλὴν γὰρ τούτου τοῦ χαλκοῦ (his instrument) οὐ κτῶμαι ἄλλο. Again in Ch. xxi. 19 we have to choose between A. V. 'in your patience possess ye (κτήσασθε) your souls,' and R. V. 'in your patience ye shall win (κτήσεσθε) your souls (lives),' both making a good sense. But in 1 Thess. iv. 4, 'that every one of you should know how to possess (κτᾶσθαι) his vessel in sanctification and honour,' the idea of *acquiring* is so remote from the common sense of the exhortation, that the Revisers have been forced to make use of the strange expression, 'to possess himself of his own vessel,' meaning, I suppose, 'to make himself master of his own body,' which before belonged to another, namely, to sin. This, at least, is St Chrysostom's explanation (T. XI. p. 460 E): ἄρα ἡμεῖς αὐτὸ κτώμεθα, ὅταν ᾖ καθαρόν· ὅταν δὲ ἀκάθαρτον, ἡ ἁμαρτία. But this seems very far fetched.

*XVIII. 13. Ὁ θεός, ἱλάσθητι] A. V. 'God be merciful'; i.e. ὁ θεὸς ἱλασθείη. It is marvellous how this erroneous punctuation (only the omission of a comma, which is rightly inserted in v. 11) should have been perpetuated through so many editions of the A. V. including (quod mireris) Dr Scrivener's Cambridge Paragraph Bible; not to mention innumerable quotations in sermons and other devotional works (some of them even pressing the point of the publican's not daring to address God directly). The only exception that I have ever met with is Le Bas's Sermons, vol. III., p. 156, though he quotes carelessly, 'Lord, be merciful &c.'

XIX. 16: παρεγένετο, 'came,' not as R. V. 'came before him[1].' It is exactly the same as ἦλθεν in the following verse, and is used by LXX. for בּוֹא 106 times. If the nobleman had dealt with his servants through an agent, instead of personally, παρεγένετο would have been equally appropriate. It is interchanged with προσέρχεσθαι Stob. Flor. T. XXIX. 78: πόνου μὲν προσερχομένου, κακὸν ἡγούμεθα προσέρχεσθαι ἑαυτοῖς· ἡδονῆς δὲ παραγινομένης, ἀγαθὸν ἡγούμεθα παραγίνεσθαι ἡμῖν[2].

XIX. 29, XXI. 37: πρὸς τὸ ὄρος τὸ καλούμενον ἐλαιῶν] 'The name, when thus put, must be accentuated ἐλαιών (Olivetum); for when it is the genitive of ἐλαία, the article is prefixed (xix. 37).'—Dean Alford. But there it is πρὸς τῇ καταβάσει τοῦ ὄρους τῶν ἐλαιῶν, which does not prove that the mount itself was not called Ὄρος ἐλαιῶν. Thus in 2 Chron. xx. 26 we read ἐπισυνήχθησαν εἰς τὸν αὐλῶνα τῆς εὐλογίας; but it follows, διὰ τοῦτο ἐκάλεσαν τὸ ὄνομα τοῦ τόπου ἐκείνου, Κοιλὰς εὐλογίας. And would it not, in the other case, be πρὸς τὸ ὄρος τὸ καλούμενον ἐλαιῶνα? comparing Acts i. 12, ἀπὸ ὄρους τοῦ καλουμένου ἐλαιῶνος. The Syriac versions are divided, the Peschito accentuating ἐλαιών (ܕܙ̈ܝܬܐ ܕܒܝܬ), and the Philoxenian ἐλαιῶν (ܕܙ̈ܝܬܐ)[3].

---

[1] [In 1 Cor. xvi. 2, 3, ὅταν ἔλθω... ὅταν παραγένωμαι are both rendered 'when I come' by A. V., R. V. 'come ...arrive.' In Acts xxviii. 21, παραγενόμενος may be rendered ' in person,' as opposed to ' by letter.']

[2] [Cf. Plut. Vit. Caes. XLVI: ἐφ' ᾧ λέγεται μὴ φαινομένῳ μὲν ἀγωνιᾶσαι

σωθέντος δὲ καὶ πραγενομένου πρὸς αὐτὸν ἡσθῆναι διαφερόντως.]

[3] [Cf. Joseph. B. J. v. 2, 3: στρατοπεδεύσασθαι κατὰ τὸ ἐλαιῶν καλούμενον ὄρος, ὃ τῇ πόλει πρὸς ἀνατολὴν ἀντίκειται.] But see Deissmann, Neue Bibelstudien (1897), pp. 36 ff. for a fresh discussion of ἐλαιών. Ed.

XIX. 44: **καὶ ἐδαφιοῦσί σε**] 'And shall lay thee even with the ground.'
R. V. 'And shall dash thee to the ground.' Besides Psa. cxxxvi. 9,
where πρὸς τὴν πέτραν is added, Hos. xiv. 1 might be referred to, where we
read, καὶ τὰ ὑποτίτθια αὐτῶν ἐδαφισθήσονται, without the addition. In the
other sense the only example quoted is from the LXX. Amos ix. 14:
πόλεις τὰς ἠδαφισμένας, a false reading of Aldus, both the Vatican and
Alexandrine MSS. having ἠφανισμένας, agreeing with the Hebrew נָשַׁמּוּ.
'To lay even with the ground' is ἰσόπεδον ποιῆσαι (2 Macc. ix. 14),
κατάγειν ἕως ἐδάφους (Isai. xxvi. 5), εἰς ἔδαφος καθαιρεῖν (Thucyd., Polyb.),
εἰς ἔδαφος καταβάλλειν (Plut.)[1]. With the places quoted above from
Psalms and Hosea we may compare Eurip. *Iph. A.* 1151: βρέφος τε
τοὐμὸν ζῶν προσούδισας πέδῳ, | μαστῶν βιαίως τῶν ἐμῶν ἀποσπάσας. Diod.
Sic. T. x. p. 105 ed. Bip.: μηδ' αὐτῶν τῶν ὑπομαζίων φειδόμενοι, ἀλλὰ
ταῦτα μὲν τῆς θήλης ἀποσπῶντες προσήρασσον τῇ γῇ[2].

XX. 20: **καὶ παρατηρήσαντες ἀπέστειλαν ἐγκαθέτους**] 'And they watched
him, and sent forth spies.' Better, perhaps: 'And watching their opportunity, they sent forth spies.' This seems to be the force of παρατηρήσαντες
absolute positum; as in the following examples. Joseph. *B. J.* II. 18, 3
(quoted by Kypke): τῇ δὲ τρίτῃ νυκτὶ παρατηρήσαντες, οὓς μὲν ἀφυλάκτους,
οὓς δὲ κοιμωμένους, πάντας ἀπέσφαξαν. Schol. ad Hom. *Od.* K 494:
ἐθεάσατο δύο δράκοντας ἐν τῷ Κιθαιρῶνι μιγνυμένους, καὶ παρατηρήσας τὴν
δράκαιναν ἀνεῖλεν.

*XXI. 13: **ἀποβήσεται ὑμῖν εἰς μαρτύριον**] Both versions: 'It shall *turn*
unto (A. V. to) you for a testimony.' Rather, 'it shall *turn out*,' as also in
Philip. i. 19. Wetstein quotes Plut. T. II. p. 299 F: ἀπέβη δὲ εἰς οὐδὲν
χρηστὸν αὐτοῖς. Thucyd. III. 93: ἔπειτα μέντοι παρὰ δόξαν αὐτοῖς ἀπέβη.
To which may be added Euseb. *H. E.* III. 23: ἀπέβη γὰρ πονηρός, 'he
turned out bad.' In Philip. i. 12 we have the same sense expressed by τὰ
κατ' ἐμὲ μᾶλλον εἰς προκοπὴν τοῦ εὐαγγελίου ΈΛΗΛΥΘΕΝ, for which a more
classical word would have been περιελήλυθεν, as Appian. *B. C.* I. 7: εἰς δὲ
τοὐναντίον αὐτοῖς περιῄει.

*XXI. 25: **συνοχὴ ἐθνῶν ἐν ἀπορίᾳ ἤχους** (T. R. **ἠχούσης**) **θαλάσσης καὶ
σάλου**] The Cod. Alex. and cursives (ap. Wetst.) join ἐν ἀπορίᾳ ἤχους, as
R. V. 'in perplexity for the roaring of the sea,' and Dean Alford, 'in
despair on account of the noise,' the genitive case being governed by
ἀπορίᾳ. But the only example of this construction quoted by the latter
(from Meyer after Wetstein) is Herodian IV. 14, 1: ἐν ἀφασίᾳ τε ἦν...καὶ
ἀπορίᾳ τοῦ πρακτέου, which is altogether different. I should prefer putting
the stop after ἀπορίᾳ (as Philox.) and making ἤχους (governed by ἕνεκα

---

[1] [And συνομαλύνειν, Plut. *Vit. Timol.* XXII.]

[2] [Cf. Dio. Chrys. *Or.* XI. p. 159,

12: ὁρώσας δὲ τὰ νήπια τέκνα πρὸς τῇ γῇ παιόμενα ὠμῶς.]

understood) to depend on the whole clause 'distress of nations with perplexity.'

XXI. 35: ὡς παγὶς γὰρ ἐπελεύσεται] The corrected text (from BDℵ, al.) followed by the Revisers is, ὡς παγίς· ἐπεισελεύσεται γάρ, which they translate, 'as a snare: for *so* shall it come upon,' &c. But (1) as to the punctuation: ἐπελεύσεται or ἐπεισελεύσεται does not seem sufficiently strong to stand alone, especially when the verb in the preceding clause, ἐπιστῇ (which is hardly distinguishable from ἐπελεύσεται) is *doubly* emphasized by 'suddenly,' and 'as a snare.' And (2) as to the double compound ἐπεισελεύσεται: the second preposition seems to have no force or propriety in this place. In 1 Macc. xvi. 16: 'So when Simon and his sons had drunk largely, Ptolemee and his men rose up, and took their weapons, and came *upon Simon into the banqueting place* (ἐπεισῆλθον τῷ Σίμωνι εἰς τὸ συμπόσιον), and slew him, and his two sons,' both prepositions exert their proper force; and, generally, when the enemy or the calamity 'breaks in upon' an assembled multitude, as Palaeph. *Incred.* XVII. 4: εὐωχουμένων δὲ αὐτῶν (Trojans) ἐπεισέρχονται οἱ Ἕλληνες. Lucian. *Asin.* 38: καὶ γέλως ἐκ τῶν ἐπεισελθόντων πολὺς γίνεται ἔξω[1]. But that is not the case here; what follows, ἐπὶ πάντας τοὺς καθημένους, being governed by the ἐπί in ἐπεισελεύσεται, not by the εἰς. On the whole, the reading of T. R. ὡς παγὶς γὰρ ἐπελεύσεται seems every way preferable, and is supported by all the ancient versions; although the *hyperbaton*, ὡς παγὶς ἐπελεύσεται γάρ would not be without example[2]. If we accept this construction, and consider ἐπεισελ. to mean no more than ἐπελ., then we come back to the A. V., as equally satisfying either reading.

*XXII. 6: ἐξωμολόγησε] A. V. 'he promised.' R. V. 'he consented.' Vulg. *spopondit*. Both Syriac versions have ولاΟᵈ⁩, which is interchanged with ἐπηγγείλατο, συνέταξε &c. But all these are the equivalents of ὡμολόγησε (as Matt. xiv. 7) not of ἐξωμ. If the preposition has any force (which can hardly be disputed), it must be that of *intensifying* the simple idea, 'he fully consented,' 'agreed out and out'; which seems to be the feeling of the Greek commentators, as Euthymius: ἐκ καρδίας ὡμολόγησε, βεβαίως ἐπηγγείλατο. In the preceding verse, it is better to join συνέθεντο αὐτῷ, 'they covenanted with him,' as Thucyd. VIII. 37: συνέθεντο βασιλεῖ. Xenoph. *H. G.* VI. 2, 34: κἀκείνοις μὲν συνέθετο. 1 Macc. xv. 27: ἠθέτησε πάντα, ὅσα συνέθετο αὐτῷ τὸ πρότερον.

*XXII. 24: φιλονεικία] A. V. 'a strife.' R. V. 'a contention.' Perhaps 'an emulation' might be sufficiently strong. In Greek writers

[1] [Id. *Philops.* 27: ἅμα ταῦτα λεγόντων ἡμῶν, ἐπεισῆλθον οἱ τοῦ Εὐκράτους υἱοὶ ἐκ τῆς παλαίστρας.]
[2] E.g. St Chrysost. T. XI. p. 25 E,

where, for περὶ γὰρ τοῦ θεοῦ ταῦτα εἰρῆσθαι λέγουσι, the MSS. give περὶ τοῦ θεοῦ ταῦτα γὰρ εἰρῆσθαι λέγουσι.

φιλονεικία and φιλοτιμία are sometimes hardly distinguishable from each other. Thus Diod. Sic. XIX. 15: πολλὴν συνέβη γενέσθαι φιλοτιμίαν ὑπὲρ τῆς ἡγεμονίας. And that φιλονεικία does not imply any unfriendly feeling appears from Aelian. V. H. I. 24: διαλύεται τὴν πρὸς τὸν Λεπρέαν ὁ Ἡρακλῆς ἔχθραν. Φιλονεικία δ' οὖν αὐτοῖς ἐμπίπτει νεανικὴ, καὶ ἐρίζουσιν ἀλλήλοις περὶ δίσκου κ.τ.έ.

XXII. 31 : ἐξητήσατο ὑμᾶς] A. V. 'hath desired *to have* you.' R. V. 'asked to have you. Or, *obtained you by asking*.' The best Greek authors distinguish between ἐξαιτεῖν, *deposcere aliquem in poenam*, and ἐξαιτεῖσθαι, *deprecari, to beg off;* but later writers do not always observe this rule. Thus Plut. *Vit. Pyrrh.* III: καὶ μικρὸν ὕστερον ἐξαιτουμένων τῶν πολεμίων (the child Pyrrhus), Κασσάνδρου δὲ καὶ διακόσια τάλαντα διδόντος, οὐκ ἐξέδωκεν. But in either case, the aorist certainly indicates the *success* of the requisition, as the following examples (from Wetstein) show. Plut. *Vit. Pericl.* XXXII: Ἀσπασίαν μὲν οὖν ἐξητήσατο (he begged off)...ἀφεὶς ὑπὲρ αὐτῆς δάκρυα, καὶ δεηθεὶς τῶν δικαστῶν. Xenoph. *Anab.* I. 1, 3: συλλαμβάνει Κῦρον, ὡς ἀποκτενῶν, ἡ δὲ μήτηρ ἐξαιτησαμένη αὐτὸν ἀποπέμπει. I add St Chrysost. T. XII. p. 137 B : ὥσπερ γὰρ εἴ τις ἄνδρα φονέα, κλέπτην, μοιχὸν μέλλοντα ἀπάγεσθαι ἐξαιτήσαιτο. An *unsuccessful* demand would have been expressed by ἐξῃτεῖτο ὑμᾶς. In the text we must have recourse to a periphrasis: 'Satan hath procured you to be given up to him.'

XXII. 37 : τέλος ἔχει] A. V. 'have an end,' i.e. 'are coming to a conclusion.' In this sense we might compare Diod. Sic. XX. 95 : τῶν τε μηχανῶν αὐτῷ τέλος ἐχουσῶν. Dion. Hal. *Ant.* X. 46: ἐπειδὴ τέλος ἑώρα τὰ τῶν πολεμίων ἔχοντα. 51 : ἐπειδὴ δὲ τὰ μὲν καθ' ἡμᾶς τέλος ἔχει (is a *fait accompli*). But since τὰ περὶ ἐμοῦ is best explained of the prophetic announcements concerning the Messiah, and τέλος ἔχει is a phrase appropriated by good Greek authors to the accomplishment of such predictions, we would so understand it here, 'are being fulfilled,' 'are receiving their accomplishment,' τελειοῦνται ἤδη (Euthym.). The following are examples of τέλος ἔχειν applied to *oracles, prophecies*, &c. Dion. Hal. *Ant.* I. 19: τέλος ἔχειν σφίσι τὸ θεοπρόπιον ὑπέλαβον. 24: εἰ δὲ δὴ καὶ τούτων λάβοιεν τὴν δικαίαν μοῖραν, τέλος ἕξειν σφίσι τὸ λογίον. 55 : ὡς τὰ πρῶτα τοῦ μαντεύματος ἤδη σφίσι τέλος ἔχοι. 56 : τέλος γὰρ τὰ μαντεύματα ἐφαίνετο ἔχειν. Pausan. *Corinth.* 16. 2: καὶ Ἀκρισίῳ μὲν ἡ πρόρρησις τοῦ θεοῦ (that Danae his daughter should give birth to a son who should kill his grandfather) τέλος ἔσχεν (he did so accidentally by throwing a *discus*). The R. V. 'hath fulfilment' is ambiguous.

XXII. 38: 'Behold, here are two swords.' Add in margin: 'Or, *knives*.' 'Chrysostom gives a curious explanation of the two swords: εἰκὸς οὖν καὶ μαχαίρας εἶναι ἐκεῖ διὰ τὸ ἀρνίον.'—*Dean Alford.* There is nothing *curious* in this: it is very probable. The μάχαιρα, as is well-known, served both purposes, those of a knife and a sword. The Dean must have forgotten his Roman History (Dion. Hal. *Ant.* XI. 37): ὡς ἐγγὺς ἦν ἐργαστηρίου μαγειρικοῦ, μάχαιραν ἐξαρπάσας ἀπὸ τῆς τραπέζης κ.τ.λ.

XXII. 44: **γενόμενος ἐν ἀγωνίᾳ**] 'Being in an agony.' The word 'agony' having become, by traditional usage, consecrated (as it were) to this particular phase of our Saviour's passion, it would be highly inexpedient to alter it; but there can be no objection to adding in the margin: 'Gr. *a great fear.*' The common notions of the meaning of the Greek word ἀγωνία are those which we are accustomed to attach to the English word 'agony,' and are so erroneous that it is necessary to discuss the noun and its cognate verb ἀγωνιᾶν at some length. FEAR then, more or less intense, is the radical idea of the word. In Diog. Laert. VII. 113 ἀγωνία is defined to be φόβος ἀδήλου πράγματος. And so Etym. M. p. 15, 42: ἀγωνία, ἐπὶ τοῦ εἰς ἀγῶνα μέλλοντος κατιέναι· καταχρηστικῶς δὲ καὶ ἐπὶ τοῦ ἁπλῶς φόβου. Viewing the words ἀγωνία and ἀγωνιᾶν in connexion with their synonyms, we find them constantly joined with other words expressive of *fear*. Thus Demosth. p. 236, 19: ἐν φόβῳ καὶ πολλῇ ἀγωνίᾳ. Joseph. *Ant.* XI. 8, 4: ἦν ἐν ἀγωνίᾳ καὶ δέει. Diod. Sic. XVI. 42: οἱ βασιλεῖς ...εἰς ἀγωνίαν καὶ μεγίστους φόβους ἐνέπιπτον. Plut. *Vit. Mar.* XLIII: ὥστε καὶ τῶν φίλων ἕκαστον ἀγωνίας μεστὸν εἶναι καὶ φρίκης, ὁσάκις ἀσπασόμενοι τῷ Μαρίῳ πελάζοιεν (because, if Marius did not return the salutation, his δορυφόροι took it as a hint to kill the person saluting). Aelian. *V. H.* II. 1: ὁ μὲν (Ἀλκιβιάδης) ἠγωνία καὶ ἐδεδίει πάνυ σφόδρα εἰς τὸν δῆμον παρελθεῖν. Stob. *Flor.* T. CVIII. 83: ὧν γὰρ ὑπαρξάντων ἄνθρωποι λυποῦνται, τούτων ἐν προσδοκίᾳ γενομένων φοβοῦνται καὶ ἀγωνιῶσι. Diod. Sic. XIII. 45: περιδεεῖς ἐγίνοντο, περὶ σφῶν ἀγωνιῶντες. XIX. 26: τοῦ δὲ περὶ ταῦτα θορυβουμένου, καὶ περὶ τοῦ μέλλοντος ἀγωνιῶντος. St Chrysost. T. VII. p. 334 B: οὕτω καὶ Μωϋσῆς πρότερον φοβεῖται τὸν ὄφιν, καὶ φοβεῖται οὐχ ἁπλῶς, ἀλλὰ μετὰ πολλῆς τῆς ἀγωνίας.

Of the phrase εἶναι or γίνεσθαι ἐν ἀγωνίᾳ I have no other example, except one from Servius to be presently quoted; but its equivalent ἐν ἀγωνίᾳ καθεστηκέναι is common: e.g. Diod. Sic. XIV. 35: διόπερ οἱ Κύρῳ συμμαχήσαντες σατράπαι καὶ πόλεις ἐν ἀγωνίᾳ πολλῇ καθειστήκεισαν, μήποτε δῶσι τιμωρίαν κ.τ.έ. XVII. 116: καὶ θεοῖς ἀποτροπαίοις θύσας, ἐν ἀγωνίᾳ καθειστήκει (Alex. M.) καὶ τῆς τῶν Χαλδαίων προρρήσεως ἐμνημόνευσε. XX. 51: (ὡς...μέλλοντες διακινδυνεύειν) ἐν ἀγωνίᾳ πολλῇ καθειστήκεισαν.

Of the versions the Peschito renders ἀγωνία by ⟨Syriac⟩, which is the common word for φόβος; the Philoxenian by ⟨Syriac⟩, and the Vulgate by *agonia*. But the Latin word most nearly corresponding to it is *trepidatio*, as we learn from Servius on Virg. *Aen.* XII. 737: 'Dum trepidat, i.e. dum turbatur, festinat, quod Graeci ἐν ἀγωνίᾳ ἐστίν.' May not this have been the word used by the old Latin version (commonly, on the precarious foundation of a doubtful[1] reading in St Augustine, called the *Itala*); to which there is probably an allusion in a passage of St Bernard, quoted in D. Heinsii *Exerc. Sacr.* p. 232: *Et quos vivificabat mors tua, tua nihilominus et* trepidatio *robustos, et maestitia laetos, et taedium alacres, et turbatio quietos faceret.*

In the Greek versions of the O. T. the verb ἀγωνιᾶν answers to יָרֵא, *timuit*, Dan. i. 10, LXX. (where Theod. has φοβοῦμαι); to חָרֵד, *trepidus*, 1 Reg. iv. 13, in an anonymous version; and to דָּאַג, *sollicitus fuit*, Jerem. xxxviii. 19 in Symmachus's version: ἐγὼ ἀγωνιῶ διὰ τοὺς Ἰουδαίους (A. V. 'I am afraid of the Jews').

XXII. 66: καὶ ἀνήγαγον αὐτὸν εἰς τὸ συνέδριον ἑαυτῶν] A. V. 'And led him into their council.' Rather, 'they brought him up before their council.' Compare Acts xii. 4: 'intending after Easter to bring him forth to the people (ἀναγαγεῖν αὐτὸν τῷ λαῷ).' 2 Macc. vi. 10: δύο γὰρ γυναῖκες ἀνήχθησαν (for having circumcised their children). Lucian. *Ver. Hist.* II. 6: ἀναχθέντες ὡς τὸν βασιλέα[2]. The Revisers have here adopted the *less* difficult reading ἀπήγαγον, 'they led him away.'

XXIII. 32: ἕτεροι δύο κακοῦργοι] A. V. 'two other malefactors,' (in recent editions sometimes pointed, 'two other, malefactors'). R. V. 'two others, malefactors.' The more probable reading of Bℵ, ἕτεροι κακοῦργοι δύο, will not admit of being so tampered with. But even in T. R., there is no occasion to separate 'other' from 'malefactors.' It is a *negligent* construction, common to all languages, and not liable to be misunderstood[3]. In the exhortation in our Communion Service, the minister says: 'If he require further comfort or counsel, let him come to me, or to some other discreet and learned minister of God's word,' without incurring the imputation of vanity or self-laudation. And so far from this text being a

---

[1] I call the reading doubtful, (1) because the *Italic* version, if such there were, would have been called *Italica*, not *Itala*; and (2) because in the printed text, 'In ipsis autem interpretationibVS ITALA caeteris praeferatur; nam est verborum tenacior cum perspicuitate sententiae,' Archbishop Potter's emendation, 'interpretationibVS VSITATA,' (or, as commonly written, 'interpretationib⁹ usitata,') is so admirable, as almost to command assent. St Augustine elsewhere speaks of 'codices ecclesiastici *interpretationis usitatae*.' [But see *Texts and Studies*,

vol. IV. No. 3. *The Old Latin and the Itala*, by F. C. Burkitt, M.A. Ed.]

[2] [Cf. Plut. *Vit. Brut.* XXXIII: ἀλλ' ἀναχθεὶς καὶ κολασθείς...; Paus. VIII. 47, 6: πρὶν ἀναχθῆναι παρὰ τὸν τύραννον ἀποκτίννυσιν ἑαυτήν; Plut. II. p. 259 c: ἤσθοντο δὲ οἱ φύλακες, καὶ συλλαβόντες ἀνήγαγον πρὸς τὸν βασιλέα; App. *B. C.* I. 60: καὶ τὸν ἐντυχόντα νηποινεὶ κτείνειν, ἢ ἀνάγειν ἐπὶ τοὺς ὑπάτους.]

[3] [Cf. Paus. VIII. 36, 3: καὶ ἐς αὐτὸ ὅτι μὴ γυναιξὶ μόναις ἱεραῖς τῆς θεοῦ, ἀνθρώποις γε οὐδενὶ ἐσελθεῖν ἔστι τῶν ἄλλων.]

stumbling-block to the intelligent reader, he should rather view in it a literal fulfilment of Isaiah's prophecy, 'And he was numbered with the transgressors.'

XXIII. 42: μνήσθητί μου] Compare Gen. xl. 14. Herod. IX. 45: ἦν δὲ ὑμῖν ὁ πόλεμος ὅδε κατὰ νόον τελευτήσῃ, μνησθῆναί τινα χρὴ καὶ ἐμεῦ ἐλευθερώσεως πέρι. Chariton. Aphrod. VI. 5: καὶ ὅταν πλουτῇς, ἐμοῦ μνημόνευε. Babr. *Fab.* L. 16: ἐρρυσάμην σε, φησίν, ἀλλά μου μνήσκου.

XXIII. 44: καὶ ἐσκοτίσθη ὁ ἥλιος] Another reading is τοῦ ἡλίου ἐκλείποντος, which the Revisers adopt, rendering: 'the sun's light failing, Gr. *the sun failing.*' Rather, 'the sun being eclipsed,' this being the common manner of describing that phaenomenon in Greek, ὁ ἥλιος ἐξέλιπε [1]. Moreover the reading ἐκλιπόντος for ἐκλείποντος is supported by Lℵ and the Philoxenian Syriac, which latter reads in text, τοῦ ἡλίου † σκοτισθέντος, and in margin † ἐκλιπόντος (not ἐκλείποντος, which would require ܐܣܟܘ ܠܐܣܐ ܂ܕ, not, as it stands, ܘܣܟܐ| ܠܐܣܐ ܂ܕ). However, as the MSS. have been divided, ever since Origen's time, between the two readings, I think it would be safer to retain the A. V., and to record in margin: 'Other ancient authorities read *the sun being eclipsed*'; as, indeed, it was κατὰ τὸ φαινόμενον.

*In answer to a remark of the *Quarterly Reviewer* (No. CCCIV. p. 343): 'In like manner τοῦ ἡλίου ἐκλείποντος, as our Revisionists are perfectly well aware, means, "*the sun becoming eclipsed*," or "*suffering an eclipse*,"' the *Two Revisers* (p. 60) reply: 'We emphatically deny that there is anything in the Greek word ἐκλείπειν when associated with the sun which involves necessarily the notion of an eclipse.' This is a most rash assertion. There can be no doubt that the phrases ἐξέλιπεν ὁ ἥλιος (ἡ σελήνη), ἔκλειψις τοῦ ἡλίου, whenever they occur in the Greek historians, necessarily describe the phaenomenon of an astronomical eclipse, and nothing else. If, therefore, St Luke really wrote τοῦ ἡλίου ἐκλείποντος (ἐκλιπόντος is the better reading) and his Greek is to be construed like that of any other Greek author, it can only be by rendering, 'the sun being eclipsed'; and the version adopted by the Revisers, 'the sun's light failing,' does NOT convey to the mind of an English reader what the original does to that of a Greek. It is no answer to this objection, to say that the obscuration was not and could not be produced by an eclipse; and that St Luke, as a member of a liberal profession, must have been well aware of this. Still, if he thought proper to describe what took place in a popular way, and as an ordinary spectator would have spoken of it, his translator is bound in faithfulness to do the same, and to trust to the good sense and information of his readers to solve the difficulty.

---

[1] [Cf. Plut. *Vit. Nic.* XXIII: ἐξέλιπεν ἡ σελήνη...τοῦ μὲν γὰρ ἡλίου τὴν περὶ τὰς τριακάδας ἐπισκότησιν....]

As St Luke was not writing as an astronomer, when he affirms the sun to have been eclipsed at or near the time of full moon, so Moses was not giving instruction in physiology, when he classed the hare among ruminating animals. Each deferred to the popular opinion.

XXIII. 51 : οὗτος οὐκ ἦν συγκατατεθειμένος κ.τ.ἑ.] 'He had not consented' &c. 'The meaning is, he had absented himself, and taken no part in their (the council's) determination against Jesus.'—*Dean Alford.* This is rather more than can be safely affirmed. He may have been present, but have *dissented* from the resolution taken ; perhaps, like Nicodemus, another secret disciple of Jesus (John vii. 50), stated his objections to it. We cannot say for certain ; but the word συγκατατεθειμένος is rather in favour of this view. If we could interrogate the 'honourable councillor' on the subject, the following dialogue (adapted from Lys. *c. Eratosth.* p. 122) might not be far from the truth : Ἦσθα ἐν τῷ βουλευτηρίῳ, ὅτε οἱ λόγοι ἐγένοντο περὶ Ἰησοῦ τοῦ Ναζωραίου; ΗΝ. Πότερον συνηγόρευες τοῖς κελεύουσιν ἀποκτεῖναι, ἢ ἀντέλεγες; ΑΝΤΕΛΕΓΟΝ.

*XXIV. 10 : ἦσαν δὲ ἡ Μαγδαληνὴ Μαρία...καὶ αἱ λοιπαὶ σὺν αὐταῖς, αἳ ἔλεγον κ.τ.ἑ.] According to the T. R., no names having been mentioned in the preceding verse, the women who returned from the sepulchre and reported what they had seen to the eleven, are only known as 'the women which had come with him from Galilee' (xxiii. 55). In this verse, three names are mentioned with others not named, who 'told these things to the Apostles.' In the text followed by the Revisers, the only change seems to be the omission of αἱ before ἔλεγον. This has strong support from the uncials ; but its effect upon the construction of the passage is most unfortunate. 'Now they [the women who returned from the sepulchre, and told all these things &c.] were Mary M. and Joanna, and Mary the *mother* of James'; then after a long stop, we are reminded of 'the other women with them,' and what they did, which differs in no respect from what the three *coryphaei* had done—'told these things to the Apostles.'

XXIV. 12 : παρακύψας] A. V. 'stooping down.' In John xx. 5, 11 A. V. gives 'stooping down *and looking in* (sic).' R. V. (ter) 'stooping and looking in.' I should prefer, in all cases, simply 'looking in,' though 'peeping in' would more accurately define the word παρακύπτειν, which means *exserto capite prospicere* sive *introspicere*[1]. So Gen. xxvi. 8 : παρακύψας διὰ τῆς θυρίδος, εἶδε τὸν Ἰσαὰκ παίζοντα κ.τ.ἑ. Prov. vii. 6 : ἀπὸ τῆς θυρίδος εἰς τὰς πλατείας παρακύπτουσα. Ecclus. xxi. 23 : ἄφρων ἀπὸ θύρας

---

[1] [Cf. Aesop. *Fab.* CCXCVII : λέων ἔν τινι αἰγιάλῳ πλαζόμενος, ὡς ἐθεάσατο δελφῖνα παρακύψαντα. Arr. Epict. I. 1, 16 : καὶ παρακύπτομεν συνεχῶς, τίς ἄνεμος πνεῖ. These two passages negative the idea of stooping down.]

παρακύπτει εἰς οἰκίαν, where A. V. 'A fool will *peep in* at the door into the house'; though this might be thought too trivial an expression in the Gospels. The *downward stooping* is rightly rejected by Casaubon against Baronius (ed. 1614), p. 693: 'Male etiam probat *humilitatem* sepulchri ex eo quod dicitur Joannes *se inclinasse;* nam Graeca veritas habet παρακύψαι, quod sive de fenestra sumatur, sive de janua, nullam inclinationem corporis designat, qualem sibi finxit Baronius, sed *protensionem colli* potius *cum modica corporis incurvatione*[1].'

*XXIV. 17: τίνες οἱ λόγοι οὗτοι, οὓς ἀντιβάλλετε πρὸς ἀλλήλους;] The A. V. 'What manner of communications are these that ye have one to another?' fairly represents the sense of the original, and the Revisers have 'passed' it without substantial change. Still the question remains, What is the literal rendering of λόγους ἀντιβάλλειν? R. V. in marg. has: 'Gr. *What words are these that ye exchange one with another?*' Another explanation is, 'which ye toss one to another,' like a ball. But ἀντιβάλλειν may also mean, 'to lay two things one against another for the purpose of comparison,' and, in fact, it is commonly so used in the subscriptions of Greek MSS., for 'to compare,' or 'collate' one MS. with another for the sake of verification. Hence we arrive at the conclusion, that ἀντιβάλλειν λόγους is neither more nor less than the Latin '*conferre sermones*' and may be added to the list of Latinisms to be found in St Luke's writings.

Ibid.: καὶ ἐστε σκυθρωποί[2]] The reading of Bℵ, and (it would appear) originally of A, is καὶ ἐστάθησαν σκυθρωποί, for which R. V. 'And they stood still, looking sad.' Apart from the testimony of the MSS., there are several reasons why we should hesitate to accept this reading. (1) The passive form σταθῆναι is not 'to stand still[3],' but either 'to be established' (Deut. xix. 15, Matt. xviii. 16), or 'reared' (as the tabernacle Num. ix. 15); or else 'to be weighed' (Job xxviii. 15, Dan. v. 27). The only exception is the participle σταθείς, which (by usage) came to be interchanged with στάς in the sense of 'standing' (Acts v. 20, xvii. 22) or even 'standing still' (Luke xviii. 40). To 'stand still,' said of a moving person or thing, is στῆναι, as ἔστη ὁ ἥλιος (Jos. x. 13, Hab. iii. 11);

[1] James Fergusson (*Essay on the Ancient Topography of Jerusalem*, p. 88) has fallen into the same error: 'I may also mention here, that the position of the cave on the Sakrah exactly corresponds with the indication in the Bible narrative; for the Evangelists all agree that those that came to look for the body of Christ "looked down into the Sepulchre," which they must have done in the Sakrah;—but in the modern building [commonly called, the Holy Sepulchre] the tomb is several feet above the pavement of the church; and if that pavement and the filling up were removed, they must have stood on their tip-toes to have looked in.'

[2] [Cf. Lucian. *Hermotim.* 18: ὃς δ' ἂν μὴ ἔχῃ ταῦτα μηδὲ σκυθρωπὸς ᾖ.]

[3] [Yet cf. Rev. viii. 3: ἄλλος ἄγγελος ἦλθε καὶ ἐστάθη ἐπὶ τοῦ θυσιαστηρίου.]

ἔστησαν, οὐκ ἀπεκρίθησαν (Job xxxii. 16); οἱ βαστάζοντες ἔστησαν (Luke vii. 14); ἐκέλευσε στῆναι τὸ ἅρμα (Acts viii. 38)¹. (2) The sentence, 'They stood still, looking sad,' must strike the English reader as singular, considering that the 'sadness' must have been depicted on their countenances both before and after their 'standing still.' In the Greek, ἐστάθησαν σκυθρωποί is open to the same remark, with the addition that 'looking sad' is not σκυθρωποί, but σκυθρωπάζοντες, as in Psa. xxxvii. 6: ὅλην τὴν ἡμέραν σκυθρωπάζων ἐπορευόμην (compare Psa. xli. 10, xlii. 2 LXX.²). (3) But why should they 'stand still' at all? We read in v. 15 that while they conversed together as they walked, 'Jesus himself drew near and went with them,' joining, of course, in their conversation. It was natural for him to ask what they were talking about so earnestly when he came up, especially as, judging from the expression of their countenances, it was a painful subject. One of them answers for both, and the conversation proceeds, still, it would appear, 'as they walked.' If they 'stood still,' the narrative would seem to imply that all the parties continued standing during the entire discussion that followed; at least there is no mention of their resuming their journey, till we read in v. 28 that they 'drew nigh unto the village whither they were going.' (4) On all other occasions similar to the present, it is not the narrator, but one of the parties concerned in the transaction, who notices 'the sadness of countenance' of the other party. Thus in Gen. xl. 7 Joseph says to his fellow-prisoners: τί ὅτι τὰ πρόσωπα ὑμῶν σκυθρωπὰ σήμερον; and in Neh. ii. 2 the king says to his cup-bearer: διὰ τί τὸ πρόσωπόν σου πονηρόν (Hex. σκυθρωπόν);³

XXIV. 18: σὺ μόνος παροικεῖς κ.τ.έ.] R. V. 'Dost thou alone sojourn in Jerusalem?' and in margin: 'Or, Dost thou sojourn alone in Jerusalem?' But the former of the two versions seems to be the idea most commonly expressed on similar occasions. Thus Dio Chrys. Or. III. p. 42 (quoted by Wetstein): σὺ ἄρα, εἶπε, μόνος ἀνήκοος εἶ τούτων ἃ πάντες ἴσασιν; Charit. Aphrod. I. 11 : μόνοι γὰρ ὑμεῖς οὐκ ἀκούετε τὴν πολυπραγμοσύνην τῶν Ἀθηναίων; Lucian. Ep. Sat. 25 : θαυμάζω γάρ σε, εἰ μόνος τῶν ἁπάντων ἀγνοεῖς, ὡς ἐγὼ μὲν πάλαι βασιλεὺς ὢν πέπαυμαι.

XXIV. 39: ψηλαφήσατέ με κ.τ.έ.] Wetstein gives a quotation (in Latin) from a Rabbinical commentary on the Book of Ruth, which (in Greek) would read thus: Ἤρξατο ὁ Βοὸς ψηλαφῆσαι τὴν κόμην αὐτῆς, καὶ εἶπε· Πνεῦμα οὐκ ἔχει κόμην.

---

¹ [Cf. Lucian. Philops. 24: ἐγὼ μὲν οὖν ἰδὼν ἔστην.]
² [Cf. Plut. Vit. Phoc. 10: τρίβωνα φορῶν ἀεὶ καὶ σκυθρωπάζων.]
³ [Canon Farrar adopts the reading of Bℵ and paraphrases it thus: 'They stopped and looked at this unknown traveller, with a dubious and unfriendly glance.' (Life of Christ, II. p. 438.) But that is not the meaning of σκυθρωποί.]

XXIV. 50: ἕως πρὸς [T. R. εἰς] Βηθανίαν] The Revisers, adopting the reading of BC¹DL℘, have translated, 'until *they were* over against Bethany'; but this sense of πρός requires confirmation. The preposition after ἕως would seem to be a mere expletive, perhaps from the Aramaic ܠ ܕܥܡܐ[1]. Ἕως εἰς occurs Lev. xxiii. 14: ἕως εἰς αὐτὴν τὴν ἡμέραν ταύτην, and is common (of places) in Polybius : ἕως πρός is found Gen. xxxviii. 1: καὶ ἀφίκετο ἕως πρὸς ἄνθρωπόν τινα Ὀδολλαμίτην[2].

---

[1] [Cf. Ezra x. 14: עַד לַדְּבָר הַזֶּה.]

[2] [Cf. Lucian. *Hermot.* 24: πορευόμενος ἄχρι πρὸς τὴν πόλιν.]

ST JOHN.

*Chap. I. 5: οὐ κατέλαβεν] R. V. 'apprehended' and in margin 'or *overcame*' with a reference to xii. 35. Blakesley would translate 'extinguished,'—see his note on Herod. I. 87: ὡς ὥρα πάιτα μὲν ἄνδρα σβεννύντα τὸ πῦρ, δυναμένους οὐκέτι καταλαβεῖν (also ἐπικρατεῖν).

I. 11: εἰς τὰ ἴδια ἦλθε, καὶ οἱ ἴδιοι αὐτὸν οὐ παρέλαβον] A. V. 'He came unto his own, and his own received him not.' By 'his own,' in *both* places, an unlearned reader cannot fail to understand 'his own people.' But the R. V. is not much less misleading: 'He came unto his own (Gr. *his own things*) and they that were his own received him not.' Why not, 'He came to his own *home*, and his own *people* received him not,' though the italics are scarcely necessary? We may appeal to the A. V. itself, which translates ἕκαστος εἰς τὰ ἴδια (John xvi. 32) by 'every man to his own (or, *his own home*)'; and ὑπέστρεψαν εἰς τὰ ἴδια (Acts xxi. 6) by 'they returned home again.' Compare also Esth. v. 10: καὶ εἰσῆλθεν εἰς τὰ ἴδια (אֶל־בֵּיתוֹ), vi. 12: 'Αμὰν δὲ ὑπέστρεψεν εἰς τὰ ἴδια (same Hebrew). 3 Esdr. vi. 31: ληφθῆναι ξύλον ἐκ τῶν ἰδίων αὐτοῦ (מִן־בַּיְתֵהּ Ezr. vi. 11). Dion. Hal. *Ant.* VIII. 57: ἀπέλυσεν ἐπὶ τὰ οἰκεῖα. *Ibid.* 63: ἀπῄεσαν ἑκάτεροι ἐπὶ τὰ σφέτερα.

I. 24: καὶ οἱ ἀπεσταλμένοι ἦσαν ἐκ τῶν Φαρισαίων] If the reading of BC¹LΧ¹, which omits οἱ, is to be followed, we would not render, 'And they had been sent from the Pharisees,' which would require παρὰ τῶν Φ., as in *v.* 6; but, 'And there had been sent *some* of the Pharisees,' ἐκ τῶν being often so used by St John, e.g. in the nom. case (as here) Ch. xvi. 17: εἶπον οὖν ἐκ τῶν μαθητῶν αὐτοῦ. vii. 40 (corrected text): ἐκ τοῦ ὄχλου οὖν ἀκούσαντες τὸν λόγον; in the accus. 2 Epist. 4: εὕρηκα ἐκ τῶν τέκνων σου περιπατοῦντας. Apoc. ii. 10; and perhaps in the gen. John iii. 25: ἐγένετο οὖν ζήτησις ἐκ τῶν μαθητῶν 'Ιωάννου, where the use of ἐκ for 'on the part of' is doubtful.

II. 9: οἱ ἠντληκότες τὸ ὕδωρ] A. V. 'Which drew (R. V. had drawn) the water.' This is generally understood of *drawing the water from the well*, as in Ch. iv. 7. So St Chrysostom: εἰ γὰρ ἔμελλόν τινες ἀναισχυντεῖν, ἠδύναντο πρὸς αὐτοὺς λέγειν οἱ διακονησάμενοι· ἡμεῖς τὸ ὕδωρ ἠντλήσαμεν· ἡμεῖς τὰς ὑδρίας ἐνεπλήσαμεν. And Nonnus: ὑδροφόρος δὲ | ᾔδει λάτρις ὅμιλος, ὃς ὑγροχύτων ἀπὸ κόλπων | ἄγγεσι λαϊνέοις μετανάστιον ᾔφυσεν ὕδωρ. But (1) it is not necessary to have actually drawn the water, in order to be assured that it was water; and (2) it is not likely that the διάκονοι had themselves drawn the water from the well, that being a different service altogether, and usually assigned to women. I would therefore translate, 'which had *drawn out* the water' (as in *v.* 8), i.e. τὸ ὕδωρ οἶνον γεγενημένον. Painters erroneously represent the servants as *pouring* the wine out of the water-pots, shaped like pitchers, into the drinking vessels; whereas both the ὑδρίαι for purifying purposes, and the κρατῆρες for mixing the wine, were *wide-mouthed* vessels, and *stationary* (Plut. *Vit. Pomp.* LXXII: καὶ κρατῆρες οἴνου προὔκειντο) in their places.

II. 10: τὸν καλὸν οἶνον τίθησι] R. V. 'setteth on the good wine.' This would seem as if the wine were placed on the table, according to our customs, instead of being drawn out from the κρατήρ with jugs or cans (οἰνοχόαι), and from the jug poured by the attendants into each man's drinking vessel (κύαθος). Nonnus's προτίθησι seems to harmonize with the A. V. 'doth set forth.'

II. 15: πάντας ἐξέβαλεν ἐκ τοῦ ἱεροῦ, τά τε πρόβατα καὶ τοὺς βόας] A. V. 'He drove them all (R. V. cast all) out of the temple, and (R. V. both) the sheep, and the oxen.' In the preceding verse two classes of *persons* are mentioned, the sellers of certain animals, and the money-changers. When therefore we are told that he made a scourge of small cords, and drove them all (πάντας) out of the temple, we cannot avoid the conclusion that the profaners of the temple are primarily intended, though, even if no more had been said, we should have had no difficulty in understanding that with the traffickers the objects and materials of their traffick were also summarily expelled. But more *is* said, and the particular manner in which each class of objects was dealt with is described. After this, it would seem the merest trifling to raise the question, whether the scourge was employed in the forcible expulsion of the dealers, or even whether they were forcibly expelled at all. Yet this is what is done by the grammatical purists of the present day. 'That our Lord,' says Dean Alford, 'used the scourge on the beasts only, not on the sellers of them, is almost necessarily contained in the form of the sentence here; the τά τε πρόβατα καὶ τοὺς βόας being merely epexegetical of πάντας, not conveying new particulars. It should therefore be rendered, "He drove all out of the temple, both the sheep and the oxen."' But the meaning (or ἐξήγησις) of πάντας being *strictly defined* by the preceding verse, it is evident that no ἐπεξήγησις of it, which is incompatible with that meaning, can be admitted. We hold therefore that τε...καί is not to be taken here as in

Matt. xxii. 10: συνήγαγον πάντας ὅσους εὗρον, πονηρούς τε καὶ ἀγαθούς (*tam malos quam bonos*), but that τε is a copula (compare Heb. ix. 1) connecting τὰ πρ. καὶ τοὺς β. with πάντας, *omnes ejecit de templo, oves quoque et boves*, which is, in fact, the rendering of the Vulgate[1].

With the remaining incident of this verse, καὶ τῶν κολλυβιστῶν ἐξέχεε τὸ κέρμα, I compare Diog. Laert. VI. 82: Μόνιμος...οἰκέτης τινὸς τραπεζίτου Κορινθίου, wishing to be dismissed that he might be able to attend Diogenes, μανίαν προσποιηθείς, τό τε κέρμα διερρίπτει, καὶ πᾶν τὸ ἐπὶ τῆς τραπέζης ἀργύριον, ἕως αὐτὸν ὁ δεσπότης παρητήσατο[2].

*II. 20: τεσσαράκοντα καὶ ἓξ ἔτεσιν ᾠκοδομήθη ὁ ναὸς οὗτος] Both versions: 'Forty and six years was this temple in building.' A learned correspondent asks: 'Can you find other good instances where the dative represents *duration of time* combined with an aorist tense? I should have thought the natural translation was: "This temple was built in 46 years," which is inconsistent with the historical date of its completion, A.D. 64.' The objection supposes that the aorist, ᾠκοδομήθη can only be used of a *completed* building. But any building which is so far advanced as to be capable of being used for the purposes of its erection is naturally spoken of by contemporaries with reference to its present state, not to some indefinite future time, when the designs of the founder or architect shall have been fully carried out. 'This temple' is the building as it was then, at the end of 46 years from its foundation; and whether we say, 'it was built in 46 years,' or, 'it was 46 years in building,' seems to make no difference as to the *sense*. And that the latter is capable of being defended on *grammatical* grounds appears from the singularly apposite quotation from Ezra v. 16: τότε Σασαβασσὰρ ἐκεῖνος ἦλθε, καὶ ἔδωκε θεμελίους τοῦ οἴκου τοῦ θεοῦ ἐν Ἱερουσαλήμ, καὶ ἀπὸ τότε ἕως τοῦ νῦν ΩΙΚΟΔΟΜΗΘΗ, καὶ οὐκ ἐτελέσθη (A. V. 'hath it been in building, and yet it is not finished').

III. 3: ἐὰν μή τις γεννηθῇ ἄνωθεν] A. V. 'Except a man be born again. Or, *from above*.' The best example for the sense of *again* (R. V. 'anew'), *de novo*, is Artemid. *Onirocr*. I. 13. A man dreams that he is being born. If his wife is pregnant at the time, this indicates that he will have a son in every respect like himself: οὕτω γὰρ ἄνωθεν αὐτὸς δόξειε γεννᾶσθαι. On the other hand it may be urged, that St John's writings furnish no example of this use of the word, and that the Hebrew

---

[1] [Cf. Babr. VII. 11, 12: πάντα τὸν γόμον λύων ἐπ᾽ αὐτὸν ἐτίθει τὴν σάγην τε τοῦ κτήνους καὶ τὴν ὀνείην προσεπέθηκεν ἐκδείρας.]

[2] Canon Farrar (*Life of Christ*, Chap. XIII) says that our Lord did not overturn the tables of the dove-sellers, lest the birds should be hurt in their cages; but a more probable reason seems to be, that the dove-sellers were not τραπεζῖται, and had no tables.

מִפְעַל is always *local.* The Syriac versions are divided, the Peschito for *denuo* (ܕܪܝܫ) ܩ) and the Philoxenian for *desuper* (ܠܥܠ ܩ)[1].

III. 15. The reading followed by the Revisers is ἵνα πᾶς ὁ πιστεύων ἐν αὐτῷ (T. R. εἰς αὐτὸν) ἔχῃ ζ. αἰ., which they translate, 'that whosoever believeth may in him have eternal life'; I suppose, because St John's usual construction is πιστεύειν εἰς αὐτόν, not ἐν αὐτῷ. But I doubt if ὁ πιστεύων is ever used by this writer *absolutè*[2]; and if it were so used here, would he not (if only for the avoiding of ambiguity) have placed ἐν αὐτῷ at the end of the sentence, as δι' αὐτοῦ (*v.* 17)?

*III. 25: ἐγένετο οὖν ζήτησις ἐκ τῶν μαθητῶν Ἰωάννου μετὰ Ἰουδαίου (T. R. -ων) περὶ καθαρισμοῦ] A. V. 'between some of John's disciples and the Jews.' R. V. 'on the part of John's disciples with a Jew.' The latter may be sustained (as by Raphel [ed. 1750]: 'orta est quaestio a discipulis; ut hi disputationis auctores fuisse intelligantur'). But the regular construction of ἐγένετο ζήτησις is with a dative, as Acts xv. 2: γενομένης δὲ...ζητήσεως οὐκ ὀλίγης τῷ Παύλῳ καὶ τῷ Βαρνάβᾳ πρὸς αὐτούς. And this construction may be obtained in this place by supposing ἐκ τῶν μαθητῶν to have the force of τισὶν ἐκ τῶν μ. as there are indubitable examples of ἐκ for τινὰς ἐκ, and τινὲς ἐκ. Of the former is Matt. xxiii. 34: ἐξ αὐτῶν ἀποκτενεῖτε; of the latter John xvi. 17: εἶπον οὖν ἐκ τῶν μαθητῶν αὐτοῦ πρὸς ἀλλήλους, and perhaps Acts xix. 33: ἐκ δὲ τοῦ ὄχλου προεβίβασαν Ἀλέξανδρον. R. V. marg. '*And* some *of the multitude*' &c. See note on Ch. i. 24.

*IV. 6: ἐκαθέζετο οὕτως] 'sat thus.' So both versions, having respect to the preceding clause κεκοπιακὼς ἐκ τῆς ὁδ., in which case οὕτως will be equivalent to ὡς μακρὰν βαδίσας ὁδόν. Another explanation of οὕτως is indicated by the margin of R. V.: 'Or, *as he was,*' and is supported by the Greek commentators (as Theoph. ἁπλῶς ὡς ἔτυχε· οὐκ ἐπὶ θρόνου, ἀλλ' οὕτως ἀφελῶς, ἐπὶ ἐδάφους), Grotius (*incuriose, ut se locus obtulerat*), Wetstein, and others. Examples of this usage might be quoted from the best Greek writers; but in such cases it will generally be found that οὕτως is explained by some other word, with which it is in combination, as Plat. *Gorg.* 506 D: οὕτως εἰκῇ, 503 D: ἴδωμεν δὴ οὑτωσὶν ἄτρεμα σκοπούμενοι. Dem. *c. Mid.* p. 553, 14: εἰσελθὼν οἴκαδε ὡς ἐκεῖνον, καὶ ἐφεξῆς οὑτωσὶ καθεζόμενος. Dio Chrys. p. 613, 6: ἐμοὶ μὲν εἰ δεῖ οὕτως (offhand) ἀποφήνασθαι φαύλως τε καὶ ἀκόμψως. Hor. *Od.* II. 11, 14: *jacentes sic temere.* Reiske says of this phrase, 'Mirifica est vis leposque particulae οὕτως sic positae'; but, perhaps, for that very reason we should hardly expect to come upon it in the writings of St John. If, however, this refinement should be preferred, we would not render 'as he was,' but 'as it chanced,'

---

[1] [Cf. Plut. ii. p. 265 A: παρασχεῖν ἑαυτὸν ὥσπερ ἐξ ἀρχῆς τικτόμενον ταῖς γυναιξὶν ἀπολοῦσαι κ.τ.ἑ.]

[2] [Cf., however, vi. 47, T. R. ὁ πιστεύων εἰς ἐμὲ ἔχει ζωὴν αἰώνιον; where R. V. omits εἰς ἐμέ.]

nullo delectu habito, or (as our common people say) 'promiscuously,' comparing Plut. *Vit. Ages.* XII: ὁ δὲ Φαρνάβαζος, αἰδεσθεὶς τὸν Ἀγησίλαον οὕτω κατακείμενον (on the grass) κατεκλίνη καὶ αὐτὸς ὡς ἔτυχεν ἐπὶ τῆς πόας χαμᾶζε.

*IV. 12. With ὃς ἜΔΩΚΕΝ ἡμῖν τὸ φρέαρ it is interesting to compare Pausan. III. 25, 3: ἔστι δὲ ἐν τῇ Πυρρίχῳ φρέαρ ἐν τῇ ἀγορᾷ, ΔΟΥΝΑΙ δέ σφισι τὸν Σίληνον νομίζουσι.

IV. 15: 'Neither come hither to draw.' For ἔρχωμαι Bℵ¹ read διέρχωμαι, which however may have arisen from a mistake in transcribing ΜΗΔΕΕΡΧΩΜΑΙ. But if not, there is no occasion to *press* the preposition, which merely implies a certain distance to be *traversed*, whether long or short, as Luke ii. 15: διέλθωμεν δὴ ἕως Βηθλεέμ; and Acts ix. 38: μὴ ὀκνῆσαι διελθεῖν ἕως αὐτῶν. The rendering, 'neither come all the way hither to draw' (as R. V. and Alford) would convey the impression, either that the well was at a longer distance from the city than usual, or that the woman regarded as a drudgery the ordinary and traditional occupation of her sex. Compare Gen. xxiv. 11 sqq.

V. 4: ὑγιὴς ἐγίνετο, ᾧ δήποτε κατείχετο νοσήματι] A. V. 'Was made whole of whatsoever disease he had.' R. V. 'Was made whole, with whatsoever disease he was holden.' Better, perhaps, 'Was made whole of whatsoever disease he was holden with.' The full construction of the Greek would be ὑγιὴς ἐγίνετο ἀπὸ τοῦ νοσήματος (cf. Mark v. 34: ἴσθι ὑγιὴς ἀπὸ τῆς μάστιγός σου) ᾧ δήποτε κατείχετο.

V. 13: ἐξένευσεν] 'had conveyed himself away.' More correctly, 'had turned aside.' Vulg. *declinavit*. S. Chrysost. ἐξέκλινεν. So Jud. iv. 18, Jael says to Sisera, 'Turn in, my lord, turn in,' where the Vat. MS. reads ἔκκλινον, but the Alex. ἔκνευσον. Plutarch (T. II. p. 577 B) has ἐκνεύσας τῆς ὁδοῦ μικρόν, and the Gloss. Vett. Ἐκνεύσεις, *diverticula*. Lastly, the Scholiast on Aristoph. *Ran.* 113 defines ἐκτροπαί to be ἐκνεύσεις τῶν ὁδῶν, ὅπου τις ἐκτραπῆναι δύναται¹. These examples are strongly against the derivation from ἐκνεῖν, 'to swim out,' which was probably the one adopted by our Translators in deference to Beza's note: "Ἐξένευσεν, *evaserat*, ad verbum *enataverat*²."

*V. 39: ἐρευνᾶτε τὰς γραφάς] 'Search the scriptures.' R. V. 'Ye search the scriptures.' On this question the 'Five Clergymen,' who, some years ago, favoured the public with a revised translation of St John's Gospel,

¹ [Cf. Lucian. *Bis Acc.* 9: ὥστε τὸ μὲν Σούνιον ἐν δεξιᾷ καταλείπωμεν, ἐς δὲ τὴν ἀκρόπολιν ἀπονεύωμεν ἤδη.]

² Dr Field here appears to summarize Beza's note. Ed.

were (like the 'five in one house' of our Lord's prophecy) 'divided three
against two and two against three'; thus, by a majority of one, τὸ εἰς
αὐτοὺς ἧκον, robbing the Christian Church, or at least the reformed part
of it, of its *raison d'être*, which has always been supposed to be bound up
with this text. It is true that the duty of 'searching the scriptures' might
be easily inferred from other texts; e.g. Acts xvii. 11, where the Bereans
are commended because they 'searched the scriptures daily, whether these
things were so'; where, however, the Greek word is not ἐρευνῶντες, but
ἀνακρίνοντες (R. V. 'examining'). Still an old favourite text is hard to
part with. And this is one. It is so compact, so directly to the point, so
musical, so fitted to be the motto of a book, the text of a sermon,
the emblazonment of a banner, the 'hand-writing on a wall,' that the
loss of it (if we must lose it) would be, perhaps, more irreparable than
that of any three words in the whole Bible. But *must* we lose it? Let
us see how the necessity is made out. If we turn to the Preface of the
work referred to, all we find is, that 'while the majority believed that the
context of *vv.* 39, 40 was decisive in favour of the indicative meaning
of ἐρευνᾶτε, two of us were equally earnest in their conviction, that the
context of the whole passage *vv.* 32—40 required that the verb should be
understood in the imperative.' A like diversity of conviction appears to
have prevailed among the members of the N. T. Revision Company, with
a similar result, the majority of two-thirds having come to the conclusion
to adopt the indicative in the text, and to relegate the imperative to the
margin. It did not fall within the plan of the Revisers to state their
reasons for retaining or rejecting any particular rendering; but since the
publication of the final result of their labours, a sort of revisional literature
has sprung up, to which we may, without any breach of confidence, appeal.
Thus, in regard to the present text, the views of the majority may be
considered to be fairly set forth in Dr Kennedy's *Ely Lectures*, pp. 52, 53.
Taking for his text John v. 39, 'Search the scriptures,' and bearing in
mind the saying, 'If the trumpet give an uncertain sound' &c., he thus
begins his discourse : 'So we read in the A. V., but wrongly: the R. V.
writes with just correctness, "Ye search the scriptures." This is mani-
festly shewn to be right by the next words, "because in them ye think ye
have eternal life."' The lecturer goes on to argue that to 'have eternal
life' is not to be taken in its best and highest sense of possessing a
personal assurance of that inestimable benefit, but in the very low and
restricted one, of being able to prove the truth of the doctrine against the
Sadducees who disputed it. If this is correct, then the words are the
reverse of commendatory; and the 'search' here spoken of is a partial
one for party purposes; not to get at the truth, but to confute the
adversary. In other words, ye search the scriptures, and ye do not
search them : ye search the scriptures diligently in support of a 'favourite
doctrine'; yet 'ye do not find in them, because ye do not search diligently
and faithfully, those many texts which bear witness of me.' This, no

doubt, *was* the case; but why not tell them so in so many words? Why not say, 'Ye do NOT search the scriptures, and therefore ye do not believe in me'?

It will have been observed that Dr Kennedy, in quoting the sequel of his text, stops short at 'eternal life,' as if ὅτι had no influence beyond those words. To this mistake it is, probably, owing that the *affirmatory* view of ἐρευνᾶτε has by some interpreters been preferred to the *hortatory*. They did not perceive that our Lord's argument, briefly stated, is this: ἐρευνᾶτε τὰς γραφὰς, ὅτι...ἐκεῖναί εἰσιν αἱ μαρτυροῦσαι περὶ ἐμοῦ. The words 'in them ye think' &c. are parenthetical; they do not give the reason why his hearers should search the scriptures, but enforce the duty from a consideration of the nature of the documents themselves. It is as if he had said, 'Search the scriptures, your own scriptures, the depositories of your faith and hope, those prophecies in which ye (rightly) think ye have eternal life—search them, I say, for they are they which testify of me.' So Beza: 'Scrutamini scripturas, quia illae testantur de me[1]'; and St Augustine: 'Scrutari enim jussit scripturas, quae testimonium perhibent de illo[2].' By adopting this construction, we need not abate one jot from the full force of ἐρευνᾶτε, which has always proved a stumbling-block to those who maintain the opposite view. Some of these (as Krebs, J. F. Schleusner) have even gone so far as to assert that there is no particular emphasis in the word, and that it may be properly used of any enquiry however superficial; in fact, that all that our Lord concedes to the Jews in this saying, is, *Vos legitis quidem litteras sacras.* Against this absurd paradox it will be sufficient to quote the comment of Euthymius Zigab. ad loc.: Ὅρα δὲ πῶς οὐκ εἶπεν, ἀναγινώσκετε, ἀλλ', ἐρευνᾶτε· ἀνεγίνωσκον μὲν γὰρ, οὐκ ἠρεύνων δέ· διὰ τοῦτο κελεύει ἐρευνᾶν. ἐπεὶ γὰρ συνεσκίαστο τὰ περὶ αὐτοῦ γεγραμμένα...ἐπιτάττει νῦν διορύττειν, ἵνα τὰ ἐν τῷ βάθει κείμενα...δυνηθῶσιν εὑρεῖν.

Although Protestant expositors, generally, may be supposed to have a bias in favour of the *imperative*, there seems a want of candour in the Ely Lecturer's concluding remark, that the Translators of 1611 probably 'chose the wrong form, because it gave a useful weapon against the practice of the Church of Rome, so far as this was supposed to forbid or condemn the study of Holy Scripture by the laity.' But the 'wrong form' had been chosen long before by Wycliffe, Tyndale, Cranmer, and the versions of Geneva and Rheims (a R. C. one); to say nothing of the ancient versions, Vet. Lat., Jerome, both Syriac (ܒܨܘ not ܚܙܘ ܐܢܬܘܢ), Memph., Armen., Aethiop.[3]

---

[1] But Beza (ed. 1598) has the following note; Cohaeret autem copula non cum ὅτι δοκεῖτε, sed cum verbo ἐρευνᾶτε, hoc modo, Vos scrutamini scripturas, et illae sunt quae testantur de me. Ed.

[2] Dr Field here appears to give a summary of St Augustine's remarks. Ed.

[3] As we have, here and elsewhere,

V. 45: εἰς ὃν ὑμεῖς ἠλπίκατε] 'in whom ye trust (or hope).' This is one of the verbs, in which the *preterite* in form is *present* in signification. Others are ἔγνωκα (Ch. viii. 52, xvii. 7), δέδοικα, ἕστηκα, πέποιθα, οἶδα (οἶδας, 'thou knowest,' not 'thou hast known,' 2 Tim. iii. 15), τεθαύμακα, τέθηπα. The same remark applies to 1 Cor. xv. 19, 2 Cor. i. 10, 1 Tim. iv. 10, v. 5 (ἤλπικε καὶ προσμένει), vi. 17 (μὴ ὑψηλοφρονεῖν μηδὲ ἠλπικέναι). In all these places ἤλπικα is *spero* (as rendered by the Vulg.) not *speravi*; 'I hope,' not 'I have hoped,' nor yet, as R. V., 'I have set my hope'; which last is merely an attempt to account for the origin of the grammatical anomaly; a matter with which the English reader has nothing to do.

*VI. 5: πόθεν ἀγοράσομεν ἄρτους;] By πόθεν is generally understood *a quibus vendentibus?* But, comparing the other Evangelists, the difficulty seems to have been one of *money*, rather than of *sellers*. Compare Lucian. *Hermot.* 71: ἦν τοίνυν ταῦτα ἐννοοῦσιν αὐτοῖς, ὁ παῖς προσελθὼν, ἔρηταί τι τῶν ἀναγκαίων, οἷον, ὅθεν ἄρτους ὠνητέον, ἢ ὅ,τι ᾖ φατέον πρὸς τὸν ἀπαιτοῦντα τοὐνοίκιον (the rent).

*VI. 10: ἦν δὲ χόρτος πολὺς ἐν τῷ τόπῳ] For similar descriptions we may compare Plut. *Ages.* XII: ὑπὸ σκιᾷ τινι πόας οὔσης βαθείας καταβαλὼν ἑαυτὸν ἐνταῦθα περιέμεινε Φαρνάβαζον. Philostr. *Imag.* I. 6: πόα δὲ ἁπαλὴ κατέχει τοὺς δρόμους, οἷα καὶ κατακλιθέντι στρωμνὴ εἶναι. Alciphr. *Fragm.* 6: ἐπὶ αὐτῆς βουλοίμην ἂν τῆς πόας κατακλιθῆναι, ἢ ἐπὶ τῶν ταπητίων ἐκείνων καὶ τῶν μαλθακῶν ὑποστρωμάτων, νὴ Δία.

VI. 51: 'And the bread that I will give is my flesh, [which I will give] for the life of the world.' Supposing ἣν ἐγὼ δώσω to be rightly ejected in deference to a great preponderance of MSS. and versions, I would still insert '*which I will give*' (in italics). But in the T. R. ὁ ἄρτος ὃν 'ΕΓΩ ΔΩΣΩ [ἡ σάρξ μου ἐστὶν ἣν 'ΕΓΩ ΔΩΣΩ] ὑπὲρ τῆς τοῦ κόσμου ζωῆς, the words within the brackets might easily have passed over; and afterwards a portion of them, ἡ σάρξ μου ἐστίν, inserted to make a tolerable sense. And it is very observable that ‫א‬ has these four words in a different place from the other uncials, namely after ζωῆς[1].

ventured to differ from the conclusions of the learned Professor, it is only fair to say that his reasonings in another question, that of *Love* v. *Charity* (pp. 63—70) are, in our humble opinion, perfectly sound and irrefragable. Here, however, the *vox populi* has a fair claim to be heard, and *that* has pronounced most strongly against disturbing the old established favourite in 1 Cor. xiii, and a few other places. It may

help to reconcile scholars to a sacrifice of their convictions in this particular instance, to remember that by this concession they are relieved at once from the infliction of that most unfortunate cadence (2 Pet. i. 7) 'and in your love of the brethren love.'

[1] [Cf. Lucian. *Scyth.* 10. Old Edd. καὶ τουτὶ γίγνεται ὅ,τι ἂν ἄριστον ᾖ τῇ πόλει. Gesner. conj. καὶ τουτὶ γίγνεται ὅ,τι ἂν (βούλονται· βούλονται γὰρ ὅ,τι

* VI. 62 : **ἐὰν οὖν θεωρῆτε**] *'What'* then if ye should behold' (R. V.). 'What' need hardly be italicized. Ἐὰν οὖν for τί οὖν ἐὰν is good Greek, an idiom, of which I have given examples in a note on S. Chrys. T. XII. p. 116 D.

* VII. 12 : **γογγυσμός**] 'murmuring,' i.e. the sound made by a number of persons conversing together in an under tone ; but not necessarily one of complaint. The proper Greek word is θροῦς. Aelian. *V. H.* II. 13 : ἀλλ' οἵ γε ξένοι· τὸν γὰρ κωμῳδούμενον ἠγνόουν· θροῦς παρ' αὐτῶν ἐπανίσταται, καὶ ἐζήτουν ὅστις ποτὲ οὗτος ὁ Σωκράτης ἐστίν. The opposite opinions of the Jews about the character of Jesus remind one of the reception of Diogenes at the Isthmian games (Dio Chrys. p. 139, 35): τινὲς μὲν οὖν αὐτὸν ἐθαύμαζον ὡς σοφώτατον πάντων· τισὶ δὲ μαίνεσθαι ἐδόκει· πολλοὶ δὲ κατεφρόνουν, ὡς πτωχοῦ τε καὶ οὐδενὸς ἀξίου.

* VII. 15 : **πῶς οὗτος γράμματα οἶδε, μὴ μεμαθηκώς;**] By γράμματα we are to understand *elementary learning,* what we pleasantly (χαριεντιζόμενοι) call the three R's. For *reading* alone we may refer to Lucian. *Dial. Mer.* X: ἀνάγνωθι λαβοῦσα, ὦ Χελιδόνιον· οἶσθα γὰρ δήπου γράμματα; for *reading* and *writing* to Stob. *Flor.* T. LXXIX. 51 : ἢ ἐπιστάμενον γράμματα οὐκ ἐπιστάμενος κελεύῃ σε γράφειν καὶ ἀναγινώσκειν μὴ ὡς ἔμαθες, ἀλλ' ἑτέρως. And that the γραμματισταί also taught arithmetic, may be inferred from S. Chrysost. T. XI. p. 711 E: ὥσπερ γάρ ἐστι παρὰ τοῖς γραμματισταῖς ὁ τῶν ἑξακισχιλίων ἀριθμός...καὶ διὰ τοῦ ἀριθμοῦ τούτου πάντα στρέφεται, καὶ ἴσασι ταῦτα ὅσοι γράμματα μεμαθήκασιν. The higher branches of education were usually called μαθήματα.

That the Jews, by their laws and traditions, long before the Christian era, attached great importance to education, we most readily admit. But we cannot go so far as Mr Mundella, who, at a banquet in aid of the Jews' Free School held in May 1884, flattered his entertainers with the notion of their co-religionists having been familiar with the principle of *compulsory* or *state* education some 2000 years ago. This he had always thought to be a novelty; but some time ago he had had a conversation with the late Emmanuel Deutsch, who poured out such a cataclysm of authorities from the Talmud and other Jewish literature, as were a revelation to him. We confess that we should like to have some more definite information on the subject before admitting into our minds the somewhat incongruous idea of a Board-school at Nazareth, or a Minister of Public Instruction at Jerusalem. Meantime we would refer *our* Minister, for the germ of such a system, to profane history, and to the laws of Charondas of Catana, who flourished about 500 years B C., and legislated for the cities of Chalcidian origin in Sicily and Italy. One of his laws, and one, says the historian (Diod. Sic. XII. 12) which had been

ἂν) ἄριστον... from the Latin version of Solanus. Solanus from MS.—ὅ,τι ἂν

(οὗτοι ἐθέλωσιν· ἐθέλουσι γὰρ ὅ,τι ἂν ἄριστον....]

overlooked by the older legislators, was this: ἐνομοθέτησε τῶν πολιτῶν τοὺς υἱεῖς ἅπαντας μανθάνειν γράμματα, χορηγούσης τῆς πόλεως τοὺς μισθοὺς τοῖς διδασκάλοις. ὑπέλαβε γὰρ τοὺς ἀπόρους τοῖς βίοις, ἰδίᾳ μὴ δυναμένους διδόναι μισθούς, ἀποστερηθήσεσθαι τῶν καλλίστων ἐπιτηδευμάτων.

*VII. 23: ὅλον ἄνθρωπον ὑγιῆ ἐποίησα] Both versions: 'I have made a man every whit whole'; joining ὅλον ὑγιῆ, as ὅλον φωτεινόν Luke xi. 36, and καθαρὸς ὅλος John xiii. 10. But it seems more natural to connect ὅλον with ἄνθρωπον, in the sense of 'a whole man,' or 'the whole of a man,' in contrast to a single member. Wetstein quotes: 'Si enim circumcisio, quae ad unum tantum membrum hominis spectat, sabbatum pellit, quanto magis periculum vitae, quod ad *totum hominem* spectat[1].'

VII. 51: ἐὰν μὴ ἀκούσῃ πρῶτον παρ' αὐτοῦ (T. R. παρ' αὐτοῦ πρότερον)] A. V. 'Before it hear him.' R. V. 'Except it first hear from himself.' Ἀκούειν παρ' αὐτοῦ is to 'hear his defence,' 'hear what he has to say.' Compare Eurip. *Heracl.* 179: τίς ἂν δίκην κρίνειεν, ἢ γνοίη λόγον | πρὶν ἂν ΠΑΡ' ἀμφοῖν μῦθον ἐκμάθῃ σαφῆ; In Acts xxv. 22, 'I would hear the man myself....To-morrow thou shalt hear him,' the preposition is wanting.

VIII. 18: ἐγώ εἰμι ὁ μαρτυρῶν περὶ ἐμαυτοῦ] A. V. 'I am one that bear witness of myself.' R. V. 'I am he that beareth witness of myself.' Ungrammatical. In the Greek ὁ μαρτυρῶν does not depend on εἰμι, but on ἐγώ. In making out the *two* witnesses, we should say in English: 'There is I (or myself) that bear witness of myself, and there is the Father,' &c. But the Greek idiom for 'There is I,' or 'It is I,' is not ἐστὶν ἐγώ, but ἐγώ εἰμι (Ch. vi. 20). Hence the A. V. (only italicizing *one*) exactly expresses what is intended.

VIII. 25: τὴν ἀρχὴν ὅ τι καὶ λαλῶ ὑμῖν] A. V. 'Even *the same* that I said unto you from the beginning.' R. V. 'Even that which I have also spoken unto you from the beginning.' In these renderings there is a difficulty in λαλῶ, which can only be got over by resolving it into λέγω ὑμῖν ἐν τῇ λαλιᾷ μου[2]. According to another construction of the Greek, ὅτι is a conjunction, and τὴν ἀρχήν has the sense of ὅλως; and we may either supply *How is it* (as R V. marg.) or consider it as an exclamation of surprise, perhaps with a corresponding gesture, 'That I should even speak to you at all!' as we sometimes say ἐν τῇ συνηθείᾳ, 'That it should come to this!' This version has the high authority of St Chrysostom: τὴν ἀρχὴν ὅτι καὶ λαλῶ ὑμῖν. ὁ δὲ λέγει τοιοῦτόν ἐστιν· τοῦ ὅλως ἀκούειν τῶν λόγων τῶν παρ' ἐμοῦ ἀνάξιοί ἐστε, μήτιγε καὶ μαθεῖν ὅστις ἐγώ εἰμι. We may

---

[1] This is in general but not verbal agreement with Wetstein's quotations. Ed.

[2] Other examples of words used by St John in a way different from other writers are χωρεῖν (Ch. viii. 37), and λαχεῖν (Ch. xix. 24).

also compare a similar construction in Ach. Tat. VI. 20, where a master, speaking to his female slave, says: οὐκ ἀγαπᾷς ὅτι σοι καὶ λαλῶ, 'Art thou not content that I even condescend to speak to thee[1]?' Still the generally received exposition commends itself by its being *just the answer we should have expected;* and the curious coincidence with Plaut. *Captiv.* III. 4, 91 : 'Quis igitur ille est? *Quem dudum dixi a principio tibi,*' is also in its favour.

*VIII. 28: ὅταν ὑψώσητε] Both versions: 'when ye have lifted up.' Better, 'when ye shall have lifted up.' Vulg. *cum exaltaveritis.* So Ch. x. 4: ὅταν ἐκβάλῃ, for which A. V. 'when he putteth forth.' R. V. 'when he hath put forth,' following the Vulg. we would adopt, 'when he shall have put forth.' The use of this tense, so rare in English, but so common and withal so convenient in Latin, is sanctioned by both versions in Luke xvii. 10: ὅταν ποιήσητε, 'when ye shall have done (all that is commanded you).'

VIII. 37: ὁ λόγος ὁ ἐμὸς οὐ χωρεῖ ἐν ὑμῖν] A. V. 'My word hath no place in you.' Other explanations of οὐ χωρεῖ are 'doth not go forward,' 'maketh no way[2].' The Revisers (while retaining the A. V. as an alternative rendering) have awarded the palm to ' My word hath not free course in you,' a rendering which brings this text into a sort of connexion with 2 Thess. iii. 1, where the Greek is τρέχῃ, and the general scope of the passage is quite different from that of our text. *There* the Apostle desires that the word of God may run, or spread rapidly, in the world: *here* our Lord's complaint is that his word does not gain an entrance into the hearts of his hearers, 'hath no room in you,' if such an use of χωρεῖν could be proved. It seems to be equivalent in sense to ὑμεῖς οὐ χωρεῖτε τὸν λόγον τὸν ἐμόν (cf. Matt. xix. 11: οὐ πάντες χωροῦσι τὸν λόγον τοῦτον) as it was certainly understood by Theophylact (διὰ τὸ τὸν λόγον τὸν ἐμον ὑψηλότερον εἶναι τῆς ὑμῶν διανοίας, καὶ μὴ χωρητὸν ὑμῖν), and both Syriac versions. That χωρεῖν to *hold, contain* (Ch. ii. 6, xxi. 25) was used with a certain elasticity is proved from Aristot. *H. A.* IX. 40: καὶ τους κηφῆνας ἀποκτείνουσιν, ὅταν μηκέτι χωρῇ αὐταῖς ἐργαζομέναις, where χωρῇ is impersonal for χώρα ᾖ. Still nothing precisely similar to the sense here required, 'hath no room in you,' has hitherto been produced; and it was reserved for the present writer, in reading Alciphron's Epistles (III. 7) to light upon a passage in which χωρεῖν is used in a way exactly parallel with St John's use of it in this place. The story is this. A parasite, having been stuffed to excess by his entertainers (πλείονα ἢ κατὰ τὸ κύτος τῆς γαστρὸς ἐσθίειν ἀναγκάζοντες) was met on his way home by Acesilaus the physician, who,

---

[1] [Cf. Aesop. *Fab.* 408: οἱ δὲ (κύκνοι) μόλις μὲν αὐτὰς (χελιδόνας) ἠξίωσαν καὶ λόγου, τῆς ἀδολεσχίας μισήσαντες· ἐπεὶ δὲ ἠξίωσαν....]

[2] [Cf. Plut. *Vit. Galba,* 10: τῷ δὲ Γάλβᾳ μετὰ τὴν Νέρωνος τελευτὴν ἐχώρει πάντα (=προὐχώρει).]

seeing his plight, took him home with him, and administered a powerful emetic, the effects of which the parasite himself thus describes: 'What vessels, λέβητας, πιθάκνας, ἀμίδας, did I fill with what I threw up! so that the doctor himself wondered ποῦ καὶ τίνα τρόπον 'ΕΧΩΡΗΣΕ τοσοῦτον ὁ τῶν βρωμάτων φορυτός, i.e. *ubi* LOCUM HABERE *tanta* (Wagner reads τοσοῦτος) *ciborum colluvies potuerit.*' Here also Bergler quarrels with the construction, and says: 'Ego verti quasi esset τίνα τρόπον ἐχώρησα τοσοῦτον βρωμάτων φορυτόν.' But the reading of all the MSS. of the witty letter-writer may be now supported by this place of St John, and the two passages mutually throw light upon each other.

*VIII. 39: Εἰ τέκνα τοῦ 'Αβραὰμ ἦτε, τὰ ἔργα τοῦ 'Αβραὰμ ἐποιεῖτε]
What Abraham was to the Jews, their great progenitor and pride, that was Hercules to the Greeks. This being understood, we may compare Plut. T. II. p. 226 A: οὐκοῦν καὶ ἡμᾶς, ὦ πολῖται, οὐδὲν ἡ παρὰ τοῖς πολλοῖς θαυμαζομένη εὐγένεια, καὶ τὸ ἀφ' 'Ηρακλέους εἶναι ὀνίνησιν, εἰ μὴ πράττομεν δι' ἃ ἐκεῖνος ἁπάντων ἀνθρώπων ἐπιδοξότερος καὶ εὐγενέστερος ἐφάνη, ἀσκούμενοι καὶ μανθάνοντες καλὰ δι' ὅλου τοῦ βίου.

*VIII. 44: καὶ ἐν τῇ ἀληθείᾳ οὐχ ἕστηκεν] A. V. 'And abode not in the truth.' R. V. 'And stood not in the truth,' with a marginal note: 'Some ancient authorities read *standeth.*' These 'ancient authorities' are, in fact, those MSS. and Edd. (Erasm. 1, R. Stephens 1550, and the T. R.) which read οὐχ ἕστηκεν, the *past* tense (in form) having a *present* signification, as Rom. v. 2, 1 Cor. xv. 1 &c. This was not understood by the Vulg. *non stetit*, or A. V. 'abode not.' The R. V. 'stood not' is owing to the error of the uncials BDℵ and others, which write ΟΥΚΕСΤΗΚΕΝ without the aspirate, a very common fault, which should be corrected in ordinary printing, instead of being exaggerated by accenting οὐκ ἕστηκεν. This, however, is what the Revisers have done, taking ἕστηκεν to be the imperfect of στήκω.

*VIII. 58: πρὶν 'Αβραὰμ γενέσθαι] Both versions: 'Before Abraham was': but, more correctly, R. V. in margin, 'Or, *was born.*' Again, Gal. iv. 4: γενόμενον ἐκ γυναικός. A. V. 'made (Vulg. *factum*) of a woman.' R. V. 'born of a woman.' So the word is often used in LXX. for יֻלַּד (as Gen. iv. 26), and also in profane authors, e.g. Dem. p. 1008 extr.: ἐκ τῆς πατρῴας οἰκίας...ἐν ᾗ καὶ ἐγενόμην καὶ ἐτράφην. Aelian. *V. H.* X. 18: γενέσθαι μὲν αὐτὸν ἐκ νύμφης. Plut. *Vit. Sert.* 1: δυεῖν δὲ ὁμωνύμων τοῖς εὐωδεστάτοις φυτοῖς πόλεων, "Ιου καὶ Σμύρνης, τὸν ποιητὴν "Ομηρον ἐν ᾗ μὲν γενέσθαι λέγουσιν, ἐν ᾗ δὲ ἀποθανεῖν. Pausan. *Arcad.* XXVI. 6: ἱερὰ δὲ 'Ασκληπιοῦ τέ ἐστι καὶ 'Αθηνᾶς, ἣν θεῶν σέβονται μάλιστα, γενέσθαι καὶ τραφῆναι παρὰ σφίσιν αὐτὴν λέγοντες. Dion. Hal. *Ant.* III. 50: ὃς μετὰ τὴν τελευτὴν τοῦ πατρὸς...γενόμενος, οὔτε τῶν πατρῴων...χρημάτων...ἐκληρονόμησε μοῖραν.

*IX. 22: ἀποσυνάγωγος γένηται] 'he should be put out of the synagogue.' Also Ch. xii. 42, xvi. 2. Might not ἀποσυνάγωγος in these places be rendered 'out of the congregation,' from the O. T. use of συναγωγή for the Hebrew עֵדָה (Exod. xii. 3, Num. xvi. 3 &c.)? In patristical writers ἡ συναγωγή is the *Jewish* church, as ἡ ἐκκλησία the *Christian*; but this same word ἀποσυνάγωγος is applied by Theodoret (*H. E.* I. 3) to Christian excommunication, thus: (Paul of Samosata) συνόδῳ καὶ κρίσει τῶν ἀπανταχοῦ ἐπισκόπων ἀποκηρυχθέντος τῆς ἐκκλησίας· ὃν διαδεξάμενος Λουκιανὸς ἀποσυνάγωγος ἔμεινε τριῶν ἐπισκόπων πολυετεῖς χρόνους. It is true that συναγωγή does not occur in the N. T. in the sense of *congregation*, unless in Apoc. ii. 9 ἡ σ. τοῦ Σατανᾶ might more conveniently be so rendered than by 'synagogue.'

*IX. 40: καὶ ἤκουσαν ἐκ τῶν Φαρισαίων ταῦτα οἱ ὄντες μετ' αὐτοῦ] A. V. 'And *some* of the Pharisees which were with him heard these things.' R. V. 'Those of the Pharisees which were with him' &c. The former is the better rendering. The nom. case to ἤκουσαν is ἐκ τῶν Φ. (see on Ch. i. 24). Literally: '*Some* of the Pharisees heard these things (namely) they which were with him.'

*X. 15: καθὼς γινώσκει με ὁ πατήρ, κἀγὼ γινώσκω] 'Even as the Father...and I know' (R. V.). 'Beware of rendering as A. V.'—Alford. But comparing Ch. xv. 9, xvii. 18, it seems impossible to resist the conclusion that καθὼς... is the *protasis* and κἀγὼ... the *apodosis*. Nonnus, however, understood this place as the Revisers: ὡς γενέτης νοέει με, καὶ ὡς νοέω γενετῆρα.

*XI. 38: 'a stone lay against it' R. V. This correction of A. V. assumes that the cave was *above ground*; but the words ἐπέκειτο ἐπ' αὐτῷ seem rather to point to a *subterranean cavern*, to which there was a descent by steps; and the only sepulchre in the neighbourhood of Bethany (still shown as Lazarus's) is of this kind.

*XI. 39: On τεταρταῖος γάρ ἐστι (contrasted with πρόσφατος νεκρὸς, *nuper defunctus*) compare Herod. II. 89: (de foeminis defunctis ad pollincturam tradendis) οὐ παραυτίκα διδοῦσι ταριχεύειν, ἀλλ' ἐπεὰν τριταῖαι ἢ τεταρταῖαι γένωνται. Xen. *Anab.* VI. 4, 9: καὶ τοὺς νεκρούς, τοὺς μὲν πλείστους ἔνθαπερ ἔπεσον ἑκάστους ἔθαψαν· ἤδη γὰρ ἦσαν πεμπταῖοι, καὶ οὐχ οἷόν τε ἀναιρεῖν ἔτι ἦν.

*XI. 44: δεδεμένος τοὺς πόδας καὶ τὰς χεῖρας κειρίαις] 'with grave-clothes'—an inadequate rendering. Moschopulus defines: κειρία· ὁ τῶν νηπίων δεσμὸς, ἤγουν ἡ κοινῶς φασκία (fascia), καὶ ᾗ δεσμοῦσι τοὺς νεκρούς: thus bringing together the two extremities of life, and affording a favourite common-place to patristic authors. Artemidorus (*Onirocrit.* I. 13) says that to dream of βρέφη ἐνειλούμενα τὰς χεῖρας, τῷ νοσοῦντι θάνατον προαγορεύει· ἐπεὶ καὶ οἱ ἀποθνήσκοντες ἐσχισμένοις ἐνειλοῦνται ῥάκεσιν, ὡς καὶ τὰ βρέφη. The Latin word σουδάριον was also naturalized in the Syrian language (סודרא, Chald. ad Ruth iii. 15) and Nonnus actually takes it for a Syrian word (σουδάριον τόπερ εἶπε Σύρων στόμα).

*XII. 3: ἡ δὲ οἰκία ἐπληρώθη ἐκ τῆς ὀσμῆς τοῦ μύρου] Compare Plut. Vit. Alex. XX: ὠδώδει δὲ θεσπέσιον οἶον, ὑπ᾽ ἀρωμάτων καὶ μύρων ὁ οἶκος (the tent of Darius). Stob. Flor. 348, 5: ἀλλὰ μέντοι τῶν γε πολυτελῶν τούτων ὀσμῶν, αἷς χρίεσθε, τοὺς πλησιάζοντας μᾶλλον οἶμαι ἀπολαύειν ἢ αὐτοὺς ὑμᾶς.

XII. 6: τὸ γλωσσόκομον εἶχε] 'Had the BAG.' It does not admit of a doubt, that γλωσσόκομον, both in its special and general sense, is not a bag, but a box, or chest, always of wood or other hard material. Hesychius defines it to be a chest (σορός), a wooden receptacle of remnants. Arrian (Periplus p. 159[1]) mentions γλωσσόκομα καὶ πινακίδια (tablets), both made of tortoise-shell. In the Greek Anthology (II. 47, 1, ed. Stephan.) we read : 'But when I look at Nicanor the coffin-maker (τὸν σοροπηγόν), and consider for what purpose he makes these wooden boxes (ταῦτα τὰ γλωσσόκομα).' Josephus (Ant. VI. 1, 2) calls by this name the coffer in which were preserved the golden emerods and mice, which the Philistines were ordered to make. Here (1 Sam. vi. 8) the Hebrew is אַרְגַז (a ἅπαξ λεγόμενον); but Aquila universally employs γλωσσόκομον for the Hebrew אָרוֹן in all its significations: as (1) the coffin in which Joseph was buried (Gen. l. 26), for which the Targum of Jonathan also has גלוסקמא, the Greek word in Hebrew characters; (2) the ark of the covenant (Exod. xxxvii. 1 ; 1 Sam. v. 1); (3) whether also for Noah's ark, is not known ; but from this translator's well-known habit of using the same Greek word for the same Hebrew in all cases, is very probable. But the most apposite example for our purpose is 2 Chron. xxiv. 8: 'And at the king's commandment they made a chest (in 2 Kings xii. 9 it is added that they bored a hole in the lid of it)...and the people cast (ἐνέβαλον) into the chest.' Here the LXX. also have translated אָרוֹן by γλωσσόκομον, though their usual rendering is κιβωτός. The ancient versions in the two places of St John take the same view. Thus the Vulgate has loculi, a box, not a bag, as is shown by the plural form, indicating several partitions ; Nonnus (on xiii. 29) δουρατέην χηλόν, ligneam arculam; the Peschito ܟܘܣܩܠܐ, which is again the Greek word in Syriac characters. [In Dr Payne Smith's Thesaurus the Syriac word is Latinized by marsupium, a purse or bag, but all his examples are of coffins, reliquaries, or other chests.] Judas therefore 'kept the BOX'; and 'carried' (?) or 'pilfered' (?) what was cast therein (καὶ τὰ βαλλόμενα ἐβάσταζε). In favour of 'bare' (A. V.) or 'carried' (R. V. marg.) may be quoted St Chrysostom, not ad loc., but in another part of his works (T. III. p. 257 A): 'Although he (Christ) had made so many

---

[1] [Periplus Maris Erythraei, ch. vii, ed. Borheck (1809). Ed.]

loaves, and was able to produce ever so many treasures by speaking the word, he did not do so, but ordered his disciples to have a box, and to *carry those things which were cast therein*, and to assist the poor therefrom.' On the other hand, the sense of *auferre*, to *carry off, take away*, is undoubted; and the only question is, whether it is properly used of a *secret* removal, *stealing* or *purloining*, as is required in this place. The most apt example of this use is Diog. Laert. IV. 59 (not noticed by Alford, and imperfectly quoted by Kuinoel and others). 'Lacydes,' he says, 'whenever he took any thing out of his storeroom, was accustomed, after having sealed it up again, to throw the ring (seal) inside through the hole, so that it might never be taken off his finger, and any of the stores be *stolen* (καί τι βασταχθείη (hence, perhaps, the gloss of Suidas: Βασταχθείη, ἀρθείη, κλαπείη) τῶν ἀποκειμένων).' Here the quotation, as usually given, ends; but what follows is still more pertinent. 'When, therefore, the servants found this out, they used to take off the seal, and *steal* whatever they pleased (μαθόντα δὲ ταῦτα τὰ θεραπόντια ἀπεσφράγιζε, καὶ ὅσα ἐβούλετο ΈΒΑΣΤΑΖΕΝ).'

XII. 7 : ἄφες αὐτήν· εἰς τὴν ἡμέραν τοῦ ἐνταφιασμοῦ μου τετήρηκεν αὐτό]
The reformed text, ἄφες αὐτὴν ἵνα εἰς—τηρήσῃ αὐτό, which is supported by all the uncials (except A) and the Vulgate, is rendered by R. V. in text: 'Suffer her to keep it against the day of my burying'; and in margin: 'Let her alone: *it was* that she might keep it,' &c. The latter is preferable, in so far as it preserves the invariable use of ἄφες αὐτήν, as a prohibition of interference; e.g. Matt. xv. 14. Mark xiv. 6 (ἄφετε αὐτήν· τί αὐτῇ κόπους παρέχετε;). 2 Kings xvi. 11. 4 Kings iv. 27; but then the remaining clause can only be rendered, 'that she may keep it,' or, perhaps (comparing Eph. v. 33: ἡ δὲ γυνὴ ἵνα φοβῆται τὸν ἄνδρα) 'let her keep it.' But however we may understand this reading, it is impossible to get over the palpable absurdity of our Lord's desiring to be kept for the occasion of his burial, that which had already been poured out upon his living person. The *correction* (supposing τετήρηκεν to be the original reading) may easily have been made by some critic-scribe, who did not understand how *that* day could be said to be the day of his ἐνταφιασμός (*pollinctura, laying out*, not *burying*); or who failed to see how the ointment could have been *kept* already, as it might more naturally be supposed to have been just purchased. The conjecture that the ointment may have been *reserved* from that used at the 'burying' of Lazarus, so far from being 'fanciful' (Dean Alford) offers an excellent example of 'undesigned coincidences'; since we should never have perceived the propriety of the ἠδύνατο πραθῆναι of the first two Gospels, if St John had not helped us out with his τετήρηκεν.

XII. 20: ἦσαν δέ τινες "Ελληνες ἐκ τῶν ἀναβαινόντων] A. V. 'And there were certain Greeks among them that came up.' This would be the rendering of ἐν τοῖς ἀναβαίνουσιν, and would include *all* worshippers, both Jews and Greeks.   The meaning is 'of the number of those (Greeks)' &c.

*XII. 40: A. V. 'He hath blinded (τετύφλωκεν) their eyes, and hardened (πεπώρωκεν) their heart.'   In the second clause, the uncials, with the exception of B², read ἐπώρωσεν.   The preterite of this verb may, perhaps, have fallen into disuse, but to insist on forcing upon the English reader such an offensive solecism as, 'He hath blinded their eyes, and he hardened their heart,' especially after so many revisions, English and American, as the R. V. is said to have undergone, is a degree of perversity almost surpassing belief.   Certainly, the present is not one of those cases 'where the combination of the aorist and the perfect shews, beyond all reasonable doubt, that different relations of time were intended to be expressed' (Revisers' Preface).

*   *ibid.* : στραφῶσι]   Probably in a *middle* sense, 'turn,' or 'turn themselves.'   Ch. xx. 14, 16: 'she turned herself.'   Matt. vii. 6: καὶ στραφέντες ῥήξωσιν ὑμᾶς, 'and turn and rend you.'   Job xli. 16 (Hebr. 25): στραφέντος δὲ αὐτοῦ (Leviathan), φόβος θηρίοις τετράποσιν.   Prov. xii. 7: οὖ ἐὰν στραφῇ ὁ ἀσεβὴς ἀφανίζεται.

*XIII. 2: καὶ δείπνου γενομένου]   'and supper being ended.'   Another reading is γινομένου, which is followed by R. V. 'and during supper.'   But as there has been no previous mention of a supper, we seem to want an announcement of the fact, like that in Ch. xii. 2: 'There they made him a supper'; for which purpose the aorist is more suitable than the present, καὶ ἐγένετο δεῖπνον, 'and a supper was holden.'   We would therefore render, 'And a supper being holden, Jesus...riseth from THE supper (ἐκ τοῦ δείπνου).'

XIII. 24: νεύει οὖν τούτῳ Σίμων Πέτρος]   'Simon Peter therefore beckoneth to him.'   Thus far all the MSS.   Then for the T. R. πυθέσθαι τίς ἂν εἴη περὶ οὗ λέγει, which is supported by AD and both Syriac versions, modern critics have adopted that of BCLX and Vulg. καὶ λέγει αὐτῷ· εἰπὲ τίς ἐστιν περὶ οὗ λέγει, 'and saith unto him, Tell *us* who it is of whom he speaketh.'   On which Dean Alford comments: 'Peter supposes that John would know without asking; but he did not, and asks.'   In favour of the old reading it may be observed, (1) that νεύει occurs twice only in the N. T., here and Acts xxiv. 10, and in both places is followed by a verb in the infinitive mood ; (2) that ἐπύθετο παρ' αὐτοῦ is used by St John, Ch. iv. 52; (3) that this reading must be older than ℵ, because that MS. has a *double* reading; first, the received one (only with ἔλεγεν for λέγει) and then the one proposed to be substituted for it.   With regard to this latter (not to insist upon the absurdity of Peter asking John for the explanation of an announcement which was made to all in common) we may remark that it is inconsistent with itself, as *making signs* and *speaking* never go together, but are always opposed to each other, νεύειν being equivalent to *nutu tacite significare*, as in Luke i. 62 : ἐνένευον δὲ τῷ πατρὶ αὐτοῦ τὸ τί ἂν θέλοι καλεῖσθαι αὐτό. From a number of examples which I had collected for this purpose, I select the following. Alciphr. *Ep. Fragm.* 5 : καὶ οἱ κωφοὶ διανεύουσιν ἀλλήλοις τὸ ἐκείνης (Λαΐδος) κάλλος. Stob. *Flor.* T. XXXVI. 27 : ἐριστικοῦ ἀνδρὸς ἐρωτῶντος αὐτόν, εἰ ἡ ἀρετὴ ὠφέλιμος, ἀνένευσεν (he shook his head), οὐ βουλόμενος παρασχεῖν αὐτῷ ἐκ τῆς ἀποκρίσεως ἀφορμὴν εἰς ἔριν. Plut. *Vit. Mar.* XLIII : οὗτοι πολλοὺς μὲν ἀπὸ φωνῆς, πολλοὺς δ' ἀπὸ νεύματος ἀνῄρουν, προστάσσοντος αὐτοῦ. So the Latin *innuo*, as Auctor *ad Herenn.* IV. 26 : 'Quod si iste suos hospites *rogasset*, immo *innuisset* modo.' We conclude, therefore, that the shorter is the genuine text, and that it was tampered with by some one who found a *difficulty* in Peter's being able to indicate by beckoning alone the particular service which he wished John to perform.

   * If we apply the ordinary *criteria*, or critical canons, to the passage before us, the rule, 'Brevior lectio praeferenda est verbosiori,' is confessedly in favour of the T. R. On the other hand the advocates for the Vatican text might argue that their reading is the more *difficult* of the two, and therefore, according to another well-known, but much-abused canon, the more likely to have invited a copyist to exercise his 'critical acumen' upon it. But supposing such an one to have found in his copy, καὶ λέγει αὐτῷ· εἰπὲ τίς ἐστιν περὶ οὗ λέγει, and to have been justly offended by John's being required to *tell* what he had no means of knowing, would he not have had recourse to the simplest of all corrections, by substituting ἐρώτησον for εἰπέ? Again, if our critical friend had come across the reading νεύει οὖν τούτω Σ. Π. πυθέσθαι κ.τ.έ., might he not have found a *difficulty* in Peter's being able to indicate by beckoning alone the particular service which he wished John to perform; and so, to make all perfectly plain, have remodelled the text according to his own idea, though he would have done better if he had merely inserted καὶ λέγει αὐτῷ before πυθέσθαι?

   * *ibid.* : νεύει] Signs are easily translated into words. Thus Aelian *V. H.* XIV. 22 : (A tyrant forbidding his subjects to speak to each other) ἐσοφίσαντο τὸ τοῦ τυράννου πρόσταγμα, καὶ ἀλλήλοις ἔνευον, καὶ ἐχειρονόμουν πρὸς ἀλλήλους. Ach. Tat. V. 18 : ἐστιωμένῳ δέ μοι μεταξὺ σημαίνει νεύσας ὁ Σάτυρος προανίστασθαι. Aristaen. *Ep.* I. 22 : ἡ δὲ μαστροπός, λαθραίως μειδιῶσα, διένευσε τῇ Γλυκέρα· ἐδήλου δέ πως τὸ νεῦμα· Ἐγώ σοι μόνη τὸν ὑπερήφανον ὑπέταξα τοῖς ποσίν.

   *XIV. 4: καὶ ὅπου ἐγὼ ὑπάγω οἴδατε, καὶ τὴν ὁδὸν οἴδατε] So T. R., for which the Revisers prefer the shorter reading, καὶ ὅπου ἐγὼ ὑπάγω οἴδατε τὴν ὁδόν, 'and whither I go ye know the way.' Since Thomas in his reply distinguishes, in the clearest manner, between the *place whither*, and the *way by which* his Lord was going, a plain reader would naturally expect to find the same distinction in the saying which drew forth this reply, as it is actually found according to the T. R. 'But,' say the 'Two Members of the N. T. Company,' (p. 61) 'a careful consideration of the clause and of the context leads us at once to surmise that we may here recognize the enfeebling hand of some early interpolator, who broke up the vigorous sentence, καὶ ὅπου ἐγὼ ὑπάγω οἴδατε τὴν ὁδόν, into two clauses, answering to the two clauses in the ensuing question of the Apostle.' Is it not a more probable 'surmise,' that the clause καὶ τὴν ὁδὸν οἴδατε was omitted on account of the ὁμοιοτέλευτον? and that then (since the Apostle's question seemed rather to turn upon the *way* than the *end*) the 'rough and ready' remedy was applied of tacking on τὴν ὁδὸν to the end of the mutilated clause? Without describing the result as 'really almost nonsense' (*Q. R.* No. 304, p. 348) we may fairly ask why the sentence thus tinkered should be characterized as 'vigorous,' and the T. R. denounced as 'feeble'; unless those terms are to be taken as synonymous with 'ungrammatical' and 'grammatical.' So at least we shall continue to call them, until an example shall turn up of the hitherto unheard-of construction, τὴν ὁδὸν ὅπου ὑπάγω, for τὴν ὁδὸν ἥν (or *Hellenisticè* ἐν ᾗ) ὑπάγω.

*XIV. 12: 'And greater works (R. V. *works*) than these shall he do.' Since it is not expressly said that the Apostles should perform *greater*, i.e. more wonderful, *miracles* than Christ, it would be better, perhaps, to render μείζονα τούτων 'greater things than these,' comparing the *results* of the respective ministries of the two parties, rather than the *modus operandi*.

*XIV. 16: ἐρωτήσω τὸν πατέρα] xvii. 9: ἐγὼ περὶ αὐτῶν ἐρωτῶ. 'There are two words in the Greek, which in our A. V. are both translated by the word "pray" or "prayer." The one of them (αἰτεῖν) represents the prayer of an inferior to a superior, as, for instance, the prayer of the beggar who asked alms of them that entered into the temple (Acts iii. 2). Or, again, the prayer of a child to its father (Matt. vii. 9). The other (ἐρωτᾶν) expresses a request made by a person on a level with us, and not by an inferior, as, for example, where it is said (Luke xiv. 32) that one king sends an ambassador to another king, and "*requests* that he would make conditions of peace (ἐρωτᾷ τὰ πρὸς εἰρήνην)." Now it is very noticeable that our Blessed Lord, in speaking of his own prayers, never uses the former word, but always the latter.' Whence the writer from whom I quote draws the inference, that the prayers in question were no prayers of a creature, or of one dependent upon God, but of 'the man that is my fellow, saith the Lord of Hosts.'—The instances chosen by this writer are unfortunate, since in the place from the Acts, τοῦ αἰτεῖν ἐλεημοσύνην in *v.* 2 is immediately followed in *v.* 3 by ἠρώτα ἐλεημοσύνην λαβεῖν: and the king who sends the embassy by the very act of '*asking* (*sic* R. V.) conditions of peace' acknowledges that he is not the equal of the rival potentate, but his inferior. But, in fact, the distinction sought to be imposed upon the unlearned reader is perfectly groundless. Every *tiro* knows that in good Greek αἰτεῖν is to make a request, and ἐρωτᾶν to make an enquiry; but that Hellenistic writers, and St John in particular, frequently use the latter word in a sense not distinguishable from the former. The writer's mistake would not have been worth noticing, if he had not attempted to prop up a most true and irrefragable doctrine by a shaky pseudo-philological argument.

*XIV. 16: παράκλητον]   A. V. 'Comforter.'   R. V. 'Comforter, or, *Advocate*, or, *Helper*.' The primary meaning of παρακαλεῖν is, undoubtedly, *arcessere*, *advocare*, to call or send for a person, in which sense it is used in the best Greek authors (as Plat. *Lach*. 3: παρακαλεῖν τινα σύμβουλον, to call some one in as an adviser), and in Acts xxviii. 20 (A. V.) 'For this cause therefore have I called for you.' Hence comes παράκλητος, 'one sent, or called, for,' a noun passive in form, but active in sense, according to the particular service which he is called in to perform.

According to our use of the term, the office of an Advocate is well understood, and harmonizes perfectly with 1 John ii. 1 : 'If any man sin, we have an Advocate with the Father, Jesus Christ the righteous,' who has the best right to plead our cause, as being himself 'the propitiation for our sins.' The Latin *advocatus* is somewhat different, as we learn from Asconius ad Cic. in *Q. Caecil.*, who says : 'Qui defendit alterum in judicio, aut *patronus* dicitur, si orator est; aut *advocatus*, si aut jus suggerit, aut praesentiam suam commodat amico.' But the Rabbinical writers make use of their פְּרַקְלִיטָא precisely in the same way as St John in his Epistle, and as the Latin *patronus*, which they also adopt (פטרון). In classical Greek παράκλητος, as a judicial term, is not an 'advocate' in our sense of the word, but a friend of the accused person, called to speak to his character, or otherwise enlist the sympathy of the judges (or, as we should call them, the jury) in his favour; in the words of Asconius, 'qui praesentiam suam commodat amico.' Even in this sense it is of very rare occurrence, as Dem. *de F. L.* init. (p. 341, 10), where it is used *in malam partem*: ἐνθυμουμένους ὅτι ταῦτα μὲν (τὸ δίκαιον καὶ ὁ ὅρκος) ἐστὶν ὑπὲρ ὑμῶν καὶ ὅλης τῆς πόλεως, αἱ δὲ τῶν παρακλήτων (partizans?) αὗται δεήσεις καὶ σπουδαὶ τῶν ἰδίων πλεονεξιῶν ἕνεκα γίγνονται. Nearly similar is Diog. Laert. *Vit. Bionis* IV. 50; where to a prating fellow who besought his aid, the answer of the philosopher is : τὸ ἱκανόν σοι ποιήσω, ἐὰν παρακλήτους (a deputation) πέμψῃς, καὶ μὴ αὐτὸς ἔλθῃς. We will give one more instance of a different kind from Philo *de Opif. M.* § 6 (quoted by Loesner): οὐδενὶ δὲ παρακλήτῳ—τίς γὰρ ἦν ἕτερος;—μόνῳ δὲ ἑαυτῷ χρησάμενος ὁ θεός, ἔγνω δεῖν εὐεργετεῖν...τὴν ἐξ ἑαυτῆς ἐπιλαχεῖν οὐδενὸς ἀγαθοῦ δυναμένην (φύσιν). Here the office intended is that of a *monitor* or *adviser* (recalling the Apostle's τίς γὰρ ἔγνω νοῦν κυρίου, ἢ τίς σύμβουλος αὐτοῦ ἐγένετο;) but still preserving the leading idea of *amicus advocatus in consilium.*

On the whole, the arguments in favour of 'another Advocate' are briefly these: (1) 'Another,' i.e. besides Myself. (2) The word is only known from St John's writings, here and 1 John ii. 1, where 'advocate' is, by general consent, 'the right word in the right place.' (3) Etymologically, 'advocate' and παράκλητος are identical. (4) This is the only rendering which accounts for the passive form.

If 'Comforter' were retained on the ground of prescription and long familiarity (a feeling which deserves the greatest respect[1]), I would still consider it as a derivative from παρακαλεῖν, 'to send for,' not from παρακαλεῖν, 'to comfort.' We send for a confidential friend on various occasions; and according to the particular service which we require from him, he is our Counsellor in difficulties, our Advocate in danger, or our Comforter in distress. But the apparent countenance given to the old favourite by the mis-translation of ὀρφανούς in *v.* 18 must certainly be given up.

*XV. 1, 2: ὁ γεωργὸς...καθαίρει αὐτό] A good parallel is Philo *De Somn.* T. III. p. 280: τοῖς δένδρεσιν ἐπιφύονται βλάσται περισσαί, μεγάλαι τῶν γνησίων λώβαι, ἃς ΚΑΘΑΙΡΟΥΣΙ καὶ ἀποτέμνουσι προνοίᾳ τῶν ἀναγκαίων οἱ ΓΕΩΡΓΟΥΝΤΕΣ.

*XV. 5: χωρὶς ἐμοῦ] A. V. 'without me.' R. V. 'apart from me.' An unnecessary refinement, here and elsewhere (especially James ii. 26: 'faith apart from works'). Ἄνευ and χωρὶς are interchangeable; as Dion. Hal. *Ant.* VIII. 22: ἔθεον ἄνευ παραγγέλματος...ἐφέροντο χωρὶς ἡγεμόνος.

* XVI. 16: 'And again a little while.' To prevent the misconception of two 'little whiles,' one succeeding the other, I would point: 'And again, a little while,' with a marginal reference to 1 John ii. 8: 'Again, a new commandment' &c. (he had just before said: 'I write NO new commandment'). So here, 'again,' introduces an *apparent* contradiction of what he had just said. Theophylact *ad loc.*: διὸ καὶ δοκοῦσιν ἐναντία τινὰ αὐτοῖς (αὐτοῖς) τὸν Ἰησοῦν φθέγγεσθαι. Compare Hom. *Il.* IX. 56: οὐδὲ πάλιν ἐρέει, and such compounds as παλινῳδία, παλιμβολία &c.

* XVI. 23: 'Or, *ask me no question.*' R. V. marg. This seems to be precluded by the position of the pronoun, ἐμὲ οὐκ ἐρωτήσετε οὐδέν (ἀλλ' ἀρκέσει ὑμῖν τὸ ὄνομά μου εἰς τὸ παρὰ τοῦ πατρὸς λαβεῖν τὰ αἰτήματα, Theophylact). Grotius: 'Nihil hoc vos turbet quod me praesentem implorare non poteritis: ipsum Patrem precibus adite.'

---

[1] Dr P. Schaff (*Companion to the Greek Testament*, p. 446) says on this text: 'After long deliberation the Revisers retained the *dear old word* (Comforter).'

* XVI. 27: αὐτὸς γὰρ ὁ πατὴρ φιλεῖ ὑμᾶς] 'For the Father himself loveth you.' Αὐτὸς is here equivalent to αὐτόματος, *ultro*, *me non commendante*. An elegant Greek use of the pronoun, traceable to Homer (*Il.* VIII. 293): τί με σπεύδοντα καὶ αὐτὸν | ὀτρύνεις; Compare also Soph. *Oed. T.* 341: ἥξει γὰρ αὐτὰ, κἂν ἐγὼ σιγῇ στέγω. Callim. *H. Apoll.* 6: αὐτοὶ νῦν κατοχῆες, ἀνακλίνεσθε, where Schol. αὐτόματοι.

* XVI. 32: ἕκαστος εἰς τὰ ἴδια] 'every man to his own,' and in margin: 'Or, *his own home.*' The latter should have been adopted by R. V. See on Ch. i. 11. Luke ii. 49; and add to examples Appian. VI. 23: ἀπέλυε τοὺς αἰχμαλώτους εἰς τὰ ἴδια. We are glad, however, to see the Revisers departing, for once, from their 'hard and fast' rule of altering 'every' into 'each,' when it stands for ἕκαστος; e.g. James i. 14: 'But each man is tempted' &c.

* XVII. 3: τὸν μόνον ἀληθινὸν θεόν] Compare Joseph. *Ant.* VIII. 13, 6: Οἱ δ' Ἰσραηλῖται τοῦτο ἰδόντες (1 Kings xviii. 39) ἔπεσον ἐπὶ τὴν γῆν, καὶ προσεκύνουν ἕνα θεὸν καὶ μέγιστον, καὶ ἀληθῆ μόνον ἀποκαλοῦντες, τοὺς δ' ἄλλους ὀνόματα κ.τ.έ. *Id.* X. 11, 7: ἐπαινῶν τὸν θεὸν ὃν Δανῆλος (Dan. vi. 26) προσεκύνει, καὶ μόνον αὐτὸν λέγων εἶναι ἀληθῆ, καὶ τὸ πᾶν κράτος ἔχοντα. Athen. VI. p. 253 C (describing the abject flattery of the Athenians in their reception of Demetrius): ὀρχούμενοι καὶ ἐπᾴδοντες, ὡς εἴη μόνος θεὸς ἀληθινός, οἱ δ' ἄλλοι καθεύδουσιν, ἢ ἀποδημοῦσιν, ἢ οὐκ εἰσίν. The last quotation will be sure to remind the reader of the taunt (μυκτηρισμός) of Elijah addressed to the prophets of Baal, 1 Kings xviii. 27.

* XVII. 11: τήρησον αὐτοὺς ἐν τῷ ὀνόματί σου, οὓς δέδωκάς μοι, ἵνα ὦσιν ἕν] So the T. R. which, however, is very feebly supported, the better class of uncials reading ᾧ for οὕς, which can only be construed by taking ὀνόματι for the antecedent, 'thy name which thou hast given me.' So Erasmus, from the Greek of Euthymius, 'Serva eos per nomen tuum omnipotens, quod et ego natura habeo; nam et ego Deus sum.' A few uncials (D, U, X), and perhaps the Syriac versions, read ὃ for ᾧ, which *may* signify precisely the same, but also admits of a construction by which the somewhat startling novelty of the Father having given his name to the Son may be avoided. Every reader of this Chapter must have noticed the peculiar way in which the neuter singular ὃ is put for the masculine plural οὕς, especially in this very phrase ὃ ἔδωκάς μοι. Thus *v.* 2: ἵνα πᾶν ὃ δέδωκάς μοι, δώσῃ αὐτοῖς ζωὴν αἰώνιον. *vv.* 11, 12 (corrected into οὕς), *v.* 24: πάτερ ὃ δέδωκάς μοι, θέλω ἵνα, ὅπου εἰμὶ ἐγώ, κἀκεῖνοι ὦσι μετ' ἐμοῦ. This last example is so curiously matched with *v.* 11, even to the correction of οὕς for ὃ, which has found its way into the T. R., that we have no hesitation in rejecting the connection ἐν τῷ ὀνόματί σου ὃ δέδωκάς μοι, and even pointing ὃ δέδωκάς μοι ἵνα ὦσιν ἕν, though this last is not absolutely necessary.

*XVII. 17, 19 : ἁγίασον αὐτοὺς...ἁγιάζω ἐμαυτόν] 'Consecrate' seems preferable to 'sanctify' on account of ἁγιάζω ἐμαυτόν, *morti me devoveo*. There is a double meaning in this word, according as it is applied to Christ or to the disciples. In Clem. Alex. *Strom.* v. 10 (p. 686 ed. Potter): ἄπορον ὡς ἀληθῶς θῦμα, υἱὸς θεοῦ ὑπὲρ ἡμῶν ἁγιαζόμενος, I would not read σφαγιαζόμενος with Bishop Kaye, p. 348.

XVIII. 22: ἔδωκε ῥάπισμα τῷ Ἰησοῦ] A. V. 'Struck Jesus with the palm of his hand.' R. V. 'Struck Jesus with his hand[1].' Both in marg. 'Or, *with a rod*.' The meaning of ῥάπισμα in the Greek Testament (here and Ch. xix. 3. Mark xiv. 65) ought not to be left any longer in doubt. Phrynichus says: "Ῥάπισμα is not in use [by Attic writers]. If you would indicate *a blow on the cheek with the open hand* (τὴν γνάθον πλατείᾳ τῇ χειρὶ πλῆξαι) say, ἐπὶ κόρρης πατάξαι, which is the Attic usage[2].' This shows clearly how the word was used in his time; and to this agrees the scriptural usage both of the Old and New Testaments. Thus Isai. l. 6 : 'I gave my back εἰς μάστιγας, and my cheek εἰς ῥαπίσματα.' Hos. xi. 4 : ὡς ῥαπίζων ἄνθρωπος ἐπὶ τὰς σιαγόνας αὐτοῦ. Matt. v. 39 : ὅστις σε ῥαπίσει ἐπὶ τὴν δεξιάν σου σιαγόνα. xxvi. 67 : καὶ ἐκολάφισαν (*pugnis caederunt*) αὐτόν, οἱ δὲ ἐρράπισαν; (which last should be compared with the celebrated passage in Demosth. *c. Mid.* p. 537, 27 : ὅταν ὡς ὑβρίζων, ὅταν ὡς ἐχθρὸς ὑπάρχων, ὅταν κονδύλοις, ὅταν ἐπὶ κόρρης). In 1 (3) Kings xxii. 24, where the LXX. have καὶ ἐπάταξε (Zedekias) τὸν Μιχαίαν ἐπὶ τὴν σιαγόνα, Josephus (*Ant.* VIII. 15, 4) puts these words into the mouth of Zedekias before striking him : 'If he be a true prophet, εὐθὺς ῥαπισθεὶς ὑπ' ἐμοῦ βλαψάτω μου τὴν χεῖρα, as Jeroboam's hand was dried up, when he put it forth against the man of God that came out of Judah.'—When ῥαπίζειν had acquired this meaning instead of the older one of ῥαβδίζειν, *to strike with a rod*, it is highly improbable that it would continue to be used in that older sense; of which I doubt if any clear instance can be found *later than Herodotus*. Schleusner, indeed, refers (for this sense) to Diog. Laert. IX. 1, and Plut. *Vit. Themist.* XI, both moderns; but the latter is an anecdote quoted from Herodotus, and the former a saying of Heraclitus, who flourished Olymp. LXIX. Another instance quoted is Diog. Laert. VIII. 36 : παῦσαι, μηδὲ ῥάπιζε (said of beating a dog); but this is from the elegiacs of Xenophanes, another old writer. Lastly, a fragment of Anacreon, ῥεραπισμένῳ νώτῳ, is quoted by the Scholiast on Hom. *Od.* ζ. 59[3]. So that in this sense ῥαπίζειν

---

[1] [Cf. Nonnus : τολμηρῇ παλάμῃ ξαθέην ἐπάταξε παρειήν.]

[2] [Cf. Aristaen. *Ep.* I. 4: καὶ τὴν δεξιὰν ἐπιτείνας οἷος ἦν ἐπιρραπίζειν με τῆς κόρρης. Plut. ii. p. 267 D : μίαν δὲ μόνην (δούλην) αἱ γυναῖκες εἰσάγουσαι,

παίουσιν ἐπὶ τῆς κόρρης καὶ ῥαπίζουσιν; ἢ τὸ μὲν ταύτην ῥαπίζεσθαι....]

[3] [Cf. Anacreon VII. 2, e Brunckiana lectione : Ὑακινθίνῳ με ῥάβδῳ χαλεπῶς ἔρως ῥαπίζων.]

would appear to be an archaic form of ῥαβδίζειν, connected with the Homeric χρυσόρραπις, an epithet of Hermes[1].

XVIII. 28: ἀπὸ τοῦ Καϊάφα] 'from Caiaphas.' Rather, 'from *the house of* Caiaphas.' So Mark v. 35: ἀπὸ τοῦ ἀρχισυναγώγου, 'from the ruler of the synagogue's *house.*' Acts xvi. 40: εἰς τὴν Λυδίαν, 'into *the house of* Lydia[2].'

XIX. 12: ἀντιλέγει τῷ Καίσαρι] 'speaketh against Caesar.' The meaning is rather, 'setteth himself against Caesar,' 'resisteth his authority.' Euthymius: ἀντιλέγει, ἤτοι ἀνταίρει, from which latter comes ἀντάρτης *a rebel;* and the *rebellion* of Korah is called his ἀντιλογία, Jude 11. To 'speak against Caesar' would probably be expressed by βλασφημεῖν or κακολογεῖν[3]. [I now see that the Revisers have given a place to this suggestion in their margin: 'Or, *opposeth Caesar.*']

XIX. 24: λάχωμεν περὶ αὐτοῦ] 'let us cast lots for it.' An improper use of the word λαγχάνειν, which in good Greek is always *to obtain something by lot.* No other example of this use is known. Schleusner's (Thucyd. III. 50: τριακοσίους μὲν (κλήρους) τοῖς θεοῖς ἱεροὺς ἐξεῖλον, ἐπὶ δὲ τοὺς ἄλλους σφῶν αὐτῶν κληρούχους τοὺς λαχόντας ἀπέπεμψαν) and Dean Alford's (Diod. Sic. IV. 63: ἔπειτα πρὸς ἀλλήλους ὁμολογίας ἔθεντο διακληρώσασθαι· καὶ τὸν μὲν λαχόντα γῆμαι τὴν Ἑλένην κ.τ.ἑ.) are both *false.*

* XIX. 29: ὑσσώπῳ περιθέντες] Without entering into the disputes of naturalists as to the particular plant denoted by this word, we may remark both in the scriptural allusions to it, and in the indigenous plants which have been identified with it, a singular inaptness to the use to which it is here applied. As to the first, we read of a 'bunch of hyssop,' and of its 'springing out of the wall,' features which sufficiently indicate its habit of growth. Of the plants which have been proposed as its modern representatives (as different species of *mint, marjoram,* and the like, and, by the most recent biblical naturalists, the *caper-plant*) nearly all are of creeping, or climbing habits, agreeing well enough with the properties of the Hebrew אֵזוֹב (LXX. ὕσσωπος) but not with the use assigned to it in this text, corresponding to that of the 'reed' in the description of the other Evangelists. The caper-plant in particular, we are told (Tristram, *N. H. of the Bible,* ed. 1868, p. 458), 'is always pendent on

---

[1] I have since found in Anton. Lib. XXIII: Ἑρμῆς δὲ...ἐρράπισεν αὐτὸν τῇ ῥάβδῳ, καὶ μετέβαλεν εἰς πέτρον; but it may be taken from an older author (as Hesiod, whose work Ἡοῖαι μεγάλαι is mentioned in the title of the chapter).

[2] [Cf. Aristoph. *Plut.* 841 ἐκ Πατρο-

κλέους γὰρ ἔρχομαι. App. *B. C.* II. 125: τὰ χρήματα τοῦ Καίσαρος εἰς τὸν Ἀντώνιον μετεκομίζετο (ubi male edebatur εἰς τὸν Ἀντωνίου).]

[3] [Or κακῶς ἀγορεύειν, Liban. I. 526: κακῶς ἀγορεύειν τοὺς θεούς.]

the rocks, or trailing on the ground.' It does not appear on what authority this plant is said to be ';capable of producing a stick three or four feet in length' (Smith's *Dict. of the Bible*) ; certainly Pliny's description of it, as *firmioris ligni frutex*, does not warrant the assertion. But the question is not whether one might cut such a stick from a particular specimen of the *capparis*, but whether sticks were commonly so cut, so that on an occasion like the present, when one was wanted for a particular purpose, the first which came to hand would be one of this kind. It adds to the improbability, that the narrator should have thought it necessary to specify the name of the shrub which furnished the stick, and also that he should have written ὑσσώπῳ for ὑσσώπου κλάδῳ, which is the ordinary usage (ἐν μύρτου κλαδὶ τὸ ξίφος φορήσω). Pressed by these difficulties, some expositors have supposed that the 'hyssop' was a bunch of the plant so called, fastened to the end of a reed (not noticed by St John) on which the sponge was placed. But of such a custom there is no trace, and the other Evangelists who relate the incident, use the very same word περιθείς to denote the attaching of the sponge to the reed without the intervention of the hyssop. Nothing remains but to call in the aid of *conjectural emendation*, which, according to one master-critic (Scrivener, *Introduction*, &c. p. 490), 'must never be resorted to, even in passages of acknowledged difficulty'; and to another (Dean Burgon, *Revision Revised*, p. 354) 'can be allowed no place whatever in the textual criticism of the N. T.' Would it not be better—instead of laying under an interdict an entire branch of verbal criticism, and that one which, in settling the text of the Greek and Roman classics, is justly held to be the crown and glory of the art—to treat each case separately on its merits, especially in regard to these two points : (1) Is some change or other a matter of absolute necessity? and (2) Is the proposed change so easy, so ingenious, so redolent of the true critical faculty, that any editor of a Greek or Roman classic, who understood his craft, would accept it as a matter of course? A very small, in fact an infinitesimal, proportion of N. T. emendations will be found to satisfy these two conditions ; but of the few, perhaps the very best is one of Joachim Camerarius on this very place. For ὑσσώπῳ περιθέντες, a perfectly unintelligible reading, write in uncial characters ΥΣΣΩΠΩΙΠΕΡΙΘΕΝΤΕΣ, expunging, as we have done, the two letters ΩΙ, repeated by a παρόραμα γραφικόν from those immediately preceding ; and the thing is done. The text becomes as clear as day : Σπόγγον οὖν μεστὸν τοῦ ὄξους ὑσσῷ περιθέντες προσήνεγκαν αὐτοῦ τῷ στόματι. The ὑσσός was the Greek equivalent for the Roman *pilum*, which is thus described by Dion. Hal. *Ant.* v. 46 : ὑσσοί...ξύλα προμήκη καὶ χειροπληθῆ, τριῶν οὐχ ἧττον ποδῶν, σιδηροῦς ὀβελίσκους ἔχοντα προυχόντας. Of these the Roman soldier carried two, and a λόγχη besides ; so that when an instrument was required for the purpose of raising the sponge to the lips of the Saviour, no readier or more convenient one could be found. It may be added that the difference is of the slightest between St John's ὑσσός and the κάλαμος of the other Evangelists, who were not eye-witnesses as he was. And, lastly, this most ingenious conjecture has stood the test of *time*, has been approved by Sylburgius, Theod. Beza, Boisius, and other critics down to the present day, when it has been revived, re-stamped and re-issued by C. G. Cobet in his *Collect. Crit.* p. 586, who says of it: 'Ex densa caligine claram lucem fecit admirabilis Camerarii emendatio ὑσσῷ περιθέντες. Nesciebant scribae veteres quid esset ὑσσῷ. Itaque notum sibi vocabulum ὑσσώπῳ substituerunt, quod abhorret prorsus a sententia.'

XIX. 34: αὐτοῦ τὴν πλευρὰν ἔνυξε] All versions: 'pierced his side,' for which I should prefer 'pricked his side,' to keep up the distinction between ἔνυξε (the *milder* word) and ἐξεκέντησε (*v.* 37). All the ancient versions vary the word, though Vulg. and Philoxenian Syriac seem to have had a different reading (ἤνοιξε). Loesner (*Observationes ad N. T. e Philone*, p. 161) suggests that this word was chosen, *ut cognosceremus non malo consilio* (δι' ὑπερβολὴν ὠμότητος, as some of the Greek commentators express it) *id fecisse militem, sed ut exploraret an Jesus vere mortuus esset.* I have lately met with a passage in Plut. *Vit. Cleom.* XXXVII, which greatly favours this idea. Cleomenes and a party of thirteen make their escape from prison, and endeavour to raise the town and get possession of the citadel; but failing, resolve to put themselves to death, one of the number, Panteus, being ordered by Cleomenes not to kill himself till he had made sure that all the others were dead. When all are stretched on the ground, Panteus goes round, and makes trial of them one by one, touching them with his dagger (τῷ ξιφιδίῳ παραπτόμενος). When he came to Cleomenes, and pricking him on the ancle (ΝΥΞΑΣ παρὰ τὸ σφυρόν) saw him contract his face, he kissed him; then sat down by him, and when he was quite dead, embracing the body, slew himself upon it[1].

* XIX. 42: ἐκεῖ οὖν—ἔθηκαν τὸν Ἰησοῦν] A. V. 'there laid they Jesus therefore' &c. Amongst the 'needless changes' introduced by the Revisers, *inversions* of the order of the A. V. to correspond with the Greek are justly complained of. A few exceptions may be noticed, of which this is one; in which the order of the original, 'There then because of the Jews' Preparation (for the sepulchre was nigh at hand) they laid Jesus,' has been properly restored by R. V.; 'a cadence suited

---

[1] [Cf. Ecclus. xxii. 19: 'He that pricketh (ὁ νύσσων) the eye will make tears to flow.' On τῷ ἀγκῶνι νύττειν see Boiss. ad Aristaen. p. 511. Cf. Plut. *Vit. Aemil.* XX: μικροῖς μὲν ἐγχειριδίοις στερεοὺς καὶ ποδήρεις θυρεοὺς νύσσοντες. id. *Vit. Anton.* LXXXVI: ἔνιοι δὲ καὶ τὸν βραχίονα τῆς Κλεοπάτρας ὀφθῆναι δύο νυγμὰς ἔχοντα λεπτὰς καὶ ἀμυδράς. id. ii. p. 255: φύλακας ἐπὶ τῶν πυλῶν κατέστησεν, οἳ τοὺς ἐκφερομένους νεκροὺς ἐλυμαίνοντο νύττοντες ξιφιδίοις καὶ καυτήρια προσβάλλοντες ὑπὲρ τοῦ μηδένα τῶν πολιτῶν ὡς νεκρὸν λαθεῖν ἐκκομιζόμενον.]

to the sacred calm in which the Evangelist brings the long sad agony to its close' (Humphry).

XXI. 5: μή τι προσφάγιον ἔχετε ;] A. V. 'Have ye any meat?' R. V. 'Have ye aught to eat?' Rather, 'Have ye taken any fish¹?' Ἔχεις τι; is the usual question addressed by a bystander to those who are employed in fishing or bird-catching, answering to our 'Have you had any sport?' This we learn from the Scholiast on Aristoph. *Nub.* 731 (quoted by Wetstein): Χαριέντως τό, ἔχεις τι; τῇ τῶν ἀγρευτῶν λέξει χρώμενος· τοῖς γὰρ ἁλιεῦσιν ἢ ὀρνιθαγρευταῖς οὕτω φασίν· ΕΧΕΙΣ ΤΙ; I add Nonnus ad Greg. Naz. *Stelit.* I. p. 138 ed. Montac.: Ἄνδρες ἀπ' Ἀρκαδίης ἁλιήτορες, ἦ ῥ' ἔχομέν τι; where the Scholiast has: ἆρα ἐθηράσαμέν τι²;

XXI. 10: ὧν ἐπιάσατε νῦν] 'which ye have now caught.' The aorist may be retained here by rendering, 'which ye caught just now.' So Ch. xi. 8 (R. V.): 'The Jews were but now seeking (νῦν ἐζήτουν) to stone thee³.'

*XXI. 18: ἐκτενεῖς τὰς χεῖράς σου, καὶ ἄλλος σε ζώσει, καὶ οἴσει ὅπου οὐ θέλεις.] Kuinöl and others will not allow that there is here any allusion to the crucifixion of St Peter, chiefly on account of the preposterous order of the arrangements, οἴσει κ.τ.ἑ. being placed last. But this may be accounted for by the circumstance of περιεπάτεις ὅπου ἤθελες coming in order after ἐζώννυες σεαυτόν; and it is not necessary to adopt Scaliger's explanation, that the criminal was led to the place of execution, tied to a *furca* or *patibulum*, before he was nailed to the cross. If St John had not furnished his own explanation, τοῦτο δὲ εἶπε σημαίνων ποίῳ θανάτῳ κ.τ.ἑ., the characteristic ἐκτενεῖς τὰς χεῖράς σου would be conclusive as to the kind of death intended by the speaker. Wetstein quotes Artem. *Onir.* I. 76: κακοῦργος δὲ ὢν σταυρωθήσεται διὰ τὸ ὕψος καὶ τὴν τῶν χειρῶν ἔκτασιν. Arrian. *Epict.* III. 26: ἵν' ἐν τῷ βαλανείῳ ἐκδυσάμενος, καὶ ἐκτείνας σεαυτὸν ὡς οἱ ἐσταυρωμένοι, τριβῇ ἔνθεν καὶ ἔνθεν. I add Dion. Hal. *Ant.* VII. 69: οἱ δ' ἄγοντες τὸν θεράποντα ἐπὶ τὴν τιμωρίαν, τὰς χεῖρας ἀποτείνοντες ἀμφοτέρας, καὶ ξύλῳ προσδήσαντες παρὰ τὰ στέρνα τε καὶ τοὺς ὤμους μέχρι τῶν καρπῶν διήκοντι, παρηκολούθουν ξαίνοντες μάστιξι γυμνὸν ὄντα.

---

¹ [Babr. IV. 1: ἁλιεὺς σαγήνην... ἀνεῖλετ'· ὄψου δ' ἔτυχε ποικίλου πλήρης.]

² [Cf. Plut. *Vit. Anton.* XXIX: ὡς δὲ ἔχειν πεισθεὶς ἀνεῖλκε...παράδος ἡμῖν, ἔφη, τὸν κάλαμον, 'when A. found that he had

caught his fish he drew up his line.' Langhorne.]

³ [Cf. Liban. II. 291: μηδὲ ἡδίω νομίζητε τούτων ἃ νῦν διῆλθον. Ubi Cobet tentat ἃ νῦν δὴ διῆλθον.]

THE ACTS OF THE APOSTLES.

Chap. I. v. 4: καὶ συναλιζόμενος] A. V. and R. V. 'And being assembled together with *them*. Or, *eating together with* them.' Neither of these versions seems admissible.

1. ' Being assembled with them' would certainly require συναλισθείς[1]. Hesychius, indeed, is appealed to, to show that συναλιζόμενος is the same as συναλισθείς; but his gloss, when fully quoted, stands thus: Συναλιζόμενος, συναλισθείς, συναχθείς, συναθροισθείς; where the explanation of συναλιζόμενος (συναθροιζόμενος) is either purposely omitted, as unnecessary,. or has dropped out. Alberti (*Glossarium Graecum in Sacros N. F. libros*, p. 61) has: Συναλιζόμενος, συναθροιζόμενος καὶ συνών [potius συνιών. So Athenaeus (II. 40) joins ἡλίζοντο καὶ συνῄεσαν] αὐτοῖς.

2. 'Eating with them.' This use of the word seems to rest entirely on the ancient versions (Vulg. Pesch.) and glossaries, from the latter of which it probably found its way into patristic commentaries. It appears to have arisen from a fanciful etymology, coupled with what is elsewhere said that the Apostles ate and drank with our Lord after his resurrection (Ch. x. 41). And of the Fathers it is observable that they always join καὶ συναλιζόμενος with the preceding verse, sometimes even inserting it after ὀπτανόμενος. The *only* instance quoted of συναλίζεσθαι in this sense is from the Hexapla on Psa. cxl. (Heb. cxli.) 4, where for the Hebrew וּבַל אֶלְחַם St Chrysostom *ad loc.* quotes: Ἄλλος· μὴ συναλισθῶ (with a various reading συναυλισθῶ[2]). But (besides the uncertainty of the reading) it by no means follows that συναλισθῶ may not be used here in its legitimate sense of *congregari*, as the LXX. render the same words by καὶ οὐ μὴ συνδυάσω (or συνδοιάσω), perhaps from the Syriac ܐܠܦ, *aptavit, concinnavit*; indeed the construction with ἐν ταῖς τερπνότησιν αὐτῶν seems almost to require this.

---

[1] [Cf. Luc. *de Luctu* 7: ἐπειδὰν συναλισθῶσι πολλοί...]

[2] [Cf. Babr. *Fab.* CVI. 5: πολὺς θηρῶν ὅμιλος συνηυλίσθη.]

The only remaining alternative is to take συναλίζεσθαι in its proper sense of *congregari* or *convenire*, insisting on the *present* participle, 'as he was assembling with them,' as he was on the way to meet them (some of them being in the same company with him) he gave them this charge. Then it follows v. 6: 'when they were (all) come together.' If it be objected that *one* person can hardly be said to be 'assembling,' the same objection would apply to the common version, 'being assembled with them' (compare also Ch. xi. 26: ἐγένετο δὲ αὐτοὺς (Paul and Barnabas) συναχθῆναι ἐν τῇ ἐκκλησίᾳ; and John xviii. 2: ὅτι πολλάκις συνήχθη Ἰησοῦς ἐκεῖ μετὰ τῶν μαθητῶν αὐτοῦ); although it cannot be denied that Hemsterhuis's conjecture συναλιζομένοις would greatly improve the text.

I. 18: ἐκτήσατο χωρίον] A. V. 'purchased a field.' R. V. 'obtained a field.' There seems no philological reason for the change. Κτᾶσθαι (Ch. viii. 20) and πωλεῖν are in common use for *buying* and *selling*. So Aristoph. *Aves* 599: γαῦλον (a ship) κτῶμαι, καὶ ναυκληρῶ; and a few lines on: πωλῶ γαῦλον, κτῶμαι σμινύην. In Acts xxii. 28 (A. V.): 'With a great sum obtained I (ἐκτησάμην) this freedom,' a similar correction might be made[1].'

*I. 21: εἰσῆλθε καὶ ἐξῆλθεν ἐφ' ἡμᾶς] 'Went in and out among us. Ἐφ' ἡμᾶς seems to be rather 'over us,' as our head. Compare Luke xii. 14. Acts vii. 27: 'Who made thee a ruler and a judge over us (ἐφ' ἡμᾶς)?' Heb. x. 21: καὶ ἱερέα μέγαν ἐπὶ τὸν οἶκον τοῦ θεοῦ. Schleusner (under ἐπὶ III. 12) gives three examples of 'among,' but none of them is to the point (e.g. 'fell among thorns,' ἐπὶ τὰς ἀκάνθας). The common resolution of the construction into 'went in ἐφ' ἡμᾶς, and went out ἐξ ἡμῶν' is objectionable, because it would seem to make the Apostles stationary, and their Lord going and returning.

II. 23: τοῦτον...ἔκδοτον λαβόντες] A. V. 'Him being delivered...ye have taken.' The last word is wanting in the oldest MSS., Vulg. and Pesch. Whoever inserted it has the merit of perceiving that ἔκδοτον, being an adjective, cannot stand by itself; and his correction is in accordance with the usage of the best Greek writers, who invariably join ἔκδοτον λαβεῖν, δοῦναι, παραδοῦναι; e.g. Diod. Sic. XVI. 3: λαβὼν παρ' αὐτῶν ἐκδότους τοὺς φυγάδας. Dion. Hal. *Ant.* VII. 53: ὡς χρὴ παραδοῦναί τινα ἔκδοτον ἐπὶ τιμωρίᾳ τοῖς ἐχθροῖς[2]. The A. V. improperly

---

[1] [Cf. 1 Kings xvi. 24: 'He bought (ἐκτήσατο) the hill Samaria...for two talents of silver.' Acts viii. 20: τὴν δωρεὰν τοῦ θεοῦ διὰ χρημάτων κτᾶσθαι. R. V. 'to obtain the gift of God with money.' A. V. 'may be purchased with money.']

[2] [Cf. Dem. 633, 28: καὶ νυνὶ τὸν ἀποκτείναντα Χαρίδημον,...ἐὰν ἀνταποκτείνωσί τινες λαβόντες ἔκδοτον. *Id.* 635, 21: ἐκ δὲ τοῦ σοῦ ψηφίσματος ὁ βουλόμενος ἄξει τὸν ἄκοντα ἀπεκτονότα, ἔκδοτον λαβών. *Id.* 648, 25: ἐὰν μὴ τὸν ἱκέτην ἔκδοτον διδῶσιν.]

separates the two words, joining λαβόντες with ἀνείλατε. Perhaps St Luke originally wrote ἔκδοτON γενόμενON, which is also a good construction, e.g. Herod. VI. 85 : ἔκδοτον γενόμενον ὑπὸ τῶν πολιητέων. Eurip. *Ion* 1251 : ἔκδοτος δὲ γίγνομαι. Symmachus ad Isai. xlvi. 1 : ἐγένετο τὰ εἴδωλα αὐτῶν ζῴοις ἔκδοτα. Compare ἔντρομος γενόμενος (Ch. vii. 32), ἔμφοβος γενόμενος (x. 4), ἔξυπνος γενόμενος (xvi. 27), σκωληκόβρωτος γενόμενος (xii. 23).

II. 24: **λύσας τὰς ὠδῖνας τοῦ θανάτου**] ''Ωδῖνας λύειν dicitur *vel* ipsa puerpera, ut S. Chrys. T. VII. p. 118 B : ὁμοῦ τε γὰρ ἐπέβη τῆς Βηθλεέμ, καὶ τὰς ὠδῖνας ἔλυσε ; *vel* id quod paritur, ut S. Chrys. T. VII. p. 375 A : εἰς ἐγέννησεν ἡμᾶς πατήρ, τὰς αὐτὰς πάντες ἐλύσαμεν ὠδῖνας ; *vel* qui partui adest et opem fert, ut LXX. Job xxxix. 2 : ὠδῖνας δὲ αὐτῶν ἔλυσας. Hinc explicandus est locus obscurus Act. Apost. ii. 24.' So I printed 42 years ago [1839] in my 'Index Graecus' to St Chrysostom's Homilies on St Matthew. The phrase λῦσαι τὰς ὠδῖνας is not uncommon (generally in the *last* of these cases) in later Greek writers, of which examples are given by L. Bos and others[1]. Although found in the LXX. version of Job, it is *not* a Hellenistic phrase, as the Hebrew is simply, 'Or knowest thou the time when they bring forth'; and the translator of Job, who was much 'better seen' in Greek than in Hebrew, rather affected such *flosculi* (as witness his *adaptation* of the names of Job's three daughters, Jemimah (Ἡμέρα), Keziah (Κασία), and Keren-happuch (Κέρας Ἀμαλθαίας!)). The meaning of the phrase in this place being certain, and recognized by St Chrysostom (especially in his Homilies on 1 Corinthians (T. X. p. 217 E): διὸ φησιν ὁ ἀπόστολος· λύσας τὰς ὠδῖνας τοῦ θανάτου· οὐδεμία γὰρ γυνὴ παιδίον κύουσα οὕτως ὠδίνει, ὡς ἐκεῖνος, τὸ σῶμα ἔχων τὸ δεσποτικόν, διεκόπτετο διασπώμενος) and others, the difficulty is to convey this sense to the English reader. 'Having loosed the pains (R. V. pangs) of death' certainly fails to suggest the idea of *death in labour, and his pains relieved by the birth of the child.* Perhaps the slight alteration, 'Having put an end to the pains[2] (Gr. *pains as of a woman in travail*) of Death' (with a capital letter), might afford a hint of the true meaning.

*II. 39: 'To all that are afar off.' Reference is made to Ch. xxii. 21 : εἰς ἔθνη μακράν. Esth. ix. 20: καὶ ἐξαπέστειλε τοῖς Ἰουδαίοις...τοῖς ἐγγὺς καὶ τοῖς μακράν. But here the Greek is πᾶσι τοῖς ΕΙΣ μακράν, which should rather be compared with 2 Sam. vii. 19: 'thou hast spoken of thy servant's house—εἰς μακρὰν, for a great while to come.' I cannot find any example in Greek authors of εἰς μακρὰν *without a negative*, though οὐκ εἰς μακρὰν for *propediem* is common.

---

[1] Theodoret (in 2 *Reg. Interr.* XLII.) not inelegantly applies this phrase to the cessation of a three years' drought: ἵλεως ὁ δεσπότης ἐγένετο, καὶ τῶν νεφελῶν ἔλυσε τὰς ὠδῖνας.

[2] [Cf. Lucian. *Hist. Conscr.* 1: τοῖς δὲ ἱδρὼς ἐπιγενόμενος πολὺς...ἔλυσε τὸν πυρετόν. Plut. ii. p. 662 C: λύειν νόσον.]

*III. 22: VII. 37: ὡς ἐμέ] Both versions: 'like unto me'; but R. V. in marg. 'Or, *as* he raised up *me.*' The order of the Hebrew (Deut. xviii· 15) is against the alternative construction. 'A prophet from the midst of thee, of thy brethren, like unto me (ּכָמֹנִי), shall raise up unto thee the LORD thy God.' The LXX. and Vulg. translate literally ὡς ἐμέ, *tanquam me*; but the other Greek versions, here and *v.* 18, ὅμοιον ἐμοί or σοί.

*IV. 25. For the T. R. ὁ διὰ στόματος Δαβὶδ τοῦ παιδός σου εἰπών, the Revisers have adopted a confused *congeries* of duplicate readings, which has found its way into ABEℵ, and a few cursives: ὁ τοῦ πατρὸς ἡμῶν διὰ πνεύματος ἁγίου στόματος Δαβὶδ παιδός σου εἰπών, which they thus attempt to *construe*: 'who by the H. G. *by* the mouth of our father David thy servant didst say.' Dean Alford observes: 'Though harsh in construction, these words are not "senseless," as De Wette terms them, στόματος Δαυεὶδ being in apposition (!) with πνεύματος ἁγίου.' But the greatest difficulty of all, the extraordinary *trajectory* described by τοῦ πατρὸς ἡμῶν, still remains. This Dr Hort gives up as a 'primitive error,' for which he proposes the desperate remedy ΤΟΙC ΠΑΤΡΑCΙΝ ἡμῶν! Even so, we cannot agree with him that 'the order of words in text presents no difficulty, David (or the mouth of David) being represented as the mouth of the H. G.' This would certainly require διὰ πν. ἁγίου ΔΙΑ στόματος Δ.

*VI. 2: διακονεῖν τραπέζαις] The English rendering 'to serve tables' is equally ambiguous with the Greek, which, perhaps, may be considered a good reason for retaining it. But as no mention has been made of *common meals* (συσσίτια), or of a *distribution in kind*, it seems better to understand by this phrase *the transaction of money matters*, in conformity with the well-known use of τράπεζα, both in Scripture (Matth. xxi. 12; Luke xix. 23), and in ordinary Greek: e.g. Plut. *Vit. Caes.* XXVIII: οἱ μὲν ἀρχὰς μετιόντες, ἐν μέσῳ θέμενοι τραπέζας, ἐδέκαζον ἀναισχύντως τὰ πλήθη. *Ibid.* LXVII: ὥστε τοὺς μὲν (on hearing of the death of Caesar) οἰκίας κλείειν, τοὺς δ' ἀπολείπειν τραπέζας καὶ χρηματιστήρια (counting-houses).

*VI. 11: ὑπέβαλον] 'they suborned.' A very rare, but undoubted, use of the word. Vulg. *submiserunt.* Pesch. paraphrases: *miserunt viros, et instruxerunt eos ut dicerent.* The only instance given by H. Steph. is Appian, *B. C.* I. 74: ἐπὶ δὲ τούτοις, ἐς ὑπόκρισιν ἀρχῆς ἐννόμου, μετὰ τοσούσδε φόνους ἀκρίτους ὑπεβλήθησαν κατήγοροι τῷ ἱερεῖ τοῦ Διὸς Μερόλᾳ. Dean Alford quotes ὑπέβαλον from Symmachus's version of Jos. xxiii. 4, but the Hebrew is, 'I have divided unto you.' St Chrysostom says that Stephen, probably, only hinted at the supersession of the Law; for if he had declared it openly, οὐκ ἔδει τῶν ὑποβλητῶν ἀνδρῶν οὐδὲ τῶν ψευδομαρτύρων.

The nearest Greek word appears to be παρεσκευάσαντο, 'they procured'; as Dem. p. 1092, 13: παρασκευασάμενός τινας τῶν δημοτῶν. Plut.

Vit. Luc. XLII: ἐν δὲ τῷ δήμῳ Λούκουλλον ὠνόμασεν, ὡς ὑπ᾽ ἐκείνου παρε-
σκευασμένος ἀποκτεῖναι Πομπήϊον.

*VI. 15. 'All that sat in the council, looking stedfastly on him,' εἶδον
τὸ πρόσωπον αὐτοῦ ὡσεὶ πρόσωπον ἀγγέλου. 'It is a question with regard
to this verse, Does it relate *any supernatural appearance, glorifying
the face of Stephen*; or merely describe the calm and holy aspect with
which he stood before the council?'—*Dean Alford*. Those who hold the
latter opinion send us to Gen. xxxiii. 10: ἕνεκεν τούτου εἶδον τὸ πρόσωπόν
σου, ὡς ἄν τις ἴδοι πρόσωπον θεοῦ. 2 Sam. xiv. 17: ὅτι καθὼς ἄγγελος τοῦ
θεοῦ, οὕτως ὁ κύριός μου ὁ βασιλεύς, τοῦ ἀκούειν τὸ ἀγαθὸν καὶ τὸ πονηρόν.
Esth. v. 2: εἶδόν σε, κύριε, ὡς ἄγγελον θεοῦ, καὶ ἐταράχθη ἡ καρδία μου
ἀπὸ φόβου τῆς δόξης σου. In the first and last of these there is a certain
verbal resemblance, which invites a comparison with the present text:
otherwise, they are all of the same kind, not *narrative*, but addressed by
an inferior to his superior by way of adulation, and throw no light at all
upon the point under discussion. On the other hand Dean Alford's
references to Luke ii. 9, Acts xii. 7 are equally inconclusive; and those
who agree with him as to the supernatural glorification of Stephen's
visage will rather rely upon the plain statement of the supposed phaenomenon, which hardly admits of being toned down to the 'calm and
holy aspect' which he presented to 'all that sat in the council.'

*VII. 4: μετῴκισεν αὐτὸν εἰς τὴν γῆν ταύτην, εἰς ἣν ὑμεῖς νῦν κατοικεῖτε]
For verbal resemblances, *si tanti est*, compare Herod. IV. 116: ἀπικόμενοι
δὲ ἐς τοῦτον τὸν χῶρον, ἐν τῷ νῦν κατοίκηνται, οἴκησαν τοῦτον. In the next
verse εἰς κατάσχεσιν, the A. V. 'for a possession,' conveys the notion
of *permanence* better than the Revisers' 'in possession,' and has a clearer
reference to the original promise (Gen. xvii. 8) εἰς κατάσχεσιν αἰώνιον, 'for
an everlasting possession.'

VII. 12. T. R. σῖτα, A. V. 'corn' (as in Gen. xlii. 1, but there the
Greek is πρᾶσις). Nearly all the uncials read σιτία, which the Revisers
follow, still retaining 'corn.' In Greek σῖτος is 'corn,' σῖτα or σιτία
'food' (βρώματα Zonaras). The LXX. use σῖτα for אֹכֶל or לֶחֶם, never
for בָּר, דָּגָן or חִטָּה. Σιτίον occurs once only in LXX., viz. Prov. xxx. 22:
καὶ ἄφρων πλησθῇ σιτίων (לָחֶם). Compare Aelian. *V. H.* v. 1: ἐπεὶ δὲ εἰς
Πέρσας ἀφίκετο (Tachos Aegyptius), καὶ εἰς τὴν ἐκείνων τρυφὴν ἐξέπεσε, τὸ
ἀηθὲς τῶν ΣΙΤΙΩΝ οὐκ ἐνεγκών κ.τ.έ.

*VII. 21: ἀνεθρέψατο αὐτόν] Here ἀνεθρέψατο seems to be used in the
wider sense of 'brought him up,' as Paul was ἀνατεθραμμένος at the feet of
Gamaliel.

*VII. 24: ἐποίησεν ἐκδίκησιν τῷ καταπονουμένῳ] Both versions, 'avenged him that was oppressed,' as if ὁ καταπονούμενος were synonymous with ὁ ἀδικούμενος, which does not seem to be the case. The latter is correctly rendered by 'he who suffered wrong,' and therefore had right on his side; whereas the former has no reference to *moral* considerations, but only to the actual result of the contest—he was *getting the worse.* The word is often used by Diod. Sic. of those who were being hard pressed in battle by superior numbers; as XV. 85: ἰσχυρᾶς δὲ μάχης γενομένης, καὶ τῶν Ἀθηναίων καταπονουμένων, καὶ πρὸς φυγὴν ὁρμησάντων. XVII. 60: τῷ τε πλήθει καὶ βάρει τοῦ συστήματος...κατεπονεῖτο τὸ τῶν Μακεδόνων ἱππικόν.

*VII. 26: καὶ αὐτοὺς συνήλασεν εἰς εἰρήνην] 'and would have set them at one again.' So both versions, although the Revisers have adopted the reading of BCDℵ συνήλλασσεν, Vulg. *reconciliabat.* Pesch. ܐܘܥܐ ܐܠܡܝܢ. Dean Alford supports the T. R., but gives up the imperfect force, 'would have set them,' and renders boldly, 'he set them at one.' But this is what he certainly did not do; especially if we insist on the proper meaning of συνήλασεν, which always implies *force*, not *persuasion*, as the following examples will show. Plut. *Vit. Sert.* XXII: συνελαυνόμενος ὑπὸ τῶν ἐχθρῶν εἰς τὰ ὅπλα. Id. *Vit. Caes.* XLI: ἐκ τούτων ἁπάντων συνελαυνόμενος ἄκων εἰς μάχην. Lucian. *Hermot.* 63: συνελαύνεις με εἰς στενόν. Diod. Sic. XVI. 50: συνήλασαν (τοὺς λοιποὺς) εἰς μέρος τι τῆς πόλεως. Dion. Hal. *Ant.* IX. 12: πολλῶν εἰς ὀλίγον συνελαθέντων χωρίον. On the whole we must give the preference to the reading adopted by the R. V., although we should be glad to find some support for the whole phrase, συναλλάσσειν εἰς εἰρήνην. *Const. Apost.* VII. 10: εἰρηνεύσεις μαχομένους, ὡς Μωσῆς, συναλλάσσων εἰς φιλίαν.

VII. 35: ἐν χειρὶ ἀγγέλου] A. V. 'by the hand of the angel.' Ἐν χειρὶ is the Hebrew and Aramaic בְּיַד, which answers to the preposition διά in Greek. So Hag. i. 1: ἐγένετο λόγος κυρίου ἐν χειρὶ Ἀγγαίου. Here R. V. renders (not very intelligibly)[1] 'with the hand'; but in Gal. iii. 19 we find A. V. 'in the hand of a mediator[2],' R. V. 'by the hand of....'

*VII. 40. 'We wot not what is become of him.' So both versions for the Greek, οὐκ οἴδαμεν τί ἐγένετο (T. R. γέγονεν) αὐτῷ. A distinction might be taken between τί ἐγένετο αὐτῷ, 'what has happened to him,' and τί αὐτὸς ἐγένετο, 'what is become of him.' (Ch. xii. 18: τί ἄρα ὁ Πέτρος ἐγένετο.) But having regard to Exod. xxxii. 1 the Revisers have judged rightly in retaining the A. V. Perhaps also in Rom. xi. 25, the A. V. 'that blindness (or, *hardness*) in part is happened (γέγονεν) to Israel,' is quite as faithful as the R. V. 'that a hardening in part hath befallen Israel.'

---

[1] [Reading σὺν χειρί.]
[2] [Cf. 1 Sam. xxviii. 15: A. V. neither 'by prophets.' Heb. 'by the

hand of prophets.' LXX. ἐν χειρὶ τῶν προφητῶν.]

VII. 45: ἦν καὶ εἰσήγαγον διαδεξάμενοι οἱ πατέρες ἡμῶν] A. V. 'Which also our fathers that came after brought in.' Other proposed renderings of διαδεξάμενοι are 'inheriting,' 'receiving it after,' 'receiving it from their predecessors' &c. I think διαδεξάμενοι, simpliciter dictum, may be taken adverbially for ἐκ διαδοχῆς, 'in their turn,' [as in the R. V.]. Compare Herod. VIII. 142: ὡς δὲ ἐπαύσατο λέγων Ἀλέξανδρος, διαδεξάμενοι ἔλεγον οἱ ἀπὸ Σπάρτης ἄγγελοι κ.τ.λ.

*Ibid. εἰσήγαγον...μετὰ Ἰησοῦ ἐν τῇ κατασχέσει τῶν ἐθνῶν] A. V. 'brought in with Jesus into the possession of the Gentiles (Vulg. in possessionem gentium).' R. V. 'brought in with Joshua, when they entered on the possession of the nations,' or as Mr Humphry explains (Comm. on R. V. 1888), 'in the taking possession of the nations, i.e. of the land of the nations.' But of the 50 examples of the same Greek word for the same Hebrew אֲחֻזָּה given by Trommius not one is to be found in which κατάσχεσις is used of the act of taking possession of a country by the expulsion of its former occupiers. In the latter case the word employed is יָרַשׁ, not אָחַז; and instead of ἐν τῇ κατασχέσει τῶν ἐθνῶν, the usage of the LXX. would require ἐν τῇ κατακληρονομήσει τῶν ἐθνῶν, or ἐν τῷ κατακληρονομῆσαι αὐτοὺς τὰ ἔθνη, as Deut. xxxi. 3: κύριος ἐξολοθρεύσει τὰ ἔθνη ταῦτα ἀπὸ προσώπου σου, καὶ κατακληρονομήσεις αὐτούς.

*Ibid. ὧν ἔξωσεν ὁ θεὸς ἀπὸ προσώπου τῶν πατέρων ἡμῶν] Grotius compares the inscription which Procopius saw in Africa, Ἡμεῖς ἐσμεν οἱ φυγόντες ἀπὸ προσώπου Ἰησοῦ τοῦ λῃστοῦ υἱοῦ Ναυή, written in Punic letters on two columns. The fugitives in question settled on the African coast near the city Tingis (Tangier).

*VII. 53: εἰς διαταγὰς ἀγγέλων] As διαταγὴ is interchanged with διάταξις in one of the significations of the latter (mandatum), I do not see why it may not be so in the more proper one of dispositio. Symmachus thrice puts ἡ διάταξις τοῦ οὐρανοῦ for the Heb. צָבָא.

VIII. 1. 'And Saul was consenting unto his death (τῇ ἀναιρέσει αὐτοῦ).' Rather, 'unto the killing (or slaying) of him.' Compare A. V. of 2 Macc. v. 13: 'Thus there was killing (ἀναιρέσεις) of young and old... slaying (σφαγαί) of virgins and infants[1].'

*VIII. 2: συνεκόμισαν δὲ τὸν Στ.] A. V. 'carried Stephen to his burial.' R. V. 'buried Stephen.' The Scholiast on Aesch. Sept. c. Theb. 1024 says: Συγκομιδή· ἡ πρὸ τοῦ τάφου πᾶσα ἐπιμέλεια. ἐκκομιδή· ἡ πρὸς τὸν

---

[1] [Cf. App. B. C. I. 96: πολλὴ δὲ καὶ τῶν Ἰταλιωτῶν ἀναιρεσίς τε καὶ ἐξέλασις καὶ δήμευσις ἦν. I. 121, ἀμφὶ τὰ ξ' (ἔτη) μάλιστα ἀπὸ τῆς ἀναιρέσεως Τιβερίου Γράκχου. Plut. Vit. Crass. IV: ἔνδηλοι ἦσαν κατιόντες οὐκ ἐπ' ἀγαθῷ τῆς πατρίδος ἐπ' ἀναιρέσει δὲ καὶ ὀλέθρῳ τῶν ἀρίστων.]

τάφον ἀπαγωγή. I would translate 'took up Stephen' or 'took up the body of Stephen,' of course for the purpose of burying him, though this is rather implied than expressed. Συγκομίζειν (said of a single person) is 'to take up a dead body, which is lying exposed,' as here, and in the often-quoted example from Soph. *Aj.* 1047: οὗτος, σὲ φωνῶ τόνδε τὸν νεκρὸν χεροῖν | μὴ συγκομίζειν, ἀλλ' ἐᾶν ὅπως ἔχει. In the case of several bodies, it also includes the notion of bringing them together into one place, as Thucyd. VI. 71: συγκομίσαντες δὲ τοὺς ἑαυτῶν νεκροὺς καὶ ἐπὶ πυρὰν ἐπιθέντες ηὐλίσαντο αὐτοῦ. Plut. *Vit. Ages.* XIX: 'Αγησίλαος δὲ... οὐ πρότερον ἐπὶ σκηνὴν ἀπῆλθεν ἢ φοράδην ἐνεχθῆναι πρὸς τὴν φάλαγγα, καὶ τοὺς νεκροὺς ἰδεῖν ἐντὸς τῶν ὅπλων συγκεκομισμένους (brought in within the camp): where the last four words have been misunderstood by Langhorne, 'borne off upon their arms,' and by Elsner ad h. l. 'buried in their arms.'

The ancient versions *in diversa abeunt.* Thus Vulg. *curaverunt.* Pesch. ܘܣܒܪܘ ܐܘ̈ܗ 'gathered and buried.' Philox. ܘܣܛܠܘ (=προέπεμψαν). Compare Luke vii. 12, ἐξεκομίζετο ܗܘ̈ܐ ܡܬܛܥܢ.

VIII. 31: πῶς γὰρ ἂν δυναίμην] 'How can I.' Rather, 'Why, how can I.' So Matt. xxvii. 23: τί γὰρ κακὸν ἐποίησε; 'Why, what evil hath he done?'

*IX. 7: ἀκούοντες μὲν τῆς φωνῆς] R. V. 'hearing [why not add 'indeed,' as in Ch. xxii. 9?] the voice. Or, *sound.*' But as 'the voice' had been already described in *v.* 4 as an articulate one, the marginal rendering is liable to the charge of being 'suggestive of differences that have no existence in the Greek' (Pref. III. 2). No doubt, if 'sound' were admissible, it would afford an easy method of harmonizing the account here given by the narrator with that of St Paul himself in Ch. xxii. 9: 'And they that were with me saw indeed the light, τὴν δὲ φωνὴν οὐκ ἤκουσαν τοῦ λαλοῦντός μοι.' But when we consider the wide range of perception between simply hearing the sound of the words, and taking in their full meaning and import,—the hearers also themselves being at the time in a confused and highly excited state of mind—there is really no contradiction between the two accounts. At all events the distinction taken by a writer in the *Quarterly Review* that ἀκούειν τῆς φωνῆς is to hear *something* of the voice, and ἀκούειν τὴν φωνήν to hear *all* of it, is perfectly puerile.

*IX. 25: διὰ τοῦ τείχους] A. V. 'by the wall.' R. V. 'through the wall.' But in the parallel place 2 Cor. xi. 33 it is διὰ θυρίδος...διὰ τοῦ τείχους, where both versions have 'through a window...by the wall.'

*IX. 30: ἐπιγνόντες] The *absolute* use of this word for *re cognita,* 'when they knew of it,' has its parallel in Diod. Sic. XVI. 10: ἀκατασχέτου δὲ τῆς ὁρμῆς τῶν ὄχλων οὔσης, ἐπιγνόντες τοὺς μισθοφόρους καὶ τοὺς τὰ τοῦ δυνάστου φρονοῦντας ἤθροισαν.

*IX. 34: στρῶσον σεαυτῷ] 'make thy bed.' Perhaps, 'make thine own bed,' an office which had been used to be done for him by others. [The name of this patient should be pronounced Aenĕas, not Aenēas, the change from Αἰνέας to Αἰνείας being a necessity induced by the laws of heroic versification.] Rev. T. Harmer (*Observations*, &c. Vol. II. p. 374, edited by Adam Clarke, LL.D., Lond. 1808) says, in opposition to the common understanding of this phrase: 'The Eastern people now do not keep their beds made: the mattresses, &c. are rolled up, carried away, and placed in cupboards, till they are wanted at night.' [But this can hardly apply to bed-ridden patients.] He therefore supposes that Aeneas is here recommended to give a feast to Peter and those that were with him on the occasion of his recovery, and to prepare his house for the reception of the company!

*IX. 38: μὴ ὀκνήσῃς διελθεῖν ἕως ἡμῶν] A courteous mode of pressing a request, of which a few examples from sacred and profane writers may not be inopportune. Of the former may be compared Num. xxii. 16: ἀξιῶ σε, μὴ ὀκνήσῃς ἐλθεῖν πρὸς μέ (A. V. 'let nothing hinder thee (Heb. *be not thou letted*) from coming unto me'). Sirac. vii. 35: μὴ ὄκνει ἐπισκέπτεσθαι ἄρρωστον ('be not slow to visit the sick'). Aelian, *V. H.* IX. 1: οὐκ ὤκνησε Σιμωνίδης, βαρὺς ὢν ὑπὸ γήρως, πρὸς αὐτὸν ἀφικέσθαι. In Diog. Laert. I. 99: Periander writes τοῖς σοφοῖς, 'I hear that last year you had a *réunion* at Sardes at the court of the Lydian (Croesus)': ἤδη ὢν μὴ ὀκνεῖτε καὶ παρ' ἐμὲ φοιτῆν τὸν Κορίνθου τύραννον.

*X. 24: τοὺς ἀναγκαίους φίλους] 'near friends.' As they are distinguished from τοὺς συγγενεῖς, we must abide by the A. V., unless we recall the version of Tyndale and his followers, 'special friends.' Generally, in the best authors, blood-relations and connexions, even the nearest, are included in the term. Festus explains the corresponding Latin term: '*Necessarii* sunt, qui aut *cognati* aut *affines* sunt, in quos necessaria officia conferuntur praeter ceteros.' Good examples of this use of the word are: Plut. *Vit. Pyrrh.* XXX: τῷ δὲ Πύρρῳ προείρητο μὲν...ὑπὸ τοῦ μάντεως ἀποβολή τινος τῶν ἀναγκαίων (who proved to be his son). Stob. *Floril.* T. CVIII. 33: οἷον, τέθνηκεν υἱὸς ἢ μήτηρ τινί, | ἢ νὴ Δί' ἄλλων τῶν ἀναγκαίων γέ τις. Diod. Sic. XIX. 43: παρὰ τοῖς πολεμίοις ὄντων τέκνων καὶ γυναικῶν, καὶ πολλῶν ἄλλων ἀναγκαίων σωμάτων.

X. 28: κολλᾶσθαι] A. V. 'to keep company (with).' R. V. 'to join himself to,' as A. V. Ch. v. 13. I prefer the former in both places, a *continued action* being intended. The other would require κολληθῆναι, as

Luke xv. 15: 'he went and joined himself (ἐκολλήθη).' Acts v. 36: 'to whom a number of men joined themselves (προσεκολλήθη)¹.'

XI. 12: **μηδὲν διακρινόμενον**] 'nothing doubting.' The MSS. usually followed by the Revisers read μηδὲν διακρίναντα (or διακρίνοντα), which they translate, 'making no distinction,' I suppose between Jews and Gentiles, but that should have been expressed, as it is Chap. xv. 9: καὶ οὐθὲν διέκρινεν μεταξὺ ἡμῶν τε καὶ αὐτῶν. Ezek. xxxiv. 17: διακρινῶ ἀναμέσον προβάτου καὶ προβάτου. Diod. Sic. XIX. 7: οὐ διέκρινε φίλον ἢ πολέμιον². We might also tolerate μηδένα διακρίνων, 'giving no one a preference,' if Ch. x. 20 were kept out of view. But comparing the two places, there seems no choice, but either to omit the clause altogether (with D, Philox.) or to bring it into harmony with its prototype.

*XI. 21: **πολύς τε ἀριθμὸς πιστεύσας** (ABℵ read ὁ πιστεύσας) **ἐπέστρεψεν ἐπὶ τὸν κύριον**] 'T. R. omits ὁ as unnecessary, not perceiving its force.' —*Dean Alford.* Without the article nothing can be simpler than the construction or clearer than the meaning of these words : 'And a great number believed, and turned unto the Lord.' What is the force of the article? The R. V. is : 'and a great number that believed turned unto the Lord'; which, however, would require ὁ πολύς τε ἀρ. ὁ πιστεύσας, with the double article. Besides, 'a great number that believed' might easily be taken to mean 'a great number of them that believed,' not the whole, as, in fact, the Vulgate has translated, *multusque numerus credentium conversus est ad Dominum* : which is not the sense intended.

XI. 29: **τῶν δὲ μαθητῶν καθὼς ηὐπορεῖτό τις, ὥρισαν ἕκαστος αὐτῶν εἰς διακονίαν πέμψαι**] 'Then the disciples, every man according to his ability, determined to send relief.' The Greek word ὥρισεν is never used in N. T. for 'determined' in the sense of 'resolved,' but always ἔκρινεν ; and if this were its meaning here, there seems no reason for adding ἕκαστος αὐτῶν, which, in fact, is omitted in the A. V., 'every man according to his ability' being no more than an adequate rendering of καθὼς ηὐπορεῖτό τις. I take the meaning to be, 'They set apart (Gr. *fixed a limit*) each of them a certain sum³.' In Gen. xxx. 28 Laban says to Jacob, 'Appoint *me* (LXX. διάστειλον, Sym. ῞ΟΡΙΣΟΝ) thy wages, and I will give it.' I would also join ὥρισαν εἰς διακονίαν, rendering the whole verse thus : 'And the disciples, as every man had to spare, set

---

¹ Here, however, the true reading is προσεκλίθη, 'whom...favoured,' or 'to whom...consented.'

² [Cf. Lucian. *Herm.* 68: τὸ τοίνυν διακρῖναι τοὺς εἰδότας ἀπὸ τῶν οὐκ εἰδότων μὲν, φασκόντων δέ...]

³ App. *B. C.* I. 21: σιτηρέσιον ἐμμηνον ὁρίσας ἑκάστῳ τῶν δημοτῶν ἀπὸ τῶν κοινῶν χρημάτων. Plut. II. p. 219 A: τῶν δὲ συμμάχων ἐπιζητούντων πόσα χρήματα ἀρκέσει, καὶ ἀξιούντων ὁρίσαι τοὺς φόρους.

apart each of them for a ministration to send unto the brethren, which dwelt in Judea.' It follows in the next verse, ὁ καὶ ἐποίησαν (sc. ἔπεμψαν).

*XII. 7 : ἐν τῷ οἰκήματι] A. V. 'in the prison.' R. V. 'in the cell.' The latter version supposes that the prison was divided into separate cells, in one of which, that in which Peter was confined, the light shone, and the other particulars took place. This *may* have been the case, but we have no authority for οἴκημα being so used. All grammarians are agreed that it is an euphemism for δεσμωτήριον; and as we have nothing corresponding to it in our language, to attempt to distinguish between the two words is only misleading. If the distinction should be insisted upon, we should prefer 'chamber' to 'cell.'

XII. 12 : συνιδών] A. V. and R. V. : 'When he had considered *the thing,*' following the Vulg. *considerans.* But συνιδεῖν never has this meaning, but invariably that of 'perceiving,' 'being ware of,' as it is rightly rendered in both versions, Ch. xiv. 6. See a host of examples in Wetstein, to which may be added Diod. Sic. XVII. 88 : ταραχῆς δὲ πολλῆς γενομένης, ὁ Πῶρος, συνιδὼν τὸ γινόμενον, κ.τ.έ. Plut. *Vit. Mar.* XXVI : καὶ συνεῖδον μὲν οἱ τῶν Ῥωμαίων στρατηγοὶ τὸν δόλον. *Vit. Syl.* IX : ὁ Σύλλας παρῆν ἤδη, καὶ συνιδὼν τὸ γινόμενον, ἐβόα τὰς οἰκίας ὑφάπτειν.

*XII. 13 : κρούσαντος τὴν θύραν...παιδίσκη ὑπακοῦσαι...εἰσδραμοῦσα ἀπήγγειλεν...ἐπέμενε κρούων] These are all familiar terms of the domestic life of the Greeks ; except that for κρούειν the purists preferred κόπτειν, and εἰσαγγέλλειν is more common than ἀπαγγέλλειν. E.g. Plut. *Vit. Pelop.* IX : ἐξαίφνης δὲ κοπτομένης τῆς θύρας, προσδραμών τις καὶ πυθόμενος, τοῦ ὑπηρέτου Χάρωνα μετιέναι παρὰ τῶν πολεμάρχων φάσκοντος, ἀπήγγελλεν εἴσω τεθορυβημένος. *Ibid.* XI : καὶ πολὺν χρόνον κόπτουσιν αὐτοῖς ὑπήκουσεν οὐδείς. Lucian. *Nigr.* 2 : καὶ κόψας τὴν θύραν, τοῦ παιδὸς εἰσαγγείλαντος, ἐκλήθην. Xen. *Symp.* I. 11 : κρούσας τὴν θύραν εἶπε τῷ ὑπακούσαντι εἰσαγγεῖλαι ὅστις εἴη. It was a mark of ἀγροικία to answer the door yourself, κόψαντος τὴν θύραν, ὑπακοῦσαι αὐτός (Theophr. *Char.*).

*XII. 17 : κατασείσας δὲ αὐτοῖς τῇ χειρὶ σιγᾶν] Compare Appian. *B. C.* II. 60 : καὶ προπηδήσας κατέσεισεν, ὡς εἰπεῖν τι βουλόμενος. σιωπῆς δὲ αὐτῷ γενομένης...

*XII. 19 : ἀνακρίνας] Although we do not find fault with the Revisers for retaining the A. V. 'he examined,' i.e. by simple interrogation, as the word is commonly used in the N. T., it ought to be understood that ἀνακρίνειν, like the Latin *quaerere* and *quaestio*, besides its general meaning, has a special reference to *examination by torture*, which is probably intended in this place. As examples of this usage, compare Plut. *Vit. Alex.* XLIX : ἐκ τούτου δὲ συλληφθεὶς ἀνεκρίνετο, τῶν ἑταίρων ἐφεστώτων ταῖς βασάνοις. *Id.* T. ΙΙ. p. 256 C: καὶ τῆς Καλβίας ἐφεστώσης... Ἀρεταφίλαν ταῖς βασάνοις ἀνέκρινε. Joseph. *Ant.* XVI. 8, 1: ἀνακρίναντι δὲ περὶ μὲν τῆς γεγενημένης πρὸς αὐτὸν κοινωνίας καὶ μίξεως ὡμολόγουν, ἄλλο δὲ οὐδὲν δυσχερὲς εἰς τὸν πατέρα συνειδέναι. βασανιζόμενοι δὲ μᾶλλον, καὶ ἐν ταῖς ἀνάγκαις ὄντες...

*XIII. 9: Σαῦλος δὲ ὁ καὶ Παῦλος] The insertion of this note in this place seems intended to account for the change of designation in St Luke's narrative, as much as to say, ' Saul, whom I shall in future call Paul'; from which we cannot certainly conclude that the change or addition took place at this time, much less that it had any connexion with the conversion of the proconsul.

*XIII. 34: τὰ ὅσια Δαβὶδ τὰ πιστά] A. V. 'the sure mercies of David.' R. V. 'the holy and sure *blessings* of David.' There is nothing about *mercies* in the Greek, nor any indication that that word is to be supplied. τὰ ὅσια Δαυὶδ (Isai. lv. 3) and τὰ ἐλέη Δαυὶδ (2 Chr. vi. 42) are *two* versions of the Hebrew חַסְדֵי. It has been attempted to show that τὰ ὅσια may mean *beneficia* by a reference to Clem. Rom. *Ep.* II. *ad Cor.* ch. I : πόσα δὲ αὐτῷ ὀφείλομεν ὅσια; τὸ φῶς γὰρ ἡμῖν ἐχαρίσατο κ.τ.λ. ; but ὅσια is here (as elsewhere) *pietatis officia* ; and there seems to be no possible way of rendering Isaiah's τὰ ὅσια Δαυὶδ τὰ πιστά except by 'the sure *pieties* (*pie facta*) of David.' But what bearing the text so understood has upon the resurrection of our Lord, it is not easy to see.

*XIV. 3 : ἱκανὸν μὲν οὖν χρόνον διέτριψαν] A. V. 'long time therefore abode they.' (R. V. 'they tarried *there*.') A good construction, as in Ch. xii. 19. But we may also join διατρίβειν χρόνον, *tempus terere*, as in the following examples : Dion. Hal. *Ant.* I. 41 : διατρῖψαι δὲ αὐτόθι πλείω χρόνον ἠναγκάσθη. *Ibid.* VI. 25 : διατριβομένου δ' εἰς ταῦτα πολλοῦ χρόνου. The same construction followed by a participle (as here) is found in Herod. I. 189 : ἤνετο μὲν τὸ ἔργον, ὅμως μέντοι τὴν θερείην πᾶσαν αὐτοῦ ταύτῃ διέτριψαν ἐργαζόμενοι.

*XIV. 4 : ἐσχίσθη δὲ τὸ πλῆθος κ.τ.έ.] Compare Diod. Sic. XII. 8 : σχιζομένων δὲ τῶν Σικελικῶν πόλεων, καὶ τῶν μὲν τοῖς Ἀκραγαντίνοις, τῶν δὲ τοῖς Συρακουσίοις συστρατευόντων. Xenoph. *Symp.* IV. 59 : ἐνταῦθα μέντοι ἐσχίσθησαν, καὶ οἱ μὲν εἶπον...οἱ δέ... Charit. Aphrod. VI. 1 : διέσχιστο δὲ ἡ πόλις· καὶ οἱ μὲν Χαιρέᾳ σπεύδοντες ἔλεγον...οἱ δὲ Διονυσίῳ σπεύδοντες ἀντέλεγον...

XIV. 6: συνιδόντες] A. V. 'they were ware of *it*.' R. V. 'they became aware of it.' Here also Prof. Scholefield would render, 'having considered *it*,' i.e. ' what was best to be done.' ' If,' he says, ' it had been an assault *meditated*, it might properly be said *they were ware of it* ; but this is superfluous, where it was an assault *made*.' But that is the question: was it actually *made*, or only *meditated*? St Chrysostom says: οὐ περιέμειναν τοίνυν, ἀλλ' εἶδον τὴν ὁρμήν, καὶ ἔφυγον. And this is agreeable to the use of the word ὁρμή, a *sudden movement*, or *impulse* (compare James iii. 4 R. V.), which might be rendered abortive, either by the timely retreat of the objects of it, as here, or by the influence of better counsels, as Diod. Sic. T. X. p. 77 ed. Bip.: τοὺς δὲ πρεσβευτὰς ἐπεβάλλοντο τοῖς λίθοις καταλεύειν· πρεσβυτέρων δέ τινων ἐπιλαβομένων τῆς ὁρμῆς τῶν ὄχλων, μόγις...τοῦ βάλλειν ἀπέσχοντο. Dion. Hal. *Ant.* VI. 16, 17: τὸ μὲν πλῆθος ὥρμησε βαλεῖν τοὺς Οὐολύσκους ὡς ἑαλωκότας ἐπ' αὐτοφώρῳ κατασκόπους· ὁ δὲ Ποστούμιος...ἐπισχὼν τὴν ὁρμὴν τοῦ πλήθους, ἀπιέναι τοὺς ἄνδρας ἐκέλευσεν[1].

*XIV. 13: ταύρους καὶ στέμματα] 'Not for ταύρους ἐστεμμένους.'— *Alford*. In his horror of the *hendiadys*, the Dean goes on to mention other purposes to which the garlands might have been applied; but there is no doubt that the principal one was the festive decoration of the animal to be sacrificed, as indicated by the following examples: Oraculum ap. Diod. Sic. XVI. 91: ἔστεπται μὲν ὁ ταῦρος, ἔχει τέλος, ἔστιν ὁ θύσων. Plut. *Vit. Ages.* VI: καὶ καταστέψας ἔλαφον ἐκέλευσεν ἀπάρξασθαι τὸν ἑαυτοῦ μάντιν. Lucian, *De Sacrif.* 12: ἀλλ' οἵ γε θύοντες, στεφανώσαντες τὸ ζῷον...προσάγουσι τῷ βωμῷ. Diod. Sic. T. X. p. 85 ed. Bip.: τούτους ἀμφοτέρους καταστέψας ἱερείου τρόπον εἰσήγαγε.

*XIV. 20: κυκλωσάντων δὲ αὐτὸν τῶν μαθητῶν] A. V. and R. V. 'as the disciples stood round about him.' Rather, 'when the disciples came round about him' (κυκλωσάντων not κυκλούντων). So John x. 24: 'the Jews came round about him' (A. V. and R. V.).

XV. 17, 18: λέγει κύριος ὁ ποιῶν ταῦτα πάντα. γνωστὰ ἀπ' αἰῶνός ἐστι τῷ θεῷ πάντα τὰ ἔργα αὐτοῦ] This is the T. R. of which the principal MSS. make sad havock. We willingly give up πάντα in the quotation from Amos ix. 12, which, though retained in the Roman text of the LXX., is wanting in II, III, XII, and many others, as well as in the Syriac version of Paul of Tela, which represents Origen's text. But, besides this, the three uncials BCℵ also omit all the words that follow αἰῶνος, leaving to be dealt with only ὁ ποιῶν ταῦτα γνωστὰ ἀπ' αἰῶνος. In which reading, whether we join γνωστὰ with ποιῶν, 'who maketh these things known,' thus affixing to the words of the prophet a meaning quite different from their proper one; or whether we accept the very lame construction, 'who doeth these things *which were* known,' in either case

---

[1] [Cf. App. *B. C.* II. 118: καὶ αὐτοῖς σκεπτομένοις ὁρμὴ μὲν ἦν ἀμύνειν τῷ Καίσαρι, τοιάδε παθόντι. Plut. *Vit. Crass.* XI: ἐφοβήθη...μὴ λάβοι τις ὁρμὴ τὸν Σπάρτακον ἐπὶ τὴν Ῥώμην ἐλαύνειν. Diod. Sic. XVI. 10: ἀκατασχέτου δὲ τῆς ὁρμῆς τῶν ὄχλων οὔσης.]

the result is equally unsatisfactory. This being acknowledged to be a *locus conclamatus*, might it not be allowable, in a version intended for general use, to pass over these three words, γνωστὰ ἀπ' αἰῶνος, altogether, as a fragment of uncertain origin, perhaps a marginal gloss on ποιῶν ταῦτα? Then in the margin might be noted: 'After *these things* the oldest authorities add, *known from the beginning of the world*. Other ancient authorities insert v. 18: *Known unto God are all his works from the beginning of the world.*' This latter insertion will be very much missed, and, whatever may be the future of the R. V., will never cease to be quoted as a portion of the word of God; therefore it is but right that some record of its existence, as such, should be preserved.

*[In the foregoing remarks, I fear I have gone too far in the way of concession to the 'oldest authorities'; and am now inclined to agree with a correspondent bearing the honoured name of BIRKS, that the words γνωστὰ ἀπ' αἰῶνος having been improperly joined to the preceding sentence, what followed was omitted by the copyists as unintelligible.]

XV. 19: μὴ παρενοχλεῖν] 'that we trouble not.' *v.* 24: ἐτάραξαν ὑμᾶς, 'have troubled you.' In the former text we might translate, 'that we disquiet not.' Compare 1 Kings (Sam.) xxviii. 15, where Samuel's ghost says: ἵνα τί παρηνώχλησάς μοι; 'Why hast thou disquieted me?'[1]

*XV. 20: τῆς πορνείας] Dr Scrivener, in pronouncing a sweeping condemnation of conjectural emendations (*Introduction*, &c. p. 491, ed. 1883) singles out as 'one of the best' that of πορκείας for πορνείας in this place, *whose* he does not say. Against which selection it may be urged: (1) No emendation is required. In the judgment of the Apostles this was one of the 'necessary things' concerning which the converts from heathenism required to be cautioned, and not the less so, because other injunctions, relating to things not of perpetual obligation, are included in the same letter. (2) Even in later times Christians were thought by the ancient Fathers to be released from the obligations of the Mosaic law, but *not* from the precepts given to Noah (Gen. ix. 4). Thus Tertullian *De Monogam.* v: 'Ut et fides reversa sit a circumcisione ad integritatem carnis illius, sicut ab initio fuit: et *libertas ciborum*, et *sanguinis solius abstinentia*, sicut ab initio fuit.' A prohibition, therefore, of the flesh of particular animals, as unclean, could not be enforced without a violation of that *libertas ciborum*, which was obscurely shadowed forth by Christ himself (Mark vii. 19), and plainly declared, as a law of the Church, to St Peter (Acts x. 14, 15). (3) For πορνείας Bentley (if we may believe Wetstein) proposed to read χοιρείας, which is not only objectionable on

---

[1] [Cf. Vulg. *Quare inquietasti.* Plut. *Vit. Phoc.* VII : παρενοχλοῦντος τοῦ νεανίσκου καὶ κόπτοντος αὐτὸν ἐρωτή- μασιν. Arrian. *Epict.* I. 9: His judges said to Socrates μηδὲ παρενοχλήσῃς (interfere with) ἡμῶν τοῖς νέοις μηδὲ τοῖς γέρουσιν.]

the ground already stated, but also *philologically*, the flesh of animals being always described in Greek by an adjective in the neuter singular or plural, κρέας or κρέα being either expressed or understood. E.g. Isai. lxvi. 17: ἔσθοντες κρέας ὕειον (Σ. τὸ κρέας τὸ χοίρειον). Herod. II. 37: κρεῶν βοέων καὶ χηνέων. Diod. Sic. I. 70: κρέα μόσχεια καὶ χηνῶν μόνον προσφερομένους. *Ibid.* 84: κρέα χήνεια. Artem. *Onir.* I. 70: βόεια, ταύρεια, χοίρεια... ὀρνίθεια καὶ χήνεια κρέα. Hence ἡ χοιρεία is a soloecism. (4) But what shall we say to ἡ πορκεία? *Quis novus hic hospes?* Not only is the word itself unknown to the Greek language, but even πόρκος, which is sometimes met with, is not the Latin *porcus*, but *an instrument used in fishing*, as Plut. T. II. p. 730C: τοσαύτην πλέοντες θάλατταν, οὐδαμοῦ καθῆκαν ἄγκιστρον, οὐδὲ πόρκον, οὐδὲ δίκτυον, ἀλφίτων παρόντων.

XV. 26: ἀνθρώποις παραδεδωκόσι τὰς ψυχὰς αὐτῶν] 'Men that have hazarded their lives.' The English expression seems to refer to *past* dangers only, whereas the Greek word implies a general determination and readiness to die for the cause, 'men that have *pledged* their lives.' Homer says of pirates: ψυχὰς παρθέμενοι, κακὸν ἀλλοδάποισι φέροντες, where the Scholiast: ἀφειδήσαντες ἑαυτῶν, παραβαλόντες. A similar phrase in Hebrew is, 'I have put my life in my hand' (Jud. xii. 3. Job xiii. 14)[1].

*XVI. 12: ἥτις ἐστὶ πρώτη τῆς μερίδος [τῆς] Μακεδονίας πόλις] A. V. 'which is the chief city of that part of M.' R. V. 'which is a city of M., the first of the district.' Philippi belonged to the first μέρος of the four into which M. was divided (Diod. Sic. T. X. p. 228, ed. Bip.); but the chief city of that μέρος was not Philippi, but Amphipolis (Livy 45, 29). This and other difficulties of the present text might be got over by reading, ἥτις ἐστι πρώτης μερίδος M. πόλις, 'which is a city of the first portion of M.,' where πρώτη, a 'primitive error,' may have been corrected πρώτη, and this correction misunderstood for πρώτη τῆς[2]. [When πρώτη means the first in point of situation (as Alford) there is always something in the context which restricts it to that sense. E.g. Appian, *B. C.* II. 35: ἥτις (Ἀρίμινος) ἐστὶν Ἰταλίας πρώτη μετὰ τὴν Γαλατίαν (ex Gallia venientibus). Herod. I. 142: πρώτη κεῖται πόλις πρὸς μεσημβρίαν. VII. 198: πρώτη πόλις ἐστὶ ἐν τῷ κόλπῳ ἰόντι ἀπ' Ἀχαίης.]

*XVI. 26: καὶ πάντων τὰ δεσμὰ ἀνέθη] The Hellenistic use of the word (Mal. iv. 2: μοσχάρια ἐκ δεσμῶν ἀνειμένα) may be traced to Hom. *Od. θ.* 359: ὡς εἰπὼν δεσμῶν ἀνίει (Martem et Venerem) μένος Ἡφαίστοιο,

---

[1] [Also Jud. v. 18: 'jeoparded their lives unto the death.' Heb. *despised*.]

[2] Professor J. Armitage Robinson has pointed out to me that Dr Field is

not alone in suggesting πρώτης. See Blass, *Philology of the Gospels*, pp. 67 f. 1898. Ed.

where Eustath.: τὸ δὲ ἀνεῖναι οὐ δεσμοῦ μόνον σημαίνει λύσιν, ὡς ἐν τοῖς ῥηθεῖσι χρᾶται ὁ ποιητής κ.τ.ἑ.   On Dio Chrys. *Or.* IV. 70, ἐπειδὰν ἀρῶσι τὸν ἄνθρωπον ἐκ τῶν δεσμῶν, Cobet (*Coll. Crit.* p. 56) notes : 'Nihil est ἀρῶσι. Nil prodest ἀνῶσι, quod Emperius, neque ἀφῶσι, quod Dindorfius conjecit. Verum est usitatissimum illud ΛΥΩΣΙ, *solvant vinculis.*' But λύωσι is the wrong tense, and the difference between αρωσι (ἀνῶσι) and αρωσι is the very slightest possible.

XVII. 14: πορεύεσθαι ὡς ἐπὶ τὴν θάλασσαν] 'to go as it were to the sea.' For ὡς the principal uncials (ΑΒΕΝ) read ἕως, whence R. V. 'to go as far as to the sea.' But ἕως ἐπὶ has not been shown to be a legitimate combination; whereas π. ὡς ἐπὶ 'to go in the direction of' a place, whether the person arrives there or not, is an excellent Greek idiom, though it may not have been familiar to those scribes who changed ὡς into ἕως. To the examples quoted by Wetstein may be added (from a single author) Pausan. *Corinth.* 11, 2 : καταβαίνουσι δὲ ὡς ἐπὶ τὸ πεδίον, ἱερόν ἐστιν ἐνταῦθα Δημητρός.   25, 9: καταβάντων δὲ ὡς ἐπὶ θάλατταν.   34, 8: ἀπὸ δὲ Σκυλλαίου πλέοντι ὡς ἐπὶ τὴν πόλιν.   *Lacon.* 20, 3: ἰοῦσιν εὐθεῖαν ὡς ἐπὶ θάλασσαν[1].

XVII. 17: πρὸς τοὺς παρατυγχάνοντας] 'with them that met with him,' as if it were περιτυγχάνοντας or ἐντυγχάνοντας. Vulg. *qui aderant,* but it is rather *qui forte aderant,* 'that chanced to be there[2].' Then 'met with him' might represent συνέβαλλον αὐτῷ *v.* 18, though 'encountered him' is not to be found fault with. Compare Dio Chrys. *Or.* IV. 59, 4: φασί ποτε Ἀλέξανδρον Διογένει συμβαλεῖν, οὐ πάνυ τι σχολάζοντα πολλὴν ἄγοντι σχολήν. Philostr. *Her.* p. 6 ed. Boiss.: οὐ γὰρ συμβάλλω ἐμπόροις, οὐδὲ τὴν δραχμὴν ὅ τι ἐστὶ γιγνώσκω, where Schol. ὁμιλῶ[3].

XVII. 22: ὡς δεισιδαιμονεστέρους ὑμᾶς θεωρῶ] A. V. 'I perceive that... ye are too superstitious.'

In the Report of S.P.C.K. for 1877, page 82, I find the following extract from a discourse lately delivered by a distinguished prelate, and published by the Society :—

'The Apostle of the Gentiles, in words that we have translated "too superstitious," called the Athenians "unusually God-fearing[4]," and thus he struck the one chord to which their hearts would vibrate.'

It is not disputed that, according to their own ideas of religion, the

---

[1] [Also *Phoc.* 19, 7: προελθεῖν δὲ ὡς ἐπὶ τὴν Ἑλλάδα οὐδὲ τότε ἐθάρρησαν οἱ Κελτοί.]

[2] [Cf. Dio Chrys. *Or.* XI. 156: καὶ οὐ μόνον γε τοὺς ἐν κοινῷ γινομένους (λόγους) καὶ παρατυγχανόντων ἁπάντων τῶν θεῶν. Plut. *Vit. Caes.* XI.VII: ἐκπλαγέντων δὲ τῶν παρατυχόντων.]

[3] [Of rival armies, App. *B. C.* I. 110: συμβάλλουσιν ἀλλήλοις περὶ πόλιν, ᾗ ὄνομα Σούκρων.]

[4] 'Unusually God-fearing' in Greek would be διαφερόντως θεοσεβεῖς, which very phrase I find in Plut. *Vit. Rom.* XXII: τὰ δ' ἄλλα τὸν Ῥωμύλον διαφερόντως θεοσεβῆ......ἱστοροῦσι γενέσθαι.

Athenians were *very religious*, as Pausanias (*Att.* 24, 3) testifies: 'Αθηναίοις περισσότερόν τι ἢ τοῖς ἄλλοις ἐς τὰ θεῖά ἐστι σπουδῆς. And that δεισιδαιμονία is occasionally used in a good sense cannot be denied in the face of such clear instances as Diod. Sic. I. 70: ταῦτα δ' ἔπραττεν, ἅμα μὲν εἰς δεισιδαιμονίαν καὶ θεοφιλῆ βίον τὸν βασιλέα προτρεπόμενος. But, undoubtedly, the general use of the word is *in malam partem*, to signify such a superstitious observance of signs, omens &c., as is described in Theophrastus's well-known character, 'Ο δεισιδαίμων; and, generally, the *religious feeling carried to excess.* In this sense it is expressly distinguished from and contrasted with εὐσέβεια, εὐλάβεια, and the like. Thus Plutarch (*Vit. Num.* extr.) says that Tullus Hostilius laughed at Numa's τὴν περὶ τὸ θεῖον εὐλάβειαν, as making men idle and effeminate; but did not continue in these swaggering notions (νεανιεύμασι), ἀλλ' ὑπὸ νόσου χαλεπῆς τὴν γνώμην ἀλλασσόμενος, εἰς δεισιδαιμονίαν ἐνέδωκεν οὐδέν τι τῇ κατὰ Νουμᾶν εὐσεβείᾳ προσήκουσαν. The same author (*Vit. Pericl.* VI) says: ἦν (ignorance of celestial phaenomena) ὁ φυσικὸς λόγος ἀπαλλάττων, ἀντὶ τῆς φοβερᾶς καὶ φλεγμαινούσης δεισιδαιμονίας τὴν ἀσφαλῆ μετ' ἐλπίδων ἀγαθῶν εὐσέβειαν ἐνεργάζεται, which Langhorne translates: 'The study of nature, which, instead of the frightful extravagances of superstition, implants in us a sober piety, supported by a rational hope.' Again, in the life of Alexander (LXXV), according to the same translator: 'When Alexander had once given himself up to superstition (ἐνέδωκε πρὸς τὰ θεῖα), his mind was so preyed upon by vain fears and anxieties, that he turned the least incident, which was any thing strange and out of the way, into a sign or prodigy....So true it is that though the disbelief of religion and contempt of things divine is a great evil, yet superstition is a greater' (δεινὸν μὲν ἀπιστία πρὸς τὰ θεῖα καὶ καταφρόνησις αὐτῶν, δεινὴ δ' αὖθις ἡ δεισιδαιμονία).

But there is another consideration which has not been sufficiently attended to in the discussion of this question, and which is really decisive of it; and that is the *comparative* form of the adjective. By a well-known idiom, common to the Greek and Latin languages, the comparative is used to indicate either a *deficiency* or *excess* (in both cases *slight*[1]) of the quality contained in the positive. In the former case, it may be expressed in English by 'somewhat' or 'rather'; in the latter, by 'too.' Our Translators have preferred the latter, 'too superstitious'; but as superstition is bad in every degree, and not only when it is excessive, the better rendering would seem to be that of R. V., 'somewhat superstitious'; which is a mild form of censure, but still of *censure*, not of *praise.* If the latter were intended to be conveyed, then it is evident

---

[1] Thus Diog. Laert. II. 132: ἦν δέ πως ἠρέμα καὶ δεισιδαιμονέστερος. In Latin the *slightness* is generally intimated by 'paulo' prefixed; of which the most apt example for our purpose is Hor. *Sat.* I. 9, 70:—Nulla mihi, inquam, | religio est. At mî: *sum paulo infirmior,*—which might almost be Grecized: δεισιδαιμονέστερός εἰμι.

that the comparative δεισιδαιμονεστέρους, 'somewhat religious[1],' would be quite out of place; and the superlative δεισιδαιμονεστάτους would be exclusively appropriate. Some critics (as H. Stephens quoted by Palairet) have considered the particle ὡς to be still further mitigatory of the censure contained in δεισιδαιμονεστέρους, as if it were the same as ὡς εἰπεῖν, *ut ita dicam* ; but this usage cannot be proved. It appears to be an abnormal construction depending on θεωρῶ, not unlike Matt. xiv. 5 : ὅτι ὡς προφήτην αὐτὸν εἶχον. 1 Cor. iv. 1 : ἡμᾶς λογιζέσθω ἄνθρωπος ὡς ὑπηρέτας Χριστοῦ. The usual construction of θεωρῶ is with a participle, as Diod. Sic. xiv. 13 : Λύσανδρος ...θεωρῶν τοὺς Λακεδαιμονίους μάλιστα τοῖς μαντείοις προσέχοντας[2].

Ibid. The supposed 'want of tact' shown by the Apostle at the very opening of his apology in characterizing his audience as 'somewhat superstitious' has been remarked upon by the Bishop of Lincoln in his 'Address on the R. V. of the N. T.' p. 29, who says: 'St Paul was too skilful an orator ('too much of a gentleman'—*Dr P. Schaff*) to open a speech to such a sensitively critical audience as an Athenian with words of censure.' It is, however, a curious coincidence that at the regular sittings of this very Court of Areopagus, it was forbidden to the parties or their advocates to use rhetorical arts, and in particular, to conciliate the goodwill of the judges by a flattering prooemium. This we learn from Lucian *De Gymnast.* xix : Οἱ δὲ ἔστ' ἂν μὲν περὶ τοῦ πράγματος λέγωσιν, ἀνέχεται ἡ βουλή, καθ' ἡσυχίαν ἀκούουσα· ἢν δέ τις ἢ φροίμιον εἴπῃ πρὸ τοῦ λόγου, ὡς εὐνουστέρους ἀπεργάσαιτο αὐτούς...παρελθὼν ὁ κῆρυξ κατεσιώπησεν εὐθύς. Although the Apostle was rather addressing a platform audience than pleading his cause before judges, we may suppose that the *genius loci* may have had some influence in inducing him to deliver his message μετὰ πάσης παρρησίας, and not 'with enticing words of man's wisdom.'

*XVII. 25 : θεραπεύεται] A. V. 'is worshipped.' R. V. 'is served.' The correction is supported by the following examples : Dion. Hal. *Ant.* II. 65: τά γέ τοι καλούμενα πρυτανεῖα παρ' αὐτοῖς Ἑστίας ἐστὶν ἱερὰ, καὶ θεραπεύεται (are served) πρὸς τῶν ἐχόντων τὸ μέγιστον ἐν ταῖς πόλεσι κράτος. *Ibid.* 67 : αἱ δὲ θεραπεύουσαι τὴν θεὸν παρθένοι (Vestales). Stob. *Floril.* T. xliv. 20 : ὡς οὐ τιμᾶται θεὸς ὑπ' ἀνθρώπου φαύλου, οὐδὲ θεραπεύεται δαπάναις οὐδὲ τραγῳδίαις...

Ibid. προσδεόμενός τινος] Both versions: 'as though he needed any thing.' We might add 'besides,' to express the full force of the preposition, as in the following passages: Stob. *Flor.* T. xliii. 134 : ἄριστον μὲν οὖν τὰν ὅλαν πόλιν οὕτως συντετάχθαι, ὥστε μηδενὸς ποτιδεῖσθαι ἔξωθεν.

---

[1] [Yet this is the result of the R. V. mg. 'Or, *religious*.']

[2] [Cf. *Id.* xiii. 86: Ἀμίλκας δὲ θεωρῶν τὰ πλήθη δεισιδαιμονοῦντα.]

Ibid. T. CVIII. 84: ὡς ὁ τοιοῦτος μάλιστα αὐτὸς αὐτῷ αὐτάρκης πρὸς τὸ εὖ ζῆν, καὶ διαφερόντως τῶν ἄλλων ἥκιστα ἑτέρου προσδεῖται. Plut. *Comp. Lys. c. Syll.* III: δεῖσθαι γὰρ ἐδίδαξε τὴν Σπάρτην ὧν αὐτὸς ἔμαθε μὴ προσδεῖσθαι. Diog. L. VI. 11: αὐτάρκη γὰρ τὴν ἀρετὴν εἶναι πρὸς εὐδαιμονίαν, μηδενὸς προσδεομένην. Dio Cass. XXXVIII. 8, 3: αὐτὸς μὲν γὰρ οὐδενὸς προσδεῖσθαι ἔλεγεν, ἀλλὰ καὶ σφόδρα τοῖς παροῦσιν ἀρκεῖσθαι ἐσκήπτετο.

*XVIII. 5: συνείχετο τῷ πνεύματι] 'was pressed in the spirit.' But the principal MSS. and versions agree in reading τῷ λόγῳ for τῷ πνεύματι, and are followed by R. V. 'was constrained by the word.' Kuinöl would understand, *totus occupatus erat in doctrina promulganda*, with whom agree Dean Alford and others: 'was earnestly (or closely) occupied in discoursing.' But this sense of συνέχεσθαι appears to be fictitious: at least, it is not defended by such phrases as συνέχεσθαι ἡδοναῖς, ὀδυρμῷ &c., where it is used *in malam partem*. Another example *Wisdom* XVII. 20: ὅλος ὁ κόσμος (except the land of Egypt) λαμπρῷ κατελάμπετο φωτὶ, καὶ ἀνεμποδίστοις συνείχετο ἔργοις, seems more to the purpose. But even here συνείχετο is not *occupabatur*, but (as Vulg. renders) *continebatur*, 'was held together,' was preserved from dissolution by the ordinary works of daily life, which went on without hindrance[1]. On the other hand, for Kuinöl's version the proper Greek would be διεσπᾶτο or ἀπησχολεῖτο, *distinebatur*. Comparing such passages as καὶ πῶς συνέχομαι—συνέχομαι ἐκ τῶν δύο—ἡ ἀγάπη τοῦ Χριστοῦ συνέχει ἡμᾶς—there can be little doubt that συνέχομαι here represents some strong internal feeling, which is further supported by the participle διαμαρτυρόμενος, 'as he testified.'

*XVIII. 17: οὐδὲν τούτων τῷ Γαλλίωνι ἔμελεν] Join οὐδὲν ἔμελεν, not οὐδὲν τούτων. Compare Dio Chrys. LXV. p. 611, 20: ἀλλ' ὅμως οὐδὲν αὐτῷ τούτων ἔμελεν. Diog. L. II. 34: εἰ δὲ φαῦλοι, ἡμῖν αὐτῶν μηδὲν μελήσει.

XVIII. 18: ἔτι προσμείνας ἡμέρας ἱκανάς] R. V. 'Having tarried after this yet many days.' In A. V. 'after this' is italicized, probably against the intention of the Translators, who have rendered προσμεῖναι ἐν Ἐφέσῳ (1 Tim. i. 3) by 'to abide still at Ephesus.' But there would seem to be no authority for this enforcing of the preposition, and it is not necessary with ἔτι. I would translate, 'having waited (or tarried) yet many days.' Compare LXX. (some MSS.) Jud. iii. 25: καὶ προσέμειναν αἰσχυνόμενοι. Aq. Job. iii. 9: προσμεῖναι εἰς φῶς, καὶ οὐκ ἔστιν. Aesop. *Fab.* XC, ed. de Fur.: προσμείνας δὲ αὐτὸν μικρὸν χρόνον[2].

---

[1] [Compare, for this use of συνέχεσθαι, S. Chrysost. T. XI. p. 576 D: δεικνύντες ὅτι οὐκ οἰκείᾳ δυνάμει, ἀλλὰ τῇ αὐτῶν φυλακῇ συνείχοντο καὶ περιεγίνοντο (*continebantur et incolumes evadebant*).]

[2] [Cf. Aesop. *Fab.* 258: διὸ δὴ προσέμενον ὡς μελλούσης αὐτῆς (ship) προσορμίζεσθαι. *Ibid.* 284: εὑρὼν δὴ τοὺς ὀλύνθους μηδέπω πεπείρους προσέμενεν ἕως σῦκα γίνωνται.]

*XVIII. 24: λόγιος] A. V. 'eloquent.' R. V. 'learned.' I prefer 'eloquent,' ὡς οἱ πολλοὶ λέγουσιν, ἐπὶ τοῦ δεινοῦ εἰπεῖν (Phryn.). So Plut. *Vit. Pomp.* LI: λόγιος ἐξ ἀφώνου γενόμενος. Philo *De Cherub.* p. 127: μικρὰ νόσου πρόφασις οὐ τὴν γλῶτταν ἐπήρωσεν; οὐ τὸ στόμα καὶ τῶν πάνυ λογίων ἀπέρραψεν; The other sense, ὁ τῆς ἱστορίας ἔμπειρος, is chiefly found in ˙Herodotus and the cultivators of the Attic dialect.

*XIX. 19: συνενέγκαντες τὰς βίβλους, κατέκαιον ἐνώπιον πάντων] The custom of the public burning of atheistical books is well known from profane history. Thus Diog. Laert. IX. 52 (of the writings of Protagoras at Athens): καὶ τὰ βιβλία αὐτοῦ κατέκαυσαν ἐν τῇ ἀγορᾷ, ὑπὸ κήρυκα ἀναλεξά-μενοι παρ' ἑκάστου τῶν κεκτημένων. Lucian. *Alex.* 47 : κομίσας (τὰ Ἐπικούρου βιβλία) ἐς τὴν ἀγορὰν μέσην ἔκαυσεν ἐπὶ ξύλων συκίνων...καὶ τὴν σποδὸν ἐς θάλασσαν ἐξέβαλεν. Magical books were treated in the same way, as we learn from Livy (XL. 29) 'Libri in comitio, igne a victimariis facto, in conspectu populi cremati sunt.'

XIX. 27: μέλλειν τε καὶ καθαιρεῖσθαι τὴν μεγαλειότητα (τῆς μεγαλειότητος ABℵ) αὐτῆς. A. V. 'And her magnificence should be destroyed.' If the T. R. were retained, I would not translate, 'and her magnifi-cence should be *destroyed*,' but 'should be *diminished*,' for which rendering the authority of H. Stephens may be claimed, who in his *Thes. L. G.* gives: 'Καθαιροῦμαι pass. *dejicior, evertor.* Item *imminuor*, ut Act. Ap. xix. 27[1].' Καθαιρεῖν in the sense of *minuere, detrahere, deprimere* (e.g. δόξαν, φρόνημα, τῦφον, ὄγκον, ἀλαζόνειαν) is very common, less so in the passive, of which an example is St Chrysost. T. IX. p. 682 A : 'Do not think that you are degraded (καθαιρεῖσθαι), because you stand in need of another person's help; for this rather exalts (ὑψοῖ) you.' But assuming τῆς μεγαλειότητος to be the true reading, I do not think this need make any difference in the sense, if we suppose the genitive to depend on τι understood. The pronoun is expressed in Diod. Sic. IV. 8: καθαιρεῖν τι τῆς τοῦ θεοῦ (Hercules) δόξης. XVIII. 4: ἵνα δὲ μὴ δόξῃ διὰ τῆς ἰδίας γνώμης καθαιρεῖν τι τῆς Ἀλεξάνδρου δόξης. If, in our text, the reading were μέλλειν τε καὶ καθαιρεῖσθαί τι τῆς μ. αὐτῆς, we should have no difficulty in translating, 'And that aught should be diminished from her magni-ficence'; but τι is sometimes omitted with verbs of a similar character. Thus Matt. ix. 16: αἴρει γὰρ τὸ πλήρωμα αὐτοῦ ἀπὸ τοῦ ἱματίου. Plut. *Vit. Marcell.* XXIV : μὴ τῆς λύπης ἀφελεῖν, ἀλλὰ τῷ φόβῳ προσθεῖναι. Id. *Vit. Cat. Maj.* XI : ἡ μὲν ἀρχὴ τῷ Σκηπίωνι, τῆς αὐτοῦ μᾶλλον ἢ τῆς Κάτωνος ἀφελοῦσα δόξης, ἐν ἀπραξίᾳ...διῆλθεν. For the same construction with καθαιρεῖν, *imminuere*, I would refer to Plut. *Vit. Gracc.* III : τοσοῦτον οὖν

---

[1] [In this sense it is opposed to αὔ-ξεσθαι. App. *B. C.* III. 64 : τὴν μὲν Πομ-πηΐου μοῖραν αὐξόντων, τὴν δὲ Καίσαρος καθαιρούντων. II. 29 : τὴν δημαρχίαν, ἐς ἀσθενέστατον ὑπὸ Σύλλα καθῃρημένην, ἀναγαγόντι αὖθις ἐπὶ τὸ ἀρχαῖον.]

ἐξεβιάσαντο τὸν δῆμον οἱ δυνατοί, καὶ τῆς ἐλπίδος τοῦ Γαΐου καθεῖλον, 'that (ὅσον) he was not first, as he expected, but fourth on the poll[1].'
Another rendering of the corrected reading is adopted by Dean Alford and the Revisers : 'And that she should be deposed from her magnificence.' Against which it may be urged that the act of *deposition* (generally from some *office* or *government*) being single, not continuous, would seem to require the aorist καθαιρεθῆναι; and also to be followed by ἀπό. Thus Luke i. 52: καθεῖλε δυνάστας ἀπὸ θρόνων. Dan. v. 20: κατηνέχθη ἀπὸ τοῦ θρόνου τῆς βασιλείας[2].

*XIX. 33: ἐκ δὲ τοῦ ὄχλου] R. V. margin : 'and *some* of the multitude instructed Alexander.' See on Matt. xiv. 8.

Ibid. κατασείσας τὴν χεῖρα] 'beckoned with the hand.' Rather, 'waved his hand,' 'beckoned' being reserved for νεύειν and its compounds. Compare Plut. *Vit. Pomp.* LXXIII : κατασείουσι τὰ ἱμάτια καὶ χεῖρας ὀρέγουσι (to attract attention at sea). Philostr. *Imag.* I. 6 (of Cupids hunting a hare): ὁ μὲν κρότῳ χειρῶν, ὁ δὲ κεκραγώς, ὁ δὲ κατασείων τὴν χλαμύδα[3].

XIX. 35: καταστείλας τὸν ὄχλον] A. V. 'had appeased (R. V. quieted) the people.' Neither of these harmonizes so well with O. T. phraseology, as ' stilled.' Thus Num. xiii. 30: ' Caleb stilled (κατεσιώπησε) the people.' Neh. viii. 11 : 'The Levites stilled the people.' Psal. lxv. 8: 'Which stilleth (Aq. καταστέλλων) the noise of the seas...and the tumult of the people.' Psal. lxxxix. 10: ' Thou stillest (Ο'. καταπραΰνεις, Sym. καταστέλλεις) them.'

Ibid. νεωκόρον] A. V. 'a worshipper,' after the Vulg. *cultricem.* R. V. 'temple-keeper,' which seems wanting in dignity. It is an official title, and might, perhaps, be rendered 'custodian of the temple (or worship)[4].'

Ibid. καὶ τοῦ Διοπετοῦς (sic)] A. V. 'And of the image which fell down from Jupiter.' R. V. the same, but gives the right rendering in the margin : ' Or, *from heaven*.' Such words as διοπετές, *de caelo delapsum*, and διοσημία, *prodigiosa tempestas*, should always be printed with a small initial letter. Compare Dion. Hal. *Ant.* II. 71 : ἐν δὲ ταῖς πέλταις ἃς οἱ σάλιοι φοροῦσι, πολλαῖς πάνυ οὔσαις, μίαν εἶναι λέγουσι διοπετῆ (afterwards

---

[1] [Cf. Dio. Chrys. *Or.* LVII. 571, 17 : καὶ ἐβούλετο ταπεινῶσαι καὶ τοῦ φρονήματος, εἰ δύναιτο, καθελεῖν—ubi Cobet requirit ἀφελεῖν.]

[2] [Cf. Lucian. *Rhet. Praec.* 3: ἦρχε μὲν γὰρ ἤδη Ἀλέξανδρος Περσῶν μετὰ τὴν ἐν Ἀρβήλοις μάχην Δαρεῖον καθῃρη-

κώς ('having deposed,' not ' post devictum Darium ').]

[3] [Cf. Lucian. *Scyth.* 11 : καὶ ἐπισεῖσαι χρὴ τὴν χεῖρα, τοῦτο μόνον...' you have only to wave your hand, and your success is ensured.']

[4] [Latin : *aedituus*.]

explained by θεόπεμπτον)[1]. Pausan. *Att.* 26, 6 (quoted by Wetstein): τὸ δὲ ἁγιώτατον...ἐστιν ᾿Αθηνᾶς ἄγαλμα ἐν τῇ νῦν ἀκροπόλει...φήμη δὲ ἐς αὐτὸ ἔχει πεσεῖν ἐκ τοῦ οὐρανοῦ. Plut. *Vit. Num.* XIII : ἱστορεῖται χαλκῆν πέλτην ἐξ οὐρανοῦ καταφερομένην εἰς τὰς Νουμᾶ πεσεῖν χεῖρας, who had eleven others made exactly like it καὶ σχῆμα, καὶ μέγεθος, καὶ μορφήν, ὅπως ἄπορον εἴη τῷ κλέπτῃ δι᾿ ὁμοιότητα τοῦ διοπετοῦς ἐπιτυχεῖν.

*XIX. 36 : μηδὲν προπετὲς πράττειν] Compare Dion. Hal. *Ant.* XI. 29: οὐδὲν οὔτε προπετὲς οὔτε βίαιον πέπρακταί μοι. Diod. Sic. T. IX. p. 389 ed. Bip.: καὶ μηδὲν ταχέως πράττειν. Charit. Aphrod. VI. 3: ὡς εἰπών τι προπετές. Stob. *Floril.* T. III. 79 (Periandri dictum): ἐπισφαλὲς προπέτεια. Diod. Sic. XIII. 23: ἢ τίς ἧττον τοῦ μὲν ὤμοῦ τὸν ἔλεον, τῆς δὲ προπετείας τὴν εὐλάβειαν ἔσχηκε; In LXX. the word is usually found in connexion with στόμα or χείλη; and in Eccles. V. 1 for μὴ σπεῦδε ἐπὶ στόματί σου Symmachus has μὴ προπετὴς γίνου τῷ στόματί σου.

*XIX. 40 : ἐγκαλεῖσθαι στάσεως πέρι τῆς σήμερον] So the preposition should be accented, according to the textual rendering of R. V. ᾿Εγκαλεῖσθαι περὶ τῆς στάσεως is a good construction (see Ch. xxiii. 29, xxvi. 7), and περὶ is often placed *eleganter* after its noun; more rarely between the noun and its epithet, as Aristoph. *Lys.* 1289: ἡσυχίας πέρι τῆς μεγαλόφρονος | ἣν ἐποίησε θεὰ Κύπρις. *Pax* 105 : ἐρησόμενος ἐκεῖνον ῾Ελλήνων πέρι | ἁπαξαπάντων ὅ τι ποιεῖν βουλεύεται.

XX. 15: παρεβάλομεν εἰς Σάμον] A. V. 'We arrived at Samos.' R. V. 'We touched at Samos.' But this is a very doubtful sense of the word. In a list of terms signifying *appellere*, J. Pollux (I. 102) includes προσβαλεῖν, but not παραβαλεῖν. Of the numerous examples given by Wetstein, *appellere* will not suit Herod. VII. 179: παρέβαλε νηυσὶ τῇσι ἄριστα πλεούσῃσι δέκα ἰθὺ Σκιάθου; nor yet Thucyd. III. 32: καὶ ἐλπίδα οὐδὲ τὴν ἐλαχίστην εἶχον, μήποτε, ᾿Αθηναίων τῆς θαλάσσης κρατούντων, ναῦς Πελοποννησίων ἐς ᾿Ιωνίαν παραβαλεῖν; in both which places it can only mean *trajicere, to cross over*, a sense which is also suitable to most of the other quotations, as well as to Joseph. *Ant.* XVIII. 6, 4: ᾿Αγρίππας δὲ εἰς Ποτιόλους παραβαλὼν ἐπιστολὴν εἰς Τιβέριον Καίσαρα γράφει .. ἀξιῶν ἔφεσιν αὐτῷ γενέσθαι εἰς Καπρέας παραβαλεῖν[2].

[1] [Cf. *Ibid.* XI. 27: πρᾶγμα ἀμήχανον ὑπελάμβανον εἶναι πολεμίους ἐπιφανῆναι τοῖς σφετέροις ἀφανεῖς ὥσπερ πτηνούς τινας ἢ διοπετεῖς.]

[2] [Cf. Plut. *Vit. Demetr.* XXXIX: ἔπειτα Κλεωνύμου τοῦ Σπαρτιάτου παραβαλόντος ἐς Θήβας μετὰ στρατιᾶς (where Langhorne absurdly, 'having *thrown* themselves into Thebes'). *Vit. Dion.* IV: θείᾳ τινὶ τύχῃ Πλάτωνος εἰς Σικελίαν παραβαλόντος (which is afterwards explained, δαίμων τις, ὡς ἔοικεν...ἐκόμισεν ἐξ ᾿Ιταλίας εἰς Συρακούσας Πλάτωνα). But in the two following examples the word seems rather to be used in the sense of *passing by* a place. Plut. *Vit. Arat.* XII: τῷ ᾿Αράτῳ γίνεταί τις εὐτυχία, ῾Ρωμαϊκῆς νεὼς παραβαλούσης κατὰ τὸν τόπον. Dio. Chrys. *Or.* XXXII. 375, 39: (the Sirens) ἐν ἐρήμῳ ἦσαν πελάγει...ἐπὶ σκοπέλου τινὸς, ὅπου μηδεὶς ῥᾳδίως παρέβαλλε.]

9—2

*XX. 20: ὡς οὐδὲν ὑπεστειλάμην τῶν συμφερόντων, τοῦ μὴ ἀναγγεῖλαι ὑμῖν καὶ διδάξαι ὑμᾶς] A. V. 'And how I kept back nothing that was profitable unto you, but have shewed you and have taught you.' R. V. 'how that I shrank not from declaring unto you anything that was profitable, and teaching you.' The A. V. is as close to the letter and spirit of the Greek as can be desired, but the latter clause might be improved by rendering, 'so as not to declare it to you, and to teach you.' The Revisers have preferred the non-biblical phrase 'I shrank not' on account of v. 27, where 'I kept not back' would not suit. But in so doing they have obliterated in v. 20 the exquisite Greek idiom, οὐδὲν ὑποστέλλεσθαι, οὐδὲν ὑποστειλάμενον εἰπεῖν, of which a few examples (out of a host) may be adduced. Thus Plut. De Adulat. XVIII. (T. II, p. 60 c): δεῖν ἐλευθέρους ὄντας παρρησιάζεσθαι, καὶ μηδὲν ὑποστέλλεσθαι μηδ' ἀποσιωπᾶν τῶν συμφερόντων (where ὑποστέλλεσθαι is synonymous with ἀποσιωπᾶν). Lucian. Pseudol. 2: καὶ μηδὲν ὑποστελουμένῳ τὸ μὴ οὐχὶ πάντα ἐξειπεῖν. Demosth. p. 54 extr.: νῦν τε ἃ γιγνώσκω πάνθ' ἁπλῶς οὐδὲν ὑποστειλάμενος πεπαρρησίασμαι. Dio. Chrys. Or. XI. 158: ὃς δ' ἂν ἀληθῶς λέγῃ τι, θαρρῶν καὶ οὐδὲν ὑποστελλόμενος λέγει.

In v. 27 οὐ γὰρ ὑπεστειλάμην τοῦ μὴ ἀναγγεῖλαι ὑμῖν, the verb being intransitive, its English equivalent must be varied, and the A. V. 'I shunned not' is at least as good as 'I shrank not.'

*XX. 23: ὅτι δεσμά με καὶ θλίψεις μένουσιν] Both versions: 'abide me.' A. V. in marg. 'Or, wait for me.' Perhaps 'await me' would be more in harmony with present usage. Palairet gives two good examples of the Greek word being so used. Anthol. I. 33, 32 (T. I, p. 125 Jacobs. 1794): παῦσαι· ἐπεί σε μένει δάκρυα καὶ κατόπιν. Ach. Tat. V. 2: ἔμενεν ἡμᾶς καὶ ἄλλο τῆς τύχης γυμνάσιον.

XX. 24: ἀλλ' οὐδενὸς λόγον ποιοῦμαι, οὐδὲ ἔχω τὴν ψυχήν μου τιμίαν ἐμαυτῷ] The reading of BCℵ¹, which is adopted by most modern editors, and followed by R. V., ἀλλ' οὐδενὸς λόγου ποιοῦμαι τὴν ψυχὴν τιμίαν ἐμαυτῷ, has every appearance of having consisted originally of two members, which, through the accidental omission of one or more words, have become fused into one. The unsuccessful attempts which have been made to construe the amalgamated sentence as a single clause plainly show this. Thus Dean Alford's 'I hold my life of no account, nor precious to me,' and the R. V. 'I hold not my life of any account, as dear unto myself,' do, in fact, break up the clause into two by the interpolation of οὐδὲ and ὡς respectively; to say nothing of the tautology. On the other hand the T. R. while yielding a faultless construction, and gets rid of the tautology, the first clause, ἀλλ' οὐδενὸς λόγον ποιοῦμαι, plainly referring to the minor evils, the δεσμὰ καὶ θλίψεις mentioned in the preceding verse, which we should have expected the speaker to allude to before expressing his contempt for death itself. The principal difficulty in this reading is, that if the words οὐδὲ ἔχω had once formed a part of the original text, there is no apparent reason for their subsequent omission. This, however, does not apply to other supplements, in which the verb is in the *middle* voice, so forming a clear ὁμοιοτέλευτον with ποιοῦμαι. In a paper printed in 1875 the present writer suggested several of these, giving the preference to ἡγοῦμαι, and quoting (besides the Pauline use of the word) several examples of τίμιον ἡγεῖσθαί τι from profane authors, and a very remarkable one of the entire phrase τιμίαν ἡγεῖσθαι τὴν ψυχήν from Dion. Hal. *Ant.* v. 30 (due to Wetstein): εἰ φίλους ἀντὶ πολεμίων, ἔφη, ποιήσαιο τοὺς ἄνδρας, τιμιωτέραν ἡγησάμενος τὴν σαυτοῦ ψυχὴν τῆς καθόδου τῶν σὺν Ταρκυνίοις φυγάδων.

The following is a copy of the Sinaitic MS. on this place, substituting λόγον for λόγου, and inserting the line supposed to be omitted:—

```
        ... ΑΛΛΟΥΔΕΝΟC
            ΛΟΓΟΝΠΟΙΟΥΜΑΙ
            ΟΥΔΕΗΓΟΥΜΑΙ
            ΤΗΝΨΥΧΗΝΤΙΜΙ
            ΑΝΕΜΑΥΤΩΩCΤΕ
```

The A. V. of οὐδενὸς λόγον ποιοῦμαι, 'None of these things move me,' though somewhat free, admirably expresses the sense and spirit of the Greek; and is so endeared to the English reader by long familiarity and frequent quotation, that it would be injudicious, not to say, irreverent, to meddle with it. Its literal counterpart may be found in Plut. *Vit. Pericl.* XXXIV : πλὴν ὑπ' οὐδενὸς ἐκινήθη τῶν τοιούτων (the importunity of his friends and the scoffs of his enemies) ὁ Περικλῆς[1].

*Ibid. οὐδενὸς λόγον ποιοῦμαι] The more common formula is οὐδένα λόγον ποιοῦμαί τινος (whether person or thing), but that of the T. R. in this place is found in Dion. Hal. *Ant.* IX. 50: πολλὰ δεομένων τῶν πρεσβευτῶν...λόγον οὐδενὸς αὐτῶν ποιησάμενος...

XX. 28: ἣν περιεποιήσατο διὰ τοῦ ἰδίου αἵματος] A. V. 'Which he [hath] purchased with his own blood.' To distinguish περιεποιήσατο from ἐκτήσατο or ἠγόρασε, we may translate, 'Which he gat him (*sibi comparavit*) through his own blood.' (Compare Eph. i. 7: 'we have redemption through his blood.') So also in 1 Tim. iii. 13 (the only other place) for 'purchase to themselves (περιποιοῦνται ἑαυτοῖς) a good degree,' may be substituted 'get themselves.' Compare Gen. xxxi. 18: 'all his goods which he had gotten (περιεποιήσατο).' Diod. Sic. XVI. 7: ἡ δὲ πόλις ἀξιόλογον ἀξίωμα περιποιησαμένη. 34: καὶ τοὺς σατράπας μεγάλαις μάχαις δυσὶ νικήσας, περιεποιήσατο μεγάλην δόξαν ἑαυτῷ τε καὶ τοῖς Βοιωτοῖς.

**XX. 34: αἱ χεῖρες αὗται] 'these hands' (stretching them out). Compare Philost. *Her.* p. 162 (ed. Boiss.): εἰπόντος γοῦν ποτε πρὸς αὐτὸν Ἀχιλλέως, Ὦ Παλάμηδες, ἀγροικότερος φαίνῃ τοῖς πολλοῖς, ὅτι μὴ πέπασαι τὸν θεραπεύσοντα, Τί οὖν ΤΑΥΤΑ, ἔφη, ὦ Ἀχιλλεῦ; τὼ χεῖρε ἄμφω προτείνας.

---

[1] [Cf. Id. *Dion.* XXXI : καὶ, τὸ μάλιστα κινῆσαν αὐτόν....]

*XXI. 1 : ἀποσπασθέντας ἀπ' αὐτῶν] A. V. 'after we were gotten from them.' R. V. 'when we were parted from them.' Perhaps 'hardly parted' might be not unsuitable to such an occasion, although the simple word is all that is required in such cases as Luke xxii. 41 : 'and he was parted (A. V. withdrawn) from them about a stone's cast.' 2 Macc. xii. 10 : ἐκεῖθεν δὲ ἀποσπασθέντων σταδίους θ̄. Polyaen. Strat. VI. 16, 4 : ὡς δὲ μακρὰν ἀπεσπάσθησαν ἄχρι πελάγους διώκοντες. Perhaps the nearest example to our place is Eurip. Alcest. 287 : οὐκ ἠθέλησα ζῆν ἀποσπασθεῖσά σου; but even this does not warrant, in a simple narration, such a sensational rendering as 'after we had torn ourselves away from them' (Grot., Hemsterh., and some English versions); not to mention that this sense is more appropriate to the *middle* than to the *passive* form : e.g. Dion. Hal. Ant. V. 55 : ἄγεσθαι ἐπὶ τὸν θάνατον, ἀποσπωμένους γυναικῶν τε καὶ παίδων καὶ πατέρων. Virg. Aen. II. 434 : *Divellimur inde* | *Iphitus et Pelias mecum.*

*XXI. 3 : ἀναφάναντες (T. R. ἀναφανέντες) δὲ τὴν Κύπρον] A. V. 'when we had discovered Cyprus.' R. V. 'when we had come in sight of Cyprus.' 'It is a nautical term for bringing the land in view by *approaching* it, and so bringing it up, as it were, above the horizon'—*Humphry.* In departing from a place the opposite effect takes place ; as Lucian. V. H. II. 38 : ἐπεὶ δ' ἀπεκρύψαμεν αὐτούς. Synes. Ep. IV : νότος λαμπρὸς, ὑφ' οὗ ταχὺ μὲν τὴν γῆν ἀπεκρύπτομεν. Virg. Aen. III. 291 : *aerias Phaeacum abscondimus arces.*

*Ibid. ἐκεῖσε γὰρ ἦν τὸ πλοῖον ἀποφορτιζόμενον τὸν γόμον] On the present part. ἀποφορτιζόμενον see on 2 Pet. ii. 9. The more common meaning of the word is 'to throw overboard,' as Philo Tom. II. p. 413 : κυβερνήτης δὲ χειμώνων ἐπιγινομένων ἀποφορτίζεται. Greg. Naz. Or. XXVII. p. 471 D (ad opulentos): ἀποφόρτισαί τι τῆς νηός, ἵνα πλέῃς κουφότερος. For 'unloading' is commonly quoted Dion. Hal. Ant. III. 44: αἱ δὲ μείζους (ὁλκάδες) ἐπ' ἀγκυρῶν σαλεύουσαι ταῖς ποταμηγοῖς ἀπογεμίζονταί τε καὶ ἀποφορτίζονται σκαφαῖς, where, however, Cod. Vat. has ἀντιφορτίζονται, 'take in a return cargo.' ἐκεῖσε=ἐκεῖ Ch. xxii. 5. Job xxxix. 29. Demosth. p. 1283, 21 : τὴν μὲν ναῦν εἰς Ῥόδον κατεκόμισε, καὶ τὸν γόμον ἐκεῖσε ἐξελόμενος ἀπέδοτο.

XXI. 7 : ἡμεῖς δὲ τὸν πλοῦν διανύσαντες ἀπὸ Τύρου] A. V. 'And when we had finished our course (R. V. the voyage) from Tyre.' From the comparison of a large number of places in Xenophon Ephesius (with whom the phrase is a very favourite one) I arrive at the correct version : 'And we, continuing our voyage from Tyre.' The following are some of the places, from the edition of Locella :—P. 19 : κἀκείνην μὲν τὴν ἡμέραν οὐρίῳ χρησάμενοι πνεύματι, διανύσαντες τὸν πλοῦν, εἰς Σάμον κατήντησαν (this was the first day's sail of a long voyage). P. 55 : ἔπλεον εἰς Ἀσίαν· καὶ μέχρι μὲν τινος διήνυστο εὐτυχῶς ὁ πλοῦς (afterwards they were wrecked). P. 86 : ὁ δὲ διανύσας τὸν ἀπ' Αἰγύπτου πλοῦν, εἰς αὐτὴν μὲν Ἰταλίαν οὐκ ἔρχεται (he was sailing from Egypt to Italy, but the wind drove him out of his course). P. 107: ἀναγόμενος, καὶ διανύσας τὸν πλοῦν, τὰ μὲν πρῶτα ἐπὶ τῆς Σικελίας ἔρχεται (only the first stage of the voyage). P. 111: ἀνήγετο, καὶ διανύσας μάλα ἀσμένως τὸν πλοῦν, οὐ πολλαῖς ἡμέραις εἰς Ῥόδον καταίρει· τῇ δ' ἑξῆς ἤδη μὲν περὶ τὸν πλοῦν ἐγίνοντο (but put it off on account of a festival). In all these cases there is no question of *finishing* the voyage, but only of *continuing* or *performing* it.

XXI. 15: ἐπισκευασάμενοι (T. R. ἀποσκ.[1])] A. V. 'We took up our carriages (baggage).' I should prefer, 'Having furnished ourselves for the journey.' Hesychius explains the word by εὐτρεπισθέντες; St Chrysostom by τὰ πρὸς τὴν ὁδοιπορίαν λαβόντες. Compare Jerem. xlvi. (Gr. xxvi.) 19: גּוֹלָה עֲשִׂי לָךְ כְּלֵי. Ο'. σκεύη ἀποικισμοῦ ποίησον σεαυτῇ. A. V. 'Furnish thyself to go into captivity.'

*XXI. 28: βοηθεῖτε] Wetstein quotes from Aristoph. *Lysist.* (sic): γείτονες, βοηθεῖτε δεῦρο, but there is no such reference in Caravella's Index Aristoph. Also from Meleager (Anthol. T. I. p. 8 Jacobs. 1794) Ὤνθρωποι, βωθεῖτε. I add Charit. Aphrod. I. 8: βοηθεῖτε. ἐπεὶ δὲ πολλάκις αὐτῆς κεκραγυίας, οὐδὲν ἐγένετο πλέον...

*XXI. 35: ὅτε δὲ ἐγένετο ἐπὶ τοὺς ἀναβαθμούς] Both versions: 'and when he came upon the stairs.' The ancient versions, more correctly, 'and when he came TO the stairs.' Vulg. *cum venisset ad gradus.* Pesch. ܟܕ ܡܛܝ ܠܕܪ̈ܓܐ. Philox. ܟܕ ܗܘܐ ܠܘܬ ܕܪ̈ܓܐ. Cf. Luke xxiv. 22: γενόμεναι ὄρθριαι ἐπὶ τὸ μνημεῖον, 'which were early at the sepulchre.'

*XXI. 37: Ἑλληνιστὶ γινώσκεις;] A. V. 'Canst thou speak Greek?' R. V. 'Dost thou know Greek?' Dean Burgon (*Revision Revised*, p. 149) instances this as a proof of the Revisers' 'want of familiarity with the refinements of the Greek language.' He rightly explains the full expression to be, 'Dost thou know [how to talk] in Greek?' and quotes (from Wetstein) the *plena locutio*, as occurring in Nehem. xiii. 24: οἱ υἱοὶ αὐτῶν ἥμισυ λαλοῦντες Ἀζωτιστί, καὶ οὐκ εἰσὶν ἐπιγινώσκοντες λαλεῖν Ἰουδαϊστί. For the elliptical form we are referred to Xen. *Cyrop.* VII. 5, 31: τοὺς δ' ἐν ταῖς οἰκίαις κηρύττειν τοὺς Συριστὶ ἐπισταμένους ἔνδον μένειν. Other examples are St Chrysost. T. IX. p. 200 E: ὅρα, Ἕλλησιν εὐαγγελίζονται. εἰκὸς γὰρ αὐτούς τε λοιπὸν εἰδέναι Ἑλληνιστί, καὶ ἐν Ἀντιοχείᾳ τοιούτους εἶναι πολλούς. Xen. *Anab.* VII. 6, 8: (Seuthes Thrax) ἐν ἐπηκόῳ εἱστήκει ἔχων ἑρμηνέα· ξυνίει δὲ καὶ αὐτὸς Ἑλληνιστὶ τὰ πλεῖστα, where the full construction would be τῶν Ἑλληνιστὶ λαλουμένων. The Vulgate has here *Graece nosti?* and *Graece scire, nescire* is the ordinary Latin idiom,

---

[1] [Cf. Plut. *Vit. Dion.* XXVI: ἀποσκευασάμενος οὖν τὰ περιόντα τῶν ὅπλων καὶ τῶν φορτίων ἐκεῖ and requesting Synalus to forward them when there was an opportunity.]

which would be not at all surprising in the mouth of the Roman 'chief captain,' as reported by the Latinizing St Luke.

XXII. 18: οὐ παραδέξονταί σου τὴν μαρτυρίαν περὶ ἐμοῦ] The reading of ABℵ (μαρτυρίαν without the article) is thus represented by R. V. 'They will not receive of thee testimony concerning me.' But this, I think, would require παρὰ σοῦ. The preposition in παραδέξονται is necessary to express *acceptance* or *favourable reception*, as Mark iv. 20 (where R. V. 'accept'), 1 Tim. v. 19; and has therefore spent its force.

XXII. 23: ῥιπτούντων τὰ ἱμάτια] A. V. 'And cast off their clothes.' R. V. 'And threw off their garments,' as preparing to stone them (Grot.). But ῥῖψαι τὰ ἱμ. is *to throw them away*, for the purpose of flight[1], or of running faster; and those who put off their garments at the stoning of Stephen did not throw away, but gave them to Saul to take care of. Amongst the gestures of an excited crowd the *shaking* or *tossing* of their garments (Lat. *jactatio togarum*) is often included. Wetstein quotes Aristaen. *Ep.* I. 26: ὁ δὲ δῆμος (to express admiration of a dancer) ἀνέστηκέ τε ὀρθὸς ὑπὸ θαύματος...καὶ τὼ χεῖρε κινεῖ, καὶ τὴν ἐσθῆτα σοβεῖ. Philostr. p. 818: καὶ οἱ μὲν τὼ χεῖρε ἀνασείουσι, οἱ δὲ τὴν ἐσθῆτα. Lucian. *De Salt.* 83 (where an ὀρχηστής overdoes the part of Ajax μαινόμενος): ἀλλὰ τό γε θέατρον ἅπαν συνεμεμήνει τῷ Αἴαντι, καὶ ἐπήδων, καὶ ἐβόων, καὶ τὰς ἐσθῆτας ἀπερρίπτουν ('ubi legere mallem ἀνερρίπτουν[2], spectatores enim non *abjecisse*, sed *succussisse, sursum jecisse* vestes credibile est.'—*Bast.*)[3]. Though there is no good example of this use of ῥιπτεῖν, it was so understood by St Chrysostom: καὶ τὰ ἱμάτια ἐκτινάσσοντες, φησί, κονιορτὸν ἔβαλον, using the same word as Nehem. v. 13, Acts xviii. 6[4].

*XXII. 25: ὡς δὲ προέτειναν αὐτὸν τοῖς ἱμᾶσιν] A. V. 'and as they bound him with thongs.' R. V. 'and when they had tied him up with the thongs.' 'Dr Bloomfield quotes from Dio. Cass. XLIX. 22 (p. 405 E): Ἀντίγονον ἐμαστίγωσε σταυρῷ προδήσας; and explains rightly, I think, the προ in both verbs to allude to the *position* of the prisoner, which was bent forward, and tied (the position?) with a sort of gear made of leather to an inclined post'—*Dean Alford*. But in the passage from Dio. Cass. προδήσας is a *vox nihili*, and the true reading is προσδήσας, as quoted by Pearson, *On the Creed*, Article IV. p. 203, ed. 1723. The force of the preposition, therefore, still remains obscure, unless we adopt Jos. Scaliger's explanation: 'Legimus in comoedia, *Ego plectar pendens* (h. e. μετέωρος).

1 [Cf. Plut. *Vit. Tim.* XXXIV: ἔθει ῥίψας τὸ ἱμάτιον διὰ μέσου τοῦ θεάτρου.]
2 [Cf. Lucian. *De Gym.* 27: ἐκεῖνο τοίνυν (discum) ἄνω τε ἀναρριπτοῦσιν εἰς τὸν ἀέρα καὶ εἰς τὸ πόρρω.]
3 See Boiss. ad Aristaen. *Epist.* p. 580. Ed.
4 [Cf. Dio. Chrys. *Or.* VII. p. 103,

40: ὥστε οἱ μὲν αὐτῶν περιτρέχοντες ἐδέοντο· οἱ δὲ τὰ ἱμάτια ἐρρίπτουν ὑπὸ τοῦ φόβου. *Or.* XXXII. p. 389, 40: (said of spectators in a theatre) πηδῶντες καὶ μαινόμενοι καὶ παίοντες ἀλλήλους, καὶ ἀπόρρητα λέγοντες...καὶ τὰ ὄντα [ἱμάτια] ῥιπτοῦντες καὶ γυμνοὶ βαδίζοντες ἀπὸ τῆς θέας ἐνίοτε.]

Illud *pendere* est ἱμᾶσι προτείνεσθαι, *funibus utrinque a terra levari*, non autem stantem funibus ad columnam alligari, ut pictorum natio somniat[1].' An extract from Ach. Tat. VII. 12 lends considerable support to this idea : ἄρτι δέ μου δεθέντος (cf. *v.* 29) καὶ τῆς ἐσθῆτος τοῦ σώματος γεγυμνωμένου, μετεώρου τε ἐκ τῶν βρόχων κρεμαμένου, καὶ τῶν μὲν μάστιγας κομιζόντων, τῶν δὲ πῦρ καὶ τροχόν....

*XXIII. 10 : εὐλαβηθεὶς μὴ διασπασθῇ] Those critics who pin their faith on the *consensus* of certain MSS. require us to believe that εὐλαβηθεὶς is a gloss on φοβηθείς, and not the reverse. We have often had occasion to notice resemblances between the diction of Diod. Sic. and that of St Luke, and we find an instance in the use of this word. As, for example, XII. 60 : Δημοσθένης εὐλαβούμενος μὴ καὶ τὸν Ναύπακτον ἐκπολιορκήσωσι. XIV. 44 : Διονύσιος...εὐλαβεῖτο μήποτε τῶν Καρχηδονίων διαβάντων εἰς Σικελίαν, ἐκείνοις προσθῶνται. XIX. 55 : ταῦτ᾽ οὖν εὐλαβηθείς. XX. 36 : τὸν ἀπὸ τῆς συγκλήτου φθόνον εὐλαβηθείς.

Examples of διασπᾶσθαι in a literal sense, from the violence of an infuriated multitude, are not wanting in the history of popular tumults. Thus in the account of the riotous proceedings which followed on the death of Julius Caesar, we read (Plut. *Vit. Caes.* LXVIII) ἄλλοι δ᾽ ἐφοίτων πανταχόσε τῆς πόλεως, συλλαβεῖν καὶ διασπάσασθαι τοὺς ἄνδρας ζητοῦντες. One of their victims was Cinna the poet (*Vit. Brut.* XX) who, ἐκκομιζομένου τοῦ σώματος αἰδούμενος μὴ παρεῖναι, προῆλθεν εἰς τὸν ὄχλον ἤδη διαγριαινόμενον, ὀφθεὶς δὲ διεσπάσθη, being taken for his namesake the conspirator[2]. Appian (*B. C.* II. 147) tells the same story with an addition by way of embellishment : Κίνναν...διέσπασαν θηριωδῶς, καὶ οὐδὲν αὐτοῦ μέρος ἐς ταφὴν εὑρέθη.

*XXIII. 14. Ἀναθέματι ἀνεθεματίσαμεν ἑαυτούς] Both versions, 'We have bound ourselves under a great curse.' Dele 'great.' It is not the Hebrew idiom (as in Deut. xx. 17 : ἀναθέματι ἀναθεματιεῖτε αὐτούς, 'ye shall utterly destroy them'), but ἀναθέματι is added ἐκ τοῦ πλεονάζοντος, like εὐχὴν εὔξασθαι, etc. Suidas[3] : ἔστι δὲ Ἀττικὸν τὸ σχῆμα, τὸ εἰπόντα τὸ πρᾶγμα ἐπαγαγεῖν τὸ ἀπὸ τοῦ πράγματος ὄνομα· ὡς τὸ ὕβριν ὑβρίζειν κ.τ.λ.[4]

*XXIII. 16 : παραγενόμενος καὶ εἰσελθὼν εἰς τὴν παρεμβολήν] A. V. 'He went and entered into the castle.' R. V. in margin proposes another rendering : 'Having come in *upon them*, and he entered.' But this would surely require ἤκουσε δέ instead of ἀκούσας δέ, and ἐπιστὰς αὐτοῖς for παραγενόμενος. As to how he came to hear of the plot, Ammonius gives the right explanation : ἤκουσεν ὡς Ἰουδαῖος ὤν, καὶ συνὼν αὐτοῖς.

[1] Scaliger, Bk II. Ep. 146. Ed.

[2] [Shakespeare *Jul. Caes.* III. 3 : 'Truly, my name is Cinna. 1st Cit. Tear him to pieces; he's a conspirator.']

[3] Dr H. Jackson points out that this

quotation is to be found *s.v.* ληρεῖς. Ed.

[4] Quoted by Vorstius, *De Hebraismis N. T. Comm.* cap. xxxv. p. 632 ed. Fischer, Lips. 1778. This reference, as well as the other in note [1], I owe to Mr W. Aldis Wright. Ed.

XXIII. 30: λέγειν τὰ πρὸς αὐτὸν ἐπὶ σοῦ] A. V. 'To say before thee what *they had* against him.' Literally, 'the things concerning him,' as τὰ πρὸς θεόν, 'the things which pertain to God' (Rom. xv. 17). But the preposition may often be rendered 'against,' when the context implies *opposition*, as Ch. xxiv. 19: εἴ τι ἔχοιεν πρός με, 'if they had aught against me[1].' Col. iii. 13: ἐάν τις πρός τινα ἔχῃ μομφήν, 'if any man have a quarrel against any.' The A. V. therefore requires no alteration, except that the words 'they had' need not be italicized. But the T. R., though yielding an excellent sense, is not exempt from difficulties on the part of the MSS., of which B simply omits τά, and Aℵ read λέγειν αὐτοὺς ἐπὶ σοῦ, supported by the Vulgate, *ut dicant apud te.* Of the Syriac versions Philox. reads τὰ πρὸς αὐτὸν (ܣܠܐܝ ܠܘܗܝ); Pesch. 'that they should come and speak with him' (ܣܠܘܗܝ ܢܐܬܘܢ ܕܐܦ), probably as B. The R. V. as usual follows the same MS. 'charging his accusers also to speak against him before thee.' If this reading *must* be adopted, since it seems superfluous to charge accusers to speak *against* the accused, I should prefer rendering, with the Peschito, 'to speak *with* him,' i.e. to say what they had against him, and to hear what he had to say in reply.

*XXIII. 35: διακούσομαί σου] A. V. 'I will hear thee.' R. V. 'I will hear thy cause.' The forensic use of this word may be illustrated from Job ix. 33: διακούων ἀναμέσον ἀμφοτέρων. Stob. *Floril.* T. XLVIII. 61: ἔργα δὲ βασιλέως τρία, τό τε στραταγὲν καὶ δικασπολὲν (to administer justice) καὶ θεραπεύεν θεούς...δικασπολὲν δὲ καὶ διακούεν πάντων τῶν ὑπ᾽ αὐτόν.... There is a story told of Philip, the father of Alexander, that when a poor old woman importuned him to hear her cause, and his answer was μὴ σχολάζειν, she promptly replied, καὶ μὴ βασίλευε. The narrator adds (Plut. T. II. p. 179 C): ὁ δὲ θαυμάσας τὸ ῥηθέν, οὐ μόνον ἐκείνης, ἀλλὰ καὶ τῶν ἄλλων εὐθὺς διήκουσεν.

*XXIV. 2: καὶ κατορθωμάτων γινομένων τῷ ἔθνει τούτῳ] A. V. 'and that very worthy deeds are done unto this nation.' R. V. (with διορθωμάτων) 'and that evils are corrected.' If διορθωμάτων is the true reading, this seems a good opportunity to confer the 'freedom' of the English Bible upon a word which would certainly have been employed by an English Tertullus on such an occasion: 'and that REFORMS are being carried out for this nation.' In partial support of this rendering we might appeal to Heb. ix. 10: μέχρι καιροῦ διορθώσεως, A. V. 'until the time of reformation.'

*XXIV. 25: Διαλεγομένου δὲ κ.τ.λ.] It may be interesting to compare with this discourse an interview between Dionysius the tyrant and Plato,

---

[1] [Cf. Lucian. *Hermot.* 85: νῦν δέ... ἔδοξεν, οὐδὲν ἐξαίρετον πρὸς αὐτὴν πρὸς τὴν στοὰν ἀποτετάσθαι ὁ λόγος ἔχων.]

related in Plut. *Vit. Dion.* v. 'The discourse turned on *virtue* (ἀρετή) in general. Afterwards they came to *fortitude* (ἀνδρεία) in particular; and the philosopher made it appear that tyrants have, of all men, the least pretension to that virtue. *Justice* (δικαιοσύνη) was the next topic; and when Plato asserted the happiness of the just, and the wretched condition of the unjust, οὔτε τοὺς λόγους ἔφερεν ὁ τύραννος ὥσπερ ἐξελεγχόμενος, ἤχθετό τε τοῖς παροῦσι θαυμαστῶς ἀποδεχομένοις τὸν ἄνδρα καὶ κηλουμένοις ὑπὸ τῶν λεγομένων.'

In describing the impression made by St Paul's argument upon Felix, for the Greek ἔμφοβος γενόμενος we would render neither 'he trembled' (ἔντρομος γ.), nor 'he was terrified' (ἐπτοήθη), but simply 'he was afraid,' as A. V. Acts x. 4, xxii. 9. We are sorry to part with the former for Felix's sake, but the sequel shows that he was not so greatly moved on this occasion as to realize the picture usually drawn of him, of a judge *trembling* before his prisoner.

*XXIV. 27 : χάριτα καταθέσθαι τοῖς Ἰουδαίοις] A. V. 'to shew the Jews a pleasure.' R. V. 'to gain favour with the Jews.' But since Felix, in retiring from his province, could have had no motive for ingratiating himself with those whom he no longer governed, but merely desired to lay them under a parting obligation, this view of the subject seems to be more correctly indicated by the A. V. 'to shew the Jews a pleasure,' than by the proposed improvement of it.

XXV. 11 : οὐδείς με δύναται αὐτοῖς χαρίσασθαι] A. V. 'No man may deliver me (R. V. give me up) unto them.' Again *v.* 16: 'It is not the manner of the Romans to deliver (give up) any man' (χαρίζεσθαί τινα ἄνθρωπον). To 'deliver' or 'give up' might be the rendering of παραδοῦναι or ἐκδοῦναι, in which the principal idea of χαρίζεσθαι is lost[1]. I would add 'as a matter of favour,' there being no single word in English equivalent to the Greek. The distinction is important, as showing the highly advanced state of the Roman criminal law, in contrast with that of Eastern nations : e.g. when Haman offered Artaxerxes 10,000 talents of silver for permission to destroy the Jews, the king (in the words of Josephus) καὶ τὸ ἀργύριον αὐτῷ χαρίζεται, καὶ τοὺς ἀνθρώπους, ὥστε ποιεῖν αὐτοὺς ὅ τι βούλεται. [I now see that R. V. offers an alternative version, 'grant me by favour.']

*XXV. 13 : κατήντησαν εἰς Καισάρειαν, ἀσπασόμενοι τὸν Φῆστον] 'to salute Festus.' So Vulg. and both Syriac versions, against the uncials, which agree in reading ἀσπασάμενοι. But how is this to be construed? Not surely as R. V. in text, 'they arrived at C. and saluted F.,' which would certainly require καὶ ἠσπάσαντο τὸν Φ. We must therefore accept

---

[1] [Cf. Plut. *Vit. Dion.* XLVII: οἱ   στρατιώταις χαρίσασθαι τὸν Ἡρακλείμὲν φίλοι παρεκελεύοντο τῷ Δίωνι...τοῖς   δην.]

the only possible alternative, 'having saluted F.,' i.e. they first saluted F. and then arrived at C. where he resided. Can anything be more childish? The participle of the aorist evidently got in here from Ch. xxi. 7, κατηντήσαμεν εἰς Πτολεμαΐδα, καὶ ἀσπασάμενοι τοὺς ἀδελφοὺς ἐμείναμεν ἡμέραν μίαν, where it is perfectly correct.

*XXV. 16: οὐκ ἔστιν ἔθος Ῥωμαίοις] A more expressive phrase would have been, οὐκ ἔστι ΠΑΤΡΙΟΝ Ῥωμαίοις, as Plut. Vit. Brut. XXVI. Dion. Hal. Ant. VI. 71. On the custom itself compare Appian. B. C. III. 54: ὁ μὲν νόμος, ὦ βουλή, δικαιοῖ τὸν εὐθυνόμενον αὐτὸν ἀκοῦσαί τε τῆς κατηγορίας, καὶ ἀπολογησάμενον ὑπὲρ αὐτοῦ κρίνεσθαι.

*XXV. 18: αἰτίαν ἔφερον] (for ἐπέφερον) is the reading of the principal uncials, adopted of course by the Revisers. Alford refers for this phrase to John xviii. 29: κατηγορίαν φέρετε, and 2 Pet. ii. 11: οὐ φέρουσι βλάσφημον κρίσιν; but neither of these is a good authority for such a writer as St Luke. Wetstein quotes a score of examples of αἰτίαν ἐπιφέρειν from writers of all ages; but only one (from Libanius) of αἰτίαν φέρειν. I add Lucian. Alex. 2: ἀλλ᾽ ἤν τις ἡμῖν ταύτην ἐπιφέρῃ τὴν αἰτίαν. Id. Apol. pro M. C. 13: ὁμόσε χωρήσας τῷ ἐπιφερομένῳ ἐγκλήματι. Ach. Tat. VI. 5: ἔγκλημα μοιχείας ἐπιφέρων. Diod. Sic. T. X. p. 40, ed. Bip.: οὐ γὰρ διέλειπεν αἰτίας ψευδεῖς ἐπιφέρων τοῖς εὐπορωτάτοις. Ibid. p. 213: περὶ τῶν ἐπιφερομένων ἐγκλημάτων ἀπολογεῖσθαι. Pausan. VIII. 46: αἰτίαν ἐπενεγκὼν Μιλησίοις, ἐθελοκακῆσαι σφᾶς...ἐν τῇ Ἑλλάδι ναυμαχήσαντας.

*XXV. 20, 21: ἀπορούμενος...εἰς τὴν τοῦ Σεβαστοῦ διάγνωσιν...] Compare Dion. Hal. Ant. III. 22: ἀπορούμενος δὲ τί χρήσεται τοῖς πράγμασι (Horatius being accused of killing his sister) τελευτῶν κράτιστον εἶναι διέγνω τῷ δήμῳ τὴν διάγνωσιν (the determination, cf. Ch. xxiv. 22 R. V.) ἐπιτρέπειν. Diod. Sic. XVI. 59: καὶ τούτῳ (concilio Amphictyonum) τὴν περὶ τῶν ὅλων διάγνωσιν ἐπιτρέψαι.

*XXV. 21: ἀναπέμψω (T. R. πέμψω) αὐτὸν πρὸς Καίσαρα] The Latin forensic word is remittere. So Plin. Epist. X. 97: 'Fuerunt alii similis amentiae, quos, quia cives Romani erant, adnotavi in urbem remittendos.' Compare Lucian. Eun. 12: ἔγνωσαν ἀναπόμπιμον ἐς τὴν Ἰταλίαν ἐκπέμψαι τὴν δίκην.

*XXV. 24: ἐνέτυχόν μοι] A. V. 'have dealt with me.' R. V. 'made suit to me.' Either of these fairly represents the Greek; as do also 'have been with me' (Tyndale), 'have called upon me' (Geneva), NOT, as Alford, 'have been urgent with me' (ἐπέκειντό μοι). A personal interview seems to be required by the following examples. Theophr. Char. 1: τοῖς ἐντυγχάνειν κατὰ σπουδὴν βουλομένοις προστάξαι ἐπανελθεῖν (to call again). Plut. Vit. Ages. VII: ἔπειτα τῶν ἐντυγχανόντων καὶ δεομένων, οὓς αἴσθοιτο Λυσάνδρῳ μάλιστα πεποιθότας, ἀπράκτους ἀπέπεμπεν. Id. Vit.

Alex. XLIX : ἐκέλευσεν εἰσάγειν αὐτοὺς πρὸς Ἀλέξανδρον, ὡς περὶ ἀναγκαίων ἔχοντας ἐντυχεῖν καὶ μεγάλων. Id. *Vit. Themist.* XXVII : βούλεσθαι δ' ἐντυχεῖν βασιλεῖ (to have an audience of the king) περὶ μεγίστων πραγμάτων. Dan. vi. 12 (LXX): τότε οὗτοι οἱ ἄνθρωποι ἐνέτυχον τῷ βασιλεῖ.]

*XXV. 27 : πέμποντα δέσμιον, μὴ καὶ τὰς κατ' αὐτοῦ αἰτίας σημᾶναι] R. V. 'in sending a prisoner, not withal to signify the charges against him.' On which Mr Humphry observes : 'This idiomatic rendering of the Greek participle is rarely so convenient as it is here.' But the English 'idiomatic rendering' is that of the A. V. and of all preceding versions till 'snuffed out' by the Revisers : 'to send a prisoner, and not withal to signify' &c.

*XXVI. 11 : ἠνάγκαζον βλασφημεῖν] A. V. 'I compelled them to blaspheme.' There seems no objection to 'compelled,' though perhaps 'constrained' (as A. V. Acts xxviii. 19, Gal. vi. 12) might be better. It is not necessarily implied in either word that the compulsion or constraint employed was successful, but only that such means *were* employed. The *imperfect*, in this case, does not indicate an unsuccessful *attempt*, but only (like ἐδίωκον in the same verse) the *frequency* of the action. There is therefore no necessity for the R. V. 'I strove to make them blaspheme,' which, taken by itself, does not even exclude moral force.

*XXVI. 26 : οὐ γάρ ἐστιν ἐν γωνίᾳ πεπραγμένον τοῦτο] A proverbial expression, for which Wetstein quotes Galen. *De loc. affect.* III : φιλοσόφοις μὲν οὖν ἐν γωνίᾳ καθημένοις ἁμαρτάνειν ἐν τῷδε τάχ' ἄν τις συγγνοίη. Lucian. *Deor. Concil.* I : μηκέτι τονθορίζετε, ὦ θεοί, μηδὲ κατὰ γωνίας συστρεφόμενοι πρὸς οὓς ἀλλήλοις κοινολογεῖσθε. I add Synes. *Ep.* 22 : τῶν πονηρῶν ἀνθρώπων τὰς ἐν σκότῳ καὶ γωνίαις ἐλπίδας. Lucian. *Pseudol.* 24 : ποῦ γὰρ ταῦτα τῶν βιβλίων εὑρίσκεις; ἐν γωνίᾳ που τάχα τῶν ἰαλέμων (melancholy) τινὸς ποιητῶν κατορωρυγμένα.

XXVI. 28 : ἐν ὀλίγῳ με πείθεις Χριστιανὸν γενέσθαι] This is the T. R. in which the only question is as to the meaning of the phrase ἐν ὀλίγῳ. All the examples of it which have been adduced by Wetstein and others may be classed under two heads : (1) *in a little time*, either understanding χρόνῳ, or taking ὀλίγῳ to be in the neuter gender, like μετ' οὐ πολύ¹; (2) in *a few words* (as Eph. iii. 3), *briefly, summatim.* Either of these will make a good sense, and not be inconsistent with the proper use of πείθω, which is not *to bring a person over to one's opinion*, but *to seek to do so².*

---

¹ [Cf. Plut. *Vit. Cor.* IX: ἰσχυρᾶς δὲ μάχης γενομένης καὶ πολλῶν ἐν ὀλίγῳ νεκρῶν πεσόντων.]

² [It seems to be used in the former of these senses by Lucian. *Philops.* 34: καὶ τέλος πείθει με, τοὺς μὲν οἰκέτας ἅπαντας ἐν τῇ Μέμφιδι καταλιπεῖν, αὐτὸν

δὲ μόνον ἀκολουθεῖν μετ' αὐτοῦ. (But here it may be the narrational present for ἔπεισε.) Plut. II. p. 185 B: μὴ πείθων δὲ τὸν Εὐρυβιάδην ἐν τοῖς στενοῖς ναυμαχῆσαι, κρύφα πρὸς τὸν βάρβαρον ἔπεμψε...On πείθω see Schäfer ad Plut. T. IV. p. 398.]

Compare Ch. xix. 8, xxviii. 23, 2 Cor. v. 11.   The A. V. 'almost' cannot be proved[1], and would require us to understand πείθω in the former sense, of *conviction* instead of *persuasion*. To which we may add, that if Agrippa had really been impressed (not to say, *almost convinced*) by the Apostle's arguments, he would hardly have used the *contemptuous* term, Χριστιανὸν γενέσθαι, in speaking of the new religion.

Unfortunately, this is not the only difficulty connected with the passage before us, as it is found in the MSS. Of these three of the oldest ABℵ (the first with πείθῃ for πείθεις) read ποιῆσαι for γενέσθαι, which is also given as a various reading by the Philoxenian Syriac. Dean Alford, who confesses that it is 'almost impossible to give any assignable meaning' to the reading of Bℵ, throws in his lot with A, ἐν ὀλίγῳ με πείθῃ Χριστιανὸν ποιῆσαι, which he translates, 'Lightly thou art persuading thyself that thou canst make me a Christian.' This sense might possibly be elicited from the Greek, if it were ἐν ὀλίγῳ με πέποιθας Χριστιανὸν ποιῆσαι, though even so the absence of δύνασθαι could hardly be excused.

How the Revisers' 'With but little persuasion thou wouldest fain make me a Christian' is to be extracted from the reading adopted by them, ἐν ὀλίγῳ με πείθεις Χριστιανὸν ποιῆσαι, seems quite inexplicable: *videant ipsi*. Re-translated into Greek, their English would be something like this: ἐν ὀλίγῃ με πειθοῖ βούλοιο ἂν Χριστιανὸν ποιῆσαι[2].

Ibid. R. V. In the good old times, when Latin was the vehicle of such lucubrations as we are now penning, we should probably have said of this desperate attempt, *Haec ex Graecis ne fidiculis extorqueas*. But before we dismiss it as utterly untenable, we will hear what one (and not the least distinguished) of the N. T. Company has to say in defence and explanation of it. 'This is a good rendering, and assuredly a true one. Literally the words are, " in a little thou usest persuasion to make me a Christian."...Agrippa in effect says, "You are such an enthusiast that you think it will take little time and few words to make me a Christian[3]."' This would be a good paraphrase, either of the T. R. with πείθεις γενέσθαι, or of the corrected (?) text, with ΠΕΙΡΑΖΕΙΣ ποιῆσαι; but by no possibility can it be brought into harmony with πείθεις ποιῆσαι. Πείθειν is not 'to use persuasion,' absolutely and without a construction, but 'to seek to persuade' some person to do something; here to persuade Agrippa to become a Christian. So the Vulgate: *in modico suades me Christianum fieri*. But if for *fieri* we substitute *facere*, then we get a sense which is little better than nonsense. The difficulty is not at all lightened by reading πείθῃ for πείθεις with Cod. A; and, if in our unwillingness to part with

---

[1] [But cf. St Chrys. II. 516 D: καὶ τὸν δικάζοντα μικροῦ μεταπεῖσαι, ὡς καὶ αὐτὸν ἐκεῖνον λέγειν, 'Εν ὀλίγῳ....]

[2] [Or ἡδέως ἄν...ποιήσαις.]

[3] [Kennedy, *Ely Lectures*, p. 60.]

ποιῆσαι, we attempt to tamper with that portion of the sentence in which the MSS. present no variation, we may take warning by the ill success of previous adventurers in the same speculative line. Dr Hort, for instance (*Notes on Select Readings*, p. 100), hazards the remark: 'Possibly ΠΕΠΟΙΘΑC should be read for ΜΕΠΕΙΘΕΙC; for the personal reference expressed by με loses no force by being left to implication (?) and the changes of letters are inconsiderable (??).' But if the personal reference is suppressed, or only not prominently put forward, what becomes of the propriety of the Apostle's rejoinder: εὐξαίμην ἂν τῷ θεῷ...οὐ μόνον ΣΕ, ἀλλὰ καὶ πάντας τοὺς ἀκούοντάς μου κ.τ.ἑ.?

*XXVII. 2: πλεῖν εἰς τοὺς κατὰ τὴν Ἀσίαν τόπους] A favourite expression of Polybius, from whom Raphel quotes p. 4, l. 14: εἴς τε τὴν Ἑλλάδα καὶ τοὺς κατὰ τὴν Ἀσίαν τόπους. p. 3, l. 28: ἐν δὲ τοῖς κατὰ τὴν Ἰταλίαν καὶ Λιβύην τόποις. p. 31, l. 6: τοῖς κατὰ τὴν Σικελίαν τόποις. Add Diod. Sic. v. 8: ἐβασίλευσε μέχρι τῶν κατὰ Ῥήγιον τόπων.

XXVII. 3: ἐπιμελείας τυχεῖν] A. V. 'to refresh himself.' R. V. adds: 'Gr. *to receive attention*.' An excellent Greek phrase, for which Wetstein quotes Schol. Apoll. Rhod. II. 390: ἐν ταύτῃ τῇ νήσῳ ναυαγήσαντες ἔτυχον ἐπιμελείας παρὰ τῶν ἡρώων. I add Dion. Hal. *Ant.* I. 33: καὶ διὰ ταῦτα πολλῆς ἐπιμελείας τυγχάνειν πρὸς τῶν ὑποδεξαμένων. Charit. Aphrod. III. 3: ἐπεὶ δὲ αὐτῷ προσηνέχθη (ποτόν), καὶ πάσης ἔτυχεν ἐπιμελείας. Plut. *Vit. Thes.* XXVII: καὶ τὰς τετρωμένας φασὶ τῶν Ἀμαζόνων εἰς Χαλκίδα λάθρα διαπεμφθείσας τυγχάνειν ἐπιμελείας[1].

*XXVII. 8: μόλις τε παραλεγόμενοι αὐτήν] Rev. J. Milner (*Voyage and Shipwreck of St Paul*, Lond. 1880) says: 'Wordsworth and others are decidedly mistaken in rendering these words, "coasting it along the southern shore of Crete"; for αὐτήν must refer to the word immediately before it, viz. Salmone. The difficulty was in working round, or (as it is called) "weathering," the projecting headland.' In answer to which we would observe (1) that in the immediately preceding clause ὑπεπλεύσαμεν τὴν Κρήτην κατὰ Σαλμώνην, the prominent idea is the name of the island under whose lee they ran, not the part of the coast which they first made. The pronoun, therefore, is rightly referred to Crete, not to Salmone. (2) It does not appear that there was any necessity for 'weathering' Cape Salmone at all, as the words κατὰ Σαλμώνην will apply to the south of the headland, as well as to the north. In fact, since the ἀκρωτήριον is by Strabo in several places called Σαλμώνιον, it is not improbable that Salmone itself was a town or village from which the cape derived its name. (3) The word παραλέγεσθαι is always used of a *coasting* voyage, and followed by the name of the country to which the

---

[1] [Of medical attendance, Hobart, p. 269; Plut. II. p. 197 E: ἵνα...   ἐπανελθόντες εἰς τὸ στρατόπεδον ἑαυτῶν ἐπιμελ ηθῶσι.]

coast belongs; e.g. Diod. Sic. XIII. 3 : κἀκεῖθεν ἤδη παρελέγοντο τὴν Ἰταλίαν. XIV. 55 : αἱ δὲ τριήρεις ἔπλευσαν εἰς τὴν Λιβύην, παρελέγοντο δὲ τὴν γῆν. (4) How St Luke would have expressed 'working round' a headland may be inferred from the following examples. Aelian. V. H. I. 15 : ὅτε ἐνταῦθα ἀπώλοντο αἱ τῶν Περσῶν τριήρεις, περικάμπτουσαι τὸν Ἄθω. Herod. VI. 44 : ἐκ δὲ Ἀκάνθου ὁρμώμενοι, τὸν Ἄθων περιέβαλλον. . Thuc. VIII. 95 : αἱ δὲ τῶν Πελοποννησίων νῆες, παραπλεύσασαι καὶ περιβαλοῦσαι Σούνιον.

*XXVII. 12 : (λιμένα) βλέποντα κατὰ λίβα καὶ κατὰ χῶρον] A. V. 'and lieth toward the S.W, and N.W.' R. V. 'looking N.E. and S.E. Gr. *looking down the S.W. wind and down the N.W. wind.*' But this force of the preposition is not supported by biblical usage, as, for instance, Ezech. xl. 23, 24, where πύλη βλέπουσα πρὸς νότον, and π. βλ. κατ' ἀνατολάς are interchanged in the sense of *looking* or *facing towards* a certain point of the compass. Mr Milner says : 'We must imagine the harbour itself to be personified,' in which case 'it will naturally look ahead of it, towards the land, and not astern, out to sea.' By way of illustration it may be mentioned that Nelson's column at Yarmouth, though on the furthest east coast of England, actually βλέπει πρὸς δυσμάς, being surmounted by a statue of the hero with his face towards the land.

XXVII. 13 : τῆς προθέσεως κεκρατηκέναι] 'That they had obtained their purpose.' Another good Greek phrase : e.g. Diod. Sic. XVI. 20 : οἱ δὲ μισθοφόροι, κεκρατηκότες ἤδη τῆς προθέσεως. Compare Lucian. *Phal. prior* 2 : ῥᾳδίως ἐκράτησα τῆς ἐπιχειρήσεως. Diod. Sic. XIII. 112 : διόπερ κεκρατηκέναι τῆς ἐπιβολῆς νομίζοντες[1].

*XXVII. 16 : μόλις ἰσχύσαμεν περικρατεῖς γενέσθαι τῆς σκάφης] A. V. 'we had much work to come by the boat.' An excellent specimen of vernacular English, for which we are indebted to Tyndale, but of which the Revisers have left not a trace in their 'we were able, with difficulty, to secure the boat.' To 'come by' is a good old idiom for 'to obtain possession of' (as Hooker, quoted by Johnson, 'Things most needful to preserve this life, are most prompt and easy for all living creatures to *come by*'), which is the exact meaning of the Greek περικρατὴς γ. or the Latin *compos fieri*. The first and hardest piece of work was to make themselves masters of the boat ; the next, to hoist it on board (*v.* 17); which done, and not before, it was 'secured.'

*XXVII. 17 : χαλάσαντες τὸ σκεῦος] 'They lowered the gear.' R. V. Compare Polyb. I. 61 : καθελόμενοι τοὺς ἱστούς.

*XXVII. 18 : ἐκβολὴν ἐποιοῦντο] A. V. 'they lightened the ship' (but see *v.* 38). R. V. 'they began to throw *the freight* overboard.' The

---

[1] [Cf. Polyb. I. 63: οὐ μόνον ἐπε-βάλοντο τῇ τῶν ὅλων ἡγεμονίᾳ, ἀλλὰ καὶ καθίκοντο τῆς προθέσεως, i.e. τῆς τῶν ὅλων ἡγεμονίας.]

proper commercial word, which may be seen every day in the 'Ship News' of the daily press, is 'they jettisoned the cargo.' As this operation is necessarily a lengthened one, there seems no occasion to insist on the imperfect tense, 'they began to do it.' Of the figurative use of this expression Wetst. quotes a pleasing example from Greg. Naz. *de Basil.* : πάντων ἐκβολὴν στέρξας ὧν τότε εἶχεν, κούφως διέπλει τὴν τοῦ βίου θάλασσαν. I add another from Stob. *Flor.* T. CXV. 28 : καταγωγῇ (a putting into harbour) γὰρ ἔοικεν ὁ γεροντικὸς θάνατος, ἐκβολὴ δὲ καὶ ναυάγιόν ἐστιν ὁ τῶν νέων.

*XXVII. 21 : μὴ ἀνάγεσθαι ἀπὸ τῆς Κρήτης, κερδῆσαί τε...] R. V. 'and not have set sail from Crete, and have gotten....' This is a legitimate construction, the negative extending to both clauses. But there is another, which is a favourite with scholars, and deserves a place in the margin, if not in the text, of the Revised Version : 'not have set sail from Crete, and *so* have been spared this injury and loss.' This is a well-known use of the word κερδαίνειν, of which the following examples are quoted by Elsner and others. Philem. p. 352 ed. Grot. et Cler. : καὶ γὰρ πένης ὢν μεγάλα κερδαίνει κακά. Joseph. *Ant.* II. 3, 2 : (Reuben) ἠξίου αὐτοὺς αὐτόχειρας μὲν μὴ γενέσθαι τοῦ ἀδελφοῦ, ῥίψαντες δὲ εἰς τὸν παρακείμενον λάκκον οὕτως ἀποθανεῖν ἐᾶσαι, καὶ τό γε μιανθῆναι τὰς χεῖρας αὐτοὺς κερδαίνειν. I add Plut. *Vit. Cleom.* XXXI : 'If it is not dishonourable for the descendants of Hercules to serve the successors of Philip and Alexander, we shall save ourselves a long voyage (πλοῦν πολὺν κερδανοῦμεν) by making our submission to Antigonus.' And so the word appears to have been understood by the Peschito, which renders ܘܠܐ݂ܣ܉ܟ݀ܡ ܡ݂ܢ ܗܘ݂ ܢܣ݂ܩܣ܉ܘ, *et immunes essemus a damno.*

XXVII. 29 : ηὔχοντο ἡμέραν γενέσθαι] For the *phrase* Wetstein quotes Long. Past. II. p. 40 ed. Schaef. : ἐπιθυμοῦσιν ἀλλήλους ὁρᾶν· διὰ τοῦτο θᾶττον εὐχόμεθα γενέσθαι τὴν ἡμέραν. *Ibid.* p. 56 : εὐχόμενος δὲ τὴν ἡμέραν γενέσθαι ταχέως...νυκτῶν πασῶν ἐκείνη ἔδοξε μακροτάτη γεγονέναι. For the *situation* compare Synes. *Ep.* IV. p. 165 : καὶ ὑφώρμει δέος οὐκ ἔλαττον, εἰ καὶ διαγενοίμεθα ἐκ τοῦ κλύδωνος, οὕτως ἔχοντας ἐν νυκτὶ πελάζειν τῇ γῇ, φθάνει δὲ ἡμέρα, καὶ ὁρῶμεν τὸν ἥλιον, ὡς οὐκ οἶδα εἴ ποτε ἥδιον[1].

*XXVII. 35 : λαβὼν ἄρτον κ.τ.έ.] Compare Diod. Sic. XI. 9 : (Leonidas, on the eve of Thermopylae) τοῖς στρατιώταις παρήγγειλε ταχέως ἀριστοποιεῖσθαι...αὐτὸς δ' ἀκολούθως τῇ παραγγελίᾳ τροφὴν προσηνέγκατο.

XXVII. 39 : κόλπον δέ τινα κατενόουν ἔχοντα αἰγιαλόν] A. V. 'They discovered a certain creek with a shore.' 'Some commentators [Kuinoel and others] suppose that it should be αἰγιαλὸν ἔχοντα κόλπον, since every creek must have a beach.'—*Dean Alford.* The true construction hardly

---

[1] [Cf. Ach. Tat. IV. 17 : μόλις ἡ πολύευκτος ἠὼς ἀναφαίνεται.]

requires confirmation, but as the two following passages have (to the best of my knowledge) escaped the researches of collectors, I will set them down. Xenoph. *Anab.* VI. 4, 4 : λιμὴν δ' ὑπ' αὐτῇ τῇ πέτρᾳ τὸ πρὸς ἑσπέραν, ΑΙΓΙΑΛΟΝ ΕΧΩΝ. Xenoph. Ephes. II. II : καὶ τῆς νεὼς διαρραγείσης, μόλις ἐν σανίδι τινὶ σωθέντες ἐπ' αἰγιαλοῦ τινος ἦλθον (where Locella has unfortunately adopted Koen's conjecture τινες for τινος).

***Ibid.* Αἰγιαλὸς is variously rendered ‘a shore,’ ‘a beach,’ ‘a sandy shore.’ It appears to be a *general* term for the sea-coast (as Diod. Sic. III. 43 : αἰγιαλὸς παρήκει κρημνώδης καὶ δυσπαράπλους for 1000 stadia, without harbour or roads), but also used *specially* (as here) for a coast which had a beach of sand or shingle between the cliffs and the water's edge (Philo Jud. T. II. p. 141 : οἱ μὲν πηξάμενοι σκηνὰς ἐπὶ τοῦ αἰγιαλοῦ, οἱ δὲ ἐπὶ τῆς αἰγιαλίτιδος ψάμμου κατακλίναντες ἐν ὑπαίθρῳ, μετ' οἰκείων καὶ φίλων ἑστιῶνται. Lucian. *Pisc.* 35 : οὐδὲν τῶν ἐν τοῖς αἰγιαλοῖς ψηφίδων διαφέρον) on which a ship might be hauled up for refitting (Herod. VII. 59 : ἐς τοῦτον τὸν αἰγιαλὸν κατασχόντες, τὰς νέας ἀνέψυχον ἀνελκύσαντες) or driven, or run aground in case of shipwreck (Lucian. *Ver. Hist.* II. 47 : χειμὼν σφοδρὸς ἐπιπεσών, καὶ προσαράξας τὸ σκάφος τῷ αἰγιαλῷ, διέλυσεν· ἡμεῖς δὲ μόλις ἐξενηξάμεθα).

**Ibid.* εἰς ὃν ἐβουλεύοντο, εἰ δύναιντο, ἐξῶσαι τὸ πλοῖον] So the Greek text is pointed both by Palmer and Scrivener ; and also (with εἰ δυνατὸν) in A. V.: ‘into the which they were minded, if it were possible, to thrust in the ship.’ But the R. V. undoubtedly reads the passage thus : εἰς ὃν ἐβουλεύοντο εἰ δύναιντο ἐξῶσαι τὸ πλοῖον, ‘and they took counsel whether they could drive the ship upon it.’ Which is right ?

In favour of the punctuation ἐβουλεύοντο εἰ δύναιντο... might be cited Luke xiv. 31 : βουλεύεται εἰ δυνατός ἐστιν ἐν δέκα χιλιάσιν ὑπαντῆσαι κ.τ.έ. But a fatal objection to this construction seems to be that, according to Greek usage, it would require εἰ δύνανται, not εἰ δύναιντο. The rule given by Hoogeveen *De Partic.* p. 226 (Ed. 1766) is : ‘In obliquis interrogationibus, notandum tironibus, non subjunctivum aut optativum sequi (post εἰ), ut apud Latinos, sed indicativum.’ Cf. Mark xv. 47 : ἐθεώρουν ποῦ τέθειται (τίθεται).

On the other hand the parenthetical εἰ δύναιντο is of frequent occurrence in the best Greek writers from Homer downwards. Thus *Il.* A. 393 : ἀλλὰ σύ, εἰ δύνασαί γε, περίσχεο παιδὸς ἑῆος. Soph. *Oed. T.* 697 : τανῦν δ' εὔπομπος γίνου, εἰ δύναιο. Thucyd. VI. 1 : ἐβούλοντο...ἐπὶ Σικελίαν πλεύσαντες, καταστρέψασθαι, εἰ δύναιντο. Plut. *Vit. Arat.* V : ἐγνωκώς, εἰ δύναιτο...πρὸς ἕνα κίνδυνον τὸ πᾶν ἀναρρῖψαι. Dio. Chrys. *Or.* LVII. p. 571, 17 : καὶ ἐβούλετο ταπεινῶσαι, καὶ τοῦ φρονήματος, εἰ δύναιτο, καθελεῖν. In the following (from Appian. *B. C.* II. 124) there is precisely the same ambiguity as in the passage before us : ἐδόκει δὲ καραδοκεῖν ἔτι τὰ γενησόμενα, καὶ τεχνάζειν, εἰ δύναιντο περισπάσαι πρὸς ἑαυτοὺς τὴν στρατιὰν τοῦ Δέκμου. So Schweigh. points, rendering, *et tentari si qua arte possent......*But here also we might join τεχνάζειν περισπάσαι, as Plut. *Vit. Fab.* XXII: ὁ Φάβιος περισπάσαι τὸν Ἀννίβαν τεχνάζων. Of the ancient versions, Vulg., as generally pointed, reads : *in quem cogitabant, si possent, ejicere navem.* Both Syriac (Pesch. with εἰ δυνατόν, and Philox. with εἰ δύναιντο) agree in joining ἐβουλεύοντο ἐξῶσαι. The false spelling ἐκσῶσαι is quite unworthy of a place in the margin of R. V.

XXVIII. 1 : Μελίτη] 'Melita.' Why not Melite? R. V. has a marginal note : 'Some ancient authorities read Μελιτήνη,' which seems to be merely a ἁμάρτημα γραφικόν. The scribe had written Μελιτηνησος for Μελιτηηνησος, omitting the article ; but, perceiving his mistake, *expunged* νη and began ηνησος again, thus : Μελιτηϋηηνησος[1].

XXVIII. 2 : 'And the barbarous people showed us no little kindness (οὐ τὴν τυχοῦσαν φιλανθρωπίαν).'

Philanthropy, according to the modern use of the term, is defined to be *the love of mankind,* and does not condescend to individuals, except as a part of mankind. In Greek there is no trace of this world-embracing virtue ; the objects of φιλανθρωπία being always individuals in distress, appealing to our common *humanity,* which word, perhaps, most accurately conveys the sense of it to the English reader[2]. This will be best seen by a few examples. Here the kindness is shown towards *shipwrecked mariners,* as it is also in Stob. *Flor.* T. XXXVII. 38, where we read that the Θύνοι (a barbarous people settled in the N.W. part of Bithynia) τοὺς ναυαγοὺς φιλανθρώπως δεχόμενοι, φίλους ποιοῦνται. Among acts of philanthropy is mentioned the *ransoming of captives* (Demosth. 107, 15 : καὶ λύσεις αἰχμαλώτων, καὶ τοιαύτας ἄλλας φιλανθρωπίας) ; the *friendly reception* of those who had escaped from the same fate by neighbouring cities (Diod. Sic. XIII. 58 : οἱ δὲ τὴν αἰχμαλωσίαν διαφυγόντες διεσώθησαν εἰς Ἀκράγαντα, καὶ πάντων ἔτυχον τῶν φιλανθρώπων. Plut. *Vit. Alex.* XIII : καὶ τοῖς καταφυγοῦσιν (of the Thebans, when their city was destroyed by Alexander) ἐπὶ τὴν πόλιν ἁπάντων μετεδίδοσαν τῶν φιλανθρώπων). Conquerors showed their philanthropy by their *humane* treatment of the vanquished, as Agathocles (Diod. Sic. XX. 17), ἑλὼν Νέαν πόλιν κατὰ κράτος, φιλανθρώπως ἐχρήσατο τοῖς χειρωθεῖσι ; and Mithridates (Id. Tom. X. p. 193 ed. Bip.),

---

[1] [The other Μελίτη, now Meleda, is called Μελιτηνή (sic) by Ptol. II. 16, § 14. Smith's Geograph. Dict.]

[2] Plato (ap. Diog. Laert. III. 98) reckons three kinds of φιλανθρωπία: (1) διὰ τοῦ προσαγορεύειν, greeting and shaking hands with every one you meet : (2) διὰ τοῦ εὐεργετεῖν, ὅταν τις

βοηθητικὸς ᾖ παντὶ τῷ ἀτυχοῦντι : (3) διὰ τοῦ ἑστιᾶν καὶ φιλοσυνουσιάξειν, giving dinners and promoting *social* intercourse. Hence correct Liddell & Scott s. v. φιλοσυνουσιάξειν. [Cf. Plut. *Vit. Crass.* III: ἤρεσκε δὲ καὶ τὸ περὶ τὰς δεξιώσεις καὶ προσαγορεύσεις φιλάνθρωπον αὐτοῦ καὶ δημοτικόν.]

πολλοὺς ζωγρήσας, ἄπαντας τιμήσας καὶ ἐσθῆσι καὶ ἐφοδίοις ἀπέλυσεν εἰς τὰς πατρίδας. διαβοηθείσης τε τῆς τοῦ Μιθριδάτου φιλανθρωπίας....Sometimes the philanthropic act was attended with danger, as the harbouring of proscribed persons in the wars of Sylla and Marius (Plut. *Vit. Syl.* XXXI : ζημίαν τῆς φιλανθρωπίας ὁρίζων θάνατον)[1]. To return to the instance before us : other barbarians besides those of Melite are commended for the exercise of this virtue. Thus the Atlantei (Diod. Sic. III. 55) φιλανθρωπίᾳ τῇ πρὸς ξένους δοκοῦσι διαφέρειν τῶν πλησιοχώρων. The Celtiberes (V. 34) are described as πρὸς τοὺς ξένους ἐπιεικεῖς καὶ φιλάνθρωποι. Of individuals, Aeolus, King of Lipara, who entertained Ulysses in his wanderings, is characterized by the historian (Diod. Sic. V. 7) as εὐσεβῆ καὶ δίκαιον, ἔτι δὲ καὶ πρὸς τοὺς ξένους φιλάνθρωπον ; and Phalaris in his defence before the Delphians (Lucian. *Phal. prior* 10), as a proof of his hospitable treatment of voyagers (ὅτι φιλανθρώπως προσφέρομαι τοῖς καταίρουσιν), says that he employed spies about the harbours, whose business it was to accost strangers, and enquire who they were and whence they came, that he might pay them such attentions as were suitable to their rank. That kind of philanthropy, which (according to Plato's definition) consisted in entertaining company, may be illustrated from Alciphr. *Ep.* III. 50, where a parasite says of his patron, κύριος γενόμενος τῆς οὐσίας, πολλὴν τὴν εἰς ἡμᾶς (professionals) φιλανθρωπίαν ἀνεδείξατο ; as well as from Lucian. *Cyn.* 6 : ἀνδρὸς πλουσίου, προθύμως καὶ φιλανθρώπως, ἔτι δὲ φιλοφρόνως ἑστιῶντος ; from which latter example we gather that φιλοφρόνως (Acts xxviii. 7) expresses a higher degree of friendliness than φιλανθρώπως. We may remark, in conclusion, that Plutarch (*Vit. Cat. Maj.* V) recommends *kindness to animals*, as a training for the higher virtue of φιλανθρωπία. 'We ought not,' he remarks, 'to treat creatures which have a living soul like shoes or household vessels, which, when worn out with service, we throw away; but if for no other reason, μελέτης ἕνεκα τοῦ φιλανθρώπου, we should habituate ourselves in these lower animals to be gentle and placable towards each other.'

XXVIII. 4: ἡ δίκη] 'Justice' (with a capital letter). To the examples collected by Wetstein may be added Dion. Hal. *Ant.* VIII. 80 : τοίγαρτοι δίκη μὲν ἐκείνοις σὺν χρόνῳ τιμωρὸς οὐ μεμπτὴ (*vindex non contemnenda*) παρηκολούθησε. Aelian. *V. H.* III. 43 : τοῖς δὲ κακῶς ῥέξασι δίκης τέλος οὐχὶ χρονιστὸν | οὐδὲ παραιτητόν (mox ἡ δὲ δίκη οὐκ ἐβράδυνε). Synes. *Ep.* 50 : τὸ μὲν οὖν ἀληθὲς οἶδεν ἡ δίκη, καὶ ὁ χρόνος εὑρήσει. Aeschyl. ap. Stob. *Flor.* T. CXXV. 7 : ἡμῶν γε μέντοι Νέμεσίς ἐσθ᾽ ὑπερτέρα, | καὶ τοῦ θανόντος ἡ δίκη πράσσει κότον. Pseudo-Lucian. *Philop.* 16 : ἐὰν κτάνῃς τὸν πλησίον, θανατωθήσῃ παρὰ τῆς δίκης. Dion. Hal. *Ant.* XI. 27 : ἀλλὰ καίπερ ἐν ἐρημίᾳ

---

[1] [Cf. Plut. *Vit. Ant.* III: οὐ διέλαθε ...ἡ πρὸς Ἀρχέλαον αὐτοῦ τεθνηκότα φιλανθρωπία which was shown in burying the body—τὸ σῶμα πεσόντος ἐξευρών, καὶ κοσμήσας βασιλικῶς ἐκήδευσεν.]

τοῦ φόνου γεγονότος...ὑπὸ τῆς ἅπαντα ἐπισκοπούσης τὰ θνητὰ πράγματα δίκης ἐξηλέγχθησαν¹.

*XXVIII. 6: μέλλειν πίμπρασθαι] 'that he would have swollen.' Compare Aelian. N. A. I. 57 (de morsu cerastae): ἐὰν πρὶν ἢ πρησθῆναι τὸ πᾶν σῶμα ἀφίκηταί τις τῶν ἐκεῖθεν (Psylli) κλητός. Diod. Sic. II. 12: εὐθὺς δὲ διοιδεῖ καὶ πίμπραται τὸ σῶμα (vapore sulfureo). Lucian. De Dips. 4: ἐκκαίει τε γὰρ καὶ σήπει, καὶ πίμπρασθαι ποιεῖ. Dio. Chrys. Or. LXXVIII. p. 655, 45: πεπρησμένον (sic conj. Cobet. pro πεπλησμένον) ὁρῶντες αὐτὸν ὑπὸ νόσου, καὶ οἰδοῦντα, καὶ ὕπουλον.

*XXVIII. 10: καὶ ἀναγομένοις ἐπέθεντο τὰ πρὸς τὴν χρείαν] A. V. 'and when we departed, they laded us with such things as were necessary.' R. V. 'and when we sailed, they put on board such things as we needed.' Grotius observes on this text, 'permisceri lectiones de navigantibus et de navi, ut fieri solet; nam ἀναγομένοις ad navigantes, ἐπέθεντο ad navim pertinere.' On this supposition the A. V. is perfectly correct, the full construction being ἀναγομένοις ἐπέθεντο ἡμῖν, and 'laded us' being a familiar phrase for 'laded our ship.' The R. V. will have precisely the same meaning, if we insert 'us' after 'put on board'; but as it stands, it is rather the rendering of ἐπέθεντο τῷ πλοίῳ, and then the other dative has nothing to govern it, and must be changed into the genitive absolute ἀναγομένων. Another objection to the common rendering is taken by Hemsterh. ad Lucian. Necyom. 9, namely that for in navem imponere the Greeks said ἐνθέσθαι not ἐπιθέσθαι²; and that St Luke's intention in the use of this word was to show the forwardness of the islanders in almost forcing their supplies upon their departing benefactors: q. d. nosque jamjam profecturos ONERARUNT rebus necessariis. If this explanation were approved, it would only be necessary in the A. V. to understand 'laded' in the sense of 'loaded,' or to adopt the latter term instead of the former, as more conformable to modern parlance. But there seems to be no occasion to depart from the common understanding of this passage.

*XXVIII. 13: περιελθόντες] R. V. 'we made a circuit,' with a note: 'Some ancient authorities read cast loose.' It would have been more correct to say: 'Some ancient authorities read περιελόντες, which some

¹ [Cf. Poll. VIII. 6: δίκη, ἥ τε θεὸς καὶ τὸ πρᾶγμα οὗ προέστηκεν ὁ δικάζων. Liban. II. 601: In bonam partem. οἷς πολλὰ ἀγαθὰ γένοιτο παρὰ τῆς δίκης ἢ τῷ Διΐ παρακάθηται. Paus. VIII. 53, 3: Λειμῶνα μὲν τοξευθέντα ὑπὸ Ἀρτέμιδος περιῆλθεν αὐτίκα ἡ δίκη τοῦ φόνου (cf. Herod. VIII. 106: ἡ τίσις περιῆλθε τὸν Πανιώνιον). Aesop. Fab. 307: ἡ

γὰρ θεία δίκη ἐφορᾷ πάντα καὶ τὸ ἴσον ἀποδίδωσι καὶ ζυγοστατεῖ.]
² The only instance of this use of ἐπιθέσθαι, which I have been able to find, is Dio. Chrys. Or. XI. p. 167, 34 (said of Paris carrying off Helen): ὥστε οὐκ ἦν ἱκανὸν αὐτῷ τὴν γυναῖκα ἀπαγαγεῖν, ἀλλὰ καὶ τὰ χρήματα προσεπέθετο.

modern interpreters explain to mean *cast loose.*' The ancient authorities
are Bℵ[1]; and περιελόντες, we are told, was a nautical term for the 'casting
loose' of the cables on leaving a port, though the only shadow of authority
for this use of the word is a supposed 'analogy' with Acts xxvii. 40, where
περιελόντες τὰς ἀγκύρας is said of 'cutting the anchors adrift,' an extraordinary manœuvre for a particular purpose, that of running the ship
aground, which has no 'analogy' with the ordinary action of 'casting
loose' the cables on putting to sea. At all events, since περιελόντες in
Ch. xxvii. 40 would have been unintelligible without the addition τὰς
ἀγκύρας, so here 'analogy' requires that τὰ ἀπόγεια, or its equivalent,
should have been expressed.

*XXVIII. 21: οὔτε παραγενόμενός τις τῶν ἀδελφῶν, ἀπήγγειλεν ἢ
ἐλάλησέ τι περὶ σοῦ πονηρόν] Badly rendered by R. V. 'Nor did any of the
brethren come hither and report or speak &c.' Better the A. V. 'any of
the brethren that came.' The best English would be: 'nor did any of
the brethren in person report &c.' See on Luke xix. 16.

*XXVIII. 25: ἀσύμφωνοι δὲ ὄντες πρὸς ἀλλήλους] Wetstein compares
Diod. Sic. IV. 1: συμβαίνει τοὺς ἀναγεγραφότας τὰς ἀρχαιοτάτας πράξεις τε
καὶ μυθολογίας ἀσυμφώνους εἶναι πρὸς ἀλλήλους. I add Synes. p. 207 D: τί
δήποτ' οὖν ἀσύμφωνός εἰμι πρὸς ἐμαυτόν; Diod. Sic. XIX. 75: οὐ δυναμένων
αὐτῶν οὐδαμῶς συμφωνῆσαι.

*XXVIII. 31. ἀκωλύτως] A. V. 'no man forbidding him.' Compare
Herodian. VIII. 2. 1 (quoted by Wetst.): διέβησαν ἀκωλύτως, μηδενὸς ἐμποδὼν
γενομένου. Another periphrasis might be μηδενὸς παρενοχλοῦντος. In Plut.
Vit. Ant. LXII. Caesar, urging his rival to a speedy settlement of their
differences, both by land and by sea, offers, in respect to a naval contest,
αὐτὸς τῷ μὲν στόλῳ (Antony's fleet) παρέξειν ὅρμους ἀκωλύτως καὶ λιμένας;
where the various reading ἀκωλύτους is to be rejected.

ROMANS.

*I. 15: οὕτω τὸ κατ' ἐμὲ πρόθυμον...εὐαγγελίσασθαι] Both versions:
'So, as much as in me is, I am ready' &c., as if the Greek were τὸ κατ'
ἐμὲ πρόθυμός εἰμι....No change is necessary, but a marginal note might be
added: 'Gr. *my good will is.*' Wetst. quotes Eur. *Med.* 178: μήτοι τό γ'
ἐμὸν πρόθυμον φίλοισιν ἀπέστω. I add Dion. Hal. *Ant.* VI. 10: καὶ ὁ
Ποστούμιος ἐπαινέσας τὸ πρόθυμον αὐτῶν...*Ibid.* 9: τὸ μὲν τῶν γερόντων
πρόθυμον...τὸ δὲ ὑμέτερον ἀκμάζον....

*I. 20: νοούμενα] A. V. 'being understood.' R. V. 'being perceived.'
Is it not rather 'conceived'—apprehended by the mind, so that we are
able to form a conception (λαβεῖν ἔννοιαν) of them? Wetst. quotes Philo
Leg. Alleg. T. I. p. 107, 3: ἐζήτησαν οἱ πρῶτοι, πῶς ἐνοήσαμεν τὸ θεῖον. εἶθ'
οἱ δοκοῦντες ἄριστα φιλοσοφεῖν ἔφασαν, ὅτι ἀπὸ τοῦ κόσμου, καὶ τῶν μερῶν
αὐτοῦ, καὶ τῶν ἐνυπαρχουσῶν τούτοις δυνάμεων, ἀντίληψιν ἐποιησάμεθα τοῦ
αἰτίου.

*Ibid. θειότης] A. V. 'Godhead.' Other versions: 'divinity.' The
attempt to distinguish between θεότης and θειότης is futile. The one is
from θεός, and the other from τὸ θεῖον, and these are precisely the same.

I. 28: οὐκ ἐδοκίμασαν] A. V. 'They did not like.' R. V. 'They
refused.' But the negative should be retained, as in all the ancient
versions. Vulg. *non probaverunt.* Pesch. ܘܠܐ ܂. Philox. ܐܠܘ ܂.
W. Wilberforce (*Practical View* &c. p. 308) gives his own version,
'They were not solicitous,' which is not the meaning of the word. Better,
'They thought not fit.' Wetstein quotes Plut. *Vit. Thes.* XII: οὐκ
ἐδοκίμαζε φράζειν αὐτόν, ὅστις εἴη, πρότερος. Joseph. *Ant.* II. 7, 4: τὰ μὲν
οὖν ὀνόματα δηλῶσαι τούτων οὐκ ἐδοκίμαζον. I add Appian. VI. 70: Οὐριάτθος
οὐ δοκιμάζων αὐτῷ συμπλέκεσθαι διὰ τὴν ὀλιγότητα[1].

---

[1] [Cf. Lucian. *Bis Accus.* 31: ὅπερ
ἐγὼ μὴ φέρων γράψασθαι μὲν αὐτὴν
μοιχείας οὐκ ἐδοκίμαζον. Himerius ap.
Aesopi *Fab.* (ed. de Furia) 406: (ἔρως)
τὸ μὲν ἁπάσαις ψυχαῖς ἐγκατοικίζεσθαι...
οὐκ ἐδοκίμαζεν. App. *B. C.* II. 114:
ὡς δὲ σφίσιν ἐδόκουν ἅλις ἔχειν, καὶ
πλέοσιν ἐκφέρειν (conjurationem) οὐκ
ἐδοκίμαζον.]

*I. 29: ἔριδος] A. V. 'debate.' R. V. 'strife.' 2 Cor. xii. 20: ἔρεις. A. V. 'debates.' R. V. (with ἔρις) 'strife.' 'Debate' is a good old word (see T. L. O. Davies *Bible English*, p. 200). Cf. A. V. Isai. lviii. 4: 'Behold ye fast for strife and debate (εἰς κρίσεις καὶ μάχας)'; where R. V. has 'strife and contention.'

*I. 30: ὑβριστάς, ὑπερηφάνους, ἀλαζόνας] A. V. 'despiteful, proud, boasters.' R. V. 'insolent, haughty, boastful.' An interesting study of these three words, by way of synonymous discrimination, may be found in Archbishop Trench's *Synonyms of the N. T.* pp. 95—101 (8th ed.). It is worthy of notice that the *order* in which he takes them, which is the reverse of that of the Apostle's description, namely, ἀλαζών, ὑπερήφανος, ὑβριστής, is the very same in which their natural sequence is presented by Callicratidas the Pythagorean philosopher (ap. Stob. *Flor.* T. LXXXV. 16): ἀνάγκα γὰρ τὼς πολλὰ ἔχοντας τετυφῶσθαι πρᾶτον, τετυφωμένως δὲ ʼΑΛΑΖΟΝΑΣ γίγνεσθαι· ἀλαζόνας δὲ γενομένως, ʽΥΠΕΡΗΦΑΝΩΣ ἤμεν...ὑπερηφάνως δὲ γενομένως, ʽΥΒΡΙΣΤΑΣ ἤμεν.

*II. 17. On the confusion of ΕΙΔΕ (ἴδε) and ΕΙ ΔΕ see on James iii. 3. It is remarkable that in both places the adoption of εἰ δέ involves a difficulty in regard to *protasis* and *apodosis*. In the present instance the *protasis* is inconveniently long[1], and the *apodosis* in *v.* 21 requires to be marked by the insertion of a particle, ὁ ΟΥΝ διδάσκων; for which a correct writer, if driven to such an expedient, would most certainly have written, ΣΥ ΟΥΝ ὁ διδάσκων, 'Thou therefore that teachest.' We are therefore compelled to differ from a writer in 'Public Opinion' for July 2, 1881: 'Εἰ δὲ σύ. An interesting, and probably secure, various reading, recorded in the Revision' &c. Our complaint is that the *false* spelling (for it is nothing more) is not *recorded*, but *adopted*, without even a marginal record of the *true*.

*II. 21: ὁ οὖν διδάσκων κ.τ.ἑ.] Wetstein's *loci communes* are ample, but not quite so apt as the following: Lucian. *Nigrin.* 25: ἠξίου γὰρ τὸν πλούτου καταφρονεῖν διδάξοντα, πρῶτον ἑαυτὸν παρέχειν ὑψηλότερον λημμάτων. Andoc. *Or.* IV. *Argum.* p. 29: εἰρήκαμεν γὰρ πολλάκις ὅτι δεῖ τὸν τοῖς αὐτοῖς ἐγκλήμασι δοκοῦντα ἐνέχεσθαι, πρῶτον ἑαυτὸν ἐλευθεροῦν, εἶτα διαβάλλειν.

III. 9: τί οὖν; προεχόμεθα; οὐ πάντως] The explanation of this text turns upon the word προεχόμεθα, for which *three* distinct versions have

---

[1] A familiar example of such a *protasis* is the 'Form of Absolution' in the Common Prayer, 'Almighty God &c. who desireth not &c.' where the deferred apodosis is indicated by the insertion of the pronoun, 'He pardoneth' &c. The American Revisers of that work, not being able to digest this construction, have struck out the *copula* before 'and hath given.' Then 'He pardoneth' &c. begins a new sentence, not connected, either logically or grammatically, with the former.

been proposed, according as it is taken in an *active, passive,* or *middle* sense.

1. A. V. 'Are we better *than they*?' This version, derived from the Vulgate, *praecellimus eos?* supposes προεχόμεθα to bear the same meaning as προέχομεν: *Num quid prae gentilibus habemus?* (Schleusner); 'Have we (Jews) the (any) preference?' (Alford). This would agree with the alternative reading, τί οὖν προκατέχομεν περισσόν; (om. οὐ πάντως), which might therefore have been a gloss upon it; but there is no example to be found of the middle form of this verb being so used.

2. R. V. 'Are we in worse case than they?' Literally, 'Are we excelled?' Here προέχεσθαι is taken to be the *passive* of προέχειν in the same sense as before. Examples of the active verb in this sense abound; e.g. Diod. Sic. XIX. 26: προέχοντος δ' Εὐμένους δύο φυλακάς (Eumenes having the start of him by two watches). *Ibid.* 34: ἡ δὲ πρεσβυτέρα δικαιότερον ἀπεφαίνετο εἶναι τὴν προέχουσαν τοῖς χρόνοις προέχειν καὶ τῇ τιμῇ. Alciphr. *Ep.* III. 55: τῶν προΰχειν δοκούντων Ἀθήνησι πλούτῳ. The use of the *passive* in this sense is, as might be expected, not so common; Wetstein, however, has a clear example from Plutarch (T. II. p. 1038 C): ὥσπερ τῷ Διῒ προσήκει σεμνύνεσθαι ἐπ' αὐτῷ τε καὶ τῷ βίῳ, καὶ μέγα φρονεῖν... οὕτω τοῖς ἀγαθοῖς πᾶσι ταῦτα προσήκει, κατ' οὐδὲν προεχομένοις ὑπὸ τοῦ Διός (*cum nulla in re a Jove superentur*).

3. R. V. in margin: '*Do we excuse ourselves?*' Προέχεσθαι is properly *to hold something before oneself,* as Herod. II. 42: τὸν Δία μηχανήσασθαι, κριὸν ἐκδείραντα, προέχεσθαί τε τὴν κεφαλὴν ἀποταμόντα τοῦ κριοῦ, καὶ ἐνδύντα τὸ νάκος, οὕτω οἱ ἑωυτὸν ἐπιδέξαι. Hence, figuratively, *to make use of anything as a pretext or excuse* (=προφασίζεσθαι); as Herod. VIII. 3: προϊσχόμενος πρόφασιν. 111: προϊσχόμενος λόγον τόνδε. Thucyd. I. 140: ὅπερ μάλιστα προΰχονται (Schol. προβάλλονται). Soph. *Antig.* 80: σὺ μὲν τάδ' ἂν προΰχοιο. Herodian. IV. 14, 3: ὁ δὲ τὸ γῆρας προϊσχόμενος παρῃτήσατο. But when προέχεσθαι is thus used, it is never *absolute positum,* as in the text, but is invariably followed by an accusative of the thing made use of as an excuse. This is a fatal objection; and we are obliged to fall back on the last number, as the best, if not the only solution of the difficulty.

*III. 25: διὰ τὴν πάρεσιν τῶν προγεγονότων ἁμαρτημάτων] A. V. 'for the remission (or, *passing over*) of sins that are past.' R. V. 'because of the passing over of the sins done aforetime.' Dean Alford says: 'Πάρεσις is not *forgiveness* (ἄφεσις), but *overlooking*,' and compares Acts xvii. 30, ὑπεριδών, 'winked at,' which is a different thing altogether. Others (as Schleusner) maintain that there is no distinction between πάρεσις and ἄφεσις. May not the distinction lie rather in the use of the words, than in the words themselves? In both cases there is a *remission*, but ἄφεσις is more commonly said of the remission or forgiveness of a sin, πάρεσις of a debt. For the latter term H. Stephens refers to Phalar. *Ep.* CXIV. p. 328: οὐ μεταμελόμενος ἐπὶ τῇ παρέσει τῶν χρημάτων...τότε μὲν ὡς πενομένους πάρεσιν αἰτεῖσθαι χρημάτων. Add (from Wetst.) Dion. Hal. *Ant.* VII. 37 : τὴν μὲν ὁλοσχερῆ πάρεσιν οὐχ εὗροντο, τὴν δὲ εἰς χρόνον ὅσον ἠξίουν ἀναβολὴν ἔλαβον.

St Chrysostom seems to understand this word in its medical sense of παράλυσις, with a transitive force ; q. d. *the paralyzing effect* ; observing, οὐδὲ γὰρ εἶπε, διὰ τὰ ἁμαρτήματα, ἀλλά, διὰ τὴν πάρεσιν, τουτέστι, τὴν νέκρωσιν· οὐκέτι γὰρ ὑγείας ἐλπὶς ἦν· ἀλλ᾽ ὥσπερ σῶμα παραλυθὲν τῆς ἄνωθεν ἐδεῖτο χειρός, οὕτω καὶ ἡ ψυχὴ νεκρωθεῖσα.

*IV. 6 : λέγει τὸν μακαρισμόν] A. V. 'describeth the blessedness.' R. V. 'pronounceth blessing upon.' Μακαρισμός is properly the act of a person who μακαρίζει, or declares the blessedness of another. Thus in the Sermon on the Mount our Lord λέγει τοὺς μακαρισμούς of the poor in spirit, the meek &c. We would retain 'blessedness' in the text, but as this is not 'described' but only 'declared,' we would correct the A. V. accordingly.

The difference between ἔπαινος and μακαρισμός is thus stated in Stob. *Flor.* T. I. 72 : γίνεται δ᾽ ὁ μὲν ἔπαινος ἐπ᾽ ἀρετᾷ, ὁ δὲ μακαρισμὸς ἐπ᾽ εὐτυχίᾳ.

*IV. 6, 8. In the A. V. we have λογίζεσθαι, throughout this Chapter, variously rendered by 'count,' 'reckon,' 'impute'; for which the Revisers, following their inexorable rule, have uniformly translated 'reckon.' This, however, seems to be a case in which some relaxation might have been admitted, so far, at least, as to retain 'impute' in *vv.* 6, 8 : 'Blessed is the man to whom the Lord will not IMPUTE sin,' taken from Psal. xxxii. 2 A. V., and not likely to be meddled with by the O. T. Revisers[1].

*IV. 20 : οὐ διεκρίθη] A. V. 'he staggered not.' R. V. 'he wavered not.' In all other places (including James i. 6) the Revisers have rendered διεκρίθη by 'he doubted.' In the present instance, having seen cause to depart from their 'hard and fast' rule, it is a pity that they should not have stuck to Tyndale's and Cranmer's 'stackered': a word which has become consecrated, so to speak, to this particular text, and which the English Bible-reader will prefer to any other.

V. 1 : T. R. ἔχομεν, 'we have.' In favour of ἔχωμεν, 'let us have,' the preponderance of MS. authority is very great ; namely, AB¹CDKLℵ¹; of the versions, Vulg. and both Syriac ; of the Fathers, Chrys. Cyril. Theodoret and many others. With respect to the Syriac versions, Dean Alford quotes the Philoxenian for ἔχομεν (wrongly) and Peschito for ἔχωμεν ('but, according to Etheridge, ἔχομεν'). Dr Scrivener is also somewhat confused about these two versions (*A plain Introduction* &c. p. 447 ed. 1861),

---

[1] Ps. xxxii. 2, R. V.: 'Unto whom the Lord imputeth not iniquity.' Ed.

assigning to the Peschito 'probably' (instead of 'certainly') ἔχωμεν (ܠܢ ܐܝܬ ܠܢ ܗܘܐ), and to the Philoxenian, 'what,' he says, 'seems to be a combination of both readings, ܐܝܬ ܠܢ ܢܗܘܐ ܠܘܬ ܐܠܗܐ.' But this is a mistake. The Syriac ܠܢ ܐܝܬ ܠܢ is ἔχωμεν, and nothing else. For ἔχομεν this version (and all others) would put ܠܢ ܐܝܬ; but when the word is in the subjunctive mood, since ܐܝܬ is indeclinable, it is a peculiarity of the Philoxenian to prefix the corresponding mood of ܢܗܘܐ, here ܢܗܘܐ. Thus ἵνα τινὰ καρπὸν σχῶ (Rom. i. 13) becomes ܐܝܬ ܠܝ ܕܦܐܪܐ ܡܕܡ ܐܩܛܘܦ ܐܦ ܒܟܘܢ ܐܝܟ ܕܐܦ ܗܘ ܕܐܝܬ ܠܝ; ἵνα ἔχητε (2 Cor. v. 12) ܐܝܬ ܢܗܘܐ ܠܟܘܢ.

In favour of the old reading (which the English reader will be most unwilling to part with, as infolding a doctrine dear to the heart of every faithful Christian) it may be urged, (1) that it is hardly within the competence of MSS.[1] to decide (especially against the strongest *internal* evidence) between such variants as ἔχομεν and ἔχωμεν, so continually are these vowels confused even in the best MSS.; (2) that ἔχομεν may have been changed into ἔχωμεν to correspond with καυχώμεθα, which was supposed to be the subjunctive mood; and (3) that there is a tendency in the copyists to turn an affirmation into an exhortation, a striking example of which is 1 Cor. xv. 49, where φορέσομεν is written φορέσωμεν in all the uncials except B.

*V. 7 : τάχα τις καὶ τολμᾷ ἀποθανεῖν] 'Peradventure some (one) would even dare to die.' For τολμᾶν in the sense of ὑπομένειν, *to submit to*, Wetst. quotes Eurip. *Alc.* 644 : ὃς τηλίκοσδ᾽ ὢν κἀπὶ τέρμ᾽ ἥκων βίου | οὐκ ἠθέλησας οὐδ᾽ ἐτόλμησας θανεῖν | τοῦ σοῦ πρὸ παιδός. Dem. *c. Aristog.* 2 : τοὺς μὲν προγόνους ὑπὲρ τοῦ μὴ καταλυθῆναι τοὺς νόμους ἀποθνήσκειν τολμᾶν. In the following from Dio. Chrys. *Or.* III. p. 48, 9 : ὑπὲρ δὲ τῆς νίκης πολλοὶ τῶν ἀγαθῶν ΚΑΙ ἀποθνήσκειν αἱροῦνται, the particle will have the same force as in text, which is explained by some grammarians (as Baver. on Thucyd. VIII. 54) to be *si usus tulerit*, εἰ δέοι, εἰ τύχοι, 'if need be.'

*VI. 5. In this somewhat difficult verse, while expositors are nearly agreed on the meaning of σύμφυτοι (not 'planted together,' but intimately united, and (as it were) 'grown together') there is room for difference as to two subsidiary points. *First*, should we understand αὐτῷ after σύμφυτοι? or should we connect σύμφυτοι τῷ ὁμοιώματι, 'united with the likeness'? The latter seems preferable, (1) because σύμφυτος has a natural affinity with a dative case ; and (2) because, if no such connexion were intended, St Paul would, probably, have guarded against misconstruction by writing ἐν ὁμοιώματι, as he has done Rom. viii. 3, Phil. ii. 7. *Secondly*, in the

---

[1] [Of such variations Cobet (*Coll. Crit.* p. 78) says : 'Saepissime libri variant in -εῖτο et -ητο....Tamen nus- quam est anceps et ambigua optio. Sententia et structura loci ubique utra scriptura sit potior plane demonstrant.']

apodosis, ἀλλὰ καὶ τῆς ἀναστάσεως ἐσόμεθα (σύμφυτοι), is τῷ ὁμοιώματι to be mentally supplied before τῆς ἀναστάσεως, or are we to join σύμφυτοι τῆς ἀναστάσεως, as St Chrysostom does, insisting much on the absence of τῷ ὁμοιώματι, and actually construing, εἰπὼν γὰρ ὅτι σύμφυτοι (=κοινωνοὶ) ἐσόμεθα τῆς ἀναστάσεως? But the construction of σύμφυτος with a genitive is not free from objection, especially when the other construction is found in close proximity to it ; although, according to Dean Alford, it could not well be said, that we shall be σύμφυτοι τῇ ἀναστάσει, because 'the dative would not be strong enough to denote the state, of which we shall be actual partakers.' But if the Apostle had actually written, ἀλλὰ καὶ τῇ ἀναστάσει ἐσόμεθα, we doubt whether such an objection would have entered into any one's head.

*VI. 17 : χάρις δὲ τῷ θεῷ] Wetst. compares Arrian. Epict. IV. 4 : τότε καὶ ἐγὼ ἡμάρτανον, νῦν δὲ οὐκέτι, χάρις τῷ θεῷ. I add Synes. Ep. VII : τῷ δὲ θεῷ χάρις, ὅτι παρέσχεν ἡμῖν ἀκοῦσαι καλλίονα. Anthol. I. 20, 2 (vol. II. p. 257, Jacobs. 1794): Πολλὴ σοί, φυτοεργέ, πόνου χάρις· εἵνεκα σεῖο | ἀχρὰς ἐν εὐκάρποις δένδρεσιν ἐγγράφομαι.

*VI. 19 : ἀνθρώπινον λέγω] 'I speak after the manner of men'; like κατὰ ἄνθρωπον λέγω Gal. iii. 15. Another version might be, 'I speak moderately,' or 'within bounds,' as 1 Cor. x. 13 : 'There hath no temptation taken you, εἰ μὴ ἀνθρώπινος (=σύμμετρος).' St Chrysostom seems to waver between the two : (1) ἀπὸ ἀνθρωπίνων λογισμῶν, ἀπὸ τῶν ἐν συνηθείᾳ γενομένων. (2) οὐδὲν ὑπέρογκον ἀπαιτεῖ, ἀλλὰ καὶ σφόδρα σύμμετρον καὶ κοῦφον.

*VII. 3 : γένηται ἀνδρὶ ἑτέρῳ...γενομένην ἀνδρὶ ἑτέρῳ] A. V. (bis) 'she be married to another man.' R. V. 'she be joined to another man.' The A. V. seems to be the more correct rendering, 'married' being understood in a popular sense, without reference to the legality of the tie. The Hebrew phrase is הָיָה לְאִישׁ. Lev. xxii. 12 (LXX.): ἐὰν γένηται ἀνδρὶ ἀλλογενεῖ, 'if she (the priest's daughter) be married unto a stranger.' In other places the same phrase ἐὰν γένηται ἀνδρὶ ἑτέρῳ is rendered 'if she become another man's' (Jerem. iii. 1), or, 'another man's wife' (Deut. xxiv. 2), the dative indicating possession. Any one of these is preferable to 'be joined to' (προσκολληθῇ), which suggests a quite different idea.

VII. 21 : τῷ θέλοντι ἐμοὶ ποιεῖν τὸ καλόν, ὅτι ἐμοὶ τὸ κακὸν παράκειται] A. V. 'That when I would do good, evil is present with me.' R. V. 'That to me who would do good, evil is present.' But this latter version takes no account of the repetition of ἐμοὶ after παράκειται ; and in v. 18 ἐμοὶ παράκειται is rendered 'is present with me,' not 'to me.' On the whole the A. V. adequately expresses the Greek, and its rhythmical superiority to that which is proposed to substitute for it is evident.

*VIII. 3: **καὶ περὶ ἁμαρτίας**] A. V. 'and for sin.' R. V. 'and *as
an offering* for sin.' Compare Heb. x. 6: ὁλοκαυτώματα καὶ περὶ ἁμαρτίας.
Περὶ ἁμαρτίας from its frequent use in the O. T. for the Hebr. חַטָּאת came
to be considered as a single word, whence were formed the derivatives
περιαμαρτίζειν, *expiare* (Οἱ λοιποί, Exod. xxix. 36, Lev. viii. 15) and
περιαμαρτισμός (Σ. Zach. xiii. 1).

VIII. 18: **οὐκ ἄξια...πρὸς τὴν μέλλουσαν δόξαν**] 'Are not worthy to be
compared with the glory.' This is, evidently, the correct version of the
Greek, the idea of *comparison* being virtually included in πρός; as
Xenoph. *Anab.* VII. 7, 41: λῆρος πάντα ἐδόκει πρὸς τὸ ἀργύριον ἔχειν.
But the construction of the whole sentence is novel, and appears to
be a confusion in the writer's mind of two others, either of which would
be free from objection. Thus he might have said, οὐκ ἄξια (for ἀντάξια)
τῆς δόξης, as Prov. iii. 15: οὐκ ἄξιον αὐτῆς; and viii. 11: πᾶν τὸ τίμιον οὐκ
ἄξιον σοφίας ἐστίν; which may be traced to the Homeric νῦν δ' οὔθ' ἑνὸς
ἄξιοί ἐσμεν | Ἕκτορος. Or he might for οὐκ ἄξια have written οὐδενὸς
ἄξια; and then we might have compared Dio. Chrys. *Or.* I. p. 12. 10:
οἱ γὰρ ἀνθρώπων λόγοι καὶ τὰ πάντα σοφίσματα οὐδενὸς ἄξια πρὸς τὴν παρὰ
τῶν θεῶν ἐπίνοιαν καὶ φήμην. This solution makes it unnecessary to give
to οὐκ ἄξια the meaning of 'insignificant,' or 'of no account,' which
cannot be proved.

VIII. 24: **τί καὶ ἐλπίζει**] 'Why doth he yet hope for?' R. V. in
margin: 'Some ancient authorities read *awaiteth*' (ὑπομένει for ἐλπίζει).
These are, according to Dean Alford's notation, 'ΑΝ¹ 47 marg. Cyr.
expectat syrr. Ambros.' By 'syrr.' we are to understand both Syriac
versions, which is not correct. The Peschito seems to have read
ὑπομένει, ܘܠܗ ܡܣܟܐ ܠܝܣܘ, as ܣܟܐ is frequently put for ὑπέ-
μεινε, προσεδόκησε &c., never for ἤλπισε. But the Philoxenian certainly
read ἐλπίζει (ܡܣܒܪ), and White's translation, *exspectat*, as well as
St Ambrose's *exspectat*, were also meant for ἐλπίζει, not for ὑπομένει,
which latter, according to N. T. use, is not 'awaiteth,' but 'endureth.'

VIII. 28: **πάντα συνεργεῖ**] 'All things work together.' So the Philoxenian Syriac ܠܗܘܢ ܡܥܕܪ ܟܠ. According to the Peschito ܒܟܠ
ܡܕܡ ܡܥܕܪ ܠܗܘܢ we must translate, 'He (God) worketh with them
in all things,' the Greek being the same, and πάντα being taken in the
sense of κατὰ πάντα. If we adopt the reading of ABN, which interpolate
ὁ Θεὸς after συνεργεῖ, the last mentioned version need not be altered.
According to this reading, Dean Alford would write συνέργει from
συνέργω, *concludo*; but this is not a biblical word; and the Apostle, if
such had been his meaning, would certainly have written συγκλείει.

IX. 6: οὐχ οἷον δὲ ὅτι ἐκπέπτωκεν ὁ λόγος τοῦ θεοῦ] 'Not (R. V. But *it is* not) as though the word of God hath taken none effect.' All English versions, following the Vulgate, *Non autem quod exciderit verbum Dei*, agree in this explanation of the unique combination of particles, οὐχ οἷον ὅτι, supposed by Dean Alford to be elliptical for οὐ τοῖον λέγω, οἷον ὅτι. But our English 'not as though' is sufficiently represented in Greek by οὐχ ὅτι (e.g. Phil. iii. 12: οὐχ ὅτι ἤδη ἔλαβον); and the question is, whether any, and what, additional force is contained in οἷον. We shall first take the well-known case of οὐχ οἷον (without ὅτι)...ἀλλὰ καί, of which Munthe (who rightly gives it the meaning of *non tantum non, sed*, or *tantum abest ut*) adduces some good examples from Diodorus Siculus ; e.g. III. 17 (of the Ichthyophagi): οὐχ οἷον ὑγρὰν τροφὴν ἐπιζητοῦσι ποτοῦ, ἀλλ' οὐδ' ἔννοιαν ἔχουσι. *Ibid.* 33: οὐχ οἷον φεύγειν βούλονται (Troglodytae) τὴν ὑπερβολὴν τῶν συμβαινόντων αὐτοῖς κακῶν (from the excessive heat of the sun), ἀλλὰ καὶ τοὐναντίον, ἑκουσίως προϊέναι τὸ ζῆν, ἕνεκα τοῦ μὴ βιασθῆναι διαίτης ἑτέρας καὶ βίου πειραθῆναι. Munthe goes on to explain the text in the same manner : 'Not only has the word of God not come to nought...but,' making the apodosis to begin at *v.* 7 : ἀλλ' ἐν Ἰσαὰκ κληθήσεταί σοι σπέρμα ; a construction (besides the insertion of ὅτι) so unlike the instances from Diodorus as to admit of no comparison. The Greek Lexicographers recognize the phrase οὐχ οἷον, not followed by ἀλλά or ἀλλὰ καί, but condemn it as a barbarism; as Phrynichus. p. 372 ed. Lobeck : Οὐχ οἷον ὀργίζομαι· κίβδηλον ἐσχάτως. , μάλιστα ἁμαρτάνεται ἐν τῇ ἡμεδαπῇ (Bithynia), οὐχ οἷον καὶ μὴ οἷον λεγόντων...λέγειν δὲ χρὴ οὐ δήπου, μὴ δήπου. Antiatt. Bekk. p. 110: Οὐχ οἷον ὁρίζομαι [ὀργίζομαι]...σὺ δέ, πολὺ ἀπέχω τοῦ ὁρίζεσθαι [ὀργίζεσθαι]. In Athen. VI. p. 244 E a parasite complains of having to keep up with his patron's pace, which he describes as flying rather than walking : πέτεται γάρ, οὐχ οἷον βαδίζει τὰς ὁδούς. From these instances it would appear that οὐχ οἷον, according to the vulgar use of it, was a strong negative, *nequaquam, ne minimum* ; and, perhaps, the sense and spirit of the whole sentence would be best conveyed to the English reader by such a translation as the following: 'Not, however, that the word of God hath come to nought, FAR FROM IT.'

IX. 30: τὰ μὴ διώκοντα...κατέλαβε...*v.* 31 : εἰς νόμον...οὐκ ἔφθασε] A. V. 'Which followed not after...have attained to...(31) hath not attained to the law.' R. V. 'Which followed not after...attained to...(31) did not arrive at *that* law.' Phil. iii. 12: διώκω δὲ εἰ καὶ καταλάβω ἐφ' ᾧ κατελήφθην...16: εἰς ὃ ἐφθάσαμεν...A. V. 'But I follow after (R. V. press on) if that I may apprehend that for which also I am (was) apprehended...(16) whereto we have already attained.'

On these versions we remark (1) that διώκειν and καταλαβεῖν are correlative terms for *pursuing* and *overtaking*. Thus Exod. xv. 9 : 'The enemy said, διώξας καταλήψομαι, I will pursue, I will overtake.' Wetstein quotes Herod. II. 30 : Ψαμμήτιχος δὲ πυθόμενος ἐδίωκε· ὡς δὲ κατέλαβε...

Lucian. *Hermot.* 77 : ὁ πρὸ σοῦ μάλα πολλοὶ καὶ ἀγαθοὶ καὶ ὠκύτεροι παρα πολὺ διώκοντες οὐ κατέλαβον[1]. (2) In the extract from Romans there is no reason why we should not translate κατέλαβε by 'overtook,' in which case we may leave 'did not attain to' as the most convenient rendering of οὐκ ἔφθασεν εἰς, agreeing with Phil. iii. 16, as represented by both versions. In Phil. iii. 12 the English 'apprehend' conveys the idea of an *arrest*, in which sense it is employed by our Translators, Acts xii. 4, 2 Cor. xi. 32 ; where, however, the Greek word is πιάσαι, not καταλαβεῖν. Some persons may be pleased with the idea of Saul's being *apprehended* or *arrested* by Jesus Christ, while on his way to apprehend others. But such an idea is foreign to the word καταλαβεῖν, and the sense is equally good, if we translate, 'I follow after, if so be that I may *overtake* that for which also I *was overtaken* of Christ Jesus.'

*X. 5 : Μωϋσῆς γὰρ γράφει τὴν δικαιοσύνην τὴν ἐκ νόμου, ὅτι ὁ ποιήσας αὐτὰ ἄνθρωπος ζήσεται ἐν αὐτῇ] This is the reading of the T. R., which is supported by B, and all uncials except A and (originally) אD, as well as by both Syriac versions (Pesch. ܇ܠܩܘܕ ܐܠܐ ܐܣܘܡ; Philox. ܐܠܐ ܠܟܐܘܘܕ). The only difficulties it presents are (1) the construction γράφει τὴν δ. (which, however, is warranted by John i. 46: ὃν ἔγραψε Μωϋσῆς...εὑρήκαμεν) and (2) the insertion of αὐτά, which is wanting in the MSS. of the LXX. (Lev. xviii. 5) though found in Ed. Rom. (but the whole text is καὶ φυλάξεσθε...πάντα τὰ κρίματά μου, καὶ ποιήσετε αὐτά, ᾿Α ποιήσας [αὐτὰ] ἄνθρωπος ζήσεται ἐν αὐτοῖς. The other reading, that of ADא[1], is : Μ. γὰρ γράφει ὅτι τὴν δ. τὴν ἐκ ν. ὁ ποιήσας ἄνθρωπος ζήσεται ἐν αὐτῇ, rendered by Vulg. *M. enim scripsit, quoniam justitiam, quae ex lege est, qui fecerit homo, vivet in ea;* and by R. V. 'For M. writeth that the man that doeth the righteousness which is of the law shall live thereby.' Against which it may be urged that Moses 'writeth' nothing of the sort. He does not even mention 'the righteousness that is of the law.' That is a phrase introduced by St Paul himself in contrast to 'the righteousness which is of faith.' True, M. 'describes' what the Apostle understands by 'the righteousness which is of the law,' when he declares that the man which doeth all the things contained in the law 'shall live by them'; but that is all. Hear St Chrysostom. Μ. γὰρ γράφει, φησί, τὴν ἐκ τοῦ νόμου δικαιοσύνην. ῾Ο δὲ λέγει, τοῦτό ἐστι. Μ. δείκνυσιν ἡμῖν τὴν ἐκ τοῦ νόμου δικαιοσύνην, ὁποία τίς ἐστι καὶ ποταπή. ποία τοίνυν ἐστί, καὶ πόθεν συνίσταται; ἀπὸ τοῦ πληρωθῆναι τὰς ἐντολάς. ὁ ποιήσας αὐτά, ζήσεται ἐν αὐτοῖς.

*XI. 8 : (πνεῦμα) κατανύξεως] A. V. 'of slumber.' R. V. 'of stupor.' The first of these is, certainly, too weak, the second, perhaps, too strong, to convey the precise sense of the original word in Isai. xxix. 10, תַּרְדֵּמָה, Ο΄. κατάνυξις. The Hexapla on that place gives a choice of renderings : ᾿Α. καταφορᾶς. Σ. καρώσεως. Θ. ἐκστάσεως. The A. V. and R. V. in Isaiah

---

[1] [Cf. Plut. *Vit. Arat.* XL : καὶ διώξαντες, ὡς οὐ κατέλαβον.]

is 'deep sleep,' which had been already used for the same word in Gen. ii. 21 : 'The LORD God caused a deep sleep to fall upon Adam.' On a final revision 'deep sleep' might be recalled in St Paul's quotation.

Other meanings of the word need not delay us, but we must be allowed to protest against Mr Humphry's derivation of the word from a verb, which means properly 'pin' or 'nail down,' and thence 'the *stupefaction* which arises from such treatment.' St Chrysostom, indeed, has something like the former part of this statement : κατανυγῆναι γὰρ (he says) οὐδὲν ἕτερόν ἐστιν ἢ τὸ ἐμπαγῆναί που καὶ προσηλῶσθαι, whence he attributes to κατάνυξις the notion of a *fixed and immoveable* state of mind, here *in malam partem* : τὸ τοίνυν ἀνίατον αὐτῶν καὶ δυσμετάθετον τῆς γνώμης δηλῶν, πνεῦμα κατανύξεως εἶπεν. But there is no authority for this use of the word ; and the sense of *stupefaction*, if correct, must be derived not from νύσσειν, 'to prick,' and so cause pain, but from the Hellenistic use of κατάνυξις in the examples quoted above.

XI. 11, 12 : 'I say then, Have they stumbled (ἔπταισαν) that they should fall (πέσωσι)? God forbid : but *rather* through their fall (τῷ αὐτῶν παραπτώματι) salvation *is come* unto the Gentiles, for to provoke them to jealousy. Now if the fall (τὸ παράπτωμα) of them *be* the riches of the world, and the diminishing (τὸ ἥττημα) of them the riches of the Gentiles, how much more their fulness (τὸ πλήρωμα)?' Besides other difficulties, there are two words in this passage which do not seem to be correctly rendered.

1. For παράπτωμα the Revisers have retained 'fall,' with a marginal note, 'Or, *trespass*.' But παράπτωμα is not an actual *fall* (which, indeed, has just been strongly denied) but a *slip* or *false step* (morally, a *trespass*), and differs from πταῖσμα only as *slipping* does from *stumbling*. In fact both Syriac versions have rendered ἔπταισαν and παράπτωμα by derivatives from the same root (Pesch. ܐܠܐܬܠܝ and ܝܐܠܬܐܠ ; Philox. ܐܟܝܐ and ܝܐܟܝܐܠ) ; and if no better word could be found, we might do the same : 'Have they stumbled...through their stumbling.'

2. The other word, ἥττημα, is more difficult, as appears from the greater variety of its proposed equivalents, 'diminishing' (from Vulg. *deminutio*), 'decay,' 'loss,' 'small number,' &c.; which, however, for the most part, seem to be mere guesses, inspired by the desire to make a good contrast with πλήρωμα. If we look only to the word itself, and its cognates ἧττα and ἡττᾶσθαι, we shall find that the only certain notion which can be assigned to them is that of being *beaten* or *defeated* in a contest, whether warlike or otherwise. Thus νίκη and ἧττα are as commonly opposed to each other as 'victory' and 'defeat.' A man may be *defeated* or *overcome* (ἡττᾶσθαι) either ὑπὸ τῶν πολεμίων, or ἐν τοῖς δικαστηρίοις (Xenoph. *Mem.* IV. 4, 17), or by his own passions and appetites (comp. 2 Pet. ii. 19). The particular form ἥττημα is peculiar to biblical Greek, and (besides the present text) is only found in Isai. xxxi. 8

and 1 Cor. vi. 7. In the former place, the phrase ἔσονται εἰς ἥττημα appears to be equivalent to ἡττηθήσονται in the next verse, though the Hebrew is different. In 1 Cor. vi. 7 : 'Now therefore there is utterly a fault (ἥττημα) among you, because ye go to law one with another,' St Chrysostom upholds the proper meaning of the word in respect to an action-at-law; as if the Apostle had said, 'You have sustained a defeat at all events, by merely going to law ; the victory would have been to suffer yourself to be defrauded.' (See more on that place.) Returning to the text, we would translate v. 12 thus : 'Now if their stumbling is the riches of the world, and their defeat the riches of the Gentiles ; how much more their fulness?' If it be objected that there is no opposition between 'defeat' and 'fulness,' we answer, why should there be, any more than between 'stumbling' and 'fulness?' and what has πλοῦτος to do with either of them? The sentence may be rhetorically faulty, but would not be much improved even if it could be shewn that ἥττημα and πλήρωμα were as opposite to each other as 'impoverishment' to 'replenishment' (Alford), or as − to + (Wetstein).

*XI. 18: οὐ σὺ τὴν ῥίζαν βαστάζεις, ἀλλ' ἡ ῥίζα σέ] A. V. 'thou bearest not the root, but the root thee.' The Revisers, perhaps with the idea of giving greater emphasis to σύ, have varied the former clause thus : 'it is not thou that bearest the root.' But in that case would not a correct English ear require in the latter clause, 'but the root *that beareth* thee'? At all events, no change was necessary.

XI. 22: ἐπὶ μὲν τοὺς πεσόντας, ἀποτομία (T. R. -ίαν), ἐπὶ δὲ σέ, χρηστότης θεοῦ (T. R. χρηστότητα sine θεοῦ), ἐὰν ἐπιμείνῃς τῇ χρηστότητι] No English reader can fail to see the awkwardness of such a sentence as the following : 'Toward them that fell, severity ; but toward thee, God's goodness.' Dean Alford says : 'The repetition of θεοῦ is quite in the manner of the Apostle. See 1 Cor. i. 24, 25.' The place is, Χριστὸν θεοῦ δύναμιν καὶ θεοῦ σοφίαν...τὸ μωρὸν τοῦ θεοῦ...καὶ τὸ ἀσθενὲς τοῦ θεοῦ. But this example would only support ἀποτομία θεοῦ...χρηστότης θεοῦ. If θεοῦ were inserted at all, it should be after both ; or if after one only, then after ἀποτομία. It has been suggested that θεοῦ was erased as unnecessary. But surely Rückert's idea is much more probable, that θεοῦ was originally a marginal note on ἐὰν ἐπιμείνῃς τῇ χρηστότητι, which might otherwise be understood in a *subjective* sense, like ἐπιμενοῦμεν τῇ ἁμαρτίᾳ (Ch. vi. 1), ἐὰν μὴ ἐπιμείνωσι τῇ ἀπιστίᾳ (Ch. xi. 23). And in this sense it seems to have been understood by St Chrysostom (T. IX. p. 650 B): διὰ τοῦτο περὶ σὲ χρηστότητα ἐπεδείξατο, ἵνα ἐπιμείνῃς· καὶ οὐκ εἶπε, τῇ πίστει, ἀλλὰ τῇ χρηστότητι· τουτέστιν, ἐὰν ἄξια τῆς τοῦ θεοῦ φιλανθρωπίας πράττῃς[1].

[1] I find ἀποτομία and χρηστότης in contrast in a passage of Diod. Sic. T. x. p. 69 ed. Bip.: ἀπονέμειν αὐτῷ (Caesari) τὸν αἰώνιον τῆς χρηστότητος ἔπαινον. τῶν γὰρ προγόνων αὐτοῦ σκληρότερον κεχρημένων τῇ πόλει, οὗτος διὰ τῆς ἰδίας ἡμερότητος διωρθώσατο τὰς ἐκείνων ἀποτομίας.

Ibid. ἐπεὶ καὶ σὺ ἐκκοπήσῃ] 'Otherwise thou also shalt be cut off.'
Dean Alford translates : 'For [otherwise] thou also shalt be cut off';
with a note : '*Otherwise* is not expressed in the original; but the
construction implies it.' He should have said : '*For* is not expressed
in the original.' Ἐπεί is either 'for' or 'otherwise,' never both, a combination which correct English also eschews. See Rom. xi. 6. 1 Cor.
xv. 29. Heb. ix. 17. Good examples of ἐπεί, *alioquin*, from Plato and
Synesius may be found in Wetstein (on xi. 6), to which add Diog. Laert.
I. 114 : (Epimenides) ἰδόντα γοῦν τὴν Μουνυχίαν παρ' Ἀθηναίοις, ἀγνοεῖν
φάναι αὐτοὺς ὅσων κακῶν αἴτιον ἔσται τοῦτο τὸ χωρίον αὐτοῖς · ΕΠΕΙ κἂν τοῖς
ὀδοῦσιν αὐτὸ διαφορῆσαι (*or else*, they would have pulled it down with their
teeth). S. Chrysost. T. XI. p. 407 D : πάλιν, ἄν τινα κατηχῇς, λέγε ἐξ
ὑποθέσεως ὑποκειμένης · ΕΠΕΙ σίγα (*or else*, be silent); where the last Paris
Editor has fallen into the same error as that noticed above, noting : 'Fort.
ἐπεὶ ἄλλως σίγα[1].'

*XII. 2 : καὶ μὴ συσχηματίζεσθε τῷ αἰῶνι τούτῳ, ἀλλὰ μεταμορφοῦσθε...]
Nothing could read better than the A. V. 'And be not conformed to this
world ; but be ye transformed.' The very alliteration, though not in the
original, is a beauty superadded to it. Granting that there is a distinction between σχῆμα and μορφή, and that this distinction is preserved by
the A. V. in other places by the appropriation of 'fashion' to the one,
and 'form' to the other, it does not follow that the inexorable rule of
uniformity should override all other considerations, whether of sound
or sense. 'Conformity to the world' is an established phrase, and much
more likely to be understood than the proposed improvement, 'And be
not fashioned according to this world.'

That μορφή and σχῆμα are contrasted with each other in Philipp. ii.
6—8, in respect to the two natures in Christ, must be allowed, but such a
distinction has no place in our text. St Chrysostom's explanation of μὴ
συσχηματίζεσθε κ.τ.έ. is this: Μὴ τυπώσῃς ἑαυτὸν κατὰ τὸ σχῆμα τοῦ παρόντος
βίου. He calls it σχῆμα, because of its unsubstantiality (τὸ ἀνυπόστατον):
it is σχῆμα μόνον καὶ ἐπίδειξις καὶ προσωπεῖον, οὐ πράγματος ἀλήθεια, οὐχ
ὑπόστασις μένουσα. In contrast to this (he says) is μορφή τις ἀληθής,
φυσικὸν ἔχουσα κάλλος, οὐ δεόμενον τῶν ἔξωθεν ἐπιτριμμάτων τε καὶ σχημάτων.
And he concludes : Ἄν τοίνυν τὸ σχῆμα ῥίψῃς, ταχέως ἐπὶ τὴν μορφὴν ἥξεις.
Perhaps this idea might be conveyed to the English reader by rendering :
'And be not outwardly conformed to this world ; but be ye inwardly
transformed by the renewing of your mind.'

XII. 10, 11 : τῇ τιμῇ...τῇ σπουδῇ] A more elegant arrangement would
be κατὰ τιμήν...κατὰ σπουδήν, which the Apostle has adopted Phil. iii. 6 :

---

[1][Cf. Paus. X. 11, 4: εἰ δέξεταί σε ἠ-
πίως τὸ ὕδωρ, ἐπεὶ ἄλλως γε χαλεπὸν ὑπὸ
ζεστότητός ἐστιν ἐμβαίνεσθαι. Plut. *Vit.*

Phoc. IX: εὐτυχεῖτε, εἶπεν, ἔχοντες στρα-
τηγὸν εἰδότα ὑμᾶς · ἐπεὶ πάλαι ἂν ἀπολώ-
λειτε.]

κατὰ ζῆλον, διώκων τὴν ἐκκλησίαν, κ.τ.λ. With the latter we may compare Diod. Sic. IX. Fragm. 8 (T. IV. p. 43 ed. Bip.): κατὰ μὲν γὰρ τὴν νομοθεσίαν ἐφαίνετο πολιτικὸς καὶ φρόνιμος· κατὰ δὲ τὴν πίστιν, δίκαιος· κατὰ δὲ τὴν ἐν τοῖς ὅπλοις ὑπεροχήν, ἀνδρεῖος· κατὰ δὲ τὴν πρὸς τὸ κέρδος μεγαλοψυχίαν, ἀφιλάργυρος.

XII. 13 : To the authorities in favour of μνείαις (for χρείαις) should be added Eusebius, who in his *History of the Martyrs in Palestine*, p. 1 (Cureton's Translation) says : 'We have been also charged in the book of the Apostles, that we should be partakers in the remembrance of the saints (ܠܩ݁ܕ̈ܝ̣ܫܐ ܕܗܘ̈ܝܢ ܘܠܐ؟).'

XII. 16 : ἀλλὰ τοῖς ταπεινοῖς συναπαγόμενοι] A. V. 'But condescend to men of low estate. Or, *be contented with mean things.*' R. V. 'But condescend to (Gr. *be carried away with*) things that are lowly (Or, *them that are lowly*).' In favour of *persons* it may be urged that both in the Old and New Testaments οἱ ταπεινοί occurs continually ; τὰ ταπεινά once only, Psal. cxxxvii. 6 : ὅτι ὑψηλὸς ὁ κύριος, καὶ τὰ ταπεινὰ ἐφορᾷ, καὶ τὰ ὑψηλὰ ἀπὸ μακρόθεν γινώσκει, where *persons* are indicated in the Hebrew. Again, the verb συναπάγεσθαι, when used in a figurative sense, may be compared with συμπεριφέρεσθαι, which is to *comply with*, humour, accommodate oneself to another, as Ecclus. xxv. 1 : γυνὴ καὶ ἀνὴρ ἑαυτοῖς συμπεριφερόμενοι. Stob. *Flor*. T. LXIV. 31 : μὴ διαμάχεσθαι (with a madman) μηδὲ ἀντιτείνειν, ἀλλὰ καὶ συμπεριφέρεσθαι καὶ συνεπινεύειν. Epict. *Enchir*. 68 (ch. XXII. ed. Wolf.) : μέχρι μέν τοι λόγου μὴ ὄκνει συμπεριφέρεσθαι αὐτοῖς. On the whole, it would be very difficult to improve upon the A. V. 'condescend to,' whether we understand by τοῖς ταπεινοῖς men of low degree, or of a meek and humble disposition.

XII. 18 : εἰ δυνατόν, τὸ ἐξ ὑμῶν] By this cumulation of conditions the difficulty of the precept is admirably brought out. In an extract from Iamblichus, quoted by Cobet (*Coll. Crit*. p. 397) : ἐκ φιλίας ἀληθινῆς ἐξαιρεῖν ἀγῶνά τε καὶ φιλονεικίαν, μάλιστα μὲν ἐκ πάσης, εἰ δυνατόν· εἰ δὲ μή, ἔκ γε τῆς πατρικῆς, few scholars will be found to accept the *dictum* of that celebrated Critic : 'Μάλιστα μέν significat εἰ μὲν δυνατόν ; itaque ridicule εἰ δυνατόν additur.' On this principle we might condemn Demosth. *Phil*. IV. p. 147, 1 : ἐὰν ὑμεῖς ὁμοθυμαδὸν ἐκ μιᾶς γνώμης Φίλιππον ἀμύνησθε[1]. With v. 21 : ἀλλὰ νίκα ἐν τῷ ἀγαθῷ τὸ κακόν, I would compare Hierocles ap. Stob. *Flor*. T. LXXXIV. 20 : ἔπειτα, κἂν ὄντως τοιοῦτος ᾖ ἀδελφὸς (σκαιὸς καὶ δυσομίλητος), ἀλλὰ σύ γε, φαίην ἄν, ἀμείνων εὑρέθητι, καὶ νίκησον αὐτοῦ τὴν ἀγριότητα ταῖς εὐποιίαις.

---

[1] [Cf. Min. Fel. *Oct*. ch. 16: Dicam equidem, ut potero, pro viribus: Dem. 715, 21: ἐν παραβύστῳ,...λάθρα τὸν νόμον εἰσήνεγκε. Plut. *Vit. Galb*. X : χαλεπῶς μὲν καὶ μόλις, ἔπεισε δ' οὖν....]

*XIII. 14 : **καὶ τῆς σαρκὸς πρόνοιαν μὴ ποιεῖσθε**] Compare Dion. Hal.
Ant. X. 1 : τῶν δ' ἐντὸς τείχους κακῶν πρόνοιαν ἐποιοῦντο. Diod. Sic. VIII.
Fragm. 6, T. IV. p. 31 ed. Bip.: καὶ τοῦ σώματος ἐποιούμην πρόνοιαν (sc. ut
ἄτρωτος evaderem). Id. XV. 23 : καὶ τῆς ἐν τοῖς ὅπλοις μελέτης πολλὴν
πρόνοιαν ἐπεποίηντο. Id. T. X. p. 218 ed. Bip.: ἐποιήσατο δὲ ὁ νομοθέτης
(Moses) τῶν πολεμικῶν ἔργων πολλὴν πρόνοιαν. Thucyd. VI. 9 : νομίζων
ὁμοίως ἀγαθὸν πολίτην εἶναι, ὃς ἂν καὶ τοῦ σώματός τι καὶ τῆς οὐσίας προνοῆται.
Since the Revisers have rendered προνοούμενα καλὰ (*v.* 17) by 'Take
thought for things honourable,' they might also, in this verse, have
translated 'Take no thought for the flesh'; though it would have been
far better to have retained 'taking thought' for μεριμνᾶν, as in A. V. See
Davies *Bible English*, p. 99.

*XIV. 6. The omission of the clause, καὶ ὁ μὴ φρονῶν τὴν ἡμέραν
κυρίῳ οὐ φρονεῖ, in some MSS. (unfortunately followed by the Revisers)
arose from the same obvious cause as that for which the latter clause of
1 John ii. 23 is wanting in the T. R. The suggestion of Dean Alford,
that it may have been *intentionally* omitted after the observance of the
Lord's day came to be regarded as obligatory, is highly improbable.
Such an intentional mutilator would have struck out the preceding clause
also.

*XIV. 7 : **ἑαυτῷ ζῇ**] Many examples of this phrase are commonly
cited, in the sense of *enjoying oneself* (Ovid's ' *Vive tibi*'), as Terent.
Ad. V. 4, 9 : 'Ille suam semper egit vitam, in otio, in conviviis…sibi
vixit, sibi sumptum fecit.' Menand. ap. Stob. *Flor.* T. CXXI. 5 : τοῦτ'
ἐστὶ τὸ ζῆν· οὐχ ἑαυτῷ ζῆν μόνον. Plut. *Vit. Cleom.* XXXI : αἰσχρὸν γὰρ
ζῆν μόνοις ἑαυτοῖς καὶ ἀποθνήσκειν. But these are all irrelevant, as St Paul
is not here speaking of our *duty*, whether as men or as Christians, but of
our *responsibility*. 'No man liveth to himself,' i.e. is his own master, is
accountable to himself alone. The following from Dion. Hal. *Ant.* III.
17 is nearer to this use of the dative, though not exactly similar : ἀλλ'
εὐσεβὲς μὲν πρᾶγμα ποιεῖτε, ὦ παῖδες, τῷ πατρὶ ζῶντες, καὶ οὐδὲν ἄνευ τῆς ἐμῆς
γνώμης διαπραττόμενοι.

XIV. 10 : **σὺ δὲ τί κρίνεις…ἢ καὶ σὺ τί ἐξουθενεῖς…**] R. V. 'But thou,
why dost thou judge…or thou again, why dost thou set at nought?' In
the A. V. the distinction between the two parties appealed to, the
abstainer and the eater, the weak and the strong, does not plainly
appear. We may compare Charit. Aphrod. I. 10 : σὺ μὲν γάρ, εἶπε,
κίνδυνον ἐπάγεις· σὺ δὲ κέρδος ἀπολλύεις. Plut. *Vit. Themist.* XXI. (from
Timocreon) : ἀλλ' εἰ τύ γε Παυσανίαν, ἢ καὶ τύ γε Ξάνθιππον αἰνεῖς, ἢ τύ γε
Λευτυκίδαν | ἐγὼ δ' Ἀριστείδαν ἐπαινέω[1].

---

[1] [Cf. Boiss. (ad Aristaen. p. 425) on Eurip. *Iph. in T.* 1079: σὸν ἔργον ἤδη
(Orestes) καὶ σόν (Pylades).]

*XV. 16: ἱερουργοῦντα τὸ εὐαγγέλιον τοῦ θεοῦ] Both versions : 'ministering the gospel of God.' R. V. in marg. 'Gr. *ministering in sacrifice.*' The A. V. has a marginal note on 'offering up' in the next clause, ' Or, *sacrificing*,' which probably belongs to 'ministering,' but has got misplaced. At all events, the passage as it is now read, 'that I should be a minister (λειτουργός) of Christ Jesus unto the Gentiles, ministering (ἱερουργοῦντα) the gospel of God,' sins against a fundamental principle of the Revisers, that two Greek words, occurring in close proximity, should not be represented by the same English word. On this principle the substitution of 'sacrificing' for 'ministering' would be a decided improvement. That *that* is the correct meaning of the term will appear from the following examples. Hesych.: Ἱερουργεῖ· θύει, ἱερὰ ἐργάζεται. We read of ἱερουργούμενοι ταῦροι, τὰ σπλάγχνα τῶν ἱερουργηθέντων etc. Philo (*Vit. Mos.* II. p. 94, 30) says : τῷ βασιλεῖ θαρροῦσιν ἤδη διαλέγεσθαι περὶ τοῦ τὸν λεὼν ἱερουργήσοντα ἐκπέμψαι τῶν ὅρων. Plut. T. II. p. 228 Ε : συνεβούλευσεν, εἰ μὲν θεὸν ἡγοῦνται (Leucotheam), μὴ θρηνεῖν· εἰ δὲ ἄνθρωπον, μὴ ἱερουργεῖν ὡς θεῷ.

XV. 20 : οὕτω δὲ φιλοτιμούμενον εὐαγγελίζεσθαι] A. V. 'Yea, so have I strived to preach the gospel.' R. V. 'Yea, making it my aim (Gr. *being ambitious*) so to preach the Gospel.' Though the word 'to strive' does not exhaust the meaning of the Greek φιλοτιμεῖσθαι, yet the English reader may accept it as adequately conveying the Apostle's meaning, both here and 2 Cor. v. 9. 1 Thess. iv. 11, where it is otherwise rendered. Dean Alford says : 'The word in the Apostle's usage seems to lose its primary meaning of *making it a point of honour.*' But this secondary meaning, *summo studio et contentione aliquid agere* (Schleusner), is by no means 'Apostolic,' but the general usage of the best Greek writers, as the following examples will shew. Polyb. I. 83 : ἀεὶ μὲν μεγάλην ἐποιεῖτο σπουδὴν εἰς πᾶν τὸ παρακαλούμενον ὑπ' αὐτῶν, τότε δὲ καὶ μᾶλλον ἐφιλοτιμεῖτο. Diod. Sic. XII. 46 : ὁ δὲ δῆμος φιλοτιμούμενος κατὰ κράτος ἑλεῖν τὴν Ποτίδαιαν. XVI. 49 : ἑκάτεροι γὰρ ἰδίᾳ διεφιλοτιμοῦντο παραδιδόναι τὰ φρούρια. Plut. *Vit. Caes.* LIV : Κάτωνα δὲ λαβεῖν ζῶντα φιλοτιμούμενος[1]. So with the noun, e.g. Diod. Sic. XII. 32 : μετὰ πολλῆς φιλοτιμίας κατεσκεύαζον τριήρεις. XVII. 83 : κατὰ τὸν πότον διηνέχθη πρός τινα τῶν ἑταίρων· τῆς δὲ φιλοτιμίας ἐπὶ πλέον προελθούσης....

*XV. 20: ἵνα μὴ ἐπ' ἀλλότριον θεμέλιον οἰκοδομῶ] A similar use of ἀλλότριος is quoted by Wetstein from Aelian. *N. A.* VIII. 2 (de cane venatico) : νεκρῷ δὲ ἐντυχὼν ἢ λαγῷ τινι ἢ συὶ οὐκ ἂν ἅψαιτο, τοῖς ἀλλοτρίοις ἑαυτὸν πόνοις οὐκ ἐγγράφων, whence the writer infers : ἔοικε δὲ ἐκ τούτων ἔχειν τι φιλοτιμίας ἐν ἑαυτῷ φυσικῆς (*a certain natural sense of honour*) ; which may also serve to illustrate the Apostle's use of φιλοτιμούμενος in

---

[1] [Cf. *Id.* II. p. 268 : Νουμᾶς...πρὸς ἔργα τῆς γῆς φιλοτιμούμενος τρέψαι τὴν πόλιν, ἀποστῆσαι δὲ τῶν πολεμικῶν.]

this verse. I add Plut. *Vit. Flamin.* XXI : ταῦτα δὴ τοῦ Σκηπίωνος οἱ πολλοὶ θαυμάζοντες ἐκάκιζον τὸν Τίτον ὡς ἀλλοτρίῳ νεκρῷ προσενεγκόντα τὰς χεῖρας (because he procured the death of Hannibal, who had been spared by his conqueror Scipio).

*XVI. 2 : προστάτις] 'a succourer.' A more honourable title, as 'protectress' or 'patroness,' might seem to be more appropriate to the technical term here used. Thus Dion. Hal. (*Ant.* II. 10) uses προστάτης and πελάτης for the Roman 'patronus' and 'cliens'; and the μέτοικοι at Athens were compelled πολίτην τινὰ 'Αθηναῖον νέμειν προστάτην (Suidas). See Elsner. ad loc. I add Diod. Sic. T. X. p. 180 ed. Bip.: τῶν γὰρ ἄλλων στρατηγῶν εἰωθότων διδόναι προστάτας τοῖς ὀρφανοῖς καὶ γυναιξὶν ἐρήμοις συγγενῶν. Lucian. *Bis Accus.* 29 : καὶ ταῦτα νῦν, ὁπότε μόνην ἐμὲ θαυμάζουσι, καὶ ἐπιγράφονται ἅπαντες προστάτην ἑαυτῶν.

*XVI. 17: σκοπεῖν τοὺς τὰς διχοστασίας καὶ τὰ σκάνδαλα...ποιοῦντας] A. V. 'mark them which cause divisions and offences.' R. V. 'mark them which are causing the divisions and occasions of stumbling.' By this time the biblical sense of 'scandals' or 'offences' should be pretty well understood by the English reader, and does not require the explanatory rendering 'occasions of stumbling.' Again, if the article designates not divisions and scandals in general, but particular ones prevalent in the Roman Church, then this should be made clear by the addition in italics '*that are among you.*'

On διχοστασίας Wetst. quotes from Plut. II. p. 479 A the proverbial saying : ἐν δὲ διχοστασίῃ καὶ ὁ πάγκακος ἔμμορε τιμῆς. I add Dion. Hal. *Ant.* V. 77 : νῦν δὲ καὶ ἐν ταῖς ἐμφυλίοις διχοστασίαις. Id. X. 13 : ἀφορμὴν δὲ διχοστασίας ἐζήτουν καὶ θορύβου. Stob. *Flor.* T. XLVI. 32 : ἀρχὴν ἔχων μὴ ἀπομνησικάκεε πρὸς τοὺς ἐν διχοστασίῃ σοι πρότερον γεγενημένους.

*XVI. 18: τῶν ἀκάκων] A. V. 'of the simple.' R. V. 'of the innocent.' An unfortunate change. *Innocence* is opposed to *guilt*: *simplicity* to *cunning.* Prov. i. 4 : ἵνα δῶ ἀκάκοις πανουργίαν (A. V. 'to give subtilty to the simple'). Wetstein quotes Dio Cocc. *Exc.* p. 722 : πανοῦργος μὲν γὰρ οὐκ ἔφυ, ἀλλ' εἴ τις ἄλλος ἀνθρώπων ἄκακος. Diod. Sic. v. 66 : διὸ καὶ τοὺς ἐπὶ Κρόνου γενομένους ἀνθρώπους παραδεδόσθαι τοῖς μεταγενεστέροις εὐήθεις καὶ ἀκάκους παντελῶς, ἔτι δ' εὐδαίμονας γεγονότας. Then in *v.* 19 ἀκέραιοι should be rendered 'harmless,' as A. V. in marg., and both versions in Matth. x. 16 : 'wise as serpents, and harmless as doves,' and Philipp. ii. 15 : 'blameless and harmless.'

I. CORINTHIANS.

*Chap. I. 10: ἦτε δὲ κατηρτισμένοι] A.V. 'but that ye be perfectly joined together.' R. V. 'but that ye be perfected together.' Unless 'perfected together' means the same as 'perfectly joined together,' it does not convey any very definite sense. It is true that the ancient versions also give prominence to the idea of perfection; as Vulg. *perfecti*, Pesch. ܡܫܬܠܡܝܢ, Philox. ܡܫܬܡܠܝܢ (both synonyms for τέλειοι). But καταρτίζειν is also applied to the *composing* of differences between individuals, or of factions in a state; e.g. Stob. *Flor.* T. I. 85 : φίλους διαφερομένους καταρτίζοιμι. Dion. Hal. *Ant.* III. 10 : ἡ δὲ ὑμετέρα πόλις, ἅτε νεόκτιστος οὖσα, καὶ ἐκ πολλῶν συμφορητὸς ἐθνῶν...ἵνα καταρτισθῇ, καὶ παύσηται ταραττομένη καὶ στασιάζουσα. In the passage before us, looking at the context, we would render : 'but that ye be COMPACTED TOGETHER in the same mind, and in the same judgment,' with a reference to Psal. cxxii. 3 (A. V.): 'Jerusalem is builded as a city that is COMPACT TOGETHER' (P. B. 'that is at unity in itself').

II. 2 : οὐ γὰρ ἔκρινά τι εἰδέναι ἐν ὑμῖν] 'For I determined not to know any thing among you.' This sense of κρίνειν, *aliquid secum statuere*, is common in biblical Greek, of which a familiar example is Tit. iii. 12 : ἐκεῖ γὰρ κέκρικα παραχειμάσαι[1]. Here, however, it is not ἔκρινα γὰρ μηδὲν εἰδέναι, but οὐ γὰρ ἔκρινά τι εἰδέναι, which requires a slight modification in the English : 'I thought not good to know' &c. Compare Diod. Sic. XV. 32 : (Agesilaus) τὸ μὲν βιάζεσθαι πρὸς ὑπερδεξίους τόπους...οὐκ ἔκρινε.

II. 4 : ἐν πειθοῖς λόγοις] Salmasius *De Hellenistica*, p. 86 : 'Πειθὸς a verbo πείθω, *qui persuadet*, ut φειδὸς, *qui parcit*, ut μιμὸς [μῖμος], *qui imitatur*, et similia.' Schleusner [2], Alford, and others, in borrowing from this source, have tacitly changed πειθὼ into πειθώ, clearly against the intention of the illustrious Frenchman, who compares the Latin *condus* from *condo*, and *promus* from *promo*. It is, however, to be observed that the analogy which connects πειθός with πειθώ also exists between φειδός, *sparing*, and φειδώ, *thrift*.

---

[1] Compare Polyb. III. 100: 'Αννίβας...κρίνας ἐκεῖ ποιεῖσθαι τὴν παραχειμασίαν.

[2] [Schleusner, 'Πειθὸς, persuasorius, ...a πείθω, persuadeo, vel a πειθὼ, ὁος ...suada, suadela.' Ed.]

*II. 13 : πνευματικοῖς πνευματικὰ συγκρίνοντες] 'Comparing spiritual things with spiritual.' So all the ancient versions. Another interpretation, mentioned by Theophylact, which understands πνευματικοῖς of persons, and συγκρίνειν in a sense in which it occurs in the LXX., 'interpreting spiritual things to spiritual men,' has been thought worthy of a place in the margin of R. V., and of an elaborate defence in the 'Ely Lectures,' p. 75 : 'Biblical scholars,' says Dr Kennedy, 'do not deny that the verb συγκρίνω can have this sense [of "explaining"] in Hellenistic Greek, though the usage is not classical.' But this use of συγκρίνειν is strictly confined to the interpretation of *dreams* (Gen. xl. 8, xli. 12, Dan. v. 12) ; and even in this sense is not accepted by Aquila and Symmachus, who substitute for it ἐπιλύεσθαι and διακρίνειν (Hex. ad Gen. xl. 8)[1]. The construction also with accusative and dative is in favour of the A. V.; as 2 Cor. x. 12 : συγκρίνοντες ἑαυτοὺς ἑαυτοῖς. Plut. *Vit. C. Gracc.* IV : τίνα ἔχων παρρησίαν συγκρίνεις Κορνηλίᾳ σεαυτόν ; *Vet. Adag.* ῥόδον ἀνεμώνῃ συγκρίνεις. The other marginal note, 'Or, *combining*' seems taken from the American R. V. '*combining spiritual things with spiritual* words (λόγοις).' So Erasm. Grot. al. '*fitting* or *attaching*.' But this sense of the word also requires confirmation.

III. 5 : διάκονοι δι' ὧν ἐπιστεύσατε, καὶ ἑκάστῳ ὡς ὁ κύριος ἔδωκεν] A. V. 'Even as the Lord gave to every man.' R. V. 'And each as the Lord gave to him.' The latter version seems to refer the clause καὶ ἑκάστῳ— ἔδωκεν to the *hearers*, not to the *teachers* ; as Dean Alford does expressly. That hearers believe, ἑκάστῳ ὡς ὁ θεὸς ἐμέρισε μέτρον πίστεως (Rom. xii. 3), is an undoubted truth ; but would not the assertion of it in this place introduce a new element into the context? St Chrysostom seems to take the other view : καὶ ἑκάστῳ ὡς ὁ θεὸς ἔδωκεν. οὐδὲ γὰρ αὐτὸ τοῦτο τὸ μικρὸν (τὸ διακόνους εἶναι) παρ' ἑαυτῶν, ἀλλὰ παρὰ τοῦ θεοῦ τοῦ ἐγχειρίζοντος. Jerem. Markland (*Conjecturae in Lysiam*, p. 560) even alters the punctuation to the same effect : '1 Cor. iii. 6 : ἑκάστῳ ὡς ὁ κύριος ἔδωκεν, ἐγὼ ἐφύτευσα, Ἀπολλὼς ἐπότισεν. Ita distinguendum.'

*IV. 4 : οὐδὲν γὰρ ἐμαυτῷ σύνοιδα] Subaudi φαῦλον vel ἄτοπον, vel simile quid, as Charit. II. 5 : οὐδὲν γὰρ σύνοιδα ἐμαυτῇ φαῦλον (V. 7, πονηρόν). Job ix. 35 : οὐ γὰρ συνεπίσταμαι ἐμαυτῷ ἄδικον. Luc. *Calum.* 23 : ἅτε μηδὲν φαῦλον ἑαυτῷ συνεπιστάμενος. Perhaps the *full* construction is that of Plut. T. II. p. 236 C : Λάκωνά τινά τις μυσταγωγῶν ἠρώτα, τί ΠΡΑΞΑΣ ἑαυτῷ σύνοιδεν ἀσεβέστατον. The omission of φαῦλον may be accounted for by the circumstance that conscience (συνείδησις) is more familiar to us as an *accusing* than as an *approving* faculty. The A. V. 'I know nothing BY myself,' though a good old English idiom, is rightly rejected by the Revisers in favour of 'AGAINST myself,' though a closer

---

[1] The technical word is κρίνειν (Herod. I. 120), whence the Ὀνειροκριτικά of Artemidorus and others.

imitation of the Greek idiom would, perhaps, be, 'I know no *harm* of myself.'

IV. 6 : ταῦτα δὲ...μετεσχημάτισα εἰς ἐμαυτὸν καὶ 'Απολλῶ] 'And these things...I have in a figure transferred to myself and to Apollos.' Instead of 'in a figure,' the meaning of the Apostle would be best conveyed to the English reader by the expression, 'by a fiction.' Μετασχηματίζειν τι is *to change the outward appearance of anything*, the thing itself remaining the same. E.g. 1 Sam. xxviii. 8 : 'Saul *disguised himself* (Sym. μετεσχη-μάτισεν ἑαυτόν) and put on other raiment.' 1 Kings xiv. 2 : 'And Jeroboam said unto his wife, Arise, I pray thee, and *disguise thyself* (Theod. μετα-σχημάτισον σεαυτόν) that thou be not known to be the wife of Jeroboam.' So, in the present case, the Apostle, in the former part of the Epistle, had been speaking the truth, but, as he now declares, *truth in disguise*. It was perfectly true that there were contentions among the Corinthians, who had attached themselves to certain favourite teachers (or, as he here expresses himself, were 'puffed up for one against another'), saying, 'I am of such an one,' and another, 'I am of such an one.' But instead of naming these leaders, or even describing them anonymously, as we have just done, St Paul, for a reason which he was now about to mention, substitutes for the names of the actual parties concerned those of himself, Apollos, Cephas, and even of Christ himself. Certainly, if we had only the earlier chapters to guide us, we should have taken it as a matter of fact, that there were parties in the Corinthian church, who ranged themselves under the banners of those distinguished Apostles, and should have found a wide field of speculation in assigning to each its distinctive tenets and prepossessions. Still further to give an air of reality to his allegations, the Apostle takes some pains to prove that he himself was free from participation or concurrence in this scandal; thanking God that he had baptized two or three individuals only out of their whole number, 'lest any should say that I baptized in mine own name.' So well is the 'fiction' kept up. For it *was* a fiction after all. Those to whom he wrote must have known it to be so from the first; but for the sake of others, he here, having accomplished his purpose, throws off the disguise, and declares plainly his object in assuming it. 'And these things, brethren, I have by a fiction transferred to myself and Apollos for your sakes, that ye might learn in us' &c.

This is the view taken by St Chrysostom at the beginning of his twelfth Homily on this Epistle. 'As when a sick child kicks and turns away from the food offered by the physicians, the attendants call the father or the tutor, and bid them take the food from the physician's hands, and bring it, so that out of fear towards them he may take it and be quiet: so also Paul, intending to find fault with the Corinthians in behalf of certain other persons (of some as being injured, of others as being honoured above measure) did not set down the persons themselves,

but conducted the argument in his own name, and that of Apollos, in
order that reverencing these they might receive his mode of cure. But
that once received, he presently makes known in whose behalf he was so
expressing himself. Now this was not hypocrisy, but *condescension* and
management (συγκατάβασις καὶ οἰκονομία). For if he had said openly,
"You are judging men who are saints, and worthy of admiration," they
would probably have taken it ill, and have started off altogether. But
now, in saying, *But to me it is a very small thing that I should be judged
of you;* and again, *Who is Paul, and who is Apollos?* he had rendered
his speech easy of reception.'

IV. 11 : καὶ ἀστατοῦμεν] A. V. 'And have no certain dwelling-place.'
Or, as we might otherwise render, 'no settled habitation,' with reference
to the primary meaning of ἄστατος, *instabilis, unsettled*. But, perhaps,
neither of these expresses the full force of the word, in which there may
possibly be an allusion to Gen. iv. 12 : 'A fugitive and a vagabond
(נָע וָנָד) shalt thou be in the earth'; where for the incorrect στένων καὶ
τρέμων of the LXX., the Hexapla gives : Σ. ἀνάστατος καὶ ἀκατάστατος. Τὸ
Ἑβραϊκὸν καὶ οἱ λοιποί· σαλευόμενος καὶ ἀκαταστατῶν· τουτέστι, μὴ μένων ἐν
ἑνὶ τόπῳ, ἀλλ' ἀλώμενος. We may also compare Isai. lviii. 7 : 'Is it not
to deal thy bread to the hungry, and that thou bring the poor that are
cast out (Or, *afflicted*) to thy house? when thou seest the naked,' &c.
Here in connexion with hunger and nakedness we find those that are
מְרוּדִים, *errabundi*, for which the LXX. have ἀστέγους, Symmachus ἀνα-
στάτους, Theodotion μεταναστάτους[1], and Aquila the very word used by
St Paul, ἀστατοῦντας. In the text, therefore, there seems no reason why
we should not translate, 'and are vagabonds,' or 'and lead a vagabond
life,' a more lively description than the other.

V. 1 : ὅλως ἀκούεται ἐν ὑμῖν πορνεία] A. V. 'It is reported commonly
that *there is* fornication among you.' The only correction required is
that of R. V. 'It is actually reported.' But Dean Alford has discovered
a new sense for ἀκούομαι, 'from missing which commentators have gone
wrong' in other respects besides the meaning of ὅλως. 'Ἀκούεται ἐν ὑμῖν
πορνεία is another way of saying ἀκούουσί τινες ἐν ὑμῖν πόρνοι, *the character
of πόρνος is borne* (by some) *among you*, or, *fornication is borne as a
character among you*.' Now it is quite true that ἀκούειν, like the Latin
audire, is sometimes followed by a noun in the nominative case, in the
sense of *dicor, appellor*; in other words, the active ἀκούειν puts on a
passive signification, and therefore ἀκούεσθαι, in this sense, would be the
passive of a passive; which is absurd. But the Dean is also wrong in
supposing that ἀκούειν, used as before, means *to bear a certain character*,
instead of *to be called by a certain name*. Thus Demosth. *de Cor.* p. 241,
12 : νῦν κόλακες, καὶ θεοῖς ἐχθροί, καὶ τἄλλ' ἃ προσήκει πάντ' ἀκούουσι, i.e.

---

[1] [Damnat hanc vocem Cobet. *Coll. Crit.* p. 62, ubi vide.]

those epithets are freely bestowed on them. Aelian. *N. A.* VII. 45 : ἔχαιρε γὰρ ἀκούων 'Αετός. Lucian. *De Merc. cond.* 35 : δεῖ 'Αδώνιδας αὐτοὺς καὶ 'Υακίνθους ἀκούειν. Hor. *Ep.* I. 7, 37 : *Rexque paterque | Audisti coram*[1].

*VI. 3 : βιωτικά] 'Things pertaining to this life.' Alford explains, 'matters relating to ὁ βίος, *a man's livelihood.*' But βιωτικὸς is derived from βίος in the wider sense of HUMAN *life,* or *the world,* and τὰ β. might be appropriately rendered 'things pertaining to common life,' 'worldly matters.' So Luke xxi. 34 : μερίμναις βιωτικαῖς. 2 Tim. ii. 4 : αἱ τοῦ βίου πραγματεῖαι. Compare Diod. Sic. T. X. p. 180 ed. Bip.: εἰς ἐπανόρθωσιν τῶν βιωτικῶν καὶ τῶν δημοσίων ἀδικημάτων, where it is equivalent to ἰδιωτικῶν.

VI. 4 : τοὺς ἐξουθενημένους...καθίζετε] If this clause is to be read interrogatively, as R. V. 'Do ye set them to judge who are of no account in the church?' it must be understood to mean, 'Do ye have recourse to the heathen tribunals?' But in that case, as the Christians had no voice in the appointment of the judges, the word καθίζετε is hardly appropriate, judging from its use in Demosth. *c. Mid.* p. 585, 26 (quoted by Wetstein): οἱ δικάζοντες, ἄν τε διακοσίους, ἄν τε χιλίους, ἄν θ' ὁπόσους ἂν ἡ πόλις καθίσῃ. I add Philostr. *Her.* p. 174 : καὶ δικαστὰς ἐκάθισεν οὓς εἰκὸς ἦν καταψηφίσασθαι τοῦ Αἴαντος[2].

*VI. 5 : οὐκ ἔστιν ἐν ὑμῖν] A. V. 'there is not among you.' R. V. reads οὐκ ἔνι for οὐκ ἔστιν; but this makes not an atom of difference in the sense; and the rendering 'there cannot be *found* among you' is equally false and absurd.

VI. 7 : ἤδη μὲν οὖν ὅλως ἥττημα [ἐν] ὑμῖν ἐστιν] A. V. 'Now therefore there is utterly a fault among you.' R. V. 'Nay, already it is altogether a defect in you (Or, *a loss to you*).' On ἥττημα see on Rom. xi. 12, where we have argued in favour of 'defeat,' whether in war, or in a court of justice. So St Chrysostom appears to have understood it in this place. 'Wherefore also Paul goes on to say, *Nay, it is already* [i.e. whatever may be the result of the lawsuit] *altogether a defeat* (ἥττημα) *to you, that ye go to law one with another.* And, *Wherefore do ye not rather suffer wrong?* For that the injured person overcomes (νικᾷ)[3] rather than he who cannot endure being injured, this I will make plain to you. He that cannot endure injury, though he drag the other party into court, though he gain the cause, yet is he then most of all defeated (κἂν περιγένηται, τότε μάλιστα ἥττηται). For that which he would not, he hath suffered, in that the

---

[1] [Cf. Boisson. ad Aristaen. p. 207.]
[2] [Cf. Galen. *Meth. Med.* I. 2 : μὴ τοὺς ὁμοτέχνους τῷ πατρί σου κριτὰς καθίσῃς ἰατρῶν, τολμηρότατε Θεσσαλέ.]

[3] [Cf. Rom. iii. 4 : καὶ νικήσῃς ἐν τῷ κρίνεσθαί σε. Dem. 711. 9 : εἰ γὰρ... τινες ἀντίδικοι παρ' ὑμῖν ἀγωνίζοιντο... ἀξιοῖ δὲ ἑκάτερος νικᾶν....]

adversary hath compelled him both to feel pain and incur a lawsuit.'
This he exemplifies in the case of Job, and asks : τίς ἐνίκησεν ἐπὶ τῆς
κοπρίας; τίς ἡττήθη; ὁ πάντα ἀφαιρεθεὶς 'Ιώβ, ἢ ὁ πάντα ἀφελόμενος διάβολος;

Ibid. διὰ τί οὐχὶ μᾶλλον ἀδικεῖσθε; διὰ τί οὐχὶ μᾶλλον ἀποστερεῖσθε;]
''Αδικεῖσθε and ἀποστερεῖσθε are not passive, but middle, *allow yourselves
to be wronged and defrauded.'—Alford.* Yet the active and passive are
very clearly set forth in this quotation from Plato's *Gorgias* (Stob. *Flor.*
T. XLV. 31): ΠΩΛΟΣ. Σὺ ἄρα βούλοι' ἂν ἀδικεῖσθαι μᾶλλον ἢ ἀδικεῖν;
ΣΩΚΡΑΤΗΣ. Βουλοίμην μὲν ἂν ἔγωγε οὐδέτερα· εἰ δὲ ἀναγκαῖον εἴη ἀδικεῖν
ἢ ἀδικεῖσθαι, ἑλοίμην ἂν μᾶλλον ἀδικεῖσθαι ἢ ἀδικεῖν.

VI. 11 : **καὶ ταῦτά τινες ἦτε**] 'And such were some of you.' On which
Dean Alford remarks : 'τινες limits the ὑμεῖς, which is the suppressed
subject of ἦτε.' Perhaps it would be more correct to say that τινες limits
the ταῦτα, which though properly said of *things*, has here for its antecedent persons (πόρνοι &c.): 'And these, one or other of them, ye were.'
This, at least, is the explanation of St Chrysostom in his fourth Homily
on Ephesians (T. XI. p. 25 E): καὶ ἐπαγαγών, βασιλείαν θεοῦ οὐ κληρονομή-
σουσι, τότε φησί· καὶ ταῦτά τινες ἦτε. οὐκ εἶπεν ἁπλῶς, ἦτε, ἀλλά, τινες ἦτε·
τουτέστιν, οὕτω πως ἦτε.

VI. 15 : **ἄρας τὰ μέλη τοῦ Χριστοῦ**] A. V. 'Shall I take the members
of Christ.' R. V. 'Shall I take away...' Alford : 'Having alienated....'
The English reader will probably prefer the first of these, being, in fact,
in exact accordance with his own familiar style, in which the word 'take'
is employed as a sort of expletive, preparatory to some other operation.
Compare Acts xxi. 11 : 'He took Paul's girdle (ἄρας τὴν ζώνην τοῦ Π.) and
bound his own hands and feet.' Ezek. iv. 1, 3, 9 : 'Take thee (λάβε
σεαυτῷ) a tile...an iron pan...wheat, barley,' &c. Matt. xiii. 33 : 'The
kingdom of heaven is like unto leaven, which a woman took and hid
(λαβοῦσα ἐνέκρυψε) in three measures of meal.' The following from Plut.
(*Vit. Fab. Max.* V) is somewhat similar : ἠρώτα τοὺς φίλους τοῦ Φαβίου,
πότερον εἰς τὸν οὐρανὸν ἄρας ἀναφέρει τὸν στρατόν, ὡς τῆς γῆς ἀπεγνωκώς [1].

VII. 16 : 'For how knowest thou (τί γὰρ οἶδας), O wife, whether thou
shalt save thy husband? or how knowest thou, O husband, whether thou
shalt save thy wife?' The only question about this argument is whether
it is intended as a reason for the parties remaining united (in continuation
of *vv.* 12—14) or for their separating (as being in immediate connexion

---

[1] [Cf. Plut. *Vit. Cor.* XXXII: ἡ
βουλὴ καθάπερ ἐν χειμῶνι πολλῷ καὶ
κλύδωνι τῆς πόλεως ἄρασα τὴν ἀφ' ἱερᾶς
ἀφῆκεν. So ἀράμενος in Lucian. *Hist.
Conscr.* 24: (Urbem) Σαμόσατα αὐτὸς
ἐν τῷ αὐτῷ βιβλίῳ ἀράμενος αὐτῇ

ἀκροπόλει καὶ τείχεσι μετέθηκεν εἰς τὴν
Μεσοποταμίαν. Compare the use of
φέρων—e.g. φέρων ἑαυτὸν ἐπιτρέπει τῷ
ποιμένι, Aesop. *Fab.* 400 (ed. de Fur.).
Babr. *Fab.* 66: ἐκ δὲ τοῦ δύω πήρας
κρεμάσαι φέροντα.]

with *v.* 15). It is argued that if the *former* had been intended, it should have been εἰ μὴ σώσεις, not εἰ σώσεις; but this is a mistake. Εἰ σώσεις is indeterminate, and holds an even balance (so to speak) between ὅτι σώσεις and ὅτι μὴ σώσεις. And that τί οἶδας εἰ τὸν ἄνδρα σώσεις is quite consistent with a *hopeful* view of the case, is abundantly proved by such examples from the O. T. as 2 Kings (Sam.) xii. 22. Joel. ii. 14. Jon. iii. 9[1]. In fact, the form under which the *latter* view is presented by Dean Alford, 'For what assurance hast thou, O wife, whether thou shalt be the means of thy husband's conversion?' is a sufficient refutation of it; philologically, because 'assurance' is incompatible with 'whether'; and morally, because if there be, not an assurance, but only a reasonable hope, of such a blessed result, it would be her bounden duty to act upon it, and not to leave her husband. St Chrysostom, who takes this view, sums up in these weighty words : 'And neither, on the one hand, doth he lay any necessity upon the wife, and absolutely demand the point of her, that he may not again do what would be too painful ; nor, on the other hand, doth he tell her to despair ; ἀλλ' ἀφίησιν αὐτὸ τῇ τοῦ μέλλοντος ἀδηλίᾳ μετέωρον.'

*VII. 20: ἕκαστος ἐν τῇ κλήσει κ.τ.έ.] A. V. 'Let every man abide in the same calling wherein he was called.' Another instance (see on John xix. 42) in which the *order* of the Greek might, with advantage, have been preserved : 'Every man in the calling wherein he was called, in that let him abide.' It is hardly necessary to observe, that by 'calling' is not here to be understood a man's calling (occupation) in life, but his calling of God, 'as God hath called each' (*v.* 17). In *v.* 21 the ambiguous phrase μᾶλλον χρῆσαι is explained by St Chrysostom μᾶλλον δούλευε, though he notices the other interpretation, εἰ δύνασαι ἐλευθερωθῆναι, ἐλευθερώθητι, but rejects it as πολὺ ἀπεναντίας τῷ τρόπῳ τοῦ Παύλου. The Peschito version ܡܐܠܐܠܐ ܠܟ ܠܐܝ, *elige tibi ut servias* (Walton), takes the same view, which seems absolutely required by the particles, ἀλλ' εἰ ΚΑΙ δύνασαι.

*VIII. 12 : ἁμαρτάνοντες εἰς τοὺς ἀδελφοὺς...εἰς Χριστὸν ἁμαρτάνετε] Compare Muson. ap. Stob. *Flor.* T. LXXV. 15 : ὥσπερ γὰρ ὁ περὶ ξένους ἄδικος εἰς τὸν Ξένιον ἁμαρτάνει Δία, καὶ ὁ περὶ φίλους εἰς τὸν Φίλιον· οὕτως ὅστις εἰς τὸ ἑαυτοῦ γένος ἄδικος εἰς τοὺς πατρῴους ἁμαρτάνει θεοὺς, καὶ εἰς τὸν Ὁμόγνιον Δία, τὸν ἐπόπτην τῶν ἁμαρτημάτων τῶν περὶ τὰ γένη.

*IX. 5 : (γυναῖκα) περιάγειν] 'to lead about.' *We* should rather say, 'to carry about.' Compare Diod. Sic. XVII. 77 : πρὸς δὲ τούτοις τὰς

---

[1] Dean Alford takes an exception to these parallels, because in all of them the verb stands in the 'emphatic position,' εἰ ἐλεήσει, εἰ ἐπιστρέψει, εἰ μετανοήσει, whereas in our text it occupies a 'subordinate place.' But there is nothing in this, which does not necessarily follow from the divergence of Hebrew and Greek syntax.

παλλακίδας ὁμοίως τῷ Δαρείῳ περιῆγε. More commonly the middle form is used, as Plut. *Vit. Anton.* IX : ὁ (γύναιον) δὴ καὶ τὰς πόλεις ἐπιὼν ἐν φορείῳ περιήγετο.

IX. 27. On Lucian. *Nec.* 4 : τὸ σῶμα καταναγκάζειν, Hemsterhuis remarks : 'Idem est quod antistiti verae salutarisque philosophiae Paulo I ad Cor. ix. 27 ὑπωπιάζειν vel ὑποπιάζειν sive ὑποπιέζειν (quarum lectionum utra sit anteferenda vix constituas) τὸ σῶμα καὶ δουλαγωγεῖν.' There is the same confusion in Plut. T. II. p. 921 F : ἀλλ᾽ ὅπερ ἀληθὲς ἦν, ἔλεγεν] ὑπωπιάζων (al. ὑποπιέζων) τὴν σελήνην, where the true reading is placed beyond doubt by the addition, σπίλων καὶ μελασμῶν ἀναπιμπλάντας. Nor is there any difficulty in the present place, where πυκτεύω immediately precedes, and ὑπωπιάζω is supported by the uncials ABCℵ. It has not, however, been remarked that the Philoxenian ܐ‍ܠ‍ܗ‍ܐ ? ܡ‍ܚ‍ܣ‍ܐ is clearly in favour of ὑποπιέζω, as I am able to prove by the following examples from the version of Paul of Tela. Jud. vi. 38 : ἐξεπίασε (ܠ‍ܥ‍ܨ‍ܐ) τὸν πόκον. Prov. xxx. 33 : ἐὰν ἐκπιέζῃς (ܠ‍ܥ‍ܨ‍ܐ) μυκτῆρας. Amos ix. 13 : Οἱ λοιποί· καὶ ὁ πιέζων (ܘ‍ܠ‍ܥ‍ܨ ܗ‍ܘ) τὰς σταφυλάς. Mic. vi. 15 : πιέσεις (ܠ‍ܥ‍ܨ‍ܐ) ἐλαίαν.

Ibid. μήπως ἄλλοις κηρύξας] Here it is disputed whether there is any allusion intended to the office of the κῆρυξ in the public games, which was (we are told) not only to call out the names of the competitors before the several contests, and of the victors after them, but also to proclaim the laws of the games, and the qualifications required in the candidates[1]. This view is supported by Wetstein, Dean Alford, and others ; but there seem to be serious, if not insurmountable difficulties in the way of it. The principal one is, that in the immediately preceding verse the Apostle speaks in the character of a combatant, between which and that of the herald who proclaimed the victor is a wide chasm, not to be bridged over by the single instance of the Emperor Nero[2], from which (quite as exceptional as that of the Emperor Napoleon I. at his coronation putting the crown on his own head) Dean Stanley would have us draw the inference that 'sometimes the victor in the games was also selected to announce his success.' If, indeed, St Paul had written ἄλλους κηρύξας, the continued allusion to the public games would have been irresistible ; but this alteration, though it has been proposed as a conjecture, is not supported by a single MS. On the whole, therefore, it is better to take κηρύξας in the sense in which it is constantly used, of the *preaching* of the

[1] St Chrysost. T. XII. p. 171 A (quoted by Wetst.): εἰπὲ δή μοι, παρακαλῶ· ἐν τοῖς Ὀλυμπιακοῖς ἀγῶσιν οὐχὶ ἕστηκεν ὁ κῆρυξ βοῶν μέγα καὶ ὑψηλόν,

εἴ τις τούτου κατηγορεῖ, λέγων, μὴ δοῦλός ἐστι, μὴ κλέπτης, μὴ τρόπων πονηρῶν;

[2] Suet. *Nero*, 24: 'Victorem autem se ipse pronunciabat.'

Gospel; as St Chrysostom comments: εἰ γὰρ ἐμοὶ τὸ κηρῦξαι, τὸ διδάξαι, τὸ μυρίους προσαγαγεῖν οὐκ ἀρκεῖ εἰς σωτηρίαν, εἰ μὴ καὶ τὰ κατ' ἐμαυτὸν παρασχοίμην ἄληπτα, πολλῷ μᾶλλον ὑμῖν.

X. 13 : ἀνθρώπινος] R. V. 'such as man can bear.' Alford : 'within the power of human endurance.' But these renderings unnecessarily raise the question of what man is able to bear, and what are the limits of human endurance. It seems impossible to improve upon the A. V. 'such as is common to man. Or, *moderate*,' as the following extracts will plainly show. Stob. *Flor.* T. XLIX. 48 : εἰ μὲν ἀνθρωπίνην (ἡδονὴν) θέλεις, ὦ Διονύσιε, πείνησον ἵνα φάγῃς, δίψησον ἵνα πίῃς· εἰ δέ...τηλικαύτην ἡλίκην οὐδεὶς πρὸ σοῦ, ἀπόθου τὴν τυραννίδα. T. CVIII. 81 : καὶ τὰ προσπίπτοντα ἀνθρώπινα νομίζοντες, καὶ μὴ μόνοις συμβαίνοντα, εὐθυμότερον διάξομεν. Epict. *Enchir.* ch. 33 (ed. Wolf.) : τέκνον ἄλλου τέθνηκεν, ἢ γυνή; οὐδείς ἐστιν ὃς οὐκ ἂν εἴποι ὅτι ἀνθρώπινον[1].

*XI. 5 : ἐν γάρ ἐστι καὶ τὸ αὐτὸ τῇ ἐξυρημένῃ] A. V. 'for that is even all one (R. V. 'for it is one and the same thing') as if she were shaven.' Literally : 'she (so Alford) is all the same with her that hath been shaven.'

XI. 22 : τοὺς μὴ ἔχοντας] A. V. 'them that have not. Or, *them that are poor*.' R. V. in marg. 'Or, *them that have nothing*.' There is the same ambiguity in Luke xxii. 36 : καὶ ὁ μὴ ἔχων, πωλησάτω τὸ ἱμάτιον αὐτοῦ, καὶ ἀγορασάτω μάχαιραν; but there ὁ ἔχων βαλλάντιον ἀράτω had immediately preceded, or with only the slight interruption, ὁμοίως καὶ πήραν; whereas here the οἰκίας, which it is proposed to supply after μὴ ἔχοντας, is in a clause which is separated from the one in question by the enunciation of a new idea, ἢ τῆς ἐκκλησίας τοῦ θεοῦ καταφρονεῖτε. Dean Alford says : 'Meyer refers in support of the meaning "the poor" to Wetst. on 2 Cor. viii. 12, where nothing on the subject is found.' The reference should have been to Wetst. on Matt. xiii. 12, where an abundance of examples may be found. Instead of selecting from them, I give *de meo penu* Neh. viii. 10 : καὶ ἀποστείλατε μερίδας τοῖς μὴ ἔχουσιν. Stob. *Flor.* T. I. 40 : ὁ γὰρ θαυμάζων τοὺς ἔχοντας καὶ μακαριζομένους ὑπὸ τῶν ἄλλων ἀνθρώπων....T. III. 18 : ἔχειν δὲ πειρῶ· τοῦτο γὰρ τό τ' εὐγενὲς | καὶ τοὺς γάμους δίδωσι τοὺς πρώτους ἔχειν. | ἐν τῷ πένεσθαι δ' ἐστὶν ἥ τ' ἀδοξία κ.τ.λ. T. XCI. 7 : ἐπίσταμαι δὲ καὶ πεπείραμαι λίαν | ὡς τῶν ἐχόντων πάντες ἄνθρωποι φίλοι[2].

---

[1] [Cf. Dio. Chrys. *Or.* XI. 157, 26 : ἀλλὰ σμικρὰ καὶ ἀνθρώπεια ψεύσματα πρὸς θεῖα καὶ μεγάλα. Plut. *Vit. Caes.* LVII : Cicero proposes honours to Caesar—ὧν ἀμωσγέπως ἀνθρώπινον ἦν τὸ μέγεθος. Soph. *Oed. C.* 598 : τί

γὰρ τὸ μεῖζον ἢ κατ' ἄνθρωπον νοσεῖς; App. *B. C.* III. 69 : πονουμένων δὲ ὧδε πάντων ὑπὲρ φύσιν ἀνθρωπίνην.]
[2] [Cf. T. XXXVIII. 6 : λιτὸς γενόμενος, τοῖς ἔχουσι μὴ φθόνει.]

*XI. 24 : τὸ ὑπὲρ ὑμῶν κλώμενον] The last word is omitted by AB and (a 1ᵐᵃ manu) Cℵ, and of the Fathers Cyr. Ath. Fulg. It is impossible that τὸ ὑπὲρ ὑμῶν can stand alone (R. V. 'which is for you'); therefore Alford and others darkly hint at an *ellipsis*, 'the filling up of which is to be sought in the foregoing ἔκλασε.' But how can an ellipsis in our Lord's speech be filled up from a word, which was not spoken, but only occurs in a narrative of the transaction? The only possible way of accounting for the omission of the participle is by supposing that the speaker did not suit the action to the word, but *substituted the action for the word*, thus : 'This is my body which is [here he breaks the bread] for you.' But this has never been suggested, and is so improbable that we are compelled, in justice to the English reader, to retain 'broken,' it matters little whether in the Roman or in the Italic character.

If we were inclined to indulge in speculations on the motives which influenced transcribers in dealing with the MSS. from which they copied, we might say that κλώμενον was dispensed with as being inapplicable to anything that was done to Christ's living body on the cross, though sometimes used of the tortures inflicted on martyrs. On the other hand, if the omission had existed in the original Epistle, copyists wishing to fill it up, would certainly have preferred διδόμενον (from Luke xxii. 19) to κλώμενον, a word not elsewhere to be found in this connexion.

*XIII. 1—3. 'Though I speak' &c. Mr Washington Moon, a great oracle in all cases of English grammar, objects to the A. V. of this passage, that the verbs are not hypothetical, as they should be, but directly affirmative. But this objection cannot be sustained. 'I speak' may be either the one or the other, according as it represents *loquor*, or *loquar*; yet practically there is no ambiguity, because the context plainly excludes the indicative mood. I cannot therefore believe that this was the reason why the Revisers changed 'Though' into 'If,' but a quite different one, which has escaped Mr Moon's perspicacity, and to which his own proposed version, 'Though I *were* to speak,' is equally liable ; namely, that although the conjunction 'though' is correctly *expressed* in the leading clause of each verse, it is incorrectly *understood* in the concluding one, common to all three verses, 'and have not charity.' To be strictly grammatical, the A. V. should have been as follows : 'Though I speak with the tongues of men and of angels, *yet if* I have not charity' &c. By substituting 'If' for 'Though,' the Revisers have avoided this difficulty. Not that I think they have done wisely in making the change, simply because no change was necessary. The A. V. as it stands, is perfectly intelligible, adequately represents the original, and the blot which I have mentioned is far too minute to be noticed by one English reader out of ten thousand.

*XIII. 3 : ἐὰν παραδῶ τὸ σῶμά μου, ἵνα καυθήσωμαι] Compare Max. Tyr. VII. 9 (quoted by Wetst.) : ἐθάρρει ἂν, οἶμαι, καὶ τῇ Αἴτνῃ αὐτοῦ παραδοὺς τὸ σῶμα. The various reading καυχήσωμαι, 'that I may glory,' though supported by the trio ABא, and mentioned by Jerome, is rightly rejected by Dean Alford. This reading supposes that the good actions here specified were performed from a corrupt motive (κενοδοξίας ἕνεκεν), which of itself would be sufficient to deprive them of all moral worth, without the superfluous addition (especially connected by an adversative particle) ἀγάπην ΔΕ μὴ ἔχω. Ostentation necessarily *implies* the absence of love. Observe also the indefiniteness of the phrase, ἐὰν παραδῶ τὸ σῶμά μου, without any hint of the *purpose*, for which the body is so given or yielded up. In Dan. iii. 28 (95 LXX.) we have παρέδωκαν τὰ σώματα αὐτῶν εἰς πῦρ (Ο'. εἰς ἐμπυρισμόν), the very counterpart of St Paul's ἵνα καυθήσωμαι. In the passage quoted by Westcott and Hort from S. Clem. Rom. 55 : πολλοὶ βασιλεῖς καὶ ἡγούμενοι παρέδωκαν ἑαυτοὺς κ.τ.έ. all ambiguity is removed by the several additions εἰς θάνατον...εἰς δεσμά...εἰς δουλείαν. Equally inconclusive is another quotation from Plut. *Vit. Demetr.* XLIX. When some one ventured to tell him, ὡς Σελεύκῳ χρὴ τὸ σῶμα παραδοῦναι, Demetrius drew his sword intending to kill himself, but was persuaded by his friends to accept the other alternative, namely, to give himself up as a prisoner to Seleucus ; which he accordingly did, and was handsomely treated by his magnanimous enemy. But what has this to do with St Paul's 'giving his body that he might glory'?

XIII. 5 : οὐκ ἀσχημονεῖ] 'Doth not behave itself unseemly.' 'Seems to be *general*, without particular reference to the disorders in public speaking with tongues.'—*Dean Alford.* This will be readily conceded ; but the difficulty remains, how this general decorousness of behaviour is connected with ἀγάπη. To obviate this difficulty, the Greek expositors have given a different turn to the word ἀσχημονεῖ, as if it were equivalent to νομίζει ἀσχημονεῖν, the very phrase used by St Paul in Ch. vii. 36. Thus Theodoret : οὐκ ἀσχημονεῖ· οὐδὲν τῶν εὐτελῶν τε καὶ ταπεινῶν τῆς τῶν ἀδελφῶν ὠφελείας ἕνεκα παραιτεῖται δρᾶσαι, ἄσχημον τὴν τοιαύτην πρᾶξιν ὑπολαμβάνων. And St Chrysostom : τί γὰρ λέγω, φησίν, ὅτι οὐ φυσιοῦται, ὅπου γε τοσοῦτον ἀπέχει τοῦ πάθους, ὅτι καὶ τὰ αἴσχιστα παθοῦσα διὰ τὸν ἀγαπώμενον, οὐδὲ ἀσχημοσύνην τὸ πρᾶγμα νομίζει; He instances in our Lord, who suffered a woman who was a sinner to anoint and kiss his feet ; in Rebecca, who felt no shame in practising a disgraceful fraud on her husband for the sake of her darling son ; in Jacob himself, who, besides the unseemliness of servitude, incurred ridicule from the trick put upon him by his father-in-law ; yet was so far from feeling himself disgraced, that the seven years 'seemed unto him but a few days for the love he had' to Rachel : ἡ γὰρ ἀγάπη οὐκ ἀσχημονεῖ, 'doth not count any thing to be unseemly.'

XIII. 7 : πάντα στέγει] 'Beareth all things.' R. V. in margin : 'Or, *covereth*,' probably with a reference to A. V. Prov. x. 12 : 'Love *covereth* all sins,' and xvii. 9: 'He that *covereth* a transgression, seeketh love.' But it does not appear that στέγειν is the proper word to be used in this connexion, but rather καλύπτειν (Psal. xxxi. 5. James v. 20. 1 Pet. iv. 8) or περιστέλλειν (see on 1 Pet. iv. 12). Acquiescing in the generally received version, 'beareth all things' (κἂν φορτικὰ ᾖ, κἂν ἐπαχθῆ, κἂν ὕβρεις, κἂν πληγαί, κἂν θάνατος, κἂν ὁτιοῦν[1]), we would substitute in the margin for 'covereth,' 'keepeth close.' This is a well-known use of the word, of which take the following examples (partly from Wetstein on 1 Cor. ix. 12). Ecclus. viii. 17: μετὰ μωροῦ μὴ συμβουλεύου, οὐ γὰρ δυνήσεται λόγον στέξαι, 'he cannot keep counsel.' Thucyd. VI. 72: ἅ τε κρύπτεσθαι δεῖ, μᾶλλον ἂν στέγεσθαι. Stob. *Flor.* T. LXII. 23: πιστὸν μὲν οὖν εἶναι χρὴ τὸν διάκονον | τοιοῦτον εἶναι, καὶ στέγειν τὰ δεσποτῶν. Lucian. *Navig.* 11: καί τοι ἐτελέσθημεν, ὡς οἶσθα, καὶ στέγειν μεμαθήκαμεν. Themist. XXVI. p. 312: στέγειν ἅττα ἂν εἰδῶσιν ἐν τῇ καρδίᾳ, καὶ μὴ ἐξαγγέλλειν. Hence the proverb: Ἀρεοπαγίτου στεγανώτερος.

XIV. 8: εἰς πόλεμον] A. V. 'to the battle.' R. V. 'for war.' See on Luke xiv. 31. The use of πόλεμος for 'battle' is common in the LXX., e.g. 2 Kings (Sam.) xi. 15: ἐξεναντίας τοῦ πολέμου τοῦ κραταιοῦ, 'in the forefront of the hottest (Heb. *strong*) battle.' Psal. xvii. (xviii.) 39: περιέζωσάς με δύναμιν εἰς πόλεμον. Eccles. ix. 11: καὶ οὐ τοῖς δυνατοῖς ὁ πόλεμος, 'nor the battle to the strong.' In the present case, it is, obviously, when the *battle* is about to be joined, that the trumpet comes into play. Wetstein quotes Dio Cass. p. 24 (ed. Leunclav. 1606): ἐγένετο δὲ ἡ μάχη τοιάδε. πρῶτον μὲν οἱ σαλπιγκταὶ πάντες ἅμα τὸ πολεμικὸν ἀπὸ συνθήματος ἐβόησαν.

*XV. 4: ἐγήγερται] A. V. 'he rose again.' R. V. 'he hath been raised.' [But as it is followed by τῇ ἡμέρᾳ τῇ τρίτῃ, the English idiom requires 'he was raised,' ἠγέρθη.] The Revisers persist in this change, so grating to the ears of the English Bible-reader, throughout the chapter, e.g. 'Now if Christ is preached that he hath been raised from the dead... But if there is no resurrection of the dead, neither hath Christ been raised: and if Christ hath not been raised...But now hath Christ been raised from the dead, the firstfruits....' That God was the agent in the resurrection of Christ, is expressly declared in *v.* 15; but is it necessary to recall this truth on every occasion that His resurrection is mentioned? And if the Apostle's argument does not require this, does the use of the passive form necessitate the proposed change? Clearly not. Both ἐγήγερται and ἐγερθήσεται are commonly used as *middle* verbs, without any

---

[1] St Chrysostom ad loc., who gives as an instance David's *forebearance* (compare 1 Thess. iii. 1) towards Absalom: τί γὰρ φορτικώτερον τοῦ υἱὸν ἰδεῖν ἐπανιστάμενον, καὶ τυραννίδος ἐφιέμενον, καὶ αἵματος διψῶντα πατρῴου; ἀλλὰ καὶ τοῦτο ἔστεγεν ὁ μακάριος ἐκεῖνος ...ἰσχυρὰ γὰρ ἦν ἡ τῆς ἀγάπης κρηπίς· διὸ καὶ πάντα στέγει.

reference to an agent; e.g. 'There hath not risen a greater prophet...' 'Many false prophets shall rise...' 'Nation shall rise against nation.' 'Unto him which died for them, and rose again (ἠγέρθη).' And so the ancient versions in this chapter: Vulg. *resurrexit*. Both Syriac ܩܳܡ.

XV. 8: ὡσπερεὶ τῷ ἐκτρώματι] 'as to one born out of due time.' Compare Diod. Sic. III. 63: (Semelem) τελευτῆσαι, καὶ τὸ βρέφος ἐκτρῶσαι πρὸ τοῦ καθήκοντος χρόνου[1]. Perhaps, for the sake of uniformity, it would be better to adopt the O. T. version of ἔκτρωμα (נֵפֶל), 'an untimely birth.' See Job iii. 16. Psal. lviii. 8. Eccles. vi. 3. In the last place only do we find the article: εἶπα ὅτι ἀγαθὸν ὑπὲρ αὐτοῦ τὸ ἔκτρωμα (הַנָּפֶל), the sentiment being a general one. In our text it might be dispensed with, unless we accept the explanation that St Paul, comparing himself with the other Apostles, describes himself as 'the *one* untimely birth' in the family. Schleusner (*Lex. N. T.* s.v.) quotes from Zonaras *Lex.* col. 661: ὁ ἐν πᾶσι τέλειος Παῦλος, ὡς ἀτελῆ ἐν ἀποστόλοις, καὶ μὴ μορφούμενον τῇ κατὰ Χριστὸν πίστει ἀπ' ἀρχῆς, ἔκτρωμά φησιν ἑαυτόν· ὡς περιττῷ ἐκτρώματι ὤφθη κἀμοί; where the singular reading, ὡς περιττῷ for ὡσπερεὶ τῷ, does not appear to have been noticed.

Ibid. American R. V. 'as to the *child* untimely born.' On this one of the American Revisers (in *Public Opinion*) comments: 'It is certainly the child born into the world prematurely, and therefore puny and weak.' On the other hand an esteemed correspondent (Dr Greenhill) writes: 'I believe ἔκτρωμα never means anything except a lifeless abortion—*not* a living child prematurely born.' While the former of these definitions does not come up to either the proper or the figurative meaning of the term, we need not press the word, as here used by St Paul, so strongly as our medical friend would seem to insist. The ἔκτρωμα may be expelled in various stages of its development; and it is not necessary to choose the lowest and most rudimental to satisfy the self-depreciating feeling of the Apostle. 'An untimely birth' fairly represents the general idea, while keeping clear of details which might offend the delicacy of the English reader. To perfectly reconcile these two qualities, *strength* and *good taste*, we must have recourse to the only language which fulfils both conditions: e.g. Theodoret. ad loc. Πάντων ἀνθρώπων ἑαυτὸν εὐτελέστερον ἀποκαλέσαι θελήσας, πάντας καταλιπὼν τοὺς ἐν τῇ μήτρᾳ τελεσιουργηθέντας, εἶτα κατὰ τὸν νόμον τῆς φύσεως γεννηθέντας, ἀμβλωθριδίῳ ἑαυτὸν ἀπεικάζει ἐμβρύῳ, ὃ τῷ τῶν ἀνθρώπων οὐκ ἐγκατείλεκται καταλόγῳ.

*XV. 47: ἐκ γῆς, χοϊκός] 'of the earth, earthy.' By 'earthy' we must understand the material of which the first man was formed, which in the

---

[1] [Cf. Galen. ap. Hubart, p. 92: γυνὴ ἔγκυος ἐκτιτρώσκει (*absolute*). Euseb. *H. E.* v. 1 § 12: οὓς ὡς νεκροὺς ἐξέτρωσε, τούτους ζῶντας ἀπολαμβάνουσα.]

Mosaic record is χοῦν (עָפָר) ἀπὸ τῆς γῆς. Unfortunately, we have no single English word which conveniently represents χοϊκός, 'dusty' being used exclusively in the sense of 'covered with dust.' 'Earthy,' being of rare occurrence, is liable to be confounded by the unlearned with 'earthly,' and, in fact, is understood by the generality of readers as merely intensive, *accentuating* (to use the *slang* of the day) the preceding description 'of the earth.' This misapprehension has given rise to a number of imitations, or rather parodies, of the phrase in question : e.g. a person or practice is said to be 'of the world, worldly,' meaning that he or it is intensely worldly. Without venturing to propose any alteration in the text, we should have no objection to see a marginal note on 'earthy': '*Gr. made of dust.*'

*XV. 49 : φορέσομεν] 'Most of the ancient MSS. read, "let us also bear" (φορέσωμεν); but the Vatican MS. and ancient Syriac version read as in our text, "we shall also bear."'—Alford (*How to Study the N. T. Epistles*, p. 98). *Both* Syriac versions read ܢܠܒܫ, which may either be 'induemus' or 'induamus.' In Rom. xiii. 12 it is for ἐνδυσώμεθα. We have already remarked (on Rom. v. 1) on the tendency of expositors (including copyists) to give a *paraenetic* turn to the sentiment in similar cases. Here St Chrysostom says : καθὼς ἐφορέσαμεν τὴν εἰκόνα τοῦ χοϊκοῦ, τὰς πονηρὰς πράξεις, φορέσωμεν καὶ τὴν εἰκόνα τοῦ ἐπουρανίου, τὴν πολιτείαν τὴν ἐν τοῖς οὐρανοῖς. On the other side Theodoret : τὸ γὰρ φορέσομεν προρρητικῶς, οὐ παραινετικῶς εἴρηκεν.

XVI. 22 : μαρὰν ἀθά] The Syriac original is ܡܳܪܰܢ ܐܶܬ݂ܳܐ, *Moran etho*, which being interpreted is not 'Our Lord cometh,' but 'Our Lord came,' or rather 'Our Lord is come,' the Syriac verb representing either ἦλθε (Jude 14) or ἥκει (Luke xv. 27. 1 John v. 20). Accordingly Theodoret and Schol. Cod. 7 explain the word to mean ὁ κύριος ἦλθεν ; Schol. Cod. 19, ὁ κύριος παραγέγονεν ; and Schol. Cod. 46, ὁ κύριος ἡμῶν ἥκει.

II. CORINTHIANS.

Chap. II. 14: τῷ πάντοτε θριαμβεύοντι ἡμᾶς] A. V. 'Which always causeth us to triumph.' R. V. 'Which always leadeth us in triumph.' The latter seems to be more agreeable to the general use of the phrase θριαμβεύειν τινά, 'to triumph over a person' (Coloss. ii. 15 : θριαμβεύσας αὐτοὺς ἐν αὐτῷ. Plut. Comp. Thes. c. Rom. IV : βασιλεῖς ἐθριάμβευσε καὶ ἡγεμόνας). But when we read of God's 'leading the Apostle in triumph,' we can only understand, with Meyer, Alford, and others, his public exhibition of him, as a conquered enemy ; an idea, which, though not incongruous in itself, does not seem suitable to the present argument, in which he thanks God for making him an instrument in 'manifesting the savour of his knowledge in every place.' We would, therefore, dismissing all reference to the Roman triumph, understand the word in a more general sense : 'Which always maketh a show (or spectacle) of us[1].' To be 'made a spectacle of' is usually considered as a disgrace, and so St Paul himself understands it in other places (1 Cor. iv. 9. Coloss. ii. 15). But viewed as a means of bringing the Apostle and his mission into greater publicity, and so tending to 'the furtherance of the Gospel,' he not only accepts, but glories in it : it is no longer a θέατρον, but a θρίαμβος. This is, substantially, the view taken of this passage by the Greek commentators ; as St Chrysostom : τῷ πάντοτε ἡμᾶς θριαμβεύοντι· τουτέστι, τῷ πᾶσι ποιοῦντι περιφανεῖς· ὃ γὰρ δοκεῖ εἶναι ἀτιμίας, τὸ πάντοθεν ἐλαύνεσθαι, τοῦτο τιμῆς ἡμῖν εἶναι φαίνεται μεγίστης. And Theodoret : ἀλλὰ διὰ πάντων ὑμνοῦμεν τὸν θεόν, ὃς σοφῶς τὰ καθ' ἡμᾶς πρυτανεύων, τῇδε κἀκεῖσε περιάγει, δήλους ἡμᾶς ἅπασιν ἀποφαίνων.

Some fanciful expositors go so far as to connect the 'savour' in the next clause with the same image of a Roman triumph. Thus Dean Alford : 'The similitude is not that of a sacrifice, but still the same as before : during a triumph, sweet spices were thrown about or burnt in

---

[1] The Peschito has ܟܣ ܢܚܠ̈ܘ ܠ, which I should render spectaculum facit nos. not, as Walton,   specimen edit nobis; nor, as Schaaf, triumphum facit nobis.

the streets, which were θυμιαμάτων πλήρεις, Plut. *Aemil.* p. 272 (cited by Dr Burton).' Both the idea and the reference to Plutarch are as old as Elsner, who mentions, in connexion with the burning of incense, 'the streets, and especially the *temples*,' but is silent as to the 'throwing about of sweet spices' during the passage of the procession. Now if we turn to the place in Plutarch, we find that the only localities described by him as 'full of fumigations' are the very ones which Dean Alford entirely omits, namely, *the temples*. His words are : πᾶς δὲ ναὸς ἀνέῳκτο, καὶ στεφάνων καὶ θυμιαμάτων ἦν πλήρης. This is all; and the Dean has 'cleckit this great muckle bird out o' this wee egg[1].'

III. 14 : τὸ αὐτὸ κάλυμμα...μένει μὴ ἀνακαλυπτόμενον, ὅ τι ἐν Χριστῷ καταργεῖται] A. V. 'Remaineth the same veil untaken away (R. V. unlifted), which *veil* is done away in Christ.' Dean Alford and R. V. in marg. point : μένει, μὴ ἀνακαλυπτόμενον ὅτι, 'The veil remaineth, it not being revealed that it is done away.' The use of ὅ τι for ὅ cannot be sustained, and forms an insuperable objection to the rendering 'which *veil*.' But neither is it possible to read μένει μὴ ἀνακαλυπτόμενον otherwise than continuously, especially when the alternative is to introduce the rare construction of the *nominative absolute*. But a compromise may, perhaps, be effected between these two renderings, by taking κάλυμμα *per synecdochem* for the *thing veiled*, which is here declared to be, the fact 'that it (the old covenant) is done away in Christ.' That there is here a transition from one to the other of these two meanings is also indicated by the use of μὴ ἀνακαλυπτόμενον, 'not uncovered,' instead of μὴ περιαιρούμενον, 'not taken away.' In the editions of St Chrysostom before that of Oxford, 1845, the pronoun ὅ τι is retained, against the tenour of his own exposition, which is : ὁ δὲ λέγει, τοῦτό ἐστι· τοῦτο αὐτὸ οὐ δύνανται συνιδεῖν, ὅτι πέπαυται (ὁ νόμος), ἐπειδὴ τῷ Χριστῷ οὐ πιστεύουσιν. And elsewhere (T. VI. p. 179): εἰπὼν γάρ, κάλυμμα ἐπὶ τῇ ἀναγνώσει τῆς παλαιᾶς διαθήκης μένει, ἐπήγαγε, μὴ ἀνακαλυπτόμενον ὅτι ἐν Χριστῷ καταργεῖται. τοῦτο αὐτό, φησίν, οὐκ ἀπεκαλύφθη, ὅτι μέλλει ἐν Χ. καταργεῖσθαι. We may, therefore, venture to translate : 'For until this day at the reading of the old covenant, the same mystery (Or, *covered thing*, Gr. *covering*) remaineth unrevealed, *namely*, that it is done away in Christ.' Or (if 'veil' must be retained) 'the same veil remaineth not taken off (Gr. *not uncovered*) *lest they should perceive* that it is done away in Christ.' In supplying the words in italics we follow the Catena on this place : μὴ ἀνακ. εἰς τὸ γνῶναι αὐτοὺς ὅτι ἐν Χ. καταργεῖται.

---

[1] [In the description of Cleopatra's sailing up the Cydnus Plutarch (*Vit. Ant.* XXVI) says: ὀδμαὶ δὲ θαυμασταὶ τὰς ὄχθας ἀπὸ θυμιαμάτων πολλῶν κατεῖχον. He also describes (*Dion.* XXIX) Dion's triumphal entrance into Syracuse: ἑκατέρωθεν παρὰ τὴν ὁδὸν τῶν Συρακοσίων ἱερεῖα καὶ τραπέζας καὶ κρατῆρας ἱστάντων καὶ καθ' οὓς γένοιτο προχύταις (flowers &c.) τε βαλλόντων.]

*IV. 17: τὸ γὰρ παραυτίκα ἐλαφρὸν τῆς θλίψεως ἡμῶν] A. V. 'For our light affliction which is but for a moment.' R. V. 'for the moment,' for the present moment. Although τὸ παραυτίκα ἐλαφρὸν is here contrasted with αἰώνιον βάρος, it must not be supposed that παραυτίκα bears the same relation to εἰς τὸν αἰῶνα as ἐλαφρὸν does to βάρος. To make the opposition exact the Apostle should have written τὸ πρὸς ὀλίγον (or πρὸς καιρὸν) ἐλαφρὸν, which might have borne out the A. V., 'which is but for a moment,' or 'but for a season.' But the correlatives of παραυτίκα are ὕστερον (Stob. Flor. T. CXIII. 5: παραυτίχ᾽ ἡσθεὶς, ὕστερον στένει διπλᾶ), ἔπειτα (Thucyd. II. 64: ἡ παραυτίκα λαμπρότης καὶ ἐς τὸ ἔπειτα δόξα), αὖθις (Eur. Orest. 909: ὅσοι δὲ σὺν νῷ χρηστὰ βουλεύουσ᾽ ἀεί, | κἂν μὴ παραυτίκ᾽, αὖθίς εἰσι χρήσιμοι), τῷ χρόνῳ (Stob. Flor. T. XXIX. 35: ῥαθυμία δὲ τὴν παραυτίχ᾽ ἡδονὴν | λαβοῦσα, λύπας τῷ χρόνῳ τίκτειν φιλεῖ). We would therefore render, 'For our light affliction, which is for the present,' or simply, 'For our present light affliction.' The best parallel is Hebr. xii. 11: πᾶσα δὲ παιδεία πρὸς μὲν τὸ παρὸν οὐ δοκεῖ χαρᾶς εἶναι, ἀλλὰ λύπης· ὕστερον δὲ κ.τ.λ.

V. 1: ἡ ἐπίγειος ἡμῶν οἰκία τοῦ σκήνους] A. V. 'Our earthly house of *this* tabernacle.' Rather, 'of the tabernacle'; and in margin, 'That is, *of the body*.' The depreciatory term σκῆνος for the human body is borrowed from the Pythagorean philosophy. Thus Democritus (ap. Stob. Flor. T. X. 66): ὧν τὸ σκῆνος χρῄζει, πᾶσι πάρεστιν εὐμαρέως ἄτερ μόχθου καὶ ταλαιπωρίης· ὁκόσα δὲ μόχθου καὶ ταλαιπωρίης χρῄζει καὶ βίον ἀλγύνει, τούτων οὐκ ἱμείρεται τὸ σκῆνος, ἀλλ᾽ ἡ τῆς γνώμης κακοηθίη. And Perictyone, a female exponent of that philosophy, in her treatise Περὶ γυναικὸς ἁρμονίας (*Ibid.* T. LXXXV. 19) says: σκῆνος γὰρ ἐθέλει μὴ ῥιγέειν, μηδὲ γυμνὸν εἶναι, χάριν εὐπρεπῆς, ἄλλου δὲ οὐδενὸς χρῄζει. We shall add two neatly-turned epigrams, belonging to the same school, the first from Spohn. *Itin.* T. II. p. 81[1]:

Σκῆνος μὲν γενετῆρες, ἐπεὶ γέρας ἐστὶ θανοῦσι,
Τιμῶντες κλαίεσκον ἀναίσθητον περὶ τύμβον.

The other is from a sepulchral bas-relief in the British Museum (also printed in Welck. *Epigr.* p. 98) over a recumbent skeleton:

Εἰπεῖν τίς δύναται, σκῆνος λιπόσαρκον ἀθρήσας,
Εἴπερ Ὕλας ἢ Θερσίτης ἦν, ὦ παροδῖτα;

*V. 11: εἰδότες οὖν τὸν φόβον τοῦ κυρίου] A. V. 'knowing therefore the terror (R. V. fear) of the Lord.' The Revisers, in adopting 'fear' from Alford, would hardly, I think, accept his explanation: 'he was inwardly conscious of the principle of the fear of God guiding and leading him.' In the sense in which this clause is usually understood, 'terror' is greatly to be preferred to 'fear,' reminding the reader of such texts as Gen. xxxv. 5: καὶ ἐγένετο φόβος θεοῦ ἐπὶ τὰς πόλεις. Job xxxiii. 7: οὐχὶ ὁ φόβος μου στροβήσει σε;

---

[1] [See Jacob Spon, *Voyage d'Italie* etc., 1724, vol. II, p. 267. Ed.]

*VI. 2 : καιρῷ δεκτῷ...καιρὸς εὐπρόσδεκτος] Of the latter term Dean Alford says that it is 'far stronger than δεκτὸς, q.d. the *very* term of *most favourable* acceptance.' But if that were so, it would be more than is required by the Apostle's argument, which insists only on this being *the* favourable time indicated by the quotation. In fact, the words δεκτὸς, προσδεκτὸς, and εὐπρόσδεκτος do not differ in sense, but the last is the only one which is in use in Greek authors, and is always preferred by St Paul, except in the single instance of θυσία δεκτὴ Phil. iv. 18, a phrase borrowed from Isai. lvi. 7. It is not desirable to vary the English word, as 'accepted...acceptable'; but since 'acceptable' is the regular rendering of εὐπρόσδεκτος, and sometimes of δεκτὸς (e.g. Luke iv. 19), it might be substituted for the A. V. 'accepted' in both places. This substitution has been adopted in the R. V.

*VII. 2 : χωρήσατε ἡμᾶς] A. V. 'Receive us.' R. V. 'Open your hearts to us.' The latter is ambiguous, and without the marginal note : 'Gr. *Make room for us*,' might be understood to mean, 'Make a full disclosure of your feelings to us.' This might be avoided by rendering, 'Take us into your heart,' which agrees with Zonaras, ἀντὶ τοῦ εἰσδέξασθε ἡμᾶς εἰς τὰς ψυχὰς ὑμῶν. St Chrysostom explains : τίς ἡμᾶς ἀπήλασε; φησί, τίς ἐξέβαλε τῆς διανοίας τῆς ὑμετέρας; πόθεν στενοχωρούμεθα ἐν ὑμῖν; (alluding to Ch. vi. 12 : στενοχωρεῖσθε ἐν τοῖς σπλάγχνοις ὑμῶν).

*VIII. 3 : ὅτι κατὰ δύναμιν, μαρτυρῶ, καὶ ὑπὲρ (παρὰ BCDFK, silente A) δύναμιν...] Of κατὰ δύναμιν in the sense of 'according to their means' good examples are Diod. Sic. I. 84: θάπτουσι δ' οὐ κατὰ τὴν ἑαυτῶν δύναμιν, ἀλλὰ πολὺ τὴν ἀξίαν τῆς ἑαυτῶν οὐσίας ὑπερβάλλοντες. Aelian. *V. H.* I. 31 : πάντες αὐτῷ (τῷ βασιλεῖ) Πέρσαι κατὰ τὴν ἑαυτοῦ δύναμιν ἕκαστος προσκομίζει. The opposite to this is ὑπὲρ (beyond) δύναμιν, and in Latin, *supra vires* ; but παρὰ (not in accordance with) δύναμιν, is also used ; as by Josephus (*Ant.* III. 6, 1) in describing the offerings for the construction of the tabernacle (quoted by Schleusner, *s. v.* δύναμις): τῆς κατὰ δύναμιν αὐτᾶ ν σπουδῆς οὐ κατελείποντο, ἀλλ' εἰσέφερον ἄργυρόν τε καὶ χρυσόν...τούτων οὖν κατὰ σπουδὴν συγκομισθέντων, ἑκάστου καὶ παρὰ δύναμιν φιλοτιμησαμένου κ.τ.λ.

*VIII. 12 : εἰ γὰρ ἡ προθυμία πρόκειται κ.τ.έ.] I compare Dion. Hal. *Ant.* X. 25 : φίλων τε καὶ συγγενῶν δωρεὰς προσφερόντων μεγάλας...ἐπαινέσας αὐτοὺς τῆς προθυμίας, οὐδὲν τῶν διδομένων ἔλαβεν.

*XI. 20 : εἴ τις λαμβάνει] A. V. 'if a man take *of you*.' R. V. 'if he taketh you *captive*.' The A. V. should certainly be recorded in the margin, being supported by the Greek commentators, the Syriac Peschito (ܢܠܟ ܕ ܢܣܒ ܡܠܟܘ), and a precisely similar use of λαμβάνειν by the best writers. Wetstein (from Elsner and others) quotes Isocr. *Panath.* p. 558: τῶν μὲν ῥητόρων πολλοὺς οὐχ ὑπὲρ τῶν τῇ πόλει συμφερόντων, ἀλλ' ὑπὲρ ὧν αὐτοὶ ΛΗΨΕΣΘΑΙ προσδοκῶσιν, δημηγορεῖν τολμῶντας. Xenoph.

Cyrop. II. 2, 12: καὶ ταῦτα φανεροῖς γιγνομένοις ὅτι τοῦ ΛΑΒΕΙΝ ἕνεκα καὶ κερδᾶναι ποιοῦσιν. Aristid. *Antonin.* p. 65 (ed. Jebb. 1722): τοὺς μὲν στρατιώτας πρὸς τοὺς πόνους καὶ τὴν ἄσκησιν ἀμείνους ἐποίησεν, οὐκέτι τῷ ΛΑΜΒΑΝΕΙΝ αὐτοὺς ἐάσας προσέχειν.

XI. 28 : ἡ ἐπισύστασίς μου ἡ καθ' ἡμέραν] A. V. 'That which cometh upon me daily.' We will first consider the claims of the rival reading ἡ ἐπίστασίς μου, which is supported by BDFℵ, to which might probably be added the Vulgate (*instantia mea quotidiana*). In Acts xxiv. 12, ἐπισύστασιν ποιοῦντα ὄχλου, the only other place in which the word is found, there is the same confusion, ἐπισύστασιν being supported by HLP and probably Vulg. (*concursum facientem turbae*), and ἐπίστασιν by ABℵ. The evidence of MSS. may therefore be said to be in favour of ἐπίστασις, but the difficulty is to assign it a meaning in this place consistent with its general use in Greek authors. It is a word of rare occurrence[1], except in Polybius, who uses it in the sense of *attention, close observation* (from the phrase ἐπιστῆσαι τὸν νοῦν, or, simply, ἐπιστῆσαι, *to attend to*), e.g. οὐκ ἐκ παρέργου, ἀλλ' ἐξ ἐπιστάσεως—ἐπιστάσεως ἀκριβοῦς δεῖται—ἄξιος ἐπιστάσεως καὶ ζήλου. Dean Alford acquiesces in the Polybian use of the word, and his rendering of this and the succeeding clause is, 'my care day by day, my anxiety for all the churches.' This gives a very poor sense even here, and in Acts xxiv. 12 none at all. The Revisers, who also adopt this reading, translate, 'that which presseth upon me daily'; but the only example approaching to this meaning of the word is Soph. *Antig.* 225 : πολλὰς γὰρ ἔσχον φροντίδων ἐπιστάσεις, where the addition of φροντίδων indicates the general sense, whatever ambiguity may attach to ἐπιστάσεις[2]. On the whole, if ἐπίστασις be the original reading in both places, it may best be explained by supposing that ἐν συνηθείᾳ, *in stylo familiari*, ἐπίστασις had come to be used in a sense not differing from that of ἐπισύστασις, about which, being a well-known biblical word, there is little room for doubt. But it seems easier to suppose that the eye of the copyist passed from the first C to the second in ΕΠΙCΥCΤΑCIC, than that having ΕΠΙCΤΑCIC before him he should have interpolated the additional syllable ΥC.

The origin of ἐπισύστασις, as a biblical word, is to be found in the rebellion of Korah and his company, Num. xvi. In *v.* 3 we read that they συνέστησαν ἐπὶ Μωϋσῆν καὶ Ἀαρών ; and in *v.* 40, after the suppression of it, a memorial is instituted, 'that no stranger, which is not of the seed of Aaron, come near to offer incense before the Lord; that he be not as Korah, and as his company (καὶ οὐκ ἔσται ὥσπερ Κορέ, καὶ ἡ ἐπισύστασις

---

[1] The only example from the LXX. is 2 Macc. vi. 3 : χαλεπὴ δὲ καὶ τοῖς ὄχλοις ἦν καὶ δυσχερὴς ἡ ἐπίστασις τῆς κακίας, where Codd. 19, 106 read ἐπίτασις.

[2] ['In deliberando moras,' Herm. 'Delays,' 'haltings,' L. and S. But it may mean only that the anxious thoughts presented themselves.]

αὐτοῦ).' Again Num. xxvi. 9 it is said of Dathan and Abiram : οὗτοί εἰσιν οἱ ἐπισυστάντες (v. l. ἐπιστάντες) ἐπὶ Μωῦσῆν καὶ Ἀαρὼν ἐν τῇ συναγωγῇ Κορέ, ἐν τῇ ἐπισυστάσει κυρίου. For the verb ἐπισυστῆναι in classical Greek we more commonly find συστῆναι ἐπί τινα, as Plut. *Vit. Lyc.* XI : καὶ συστάντας ἐπ' αὐτὸν ἀθρόους καταβοᾶν καὶ ἀγανακτεῖν. Lucian. *Dem.* 10 : καί τινες ἐπ' αὐτὸν συνέστησαν Ἄνυτοι καὶ Μέλιτοι, τὰ αὐτὰ κατηγοροῦντες ἅπερ κἀκεῖνοι τότε[1]. In all cases the object of the combination is *hostile* ; which consideration enables us to dismiss at once such interpretations as that of Schleusner, *quotidianae perturbationes ex multitudine adeuntium ortae*, or Dean Stanley, 'the concourse of people to see me'; as well as those which make the succeeding clause, 'the care of all the churches,' to be an ἐπεξήγησις of the present one, as both A. V. and R. V. The Apostle is here describing two distinct elements of the harassing and wearying life which he led ; *first*, the 'caballing' or 'conspiring against him' of those rulers or members of the church with whom he was in 'daily' communication ; and *secondly*, the interest which, from his position, he was led to take in the concerns of distant churches. Without some allusion to the former of these, no description of his Apostolical labours and sufferings would have been complete.

* St Chrysostom, who certainly read ἐπισύστασις, understands it in a more general sense than that which we have suggested : οἱ θόρυβοι, αἱ ταραχαὶ, αἱ πολιορκίαι τῶν δήμων καὶ τῶν πόλεων ἔφοδοι ; and especially of the Jews, ἐπειδὴ μάλιστα πάντων αὐτοὺς συνέχεε, καὶ μέγιστος τῆς μανίας ἔλεγχος ἦν, μεταταξάμενος ἀθρόον. But the *historical* use of the word, with which St Paul must have been familiar, seems to be against this extension.

Ἐπισύστασις is also to be found in the Alex. MS. of the apocryphal book of Esdras, ch. v. 73 : ἐπιβουλὰς καὶ δημαγωγίας καὶ ἐπισυστάσεις (Vat. συστάσεις) ποιούμενοι ἀπεκώλυσαν (the work of rebuilding the temple); and in Joseph. *c. Apion.* I. 20 (from Berosus) : ἀπολομένου δὲ τούτου, συνελθόντες οἱ ἐπιβουλεύσαντες αὐτῷ, κοινῇ τὴν βασιλείαν περιέθηκαν Ναβοννήδῳ τινὶ τῶν ἐκ Βαβυλῶνος, ὄντι ἐκ τῆς αὐτῆς ἐπισυστάσεως. The double compound verb occurs in Plut. T. II. p. 227 A : πρὸς οὖν τὰ τοιαῦτα τῶν νομοθετημάτων (Lycurgi) χαλεπήναντες οἱ ἔφοροι ἐπισυνέστησαν. But, as I have stated above, the more general phrase for *rising up* or *conspiring against* a person is συστῆναι ἐπί τινα.

*XI. 32 : ἐφρούρει τὴν Δαμασκηνῶν πόλιν] A. V. 'kept the city of the Damascenes with a garrison.' R. V. 'guarded the city.' Φρουρεῖν is either

---

[1] [Cf. Plut. *Vit. Demetr.* XLIV : οἱ τρεῖς (βασιλεῖς) συνέστησαν ἐπὶ τὸν Δημήτριον. XXVIII : τῶν γὰρ ἄλλων βασιλέων ἁπάντων συνισταμένων ἐπὶ τὸν Ἀντίγονον. *Cat. Maj.* XIX : οἱ δὲ περὶ τὸν Τίτον συστάντες ἐπ' αὐτόν. App.

B. C. I. 81 : συνίσταντο τοῖς ὑπάτοις ἐπὶ τὸν Σύλλαν μετὰ δέους. Lucian. *Phal. prior* 4 : οἱ δὲ ἤδη τε συνίσταντο ἐπ' ἐμὲ, καὶ περὶ τοῦ τρόπου τῆς ἐπιβουλῆς καὶ ἀποστάσεως ἐσκοποῦντο, καὶ συνωμοσίας συνεκρότουν.]

to watch *from the outside*, as Plut. *Vit. Cam.* XXIII : καὶ διελόντες ἑαυτούς, οἱ μὲν τῷ βασιλεῖ παραμένοντες ἐφρούρουν τὸ Καπιτώλιον; or *from the inside*, as Appian. VI. 32 : οἱ δὲ (πολῖται) τοῖς φρουροῦσι σφᾶς ἐμποδὼν οὖσιν ἐπιθέμενοι καὶ κρατήσαντες, ἐνεχείρισαν τὴν πόλιν τῷ Σκιπίωνι. Here, since the ethnarch was in possession of the city, we must understand that he placed a watch at the gates, as the word is used by Dion. Hal. *Ant.* V. 57 : καὶ τὰ περὶ τὴν ἀγορὰν ἐφρουρεῖτο ὑπὸ τῶν ἱππέων κύκλῳ, οὐδεμία τε κατελείπετο τοῖς ἀπιέναι βουλομένοις ἔξοδος.

*XII. 3 : οἶδα] A. V. 'I knew.' R. V. 'I know.' Perhaps 'I remember' would be admissible, here and 1 Cor. i. 16 : λοιπὸν οὐκ οἶδα, εἴ τινα ἄλλον ἐβάπτισα. This use of οἶδα is not unknown to classical Greek ; e.g. Lucian. *Dial. Meretr.* I. 1 : Οἶσθα αὐτὸν, ἢ ἐπιλέλησαι τὸν ἄνθρωπον; Οὐκ, ἀλλ' οἶδα, ὦ Γλυκέριον. Plut. *Vit. Eum.* XVIII : ἀλλ' οὐδενὶ κρείττονι προστυχὼν οἶδα. Pausan. VIII. 17 (3) : οἶδα ἐν Σιπύλῳ θεασάμενος (white eagles).

XII. 7 : **ἐδόθη μοι σκόλοψ τῇ σαρκί**] There is no doubt that the Alexandrine use of σκόλοψ for 'thorn' (Num. xxxiii. 55. Ezek. xxviii. 24. Hos. ii. 6) is here intended, and that the ordinary meaning of 'stake' (R. V. in marg.) must be rejected. Elsner gives several examples of this use, especially one from Artemidorus, which has been repeated by succeeding editors of the Greek Testament down to Dean Alford (who, as usual, gives the credit of it to Meyer). The following is new : Babr. *Fab.* CXXII : Ὄνος πατήσας σκόλοπα χωλὸς εἱστήκει. He meets a wolf, and appeals to him : χάριν δέ μοι δὸς ἀβλαβῆ τε καὶ κούφην, | ἐκ τοῦ ποδός μου τὴν ΆΚΑΝΘΑΝ εἰρύσας.

GALATIANS.

*Chap. I. 6 : ὅτι οὕτω ταχέως μετατίθεσθε] A. V. 'that ye are so soon removed.' R. V. 'that ye are so quickly removing.' Perhaps 'going over' would better express the change of religious views here indicated. The word is used of political changes, as Plut. *Vit. Marc.* XX : ταύτην (τὴν πόλιν) προθυμότατα καρχηδονίζουσαν, Νικίας...ἔπειθε μεταθέσθαι πρὸς Ῥωμαίους. Diod. Sic. XVI. 69 : εὐθὺς δὲ καὶ τὴν Μεσσήνην μετατιθεμένην πρὸς Καρχηδονίους ἀνεκτήσατο. Of the different sects of philosophers, as Dionysius (Athenaeus VII. p. 281 E) : καίτοι γεραιὸς ἀποστὰς τῶν τῆς στοᾶς λόγων καὶ ἐπὶ τὸν Ἐπίκουρον μεταπηδήσας, got the *cognomen* of ὁ μεταθέμενος.

*I. 18 : ἱστορῆσαι Πέτρον] A. V. 'to see Peter.' R. V. 'to visit (Or, *become acquainted with*).' St Chrysostom remarks : καὶ οὐκ εἶπεν, ἰδεῖν Πέτρον, ἀλλ', ἱστορῆσαι Πέτρον· ὅπερ οἱ τὰς μεγάλας πόλεις καὶ λαμπρὰς καταμανθάνοντες λέγουσιν. Ἱστορῆσαι differs from ἰδεῖν only as it has for its object any remarkable person or thing. Thus ἱστορῆσαι πόλιν is *to visit the curiosities of a place.* Josephus (*Ant.* I. 11, 4) speaking of Lot's wife, says : εἰς στήλην ἁλῶν μετέβαλεν· ἱστόρηκα δ' αὐτήν· ἔτι γὰρ καὶ νῦν διαμένει. Another phrase might have been, κατὰ τὴν Πέτρου ἱστορίαν, as Diog. Laert. I. 43 : πλώσαντες μὲν εἰς Κρήτην κατὰ τὴν κεῖθι ἱστορίαν. Hence ἀνιστόρητος in a passage of Epict. *Diss.* I. 6, 23 : ἀλλ' εἰς Ὀλυμπίαν μὲν ἀποδημεῖτε, ἵνα ἴδητε τὸ ἔργον τοῦ Φειδίου, καὶ ἀτύχημα ἕκαστος ὑμῶν οἴεται τὸ ἀνιστόρητος τούτων ἀποθανεῖν.

II. 11 : ὅτι κατεγνωσμένος ἦν] A. V. 'Because he was to be blamed,' from the Vulg. *quia reprehensibilis erat.* This peculiar force of the perfect participle passive is denied by Dean Alford, who renders, 'because he was condemned,' '*a condemned man,* as we say ; by whom does not appear ; possibly, by his own act, or by the Christians at Antioch....I prefer the former ; "he was self-convicted," convicted of inconsistency by his conduct.' But in this case the 'self,' being of the very essence of the charge, ought surely to have been *expressed,* as it is in Tit. iii. 11 : καὶ ἁμαρτάνει ὢν αὐτοκατάκριτος, and John viii. 9 : ὑπὸ τῆς συνειδήσεως ἐλεγχόμενοι. The R. V. 'stood condemned' is open to the same objection. In support of the Vulgate *reprehensibilis*, we will not rely upon Lucian. *de Salt.* 84; where a dancer, in representing the madness of Ajax, carried his μίμησις to such an extravagant length that some of the spectators believed he had really gone mad: καὶ αὐτὸν μέντοι φασὶν οὕτω μετανοῆσαι ἐφ' οἷς ἐποίησεν, ὥστε καὶ νοσῆσαι ὑπὸ λύπης, ὡς ἀληθῶς ἐπὶ μανίᾳ κατεγνωσμένον. But the following from Diod. Sic. T. x. p. 19 ed. Bip. seems to be quite free from ambiguity: ὅτε δὲ εἰς αὐτὸν (Antiochus Epiphanes) ἀτενίσοι, καὶ τὸ τῶν ἐπιτηδευμάτων κατεγνωσμένον, ἀπιστεῖν εἰ περὶ μίαν καὶ τὴν αὐτὴν φύσιν τοσαύτην ἀρετὴν καὶ κακίαν ὑπάρξαι δυνατόν ἐστιν : where τὸ κατεγνωσμένον can only mean the *reprehensible character*, or *blameableness* of the acts just described. We may also compare the Homeric usage (*Il.* Ξ 196): εἰ δύναμαι τελέσαι γε, καὶ εἰ τετελεσμένον ἐστίν (where τετελεσμένον = τὸ τελεσθῆναι πεφυκὸς καὶ δυνάμενον); and such familiar instances as εὐλογημένος for εὐλογητός, ἐβδελυγμένος for βδελυκτός (Rev. xxi. 8)[1].

*III. 1: τίς ὑμᾶς ἐβάσκανεν] A. V. 'who hath bewitched you.' R. V. 'who did bewitch you.' But as the effect of the bewitching still continued, the perfect is most agreeable to the English idiom, and would probably have been employed by the writer, if the perfect of βασκαίνω had been in use. A more common Greek word for the operation is καταγοητεύειν, as Alciph. III. 44: Θετταλίδα τινὰ γραῦν, ἢ 'Ακαρνανίδα φαρμακευτρίαν πεπορισμένος, καταγοητεύει τοὺς ἀθλίους νεανίσκους.

**Ibid.* προεγράφη] A. V. 'hath been evidently (R. V. openly) set forth.' The Syriac versions understand γράφειν here in the sense of ζωγραφεῖν. Thus Pesch. *quasi pingendo depictus erat*; Philox. *prius depictus est*. Retaining the undoubted force of πρό in composition for *publice*, we would render, 'was evidently pourtrayed,' as it appears to have been understood by St Chrysostom, who enlarges eloquently upon the several details of the picture : ὃν εἶδον ὑπὲρ αὐτῶν γυμνωθέντα, ἀνεσκολοπισμένον, προσηλωμένον, ἐμπτυόμενον, κωμῳδούμενον, ποτιζόμενον ὄξος, κατηγορούμενον ὑπὸ λῃστῶν, λόγχῃ νυττόμενον· ταῦτα γὰρ πάντα ἐδήλωσε διὰ τοῦ εἰπεῖν, προεγράφη ἐν ὑμῖν ἐσταυρωμένος. All these things had been so vividly placed before their minds by the preaching of Christ crucified, that they could see them with the eyes of faith even more plainly than if they had been among the actual spectators.

III. 28 : οὐκ ἔνι] A. V. 'there is.' R. V. 'there can be.' See on 1 Cor. vi. 5.

V. 1. A. V. 'Stand fast therefore in the liberty' &c. The accidental omission of ᾗ before ἡμᾶς has thrown the whole sentence into confusion :

---

[1] [Cf. Plut. *Vit. Demetr.* 1: εἰ μηδὲ τῶν φαύλων καὶ ψεγομένων βίων ἀνιστορήτως ἔχοιμεν.]

'With freedom did Christ set us free: stand fast therefore.' So the Revisers; but if τῇ ἐλευθερίᾳ ἠλευθέρωσεν be meant for a Hebraism (like ἐπιθυμίᾳ ἐπεθύμησα Luke xxii. 15) the article is in the way. The only objection to the T. R. is the construction of στήκετε with a dative, instead of a preposition (as Rom. v. 2: εἰς τὴν χάριν ταύτην ἐν ᾗ ἑστήκαμεν; 1 Cor. xvi. 13: στήκετε ἐν τῇ πίστει) but this may, perhaps, be accounted for by the noun τῇ ἐλευθερίᾳ standing at the head of a sentence, of which the writer had not forecasted the governing verb. Instead of στήκετε he might have used ἐπιμένετε.

*VI. 1: ἐὰν καὶ προληφθῇ ἄνθρωπος ἔν τινι παραπτώματι] A. V. 'If (Or, *although*) a man be overtaken in a fault.' This use of the word προληφθῇ, in its moral aspect, is entirely passed over by the great Lexicographers; but there is no doubt that it is accurately represented, both physically and morally, by the English 'overtaken.' Thus, physically, a man is said to be 'overtaken' by the Egyptian plague of darkness, Wisdom xvii. 17: 'For whether he were husbandman, or shepherd, or a labourer in the field, he was overtaken, and endured that necessity, which could not be avoided' (προληφθεὶς τὴν δυσάλυκτον ἔμενεν ἀνάγκην): and Arrian. *Peripl. Mar. Erythr.* (quoted by Kypke): διὸ καὶ τὰ προληφθέντα πλοῖα τῇ 'Ἰνδίᾳ, πλαγιασθέντα ὑπὸ τῆς ὀξύτητος τοῦ ῥοὸς, ἐποκέλλει τοῖς τενάγεσι καὶ ἀνακλᾶται. In a moral sense, St Chrysostom (whose commentary on this place is: οὐκ εἶπεν, ἐὰν πράξῃ, ἀλλ', ἐὰν προληφθῇ, τουτέστιν, ἐὰν συναρπαγῇ) will furnish several examples; as T. VII. p. 526 D: Τί οὖν, ἐὰν προληφθῶ; φησίν. T. IX. p. 455 D: 'Τὴν ἀσχημοσύνην κατεργαζόμενοι'... Οὐκ εἶπεν, παρασυρέντες, ἢ προληφθέντες, ὅπερ ἀλλαχοῦ φησίν. T. XII. p. 220 C: πολλοὶ δὲ καὶ προληφθέντες, τὴν αἰσχύνην οὐ φέροντες, καὶ ἀπήγξαντο. Other meanings which have been assigned to the word in this place, *Siquis antea* (before this Epistle reaches you) *deprehensus fuerit; Etiam siquis antea deprehensus fuerit in peccato, eum tamen* (iterum peccantem) *corrigite; Siquis vel flagrante delicto deprehensus fuerit*[1], are all destitute of any authority from the usage of Greek authors, and would never have been thought of, if it had not been for the emphatic καί prefixed to προληφθῇ. This is certainly a difficulty; but if we suppose the καί to attach to the whole sentence (as if the Apostle had intended to write ἐὰν καὶ παραπέσῃ ἄνθρωπος ἔν τινι π., but, on consideration, substituted the milder term) then we may connect this verse with Ch. v. 25: 'If we live in the Spirit, let us also walk in the Spirit....But and if any man professing so to walk, should, by reason of the frailty of his nature, fall into grievous sin, then do ye which are spiritual' &c.

---

[1] ['This sense,' says Dean Alford, 'though unusual, seems justified by Wisdom xvii. 17.' This is the place which we have quoted above; and the reader may judge how far it justifies the sense of being 'taken in the very act' (καταληφθῆναι ἐπαυτοφώρῳ Joh. viii. 4).]

VI. 10: ὡς καιρὸν ἔχομεν] 'While we have time.' So the Prayer-book, and all English versions prior to A. V. It is also the rendering of Vulg. (*dum tempus habemus*); of Peschito (ܠܐ ܐܠܐ ܐܡܕܐ (ἕως) ܠܐ) and of Philox. (ܠܐ ܐܠܐ ܐܡܕܐ (ὡς) ܡ). The use of ὡς for ἕως, in this and similar phrases, is undoubted[1]. Thus St Chrysost. T. IV. p. 315 E : ὡς ἔτι καιρὸν ἔχομεν. T. VII. p. 754 D : ὡς ἔστι καιρός. T. VIII. p. 148 A : ὡς ἔτι καιρός. T. XI. p. 458 D : ὡς ἔτι ζεῖ τῇ μνήμῃ τῶν ἁγίων ἡ καρδία. Sym. Psal. cxviii. (cxix) 147 : ἐγειρόμενος ὡς ἔτι σκότος. In John xii. 35, 36, 'While ye have the light,' nearly all the uncials read ὡς for ἕως. The alternative rendering, 'As we have opportunity,' would seem to require ὡς ἂν καιρὸν ἔχωμεν, comparing Thucyd. VIII. 1 : οἵτινες περὶ τῶν παρόντων ὡς ἂν καιρὸς ᾖ προβουλεύσουσι[2]. It is also obvious to remark, that 'as we have opportunity' is as often an excuse for *not* doing good, as an argument for doing it, like Felix's καιρὸν δὲ μεταλαβὼν μετακαλέσομαί σε ; whereas 'while we have time,' by reminding us of the shortness of our time here on earth, sets us upon *seeking* opportunities of doing good, instead of waiting for them. This is St Chrysostom's reflexion on our text : ἄρ' οὖν, ὡς καιρὸν ἔχομεν, ἐργαζώμεθα τὸ ἀγαθόν. ὥσπερ γὰρ οὐκ ἀεὶ τοῦ σπείρειν ἐσμὲν κύριοι, οὕτως οὐδὲ τοῦ ἐλεεῖν. ὅταν γὰρ ἐντεῦθεν ἀπενεχθῶμεν, κἂν μυριάκις βουληθῶμεν, οὐδὲν περανοῦμεν πλέον.

VI. 11 : Ἴδετε πηλίκοις ὑμῖν γράμμασιν ἔγραψα τῇ ἐμῇ χειρί] A. V. 'Ye see how large a letter I have written unto you with mine own hand.' The only possible rendering of πηλίκοις γράμμασιν, 'in what large letters,' is now generally accepted. St Paul was a very indifferent penman, and when he did not employ an amanuensis, was obliged to write in very large and, probably, ill-shaped characters. St Chrysostom is inclined to the latter hypothesis : τὸ δὲ πηλίκοις ἐμοὶ δοκεῖ οὐ τὸ μέγεθος, ἀλλὰ τὴν ἀμορφίαν τῶν γραμμάτων ἐμφαίνων λέγειν. But no doubt the *size* of the letters was their principal feature, as in a curiously parallel passage from Plutarch's life of Cato the elder (T. I. p. 348 B), which was first pointed out by the present writer in his edition of St Chrysostom's Commentary on this Epistle, Oxon. 1852. In describing Cato's method of educating his son, the historian tells us that he wrote histories for him *with his own hand, and in large characters* (ἰδίᾳ χειρὶ καὶ μεγάλοις γράμμασιν)[3].

The connexion of this verse with the next seems to have been rightly understood by Dean Alford. 'My indifferent penmanship is a type of my general character. I do not set much value upon outward appearances. I am not one of those who "desire to make a fair show in the flesh."'

---

[1] [Cf. Clem. Rom. II *ad Cor.* ix: ὡς ἔχομεν καιρὸν τοῦ ἰαθῆναι ἐπιδῶμεν ἑαυτοὺς τῷ θεραπεύοντι θεῷ.]

[2] [Cf. 1 Cor. xii. 2: ὡς ἂν ἤγεσθε. A. V. 'even as ye were led.' R. V.

'howsoever ye might be led.']

[3] [Cf. Lucian. *Hermot.* 11: πινάκιον γάρ τι ἐκρέματο ὑπὲρ τοῦ πυλῶνος, μεγάλοις γράμμασι λέγον, τήμερον οὐ συμφιλοσοφεῖν.]

EPHESIANS.

*Chap. IV. 15 : ἀληθεύοντες] A. V. 'Speaking the truth. Or, *being sincere.*' Other renderings are, 'Being truthful,' 'Being followers of truth' (Alford), 'Cultivating truth' (Alex. Knox); all which lay the chief stress on the inward disposition, as distinguished from the practice of truth. On the other hand, the Vulgate *veritatem facientes* seems to be too strongly contrasted with *vera dicentes*, which will always be the principal use of ἀληθεύειν. Perhaps our biblical phrase 'dealing truly' (from the Hebrew עָשָׂה אֱמֶת), to which the Revisers have given a place in the margin, is free from both objections. The following extract from Aristot. *Eth. Nic.* IV. 13, 7 may serve to throw light upon this use of the word : Περὶ ἑκατέρου δ᾽ εἴπωμεν, πρότερον δὲ περὶ τοῦ ἀληθευτικοῦ, οὐ γὰρ περὶ τοῦ ἐν ταῖς ὁμολογίαις ἀληθεύοντος λέγομεν, οὐδ᾽ ὅσα εἰς ἀδικίαν ἢ δικαιοσύνην συντείνει...ἀλλ᾽ ἐν οἷς μηθενὸς τοιούτου διαφέροντος (nothing of this kind being concerned) καὶ ἐν λόγῳ καὶ ἐν βίῳ ἀληθεύει τῷ τὴν ἕξιν τοιοῦτος εἶναι.

IV. 29 : ἀλλ᾽ εἴ τις ἀγαθὸς πρὸς οἰκοδομὴν τῆς χρείας] A. V. 'But that which is good to the use of edifying. Or, *to edify profitably.*' The first of these is the translation of πρὸς χρείαν τῆς οἰκοδομῆς, with which we are not concerned. Dean Alford gives a servile rendering of the Greek, 'Whatever is good for the building up of the need,' understanding by 'need' some want or defect to be supplied by the discourse recommended. The translation of Tyndale, 'to edifye withall when nede ys' (Cranmer, 'as oft as nede is') has been lately revived by R. V. 'for edifying as the need may be'; and, in spite of the Dean's anathemas, might be simplified by the use of the 'miserable hendiadys' into 'that which is good for needful edification.' Or, taking χρεία in the sense of any special *occasion* or *matter in hand* (as Acts vi. 3 : οὓς καταστήσομεν ἐπὶ τῆς χρείας ταύτης. Plut. *Vit. Pericl.* VIII : μηδὲ ῥῆμα μηδὲν ἐκπεσεῖν ἄκοντος αὐτοῦ πρὸς τὴν προκειμένην χρείαν ἀνάρμοστον) and giving to οἰκοδομή the somewhat modern, but not inappropriate sense of 'improvement' or 'turning to good account,' we might translate : 'That which is good for the IMPROVEMENT OF THE OCCASION[1].'

---

[1] [For further illustration of χρεία, cf. App. *B. C.* III. 84 : καὶ ἀπιστοῦντα ἐκέλευε τὴν στρατιὰν εἰς πολλὰ διελόντα ἐκπέμψαι κατὰ δή τινας χρείας. Lucian. *Bis. Accus.* 10 : τίς δὲ ὑμᾶς, ὦ Ἑρμῆ, δεῦρο χρεία ἤγαγεν; Plut. *Vit. Crass.* XII : δεξά-μενος δὲ (Pompeius) τὴν χρείαν (Crassi) ἀσμένως (Crassus soliciting his good offices). Id. *Brut.* XXXVI : εἰ δὲ συνέλοι καὶ κατοικονομήσειε τὴν περὶ ταῦτα (τὰ κατεπείγοντα τῶν πραγμάτων) χρείαν.]

PHILIPPIANS.

*Chap. II. 6 : οὐχ ἁρπαγμὸν ἡγήσατο] A. V. 'thought it not robbery.' R.V. 'counted it not a prize,' with a marginal note on 'prize': 'Gr. *a thing to be grasped.*' But ἁρπάζειν is not to 'grasp,' but to 'snatch,' and is so rendered by R. V. in John x. 12 : 'the wolf snatcheth them.' Read therefore : 'Gr. *a thing to be snatched.*' As a biblical curiosity the Rev. J. A. Beet's rendering of this phrase (quoted in the *Church Q. R.* for January, 1883, p. 366) is worth recording : 'Not high-handed self-indulging did he deem his equality with God.'

II. 16: λόγον ζωῆς ἐπέχοντες] A. V. 'holding forth the word of life.' Nearly all our recent translators agree in this version, or vary only between 'holding forth' and 'holding fast.' The popular idea of the context is that the Apostle compares the Philippian church to *lights* or *luminaries* (probably the heavenly luminaries (φωστῆρες) described in Gen. i. 14 were in his mind ; certainly *not* such lights as the Pharos of Alexandria (Doddridge), to which the term is never applied) in which character they were to 'hold forth' to the benighted world 'the word of life,' the preaching of salvation by Jesus Christ. But, not to mention the absence of the articles (compared with 1 John i. 1), the employment of ἐπέχειν in this sense is not supported by any sound example, the Homeric usage of *offering* (wine, the breast[1], &c.) being too remote to be brought into the comparison. If now we turn to the Greek expositors, we shall find Theodoret alone favouring the popular explanation of the words, ἀντὶ τοῦ, τῷ λόγῳ προσέχοντες τῆς ζωῆς, and he puts himself out of court by quoting in support of it 1 Tim. iv. 16: ἔπεχε σεαυτῷ καὶ τῇ διδασκαλίᾳ, where both the meaning of ἐπέχειν and its construction are different. St Chrysostom entirely ignores 'the word of life,' and considers the words to contain not an exhortation to future action, but a reward for past exertions (ὅρα πῶς εὐθέως τίθησι τὰ ἔπαθλα). He goes on: τί ἐστί, λόγον ζωῆς ἐπέχοντες; τουτέστι, μέλλοντες ζήσεσθαι, τῶν σωζομένων ὄντες...οἱ φωστῆρες, φησί, λόγον φωτὸς ἐπέχουσιν, ὑμεῖς λόγον ζωῆς. τί ἐστί, λόγον ζωῆς; σπέρμα ζωῆς ἔχοντες, τουτέστιν, ἐνέχυρα ζωῆς

---

[1] [Cf. Lucian. *Zeux.* 4: καὶ τρέφει ἀνθρωπικῶς, ἐπέχουσα (female hippocentaur) τὸν γυναικεῖον μαστόν.]

ἔχοντες, κατέχοντες τὴν ζωήν· τουτέστι, σπέρμα ζωῆς ἐν ὑμῖν ἔχοντες· τοῦτο λέγει, λόγον ζωῆς. This redundancy of explanation probably arose from the Commentator's setting down a variety of glosses, as he found them in the margin of his Greek Testament; which is known to have been a common practice with him. They all seem to point, as he had before remarked, to some benefit to be enjoyed by themselves, and not (as the context requires) conferred by them upon the world at large. How is this latter point to be made out consistently with sound philological principles?

The phrase λόγον ἐπέχειν τινός is not unknown to later Greek authors, and has been illustrated, as far as examples go, by Wetstein, from whose collection we quote Nemes. *de Anima* II (p. 32, ed. Antverp. 1565): ἐρωτητέον ποία κρᾶσις ἐστὶν ἡ ποιοῦσα ζῷον, καὶ ψυχῆς λόγον ἐπέχουσα. Diog. Laert. VII. 155: ἀρέσκει δὲ αὐτοῖς καὶ τὴν διακόσμησιν ὧδε ἔχειν· μέσην τὴν γῆν, κέντρου λόγον ἐπέχουσαν. St Basil. *Hexaëm.* IX. (T. I. p. 83 E): κακὸν δὲ πᾶν ἀρρωστία ψυχῆς, ἡ δὲ ἀρετὴ λόγον ὑγιείας ἐπέχει. I add Aristid. T. II. p. 41: ὥστε καὶ τὸν τῆς μαντικῆς ἐπέχει λόγον (ἡ ῥητορική) καὶ τὸν τῆς στρατηγικῆς. In all these places the sense required is that of *corresponding*, or *being analogous to*, in which it has a close affinity with the better-known phrases, τάξιν, or τόπον, ἐπέχειν τινός (e.g. Theodoret. T. III. p. 489: ἡ εὐαγγελικὴ πολιτεία σώματος ἐπέχει τάξιν, ὁ δὲ νόμος σκιᾶς); and in this sense it was undoubtedly understood by the older Syriac translator, whose version is ܐܝܟ ܕܘ

ܗܘܝܬܘܢ ܒܕܘܟܬ ܚܝ̈ܐ, *quibus estis loco vitae.* Conformably to which, and in accordance with all the known examples of the phrase, I would render the whole passage thus: 'That ye may be blameless and harmless...in the midst of a crooked and perverse generation, among whom ye appear as lights in the world, BEING (TO IT) IN THE STEAD OF LIFE.' To the last clause a marginal note might be added: 'Gr. *holding the analogy of life.*' We are reminded of a portion of the Sermon on the Mount (Matt. v. 13, 14) in which ὑμεῖς ἐστε τὸ φῶς τοῦ κόσμου—τὸ ἅλας τῆς γῆς would be, according to the Apostle's phraseology, ὑμεῖς φωτὸς (ἅλατος) λόγον ἐπέχετε ἐν τῷ κόσμῳ (ἐν τῇ γῇ).

COLOSSIANS.

*Chap. II. 1 : ἡλίκον ἀγῶνα ἔχω περὶ ὑμῶν] A. V. 'what great conflict (Or, fear or care) I have for you.' R. V. 'how greatly I strive for you,' with reference to the preceding verse, 'striving (ἀγωνιζόμενος) according to his working.' But the former rendering, besides being more expressive, has the advantage of being closer to the original phrase, which may have been borrowed from Isai. vii. 13 : μὴ μικρὸν ὑμῖν ἀγῶνα παρέχειν ἀνθρώποις, καὶ πῶς κυρίῳ παρέχετε ἀγῶνα; I compare Plut. Vit. Flam. XVI : πλεῖστον δ' ἀγῶνα καὶ πόνον αὐτῷ παρεῖχον αἱ περὶ Χαλκιδέων δεήσεις πρὸς τὸν Μάνιον (Langhorne : 'But he had much greater difficulties to combat, when he applied to Manius in behalf of the Chalcidians.') Alciphr. II. 1 : τὰ Ἀφροδίσια ποιῶ κατ' ἔτος, καὶ ἀγῶνα ἔχων εἰ τὰ πρότερα τοῖς ὑστέροις νικῶ (Corrige, fere ut Arnaldus : ἀγῶνα ἔχω ἀεὶ τὰ πρότερα τοῖς ὑστέροις νικᾶν).

II. 8 : βλέπετε μή τις ὑμᾶς ἔσται ὁ συλαγωγῶν] A. V. 'Beware lest any man spoil you.' For 'spoil' (which might easily be taken for 'mar,' and, in fact, has been so taken by our great English Lexicographer) the R. V. substitutes, 'make spoil of,' Dean Alford, 'lead you away as his prey'; both of which, especially the latter, convey the idea of the Colossians themselves being carried off, instead of their (spiritual) treasures. There can be no better rendering than, 'lest any man *rob* you,' which is quite justified by Aristaen. *Ep.* II. 22 : τοῦτον κατέλαβον, ἄνερ, ἐγχειροῦντα συλαγωγῆσαι τὸν ἡμέτερον οἶκον. Dean Alford's objection is curious : 'The meaning *to rob* hardly appears suitable on account of the κατά...κατά, which seems to imply motion[1].'

II. 14 : προσηλώσας αὐτὸ τῷ σταυρῷ] The popular explanation of these words is derived from a supposed 'ancient custom' of cancelling a bond

---

[1] St Chrysostom (on the word βλέπετε) supposes the συλαγωγία to be conducted secretly, and so as μηδὲ αἴσθησιν παρέχειν. The householder finds himself losing his goods every day, and a friend warns him, 'Take heed lest there be somebody,' and shows him by what way the robber may have gained an entrance, διὰ τοῦδε τοῦ δωματίου, answering to the Apostle's διὰ τῆς φιλοσοφίας κ.τ.λ.

by driving a nail through it. Wolf refers for this custom to Grot. ad loc., Le Moyne *Var. Sacr.* p. 508, and Pearson on the Creed [Vol. I. p. 317, ed. Oxf. 1797]. Of these the last merely asserts the existence of such a custom, without giving any authority for it. Most probably it has no other foundation than this very passage; just as the existence of a low gate in the wall of Jerusalem, called 'The needle's eye,' through which a camel could not pass without being unloaded, rests on a false interpretation of Matt. xix. 24. St Chrysostom connects the 'nailing' with the cancelling of the bond, only as *making a rent* in it : καὶ οὐδὲ οὕτως ἐφύλαξεν, ἀλλὰ καὶ διέρρηξεν αὐτό, προσηλώσας τῷ σταυρῷ. But since the cancelling of the 'handwriting that was against us' is already amply secured by its being 'blotted out' and 'taken out of the way,' may there not, in this seemingly superfluous addition of nailing it to the cross, be an allusion to another undoubted custom, of hanging up spoils taken in war in the temples of the gods? Thus we read in Diod. Sic. XI. 25 : τῶν δὲ λαφύρων τὰ καλλιστεύοντα παρεφύλαξε, βουλόμενος τοὺς ἐν ταῖς Συρακούσαις νεὼς κοσμῆσαι τοῖς σκύλοις· τῶν δὲ ἄλλων πολλὰ μὲν ἐν Ἱμέρᾳ προσήλωσε τοῖς ἐπιφανεστάτοις τῶν ἱερῶν. Id. p. 152 D (Munthe): κατέσπασεν ἐκ τῶν νεὼν τὰς προσηλωμένας πανοπλίας, ἃς οἱ πρόγονοι σκῦλα τοῖς θεοῖς ἦσαν ἀνατεθεικότες.

II. 18 : **μηδεὶς ὑμᾶς καταβραβευέτω**] A. V. 'Let no man beguile you of your reward. Or, *judge against you.*' R. V. 'Let no man rob you of your prize.' There is no doubt that the judge who assigned the prizes at the games was technically called βραβεύς or βραβευτής, and the prize itself βραβεῖον (1 Cor. ix. 24. Philip. iii. 14). Hence βραβεύειν would properly signify to *act as* βραβεύς or *umpire,* and award the prize to the most meritorious candidate. But it so happens that in the examples that we have of this verb and its compounds, the *prize* itself never comes into view, but only the *award* or *decision,* and that not so much in its proper agonistical, as in an applied and general sense. Thus Isocr. p. 144 B : ἐν μὲν γὰρ τῇ κληρώσει (election of magistrates by lot) τὴν τύχην βραβεύσειν (Fortune will decide). Demosth. p. 36, 7 : ἐξὸν ἡμῖν καὶ τὰ ἡμέτερα αὐτῶν ἀσφαλῶς ἔχειν, καὶ τὰ τῶν ἄλλων δίκαια βραβεύειν (to arbitrate upon the rights of others). Diod. Sic. XIII. 53 : ὥσπερ τῆς τύχης οὐκ ἐναλλὰξ εἰθισμένης βραβεύειν τὰ κατὰ πόλεμον προτερήματα (to adjudge to either side by turns the successes of war); or, as the same sentiment is expressed by Josephus (*Ant.* XIV. 9, 5): ὡς εἰ καὶ πολέμου ῥοπὰς βραβεύει τὸ θεῖον[1].

Of καταβραβεύειν the examples are very rare, and must therefore be separately considered. The first is Eustath. on *Il.* A. 402 sqq. (T. I. p. 124, 2 ed. Rom.). He had before explained that Heré, Posidon, and Pallas Athené had conspired against Zeus, and would have bound him ;

---

[1] [Cf. Dio. Chrys. *Or.* XXXI. p. 344, 36 : βραβεύειν τὸν ἀγῶνα. Plut. *Vit.* *Brut.* XL: θεοῦ καλῶς τὰ παρόντα μὴ βραβεύσαντος.]

but Briareus, the son of Posidon, at the invitation of Thetis, came to his
assistance, and for fear of him the three celestials ceased from their
attempt. On which the Commentator remarks : ὅρα δὲ ὅπως, ὡς ἐν
ἀνθρώποις εἰσὶ πολλάκις παῖδες οὐχ ὅμοιοι, ἤγουν ὁμονοητικοί, τῷ πατρί,
οὕτως οὐδὲ ὁ μυθικὸς Βριάρεως φίλα φρονεῖ τῷ πατρί, ἀλλὰ καταβραβεύει
αὐτόν, ὡς φασιν οἱ παλαιοί, τοῦ φυσικοῦ θεσμοῦ προθέμενος τὸ δίκαιον. In
other words, Briareus decides, or takes part against his own father, preferring the claims of right to those of natural affection[1].

The only other example that is commonly quoted is from Demosth.
c. Mid. p. 544 ; where one Straton, who had been chosen arbitrator in a
cause between Demosthenes and Midias, in the absence of the latter
condemns him by default; but is afterwards himself in his absence
accused by Midias, and, by the aid of artifice and stratagem, condemned,
and branded with ἀτιμία. In speaking of this latter condemnation, the
witnesses conclude their statement of facts by saying: καὶ διὰ ταύτην τὴν
αἰτίαν ἐπιστάμεθα Στράτωνα ὑπὸ Μειδίου καταβραβευθέντα (damnatum) καὶ
παρὰ πάντα τὰ δίκαια ἀτιμωθέντα.

On the whole, comparing the phraseology of v. 16: μὴ οὖν τις ὑμᾶς κρινέτω
ἐν βρώσει κ.τ.ἑ. with that of v. 18: μηδεὶς ὑμᾶς καταβραβευέτω ἐν ταπεινοφρο-
σύνῃ κ.τ.ἑ., we arrive at the conclusion that the two verbs are of cognate
signification, but the second (as we might expect) the more forcible and
emphatic of the two : 'Let no man judge you,' 'Let no man condemn you.'
This agrees with the definition of Phavorinus : Καταβραβευέτω· παραλογι-
ζέσθω καὶ κατακρινέτω (Phot. καταλογιζέσθω, κατακρινέτω, καταγωνιζέσθω); as
well as with the Syriac translators, of whom the older has: 'Nequis
velit ἐν ταπ. damnare vos (ܘܢܚܣܘܢܟܘܢ),' and the later : 'Nemo
vos condemnet (ܢܚܣܘܢ) volens,' the Syriac word being usually the
rendering of κατακρίνειν and καταδικάζειν. Theodoret defines καταβραβεύειν
by τὸ ἀδίκως βραβεύειν, but this is rather παραβραβεύειν (Plut. T. II. p. 535 C :
οἱ παραβραβεύοντες ἐν τοῖς ἀγῶσιν). If any by-sense was in the Apostle's
mind in choosing this word in preference to κατακρίνειν, it may, possibly,
have been that of assumption and officialism, as it follows, εἰκῆ φυσιού-
μενος.

*Ibid. T. R. ἃ μὴ ἑώρακεν ἐμβατεύων] A. V. 'intruding into those
things which he hath not seen.' For the sense of 'intruding into'
Wetstein quotes Aristid. c. Phil. p. 486 (ed. Jebb, 1722): ἐμβατεύων εἰς
τὰ τῶν Ἑλλήνων, but the more familiar use of the word for 'searching
into' (Phavorinus: ἐμβατεῦσαι· τὰ ἔνδον ἐξερευνῆσαι ἢ σκοπῆσαι) seems
to suit the place equally well. So the Philoxenian Syriac: (ἐρευνῶν)
ܡ ܚܙܳܐ ܕܠܐ ܒܝ ܠܗܘ ܕܝ. And for the biblical terms πάσας καρδίας

---

[1] [Cf. καταδιαιτᾶν. Lucian. Hermot.   νώσκειν οὐδὲ ἐρήμην ἡμῶν καταδιαιτᾶν
30: ὥστε οὐκ ἐχρῆν ἀπάντων καταγιγ-   (to give judgment in default against us).]

ἐξετάζει κύριος (1 Paral. xxviii. 9), ὁ δὲ ἐρευνῶν τὰς κ. (Rom. viii. 27), St Chrysostom's stereotyped phrase is ὁ τὰς ἁπάντων ἐμβατεύων καρδίας (T. I. p. 371 E. Cf. 472 C: οἱ τὴν μακαρίαν ἐκείνην φύσιν ἐμβατεύειν ἐπιχειροῦντες, and T. IX. p. 437 D: τὸν ἐμβατεύοντα ταῖς καρδίαις). The Revisers' 'dwelling in' and (in marg.) 'taking his stand upon' are very doubtful. But the main difficulty lies in the omission of the negative, ἃ ἑόρακεν ἐμβατεύων, which is the reading adopted by nearly all modern Editors, and has driven expositors to such extremities that they have actually called in the aid of conjectural emendation, to which the fortuitous occurrence of κεν before ἐμβατεύων has opened a door. But all such attempts, including the most approved of them, ἀέρα κενεμβατεύων (*Journal of Philology*, No. 13, p. 130), are liable to the fatal objection that κενεμβατεύων is a *vox nulla*, the inviolable laws regulating this class of composite verbs stamping κενεμβατεῖν as the only legitimate, as it is the only existing, form.

I. THESSALONIANS.

Chap. II. 6: δυνάμενοι ἐν βάρει εἶναι] 'When we might have been burdensome.' Another understanding of the Greek phrase is suggested by the marginal versions, 'Or, *used authority*' (A. V.), 'Or, *claimed honour*' (R. V.). It is true that βάρος, like our English 'weight,' is sometimes used in the sense of *importance, preponderating influence;* but in such cases it is always something inherent and intrinsic that is intended, not any outward manifestation of respect. Thus we find ἐν τιμῇ εἶναι, ἐν δόξῃ εἶναι, ἐν ἀξιώματι εἶναι, but never ἐν βάρει εἶναι. In this sense, though the Apostle had been ever so averse to 'seeking glory of men,' he could not help being ἐν βάρει, in a condition of weight and influence, from the mere force of character and position. Hence those who adopt this view are forced to give a turn to their renderings, which is not in the original; 'though I might have *claimed* honour'; 'though I might have *stood upon* my dignity.' But however this may be, the instances of ἐπιβαρῆσαι (*v.* 9. 2 Thess. iii. 8), καταβαρῆσαι (2 Cor. xii. 16), and especially ἀβαρῆ ἐμαυτὸν ἐτήρησα (2 Cor. xi. 9), are so strongly in favour of the Vulgate, *cum possemus vobis oneri esse*, as to leave no reasonable doubt[1]. Dean Alford, who understands ἐν βάρει to be equivalent to ἐν τιμῇ, appeals to St Chrysostom: καίτοιγε εἰ καὶ ἐζητήσαμεν, οὐδὲ οὕτως ἦν ἔγκλημα· εἰκὸς γὰρ τοὺς παρὰ θεοῦ πρὸς ἀνθρώπους ἀποσταλέντας, ὡσανεὶ ἀπὸ τοῦ οὐρανοῦ νῦν ἥκοντας πρέσβεις, πολλῆς ἀπολαῦσαι τιμῆς. But the words εἰ καὶ ἐζητήσαμεν (passed over by the Dean) plainly shew that he is referring to the former part of the verse, οὔτε ζητοῦντες κ.τ.έ.; and his understanding of the latter part must be gathered from his concluding remark: ἐνταῦθα δὲ καὶ περὶ χρημάτων φησί, δυνάμενοι ἐν βάρει εἶναι ὡς Χριστοῦ ἀπόστολοι.

*II. 17: ἀπορφανισθέντες ἀφ' ὑμῶν] A. V. 'being taken from you.' R. V. 'being bereaved of you.' Mr Humphry comments: 'The Apostle,

---

[1] [In ii. 9 πρὸς τὸ μὴ ἐπιβαρῆσαί τινα ὑμῶν A. V. translates 'because we would not be chargeable.' R. V. 'Burden any.' A better translation would be, 'be burdensome to,' as R. V. in 2 Sam. xiii. 25, where A. V. has 'be chargeable unto thee.' But no change is necessary. Cf. Neh. v. 15, 'were chargeable,' both A. V. and R. V., for LXX. ἐβάρυναν ἐπ' αὐτούς.]

having reminded them of his parental tenderness and care (*vv.* 7, 11), now speaks of his parental sorrow. A. V. misses the point of this allusion.' St Chrysostom has a similar remark : ἐπειδὴ εἶπεν ἀνωτέρω, ὡς πατὴρ τέκνα, ὡς τροφός, ἐνταῦθα ἕτερόν φησιν, ἀπορφανισθέντες; which is open to the objection (as he says himself) καὶ μὴν ἐκεῖνοι ἀπωρφανίσθησαν, not the Apostle, who would rather have used the proper equivalent of 'bereaved,' ἀτεκνωθέντες. It is also to be observed that the R. V. is the rendering of ἀπορφανισθέντες ὑμῶν, which (not ἀφ' ὑμῶν) is the regular construction of the word. Dropping the idea of orphanhood, and taking ἀπορφανισθέντες in the general sense of χωρισθέντες, we would translate 'being separated from you,' which also harmonizes better with what follows, 'for a short season, in presence, not in heart.' The older versions have 'being kept from you,' which was altered by the Revisers of 1611, perhaps (as a parent is commonly said to be 'taken from' his orphan family) for the sake of retaining the very allusion which they are said to have 'missed.'

*IV. 1 : καθὼς παρελάβετε παρ' ἡμῶν τὸ πῶς δεῖ ὑμᾶς περιπατεῖν καὶ ἀρέσκειν θεῷ, ἵνα περισσεύητε μᾶλλον] After θεῷ the uncials ABD¹Fℵ insert καθὼς καὶ περιπατεῖτε. To these authorities Dean Alford adds (among other versions) the Vulgate and Philoxenian Syriac. In the latter the words are ܐܝܟܢܐ ܕܡܗܠܟܝܬܘܢ ܘ, which White translates, *ut ambulantes*; but it should be, *ut ambulatis*, καθὼς περιπατεῖτε (omitting the καί). But the Vulg. is, *sic et ambuletis* (=οὕτως καὶ περιπατῆτε), the very words which, according to Alford, the Apostle intended to write, but changed his mind. All things considered, it seems most probable that the shorter, and seemingly defective, reading is the original, which was afterwards supplemented after the pattern of *v.* 10, where a like testimony is borne to the Thessalonians, that they are already doing the thing required, before they are exhorted to 'abound more and more.'

V. 4 : ἵνα ἡ ἡμέρα ὑμᾶς ὡς κλέπτης καταλάβῃ] 'That that day should overtake you as a thief.' 'Some ancient authorities [AB Copt.] read, *as thieves* [ὡς κλέπτας]¹.' The marginal reading does not appear to have received so much attention as it deserves. If genuine, following so soon after *v.* 2, ἡ ἡμέρα κυρίου ὡς κλέπτης ἐν νυκτὶ οὕτως ἔρχεται, it is no wonder that it should have been tampered with; rather we may be surprised that it has escaped correction in two of the most ancient and representative MSS. With respect to internal evidence, we may observe that 'a thief in the night' is a well-known illustration of any thing that happens at a time when it is not expected (compare Matt. xxiv. 43), and so cannot be guarded against². Still it cannot be said, in such a case, that the thief *overtakes* the inmates, seeing it is his object not to disturb them, but to

¹ [R. V. margin.]
² [Cf. Hom. *Il.* III. 10: ὀμίχλην ποιμέσιν οὔτι φίλην, κλέπτῃ δέ τε νυκτὸς ἀμείνω.]

begin and end his operations under cover of the night. Should he fail in this, should 'the day' (not 'that day') 'overtake him,' then he furnishes an illustration of the manner in which the day of the Lord would overtake those who were not prepared for it. The phrase occurs in Plut. *Vit. Ages.* XXIV [1], in the account of a nocturnal expedition of Sphodrias to seize on the Piraeus: ἡμέρα γὰρ αὐτὸν ἐν τῷ Θριασίῳ πεδίῳ κατέλαβε καὶ κατέλαμψεν, ἐλπίσαντα νυκτὸς προσμίξειν τῷ Πειραιεῖ (where I would retain καὶ κατέλαμψεν against Cobet's opinion (*Collect. Crit.* p. 580): 'Dittographiam vides manifestam [2]').

[1] [Cf. Plut. *Vit. Crass.* XXIX: τὸν δὲ Κράσσον ἡμέρα κατελάμβανεν...περὶ τὰς δυσχωρίας καὶ τὸ ἕλος. Ibid. *Cor.* XVII: τότε μὲν οὖν ἑσπέρα καταλαβοῦσα τὴν ταραχὴν διέλυσεν. Paus. X. 23, 7: καὶ οἱ μὲν ἐστρατοπεδεύσαντο ἔνθα ἡ νὺξ κατελάμβανεν ἀναχωροῦντας.]

[2] [For similar repetition see Plut. *Vit. Otho.* VII: κἂν συνάψωσιν οἱ πολέμιοι κατὰ μικρὸν ἀναχωρεῖν καὶ ἀναφεύγειν. For καταλάμπειν see Ael. *V. H.* XIII. 1: τοσαύτη μετὰ τῆς ὥρας κατέλαμπεν αἴγλη τοὺς ὁρῶντας (the beauty of Atalante). *Wisdom* XVII. 20: ὅλος ὁ κόσμος λαμπρῷ κατελάμπετο φωτί. Compare Plut. *Vit. Arat.* XXII: ἡμέρας ἤδη διαυγούσης, ὅ τε ἥλιος εὐθὺς ἐπέλαμπε τῷ ἔργῳ.]

II. THESSALONIANS.

*Chap. II. 2: μήτε δι' ἐπιστολῆς ὡς δι' ἡμῶν] 'Nor by letter, as from us.' No satisfactory account has been given of this use of the preposition. Dean Alford explains, 'as by agency of us'; but if St Paul was the *agent*, who was the *principal*? In the subscriptions to the Epistles, διὰ indicates the *bearer* of the letter, as: Πρὸς Κολασσαεῖς ἐγράφη ἀπὸ Ῥώμης διὰ Τυχικοῦ καὶ Ὀνησίμου. Perhaps the Apostle wrote, ὡς δὴ ἡμῶν, 'as pretending to be ours.' 'Cum irrisione quadam plerumque ponitur ὡς δή.'—Ast. *Lex. Plat.* T. II. p. 586. Among other examples he quotes *Prot.* 342 D : ὡς δὴ τούτοις κρατοῦντας τῶν Ἑλλήνων τοὺς Λακεδαιμονίους. *Phaedr.* 228 C : ἐθρύπτετο, ὡς δὴ οὐκ ἐπιθυμῶν λέγειν. *Conv.* 222 D : ὡς ἐν παρέργῳ δὴ λέγων. *Pol.* I. 337 C : ὡς δὴ ὅμοιον τοῦτο ἐκείνῳ.

I. TIMOTHY.

Chap. I. 3: ἵνα παραγγείλῃς τισὶν μὴ ἑτεροδιδασκαλεῖν] 'The compound ἑτεροδιδασκαλεῖν, not -διδάσκειν, brings in the sense of "acting as a teacher," *not to be teachers of strange things.'—Alford.* On which it is sufficient to observe, that ἑτεροδιδάσκειν is not a legitimate Greek formation, any more than κακοδιδάσκειν or λαθροδιδάσκειν, which were long ago exploded by Lobeck *ad Phryn.* p. 623. In the indefinite pronoun τισίν, which has been characterized as 'slightly contemptuous,' we would rather recognize, with St Chrysostom, an amiable feeling towards the offenders ; οὐ τίθησιν αὐτοὺς ὀνομαστί, ἵνα μὴ ἀναισχυντοτέρους ἐργάσηται τῇ τοῦ ἐλέγχου περιφανείᾳ.

I. 15: πιστὸς ὁ λόγος] A. V. 'This is a faithful saying.' 2 Tim. ii. 11 : '*It is* a faithful saying.' The latter might be adopted in all places. To insist upon retaining the order of the Greek text, 'Faithful is the saying' (R. V.), is mere pedantry[1]. Compare 1 Kings x. 6: Ἀληθινὸς ὁ λόγος ὃν ἤκουσα ἐν τῇ γῇ μου. A. V. 'It was a true report that I heard in mine own land.'

Ibid. καὶ πάσης ἀποδοχῆς ἄξιον] 'And worthy of all acceptation.' In this case the Revisers have (not improperly, on the ground of *prescription*) retained the old word, though, perhaps, 'approbation' or 'admiration' would more correctly represent the Greek. Wetstein says: 'Erotianus ἀποδοχήν opponit τῇ μέμψει, Sextus Empiricus τῇ ἐπιτιμήσει.' The word is a favourite one with later Greek authors, especially with Diodorus Siculus, generally in the phrases ἀποδοχῆς ἄξιος, ἀξιοῦσθαι, τυγχάνειν. We subjoin a few examples. Diog. Laert. v. 64: αὐτὸς δὲ ὁ Στράτων ἀνὴρ γέγονε πολλῆς τῆς ἀπ. ἄξιος. Diod. Sic. I. 47: τὸ δ' ἔργον τοῦτο μὴ μόνον εἶναι κατὰ τὸ μέγεθος ἀπ. ἄξιον, ἀλλὰ καὶ τῇ τέχνῃ θαυμαστόν. I. 51 : μεγάλης ἀπ. ἀξιούμενον ὑπὸ πάντων. I. 69 : οὐ μόνον παρὰ τοῖς ἐγχωρίοις ἀπ. ἔτυχεν, ἀλλὰ καὶ παρὰ τοῖς Ἕλλησιν οὐ μετρίως ἐθαυμάσθη. V. 31 : ἀπ. μεγάλης ἀξιοῦντες αὐτούς. XI. 40: ὁ δὲ Θεμιστοκλῆς, τοιούτῳ στρατηγήματι τειχίσας τὴν πατρίδα...μεγάλης ἀπ. ἔτυχεν παρὰ τοῖς πολίταις. XII. 15 : νόμον ἀπ. ἀξιούμενον ἔγραψεν. XV. 35 : κατέπλευσε μετὰ πολλῶν λαφύρων εἰς τὸν Πειραιέα, καὶ μεγάλης ἀπ. ἔτυχε παρὰ τοῖς πολίταις.

---

[1] [In 1 Cor. x. 13 the R. V. has, for πιστὸς δὲ ὁ θεός, 'But God is faithful.']

* I. 20: οὓς παρέδωκα τῷ Σατανᾷ, ἵνα παιδευθῶσι μὴ βλασφημεῖν] 'Whom I have delivered unto Satan, that they may learn not to blaspheme.' R. V. 'Whom I delivered...that they might be taught....' Dean Alford says: 'The subjunctive after the aorist indicates that the effect of what was done (when he was last at Ephesus) still abides; the sentence was not yet taken off.' This is precisely what is conveyed to the English reader by the substitution of the perfect tense for the aorist. Nor is anything gained by the correction, 'be taught' (Alford adds 'by chastisement') for 'learn': on the contrary, there is a sort of irony in the choice of the latter word, which is very expressive. Let the reader compare Ach. Tat. VI. 20: ταύτην ξανθῆναι μάστιξι δεῖ...ὡς ἂν μάθῃ δεσπότου μὴ καταφρονεῖν. Lucian. Pisc. 2: ἐς τοὺς κρατῆρας ἐμπεσεῖν αὐτόν, ὡς μάθοι μὴ λοιδορεῖσθαι τοῖς κρείττοσι.

III. 1: ὀρέγεται...ἐπιθυμεῖ] A. V. 'desire...desireth.' R. V. 'seeketh... desireth.' Though the two words are nearly synonymous (Hesych. Ὀρέγεται· ἐπιθυμεῖ) the former has a special application to such objects as a man is commonly said to aspire to. Thus Diod. Sic. XI. 86: φανερὸς ὢν ὅτι δυναστείας ὀρέγεται. XV. 50: φρονήματος ἦν πλήρης, καὶ μεγάλων ὠρέγετο πραγμάτων. XVI. 65: πάλαι μὲν ἦν φανερὸς τυραννίδος ὀρεγόμενος (tyrannidem affectans). Thucyd. VI. 10: καὶ ἀρχῆς ἄλλης ὀρέγεσθαι, πρὶν ἣν ἔχομεν βεβαιωσώμεθα. Plut. Vit. Artox. VIII. (quoted by Wetst.): σὺ κελεύεις με τὸν βασιλείας ὀρεγόμενον ἀνάξιον εἶναι βασιλείας[1]. We would therefore render: 'If a man aspire to the office of a bishop'; at the same time repudiating the idea of an ambitious seeking, which does not belong either to the word itself or to its connexion.

*III. 16: Ὅς or Θεός][2] Although not of the number of those who lightly estimate or altogether deny the doctrinal results of the Revision, I cannot help thinking that the extent and importance of them has been greatly exaggerated both by advocates and impugners of the Catholic faith. To take the articles of the Holy Trinity and of our Lord's divinity, the only alterations which can be said to detract from the scriptural arguments in favour of these doctrines are 1 John v. 7 and 1 Tim. iii. 16; and of these the first cannot fairly or reasonably be said to be a 'result of the Revision.' The change was virtually made long ago; the Revisers had only to register it. If they have not even done this, but preserved an absolute silence as to the existence of a lis no longer sub judice, I would account for it by their desire to make a broad distinction between this particular corruption of the sacred text and all others, and not from any idea of

---

[1] [Plut. Vit. Comp. Timol. c. Aemil. II: καίτοι Δίωνα πολλοὶ μοναρχίας ὀρέγεσθαι ὑπενόουν. Id. Comp. Nic. c. Crasso IV: ἥμαρτεν, ὠρέχθη δὲ μεγάλων. App. B. C. III. 89: οὐ γάρ πω σαφοῦς ὄντος, ὅτι μόνης ὀρέγοιτο ὑπατείας (Oct. Caesar).]

[2] This note appeared in the Christian Opinion and Revisionist, March 25, 1882. Ed.

bringing it to what one of their number has described as an 'ignominious end.' It should never be forgotten that the text 1 John v. 7 stands single and alone in the history of N. T. criticism: it has nothing *simile aut secundum.* Nothing can be more disingenuous than, by including this confessedly spurious text in the same category with some other which it is desired to get rid of, to procure the summary condemnation of both. Yet this is a charge to which more than one of the Revisers have laid themselves open. Professor Palmer, for instance, at the Newcastle Church Congress, is reported to have said: 'I will give two examples, but they shall be examples of the first importance. ONE is the famous text of the "Three heavenly witnesses"; the OTHER is 1 Tim. iii. 16....In BOTH of these cases the consensus of critics is remarkable.' This is (unintentionally no doubt) a most unfair and misleading representation of the facts of the case. It is, Mezentius-like, coupling the living with the dead— 'Mortua quin etiam jungebat corpora vivis.' It is not correct to say that there is the same consensus of critics in regard to 1 Tim. iii. 16 as there is in the other case, nor anything like it. Exactly a century ago (Riga, 1782) Matthæi, the most careful and conscientious of textual critics, and a good Greek scholar to boot, summed up the controversy in favour of the T. R., both on external and internal grounds. As to the latter, his judgment (as we shall presently show) requires no modification: 'Lectiones ὃς et ὃ nec συνάφεια contextus, nec sententia, nec ratio grammatica admittere potest[1].' And with respect to documentary proofs, if the lapse of a century has brought to light *one* MS. of the greatest importance, it should be borne in mind that the oldest witness of all still remains dumb, and that the facilities for ascertaining by inspection the original reading of another cannot have been improved by the incessant handling, lensing, and microscoping to which the Alexandrine MS. has been subjected. And accordingly we find that (speaking broadly) those critics who inspected the MS. in the last century (Young, Mill, Woide, Berriman) believed that ΘC was written *by the first hand*; whereas those who have recently repeated the experiment, when the leaf in question was 'very thin and falling into holes' (Tregelles, Ellicott, Alford, and others), have arrived at the opposite conclusion.

But to return to the alleged 'consensus of critics.' Dr Kennedy in his *Ely Lectures*, p. 15, sanctions the same ill-omened conjunction between 1 John v. 7 and 1 Tim. iii. 16 in these words: 'Do we not still see the spurious verse in St John's first epistle cited as genuine by writers of slender learning?...Is not St Paul's evidence still quoted in terms which he did not use, "*God* was manifest in the flesh"?' And again at p. 90, referring to the latter text: '"Ὃς is now allowed by all wise and candid divines of our Church to be the true reading.' But (alas for critical unanimity!) between his Appendix I. and Postscript a certain bombshell

---

[1] Praefat. ad Epist. Cathol. p. XLVI.

had fallen upon the devoted heads of the N. T. Company of Revisers, which obliged our Ely Lecturer to qualify his previous statements. 'I really thought,' he says (p. 159), 'that when a divine at once so learned and conservative as Bishop C. [Christopher] Wordsworth had forsaken it [the reading $\overline{\Theta C}$], there was no further chance of support for it in our Church. I find myself mistaken.' In other words, the question is still an arguable one; an admission which severs at once the Mezentian tie between this text and the defunct 1 John v. 7, and destroys the monopoly of wisdom and candour claimed for those who maintain that St Paul did not and could not say of our Lord Jesus Christ, 'in express predication,' that HE IS GOD.

The Revisers (as we have already remarked) as a body have very properly made a distinction in their modes of dealing with the two texts under discussion. While they wholly ignore 1 John v. 7, and treat it as non-existent, on the other text they have recorded in the margin: '*The word* God *in place of* He who, *rests on no sufficient ancient evidence.*' The word 'ancient,' while it includes the testimony of MSS., versions, and quotations from the Fathers, excludes proofs from internal evidence, to which the Revisers, in common with the majority of textual critics, seem to have assigned a very subordinate place, if any at all, in the determination of the readings which they have adopted. By *internal* evidence I understand that which begins and ends within the compass of the passage itself, so that if it could be incontestably shown that St Paul has nowhere spoken of our Lord as God, *that* would not come within the scope of the present inquiry. Applying this criterion to the case before us, we ask: Which of the two readings, OC or $\overline{\Theta C}$, makes the better sense? Which offers the greatest facility in regard to grammatical construction? Which vocable is the more worthy of the dignified post assigned to it, at the head and front of a recital, the like of which, from the inherent grandeur of its topics, and the exquisite symmetry of its arrangement, is not to be found, and which is introduced by a proëm or preface, expressly designed to enhance the importance of the elaborate statement which is to follow, but distinct from that statement, as the porch from the temple, or the Propylæa from the Parthenon: 'Without controversy great is the mystery of godliness'?

1. $\overline{\Theta C}$ is entirely free from objection on grounds of internal evidence. If there had been no other reading known, assuredly no other would have been sought. The sense is perfect. The construction is easy and natural, flowing in a full majestic stream, without break or eddy, from beginning to end. It is also self-contained; it has a relation of order and comeliness with its preface, but is not dependent on it. If it be objected that the clauses after the first are more strictly applicable to Christ than to God, the answer is—that, after the leading enunciation, 'God was manifested in the flesh,' the notion of an incarnate Deity is so firmly established

in the mind of the reader that this complex idea, not the simple one of God only, is naturally taken as the subject to all the verbs that follow.

2. The claims of ΟΣ to occupy the post of honour at the head of this compendium of Christian faith come now to be considered. Ὅς is a *relative* pronoun, and has no significance at all, no *locus standi* (or, to use the fashionable phraseology, no *raison d'être*), without an antecedent. Now, if we ask, Where is the antecedent to ὃς ἐφανερώθη, the answers usually furnished are various, but all open to grave objections. (1) Bishop Ellicott (as quoted by Alford) says, "Ὅς is a relative to an omitted, though easily recognised, antecedent, namely, Christ.' But in the whole compass of St Paul's writings can any instance of such a *suppression of the antecedent* be found? In the similar passage, Col. i. 27, 'To make known what is the riches of the glory of this mystery among the Gentiles,' there follows, ὅ ἐστιν Χριστὸς ἐν ὑμῖν ἡ ἐλπὶς τῆς δόξης. If such had been the design of the Apostle here, would he not have written τὸ τῆς εὐσεβείας μυστήριον, ὅ ἐστιν Χριστός, ὃς ἐφανερώθη, which is, in fact, the identical device adopted by St Cyril to help out the imperfect reading which he had before him, and which, he rightly judged, could not stand without such an interpolation? (2) Dean Alford, taking the text Col. i. 27 for his 'key-note,' also agrees that 'the mystery of godliness' is Christ, but says, in explanation, that the Apostle 'joins the deep and latent thought with the superficial and obvious one, and, without saying that the mystery *is in fact* Christ, passes from the mystery to the person of Christ, as being one and the same,' an explanation which seems to belong to the class pointed at in the proverb— *Obscurum per obscurius.* (3) The Revisers have endeavoured to palliate the constructive difficulty by rendering ὃς ἐφανερώθη, 'HE WHO was manifested'; but if this use of ὃς (analogous to the Latin *qui*) could be proved, then all the clauses after the first must bear to it the relation of the *apodosis* to the *protasis*, and we must translate, 'He who was manifested in the flesh WAS justified in the spirit,' &c. But, in fact, no such use of ὃς (except in the oblique cases, as ὃν φιλεῖς ἀσθενεῖ) is known; and if such had been the construction intended by St Paul, he would certainly have written, Ὁ φανερωθεὶς ἐν σαρκὶ ἐδικαιώθη, κ.τ.λ. (4) The latest apologist for ὃς, and for the construction involved in it, is Dr Kennedy, who after the words already quoted, '"Ὅς is now allowed by all wise and candid divines of our Church to be the true reading,' adds jauntily, 'Since the μυστήριον [μ. θεότητος he repeatedly quotes from our text, instead of μ. εὐσεβείας, probably by accident, but the change is not without its significance] is Christ Himself, there is not the very slightest difficulty in its being referred to by a masculine relative.' Others, however, have found considerable difficulty in this reference, and amongst them the *Quarterly* Reviewer, who, whatever else he may be, is certainly not a contemptible grammarian. He is, therefore, fairly entitled to one more 'last word' from the Ely Lecturer, for which the 'Postscript' offers an appropriate place (p. 160): 'I will only add that when the Reviewer

calls μυστήριον ὅς a "patent absurdity," he seems to have forgotten the facts of grammar. If μυστήριον means Christ (and it does), the reference to it by the masculine ὅς is one of the simplest examples of *synesis*, a construction which abounds in Greek and Latin, and becomes, in this place, inevitable.' In other words, the construction is *synesis*, or nothing. If *synesis* fails, we must either recall Θ͞C, or retain a 'patent absurdity.' Of course the reader knows what *synesis* is; but if not, we will tell him. It is a grammatical figure, also called σχῆμα πρὸς τὸ σημαινόμενον, according to which (amongst other cases) the relative pronoun is made to agree in gender with the *sense* (σημαινόμενον) of the antecedent, and not with its verbal representative. For example, Homer says, φίλον θάλος ὃν τέκον αὐτή. Here θάλος is a *young shoot* or *scion*, and neuter; but it is perfectly plain that a *male child* is intended, and therefore the construction κατὰ σύνεσιν (ὃν for ὃ) is rightly used. Again, βίη Ἡρακληείη is a well-known periphrasis for Hercules himself, and there is, therefore, no difficulty in its being construed with ἐλθὼν instead of ἐλθοῦσα (*Il.* XI. 690). But such instances as these, even if they 'abounded in Greek and Latin' (which they do not), have nothing in common with the case before us. The peculiar characteristic of *synesis*, the clearly recognisable *personality* of the antecedent, is wanting. When we read, 'Great is the mystery of godliness,' we do not ask, Who is it? but, What is it? To pronounce dogmatically, ' Since the mystery is Christ Himself,' ' If μυστήριον means Christ, AS IT DOES,' is to beg the question altogether. To say that ὅς is grammatically correct, because its antecedent, the mystery of godliness, is a person; and when pressed on this latter point to reply that the mystery of godliness must be a person, because its relative is a masculine pronoun—if this is not to argue in a circle, I know not what is.

IV. 4: οὐδὲν ἀπόβλητον] A proverbial saying, founded on Homer's γνώμη (*Il.* Γ. 65): οὔ τοι ἀπόβλητ᾽ ἐστὶ θεῶν ἐρικυδέα δῶρα. Compare Lucian. *Tim.* 37: οὔ τοι ἀπόβλητά εἰσι τὰ δῶρα τὰ παρὰ τοῦ Διός. Stob. *Flor.* T. CXXIV. 33: παραινοῦσι δὲ ἄλλοι τε σοφοὶ καὶ οὐχ ἥκιστα Ὅμηρος λέγων, μηδαμῇ ἀπόβλητα εἶναι ἀνθρώποις τὰ θεῶν δῶρα, καλῶς ὀνομάζων τὰ δῶρα τὰ ἔργα τῶν θεῶν, ὡς ἅπαντα ἀγαθὰ ὄντα, καὶ ἐπ᾽ ἀγαθῷ γιγνόμενα. Dio. Chrys. *Or.* IV. p. 74, 20: (φιλάργυρος) περὶ πάντα λυττῶν κτήματα, καὶ οὐδὲν ἀπόβλητον ἡγούμενος. Galen. *de Compos. Med.* (quoted by Wetstein): πιστεύσαντες οὖν ἐμοί, τῶν εἰρημένων...φαρμάκων οὐδὲν ἀπόβλητον ὑπάρχειν, ἀσκεῖτε τὴν μέθοδον τῆς χρήσεως αὐτῶν.

IV. 6: ταῦτα ὑποτιθέμενος τοῖς ἀδελφοῖς] A. V. 'If thou put the brethren in remembrance (R. V. in mind) of these things.'[1] Ὑποτίθεσθαι does not appear to contain the idea of *reminding* a person of something that he knew before, but simply of *suggesting* or *advising*. Both Thom. M. and

---

[1] [' Put in remembrance'=ὑπομίμνησκε, 2 Tim. ii. 14. Tit. iii. 1.]

Hesych. explain it by συμβουλεύειν. So in all Wetstein's examples, to which add Dion. Hal. *Ant.* IX. 23: καταφρονήσας τῶν τὰ συμφέροντα ὑποτιθεμένων. Diod. Sic. T. X. p. 163 ed. Bip.: πλὴν ἐπεκράτησεν ἡ γνώμη τῶν μέχρι τελευτῆς ὑποθεμένων ἀγωνίσασθαι¹.

*IV. 12: μηδείς σου τῆς νεότητος καταφρονείτω] Compare Appian. *Bell. Hisp.* VI. 8: ὡς ἔμαθον αὐτοὺς (Barca and Hasdrubal) τεθνεῶτας, Ἀννίβα κατεφρόνουν ὡς νέου. Diod. Sic. XVII. 2: νέος γὰρ ὢν παντελῶς (Alex. M.) καὶ διὰ τὴν ἡλικίαν ὑπό τινων καταφρονούμενος. 7: Φιλίππου δὲ τελευτήσαντος, ἀπελύθη τῆς ἀγωνίας, καταφρονήσας τῆς Ἀλεξάνδρου νεότητος. The last example may be appealed to in defence of the construction, 'Let no man despise thy youth,' against those who would construe, 'Let no man despise thee on account of (thy) youth'; as may also the following, Plut. *Vit. Pericl.* XXVI: καταφρονήσας τῆς ὀλιγότητος τῶν νεῶν ἢ τῆς ἀπειρίας τῶν στρατηγῶν. Herodian. I. 3, 14 (quoted by Wetstein): ὑπώπτευεν μὴ τῆς ἡλικίας αὐτοῦ καταφρονήσαντες ἐπιθῶνται αὐτῷ.

*IV. 15: ταῦτα μελέτα] A. V. 'Meditate on these things.' R. V. 'Be diligent in these things.' The best rendering seems to be Prof. Schole-field's, 'Exercise thyself in these things,' who quotes Psal. i. 2: ἐν τῷ νόμῳ αὐτοῦ μελετήσει, 'in his law will he exercise himself' (P. B.); and Thucyd. I. 142, where he speaks of the Athenians having obtained their naval pre-eminence by *long training and practice*; μελετῶντες αὐτὸ εὐθὺς ἀπὸ τῶν Μηδικῶν. I add Diog. L. *Sol.* XII: τὰ σπουδαῖα μελέτα. Epict. *Diss.* I. 1, 25: ταῦτα ἔδει μελετᾶν τοὺς φιλοσοφοῦντας, ταῦτα καθ' ἡμέραν γράφειν, ἐν τούτοις γυμνάζεσθαι. J. Pollux VIII. 105: περίπολοι ἔφηβοι περιῄεσαν τὴν χώραν φυλάττοντες, ὥσπερ ἤδη μελετῶντες τὰ στρατιωτικά.

V. I: πρεσβυτέρῳ μὴ ἐπιπλήξῃς, ἀλλὰ παρακάλει (A. V. 'intreat,' R. V. 'exhort') ὡς πατέρα] The following extract from Hierocles, ἐκ τοῦ, πῶς χρηστέον τοῖς γονεῦσιν (Stob. *Flor.* T. LXXIX. 53), furnishes a good illus-tration of both verbs: κἂν εἴ τι που γένοιντο παραμυρτάνοντες...ἐπανορθωτέον μέν, ἀλλ' οὐ μετ' ἐπιπλήξεως, μὰ Δία, καθάπερ ἔθος πρὸς τοὺς ἐλάττονας ἢ ἴσους ποιεῖν, ἀλλ' ὡς μετὰ παρακλήσεως (but as it were by way of intreaty). The reason why the Revisers (who have not altered 1 Cor. iv. 13: 'Being defamed, we *intreat*') have here preferred 'exhort' is, probably, because exhortation is more suitable to the other persons to be dealt with, 'the younger men as brethren' &c. Dean Alford even goes so far as to make the prohibition μὴ ἐπιπλήξῃς extend to all the classes described in *vv.* 1, 2; as if the younger men, for instance, were never to be rebuked: to avoid which absurdity, he is compelled to give to ἐπιπλήσσειν the sense of 'rebuking sharply,' which cannot be proved².

¹ [Cf. Lucian. *Harm.* 2: ὡς δὲ ποιήσας γνωσθήσῃ αὐτοῖς, καὶ ἐπὶ τὸ πέρας ἀφίξῃ τῆς εὐχῆς, ἐγὼ καὶ τοῦθ' ὑποθήσομαί σοι.]

² [Cf. Themist. *Or.* XXII. p. 277 A: πάμπολυ γὰρ διαφέρει νουθεσία μὲν λοιδορίας, ἐπίπληξις δὲ ὀνείδους.]

K.   14

V. 13: ἀργαὶ μανθάνουσι] 'They learn *to be* idle.' 'A harsh construction, but, it is said, not without example: however, the only one cited is Plat. *Euthyd.* p. 276 B: οἱ ἀμαθεῖς ἄρα σοφοὶ μανθάνουσιν...ἀλλ' οὐχ οἱ σοφοί, where the first σοφοί does not occur in Bekker's text' [it is inserted by Winckelmann from two excellent authorities, Bodl. and Vat. Θ].—*Alford*. Although the reading in Plato may be doubtful, there is no doubt of the agreement of St Paul's construction with *later* usage, especially if we take ἀργαί, φλύαροι, περίεργοι as *nouns*, 'idlers,' 'tattlers,' 'busybodies.' Winckelmann compares Dio. Chrys. T. II. p. 283 (*Or.* LV.): Σωκράτης... παῖς ὢν ἐμάνθανε λιθοξόος τὴν τοῦ πατρὸς τέχνην: to which I add S. Chrysost. T. VII. p. 699 A: τί οὖν; ἂν παλαιστὴς μανθάνῃς; T. IX. p. 259 B: εἰ ἰατρὸς μέλλοις μανθάνειν. Aesop. *Fab.* CXL, ed. de Furia: τί γάρ, τοῦ πατρός με μάγειρον διδάξαντος, ἰατρικὴν τέχνην ὑπελαβόμην; Examples similar to the last, διδάξαι (or διδάξασθαι) τινὰ τεκτόνα, χαλκέα, ἱππέα, ῥήτορα, are to be found in the best writers, as has been shown by Hemst. on Aristoph. *Plut.* p. 4: ΥΠΟΘΕΣΙΣ...ἀφικνεῖται εἰς θεοῦ, χρησόμενος πότερον τὸν παῖδα σωφρόνως ἀναθρέψειε, καὶ ὅμοιον ἑαυτῷ τοὺς τρόπους διδάξειεν, ἢ φαῦλον, ὡς τῶν φαύλων τότε εὐπραγούντων.

*V. 23: μηκέτι ὑδροπότει] A. V. 'Drink no longer water.' R. V. 'Be no longer a drinker of water.' Better, 'a water-drinker.'

VI. 2: ὅτι πιστοί εἰσι καὶ ἀγαπητοὶ οἱ τῆς εὐεργεσίας ἀντιλαμβανόμενοι] The subject is, undoubtedly, οἱ...ἀντιλαμβανόμενοι, which requires the A. V. to be read, 'Because they that are partakers of the benefit are faithful (Or, *believing*) and beloved.' The 'benefit' is the improved quality of the service, and 'they that partake of it' are the masters. There is some difficulty in this applied sense of ἀντιλαμβάνεσθαι, the proper meaning of which is 'to lay hold of.' We cannot accept Dean Alford's version, 'receive in exchange,' because that is ἀντιλαμβάνειν, and his three instances from Euripides and Theognis are all of the active form, ἀντιλήψεται with an accusative case being *active*, not *middle*. The regular biblical meaning of the word, to *help* or *support* (Luke i. 54, Acts xx. 35, Sirac. ii. 6), though adopted by the Philoxenian Syriac, yields no tolerable sense. On the whole, we are disposed to acquiesce in the usual translation, 'they that *partake of*, or enjoy the benefit,' from the Vulgate, *qui beneficii participes sunt*. The older Syriac gives the sense very well, ܘܣܛܐܒܣܘܐܟ ܡܬܬܢܝܚܝܢܒܗܘܢ, which might be re-translated into Greek, οἱ ἀναπαυόμενοι τῇ θεραπείᾳ αὐτῶν. This use of the word is nearly allied to that in which a person is said to be *sensible of* any thing which acts upon the senses, as in the following examples: Alex. Aphr. *Probl.* (quoted by Budaeus): ἡ ψυχὴ πλέον ἀντιλαμβάνεται τῶν σωματικῶν παθῶν κατὰ τὴν ἁπτικὴν αἴσθησιν. Artemid. *Onirocr.* I. 81: διὰ τὸ τοὺς καθεύδοντας μὴ ἀντιλαμβάνεσθαι πόνων. S. Chrysost. T. IV. p. 725 B: ῥόδον...οὗ τῆς εὐωδίας ἅπαντες οἱ κατὰ τὴν οἰκουμένην ἀντιλαμβάνονται (*potiuntur*) μέχρι τήμερον.

*VI. 3 : καὶ μὴ προσέρχεται ὑγιαίνουσι λόγοις] A. V. 'And consent not to wholesome words.' Vulg. *et non acquiescit sanis sermonibus*. This seems to be the only meaning suitable to the connexion ; but it is not borne out by the very few examples usually quoted in support of it. For instance, Diod. Sic. I. 95 (in an enumeration of the legislators of Egypt): μετὰ δὲ τοῦτον προσελθεῖν λέγεται τοῖς νόμοις Ἄμασιν τὸν βασιλέα, i.e. as we should say, 'took his turn at law-making.' Philo Jud. *De Gigant*. 9 (p. 267, ed. Mangey): μαθέτωσαν δὴ πάντες οὗτοι μηδενὶ προσέρχεσθαι γνώμη τῶν εἰρημένων (riches, honour, strength, the *involuntary* possessors of which are warned not to *approach to them in their mind*), τοῦτο δέ ἐστι, μὴ θαυμάζειν αὐτὰ καὶ ἀποδέχεσθαι πλέον τοῦ μετρίου, where the use of the word προσέρχεσθαι is to be explained by a reference to the text (Lev. xviii. 6) of which the whole passage is an allegorical exposition : ἄνθρωπος πρὸς πάντα οἰκεῖον σαρκὸς αὐτοῦ οὐ προσελεύσεται.

Bentley's conjecture προσέχει[1] occurs in a similar connexion ch. i. 4, where the Philoxenian has "ܒ ܡܝܩܠ, the very word which the same translator has employed in this place ("ܒ ܢܝܕ).

*VI. 4 : The *structure* of the sentence ζητήσεις καὶ λογομαχίας, ᾽ΕΞ ῟ΩΝ γίνεται φθόνος, ἔρις... is curiously paralleled by Stob. *Flor*. T. x. 78 : εὐθὺς στάσεις, λοιδορίαι, καὶ πόλεμος ἄσπονδος, ᾽ΕΞ ῟ΩΝ ψευδεῖς διαβολαί, καὶ πᾶν εἶδος ἐπιβουλῆς.

*VI. 5 : διαπαρατριβαί] R. V. 'wranglings.' The T. R. παραδιατριβαί has no support from MSS. Those who introduced it were not so familiar with the use of the word παρατριβαί, *frictions, irritations*, as with that of διατριβαί. The prefix διά has been thought to give the sense of *continuance*, 'incessant quarrels'; but comparing διαμάχεσθαι, διαφιλοτιμεῖσθαι, &c., I should prefer that of *reciprocity*, 'mutual irritations,' which seems to have been the opinion of our Translators, who, having adopted παραδ., 'perverse disputings,' in their text, have given their version of διαπ. in the margin : ' Or, *gallings one of another*.'

*Ibid. νομιζόντων πορισμὸν εἶναι τὴν εὐσέβειαν] A. V. 'Supposing that gain is godliness.' The Greek undoubtedly requires 'that godliness is gain.' Πορισμὸς is properly 'a means of gain,' which might be noted in the margin, 'gain' being retained in the text on account of the next verse. Cato the elder used to say that he had only two ways of making money (πορισμοί), *husbandry* and *thrift* (γεωργία καὶ φειδώ). In the text, instead of πορισμὸν a Greek classic would probably have used πρόσοδον or χρηματισμόν. Thus Lucian. *Saturn*. 8 : ἀλλὰ πρόσοδον οἱ πολλοὶ πεποίηνται

---

[1] ' If some MSS. then should have it προσέχεται or προσίχεται [προσίσχεται?], *cleaves and adheres to the wholesome words*, who has reason to be angry at that variation? But I should sooner expect to find προσέχει; because προσέχειν λόγοις, *to give heed, attend*...is a known phrase as well in sacred as profane authors.' *Remarks on Freethinking*, p. 107 (7th ed. 1737).

τὴν ἑορτήν. Dion. Hal. *Ant.* III. 5 (quoted by Wetstein): οἱ δὲ χρηματισμὸν ἡγούμενοι τὸν πόλεμον. We have a vulgar phrase of 'making capital' of any thing.

VI. 7: οὐδὲν γὰρ εἰσηνέγκαμεν εἰς τὸν κόσμον, [δῆλον] ὅτι οὐδὲ ἐξενεγκεῖν τι δυνάμεθα] Δῆλον is wholly wanting in AFℵ. In other authorities we find some substitute for it, as ἀληθές (D), *haud dubium* (Vulg.), *vere* (Philox. in marg. Both Syriac versions have δῆλον (ܫܪܝܪ) in text). These variations clearly show that δῆλον is spurious; but they further indicate that something is wanting to complete the sense, which something those who felt the deficiency had recourse each to his own critical faculty to supply. The most natural solution of the problem is, that there is an ellipsis of δῆλον, or that ὅτι is for δῆλον ὅτι. L. Bos adduces but one example of this ellipsis, 1 Joh. iii. 20: ὅτι ἐὰν καταγινώσκῃ ἡμῶν ἡ καρδία, ὅτι μείζων ἐστὶν ὁ θεὸς τῆς καρδίας ἡμῶν; in which, if an ellipsis of δῆλον before the second ὅτι were admissible, it would seem to offer an easy explanation of that difficult text. I venture to add two examples from St Chrysostom (T. X, p. 38 BD): Εἰ γὰρ μὴ ἐγένετο τὰ γεγενημένα... (supply δῆλον) ὅτι ταῦτα πλάττειν φιλονεικοῦντες ... καὶ τῷ θεῷ προσκρούειν ἔμελλον, καὶ μυρίους ἄνωθεν προσδοκᾶν κεραυνούς ... Εἰ γὰρ μαινόμενοι ἦσαν ... οὐδὲν ὅλως κατορθῶσαι ἔδει, οὐδεὶς γὰρ μαινομένοις πείθεται· εἰ δὲ κατώρθωσαν, ὥσπερ οὖν κατώρθωσαν, καὶ δείκνυσι τὸ τέλος (supply δῆλον) ὅτι πάντων ἦσαν σοφώτεροι· εἰ δὲ πάντων ἦσαν σοφώτεροι, ΕΥΔΗΛΟΝ ὅτι οὐκ ἂν ἁπλῶς ἦλθον ἐπὶ τὸ κήρυγμα.

Those who reject the idea of an ellipsis, take ὅτι for *quia*, and demand our acquiescence in such a preposterous sentiment as the following: 'For we brought nothing into this world, for (because) neither can we carry anything out'; in other words: 'It was the ordinance of God, that we should bring nothing into the world, to teach us to remember that we can carry nothing out.'

VI. 10: ῥίζα γὰρ πάντων τῶν κακῶν ἐστὶν ἡ φιλαργυρία] A. V. 'For the love of money is THE root of all evil.' Recent translators (with the exception of Dean Alford) have ascribed to St Paul the very tame and unrhetorical sentiment: 'The love of money is A root of all evil.' 'This passage,' say the Authors of the *Temperance Bible Commentary*[1], 'has been strangely cited in opposition to the statement that strong drink is the source of much of the evil which afflicts and demoralizes society.' And again: 'St Paul's words are, "For covetousness is *a* root of all the evils," i.e. of all the evils mentioned in the preceding verse[2], but not the exclusive root

---

[1] Instead of 'Rightly dividing the Word of Truth,' the present 'motto' of this work, I would suggest the following from Menander:

°Ο βούλεται γὰρ μόνον ὁρῶν καὶ προσ-
δοκῶν,

ἀλόγιστός ἐστι τῆς ἀληθείας κριτής.

[2] Another mis-translation, as if the Greek were πάντων τῶν προειρημένων κακῶν. Compare Gen. xlviii. 16: ὁ ἄγγελος ὁ ῥυόμενός με ἐκ πάντων τῶν κακῶν (A. V. 'from all evil').

of even these;—a much more moderate proposition.' Moderate enough, but (as we have before hinted) *not rhetorical.* If St Paul had been elsewhere declaiming against intemperance, as here against covetousness, he might have said, ῥίζα γὰρ πάντων τῶν κακῶν ἡ φιλοινία, without being chargeable with inconsistency. From an animated and vehement speaker or writer we naturally look for strong and highly coloured denunciations of that particular folly or vice which comes under his lash, leaving out of sight for the time others which may equally deserve castigation.

With respect to the absence of the article, we take the following examples from Wetstein (who collected them for another purpose), in all of which the English idiom requires its insertion. Athenaeus VII. p. 280 A : ἀρχὴ καὶ ῥίζα παντὸς ἀγαθοῦ ἡ τῆς γαστρὸς ἡδονή. Diog. Laert. VI. 50: τὴν φιλαργυρίαν εἶπε (Diogenes Cynicus) μητρόπολιν πάντων τῶν κακῶν. From our own observation we add: Stob. *Flor.* T. X. 38: Βίων ὁ σοφιστὴς τὴν φιλαργυρίαν μητρόπολιν ἔλεγε πάσης κακίας εἶναι. Philostr. *Her.* p. 24, ed. Boissonade : μὴ τιμῶν ἀλήθειαν, ἣν ἐκεῖνος μητέρα ἀρετῆς ὀνομάζειν εἴωθεν. Synes. *Ep.* 115 : τὴν ἔνδειαν ἔφη ὑγείας εἶναι μητέρα. Aeschin. *Ep.* 5 : ἀρχὴ δοκεῖ μοι τοῦ βίου ἡ ἀπαλλαγὴ τῆς αὐτόθι πολιτείας. Diod. Sic. T. IX. p. 350, ed. Bip.: ἡ γὰρ ἀδικία, μητρόπολις οὖσα τῶν κακῶν ... τὰς μεγίστας ἀπεργάζεται συμφοράς[1].

VI. 17 : **τῷ παρέχοντι ἡμῖν πλουσίως πάντα**] A more elegant Greek phrase would have been, τῷ δαψιλῶς ἡμῖν ἅπαντα χορηγοῦντι (Diod. Sic. XIX. 3). The addition εἰς ἀπόλαυσιν may mean *ad fruendum, non ad accumulandum,* though as we cannot accept Dean Alford's understanding of ἀπόλαυσις, 'the reaping enjoyment from, *and so having done with,*' for which he claims the analogy of ἀπέχω, and other verbs in which ἀπό exerts this force, which does not hold when the simple verb, as in ἀπολαύειν, is not in use. But, more probably, εἰς ἀπόλαυσιν is an *epexegesis* of πλουσίως, intended to emphasize the prodigality of the Giver of all good, as in the following passages : Lucian. *Cyn.* 5 : ὥστ' ἔχειν ἡμᾶς πάντα ἄφθονα, μὴ πρὸς τὴν χρείαν μόνον, ἀλλὰ καὶ πρὸς ἡδονήν. Diod. Sic. XI. 25 : ἰχθυο-τροφεῖον ἐγένετο, πολλοὺς παρεχόμενον ἰχθῦς εἰς τρυφὴν καὶ ἀπόλαυσιν. V. 40 (quoted by Wetstein): καρπῶν ἀφθονίαν ἔχουσιν, οὐ μόνον πρὸς τὴν ἀρκοῦσαν διατροφήν, ἀλλὰ καὶ πρὸς ἀπόλαυσιν δαψιλῆ καὶ τρυφὴν ἀνήκουσαν.

VI. 18 : **εὐμεταδότους...κοινωνικούς**] 'Ready to distribute, willing to communicate.' For 'distribute' (which is rather διαδιδόναι, Luke xviii. 22, Acts iv. 35) a better word would be 'impart,' as A. V. Luke iii. 11, Rom. i. 11, 1 Thess. ii. 8. Compare Schol. Platon. Ruhnk. p. 68 : κοινὰ τὰ τῶν φίλων· ἐπὶ τῶν εὐμεταδότων. S. Basil. T. II.‿ p. 620 C : ἠδύνατο γάρ μοι εἰπεῖν ὁ φειδωλός...ὅτι μιμοῦμαι τὸν μύρμηκα· ἀμετάδοτον γὰρ τὸ ζῷον· ἑαυτῷ μὲν συνάγει, ἑτέρῳ δὲ οὐ θησαυρίζει. As 'imparting' and 'communicating'

---

[1] [Cf. Phot. Cod. CLXVI. p. 189 : καὶ γὰρ τοῦ περὶ ἀληθῶν διηγημάτων Λου- κιανοῦ, καὶ τοῦ περὶ μεταμορφώσεων Λου-κίου, πηγὴ καὶ ῥίζα ἔοικεν εἶναι τοῦτο.]

are virtually the same thing, to avoid tautology, another sense of κοινωνικούς has been thought to be here intended, as St Chrysostom explains ὁμιλητικούς, προσηνεῖς ; Theodoret ἄτυφον ἦθος ἔχοντας ; A. V. 'Or, *sociable*' ; R. V. 'Or, *ready to sympathize*' ; all of them fairly within the scope of the term. But Gal. vi. 6 and Heb. xiii. 16 are in favour of the common interpretation, in support of which Wetstein also adduces Lucian. *Tim.* 56: πρὸς ἄνδρα οἷον σέ, ἁπλοϊκὸν καὶ τῶν ὄντων κοινωνικόν. Id. *Pisc.* 35: ὅταν μὲν οὖν αὐτούς τι δέῃ λαμβάνειν, πολὺς ὁ περὶ τοῦ κοινωνικὸν εἶναι δεῖν λόγος, καὶ ὡς ἀδιάφορον ὁ πλοῦτος. I add Alciphr. *Ep.* III. 19: κοινωνικὸς ὢν καὶ φιλέταιρος ὄναιο σαυτοῦ. Diotogenes Pythagoricus ap. Stob. *Flor.* T. XLVIII. 62 : A true king should be σώφρων μὲν περὶ τὰς ἁδονάς, κοινωνατικὸς δὲ περὶ τὰ χρήματα, φρόνιμος δὲ καὶ δεινὸς περὶ τὰν ἀρχάν.

II. TIMOTHY.

Chap. II. 2 : καὶ ἃ ἤκουσας παρ' ἐμοῦ διὰ πολλῶν μαρτύρων] A. V. 'Among (Or, *by*) many witnesses.' The sense of 'among' seems to be confined (or nearly so) to the phrase διὰ πάντων, as Homer, ὁ δ' ἔπρεπε καὶ διὰ πάντων, or Herodotus, θέης ἄξιον καὶ διὰ πάντων τῶν ἀναθημάτων. The best Greek writers prefer ἐπὶ μαρτύρων[1] to signify that anything was done *adhibitis testibus*, in the presence of witnesses; but διὰ μαρτύρων is also used in the same way, as was long since observed by H. Stephens, s. v. μάρτυρ; and the single example which he adduces might, perhaps, lead us to suppose that it was a *legal* term. It is to be found in Plut. T. II. p. 338 F, where Darius is made to say : ' I pray that I may be fortunate, and victorious in war ; but if I am ruined, ὦ Ζεῦ πατρῷε Περσῶν καὶ βασίλειοι θεοί, may no other than Alexander sit on the throne of Cyrus !' 'This,' adds the Author, 'was an act of adoption (εἰσποίησις) of Alexander in the presence of the gods as witnesses (διὰ θεῶν μαρτύρων).' And so the phrase was understood by St Chrysostom: Τί ἐστι, διὰ πολλῶν μαρτύρων; ὡς αν εἰ ἔλεγεν· οὐ λάθρα ἤκουσας, οὐδὲ κρυφῇ, ἀλλὰ πολλῶν παρόντων, μετὰ παρρησίας.

II. 20 : εἰς τιμὴν...εἰς ἀτιμίαν] To the former class belonged the *table*, to the latter the *footstool*, according to Diod. Sic. XVII. 66 : ἤλγηκα ἰδὼν τὸ παρ' ἐκείνῳ μάλιστα τιμώμενον (τὴν τράπεζαν) νῦν ἄτιμον γεγονὸς σκεῦος (ὑπόβαθρον); also the ποδανιπτήρ, which was used ἐνεμεῖν τε καὶ ἐνουρέειν καὶ πόδας ἀπονίζεσθαι (Herod. II. 172[2]). In the next verse εὔχρηστον τῷ δεσπότῃ might be translated, 'meet for the *owner's* use,' as Lucian. *Demon.* 17 : γραμμάτιον ἐν ἀγορᾷ προτιθείς, ἠξίου τὸν ἀπολέσαντα, ὅστις εἴη τοῦ δακτυλίου δεσπότης, ἥκειν καὶ ... ἀπολαμβάνειν. Synes. *Ep.* 42 : ἐπανίτω τοίνυν Ἀσφάλιος εἰς τὸ δεσπότης εἶναι τῶν κεραμίων (potteries) τῇ τοῦ πατρὸς διαθήκῃ[3].

II. 25 : τοὺς ἀντιδιατιθεμένους] All English versions : 'those that oppose themselves.' Vulg. *eos qui resistunt veritati*. Dean Alford quotes from Ambrosiaster, 'eos qui diversa sentiant,' but puts it aside with the remark : ' To take the general meaning of διατίθεσθαι satisfies the context better

---

[1] [Ἐπὶ μάρτυσι is found App. *B. C.* III. 14: ἔθος γάρ τι Ῥωμαίοις τοὺς θετοὺς ἐπὶ μάρτυσι γίγνεσθαι τοῖς στρατηγοῖς.]

[2] [Compare the saying of Themistocles Ael. *V. H.* XIII. 40 (of the Athenians who first disgraced him and then recalled him to power): Οὐκ ἐπαινῶ

τοὺς τοιούτους ἄνδρας, οἵτινες τὴν αὐτὴν ἀμίδα καὶ οἰνοχόην ἔχουσι. See Synes. *Ep.* 57, p. 192 B: οὕτω δὲ σκεῦος τὸ μὲν ἄτιμον τὸ δὲ τίμιόν ἐστί τε καὶ νομίζεται.]

[3] [Cf. Lucian. *Scyth.* 1: οἱ ὀκτάποδες καλούμενοι· τοῦτο δέ ἐστι, δύο βοῶν δεσπότην εἶναι, καὶ ἀμάξης μιᾶς.]

than to supply τὸν νοῦν.' He evidently takes διατίθεσθαι to be the *middle* form, of which the 'general meaning' is *disponere* (aliquid), never that I am aware of *disponere se*, which is what is required to make ἀντιδιατίθεσθαι bear the sense of *opponere se*. Nor, if we accept the version of Ambrosiaster, is it necessary to supply τὸν νοῦν, since διατίθεσθαι may well be *passive*, as it certainly is in such phrases as δυσκόλως or χαλεπῶς διατίθεσθαι πρός τινα, differing in no respect from διακεῖσθαι. Here, instead of a qualifying adverb, we have the compound form ἀντιδιατίθεσθαι, which may therefore be considered as equivalent to ἐναντίως διατίθεσθαι, 'to be *contrariwise* or *adversely affected*,' which brings us back to the rejected version, 'eos qui diversa sentiunt.'

The only other example of the compound verb is to be found in Longinus περὶ ὕψους XVII. 1. The Author is speaking of the too free use of figures (σχήματα) in pleading before an arbitrary judge, who might be apt, in such a case, to think the orator was treating him like a child, and trying to take advantage of his simplicity; and so he either turns quite savage (ἀποθηριοῦται τὸ σύνολον), or if he should suppress his wrath, *he is sure to be adversely affected towards the persuasive force of the pleadings* (πρὸς τὴν πειθὼ τῶν λόγων πάντως ἀντιδιατίθεται).

II. 26: ἐζωγρημένοι ὑπ' αὐτοῦ εἰς τὸ ἐκείνου θέλημα] Literally, 'having been caught by him unto his will.' If the second pronoun had been αὐτοῦ as well as the first, there would have been no difficulty in referring both to ὁ διάβολος. But the change of pronouns would lead us to look out for another and more remote person for ἐκείνου, and this could be none other than ὁ θεὸς in *v.* 25. But if *God's* will were the object in view, the agent could no longer be the devil, and we should have to go back to δοῦλος κυρίου in *v.* 24 for the antecedent of αὐτοῦ; in which case the words before us could only be made intelligible by the insertion of explanatory notes in the text, as R. V. 'having been caught by him (the Lord's servant) unto his (God's) will[1].' To avoid this, the question has been raised whether the two pronouns must *necessarily* be assigned to different persons. It is allowed that if their places had been reversed, ὑπ' ἐκείνου εἰς τὸ αὐτοῦ (= ἑαυτοῦ) θέλημα, there would have been nothing abnormal in the phrase; the devil, having been just mentioned by name, might properly be referred to as 'that person' (compare Tit. iii. 7, 2, Pet. i. 16). Here, however, it is, 'having been caught by him unto that person's will'; which, though certainly a clumsy mode of putting it, is one which might slip from the pen of the most practised writer in the fervour of composition. Examples, coming more or less near to that of the text, are not wanting; but the following from Xenoph. *Cyrop.* IV. 5, 20 seems to have escaped observation: ἐπειδὰν δὲ αἴσθηται (Cyaxares) πολλοὺς μὲν τῶν πολεμίων ἀπο-

---

[1] [R. V. 'by the Lord's servant unto the will of God.' In Heb. iii. 2, 5: ἐν ὅλῳ τῷ οἴκῳ αὐτοῦ is translated 'in all his house,' with a marginal note 'That is, God's house.']

λωλότας, πάντας δὲ ἀπεληλαμένους ... γνώσεται ὅτι οὐ νῦν ἔρημος γίνεται, ἡνίκα
οἱ φίλοι ΑΥΤΟΥ τοὺς ΕΚΕΙΝΟΥ ἐχθροὺς ἀπολλύουσιν[1].

*III. 6: σεσωρευμένα ἁμαρτίαις] 'Laden with sins.' Dean Alford
(after De Wette) says: 'They are burdened, their consciences oppressed,
with sins, and in this morbid state they lie open to the insidious attacks
of these proselytizers' &c.   But σεσωρευμένα is rather 'overwhelmed' than
'burdened' (βεβαρημένα) and so it was understood by the Syriac translators, who render it by ܪܰܡܝܳܢ, which is the equivalent of such Greek
words as κατακεχωσμένα, κατορωρυγμένα, &c.   St Chrysostom says of this
word: τὸ πλῆθος τῶν ἁμαρτιῶν παρίστησι, καὶ τὸ ἄτακτον, καὶ τὸ συγκεχυμένον.

IV. 13: τὸν φελόνην] 'the cloke.'   On the φελόνης (φαινόλης, paenula)
see Wetstein.   His best examples are Artemid. Onirocr. II. 3: χλαμὺς ...
θλῖψιν καὶ στενοχωρίαν ... μαντεύεται, διὰ τὸ ἐμπεριέχειν τὸ σῶμα· τὸ δὲ αὐτὸ
καὶ ὁ λεγόμενος φαινόλης.   Ael. Lamprid. Alexandro Severo: Paenulis
intra urbem frigoris causa ut senes uterentur permisit; cum id vestimenti
genus semper itinerarium aut pluviae fuisset.   For the benefit of those
who hold with the late Dr Neale, that the cloke which St Paul left behind
him at Troas, and which he desires Timothy to bring with him, was a
liturgical vestment or chasuble, I will point out a curious coincidence
from profane history, in a story told of Hercules by Diod. Sic. IV. 38:
Ἐνταῦθα δὲ θυσίαν ἐπιτελῶν, ἀπέστειλε τὸν ὑπηρέτην εἰς Τραχῖνα πρὸς τὴν
γυναῖκα Δηϊάνειραν· τούτῳ δὲ προστεταγμένον ἦν, αἰτῆσαι χιτῶνα καὶ ἱμάτιον,
οἷς εἰώθει χρῆσθαι πρὸς τὰς θυσίας.

As the subject of VESTMENTS possesses a certain interest at the
present time[2], it may be worth while to notice one or two passages from
patristical writers, which have been thought (quite groundlessly) to favour
the idea that St Paul's cloke was a chasuble.

The first, in order of time, is that of Tertullian, Lib. de Oratione, c. 12:
'We will here notice certain other observances, which may be justly
charged with vanity, as being practised without any authority of Christ or
his Apostles.   For instance; it is the practice of some persons to lay
aside their clokes before they pray (positis penulis orationem facere), a
rite borrowed from heathen worship; which if it were proper to be done,
the Apostles who have given directions about the dress to be used in
prayer (de habitu orationis) would not have omitted: unless any one
should claim St Paul's own example in favour of the custom, supposing

---

[1] [This passage from Xenoph. is
quoted by Stallbaum in his note on Plat.
Phaedo 106 B. Cf. Dem. p. 633, 12:
τὸν γὰρ φυγάδα τὸ τῆς πόλεως οὐ προσεῖπεν
ὄνομα, ἧς οὐκ ἔστι μετουσία αὐτῷ (τῷ φ.),
ἀλλὰ τὸ τοῦ πράγματος (τὸν ἀνδροφόνον)
ᾧ κατέστησεν αὐτὸν ἐκεῖνος ἔνοχον.
Lucian. Zeux. 8: ταῦτα ὁρῶν (Antiochus)
πάνυ πονηρὰς εἶχε τὰς ἐλπίδας, ὡς ἀμάχων

ὄντων ἐκείνων (Galli) αὐτῷ. ἐκεῖνος γάρ
(Antiochus) κ.τ.ἑ. The Bishop of Here-
ford, in a letter, quotes Plat. Protag.
310 D: ἂν αὐτῷ (Protagorae) διδῷς ἀργύριον καὶ πείθῃς ἐκεῖνον...where Stallb.
refers to his note on Phaed. 106 B.]

[2] The Otium Norv. Pars Tertia
was published in 1881. Ed.

that he left his cloke with Carpus, while he was at prayer.' The sentence
in italics (which is evidently a sort of banter) in the original is only, 'nisi
si qui putant Paulum penulam suam in oratione penes Carpum reliquisse';
but the writer's meaning is undoubtedly what I have expressed.   Thus
understood, the passage, instead of favouring, is so plainly opposed to the
'chasuble theory,' as to elicit from one of its advocates[1] the following
remark: 'The passage is rhetorical, and the *lacuna* (sic) seems to require
filling up in this way—"an opinion too absurd to be maintained by reason
of the φαινόλης not being a cloke."'   This is 'filling up' with a vengeance!

The next authority is that of St Chrysostom, who, however, is not
claimed as a witness in favour of the 'chasuble theory,' but only as
neutral, and not to be cited on the other side; first, because he is
undecided whether the φελόνης was a cloke, or a case wherein books were
kept; and, secondly, because the use of a general term (ἱμάτιον) does not
exclude the particular kind of vestment called a chasuble.   In reply we
would remark, that although St Chrysostom was bound to mention the
'portfolio theory,' as being held by some (his words are: ἱμάτιον ἐνταῦθα
λέγει· τινὲς δέ φασι τὸ γλωσσόκομον, ἔνθα τὰ βιβλία ἔκειτο) his own opinion
was, evidently, the one first stated, as he goes on to remark: 'But he
sends for the φελόνης, that he may not have to procure it from others,
according to his own saying, "Ye know that these hands have ministered
to my necessities"; and again, "It is more blessed to give than to
receive."'   But there is another passage of St Chrysostom, which has
never been quoted in connexion with this controversy, but which is quite
conclusive, as far as his opinion goes.   It is in his first homily on the
Philippians, where he is replying to the objection of some mean persons,
who excused themselves from providing a suitable maintenance for their
spiritual pastors on the ground of such texts as Matt. x. 9, 10: 'Provide
neither gold, nor silver, nor brass in your girdles, nor scrip for your
journey, *neither two coats*, neither shoes,' &c.   'What?' he says, 'had
not Peter a girdle, and a cloke, and shoes (Acts xii. 8)?   And Paul too,
when he writes to Timothy, "Do thy diligence to come before winter";
and then gives him instructions, "The cloke which I left at Troas" &c.
There now! he says, *the cloke;* and no one would pretend to say that he
had not a second, namely, the one he was wearing.   For if he was not in
the habit of wearing one, it would be superfluous for him to bid Timothy
bring this one; but if he did wear one, and could not help wearing one,
it is clear that he had another besides.'

After this, I think there can be no doubt what this early Greek father
understood by St Paul's φελόνης, namely, not a portfolio (though that
explanation has some support from antiquity, especially from both Syriac
versions) but a cloke, perhaps of some particular make or material which
procured it a peculiar name, but still a garment for ordinary wear, or as
an additional protection against the winter.

[1] Rev. J. R. Lunn, in the *Report of*   *Exhibition, held at York in October,*
the Proceedings of the Ecclesiastical Art   1866.

TITUS.

*Chap. I. 5: ἵνα τὰ λείποντα ἐπιδιορθώσῃ] 'That thou shouldest set in order' &c. Dean Alford, in his *New Testament*, gives the more correct rendering, 'That thou shouldest further set in order' &c. So St Chrysostom, who urges it as a proof of the Apostle's freedom from jealousy, that he leaves to Timothy the appointment of elders, καὶ τὰ ἄλλα πάντα ὅσα ἐδεῖτό τινος ἐπιδιορθώσεως, ὡς ἂν εἴποι τις, πλείονος καταρτισμοῦ. Then he goes on: τί λέγεις, εἰπέ μοι; τὰ σὰ προσδιορθοῦται;

I. 7: μὴ αὐθάδη] 'not self-willed.' 2 Pet. ii. 10: τολμηταί, αὐθάδεις, 'presumptuous *are they*, self-willed.' A *self-willed* person is one who follows his own will or opinion, and does not yield to the wishes or opinions of others. Perhaps he is best represented by the Greek ἰδιογνώμων and δυστράπελος. Αὐθάδης, though nearly related to these, is, properly, *sibi placens*, that is, not one who *pleases himself*, but who *is pleased with himself*, and holds other people cheap, in one word, *self-satisfied*. This is the strict meaning of the word, but it is commonly used in a wider sense, best expressed by the English 'arrogant,' which is also etymologically appropriate (*arrogans, qui sibi aliquid arrogat*). Aristotle (*Eth. Magn.* I. 29) says that σεμνότης ἐστὶν αὐθαδείας ἀναμέσον τε καὶ ἀρεσκείας, which H. Stephens correctly renders, *Gravitas est medium inter arrogantiam et placendi studium*. It should also be observed that *self-will* or *wilfulness* usually displays itself in the disposition and actions; while αὐθάδεια is chiefly concerned with a man's manners and outward behaviour[1].

The Philoxenian version of the N. T., and the Syro-hexaplarian of the O. T., render αὐθάδης by ܠܘܝܨܐ, which they also use for θρασύς, προπετής, and ἰταμός. Compare Archbishop Trench's *Synonyms of the N. T.*, p. 350, ed. 9.

---

[1] [Cf. Plut. *Vit. Cor.* XV: οὐδὲ τὴν ἐρημίᾳ ξύνοικον, ὡς Πλάτων ἔλεγεν, αὐθάδειαν εἰδὼς ὅτι δεῖ μάλιστα διαφεύγειν ἐγχειροῦντα πραγμασι κοινοῖς καὶ ἀνθρώ- ποις ὁμιλεῖν. See also *Id. Dion* VIII. and *Comp. Alcib. c. Cor.* IV: ὧν αἴτιον ἁπάντων τὸ ἀνομίλητον τοῦ τρόπου καὶ λίαν ὑπερήφανον καὶ αὐθαδες.]

*II. 3: ἐν καταστήματι] A.V. 'in behaviour.' Alf. 'in deportment.' R.V. 'in demeanour.' Either of these two is to be preferred to the A. V. Κατάστημα expresses a man's outward bearing, including *gait, posture, expression of countenance, dress*, &c. The following descriptions have been previously quoted: Porphyr. *De Abstin.* IV. 6: τὸ σεμνὸν κἀκ τοῦ καταστήματος ἑωρᾶτο. πορεία τε γὰρ ἦν εὔτακτος, καὶ βλέμμα καθεστηκὸς ἐπετηδεύετο ... γέλως δὲ σπάνιος, εἰ δέ που γένοιτο, μέχρι μειδιάσεως· ἀεὶ δὲ ἐντὸς τοῦ σχήματος χεῖρες. Joseph. *Ant.* XV. 7, 5: αὕτη (Mariamne) γε μὴν ἀτρεμαίῳ τῷ καταστήματι καὶ τῇ χρόᾳ τῆς σαρκὸς ἀμεταβλήτῳ πρὸς τὸν θάνατον ἀπῄει. I add Ignat. *ad Trall.* 3: ἐν τῷ ἐπισκόπῳ ὑμῶν, οὗ αὐτὸ τὸ κατάστημα μεγάλη μαθητεία. It should, however, be observed that both κατάστημα and κατάστασις, even without an epithet, involve the idea of *calmness* and *composure.* Thus, from the former we get the adjective καταστηματικὸς, which is used by Plutarch in contrasting the characters of the two Gracchi (*Vit. T. Gracc.* II): πρῶτον μὲν οὖν ἰδέᾳ προσώπου καὶ βλέμματι καὶ κινήματι πρᾷος καὶ καταστηματικὸς ἦν ὁ Τιβέριος, ἔντονος δὲ καὶ σφοδρὸς ὁ Γάιος. For κατάστασις I would instance in St Chrysostom (T. X. p. 259 D), in describing the difference between the prophet and the μάντις: ὁ δὲ προφήτης οὐχ οὕτως, ἀλλὰ μετὰ διανοίας νηφούσης, καὶ σωφροσύνης, καὶ καταστάσεως, καὶ εἰδὼς ὃ φθέγγεται, ἅπαντά φησιν: where for κατάστασις the Syriac version has ܠܩܘܡܣܐ, the very word which the Philox. puts for κατάστημα in this place, and the Syriac translator of Lagarde's *Rel. Juris Eccles.* for εὐταξία (p. ܣܟܡ, 16).

II. 5: οἰκουρούς] 'Keepers at home.' This is the old reading, which has lately been ousted on the authority of ACF and (before correction) אD, which read οἰκουργούς, i.e. according to R. V. 'workers at home.' The only authority for this word is Soranus of Ephesus, a medical writer (not earlier than the 2nd century) from whose work Περὶ γυναικείων παθῶν (published at Berlin 1838) Boissonade quotes οἰκουργὸν καὶ καθέδριον (sedentary) διάγειν βίον, where οἰκουρόν would suit at least equally well. The *verb* is quoted from Clem. Rom. Ep. ad Cor. I. 1: ἔν τε τῷ κανόνι τῆς ὑποταγῆς ὑπαρχούσας, τὰ κατὰ τὸν οἶκον σεμνῶς οἰκουργεῖν ἐδιδάσκετε πάνυ σωφρονούσας[1]. The ancient versions have, Vulg. *domus curam habentes*; Pesch. ܒܢ̈ܝ ܒܝܬܗܝܢ; Philox. ܝܨ̈ܦܢ ܕܒ̈ܬܐ; all for οἰκουρούς. But the strongest argument for the old reading is, that it is improbable, not to say incredible, that in his exhaustive description of the female character, the Apostle should have omitted this particular feature. 'Graecae mulieris' (to quote Valcken. ad Herod. IV. 114) 'prima virtus habebatur τὸ ἔνδον μένειν καὶ οἰκουρεῖν.' Such was Sarah, צנועה (*abscondita, domi sedens*) according to Raschi on Gen. xviii. 9; Dinah,

---

[1] [Cf. Dio. Chrys. *Or.* III. p. 48, 34: ἀλλ' ἐκείναις μὲν τὰ πολλὰ τῶν ἔργων κατ' οἰκίαν ἐστί. Lucian. *Herc.*   1: διακεκαυμένος εἰς τὸ μελάντατον, οἷοί εἰσιν οἱ θαλαττουργοὶ γέροντες.]

on the contrary, is described as יצאנית (*exiens extra aedes*, φιλέξοδος[1]) in allusion to Gen. xxxiv. 1. And there is scarcely a single passage of ancient writers, from Solomon downwards, in praise of a virtuous wife, in which this feature is not specially set forth. From Wetstein's ample store and other sources we select the following. Dio. Cass. LVI. p. 391: γυνὴ σώφρων, οἰκουρός, οἰκονόμος, παιδοτρόφος. Philo Jud. *de Maled.* T. II. p. 431: γυναῖκας ἃς ἠγάγοντο κουριδίας ἐπὶ γνησίων παιδῶν σποράν, σώφρονας, οἰκουρούς, καὶ φιλάνδρους. Plut. *Conjug. Praec.* 32 (T. II. p. 142 D): τὴν Ἠλείων ὁ Φειδίας Ἀφροδίτην ἐποίησεν χελώνην πατοῦσαν, οἰκουρίας σύμβολον ταῖς γυναιξὶ καὶ σιωπῆς. Alciphr. *Ep.* III. 58: ἔλεγεν γὰρ γαμεταῖς ἐπικλήροις οἰκουρίας πρέπειν καὶ τὸν σεμνὸν βίον, τὰς ἑταίρας δὲ δεῖ εἶναι πάντων ἀναφανδόν. [Compare Prov. vii. 11: ἐν οἴκῳ οὐχ ἡσυχάζουσιν οἱ πόδες αὐτῆς (*meretricis*).] *Ibid.* 25: ἐγὼ δὲ οἰκουρῶ μόνη μετὰ τῆς Σύρας ἀγαπητῶς, τὰ παιδία βαυκαλῶσα (singing to sleep). Stob. *Flor.* T. LXXIV. 61: ἴδια μὲν ἀνδρός, τὸ στραταγέν, καὶ πολιτεύεσθαι, καὶ δαμαγορέν· ἴδια δὲ γυναικός, τὸ οἰκουρέν, καὶ ἔνδον μένεν, καὶ ἐκδέχεσθαι καὶ θεραπεύεν τὸν ἄνδρα. Artemid. *Onirocr.* II. 32: λήψεται γυναῖκα εὔμορφον, ἠρέμα πλουσίαν, πιστικὴν καὶ οἰκουρὸν καὶ πειθομένην τῷ ἀνδρί. Orell. *Inscrip. Lat.* 4639: 'Hic sita est Amymone Marci, optima et pulcherrima, lanifica, pia, pudica, frugi, casta, *domiseda. Ibid.* 4848: Nomen parentes nominarunt Claudiam, | suum maritum corde dilexit suo | ... | domum servavit, lanam fecit. Dixi; abi[2].'

Two distinct meanings have been correctly assigned to οἰκουρός and its derivatives: first, *domi se continens*[3], and secondly, *rem familiarem curans*. As might have been expected, and as may be seen in some of the above examples, they are apt to run into each other. The Vulgate and Syriac versions have taken the word in the second sense, which is etymologically the more correct of the two, as Hesychius: Οἰκουρός, ὁ φροντίζων τὰ τοῦ οἴκου καὶ φυλάττων· οὖρος γὰρ ὁ φύλαξ λέγεται. But, without an epithet, it seems more natural to understand οἰκουρός as significant of a *moral* quality, which, in the mistress of a family, 'keeping at home' undoubtedly is. If, however, with Theophylact and the elder Syriac, we point οἰκουροὺς ἀγαθάς, 'good housekeepers,' we may then include *both* senses of οἰκουρός, our English word 'housekeeper'

---

[1] Epicharm. ap. Stob. *Flor.* T. LXIX. 17: εἰ δὲ καὶ φιλέξοδόν τε καὶ λάλον καὶ δαψιλῆ, | οὐ γυναῖχ᾽ ἕξεις, διὰ βίου δ᾽ ἀτυχίαν κοσμουμέναν. [Plut. II. 242 E: καθάπερ τὸ σῶμα καὶ τοὔνομα τῆς ἀγαθῆς γυναικὸς οἰόμενος δεῖν κατάκλειστον εἶναι καὶ ΑΝΕΞΟΔΟΝ. Ps. lxviii. 13: וּנְוַת בַּיִת 'she that tarried at home divided the spoil.' *Mater familias.*]

[2] A shorter and better-known epitaph on a good wife is 'Domum mansit; lanam fecit,' the source of which I have

not been able to find. That these two ideas were generally associated appears from Plutarch's (*Vit. Anton.* X.) description of the character of Fulvia, the wife of Antony, 'who had a soul above wool-spinning and housekeeping' (οὐ ταλασίαν οὐδὲ οἰκουρίαν φρονοῦν γύναιον).

[3] [Said of men. Plut. *Vit. Caes.* XIV: τί οὖν...οὐ καὶ σὺ ταῦτα δεδιὼς οἰκουρεῖς; (instead of going to the senate).]

having precisely the same twofold acceptation. At all events, we trust we have successfully vindicated the old and cherished reading against the proposed unnecessary and most tasteless innovation. We shall be told that it is hardly possible that for so well-known a word as οἰκουρός the copyists should have substituted one, of which the existence is extremely doubtful. But to this it may be replied: if οἰκουρός was familiar to the copyists, *a fortiori* it must have been familiar to the Apostle; and, in writing on such a subject, must have been (so to speak) *at his fingers' ends;* how came he then to give the preference to a barbarous, scarcely intelligible ἅπαξ λεγόμενον, if not *vox nulla*, like οἰκουργός?

III. 4: ὅτε δὲ ἡ χρηστότης καὶ ἡ φιλανθρωπία ἐπεφάνη τοῦ σωτῆρος ἡμῶν θεοῦ] In a note on Acts xxviii. 2 we have said that *philanthropy*, as felt and exercised by a human being towards mankind in general, is a novel use of the word; but this does not apply to beings of a superior nature. Indeed Thomas Magister (p. 896) places in the very front of his definition of φιλανθρωπία, οὐ μόνον ἡ ἀπὸ τῶν ὑπερεχόντων εἰς τοὺς ἐλάττους εὐμένεια, ὡς ἡ τοῦ θεοῦ φιλανθρωπία περὶ ἡμᾶς...ἀλλ' ἥ τινος ἁπλῶς πρὸς ὀντινοῦν φιλία. In this special sense the word is used by Plutarch (*Vit. Num.* IV): καί που λόγον ἔχει, τὸν θεὸν οὐ φίλιππον, οὐδὲ φίλορνιν, ἀλλὰ φιλάνθρωπον ὄντα, τοῖς διαφερόντως ἀγαθοῖς ἐθέλειν συνεῖναι[1]. And when it is said of Prometheus, a heroic if not a divine personage, that he was καθ' ὑπερβολὴν φιλάνθρωπος (Lucian. *de Sacrif.* 6), no doubt it is the whole race of mankind that he embraced in his beneficent views. To this class is usually supposed to belong St Paul's use of the word in Tit. iii. 4. The A. V. 'But after that the kindness and love (Or, *pity*) of God our Saviour toward man appeared,' is faulty because it seems to connect 'kindness' with 'toward man,' as well as 'love,' which the Greek does not. This may be avoided by rendering 'the kindness and love-toward-man of God our Saviour,' or (as R. V.) 'the kindness of God our Saviour, and his love toward man.' But in fact, the combination of χρηστότης καὶ φιλανθρωπία, 'kindness and humanity,' is so familiar to all readers of Greek, that it seems unlikely that the Apostle should have used this formula in any other way than that which has obtained the stamp of literary currency. The following examples, partly original, and partly from Wetstein's collection, may suffice. Stob. *Flor.* XLVI. 76: ἀλλ' ὅταν χρηστότητι καὶ φιλανθρωπίᾳ κραθῇ τὸ σεμνὸν καὶ αὐστηρὸν τῆς ἐπικρατείας[2]. Liban. *Progymn.* p. 52 B: χρηστότητα ἄσκει, φιλανθρωπίαν μελέτα. Lucian. *Tim.* 8: χρηστότης ἐπέτριψεν αὐτόν, καὶ φιλανθρωπία, καὶ ὁ πρὸς δεομένους ἅπαντας οἶκτος. Id. *Scyth.* 10:

---

[1] [Cf. Lucian. *Bis Acc.* 1: πάντα γὰρ ταῦτα ὑπὸ φιλανθρωπίας οἱ θεοὶ πονοῦσι. Philo de Abr. § 36 (Mangey, p. 29): τῷ δὴ τὴν ἀληθῆ ταύτην ὁμολογίαν ὡμολογηκότι τρόπῳ, χρηστὸς ὢν καὶ φιλάνθρωπος ὁ θεός...προσηκόντως ἀντιχαρίζεται τὸ δῶρον.]

[2] [Cf. Plut. *Vit. Demetr.* L: μετὰ τῶν ἄλλων καλῶν αὐτῷ φιλανθρωπίας καὶ χρηστότητος ἐπίδειξιν διδούσῃ.]

τὴν μὲν γὰρ χρηστότητα, καὶ τὴν πρὸς τοὺς ξένους φιλανθρωπίαν. Diod. Sic. T. X. p. 122, ed. Bip.: καὶ γὰρ ἐκεῖνοι, χρηστότητι καὶ φιλανθρωπίᾳ χρώμενοι, ταῖς βασιλείαις ἐνευδαιμόνησαν. Joseph. Ant. X. 9, 3: κατανοήσαντες δὲ...τὴν τοῦ Γοδολίου χρηστότητα καὶ φιλανθρωπίαν. Aristid. p. 335 C: ἧς φιλανθρωπίας καὶ χρηστότητος ἔτι πολλὰ καὶ καθ᾽ ἡμᾶς ἡ πόλις ἐκφέρουσα δείγματα θαυμάζεται. So with the adjectives, as Stob. Flor. T. XLVIII. 67: ἔτι δὲ εὐεργετικός, φιλάνθρωπος, χρηστός. Plut. Vit. Luc. XVIII: ταῦτα μὲν οὖν φύσει χρηστὸν ὄντα καὶ φ. ἡνία τὸν Λούκουλλον. Lucian. Ep. Sat. 33: πρὸς γὰρ τῷ χρηστοὺς καὶ φ. ἀκούειν. Charit. Aphrod. II. 2: Διονύσιος γὰρ ὁ δεσπότης ἡμῶν χρηστός ἐστι καὶ φ. Herodian. IV. 3, 6: χρηστός τε ὢν καὶ φ. τοῖς συνοῦσι. Onosander 38: ταῖς δὲ προσχωρούσαις·πόλεσι...φιλανθρώπως καὶ χρηστῶς προσφερέσθω. Sed manum de tabula.

III. 8, 14: **καλῶν ἔργων προΐστασθαι**] A. V. 'To maintain good works.' And on v. 14: 'Or, *profess honest trades.*' The marginal version has been advocated by Grotius (on v. 14 only) and Clericus; and recently by A. H. Wratislaw in the *Journal of Philology*, Vol. III. p. 258 sq. We will first enquire how the verb προΐστασθαι comes to be used in the sense of *professing or practising* a particular calling or business.

Comparing the Latin *prostare*, it appears probable that this use of the word arose from the practice of the workman or tradesman *standing before* his shop for the purpose of soliciting customers. We have an example of this primary use in a passage of St Chrysostom (T. IX. p. 443 C), who says of St Paul: καὶ οὐδὲ ἐν τῷ κηρύττειν τῆς τέχνης ἀπέστη, ἀλλὰ καὶ τότε δέρματα ἔρραπτε, καὶ ἐργαστηρίου προεϊστήκει. Of course it is a rhetorical flourish to say that Paul *stood before the workshop;* but less so than if we were to understand the phrase (as St Chrysostom's translators have done) of his being the manager or foreman of a tent-manufactory. However, there is *one* kind of occupation (τῶν ἐπὶ μισθῷ πωλουσῶν τὰ Ἀφροδίτης) to which the word has always been applicable in its literal sense; which is sufficiently indicated by the well-known phrases ημυεστηκέναι οἰκήματος, τέγους, or simply προεστηκέναι, *prostare.* Thus Xenoph. Ephes. v. 7 : ὁ δὲ πορνοβοσκὸς...ἠνάγκασεν αὐτὴν οἰκήματος προεστάναι· καὶ δὴ...ἦγεν ὡς προστησομένην τέγους. S. Chrysost. T. II. p. 559 D: τὰς ἀπὸ τοῦ τέγους γυναῖκας ἀνεστήσας ἀπὸ τῶν οἰκημάτων ἐν οἷς προειστήκεσαν. T. X. p. 154 E: καὶ γὰρ πάσης πόρνης αἰσχρότερον προειστήκει ἡ ἡμετέρα φύσις. Macrob. *Somn. Scip.* I. 2: 'Visas sibi esse Eleusinias Deas habitu meretricio ante lupanar ludere *prostantes.*' From this primary meaning is naturally derived that of *exercising a calling* or *profession,* whether *discreditable,* as Plut. *Vit. Pericl.* XXIV: καίπερ οὐ κοσμίου προεστῶσαν ἐργασίας οὐδὲ σεμνῆς, ἀλλὰ παιδίσκας ἑταιρούσας τρέφουσαν ; Julian. *Ep.* XLIX: ἢ τέχνης τινὸς καὶ ἐργασίας αἰσχρᾶς καὶ ἐπονειδίστου προΐστασθαι; or *respectable,* as προΐστασθαι ῥητορικῆς, ἰατρικῆς etc. Hence, by an easy transition, we arrive at the general meaning of *conducting* or *managing any matter of business;* as Stob. *Flor.* T. CXVI. 49: οὔτε μὴν ἀρχῆς οἷός τέ ἐστι προΐστασθαι (ὁ γέρων). Dion. Hal. *Ant.* III. 36: ἐμέμφετο δὲ τοὺς κακῶς προϊσταμένους τῶν ἰδίων [κτημάτων], ὡς οὐ βεβαίους πολίτας. V. 17: ἐάν τε πολέμων ἡγεμονίας λαβόντες, ἐάν τε πολιτικῶν ἔργων προστασίας. Xenoph. *Mem.* III. 2, 2: οὐκ εἰ μόνον τοῦ ἑαυτοῦ βίου καλῶς προεστήκοι. There is, therefore, no objection, as far as προΐστασθαι is concerned, to either of the proposed interpretations.

The advocates of *honest trades* or *occupations* insist strongly on the context in both places: in the former ταῦτά ἐστι καλὰ καὶ ὠφέλιμα τοῖς ἀνθρώποις; in the latter, εἰς τὰς ἀναγκαίας χρείας[1]; but these are general expressions, which are capable of being so explained as to suit either interpretation. Even if *honest trades* were intended, the 'necessary uses' may still be those of the Church, not of the individual, especially when it is added, 'that they be not *unfruitful*,' that is, 'that they may bring forth fruit unto God' (Rom. vii. 4).

But the true solution of the question turns upon another point, namely, what is the idea most naturally suggested by the words καλῶν ἔργων? Can any instance be found of καλὰ ἔργα being said of *honest occupations* or *crafts*, δίκαιοι πόνοι, as St Chrysostom invariably calls them? The example adduced from 1 Tim. iii. 1, where the office of a bishop is said to be a καλὸν ἔργον, rather tells the other way, since it would be absurd to say that if a man aspires to such an office, he desires an *honest occupation*. Again we ask, what are καλὰ ἔργα in the common acceptation of the term? For an answer to this we need go no further than the pastoral epistles. Thus 1 Tim. v. 10, a widow should be ἐν ἔργοις καλοῖς μαρτυρουμένη; vi. 18, the rich are to be exhorted to be rich ἐν ἔργοις καλοῖς; and Titus (ii. 7) is to shew himself τύπον καλῶν ἔργων. These examples are sufficient to shew St Paul's practice in the use of this phrase, from which it is incredible that he should have departed in the two instances before us. By way of corollary I add the following from classical sources. Plut. *Vit. Pelop.* XIX: οὕτως ᾤετο τοὺς ἀγαθούς, ζῆλον ἀλλήλοις καλῶν ἔργων ἐνιέντας, ὠφελιμωτάτους εἰς κοινὸν ἔργον εἶναι καὶ προθυμοτάτους. Id. *Vit. Mar.* IX: ἅτε δὴ μηδ' αὐτοὺς δι' εὐγένειαν, ἀλλ' ἀπ' ἀρετῆς καὶ καλῶν ἔργων ἐνδόξους γενομένους. Id. *Vit. Alex.* XXXIV: οὕτω τις εὐμενὴς ἦν πρὸς ἅπασαν ἀρετήν, καὶ καλῶν ἔργων φύλαξ καὶ οἰκεῖος. Diod. Sic. T. X. p. 196, ed. Bip.: τῶν καλῶν ἔργων ὀρεχθείς. Isocr. *ad Demon.* 48: μάλιστα δ' ἂν παροξυνθείης ὀρεχθῆναι τῶν καλῶν ἔργων, εἰ καταμάθοις ὅτι καὶ τὰς ἡδονὰς ἐκ τούτων μάλιστα γνησίους ἔχομεν.

---

[1] [Cf. Dem. 668, 28: ὅτι αἱ ἀναγκαῖαι χρεῖαι τοὺς τοῦ τί πρακτέον ἢ μὴ λογισμοὺς ἀναιροῦσιν ἅπαντας.]

PHILEMON.

* Verse 12: Corrected text: ὃν ἀνέπεμψά σοι, αὐτόν, τουτέστι, τὰ ἐμὰ σπλάγχνα] R. V. 'whom I have sent back to thee in his own person, that is &c.' One is tempted to ask, how else could he have sent him back, if not *in his own person?* Dean Alford sets up an anacoluthon, the writer going off into the relative clause, ὃν ἐγὼ ἐβουλόμην κ.τ.έ., and losing sight of the construction with which he began, and which he takes up again at *v.* 17. This was also the opinion of those who interpolated σὺ δὲ before αὐτὸν, and προσλαβοῦ after σπλάγχνα. But αὐτὸν seems to be merely a repetition of ὃν before τουτέστι; 'him, *I say*, that is, mine own bowels.' In *v.* 17 προσλαβοῦ αὐτόν is not 'receive him,' but 'take him unto thee,' as correctly rendered Acts xviii. 26. St Chrysostom, commenting on *v.* 12, according to the T. R., remarks: Οὐκ εἶπεν, ἀπόδεξαι...ἀλλὰ προσλαβοῦ· τουτέστιν, οὐχὶ συγγνώμης, ἀλλὰ τιμῆς ἐστιν ἄξιος.

*13: ὑπὲρ σοῦ] A. V. 'in thy stead.' R. V. 'in thy behalf.' The A. V. might be defended from Ael. *V. H.* XII. 45: Πινδάρῳ...μέλιτται τροφοὶ ἐγένοντο ὑπὲρ τοῦ γάλακτος παρατιθεῖσαι μέλι.

*14: χωρὶς τῆς σῆς γνώμης] See the quotation from Dion. Hal. in the note on Rom. xiv. 7.

* 19: προσοφείλεις] 'thou owest besides.' The force of the preposition is that, instead of Philemon's being the Apostle's creditor, he was, in fact, his debtor; not only was the debt cancelled, but the balance was turned *against* Philemon. Compare Demosth. *c. Aphob.* I. p. 825, 17: αὐτὰ δὲ τὰ ἀρχαῖα πάντα ἀναλωκέναι φασὶ σὺν ταῖς ὂζ μναῖς. Δημοφῶν δὲ καὶ προσοφείλοντας ἡμᾶς ἐνέγραψεν. Adag. e Suid. collect. Cent. X. 72: ὁ ἐν Τεμέσῃ ἥρως· ὅταν τις ἀπαιτῶν τι, μᾶλλον προσοφείλων εὑρεθῇ.

HEBREWS.

Chap. I. 6: ὅταν δὲ πάλιν εἰσαγάγῃ] A. V. 'And again, when he bringeth in.' R. V. 'And when he again bringeth in.' The *supposed* transposition of πάλιν may easily be avoided, in reading the Greek by making a slight pause after πάλιν, so as to separate it from εἰσαγάγῃ; and in English by a slight correction of the A. V. 'And when, again, he bringeth in.' Dean Alford claims St Chrysostom in favour of the construction πάλιν εἰσαγάγῃ; but I can find nothing in that author to justify the assertion. He speaks of one εἰσαγωγή, and only one; εἰσαγωγὴν ταύτην λέγων, τὴν τῆς σαρκὸς ἀνάληψιν. And further on: 'If he was in the world, and the world was made by him, as St John says, πῶς ἑτέρως εἰσάγεται, ἀλλ' ἢ ἐν σαρκί;' One would also have expected, if a *second* εἰσαγωγή were intended, that some mention would have been made of a *previous* one, of which there is not the slightest hint, and the reader is left to speculate upon the time and manner of these two introductions without any assistance from the context.

IV. 2: A. V. 'Not being mixed with faith (μὴ συγκεκραμένος τῇ πίστει) in them that heard it. Or, *because they were not united by faith* (μὴ συγκεκρασμένους τῇ π.) *to* (R. V. with) *them that heard it.*' The latter reading and version is that adopted by R. V. The Syriac Peschito certainly read συγκεκραμένος, but it is disputed which of the two *constructions* of this word can lay claim to its authority.

Dean Alford gives as the sense of this version: *quoniam non commixtus erat per fidem cum iis qui eum audierant.* On the other hand, the Latin version of Schaaf's Syriac N. T. has: *quia non contemperabatur cum fide illis qui audiverunt ipsum.* Which is right? The words are ܠܐ ܡܡܙܓܐ ܗܘܐ ܒܝܕ ܗܝܡܢܘܬܐ ܠܗܢܘܢ ܕܫܡܥܘܗܝ. We have therefore to enquire, what is the construction of ܡܙܓ, ἐκέρασε, when one thing is mixed with another. A good example is 2 Macc. xv. 39: οἶνος ὕδατι συγκερασθείς, for which the Syriac is ܐܝܟ ܚܡܪܐ ܕܡܙܝܓ ܒܡܝܐ. In the LXX. version of Dan. ii. 43 for συγκραθῆναι τῷ ὀστράκῳ the Syriac is ‏ܠܘܬ ܣܘܣ ܕܝܠܗ‎. The same two-fold construction with ‏ܠ‎ and ‏ܣܘܣ‎ (but more frequently with the former) is found with ‏ܐܠܟܣ‎, ἔμιξε (see Payne Smith's *Thes. Syr.* s. v.). On the other hand, in Apoc. xviii. 6, for κεράσατε αὐτῇ διπλοῦν we have ‏ܐܘܟܠܘ‎

‏ܦܠܓ ܥܠ‎, where ‏ܥܠ‎ indicates the *dativus commodi* (αὐτῇ), as ‏ܕܥܠ‎ in our text. The Peschito, therefore, is rightly rendered by Schaaf, and is in favour of A. V.

*VII. 18, 19: ἀθέτησις μὲν γὰρ γίνεται προαγούσης ἐντολῆς...οὐδὲν γὰρ ἐτελείωσεν ὁ νόμος, ἐπεισαγωγὴ δὲ κρείττονος ἐλπίδος] A. V. 'For there is verily a disannulling of the commandment going before...For the law made nothing perfect, but the bringing in of a better hope *did*.' The error of the A. V., in contrasting 'the law' with 'the bringing in of a better hope,' has often been pointed out. Most critics are agreed in rendering: 'For there is, on the one hand, a disannulling &c. (for the law made nothing perfect) and, on the other, a bringing in &c.' From a morbid anxiety to reproduce in the translation every 'shade of meaning' which they conceive to be contained in the original, some critics have proposed to render ἐπεισαγωγή by 'a bringing in besides' or 'thereupon' (R. V.), relying on such instances as Hippocr. p. 27, 20 (Ed. Anut. Foes. 1624): ἑτέρων ἰητρῶν ἐπεισαγωγήν; or Joseph. *Ant.* XI. 6, 2: σβέννυσθαι γὰρ τὸ πρὸς τὴν προτέραν (γυναῖκα) φιλόστοργον ἑτέρας ἐπεισαγωγῇ. But the analogy does not hold good; because the 'foregoing commandment' did not remain (as the first wife, or the first physician), but was 'disannulled.' The Syriac version, indeed, has expressed ἐπι- by ‏ܚܠܦܝܗ‎, *pro ea*; but that would rather represent ἀντεισάγειν, which is the very word used by St Chrysostom (T. XII. p. 142 C) of the two covenants: πόθεν τοῦτο δῆλον; ἐξ ὧν αὕτη μὲν ἐξεβλήθη, ἐκείνη δὲ ἀντεισήχθη.

VIII. 1: κεφάλαιον δὲ ἐπὶ τοῖς λεγομένοις] A. V. 'Now of the things which we have spoken, *this is* the sum.' R. V. 'Now in the things which we are saying the chief point is this.' The A. V. exactly represents the formula used by Isocrates (*Nicocl.* p. 39 D) in summing up his preceding discourse: κεφάλαιον δὲ τῶν εἰρημένων, which resembles that of the Apostle in its construction *per asyndeton*, but differs in other particulars. Nearer to our text, and, perhaps, modelled upon it, is the following from St Basil (T. II. p. 7 E): κεφάλαιον δὲ ἐπὶ τοῖς εἰρημένοις· ὁ κύριος ἡμῶν νηστείᾳ τὴν σάρκα, ἣν ὑπὲρ ἡμῶν ἀνέλαβεν, ὀχυρώσας, κ.τ.έ.; where, however, he is not summarizing his former arguments, but introducing, by this formula, a new and stronger reason, drawn from the example of our Lord himself. By ἐπὶ τοῖς εἰρημένοις, therefore, in St Basil, we must understand 'besides what has been said' (as Luke xvi. 26: καὶ ἐπὶ πᾶσι τούτοις); and by κεφάλαιον, not the *sum*, but the *main point, palmarium argumentum,* as in Thucyd. VI. 6: λέγοντες ἄλλα τε πολλά, καὶ κεφάλαιον· εἰ Συρακόσιοι...τὴν ἅπασαν δύναμιν τῆς Σικελίας σχήσουσι, κίνδυνον εἶναι κ.τ.ἑ.[1] Returning to the text, there might seem to be a difficulty in the use of the *present* participle, ἐπὶ τοῖς λεγομένοις; which, however, may easily be explained by the consideration that the discourse is continuous, and that what the writer had said just before, he might be considered as still saying. Compare Acts xxvii. 11: τῷ ναυκλήρῳ ἐπείθετο μᾶλλον ἢ τοῖς ὑπὸ τοῦ Παύλου λεγομένοις. Job xli. 1 (Heb. 9): οὐχ ἑώρακας αὐτόν, οὐδὲ ἐπὶ τοῖς λεγομένοις τεθαύμακας[2]. We would, therefore, render the whole passage thus: 'Now to crown (Or, *sum up*) our present discourse: We have such a high priest' &c.

IX. 1: τό τε ἅγιον κοσμικόν] A. V. 'And a worldly sanctuary.' The absence of the article before κοσμικόν was a stumbling-block to Bishop Middleton, who having discovered[3] in a certain Rabbinical writing the word קוזמיקין meaning (it would appear) 'a woman's toilet' (*mundus muliebris*), hastily imported this exotic use of the word into the Greek Testament, in the general sense of 'furniture.' What is still more surprising, this bold innovation has been endorsed by Professor Scholefield (*Hints* &c., p. 99) who settles the matter in a very few words: 'Both ἅγιον and κοσμικόν being adjectives, one of them must be taken substantively; and the position of the article determines that that one must be κοσμικόν.' But, surely, in such a case the better plan is to enquire, whether either and which of the two adjectives is commonly used as a substantive; and the result would be wholly in favour of ἅγιον (Joseph. *Ant.* III. 6, 4: ὁ μὲν πᾶς νεὼς ἍΓΙΟΝ ἐκαλεῖτο) and against κοσμικόν. In fact, even as an adjective, κοσμικόν is never connected with κόσμος, *ornatus*, but always with κόσμος, *mundus*.

The omission of the article will appear to be quite regular, if we consider it to be added ἐπεξηγητικῶς, by way of explanation, τό τε ἅγιον, scilicet κοσμικόν, or τό τε ἅγιον κοσμικὸν ὄν. Out of a number of examples which I had collected for this construction, I select the following in which

[1] [Cf. Lucian. *Tyran.* 17: νῦν δὲ καὶ τὸ κεφάλαιον αὐτὸ ἐννοήσατε. Dio Chrys. *Or.* XI. p. 158, 30: ᾔδει τἀναντία λέγων τοῖς οὖσι, καὶ τὸ κεφάλαιον αὐτὸ τοῦ πράγματος ψευδόμενος. Lucian. *Philops.* 6: ὅ,τι περ τὸ κεφάλαιον αὐτὸ ἐξ ἑκάστης προαιρέσεως (school of philosophy). Liban. 1. 694 (ed. Reiske, 1791): αὐτῶν δέ γε τῶν λεγομένων τὸ κεφάλαιον· τὰ τήνδε μέλλοντα τὴν πόλιν ἐπικλύσειν ἔστησας.]

[2] [Cf. Plut. *Vit. Nic.* XI: ὡς μᾶλλον ἐν τοῖς περὶ ἐκείνου (Alcibiades) γραφομένοις δηλοῦται. App. *B. C.* III. 88: ὧν λεγομένων ἥ τε στρατιὰ προθύμως ἐπεβόησε.]

[3] The original discoverer was Schoettgen, *Horae Hebr.* p. 973, from which work, in Hugh James Rose's edition of Middleton, *On the Greek Article*, p. 414, for טיני תבשימין read מיני תבשיטין.

the article is omitted before this identical adjective : Euseb. *de Mart. Pal.*
IV: πρῶτον μὲν οὖν τῆς Ἑλλήνων παιδείας ἕνεκα ΚΟΣΜΙΚΗΣ[1].

IX. 11: οὐ ταύτης τῆς κτίσεως] A. V. 'Not of this building.' R. V.
'Not of this creation.' By ταύτης I understand *vulgaris, quae vulgo
dicitur.* Wetstein rightly explains : *habitacula super terram in usus
hominum ab illis exstructa,* comparing Ch. VIII. 2: σκηνῆς ἣν ἔπηξεν
ὁ κύριος, καὶ οὐκ ἄνθρωπος, in other words, οὐ ταύτης τῆς πήξεως[2]. I have
called attention to this use of οὗτος in a note on S. Chrysost. T. VII.
p. 376 B. To the examples there given may be added from the same
author T. V. p. 208 E : ἐν μὲν οὖν τούτοις τοῖς δικαστηρίοις. *Ibid.* p. 280 B :
εἶχον μὲν γὰρ τὴν δόξαν τὴν παρὰ τοῦ θεοῦ· εἵπετο καὶ αὕτη (*mundana*).
T. IX. p. 736 E: λύκοι τούτων πολὺ πικρότεροι. T. XII. p. 213 C: τί ἐστι,
τὴν τοὺς θεμελίους ἔχουσαν πόλιν; οὗτοι (*quae apud nos sunt*) γὰρ οὐκ εἰσὶ
θεμέλιοι. As this usage seems to have been overlooked by Lexicographers, I will add two examples from classical Greek. Stob. *Flor.*
T. XCIII. 1 : ψυχὴν ἔχειν δεῖ πλουσίαν· τὰ δὲ χρήματα ΤΑΥΤ (*quae vulgo
appellantur*) ἐστὶν ὄψις. Lucian. *Nec.* 4: ἀτεχνῶς οὖν ἔπασχον τοῖς νυστά-
ζουσι ΤΟΥΤΟΙΣ ὅμοιον, ἄρτι μὲν ἐπινεύων, ἄρτι δὲ ἀνανεύων ἔμπαλιν. This
being understood, there is no occasion to take κτίσις in any other sense
than that in which κτίζειν is commonly applied to a city (3 Esdr. iv. 53 :
κτίσαι τὴν πόλιν) or to the tabernacle itself (Lev. xvi. 16: οὕτω ποιήσει τῇ
σκηνῇ τῇ ἐκτισμένῃ αὐτοῖς)[3].

IX. 16, 17 : A. V. 'For where a testament *is*, there must also of
necessity be (Or, *be brought in*) the death of the testator; for a testament *is* of force after men are dead (ἐπὶ νεκροῖς): otherwise it is of no
strength at all while the testator liveth.' R. V. the same, with a few
verbal alterations. We agree with Dean Alford, that 'it is quite vain to
deny the *testamentary* sense of διαθήκη in this passage[4].' If the question
were put to any person of common intelligence, 'What document is that,
which is of no force at all during the lifetime of the person who executed

---

[1] [Cf. Plut. *Vit. Aristid.* XVIII :
ἀντιλαμβανόμενοι τῶν δορατίων ταῖς χερσὶ
γυμναῖς (sc. οὔσαις). Diod. Sic. XI. 37:
τοὺς δὲ συμμάχους διαποντίους (sc. ὄντας)
μὴ δύνασθαι τὰς βοηθείας εὐκαίρους αὐτοῖς
ποιήσασθαι. *Id.* XIII. 43: ἅμα μὲν γὰρ
ἐπεθύμουν παραλαβεῖν τὴν πόλιν εὔκαιρον
(sc. οὖσαν). Charit. VI. 6: καὶ ἑαυτὸν
ἐλαφρῦναι τῆς διακονίας δυσχεροῦς (sc.
οὔσης).]

[2] [Wetstein (ed. 1752) compares
1 Pet. ii. 17 (?iv. 17), Apoc. xiii. 6, Ps.
cxv. 16, Rom. viii. 21. Ed.]

[3] [Cf. also Synes. *Ep.* 103, p. 242 B:
σὺ μὲν ἐργάζῃ ῥητορικήν· καὶ συγχωρῶ
σοι μὴ ΤΑΥΤΗΝ ἐπιτηδεύειν, ἀλλὰ τὴν
ὀρθὴν καὶ γενναίαν. Dio. Chrys. *Or.*
XXXI. p. 356, 35: ὁμοίως δίδοτε τοὺς
ἀνδριάντας ὥσπερ οἱ τὰς κόρας ΤΑΥΤΑΣ
ὠνούμενοι τοῖς παισίν. Orig. (Burgon,
Revision Revised, p. 185) neque de hoc
quod oculis intuemur unguento, sed de
nardo spirituali.]

[4] [Compare John iii. 8, where πνεῦμα
is used in two senses (1) wind, (2) The
Holy Spirit.]

it?' the answer can only be, 'A man's *will* or *testament*.' A covenant is out of the question; partly, because there must be two parties to it, and also because the validity of a covenant, unless otherwise expressed, depends rather upon the life than the death of the parties; so that, in this case, we should have expected the 17th verse to run thus: διαθήκη γὰρ ἐπὶ ζῶσι βεβαία, ἐπεὶ μήποτε ἰσχύει ὅτε τέθνηκεν ὁ διαθέμενος. As to the word itself, it should be observed that διαθήκην διέθετο is generally used in classical Greek of making a testament, not a covenant, which latter is rather συνθήκην συνέθετο[1]. It is true that the LXX. for בְּרִית, as between God and man, have invariably put διαθήκη, probably on account of the disparity of the parties to the covenant; but not without a protest from the other Greek translators, as we constantly find in the Hexapla, οἱ λοιποί· συνθήκην.

Such attempts as that of Prof. Scholefield: 'For where a covenant is, there must of necessity be brought in the death of the mediating *sacrifice*. For a covenant is valid over dead *sacrifices*; since it is never of any force while the mediating *sacrifice* continues alive,' hardly deserve a serious refutation, especially as the Professor admits that 'he must be a man of strong nerve, who feels no difficulty in translating ὁ διαθέμενος in any sense but that of the party who makes the covenant' (or testament).

In any case, there is a little difficulty about the precise meaning of φέρεσθαι. Wetstein explains: 'Necesse est afferri testimonia de morte testatoris.'[2] Perhaps the idea may be that of being publicly known, carried from mouth to mouth[3]; as in the case of a deceased author's works, of some it is said φέρονται (i.e. from hand to hand), of others οὐ φέρονται, according as they are still extant, or have not come down to us. Compare the Latin *Fertur*, 'It is reported.'

X. 24: εἰς παροξυσμὸν ἀγάπης] 'To provoke unto love.' There is no difficulty in the use of παροξύνειν *in bonam partem*, for which the following

---

[1] A clear exception to this rule is Aristoph. *Av.* 432: ἢν μὴ διάθωνταί γ' οἵδε διαθήκην ἐμοί, | ἥνπερ ὁ πίθηκος τῇ γυναικὶ διέθετο, | μήτε δάκνειν τούτους ἐμὲ κ.τ.λ. But this use may generally be distinguished from the other by the mention of *two* parties.

[2] [Plut. *Vit. Cat. Min.* XIX: δίκη τινὶ μαρτυρίας μιᾶς φερομένης, 'when only one witness was produced.' Langhorne.]

[3] [See Lidd. and Sc. φέρω, A. VIII. Cf. Paus. VIII. 43, 5: δόξῃ δὲ ἐμῇ καὶ τὸ ὄνομα τοῦ Κύρου φέροιτο ἄν...πατὴρ

ἀνθρώπων καλούμενος. (Also περιφέρεσθαι: Plut. *Vit. Ant.* LXX: τὸ δὲ περιφερόμενον Καλλιμάχειόν ἐστι.) Plut. *Vit. Brut.* LIII: καίτοι φέρεταί τις ἐπιστολὴ Βρούτου πρὸς τοὺς φίλους.] Note also Plut. *Vit. Arat.* XXXIX: καὶ ἐφέροντο (were bandied about) λοιδορίαι καὶ βλασφημίαι...ἀλλήλους κακῶς λεγόντων (Cleomenes and Aratus). App. *B. C.* II. 143: διαθῆκαι τοῦ Καίσαρος ὤφθησαν φερόμεναι (qu. being brought to the assembly?) καὶ εὐθὺς αὐτὰς τὸ πλῆθος ἐκέλευον ἀναγινώσκεσθαι.

examples have been adduced. Xenoph. *Mem.* III. 3, 13: φιλοτιμία ἥπερ μάλιστα παροξύνει πρὸς τὰ καλὰ καὶ ἔντιμα. Isocr. *ad Demon.* 48: μάλιστα δ' ἂν παροξυνθείης ὀρεχθῆναι τῶν καλῶν ἔργων. I add Diod. Sic. XVI. 54: μάλιστα δ' αὐτοὺς παρώξυνε προστῆναι τῆς Ἑλλάδος Δημοσθένης ὁ ῥήτωρ. Since παροξύνειν is used by the LXX. for 'to sharpen' (Deut. xxxii. 41, Prov. xxvii. 17), we might understand by παροξυσμός the 'sharpening' or 'quickening' of love; but this does not apply so well to 'good works,' and the explanation usually given is the better one, namely, that εἰς παροξυσμὸν ἀγάπης is equivalent to εἰς τὸ παροξύνειν (ἀλλήλους) πρὸς ἀγάπην, 'to incite, or *provoke* (used in a good sense here and 2 Cor. ix. 2) unto love.' The least probable rendering of all is that proposed by a distinguished living prelate, 'a paroxysm of love and good works,' the English reader knowing but one use of the word *paroxysm*, namely, the sudden and violent exacerbation of a *disease*. And that the Apostle does not contemplate such love as exerts itself by fits and starts, but by a sustained and continued action, is evident from the means suggested to promote it, 'Let us consider one another[1].'

X. 27: φοβερὰ δέ τις ἐκδοχὴ κρίσεως] A. V. 'But a certain fearful looking for (R. V. expectation) of judgment.' Dean Alford denies the meaning of 'looking for' attributed to ἐκδοχή, and renders it by 'reception' (i.e. *meed, doom*), against the Vulg. *expectatio*, and the Philox. Syriac ܠܣܘܡ (elsewhere interchanged with προσδοκία). And so Hesychius: Ἐκδοχή· προσδοκία; and the use of ἐκδέχεσθαι for ἀναμένειν is undoubted, e.g. John v. 3, Acts xvii. 16, Heb. x. 13, xi. 10. [In the last instance the Dean explains that 'the preposition intensifies the expectation'; but how can that be, seeing that δέχομαι is not 'to expect' at all?][2] At all events the meaning of 'reception,' as equivalent to *meed* or *doom*, is equally unsupported by usage.

X. 35: μὴ ἀποβάλητε οὖν τὴν παρρησίαν ὑμῶν] A. V. 'Cast not away therefore your confidence' (R. V. boldness). The rendering of the Vulgate is *Nolite amittere*, which is the more common meaning of the word, 'Lose not, let not go,' the opposite of which is κατασχεῖν τὴν π. (Ch. iii. 6). The following (from Wetstein) is strongly in favour of the change: Dio. Chrys. *Or.* XXXIV. p. 425: δέδοικα μὴ τέλεως ἀποβάλητε τὴν παρρησίαν. I add

---

[1] The prelate alluded to, on the occasion of his consecrating four churches at once, had let fall the expression, 'a paroxysm of building churches,' which was mildly censured by the 'Times,' as 'somewhat irreverent.' Whereupon the Archbishop replies: 'If so, what becomes of the "paroxysm of love and good works" in Heb. x. 24, veiled from the English reader by the paraphrase "provoking one another"?'

[2] [But see L. and S. s. v. II. 4. A better example is Plut. *Vit. Brut.* XVIII: διέτρεσαν καὶ τὸ μέλλον ἐδέχοντο κόσμῳ καὶ σιωπῇ. But Schaf. *ad loc.* proposes ἀνεδέχοντο.]

Diod. Sic. XVI. 64: αἱ πόλεις...ὕστερον ὑπὸ Ἀντιπάτρου καταπολεμηθεῖσαι, τὴν ἡγεμονίαν ἅμα καὶ τὴν ἐλευθερίαν ἀπέβαλον. Dion. Hal. Ant. VIII. 86: νῦν δὲ τοῦ πλείονος ὀρεγόμενοι, καὶ τὴν ἐκ τῆς προτέρας νίκης δόξαν ἀπέβαλον[1].

XI. 11: **πίστει καὶ αὐτὴ Σάρρα δύναμιν εἰς καταβολὴν σπέρματος ἔλαβεν**] A. V. 'Through faith also Sara herself received strength to conceive seed.' There appear to be several difficulties in these words. (1) Πῶς πίστει ἡ γελάσασα; This objection is noticed by St Chrysostom, who gets over it by saying that her laughing was through unbelief, but her afterwards denying it was 'by faith.' (2) The faith of Abraham in believing that a son should be born to him παρὰ καιρὸν ἡλικίας is here entirely passed over, though in Rom. iv. 18 it is particularly dwelt upon, and Sarah is mentioned only for the purpose of setting it off. (3) The καταβολὴ σπέρματος belonged to the male. Thus Galen De Semine I. (quoted by Wetstein): τὸ τοῦ ἄρρενος σπέρμα τὸ καταβαλλόμενον εἰς τὰς μήτρας τοῦ θήλεως; and Lucian. Amor. 19 (quoted by L. Bos): τοῖς μὲν γὰρ ἄρρεσιν ἰδίας καταβολὰς σπερμάτων χαρισαμένη (ἡ τῶν ὅλων φύσις), τὸ θῆλυ δ' ὥσπερ γονῆς τι δοχεῖον ἀναφήνασα. Hence the Greek commentators are forced to explain καταβολὴ as if it were ὑποδοχή, as St Chrysostom, εἰς τὸ κατασχεῖν τὸ σπέρμα, εἰς τὴν ὑποδοχὴν δύναμιν ἔλαβεν; and Oecumenius, ἐνεδυναμώθη εἰς τὸ ὑποδέξασθαι παιδοποιὸν σπέρμα[2].

If we suppose καὶ αὐτὴ Σάρρα to be an interpolation from the margin, the 11th and 12th verses will be continued to Abraham without interruption, and leave nothing to be desired. For though it follows in the T. R. καὶ παρὰ καιρὸν ἡλικίας ἔτεκε, A. V. 'and was delivered of a child when she was past age,' ἔτεκε is an acknowledged insertion, being wanting in A (B hiat) D[1] and א[1].

XI. 29: **ἧς πεῖραν λαβόντες οἱ Αἰγύπτιοι**] A. V. 'Which the Egyptians assaying to do.' 36: ἐμπαιγμῶν καὶ μαστίγων πεῖραν ἔλαβον. A. V. 'Had trial of cruel mockings and scourgings.' R. V. the same, omitting cruel. In both places we should prefer, 'had experience of.' In v. 29 the antecedent of ἧς is the Red sea; and the words πεῖραν ἔλαβον τῆς θαλάσσης are intended to state the fact, not merely that they assayed to pass it, but that they had woeful and disastrous experience of it. So in v. 36, the only distinction between the two cases being that in the first the experience was voluntary, in the second compulsory. The full force of the Greek phrase is best seen by examples, of which the following (partly from Wetstein) may suffice. Diod. Sic. XII. 24: ἵνα μὴ

---

[1] [Cf. Dio. Chrys. Or. XXXI. p. 345, 1: τὴν ἐλευθερίαν ἀποβαλεῖν. Plut. Vit. Tim. XXXVII: ἀποβαλεῖν τὴν ὄψιν ὑπὸ γήρως ἀπομαρανθεῖσαν. Id. Aemil. XXI: ἔνθα δὴ καὶ Μάρκος ὁ Κάτωνος υἱός...πᾶσαν ἀλκὴν ἐπιδεικνύμενος ἀπέβαλε τὸ ξίφος.]

[2] [Cf. H. Steph.: 'vim ad jaciendum sive emittendum semen accepit, nam καταβολήν interpretari conceptionem violentum esse videtur.']

τῆς ὕβρεως λάβῃ πεῖραν, τὴν θυγατέρα ἀπέκτεινεν. XIII. 52: παρὸν μηδ᾽ ὅλως ἀτυχίας λαβεῖν πεῖραν. XV. 88: (ἡ πατρὶς αὐτοῦ) ἀνδραποδισμοῦ καὶ κατασκαφῆς ἔλαβε πεῖραν. Charit. Aphrod. VIII. 4: μὴ λάβῃ δὲ πεῖραν μητρυιᾶς. Plut. *Vit. Pomp.* LXXIII: ἥττης δὲ καὶ φυγῆς τότε πρῶτον ἐν γήρᾳ λαμβάνοντα πεῖραν. Pausan. *Corinth.* 33, 3: Δημοσθένει δὲ φυγῆς τε συνέπεσεν ἐν γήρᾳ λαβεῖν πεῖραν. Ach. Tat. VI. 20: ἀλλ᾽ ἐπειδὴ μὴ θέλεις ἐραστοῦ μου πεῖραν λαβεῖν, πειράσῃ δεσπότου. Aesop. *Fab.* CXXXII, ed. de Fur.: ὁ μῦθος δηλοῖ, ὅτι μάλιστα τοὺς πρώτους δεσπότας τότε ποθοῦσιν οἱ οἰκέται, ὅταν πεῖραν λάβωσιν ἑτέρων[1]. In the following the same idea is expressed by a single word, πειραθῆναι. Dio Chrys. *Or.* III. p. 158, 25: πολλάκις δὲ καὶ λιμοῦ καὶ δίψους πειραθῆναι. Diod. Sic. T. x. p. 113, ed. Bip.: ἐπειράθησαν τῶν μεγίστων ἀτυχημάτων. Charit. Aphrod. VII. 5: ὃ μόνον ἔλιπέ μου ταῖς συμφοραῖς, ἤδη καὶ πολέμου πεπείραμαι. This leads us to offer a speculation on the very difficult word ἐπειράσθησαν, 'they were tempted,' placed between two kinds of capital punishment, ἐπρίσθησαν and ἐν φόνῳ μαχαίρας ἀπέθανον. Dean Alford says: '*If any conjecture is to be made*, I would say that either the omission, or ἐπρήσθησαν (they were burned) would appear to be the most probable.' But no good writer would have brought two words hardly distinguishable in sound, ἐπρίσθησαν, ἐπρήσθησαν, into juxta-position, and the biblical use of ἐπρήσθησαν (Num. v. 27[2]) is something quite different. It is entirely omitted by the Peschito, and inserted *before* ἐπρίσθησαν by Lℵ, 17. Supposing it to be a gloss which has crept in from the margin, it can hardly, in its present form, be assigned to any particular word; but if we conceive it to have been originally written ἐπειράθησαν, it may then have been intended to explain πεῖραν ἔλαβον in the same verse[3].

XII. 23: **πνεύμασι δικαίων τετελειωμένων**] A. V. (Ye are come) 'to the spirits of just men made perfect.' To avoid ambiguity, a slight change is necessary; namely, 'to the spirits of just men who have been made perfect.' It is the *just men*, not their *spirits*, that are made perfect, and that not in the future state, but here on earth, where alone they can be subject to those trials and conflicts, by the patient endurance of which they are prepared for a higher state of being.

That the common translation is often misunderstood will be seen by a few examples. Thus Archbishop Sumner in his *Exposition on Ephesians*, p. 17, (*On the Epistles*, 1845, p. 244), says: 'To know them fully...

---

[1] [Cf. Plut. *Vit. Ant.* XVIII: τὸν στρατὸν ἔχων ἀπεπειρᾶτο τοῦ ποταμοῦ. καὶ πρῶτος αὐτὸς ἐμβὰς ἐπορεύετο πρὸς τὴν ἀντιπέρας ὄχθην. The phrase is used *in bonam partem* in Dem. 663, 19: καὶ λαβὼν ἔργῳ τῆς ἐκείνου φιλίας πεῖραν. Ael. *V. H.* XII. 22: ἐβούλετο λαβεῖν αὐτοῦ ἰσχύος πεῖραν. Plut. *Vit. Otho*

XII: οἱ μὲν οὖν Ὄθωνος ἄνδρες ἦσαν εὔρωστοι καὶ ἀγαθοί, πολέμου δὲ καὶ μάχης τότε πρῶτον πεῖραν λαμβάνοντες.]

[2] [Cf. also Acts xxviii. 6.]

[3] [Boiss. ad Aristaen. p. 361 seems to say that πειραθῆναι and πειρασθῆναι are both in use, *Ep.* II. 18: νῦν πρῶτον ἔρωτος πειρασθεῖσα.]

will be the high privilege of "the spirits made perfect."' *Ibid.* p. 11 : 'The inheritance of the purchased possession, when "the spirits of just men" will be "made perfect," no longer clouded by the pains and anxieties which attend a fallen state.' And Sir Theodore Martin, in the concluding sentence of his *Life of the Prince Consort,* says of the heavenly state, 'where there is rest for the weary, and where "the spirits of the just are made perfect."'

*XII. 25 : μὴ παραιτήσησθε τὸν λαλοῦντα] ܐܠ܌ܐ. Both Versions : 'refuse not.' Is it not rather (with τινὰ) 'to beg to be excused'? Cf. Plut. *Vit. Tim.* XXXVII : ὡς δὲ ἐπανῆλθεν εἰς Συρακούσας, εὐθὺς ἀποθέσθαι τὴν μοναρχίαν καὶ παραιτεῖσθαι τοὺς πολίτας—on account of his blindness 'excused himself to the people' from any further service.

*XII. 28 : ἔχωμεν χάριν] A. V. 'Let us have grace.' For 'grace' Dean Alford and others would translate 'thankfulness.' But χάριν ἔχειν is not 'to have thankfulness,' but 'to thank,' and then only when it is followed by a dative. Schleusner s. v. χάρις num. 7, gives '*gratiarum actio,* εὐχαριστία'; but of his eleven examples from N. T. in three χάρις is 'grace'; five are of χάρις τῷ θεῷ, 'God be thanked'; and in the others there is a dative expressed. In the following from Xenoph. *Anab.* VI. 1, 26, the dative, though not expressed, is easily supplied : Ἐγώ, ὦ ἄνδρες, ἥδομαι μὲν ὑπὸ ὑμῶν τιμώμενος...καὶ χάριν ἔχω, καὶ εὔχομαι δοῦναί μοι τοὺς θεοὺς αἴτιόν τινος ὑμῖν ἀγαθοῦ γενέσθαι.

*XIII. 2 : τῆς φιλοξενίας μὴ ἐπιλανθάνεσθε] A. V. 'Be not forgetful to entertain strangers.' R. V. 'Forget not to show love unto strangers : for thereby &c.,' which ruins the connexion between the two clauses. Rom. xii. 13 : τὴν φιλοξενίαν διώκοντες. A. V. 'given to hospitality.' Not altered by R. V. but the margin has 'Gr. pursuing.' Φιλόξενος 1 Tim. iii. 2, A. V. 'given to hospitality,' and so R. V. Tit. i. 8, A. V. 'a lover of hospitality.' R. V. 'given to hospitality.' 1 Pet. iv. 9 both A. V. and R. V. 'using hospitality.'

With this command we may compare Plato *Legg.* p. 953 A : χρὴ καταλύσεις πρὸς ἱεροῖς εἶναι φιλοξενίαις ἀνθρώπων παρεσκευασμένας. Synes. *Ep.* 57, p. 192 C : καὶ τὸν Ἀβραὰμ ἡ φιλοξενία θεοῦ πεποίηκεν ἑστιάτορα.

JAMES.

*Chap. I. 4: ἐν μηδενὶ λειπόμενοι] A. V. 'wanting nothing.' R. V. 'lacking in nothing.' Λείπεσθαι ἔν τινι πράγματι is a doubtful construction, except when λείπεσθαι is used in the sense of *inferiority*, with or without a genitive of the person compared. Thus Diod. Sic. XX. 23: λειφθέντες (beaten) ἐν τῇ μάχῃ. Polyb. (quoted by Raphel) p. 1202, 15 (Ed. Amstelodami, 1670): ἐν τῇ πρὸς Ῥωμαίους εὐνοίᾳ παρὰ πολὺ τἀδελφοῦ λειπόμενος (inferior to his brother). Plut. *Vit. Mar.* V: ὡς οὖν ὁ Μάριος φανερὸς ἦν λειπόμενος ἐν ἐκείνῃ (the curule aedileship) ταχὺ μεταστὰς αὖθις ᾔτει τὴν ἑτέραν (the plebeian). St Paul has the same construction with ὑστερεῖσθαι I Cor. i. 7: ὥστε ὑμᾶς μὴ ὑστερεῖσθαι ἐν μηδενὶ χαρίσματι. Another construction of λείπεσθαι, with a genitive of the thing wanting, which occurs James i. 5, ii. 15, is only found in very late writers (as Libanius quoted by Wetstein). The regular construction is λείπεσθαί τινός (personae) τινι (rei); as Aelian. *V. H.* I. 23: τῇ δὲ σοφίᾳ τοσοῦτον ἐλείποντο (αὐτῶν) ὅσον ἀνδρῶν παῖδες.

*I. 14: ὑπὸ τῆς ἰδίας ἐπιθυμίας ἐξελκόμενος καὶ δελεαζόμενος] Dean Alford, amongst other parallels, quotes (from Huther) as 'the nearest correspondence of all,' Plut. *de Sera Num. Vind.*: τὸ γλυκὺ τῆς ἐπιθυμίας ὥσπερ δέλεαρ ἐξέλκειν [ἀνθρώπους]. But when we turn to the place (Plut. T. II. p. 554) we find, instead of the words given above, the following: τὸ γλυκὺ τῆς ἀδικίας, ὥσπερ δέλεαρ, εὐθὺς ἐξεδήδοκε (!). I have since found the same glaring mis-quotation (with ἐξέλκειν) in Schneckenburger *Annot. ad Ep. Jac.* (1832) p. 25.

*I. 22: παραλογιζόμενοι] A. V. 'deceiving your own selves.' R. V. 'deluding.' Col. ii. 4, A. V. 'Lest any man should beguile (R. V. delude) you.' But 'beguile' is used by A. V. of the wily act of the Gibeonites in Jos. ix. 22, where the LXX. have διὰ τί παρελογίσασθέ με; 'why have ye beguiled me?'

I. 25: ὁ δὲ παρακύψας εἰς νόμον τέλειον] I Pet. i. 12: εἰς ἃ ἐπιθυμοῦσιν ἄγγελοι παρακύψαι. On the *proper* meaning of παρακύψαι see on Luke

xxiv. 12. When used figuratively, as here, the same idea of 'looking in' or 'into' holds good, but without the intensive force which is usually claimed for it, of 'looking closely into' (Alford), *diligenter considerare* (Schleusner), *intentis oculis acerrime contemplari* (Elsner). On the contrary, 'to peep' or 'look sideways,' which is its original meaning, is rather to cast a careless or hurried glance on anything, than to submit it to close examination; as may be shown from the very passage which Elsner appeals to in favour of the latter view, namely, Lucian. *Pisc.* 30: κἀπειδὴ μόνον παρέκυψα ἐς τὰ ὑμέτερα, σὲ μὲν (ὦ Φιλοσοφία)... ἐθαύμαζον κ.τ.ἑ. I add S. Chrysost. T. x. p. 54 D: αὕτη γὰρ (ἡ ἔξωθεν σοφία) οὐκ ἀφείθη ἔνδον εἰσελθεῖν, καὶ παρακύψαι εἰς τὰ δεσποτικὰ μυστήρια[1].

II. 3: καλῶς] 'in a good place.' The classical phrase is ἐν καλῷ, as Alciphr. *Ep.* III. 20: ἄγει μέ τις λαβὼν εἰς τὸ θέατρον, καθίσας ἐν καλῷ. Philostr. *Her.* p. 10: βέλτιον δὲ καὶ ἐν καλῷ τοῦ χωρίου ἱζῆσαι. Aelian. *V. H.* II. 13: καὶ γάρ τοι καὶ παρῆν (Socrates) οὐκ ἄλλως οὐδὲ ἐκ τύχης, εἰδὼς δὲ ὅτι κωμῳδοῦσιν αὐτόν· καὶ δὴ καὶ ἐν καλῷ τοῦ θεάτρου ἐκάθητο[2].

II. 6: ἠτιμάσατε τὸν πτωχόν] A. V. 'ye have despised the poor.' R. V. 'ye have dishonoured the poor man.' The former rendering has good authority in its favour; e.g. Schol. ad Philostr. *Her.* p. 420: ἀτιμάζω· τὸ παραβλέπω, τὸ ἄτιμον ἡγοῦμαι. Fragm. Lex. Gr. ap. Hermann. *De Emend. Gr. Gr.* p. 340: ἀτιμάζω· τὸ περιφρονῶ παρὰ Λιβανίῳ· μὴ ἀτίμαζε τὸν γάμον. Compare Lucian. *Nec.* 20: ΨΗΦΙΣΜΑ. Ἐπειδὴ πολλὰ καὶ παράνομα οἱ πλούσιοι δρῶσι...ἁρπάζοντες καὶ βιαζόμενοι καὶ πάντα τρόπον τῶν πενήτων καταφρονοῦντες.

II. 15: τῆς ἐφημέρου τροφῆς] 'of daily food.' More correctly, 'of the day's supply of food,' as distinguished from τῆς καθ' ἡμέραν τροφῆς. J. Pollux defines ἐφήμερον to be τὸ εἰς τὴν ἐπιοῦσαν μὴ μένον. Wetstein quotes Aristid. T. II. p. 398: ἂν δ' αὐτὸς προσαιτῶν, καὶ τῆς ἐφημέρου τροφῆς ἀπορῶν, καὶ βλέπων εἰς β καὶ γ ὀβολούς. Dion. Hal. *Ant.* VIII. 41: ἀπῆλθεν ἐκ τῆς οἰκίας μόνος...ἄδουλος, ἄπορος, οὐδὲ τὴν ἐφήμερον ὁ δύστηνος ἐκ τῶν ἑαυτοῦ χρημάτων τροφὴν (*ne unius quidem diei viaticum*) ἐπαγόμενος. I add Aelian. *V. H.* III. 29 (probably from some Tragic writer, though Perizonius does not print it as verse) πλάνης, ἄοικος, πατρίδος ἐστερημένος, | πτωχός, δυσείμων, βίον ἔχων [τὸν] ἐφήμερον. Menand. ap. Stob. *Flor.* T. LIII. 2: στρατεία δ' οὐ φέρει περιουσίαν | οὐδεμί', ἐφήμερον δὲ καὶ προπετῆ βίον. S. Chrysost. T. IX. p. 677 B: ἀλλ' ὁ μὲν

---

[1] [Cf. Liban. I. 511: ἀλλ' ὥσπερ παρακύψασαν τὴν ἀγαθὴν τύχην εὐθὺς οἴχεσθαι φεύγουσαν. Lucian. *Hermot.* 2: πόθεν, ὦ Λυκῖνε, ὃς νῦν ἄρχομαι παρακύπτειν ἐς τὴν ὁδόν;]

[2] [Cf. *Ibid.* XIII. 22: Πτολεμαῖος ὁ Φιλοπάτωρ κατασκευάσας Ὁμήρῳ νεών, αὐτὸν μὲν καλὸν καλῶς ἐκάθισε, κύκλῳ δὲ τὰς πόλεις περιέστησε τοῦ ἀγάλματος, ὅσαι ἀντιποιοῦνται τοῦ Ὁμήρου.]

δεσπότης σου καὶ ἥλιον αὐτῷ ἀνατέλλει, σὺ δὲ καὶ τῆς ἐφημέρου τροφῆς ἀνάξιον αὐτὸν κρίνεις [1].

III. 3: ἰδοὺ τῶν ἵππων κ.τ.ἑ.] 'Behold, we put bits' &c. For ἰδοὺ (which is unsupported) the MSS. are divided between ἴδε and εἰ δὲ (or rather ΕΙΔΕ), the latter being contained in ABKL and א (with ΕΙΔΕ-ΓΑΡ). Of the versions, the Vulg. has si autem, the old Syriac ecce enim, and the Philoxenian ecce. Modern critics adopt the reading of the principal uncials, and make the apodosis begin from καὶ ὅλον, thus: 'But if we put bridles into the horses' mouths, that they may obey us, we turn about their whole body also.' This is objectionable for several reasons, especially the insertion of the clause, εἰς τὸ πείθεσθαι ἡμῖν αὐτούς, in presence of which we should rather have expected such an apodosis as this: 'in the same manner, when our object is that our own bodies should obey us, let us begin by restraining that member which corresponds to the horses' mouths, namely, the tongue.'

It should be borne in mind that ΙΔΕ and ΕΙΔΕ are rather different spellings than different readings. To take only the Sinaitic MS.: in Luke xxiii. 15 we have ειδου for ἰδού; in Luke xxiv. 39 and 1 Joh. iii. 1, ειδετε for ἴδετε; while in Rom. ii. 17, instead of the old reading ἴδε σὺ 'Ιουδαῖος ἐπονομάζῃ most of the uncials have ΕΙΔΕ, which has been (as in this place) assumed to be εἰ δέ, and so introduced into the text, involving it in the same difficulty with regard to an apodosis, as we have seen in St James.

In this very Epistle (v. 11), εἴδετε (T. R.) is supported by B¹Kא against ἴδετε, which is found in AB²L. In this case, however, εἴδετε, being coupled with ἠκούσατε, is undoubtedly the true reading.

*III. 6: φλογίζουσα τὸν τροχὸν (A. V. 'the course') τῆς γενέσεως] Without attempting to deal with the various explanations which have been given of this obscure phrase, we think that the word 'wheel' should be retained, and that Beza's idea is correct: 'Jacobus mihi videtur alludere ad rapiditatem circumactae rotae, suo motu flammam concipientis.' Strongly in favour of this idea is a passage quoted by Wetstein from Achmet. Onir. 160: εἰ δὲ ἴδῃ ὅτι ἤλαυνεν ἐν τῷ δίφρῳ, καὶ οἱ τροχοὶ ἐφλογί-σθησαν ἐκ τῆς ἐλάσεως, εὑρήσει νόσον.

III. 7: δαμάζεται] 'is tamed.' This meaning more properly belongs to ἡμεροῦται or τιθασεύεται; and perhaps the proposition itself, so stated, over-rates the 'taming' power of man. If we substitute 'subdued' for 'tamed,' both objections will be obviated. So the word is rendered Dan.

---

[1] [Cf. Ael. V. H. XIV. 6: προσέταττε δὲ ἐφήμερον τὴν γνώμην ἔχειν. Plut. Vit. Aemil. XXVII: τοὺς ἄρτι μυριάσι πεζῶν...ὁπλοφορουμένους βασιλεῖς ἐκ τῶν πολεμίων χειρῶν ἐφήμερα σιτία καὶ ποτὰ λαμβάνοντας.]

ii. 40: ὁ σίδηρος δαμάζει πάντα, 'iron subdues all things.' For the sentiment we may compare a beautiful fragment of the Aeolus of Euripides,
preserved by Plutarch, T. II. p. 959 C:

> Ἦ βραχύ τοι σθένος ἀνέρος·
> ἀλλὰ ποικιλίᾳ πραπίδων
> δαμᾷ φῦλα πόντου,
> χθονίων τ᾽ ἀερίων τε παιδεύματα.

IV. 9: **εἰς κατήφειαν**] 'to heaviness.' But 'heaviness' (λύπη Rom.
ix. 2, 2 Cor. ii. 1), we know, is 'in the heart of a man'; and it is the
outward expression of it in the countenance, 'gloominess,' which is
indicated by this word, as will appear from the following examples.
Plut. *Vit. Pelop.* XXXIII: σιγὴν δὲ καὶ κατήφειαν εἶναι τοῦ στρατοπέδου
παντός (on the death of Pelopidas). Dion. Hal. *Ant.* X. 59: εἰς πολλὴν
ἦλθε δυσθυμίαν καὶ κατήφειαν (despondency and dejection). Charit.
Aphrod. VI. 8: πρὸς δὲ τὴν φήμην κατήφεια πᾶσαν ἔσχε Βαβυλῶνα (these
tidings cast a gloom over the whole city[1]).

IV. 11: **μὴ καταλαλεῖτε ἀλλήλων**] A. V. 'Speak not evil one of
another.' R. V. 'Speak not one against another.' On behalf of the
former it may be urged, that to 'speak against another' may be said
of open accusations; whereas καταλαλεῖν is defined to be τὸ εἰς ἀπόντα
ὑπό τινων βλασφημεῖν, and κατάλαλοι are οἱ διαβολαῖς κατὰ τῶν ἀπόντων
ἀδεῶς κεχρημένοι. Hence καταλαλιαί is rightly rendered 'evil-speakings,'
1 Pet. ii. 1; 'backbitings,' 2 Cor. xii. 20; and κατάλαλοι 'backbiters,' Rom.
i. 30.

---

[1] [Cf. Dio Chrys. *Or.* XI. p. 174,
28: τήν τε νύκτα ἐκείνην τὴν χαλεπήν, καὶ
τὴν ἐν τῷ στρατοπέδῳ (of the Greeks at
Troy) κατήφειαν. Synes. *Ep.* 79, p.
227 C: ἀπάλλαξον κατηφείας Πτολεμαΐδα.]

I. PETER.

Chap. II. 5 : οἰκοδομεῖσθε] A. V. 'are built up. Or, *be ye built up*.' Dean Alford decides for the imperative, '*against* the Peschito Syriac (Etheridge : 'you also as living stones are builded') but *with* the same version (as commonly quoted).' The Syriac is ܠܒ̈ܢܐ ܗܝ̈ܟܠܐ ܗܘܘ ܐܬܒܢܘ, *aedificamini, et estote templa spiritualia.* Etheridge's translation would require ܐܬܒܢܘܬܘܢ.

IV. 12 : μὴ ξενίζεσθε τῇ ἐν ὑμῖν πυρώσει πρὸς πειρασμὸν ὑμῖν γινομένῃ] A. V. 'Think it not strange concerning the fiery trial which is to try you.' R. V....'concerning the fiery trial among you, which cometh upon you to prove you.' A better order would seem to be : τῇ πυρώσει (τῇ) γινομένῃ ἐν ὑμῖν πρὸς πειρασμὸν ὑμῖν (ὑμῶν). 'Be not surprised at the fiery trial which is taking place among you for to prove you.' On *v.* 8 ἡ ἀγάπη καλύπτει κ.τ.έ. I compare Prov. x. 12 : Ἀ. Θ., καὶ ἐπὶ πάσας ἀθεσίας καλύψει ἀγάπη. Stob. *Flor.* T. XXXVII. 27 : ΣΩΚΡΑΤΟΥΣ. Ἡ μὲν ἐσθὴς τὴν ἀρρυθμίαν, ἡ δὲ εὔνοια τὴν ἁμαρτίαν περιστέλλει (Hesych. Περιστέλλει· καλύπτει)[1].

---

[1] [Cf. Dio. Chrys. *Or.* LXVI. p. 604, 10: ὀψοφαγῶν μὲν ἢ πίνων ἢ ἐρῶν τινος αἰσχύνεται καὶ περιστέλλει τὴν ἀκρασίαν.]

II. PETER.

Chap. I. 1: τοῖς ἰσότιμον ἡμῖν λαχοῦσι πίστιν] A. V. 'To them that have obtained like precious faith with us.' R. V. agrees, with 'a like' for 'like,' and in marg. 'Gr. an equally precious.' Alford : 'of equal value.' All these renderings suppose that ἰσότιμος is a derivative of τιμή in the sense of *pretium*, like πολύτιμος, whereas both ἰσότιμος and ὁμότιμος invariably borrow their meaning from τιμή, *honor*. In ἰσότιμος the emphatic idea is *equality*. Ἰσοτιμία is properly *aequalitas honoris*, but comes to be used for *equality* in general, *par conditio et jus*[1]. Wetstein quotes from Joseph. *Ant*. XII. 3, 1: ἐν αὐτῇ τῇ μητροπόλει Ἀντιοχείᾳ πολιτείας αὐτοὺς (Judaeos) ἠξίωσε, καὶ τοῖς ἐνοικισθεῖσιν ἰσοτίμους ἀπέδειξε Μακεδόσι καὶ Ἕλλησι. On 1 Cor. vii. 4: ὁ ἀνὴρ τοῦ ἰδίου σώματος οὐκ ἐξουσιάζει, St Chrysostom's reflexion is: πολλὴ ἡ ἰσοτιμία, καὶ οὐδεμία πλεονεξία; and on Luke ii. 26: καὶ ἦν αὐτῷ κεχρηματισμένον ὑπὸ τοῦ πνεύματος, he remarks: ὁρᾷς τοῦ πνεύματος τὸ ἰσότιμον; ὥσπερ γὰρ ὁ θεὸς χρᾷ, οὕτω καὶ τὸ πνεῦμα τὸ ἅγιον. This being the only recognized meaning of the word, we must render, 'to those who have obtained an equal faith with us,' understanding by 'equal,' *equally privileged*, a faith which puts them on an equality with us, whether *us*, the Apostles, or, if addressed to Gentiles, *us* Jews. In the latter case, there seems to be an allusion to St Peter's action in the admission of the Gentiles to the privileges of the Gospel. See Acts xi. 17, xv. 9.

I. 12: διὸ οὐκ ἀμελήσω ὑμᾶς ἀεὶ ὑπομιμνήσκειν περὶ τούτων] The reading of the uncials ABCℵ is διὸ μελλήσω, which R. V. renders 'I shall be ready,' and Alford 'I will be sure'; but no example of any such use of μελλήσω is forthcoming. The Vulg. *incipiam* is open to the same objection. I think it not improbable that St Peter wrote διὸ μελήσω, 'I will take care,' a rare, but not unexampled construction for διὸ μελήσει μοι. The reading μελλήσω would then be a very common clerical error, and that of KL, οὐκ ἀμελήσω, a correction either for the unusual personal form μελήσω, or for the unintelligible μελλήσω, 'I will delay.' There is the same confusion about this word in the Greek Lexicographers. Thus Suidas has, correctly: Μελήσω· σπουδάσω, φροντίσω; but Hesychius: Μελλήσω· σπουδάσω ἢ ὑπερθῶμαι, and Photius: Μελλήσω· σπουδάσω, φροντίσω.

[1] [Cf. Lucian. *Hermot*. 24: αὐτίκα μάλα πολίτην ὄντα τοῦτον, ὅστις ἂν ᾖ, καὶ ἰσότιμον ἅπασιν.]

I. 19: καὶ ἔχομεν βεβαιότερον τὸν προφητικὸν λόγον] A. V. 'We have also a more sure word of prophecy.' R. V. 'And we have the word of prophecy *made* more sure.' Wetstein's explanation (from the Greek expositors) seems to agree with this: ' Sermo propheticus nunc firmior est, postquam eventu comprobatus fuit, quam ante eventum.' But as the phrase itself has not yet been illustrated from Greek authors, the following examples may be compared. Charit. Aphrod. III. 9: κἀγὼ βεβαιότερον ἔσχον τὸ θαρρεῖν. Chaeremon ap. Stob. *Flor.* T. LXXIX. 31 : βεβαιοτέραν ἔχε τὴν φιλίαν πρὸς τοὺς γονεῖς. Isocr. *ad Demon.* p. 10 A: ὥστε σοι συμβήσεται παρά τε τῷ πλήθει μᾶλλον εὐδοκιμεῖν, καὶ τὴν παρ' ἐκείνων (τῶν βασιλέων) εὔνοιαν βεβαιοτέραν ἔχειν. These instances are in favour of construing βεβαιότερον in the text as an adjective; but if we should prefer to take it as an adverb, we may do so without any perceptible alteration in the sense. At least the distinction taken by Dean Alford between the adjective, 'we possess a thing more secure,' and the adverb, 'we hold it faster,' is not borne out by the following examples of the latter construction. Demosth. p. 99. 29: οἵδε γὰρ ἀκριβῶς ὅτι οὐδ' ἂν πάντων τῶν ἄλλων γένηται κύριος, οὐδὲν ἔστ' αὐτῷ βεβαίως ἔχειν, ἕως ἂν ὑμεῖς δημοκρατῆσθε. Stob. *Flor.* T. CV. 55 : εἰ δέ τις ὑπείληφε βεβαίως ἔχειν τὸν πλοῦτον. Dion. Hal. *Ant.* XI. 40: ὧν ὑμῖν οὐδὲν ἔξεστι βεβαίως ἔχειν, ἕως ἂν ὑπὸ τῶν δέκα τυραννῆσθε.

II. 4: σειραῖς ζόφου] 'into chains of darkness.' For σειραῖς (Vulg. *rudentibus*, Pesch.]Δ‥ـ‥ـ, Philox. ‥ܘܘܣܪ‥ܩ (= σειρες i.e. σειραις)) the uncials ABCℵ read σειροῖς, from σειρός, σιρός, or σιρρός, 'a pit,' or 'excavation,' properly for the storage of grain, as Demosth. p. 100, 28: ἀλλὰ ταῦτα μὲν ἐάσειν ὑμᾶς ἔχειν, ὑπὲρ δὲ τῶν μελινῶν καὶ τῶν ὀλυρῶν τῶν ἐν τοῖς Θρᾳκίοις σιροῖς ἐν τῷ βαράθρῳ χειμάζειν; where the Scholiast: τοὺς θησαυροὺς καὶ τὰ ὀρύγματα, ἐν οἷς κατετίθεντο τὰ σπέρματα, σιροὺς ἐκάλουν οἱ Θρᾶκες καὶ οἱ Λιβύες. Philo *de Tel. Constr.* p. 86: τὰς δὲ κριθὰς δεῖ καὶ τοὺς πυροὺς ὡς βέλτιστα καθάραντας, καὶ σειροὺς ὡς βαθυτάτους ὑπαιθρίους ὀρύξαντας κ.τ.έ. And J. Pollux joins κατάγειοι οἰκήσεις, καὶ σειροί, καὶ φρέατα, καὶ λάκκοι. Dean Alford wrongly translates 'dens,' and says: 'The word is used for a *wolf's den* by Longus, I. 11': but he can never have read the passage, in which the method of trapping a she-wolf is thus described: συνελθόντες οὖν οἱ κωμῆται νύκτωρ, σιρροὺς ὀρύττουσι τὸ εὖρος ὀργυιᾶς, τὸ βάθος, τεσσάρων...ξύλα δὲ ξηρὰ μακρὰ τείναντες ὑπὲρ τοῦ χάσματος, τὸ περιττὸν τοῦ χώματος κατέπασαν κ.τ.έ.

II. 8: βλέμματι καὶ ἀκοῇ] 'in seeing and hearing.' This seems to be the only admissible interpretation, though quite at variance with the use of βλέμμα in good writers. Thus Demosthenes joins τῷ σχήματι, τῷ βλέμματι, τῇ φωνῇ, and for epithets we find βλέμμα κατεσταλμένον, μειλίχιον, δριμύ, ἥμερον, φαιδρόν. St Peter should have written either ὁράσει καὶ ἀκοῇ, or βλέπων καὶ ἀκούων.

K.　　　　　　　　　　　　　　　　　　　　　　　　　　16

II. 9: ἀδίκους δὲ εἰς ἡμέραν κρίσεως κολαζομένους τηρεῖν] A. V. 'And to reserve the unjust unto the day of judgment to be punished.' R. V. 'And to keep the unrighteous under punishment unto the day of judgment.' And so Dean Alford explains: 'Actually in a penal state, and awaiting their final punishment.' But if they are 'reserved unto the day of judgment,' it seems paradoxical to say that they are punished in the meantime; and *v.* 4, which is usually appealed to in defence of this paradox, only speaks of their *detention in prison* till the time of trial, an arrangement which is in accordance with the administration of justice amongst ourselves. The solution of the difficulty seems to be the same which Dean Alford himself has recourse to in another place (Ch. iii. 11: τούτων πάντων λυομένων, 'seeing that all these things are to be dissolved'), namely, that the present participle implies *destiny*. So, at least, the Vulg. understood its force in both texts—'iniquos vero in diem judicii reservare *cruciandos*'—'cum igitur haec omnia *dissolvenda* sint.' I compare Diod. Sic. XII. 17, where Charondas is said to have made a law that any person proposing to amend an existing law, should come forward with a halter round his neck, and so continue ἄχρις ἂν ὅτου τὴν κρίσιν ὁ δῆμος περὶ τοῦ διορθουμένου νόμου (the law to be amended) ποιήσηται.

*III. 5: καὶ γῆ ἐξ ὕδατος καὶ δι' ὕδατος συνεστῶσα] A. V. 'And the earth standing (Gr. *consisting*) out of the water and in the water.' R. V. 'And an earth compacted out of water and amidst (Or, *through*) water.' Neither of these is satisfactory. Συνεστῶσα is 'consisting,' as in Col. i. 17: 'by him all things consist (συνέστηκε),' not 'compacted' (συμβιβαζόμενον, Eph. iv. 16). Compare Diog. Laert. III. 1, 73: συνεστάναι δὲ τὸν κόσμον ἐκ πυρός, ὕδατος, ἀέρος, γῆς. Stob. *Flor.* T. LXXX. 14: τί μοι μέλει, φησί, πότερον ἐξ ἀτόμων, ἢ ἐξ ἀμερῶν, ἢ ἐκ πυρὸς καὶ γῆς συνέστηκε τὰ ὄντα; If we translate, 'And the earth consisting out of water and by means of water,' we must understand 'consisting' with a slight difference of meaning, *put together* and *held together*, according as it is construed with ἐξ ὕδατος or δι' ὕδατος. Oecumenius explains the matter thus: Ἡ γῆ ἐξ ὕδατος μέν, ὡς ἐξ ὑλικοῦ αἰτίου· δι' ὕδατος δέ, ὡς διατελικοῦ (I would read διὰ τελικοῦ SC. αἰτίου)· ὕδωρ γὰρ τὸ συνέχον τὴν γῆν, οἷον κόλλα τις ὑπάρχον αὐτῇ. Or we may understand δι' ὕδατος, not of the conglutinating power of water upon the particles of which the earth is composed (as Oecumenius), but of its external pressure upon the mass of the earth.

III. 8: ἐν δὲ τοῦτο μὴ λανθανέτω ὑμᾶς] A. V. 'Be not ignorant of this one thing.' R. V. 'Forget not this one thing.' The very common formula, μηδὲ τοῦθ' ὑμᾶς λανθανέτω, is not one of reminding the hearers of something they knew already, but serves as an introduction to a new topic, to which the orator is desirous to call their attention: literally, 'let it not escape your notice.' The A. V. therefore seems here preferable to the corrected rendering.

I. JOHN.

*Chap. III. 1: ἵνα τέκνα θεοῦ κληθῶμεν + καὶ ἐσμεν] R.V. 'and *such* we are.' Alford 'and we are *so*.' But it seems a gloss. Hort and Westcott adopt it, but without annotation. Philox.: ܘܢܗܘܐ ܐܝܬܝܢ ܐܠܗܐ (καὶ ὦμεν). Pesch. *qui filios vocavit nos* (ܩܪܢ) *et fecit nos* (ܘܥܒܕܢ). Compare Just. Mart. *Dial. c. Try.* 123: καὶ θεοῦ τέκνα καλούμεθα καί ἐσμεν. Synes. *Ep.* 57, p. 192 C: ἐστίν τε καὶ νομίζεται.

III. 20: ὅτι ἐὰν καταγινώσκῃ ἡμῶν ἡ καρδία, ὅτι μείζων ἐστὶν ὁ θεὸς κ.τ.ἑ.] The difficulty is in the second ὅτι, which is ignored by the Vulgate and A. V. The Revisers (after Hoogeveen, *De Partic.* p. 589 ed. Schütz. and others) point ὅ,τι ἐὰν in the first clause, which they join with the preceding verse: 'and shall assure our heart before him, whereinsoever our heart condemn us; because God' &c. But this is quite inadmissible, since nothing can be plainer than that ἐὰν καταγινώσκῃ (*v.* 20) and ἐὰν μὴ καταγινώσκῃ (*v.* 21) are both *in protasi*, and in strict correlation with each other. Dean Alford suggests an ellipsis of the verb substantive before the second ὅτι, and would translate: 'Because if our heart condemn us, (it is) because God' &c. He instances such cases as εἴ τις ἐν Χριστῷ, (he is) καινὴ κτίσις, which are quite dissimilar; but the following from St Chrysostom (T. X. p. 122 B) fully bears out this construction: Ὁ ζυγός μου χρηστὸς κ.τ.ἑ., εἰ δὲ οὐκ αἰσθάνῃ τῆς κουφότητος, ΟΤΙ προθυμίαν ἐρρωμένην οὐκ ἔχεις; where I have expunged δῆλον before ὅτι on the authority of three out of four MSS. collated for these Homilies, the fourth, with the old Latin version, for ὅτι προθυμίαν reading μὴ θαυμάσῃς· προθυμίαν γάρ. In my note on that place I have pointed out that the ellipsis is not of δῆλον, but of τὸ αἴτιον, *causa est, quia*. So in the present instance we might translate: 'For if our heart condemn us, (the reason is) because God is greater' &c., were it not for the difficulty of explaining how the fact of God's being greater than our heart can be valid reason for our heart condemning us. I would, therefore, take the second ὅτι for *quod*, not *quia*, and suppose an ellipsis of δῆλον, as in 1 Tim. vi. 7, where see note.

JUDE.

Verse 9: οὐκ ἐτόλμησε κρίσιν ἐπενεγκεῖν βλασφημίας] Comparing this text with 2 Pet. ii. 11: οὐ φέρουσι κατ᾽ αὐτῶν βλάσφημον κρίσιν, all our English translators have arrived at the same conclusion, that Michael the archangel 'durst not bring a railing accusation' against the devil on the occasion alluded to. Even Dean Alford, whose antipathy to 'silly hendiadyses' and 'wretched adjectival renderings' is so marked, is here forced to give way, explaining κρίσιν βλασφημίας to be 'a sentence savouring of, or belonging to, βλασφημία, a railing accusation,' adding (against Calovius, who translates 'ultionem de blasphemia sumere') that 'the blasphemy is not one spoken by, but against the devil.' But if (as the Dean justly observes with reference to σπιλάδες (v. 12) and σπίλοι (2 Pet. ii. 13)) 'each passage must stand on its own ground,' we have only to enquire what is the meaning conveyed by the Greek phrase ἐπενεγκεῖν κρίσιν (αἰτίαν, δίκην) τινὶ (κατά τινος). This is, undoubtedly, 'to bring an accusation, or lay an information, against any one.' Compare (besides Acts xxv. 18) the following examples, furnished by a single Greek author. Diod. Sic. XVI. 29: (Θηβαῖοι) δίκην ἐπήνεγκαν εἰς ᾿Αμφικτύονας κατὰ τῶν Σπαρτιατῶν (laying the damages at 500 talents). XX. 10: καὶ κρίσεις ἀδίκους ἐπιφέροντες διὰ τὸν φθόνον, τιμωρίαις περιβάλλουσι. 62: ὁ δὲ φοβηθεὶς τὰς ἐπιφερομένας εὐθύνας καὶ κρίσεις, ἀπεχώρησεν εἰς τὴν Γέλαν. Id. T. X. p. 171, ed. Bip.: οἱ καθυβρισθέντες ἐπήνεγκαν κρίσιν τῷ Σατουρνίνῳ περὶ τῆς εἰς αὐτοὺς ὕβρεως. In the last case the accusation might be described as a κρίσις ὕβρεως; here it is a κρίσις βλασφημίας. To understand wherein the 'blasphemy' consisted, we should have to enter into the fruitless enquiry, which, among the various traditions relating to this subject, was the one followed by the Writer of this Epistle. Several of these are to be found in Cramer's Catena, as, for instance, that the devil claimed the body as being lord of matter (ὅτι ἐμὸν τὸ σῶμα, ὡς τῆς ὕλης δεσπόζοντι); that he charged Moses with being a murderer, because he slew the Egyptian &c. We have said enough to show that the literal rendering, 'durst not bring against him an accusation of blasphemy,' is the true one; and that instead of bringing St Jude's phraseology into conformity with St Peter's, it would be better to explain βλάσφημον κρίσιν in the sense which we have now asserted for κρίσιν βλασφημίας.

REVELATION.

*Chap. XIX. 5: αἰνεῖτε τὸν θεὸν ἡμῶν, πάντες οἱ δοῦλοι αὐτοῦ, καὶ οἱ φοβούμενοι αὐτόν, καὶ οἱ μικροὶ καὶ οἱ μεγάλοι] A. V. 'Praise our God, all ye his servants, and ye that fear him, both small and great.' For this incomparable rendering, the Revisers have given us: 'Give praise to our God, all ye his servants, ye that fear him, the small and the great': thus illustrating the two principal faults with which they have been charged, *unnecessary changes*, and *want of ear*. As to the latter, the most un-practised reader cannot fail to be sensible of the rhythmical inferiority of the revised rendering; and the sole ground for the necessity of the change rests upon a various reading of τῷ θεῷ for τὸν θεόν, a rare construction of αἰνεῖν with the dative, which makes no difference at all to the English reader, and for which a Greek writer would probably have said ΔΟΤΕ ΑΙΝΟΝ ΤΩΙ ΘΕΩΙ.

IS 'CONVERSION' A SCRIPTURAL TERM?[1]

Non aliunde dissidia in religione dependent, quam ab ignoratione grammaticae.
JOSEPHUS SCALIGER.

IT is remarkable that the word CONVERSION, which, in the religious phraseology of the day, meets us at every turn, occurs but once in the Authorised Version (A. V.) of the canonical Scriptures; and then not of individuals, as now commonly used, but of an entire class, one, in fact, of the two great classes, into which, in regard to their religious condition, the whole world was divided. We read in Acts xv. 3, that Paul and Barnabas, on their way from Antioch to Jerusalem, 'passed through Phenice and Samaria, declaring *the conversion of the Gentiles;* and they caused great joy unto all the brethren.' The Greek word (ἐπιστροφή) signifies *a turning;* and what kind of a turning is intended, is expressly declared in ver. 19: 'Wherefore my sentence is, that we trouble not them, which from among the Gentiles *are turning* (ἐπιστρέφουσιν, not ἐπέστρεψαν) *to God.*' All our English versions, from Tyndale to A. V., agree in the use of the word in this place; and there seems no objection to the retaining of it, if it be clearly understood that this conversion was the act of the Gentiles themselves, who, under the influence of the Holy Spirit (which in this whole enquiry must never be lost sight of) and the preaching of the two Apostles, '*turned* (ἐπέστρεψαν) to God from idols, to serve the living and true God, and to wait for his Son from heaven' (1 Thess. i. 9, 10).

But (it may be said) although the noun itself is nowhere to be found with reference to the conversion of a sinner, yet the verb with which it is connected is often so employed; and one text in particular (Matt. xviii. 3) is sure to be brought forward in connexion with this subject: 'Except ye BE CONVERTED, and become as little children, ye shall not enter into the kingdom of heaven.' As this text is clearly distinguishable from all others which will come under our consideration in this paper, it may be as well to dispose of it in the first instance.

It is distinguishable, first, in the use of the general word στραφῆτε instead of the special term ἐπιστρέψητε; and, secondly, in the *limited*

---

[1] Cf. note on Matt. xiii. 15. Ed.

nature of the so-called conversion, which is here intended. The *verbal* distinction was recognized by our older translators; as Wycliffe, 'but ye be turned'; Coverdale, Cranmer, and Geneva, 'except ye turn'; the Rhemish (a Roman Catholic) version alone, following the Vulgate, and unfortunately followed by A. V., 'except ye be converted.' In deciding between the two renderings, 'except ye *turn*,' and 'except ye *be turned*,' the *passive* form of the original word might be urged in favour of the latter. But this would be a mistake. Though ἐστράφην, according to the grammarians, is the second aorist *passive*, the *usus loquendi*, from which there is no appeal, has determined otherwise, and assigned to this passive form what is technically called a *middle* force, the agent being himself the object of the action performed[1]. We must therefore translate: 'Except ye *turn*, and become as little children.'—But a still more important objection to the use of the word *conversion* in this place, is the *partial* nature of the change proposed, not from sin to holiness, but from the self-seeking and ambitious views which prompted the question, 'Who is the greatest in the kingdom of heaven?' to the opposite dispositions. Theophylact explains this change from φιλοδοξία to ταπεινοφροσύνη as a *going back* to their former state of mind, when they were children: δεῖ οὖν στραφῆναι πάλιν ἐκεῖσε. Later expositors, who retain the word *converted*, explain it in a similar sense. Thus the good old nonconformist Doddridge: '*Except ye be converted*, and turned from these ambitious and carnal views, *and become*, &c.'; and the evangelical Thomas Scott: 'Though all the Apostles, except Judas, were at this time regenerate, and "converted" in the general sense of the word, yet they all needed a very great change in respect of their ambition and carnal emulation.'

[1] E.g. Matt. vii. 6: 'Lest they *turn again* and rend you (στραφέντες ῥήξωσιν).' Luke vii. 9: 'He *turned him about*, and said (στραφεὶς εἶπεν).' Joh. xx. 14: 'She *turned herself* back (ἐστράφη εἰς τὰ ὀπίσω).' Acts vii. 39: 'And in their hearts *turned back again* (ἐστράφησαν) into Egypt.' The usage of the Septuagint version of the O. T. is the same; as Job xli. 16 (Heb. 25): 'When he (Leviathan) *turneth himself* (στραφέντος αὐτοῦ), the four-footed wild beasts are afraid.' 1 Kings (Sam.) xiv. 47: 'Whithersoever he *turned himself* (οὗ ἂν ἐστράφη), he vexed them.' A notable example is Psal. cxiv. 3: 'The sea saw it, and fled; Jordan *was driven back* (בֹּסֹי).' So A. V.; but LXX., ἐστράφη εἰς τὰ ὀπίσω, turned back *again;* and that Jordan (personified) was himself the agent, appears not only from the parallel word 'fled,' but also from ver. 5: 'What ailed thee, O thou sea, that thou fleddest? thou, Jordan, that thou turnedst back?' The Hebrew בֹּסֹי is also reflective, *vertit se;* as in Prov. xxvi. 14: 'As the door *turneth* (בֹּסֹי, στρέφεται) upon its hinges &c.'—An exception may be noted, when the verb is followed by εἰς with a noun expressing that *into* which any thing *is changed;* as Exod. vii. 15: 'The rod which *was turned* to a serpent (τὴν στραφεῖσαν εἰς ὄφιν)'; and 1 Kings (Sam.) x. 6: 'Thou shalt *be turned* into another man (στραφήσῃ εἰς ἄνδρα ἄλλον).'

Returning to ἐπιστρέψαι, we observe that the cardinal text on which this enquiry turns is Isai. vi. 10: 'Lest they see with their eyes, and hear with their ears, and understand with their heart, and *convert* (ἐπιστρέψωσι), and be healed.' This is three times quoted in the N. T., Matt. xiii. 15, John xii. 40 (with ἐπιστραφῶσι or στραφῶσι), and Acts xxviii. 27. In all three places A. V. substitutes 'be converted' for 'convert,' herein agreeing with the older English versions, except that in the first place Tyndale has 'should turn,' and Geneva 'should return.' Now with respect to the usage of the LXX., we find that the Hebrew words שׁוּב, *to return*, and הָשֵׁב, *to cause to return*, are both rendered by ἐπιστρέψαι, which is, therefore, to be taken in the former case in an *intransitive*, and in the latter in a *transitive* sense, as is also common in classical Greek. Occasionally both senses are found in the same sentence; as 2 Kings (Sam.) xvii. 3: 'I will *bring back* (ἐπιστρέψω) all the people unto thee, as a bride *returns* (ἐπιστρέφει) to her husband'; and Jerem. xxxviii. (xxxi.) 18: Ἐπίστρεψόν με, καὶ ἐπιστρέψω. In the texts before us we are concerned only with the *intransitive* sense, which is found in the following places, selected with a view to the variety of renderings adopted by our Translators. Zach. i. 3: '*Turn* (ἐπιστρέψατε) ye unto me, and I will *turn* unto you.' Ezek. xviii. 32: '*Turn yourselves* (ἐπιστρέψατε), and live ye.' Mal. iii. 7: '*Return* (ἐπιστρέψατε) unto me, and I will *return* unto you.' 1 Kings viii. 33: 'When thy people Israel be smitten down before the enemy, because they have sinned against thee, and shall *turn again* (ἐπιστρέψουσι) to thee, and confess thy name, and pray.'—In all these places A. V. is in accordance with the Hebrew and Greek in representing the act as that of a free agent; not so in Jerem. xxxi. 18: 'Turn thou me, and so shall I *be turned*.' For this 'being turned' has the obvious effect of removing the act from the province of the Will, and making the latter clause identical with the former, from which it is plainly intended to be distinguished. When I pray to God, 'Turn thou me,' I make a clear acknowledgment of the necessity of divine influence, or (as it is expressed in Art. X.) of 'the grace of God preventing me that I may have a good will'; and when I add, 'and so shall I *turn*,' I assert the freedom of my own will, against the unscriptural notion of the *irresistible operation of divine grace*. The same remark applies even more strongly to the A. V. of Matt. xiii. 15, 'and should understand with their heart, and *be converted*,' inasmuch as this expression, from its being employed in this and similar passages, has acquired a more technical and dogmatical sense than the other, and is therefore more liable to misconstruction. For all these reasons it seems desirable, that both in the original passage [1], and

---

[1] In the original passage of Isaiah, our Translators (or rather Coverdale, who preceded them) seem to have used the verb 'to convert' in an intransitive sense, in close imitation of the Greek ἐπιστρέψαι; and so Cranmer's version of Acts iii. 19: 'Repent and *convert* (ἐπιστρέψατε).' But this usage is now obsolete.

in the N. T. citations of it, we should adopt one or other of the more familiar renderings, 'and should *turn, return,* or *turn again.*' Even so the honour due to 'God our Saviour' is fully reserved. *Finis coronat opus.* All that has preceded is only preparatory to the final consummation, 'and I SHOULD HEAL them[1].'

The few remaining texts in which this word is introduced may be conveniently taken in the order in which they occur in the Old and New Testaments.

Psal. xix. 7: 'The law of the Lord is perfect, *converting the soul.*' In the Hebrew this is a peculiar combination, which has nothing to do with the conversion of a sinner. A better translation, *restoring the soul,* has a place in the margin here, and in the text of Psal. xxiii. 3. The literal rendering, 'making the soul to come again,' may be seen in the margin of Lam. i. 11.

Psal. li. 13: 'Sinners shall *be converted* (ἐπιστρέψουσιν) unto thee.' This case follows the determination of Isai. vi. 10.

Isai. lx. 5: 'The abundance of the sea shall *be converted* unto thee.' Here both Hebrew and Greek (יֵהָפֵךְ, μεταβαλεῖ) are different from former examples. We may translate 'shall be turned unto thee,' in the sense of 'shall be transferred unto thee,' comparing Lam. v. 2: 'Our inheritance *is turned* (נֶהֶפְכָה) unto strangers.'

Luke xxii. 32: 'And when thou *art converted* (ἐπιστρέψας) strengthen thy brethren.' Here some Roman Catholic expositors (as Maldonatus, refuted by Casaubon in his *Exercitationes Anti-Baron.* p. 640 [p. 520, ed. 1615]), to avoid the application to the chief of the Apostles of what might seem a derogatory term, would join ἐπιστρέψας στήρισον, *return and strengthen,* i.e. by a common Hebraism, *again strengthen,* comparing Psal. lxxxiv. (lxxxv.) 6: σὺ ἐπιστρέψας ζωώσεις ἡμᾶς. This is a legitimate construction, but unnecessary in the present instance. The meaning is perfectly plain, 'when thou art come to thyself,' *quum ad sanam mentem redieris,* ἀποκαταστὰς (says Euthymius Zigabenus) πάλιν εἰς τὴν πρώτην τάξιν.

There remains only James v. 19, 20: 'If any of you do err (πλανηθῇ) from the truth, and one *convert* (ἐπιστρέψῃ) him; let him know that he which *converteth* (ἐπιστρέψας) a sinner from the error (πλάνης) of his way &c.' Here we have an instance of the *transitive* use of ἐπιστρέψαι

---

[1] In John xii. 40 the substitution by the Evangelist of ἐπιστραφῶσι or στραφῶσι for ἐπιστρέψωσι might seem to favour, in that passage at least, the version 'be turned,' or 'be converted.' But what has been said of the *middle* force of στραφῆναι is equally true of ἐπιστραφῆναι, the use of which in the LXX. is in no respect distinguishable from the *intransitive* use of ἐπιστρέψαι. Thus in Lam. v. 21 instead of καὶ ἐπιστρέψομεν we have καὶ ἐπιστραφησόμεθα; and in Zach. i. 3, and Mal. iii. 7, God says: ἐπιστρέψατε πρὸς μέ, καὶ ἐπιστραφήσομαι πρὸς ὑμᾶς. Compare also Amos iv. 6 with verse 8 in the Hebrew and Greek.

(Heb. הָשֵׁב), *to cause another to return*, which is also found in Luke i. 16: 'And many of the children of Israel shall he *turn* (ἐπιστρέψει) to the Lord their God'; and in Acts xxvi. 18: 'To *turn* (ἐπιστρέψαι) them from darkness to light.' Being here used in connexion with *going astray*, we are reminded of the figure of a lost sheep, which is to be *brought back* to the fold, either by (ὑπὸ) the Great Shepherd himself, as the *primary*, or by (διὰ) one of those employed by him, as the *secondary* or *instrumental* agent in his restoration. In the latter case (which is here intended) we may aptly compare Ezek. xxxiv. 4, where it is laid to the charge of the shepherds of Israel, τὸ πλανώμενον οὐκ ἐπεστρέψατε, 'neither have ye *brought again* that which was lost.' Although the use of the word 'to convert' is not here liable to the same theological objection as before (since no one would think of attributing an irresistible power to mere human agency) we cannot help thinking that a more familiar term, as *bringing back*, would be more appropriate to the words πλάνη and πλανᾶσθαι; in which opinion we find ourselves anticipated by an expositor who cannot be supposed to have had any prejudice against the popular idea of conversion, Doddridge, who thus paraphrases the passage: 'If any of you do wander from the truth, and one *turn him back* to it, let him know that he that *turneth back* a sinner &c.'

On the whole, while protesting against that indiscriminate and fanatical use of the word, which is now so much in vogue, we would not be understood to deny that CONVERSION itself is a real fact, and the term, when rightly understood, both convenient and appropriate. We will not say, *indispensable*, because we find that in many cases, to which, in later phraseology, the word would be thought specially applicable, the writers of Scripture, if they do not avoid the use of it, have certainly employed other words in preference. Thus, we do not read that Zacchaeus was *converted* by the preaching of Christ, or the three thousand on the day of Pentecost by that of Peter, or 'a great company of the priests' by that of Stephen, or the gaoler by the stirring appeal of Paul, or Lydia by his more argumentative discourse. Even the conversion of Paul himself, though fulfilling every possible condition of a genuine conversion, is not described by that particular term in any one of the many places of Holy Writ in which it is alluded to. Yet in this and other instances, even up to the present day, of sudden and extraordinary changes in the state of mind of individuals in regard to religion, we certainly want a name to distinguish such cases from the experience of ordinary Christians; and we may therefore without impropriety, on a worthy occasion, allude to a conversion from infidelity, or a conversion from sin. Again, to speak of the conversion of the heathen, or the conversion of the Jews, or of any body of men, whom it is sought to bring over from their former ignorance or error to the true faith, if it be 'done with charity,' should give no offence. But when conversion is insisted upon as universally necessary in order to a state of salvation—when preachers divide their hearers, being believers in a common Christianity, into the two classes of 'converted' and 'unconverted'—when the former class are led to cherish overweening ideas of their acceptance with God, and of their assurance of eternal salvation; and the latter are either driven to despair of their spiritual state, or else, without any real change of heart, to adopt the phraseology and exhibit the outward signs and badges of the 'converted';—a candid enquiry, how far such views of CONVERSION are consistent with a 'discreet and learned' ministration of the Word of God, can never be deemed superfluous or inopportune[1].

---

[1] This note was printed in form of a pamphlet in October, 1876. See p. xv. Ed.

ACTS OF THE APOSTLES.

*XX. 24[1]: 'Αλλ' οὐδενὸς λόγον ποιοῦμαι, οὐδὲ ἔχω τὴν ψυχήν μου τιμίαν ἐμαυτῷ, ὡς τελειῶσαι τὸν δρόμον μου κ.τ.ἑ.] A. V.: 'But none of these things move me, neither count I my life dear unto myself, so that I might finish my course' &c.

The variations of the principal MSS. are as follows :—

B, C, א[1]: ἀλλ' οὐδενὸς λόγου ποιοῦμαι τὴν ψυχὴν τιμίαν ἐμαυτῷ.

A, D, א[3]: ἀλλ' οὐδενὸς λόγον ἔχω [+μοι D] οὐδὲ ποιοῦμαι τὴν ψυχὴν (+μόυ D) τιμίαν ἐμαυτῷ (-τοῦ D[1]).

E, H, L, P agree with T. R., except that L, P omit μου after ψυχήν.

Of the Latin versions Lucifer Calaritanus (A.D. 354–367) has the shorter reading: *Sed pro nihilo aestimo animam meam caram esse mihi;* Cod. D the longer : *Sed nihil horum cura est mihi, neque habeo ipsam animam caram mihi.* The Vulgate (whose authority Dean Alford unaccountably claims for the absence of οὐδὲ ἔχω) has : *Sed nihil horum vereor[2], nec facio animam meam pretiosiorem quam me;* a free translation (it would appear) of the reading of A or D.

The Syriac Peschito version is the shortest of all: *Sed mihi nihili aestimatur anima mea* (ܐܢ̈ܐ ܚܝܐ ܠܐ ܠܝ ܚܫܝܒܐ ܗܘܐ ܡܕܡ). Still the translator may have had before him the whole reading of B, because the words τιμίαν ἐμαυτῷ add nothing to the sense contained in the preceding part of the clause. The Philoxenian Syriac agrees with T. R., somewhat more freely translated than is usual with this version : ܐܢ̈ܐ ܘܠܐ

ܣܪܝ ܡܕܡܐܟܐ ܚܕ ܐܢܐ ܐܦܠܐ ܚܫܝܒܐ ܠܝ ܢܦܫܐ ܕܝܠܝ ܡܕܡ ܝܩܝܪܐ, which may be thus Graecised : ἀλλ' οὐδένα (not οὐδενὸς, as White) λόγον ποιοῦμαι, οὐδὲ λελόγισταί μοι ψυχή μου τι τίμιον.

St Chrysostom, in his Commentary on the Acts (A.D. 401), quotes vv. 22–24 in exact accordance with T. R., from which, however, no certain conclusion can be drawn, since we do not possess a critical edition of this work, and Matthaei found no MS. of it in the Moscow collection. Still there is no reason to doubt that his text agreed with

---

[1] Cf. p. 132 f. The note here re-printed appeared in form of a pamphlet in March, 1875. See p. xv. Ed.

[2] As St Jerome here translates λόγον ποιοῦμαι (or ἔχω) by *vereor*, so in his Latin translation of the LXX. version of Job (xxii. 4), as the equivalent for λόγον σου ποιούμενος ἐλέγξει σε, he gives: *timens te arguet te.*

T. R. at least as far as relates to the clause, οὐδὲ ἔχω κ.τ.ἑ., since he twice repeats those words with a slight variation (οὐκ ἔχω τιμίαν τὴν ἐμαυτοῦ ψυχήν) in his explanation of the passage (Opp. T. IX. pp. 332 C, 334 B).

In support of the longer reading it may be argued a priori, that it suits the context better. In the preceding verse the speaker had mentioned δεσμά and θλίψεις, but not death. It seems probable, therefore, that before expressing his contempt for life itself, he should have alluded to these minor evils ; just as in the next chapter (xxi. 13), upon Agabus foretelling his imprisonment at Jerusalem, he replies: *I am ready not to be bound only, but also to die* &c.

Modern critics, however, in deference to the authority of the older MSS., and to certain critical canons, which prescribe that preference should be given to the *shorter* and *more difficult* reading over the *longer* and *easier* one, have decided that the T. R. in this passage is to be replaced by that which is contained in those older MSS.

I. In regard to the *difficulty* of this reading, that term seems hardly applicable to the present case. A *difficult* reading is one which presents something apparently incongruous in the sense, or anomalous in the construction, which an ignorant or half-learned copyist would endeavour, by the use of such critical faculty as he possessed, to remove; but which a true critic is able, by probable explanation, and a comparison of similar cases, to defend against all such fancied improvements. In the reading before us, ἀλλ' οὐδενὸς λόγου ποιοῦμαι τὴν ψυχὴν τιμίαν ἐμαυτῷ, it is the construction, and not the sense, which is in question ; and this is not simply *difficult*, but *impossible*. There is really no way of getting over it; it baffles novices and experts alike. Let us see how it has fared with the latter.

1. Dr Tischendorf, in his edition of the A. V. (Tauchnitz, 1869), has this curious note on the place : 'S V [i.e. ℵ, B] : *But on no account do I hold my life dear unto myself, that I might finish my course.*' The error is excusable in a foreigner ; but his English assistant ought to have informed him, that 'ON no account' and 'OF no account' bear a totally different meaning ; and that the Greek answering to his proposed version would be : ἀλλ' οὐδαμῶς ποιοῦμαι τὴν ψυχὴν τιμίαν ἐμαυτῷ.

2. Dean Alford, in his *Revision of the A. V.* (London, 1870), translates the shorter reading thus : *But I count my life of no value unto myself, so that I finish* &c.; a version which (as was remarked of the Peschito) is not more than is required to satisfy the Greek, ἀλλ' οὐδενὸς λόγου ποιοῦμαι τὴν ψυχήν, the words τιμίαν ἐμαυτῷ being left untranslated. In the notes to his Greek Testament he says : 'The best rendering in English would be, *I hold my life of no account, nor precious to me;*' in which, if the tautology might be pardoned, the interpolation of the copula

before τιμίαν shows clearly that this reading cannot be construed as a *single* clause, but must be broken up into two ; and if by οὐδέ, why not by οὐδὲ ἔχω? He also suggests, in explanation of the constructional difficulty, that 'the clause in question is a combination of *two* constructions, οὐδενὸς λόγου ποιοῦμαι τὴν ψυχὴν ἐμαυτοῦ, and οὐ ποιοῦμαι τὴν ψυχὴν τιμίαν ἐμαυτῷ.' Such combinations, no doubt, are to be found, a simple instance of which is Acts xi. 17 : ἐγὼ δὲ τίς ἤμην δυνατὸς κωλῦσαι τὸν θεόν; which is an amalgamation of two forms in which the question might have been put : τίς ἤμην ἵνα κωλύσαιμι τὸν θεόν, and πῶς ἤμην δυνατὸς κωλῦσαι τὸν θεόν. But the present example is quite different. In it the original construction is not only begun, but concluded. After ἀλλ' οὐδενὸς λόγου ποιοῦμαι τὴν ψυχήν nothing more is required ; and the other two words τιμίαν ἐμαυτῷ are a mere *pannus assutus*, spoiling the construction without adding anything to the sense.

II. The *shortness* of a reading may arise from two causes. Either the reading with which it is compared may have been interpolated for reasons which generally appear on the face of it ; or some words may have accidentally dropped out from the longer text, which usually happens from the similar endings of two words not far distant from each other, the eye of the copyist passing over the intermediate words. Such an accident commonly betrays itself by the want of coherence in the parts of the sentence thus improperly brought into contact ; they do not *join on* together. This is just what we observe in the case before us. An accomplished critic, even if he knew of no other reading, would pronounce at once : *Mendi aliquid hic latet, lacunam suspicor.* He would probably detect the source of the error, the fusion of two members into one; of which he would be pretty sure that ἀλλ' οὐδενὸς λόγου ποιοῦμαι belonged to the first, and τιμίαν ἐμαυτῷ to the second ; leaving it doubtful to which of the two τὴν ψυχήν should be assigned. Now let him be informed that the MSS. which he has been using are not the *only* authorities for settling the text, but that there are other ancient MSS. which confirm his suspicion, and make the construction *sartam tectam* by the insertion of two words *before* τὴν ψυχήν ; and I think he would hardly entertain a doubt, that the accidental omission, if not of these identical words, at least of *something similar to them*, furnished the true solution of the difficulty.

Assuming, then, the probable existence of a *lacuna* between ποιοῦμαι and τὴν ψυχήν, we may proceed to enquire how it may most satisfactorily be supplied.

No shorter or easier method can be proposed than that which is suggested by the reading of the other uncials ; a *negative copula*, and a *verb*, the latter in the same mood, tense, &c. as that in the former clause. Is ἔχω that verb? As far as the language is concerned, there can be no objection to it. Some critics have denied that ἔχω *per se* is ever used in the sense of *aestimo*[1]; but all they seem to contend for is, that the idea of *possession* is not to be excluded from such examples as ὅτι ὡς προφήτην αὐτὸν εἶχον—εἰ οὖν ἐμὲ ἔχεις κοινωνόν—καὶ τοὺς τοιούτους ἐντίμους ἔχετε (*tales doctores* possidete *ita ut eos honoretis*)[2]; which may be easily conceded so long as the use itself is not disputed. We have the very phrase τίμιον ἔχειν in Dion. Hal. *Ant. Rom.* x. 5 : Οἱ μὲν οὖν πατρίκιοι τίμιον αὐτὸν ἐπὶ τούτοις εἶχον· οἱ δ᾽ ἐκ τοῦ δήμου πάντων δὴ μάλιστα αὐτὸν ἀνθρώπων ἐμίσουν. To which it may be added that if this use of ἔχειν should be held to be not of the purest Greek, it is not on that account less likely to have found a place, along with ἔχε με παρῃτημένον, and other undoubted Latinisms, in the writings of St Luke. The real obstacle to our acquiescing in the reading of T. R. is, that if the words οὐδὲ ἔχω had once formed a part of the original text, there is no possibility of accounting for the subsequent omission of them. This is an insuperable objection, but it does not apply to other supplements in which the verb is of the *middle* voice, so forming a clear ὁμοιοτέλευτον with ποιοῦμαι. Of these there are at least *four* : ποιοῦμαι, λογίζομαι, τίθεμαι, and ἡγοῦμαι.

1. If St Luke originally wrote, ἀλλ᾽ οὐδενὸς λόγον **ποιοῦμαι**, οὐδὲ **ποιοῦμαι** τὴν ψυχὴν τιμίαν ἐμαυτῷ, the cause of the *lacuna* in B, C, א is patent ; and we might then have accounted for the readings of the other uncials by supposing that the copyists, for the sake of variety, had substituted ἔχω for ποιοῦμαι in one or other of the two clauses. Still it must be confessed to be highly improbable that so correct a writer as the author of the Acts of the Apostles, in this, one of the most finished portions of his work, should have repeated the same word, when he had others equally suitable at his command.

2. One of these is λογίζομαι, a word frequently used in similar phrases in the Greek Bible[3]. But if this had been the word, we might, perhaps, have expected (though not absolutely necessary) the insertion of ὡς before τιμίαν, or of εἶναι after it, agreeably to St Paul's use, οὕτως ἡμᾶς λογιζέσθω ἄνθρωπος ὡς ὑπηρέτας Χριστοῦ—λογίζεσθε ἑαυτοὺς νεκροὺς μὲν εἶναι τῇ ἁμαρτίᾳ[4]—and in other places.

3. The use of τίθεμαι in such phrases as μέγα τίθεσθαι, παρ᾽ οὐδὲν τίθεσθαι, δεύτερον τίθεσθαί τι τινός &c. is well known ; and with respect to this word it is worthy of observation that St Chrysostom in his Homilies on the Epistle to the Hebrews, in alluding to this very text, actually employs it in preference to ἔχω. His words are (Opp. T. XII. p. 45 C): ἀλλὰ ταῦτα μικρὰ τῷ μηδὲ τὴν ψυχὴν τιμίαν τιθεμένῳ, κατὰ τὸν μακάριον Παῦλον. But since we have seen reason to believe that St Chrysostom

---

[1] E.g. C. F. A. Fritzsche in his Commentary on St Matthew, p. 487, where he quotes our text without any suspicion of its genuineness, explaining it, *nec vitam meam* possideo *mihi caram*, h.e. *ut sit mihi cara.*

[2] Matt. xiv. 5, Philem. 17, Phil. ii. 29.

[3] E.g. Deut. ii. 11, Nehem. xiii. 13.

[4] 1 Cor. iv. 1, Rom. vi. 11.

read the words alluded to exactly as they stand in T. R., all that can be certainly concluded from this passage is, that if St Luke had written οὐδὲ τίθεμαι τὴν ψυχὴν τιμίαν ἐμαυτῷ, he could not have expressed himself with greater propriety.

4. There remains yet one more word, which besides being equally appropriate with any of the others, better fulfils the condition of *rhyming* (so to speak) with ποιοῦμαι; that is, ἡγοῦμαι. This is quite in the style of St Paul, e.g. ἀλλήλους ἡγούμενοι ὑπερέχοντας ἑαυτῶν—ὅτι πιστόν με ἡγήσατο —τοὺς ἰδίους δεσπότας πάσης τιμῆς ἀξίους ἡγείσθωσαν—τὸ αἷμα τῆς διαθήκης κοινὸν ἡγησάμενος[1]. Turning to profane authors, and confining ourselves to examples of τίμιον ἡγεῖσθαί τι, we have τὸ ἐν ταῖς ψυχαῖς κάλλος τιμιώτερον ἡγήσασθαι τοῦ ἐν τῷ σώματι—ὅταν...μήτε ταῦτα ἡγῆται τίμια καὶ οἰκεῖα[2]. Lastly, we find the entire phrase τιμίαν ἡγεῖσθαι τὴν ψυχήν in Dion. Hal. *Antiq. Rom.* V. 30 (quoted by Wetstein): εἰ φίλους ἀντὶ πολεμίων, ἔφη, ποιήσαιο τοὺς ἄνδρας, τιμιωτέραν ἡγησάμενος τὴν σαυτοῦ ψυχὴν τῆς καθόδου τῶν σὺν Ταρκυνίοις φυγάδων. We may add St Chrysostom *ad loc.*: Οὐκ εἶπεν ὅτι ἀλγῶμεν (fort. ἀλγῶ μὲν), ἀνάγκη δὲ φέρειν· ἀλλ' οὐδὲ ἡγοῦμαι.........ὡσεὶ ἔλεγεν· οὐ φιλῶ αὐτὴν πρὸ ταύτης· προτιμότερον [fort. οὐ φιλῶ αὐτήν· πρὸ ταύτης προτιμότερον] ἡγοῦμαι τὸ τελέσαι τὸν δρόμον, τὸ διαμαρτύρασθαι[3]. It is unnecessary to point out how easily the words οὐδὲ ἡγοῦμαι may have dropped out in transcribing, especially if (as is very probable) they occupied a whole line in the MS. The following is a copy of the Sinaitic MS. on this place, substituting λόγον for λόγου, and inserting the line supposed to have been omitted :—

   ... ΑΛΛΟΥΔΕΝΟC
   ΛΟΓΟΝΠΟΙΟΥΜΑΙ
   ΟΥΔΕΗΓΟΥΜΑΙ
   ΤΗΝΨΥΧΗΝΤΙΜΙ
   ΑΝΕΜΑΥΤΩΩCΤΕ

The third line having been passed over, it became necessary to rectify the construction by changing λόγον into λόγου, whence we get the reading of B, C, ℵ. The T. R. (which is at least as old as St Chrysostom) arose from a fairly successful attempt to supply the obvious deficiency of the mutilated reading by the insertion of οὐδὲ ἔχω before τὴν ψυχήν. And, lastly, the reading of A, D would be derived from the last by changing the places of ποιοῦμαι and ἔχειν; the author of this change being less familiar with the use of ἔχειν for *aestimare* than in the common combination, λόγον ἔχειν.

[1] Phil. ii. 3, 1 Tim. i. 12, vi. 1, Heb. x. 29.

[2] Platonis Opp. (*Conv.*) p. 210 B, (*Pol.*) 538 E. [Cf. Herod. IV. 2: καὶ τὸ μὲν αὐτοῦ ἐπιστάμενον ἀπαρύσαντες ἡγεῦνται εἶναι τιμιώτερον.]

[3] For λόγον ποιοῦμαι the following passages may be compared. Herod. IV. 65: ξείνων δέ οἱ ἐλθόντων τῶν ἂν λόγον ποιήται. Anton. Liberalis XXX: ἡ δὲ τῶν μὲν (μνηστήρων) λόγον ἐποιεῖτο βραχύν. Paus. *Mess.* XVI. 10: 'Αριστομένους δὲ ἀπείργοντος...ὐδένα ἐποιοῦντο λόγον.]

LIST OF THE NOTES.

K.

17

SUPPLEMENTARY INDEX OF PASSAGES AND SUBJECTS DISCUSSED OR ILLUSTRATED.

INDEX OF GREEK WORDS.

K.

18

προσέρχεσθαί τινι (=to consent to) 211
προσλαμβάνεσθαί τινα 225
προσοφείλειν 225
προστάτης (=patronus) and -τις 166
προτείνειν (τινὰ ἱμᾶσιν) 136 f.
πρῶτος (of geographical situation) 124
πυγμῇ 30
πῶς γὰρ...; 117

ῥαπίζειν, -σμα 40, 105
ῥαπίσμασι βάλλειν, λαβεῖν 40
ῥιπτεῖν ἱμάτια 136

σειρός (σιρός, σιρρός) 241
σινδών 40
σῖτος, σῖτα, σιτία 114
σκῆνος (of the body) 183
σκόλοψ 187
σκυθρωπός, -άζειν 82
σουδάριον 97
σταθῆναι, στῆναι 81
στέγειν 177 f.
στέμματα (in sacrifices) 122
στήκω (with dative) 190
στῆσαι (= ζυγοστατῆσαι) 19 f.
στρατευόμενος and στρατιώτης 56
στραφῆναι 247
στρέφειν and ἀποστρέφειν 21
συγκομίζειν 116 f.
συγκρίνειν 168
συκοφαντεῖν 56 f.
συλαγωγεῖν (=rob) 195
συλλαμβάνεσθαι (=help) 57
συμβάλλειν τινί (εἰς πόλεμον) 67, 125
συμπεριφέρεσθαι 163
σύμφυτος 155 f.
συναγαγών (=ἐξαργυρίσας) 68
συναλίζεσθαι 110 f.
συναπάγεσθαι 163
συνειδέναι (οὐδὲν ἑαυτῷ) 168
συνελαύνειν εἰς... 115
συνέρχεσθαί τινι 40
συνεστηκέναι 242
συνέχεσθαι 128
συνιδεῖν 120 f.
συσχηματίζεσθαι 162
σχῆμα and μορφή 162
σχίζεσθαι (of multitudes) 121
σωρεύεσθαι 217

τὰ παρά τινος 27
τε...καί 85 f.
τέλος ἔχειν (of prophecies) 76
τεταρταῖος (of dead bodies) 96
τηλαυγῶς 33
τί ἔσται τινι...; (what reward...?) 15
τί οἶδας εἰ... 172 f.
τίς τί (ἄρη); 43 f.
τὸ κατ' ἐμὲ πρόθυμον 151
τολμᾶν (=ὑπομένειν) 155
τολμήσας εἰσῆλθε 44
τραπέζαις διακονεῖν 113
(μετὰ) τρεῖς ἡμέρας 13
τῇ τρίτῃ ἡμέρᾳ 11 ff.
τροχὸς (γενέσεως) 237

ὑγιὴς ἀπό... 88
ὑπὲρ (=instead of) 225, (ὑπ. δύναμιν) 184
ὑποβάλλειν (=suborn) 113
ὑπολῦσαί τινα 24
ὑποστέλλεσθαι (οὐδέν) 132
ὑποτίθεσθαι 208 f.
ὑπωπιάζειν 71, 174
ὑσσός 107 f.
ὕσσωπος 106 ff.

φελόνης 217 f.
φέρεσθαι 230
φέρων (colloquial) 172
φιλανθρωπία 147 f.
φιλονεικία 75 f.
φιλοτιμεῖσθαι 165
φόβος, ὁ φ. τοῦ κυρίου 183
φρουρεῖν 186 f.

χάριν ἔχειν 234
χάρις τῷ θεῷ 156
(ἐν) χειρί=διά 115
χοϊκός 179 f.
χρεία 192
χρηστότης 161, (and φιλανθρωπία) 222 f.
χωρεῖν 14, 94, 184
χωρίς (=ἄνευ) 103

ὠδῖνας λύειν 112
ὡς (with nouns) 127, (=ἕως) 191
ὡς δὴ 202
ὡς ἐπί... 125
ὠφελεῖν (=prevail) 21